HISTORY

OF

MIDDLE TENNESSEE;

OR,

LIFE AND TIMES

OF

GEN. JAMES ROBERTSON.

BY
A. W. PUTNAM, Esq.,
PRESIDENT OF THE TENNESSEE HISTORICAL SOCIETY.

NASHVILLE, TENN.:
PRINTED FOR THE AUTHOR.
1859.

STEREOTYPED AND PRINTED BY A. A. STITT, SOUTHERN METHODIST
PUBLISHING HOUSE, NASHVILLE, TENN.

Printing Statement:

Due to the very old age and scarcity of this book, many of the pages may be hard to read due to the blurring of the original text, possible missing pages, missing text and other issues beyond our control.

Because this is such an important and rare work, we believe it is best to reproduce this book regardless of its original condition.

Thank you for your understanding.

APOLOGY.

OUR personal friends know that we are entitled to indulgent consideration and criticism, because of the circumstances affecting us while preparing much of this work.

To others, we say that, as we correct our proof-sheets, we discover the omission of the names of perhaps twenty sufferers by the Indian wars here; as also of several incidents, which we had intended to introduce into our narrative.

We must also admit that very recently some information has reached us, which we should have been pleased to have used in appropriate time and place; and that we are aware of the existence of some manuscripts and documents, (but to which access could not now be had,) by which a few of our statements might have been extended or slightly modified.

We know of nothing, however, to cause us to doubt the general accuracy of our narration. We have something more in confirmation and illustration. A future day and inducements may, or may not, call for these. A volume of Biographies can readily be prepared.

A few paragraphs appear in the body of our work which should have been omitted, or inserted as notes.

This is the extent of our apology.

PREFACE.

Uncertain of our footing, we pause: discerning not all our surroundings, doubtful whither a step will lead, we ask, "Shall we go forward?" In the "palpable obscure" we stand: no pathway is discernible; no human, guiding voice is heard; no helping hand is felt. Our first step is into the wilderness and gloom. No pillar of fire opens and defends the way: silence reigns.

In unknown ages the heathen were here; these wild woods were once inhabited, or the race of man was before these forests. The bones of thousands rest beneath the very roots of our gigantic oaks. Here are the cemeteries of old, "the treasures of darkness," the sleep of a lost race. "The dead know not any thing," "they tell no tales," their voice is hushed, their "light is as darkness, as darkness itself."

> *"Mors veritatem in profundo abstrusit."*
> Dark ages close up the vision: death reigns.

But again the living are here; tumuli and earth-works are throughout the land. But when came the one, or wherefore the others, none can tell. Our questions obtain answers obscure as those given by the pyramids and their builders. And yet we hear no utterance—

> *"Procul, ô procul este, profani."*

Tenebras intramus, and pray and look for flashes and streaks of light and coming dawn, as we venture cautiously to gather up some relics of the past.

We go out with the hunters, we lodge in the rank grass, we kindle our camp-fires at the foot of the venerable tree, we herd with the wild beasts, we fight with the wild Indians. "The battle of life" hath many blows and phases—retreat is made impossible. Whether "the wolf be at our back, or a precipice at our feet," the impulse and command is, "Go forward."

We tread in the trail of the buffalo, we find their haunts —"the waters which they love;" and here we supply our table, and refit our wardrobe. We gaze upon the grandeur of the mountains, we admire the beauty of the plains, and we spy out the richness of the valleys. We discover places suitable for farms, and cities, and lovely homes. The mountain barriers are passed, the uplands are explored, the lowlands "plotted out."

Here are places for habitation. We cut down the cane, we deaden the forests, open our grounds, cast round the rude fence, build up the log-hut, construct the wood-fort, plant the sharp palisades, and fancy ourselves secure—that "every man may dwell safely under his vine, and under his fig tree."

Will this be so? Can such a hope be realized? Will no storms desolate this land?

Here are defences—proofs of doubtful safety; here are arms—threatening or apprehending war. There stand the sentinels upon the look-out stations; yonder go the rangers, scouting through the woods; spies tread stealthily in the cane, or dodge from tree to tree. The tangled brush is a covert for some foe. The grand old oak serves for defence or place of assault.

This is an enemy's country; on every side are piercing eyes, and weapons uplifted for the slaughter. Who can elude or foil weapons in the dark? Can such foes be pacified? Need we ask, "Will they give their sons and their daughters for men-servants and maid-servants?" Wild beasts domesticated! Shall Saxon blood and the blood of savages course freely and healthily in the same veins? Or is this the decree which has gone forth: "Drive ye out the heathen; go ye in and possess the land?"

It cannot be without a struggle. Distant thunder is heard, the heavens gather blackness, the storm bursts in fury; there is terror, wasting, and desolation; and then, the storm hath spent its fury, the shadows are over and gone. And now the annalist, the sketcher, and the antiquary find a field whereon they gather much for admonition, illustration, and gratification.

Hunters and explorers have been here. The race of pioneer settlers is "westward-bound." A conquering, all-conquering race are these. Forests and foes they dread not, but hasten to subdue them both; danger and toil they esteem as pleasure. They come to test mental and physical endurance; and these by watchfulness, privation, and hardship. These are the virtues to be tried, the lessons to be learned, the experiences to be endured.

They must be wise and great men who can find pleasure in these, and from much real evil educe great and lasting good. This is an art divine; dull minds can never learn it, the vulgar never appreciate it, the listless and the weak can never practice it.

Summa perfectio virtutis—this consummation of dignity springs not from sordid souls; graces not the vile and profligate: "it rejoices not in iniquity, but rejoiceth in the truth," in noble sentiments and noble deeds. "These defile not the man." To have in view some great aim, and press toward it; to encounter obstacles and overcome them; to know the path of duty, and steadily pursue it, is not a wisdom or a favor granted to all men.

It is, *Deo juvante*, by the smile of Heaven.

Pioneers on the Watauga and Sewanee* had their trials, and proved themselves rich in virtues. Like gold in the alembic, they passed the refiner's fire, leaving the dross in deposit or cast away. The leaders were in the cupel for a life-time; others were called to a fellowship in suffering.

And now, it is to the consideration of such times, such persons, and such sufferings, that our attention is directed.

Our immediate forefathers were these adventurers. Not long have they slept in the dust of death. The man of three-score years and ten was a lad when perilous times were here.

---

* Cumberland.

The octogenarian lived through the fifteen years of murderous warfare, and may have fought at Nickojack and Running Water.

The living have seen Tucalatagoo and McGillivray, the great men of the Creeks; Ocon-os-to-ta, Eskaqua, and Atta-culla-culla, of the Cherokees; Piomingo and Chin-nubbe, of the Chickasaws.

Their chiefs, their descendants, and their nations, have passed away. So will all earthly greatness and sublunary glory—

" So die the waves along the shore."

The ocean cannot always rest; it heaves and surges high, then billows rise. Vessels richly freighted and wisely helmed, or goods, "jetson or flotson," may be borne to a destined harbor, or to an unknown shore.

Life and mind are yet more restless and urgent. Races from another continent are here. They possess this land, and no ebb-tide can take them hence: " The bow in the cloud is set, and the waters shall no more become a flood to destroy all flesh."

From England and Ireland, from France and from Germany, the living have come. They came to change the face of nature ; to make these lands yield their increase, these streams serviceable to commerce: they came to plant, and build, and beautify. Dwellings for domestic happiness; temples with devout worshippers; institutions of learning; homes of charity; places of art and mart—farms, and towns, and cities, are throughout the land.

Society is here, religion is here; intelligence and industry are here. The mind and energy of another people control the elements of nature, and produce these changes. The consummation is not yet; the future is not all in view; mortal ken cannot pierce to the utmost limit. Perfection, the acme of effort and desire, like the ultimate glory, shall only be " hereafter."

But what are the influences now at work; what the attainments already made; what the tendency, and what the opening prospect? These are questions for the divine, the historian, the philosopher, and the statesman. But who can count them all, estimate their forces, detect their combinations, and declare their results in the undiscovered future? Here again we approach the "palpable obscure." We know not what shall be hereafter.

But the past, the present, and the future, touch each other. The record of the past is not all obliterated; current events are tangible; the future is foretold, or in inferential sequences. The same light shines upon them all, but we look at them through different mediums. In every existing object or condition we easily find some relation and connection to the past. It gives pleasure in our researches when we discover in any community the elements essential to improvement; the moral principles, the religious sentiments, and the intellectual vigor, which are sure to elevate and refine.

To find these in the earliest settlements made in the forests, among savages and wild beasts, (and in despite of these, and all other hindrances,) is interesting and gratifying to the student of American history. We have originated, developed, and improved; but we have not been wholly independent and original. We are glad when we trace in the best principles and best lives in our own day, strong alliances to the wise, the good, and the great of the past, whom we may well venerate and admire. Such traceries run back to our ancestors on this continent, and even into the dark ages upon another.

We believe that life is immortal; that truth communicated to that life is sempiternal. We admit that the elements of light and knowledge may be neglected and obscured, but are indestructible; that the utmost influence of these principles is not felt or limited to any one generation; that the past, the present, and the future constitute (not only in the Divine mind) an ever-present moment—an eternal τὸ παρόν—but to all the race of man, an unbroken series of interesting and instructive relations.

We, indeed, know not who, of all their countless descendants, bears most resemblance to "the original pair in Eden;" but we do all retain, more or less, the form and features of our more immediate progenitors. These identities or resemblances are not altogether physical; there are mental, if not

The *men* and the *times* came together; were partly productive of each other; yet not wholly so; for we hold that it
is as true in providence as in morals, in nature as in grace,
that there are no results without causes; that *the events* and
the men of our day are in covert or in manifest alliance with
those which have preceded; as well as in actual and momentary contact with passing events. The occurrences of life, like
the succession of beings, form continuous *chains*—not separate,
disconnected *links;* nor even united in two distinct chains,
which have no contact with and no influence upon each
other. They each and all occur, appear and disappear, by
ordination of the Great Governor of the material and immaterial world—of matter and of mind. They have their signification, their connection, influence, end. *They utter their voices.*
Is it not as philosophically true that events have signification,
and teach their inaudible meanings, as to say, *"Men speak!"*
Do not

> "Acts speak louder than words?"

> "Day unto day uttereth speech."

The sweet singer of Israel announced the sentiment we hold.
He gathered up the events of many generations, and, in words
of beautiful simplicity, reiterated the lessons of God's providence: "Their line is gone out through all the earth, and
their words to the end of the world." Such a line (impulse,
influence, purpose) there is—continuous from the beginning
—bringing down intelligence, sentiment, principle, example,
from "before the flood," through the middle and dark ages,
amidst the revolutions of kingdoms, the convulsions and
desolations of the earth. *This is history!* And this shall continue and transmit words and deeds, with signification, down
to the

> "Last syllable of recorded time."

The light and influence of the sun were not designed to be
seen and felt in that orb alone. Relation and influence are
laws operative throughout the planetary system. So in other
systems. If, "in the course of human events," one and
another individual is brought out of darkness and obscurity,

it is not that he may run alone, or without spectators, or without a goal, nor yet without his guerdon. They all have their spheres, their relations, and their sequences.

It is the pleasure of the student to examine these in their inception, nature, bearings, and results; and of the historian to present all these features in one condensed, yet appropriately illustrated and luminous panorama.

The lessons of history have their "inspiration," and are full of profitable teaching. The prudent and the wise will listen, reflect, and learn.

We need to hear the voices from the dead. The leading events of a nation and of a century are within the grasp of common minds; but we may all be pardoned for a strong desire to possess reliable information of the thousand "common occurrences" among the people who have "just passed on before us."

It is a duty to study the lives and times of immediate predecessors; and this, whether there may be reason to be proud or ashamed of them. The fame of our public men, the good name of our people, the character and worth of our institutions, civil, literary, benevolent, and religious, is involved in this question of history.

The character of our State, high and illustrious as it unquestionably is, demands attention to the men and their deeds —to the principles and the tendencies which constitute the very elements of that reputation. True, we have a distinguished position politically and otherwise. We think sufficiently well of ourselves, and are quite favorably regarded by others. Yet there are items of information not generally known, even here at home, which ought to be preserved and communicated. There are "baskets full of scraps, which ought to be gathered up, that nothing be lost." In this we have been engaged for a few months; of course, our collection consists chiefly of broken pieces—many bones—but with sufficient meat for a tolerable repast to one who is hungry, and not too dainty.

Our children, and children's children, and all the children of worthy people, will delight to read the history and biographies of such times and ancestors as distinguished the last quarter of the last century in America. The occurrences in our early history here (limited in its theatre and its actors as it was) are pregnant with that which is curious and interesting: "it is stranger than fiction"—it is better than apologue. It is not only "philosophy teaching by example," but example inculcating and enforcing the best lessons of a sound philosophy.

Here is one fact, a truth, which conducts us up to a very distinguished source of favor; and, whether their immediate successors acknowledge it or not, it certainly is true, that our pioneer fathers did gratefully acknowledge it. 'Tis *this:* they "got not this goodly land by their own righteousness, but by the favor of the Lord and his mighty arm." This is historically and religiously true.

Their spirit and character were, to a needed extent, conformed to and influenced by the exigencies and events of the times; but they also, in some degree, moulded and directed those events. And yet, in all, they publicly, and by record, acknowledged a "Divine Providence." If any of their descendants discard this salutary and sustaining doctrine, we cannot but suggest that they have never wisely read the best words in Holy Writ, nor understood the lessons of history. We certainly have felt proud so often to meet with the frank recognition of this great dogma. We should be unfaithful to "the truth of history," and unjust to their memories and merits, were we to ignore or disguise a fact so often and so prominently presented by these pioneer settlers. As we are pleased to look upon rich tracery in architecture, so may we, with pleasure, behold in Tennessee character and institutions that which is most ornamental and valuable. And now we say that, in our short chapter of history, we have discovered well-known features. We have been looking into the faces and upon the forms, listening to the words and scrutinizing the acts of our own parents, and their neighbors and associates, (so nearly do we feel identified,) and with our most impartial eye we discern much for admiration and imitation —though some things for warning and avoidance. This is just as we may expect it will be with those who shall come after ourselves.

The privilege and duty of each generation is, to imitate and perfect whatsoever is virtuous and commendable, and avoid the wrong and hurtful. So shall we best and most wisely live in our own day, and perpetuate ourselves and our virtues in those whom we love and leave.

There are incidents, notable and curious; there are plots and counter-plots; there are alarms and troubles; there are fears and fightings; there are revolutions, and even treasons; there are outlawries and confiscations; there are civil and religious commotions; there are political and belligerent excitements and conflicts.

Every age has them, (unless torpid and dying,) and will have them, until that consummation when truth, and righteousness, and peace shall reign triumphant, and no more change be needed or desired. And this, He whose right and wisdom it is will hasten in his own time. *Festina lente* is his law, and no impatience or violence, cavilling or commentary, on man's part, will ever change or improve his purposes.

Upon the limited space here opened in 1780, the actors came out in full character and costume. But they have disappeared. The curtain is still uprolled, though the *dramatis personæ* have dropped from off the stage. The theatre—the arena—is still occupied; but by a new set of dramatists, who also will be allowed to "strut and fret," and act their brief part, and then, *Exeunt omnes.*

Rotulæ in rota fortunæ: the smaller wheels within the wheel of fortune, are but parts and operations of one pervading whole; a providence to which they all belong, or could not at all exist. Many are not entitled to *particular* notice; while others, however small and seemingly insignificant, may, from their peculiar structure, position, or velocity of motion, merit the most careful examination and regard.

The historian is called upon to consider and explain the connections, forces, operations, and results of much of this extensive and complicated machinery. With its movements the whole human family is concerned. By and with it, States, families, and individuals are carried forward to results devoutly to be wished, or sadly to be deplored.

In the preparation of this volume, we have usually and sufficiently indicated the sources whence our information has been derived. That we have had access to some original, valuable, and hitherto unpublished documents, will also be evident to the reader.

We could have made use of many oral statements, and the rehearsal of colloquies, which, to us, have been interesting and instructive. We have, however, refrained from inserting the most of them, lest we should awake distrust as to the credibility of the few.

The biographer and the eulogist identifies himself with the person and deeds he commends. But by other ties than these are we interested in the early great men and the history of Tennessee and Kentucky.

Vinculi foti, a cœlo ad cœlum. We have had and have such cherished ties—inheritances from the past, dear alliances of the present—garnered and enriching in heaven. These ties are not sundered; all that was pure, and truthful, and lovely here, is brightened and kept in store there.

As we close this little work, though our heart is desolate and family bereaved, our treasures and hopes are enhanced for the life to come. We have a stronger love for the excellent of earth, and the pure in heaven.

May some such service be rendered by what we now tender to the posterity of a worthy race, and for the perusal of all who may desire to find excellences in the lives of hardy pioneers, equal to those we admire in the living, and commend to all coming time. Virtues and beauty are heaven-born, and, when they cease below, reäppear in their native home. The storm-cloud may obscure the sun, but he still abides in strength, dominion, and glory.

WAVERLY PLACE, (Suburbs of Nashville,) November, 1858.

HISTORY

O F

MIDDLE TENNESSEE.

CHAPTER I.

1742—1774.

THE purpose which we wish to accomplish is, to give a history of the early settlements in Middle Tennessee.

In the prosecution of this object, we shall find it our pleasure, as well as essential to the attainment of the end in view, to present the acts and characters, the manners and habits, of the pioneers and early stationers on the Cumberland river.

As General Robertson was the recognized leader in these settlements, and during all his life acted a most useful and distinguished part here, we deem it no disparagement to others, nor more than due to him, to add his name in the title-page. The fact is, that no just history of this section of country could be given without presenting him at the head of affairs; nor could a faithful biography of Robertson be written which should not, at the same time, identify him with all that is interesting in the events which transpired here, from the planting of corn in 1779, the planting of a colony in 1780, to the close of the last century.

The country in which most of the scenes transpired to which we shall invite attention is chiefly embraced in the present counties of Davidson, Sumner, Robertson, and Montgomery: a country of rich lands, and then of unbroken forests. Prior to the American Revolution it was almost unknown to the white people, and, until the emigration of the Robertson party, was wholly unoccupied, unexplored, and untrodden but by wild beasts. These were in countless herds, and occasionally there came the wild Indian from distant tribes to kill the game.

2   (17)

The multitudinous race of people which some centuries ago must have possessed these lands, who built its mounds, cast up the varied and inexplicable earth-works, and whose extensive cemeteries, with their thousands of rude stone tombs and skeletons, are to be found in many portions of Middle Tennessee, had disappeared at a date and by such causes as none can now determine.

We would gladly make researches into those " dark ages," but whatever steps could possibly be taken in the right direction would lead far beyond the appropriate limits of our history. We write of men and deeds whereof we have records and yet some living witnesses.

The charter of Carolina included all of this region of country, but until the period at which the "stirring events" of our history commenced there had been no surveys of boundaries undertaken or settlements contemplated.* A few adventurous hunters had indeed followed some of the traces of buffaloes and discovered some of the sulphur springs. James Robertson came as a pioneer settler.

He was born in Brunswick county, Virginia, June 28th, 1742, and died at the Chickasaw Agency (now in West Tennessee) September 1st, 1814. In 1825 his remains were reïnterred at Nashville, with marked honors by the citizens, and an appropriate eulogium by Judge Haywood, the earliest historian of the State.

When Robertson was but a youth, his parents removed and settled in Wake county, North Carolina, where he early married Miss Charlotte Reeves, by whom he had eleven children—seven sons and four daughters.*

We hasten to bring up the records of the lives of those parents, and of the lives of others, their worthy compeers, co-laborers, and pioneers, that the living, their descendants and friends, may affix the seal of truth and approval to what we write, and the ways of Providence be vindicated and admired. We pretend not to do full justice to all, but we claim to do injustice to none.

Our relation will set forth the native forests and the wild woods as the pioneers found them, when, by the introduction of the woodman's axe and the farmer's plough, the changes began which have resulted in the great improvements we now behold in city, town, and country.

The perils, hardships, and sufferings endured by the first settlers on the Cumberland would be deemed fabulous by many persons born and

---

* Two sons were killed by the Indians, one daughter died at two years of age; four children, two sons and two daughters, yet live. One of these, Dr. Felix Robertson, ever highly honored, was the first male child born at the Bluffs, or Nashville. He was regarded as a New Year's gift, presented on 11th January, 1781. *Filiorum felix Nashvilliensis primævus.*

living in the enjoyment of the peace and luxuries of the present day; therefore we have taken the more pains to give names, places, and circumstances, which, indeed, we consider but due to the actors themselves, the verification and interest of our narration. Facts require time and place as well as actors.

The "Old County of Orange" embraced an extensive region of country, and in this year was reduced and changed in its limits by the erection of two other counties. The new county of Wake was organized. Raleigh, the capital of the State, is in this county. Here, and around this central position, were an intelligent people, "studious of their rights, bold to avow, and brave to maintain them." It was among the inhabitants of this portion of the State that the celebrated organization of "Regulators," under Herman Husbands, had its origin and chief support.

Robertson was personally acquainted with the leading men of the country, and was intimate with many of the young men who had resolved to sustain the measures, suggested by older heads, to resist the extortions and tyranny under which the whole community had groaned for years. He heartily approved the sentiments of independence, "the breaking in of the dawn of freedom."

The "Impartial Relation," that amazingly curious and interesting book of that extraordinary man, Husbands, was, in 1770, published and widely circulated. Robertson had often heard it read, and treasured in his very heart its choicest truths and most impressive statements. He hated the very shadow of oppression. In the "Impartial Relation," Husbands had "showed up the intolerable abuses heaped upon the people."

"Allegiance to the king, and to the King of kings, enjoins resistance to wrongs." This was the political sentiment thus early scattered broadcast over that population.

Robertson, when a youth, had seen Washington and other wise and good men in Virginia; but whatever of political opinions he may have then heard, he now was old enough to listen profitably, and form and express his own. He found himself among men of education, in every way worthy peers of the wisest and best of his native State.

The spirit of resistance to oppression was on the increase, and it spread rapidly and extensively, until the resolution was taken "to resist unto blood." This was a novel and daring avowal, a step hitherto not taken. The result was the bloody battle of the Alamance, in which "The great He-Wolf," William Tryon, the Governor, at the head of eleven hundred well-armed troops, some of them thoroughly drilled soldiers, attacked a body of two thousand citizens, on the 16th day of May, 1771.

The citizens, Independents or Regulators, were hastily assembled, poorly equipped, commanded by Husbands, who had no experience in military tactics, and had not taken an active part in the measures until he was personally assailed by the "Bums and Bumpkins of Tyranny."

The Battle of the Great Alamance, which terminated in the defeat of the citizens, with a slaughter of two hundred on their part, and of sixty odd of the "regular army," may properly be regarded as the first battle of the American Revolution. A Revolution had commenced, it was progressing, and it went forward, assisted by every act of extortion and oppression on the part of its enemies.

The battles of Lexington and Bunker Hill came in after years, but the ball was set in motion as early and by as pure hearts and resolute hands in North Carolina as in Massachusetts; and here, as well as there, was a people indoctrinated, religiously educated in the great truths of the Bible, the rights of conscience, and the right of property. For three years warm discussions had been conducted between the Royalists and the Regulators, and the Governor threatened a resort to force; but no collision had as yet taken place. The people desired peace.

In the spring of the year, (1770,) and at a time when the opposing parties were at a sullen pause, there were a number of hardy men equipped for a hunting-tour, and for the purposes of exploration among the Appalachian mountains and the head-waters of the streams which form the Cheràke or great Tennessee river.

Daniel Boone and others had been employed by Colonel Richard Henderson and his associates to examine the same country; they had passed beyond the mountains, and discovered the rich lands upon the Cumberland and Kentucky rivers, and the extensive barrens, or open lands, in Kentucky. Their report of the beauties and richness of the country, and of its attractive features, came indeed like "good news from a far country." The accounts given of the quantity of wild game—"herds of deer and droves of buffaloes, thousands and thousands"—seemed incredible; yet they were true. The fact needed no coloring, no exaggeration.

The thoughts of some were, "'Tis better to fly to ills we know not of, than suffer the daily repetition of a thousand petty annoyances which sting us as the flies:" better to take up our abode in the wilderness, and live a hunter's and a hunted life among the wild beasts there, than be continually "set on" and preyed upon by "the great He-Wolf of Carolina." "The minions of royalty," "the imps of power," and "the feed lawyers," seemed to make "a pleasure and a pastime to exact upon the people."

It was strangely but wisely ordered that "the most tyrannical and proud of the representatives of a kingly government" should have made forced contributions by the people wherewith to build for himself "a palace, a magnificent palace," and that his "petty officers should prick and prick and worry the people, until they were made *sore all over* and *inflamed all through.*" There was a large infusion of the bitter in the cup daily commended to their lips. They would not drink it to its dregs. They were compelled to study the compound—to analyze and consider its adaptation to their well-being. They reluctated, they loathed, they determined to reject it.

But, as we have intimated, there was a calm, like that oppressive and premonitory quiet which often precedes the outbursting of the destructive storm. No man felt secure, and no one had any particular anticipation of coming events.

It was at this time that Robertson accompanied or led a small party into the distant mountains and across to the Watauga. There is good reason to believe that Boone himself conducted this party, or that they at least availed themselves of information received from him as to the route to be pursued, and followed close "upon his trail;" for Boone and Robertson were on the Watauga and Holston at the same time in this year. Boone had been here ten years before, and had cut into the bark of a beech tree yet standing upon the east side of the present stage-road leading from Jonesboro' to Blountsville, in the valley of Boone's Creek, (a branch of Watauga,) this record:

D. Boon

CillED   A. BAR   on

Tree

in   ThE

yEAR

1760.

Robertson had killed many "A. BAR," but had not yet learned to write or cut letters. He had been married not yet two years, was the proud father of one son, Jonathan Friar Robertson, and had been "learning his letters and to spell" under the tuition of his well-educated wife. This eldest son was born in June, 1769. When Robertson started on this hunt, it was with the avowed intention to find a home for himself, his wife, and child. He had made promises to many of his friends to look out for them desirable locations near to his own.

"Be sure to find good springs and rich lands, and enough of both to accommodate us all," was the injunction of these neighbors, who had a desire to emigrate and form a community of relatives and friends in the

vast wilderness, that they might enjoy political freedom and the rights of
conscience. They had already confidence in this young man, of which
he showed, in all his public and private life in after days, great worthiness.
He had often given assistance in the survey of lands; "could run a line
as accurately as anybody; could calculate and sum up figures or numbers
and courses and distances 'in his head,' in less time than others could do
the same if they had all written down." He had also been taking lessons
in arithmetic.

The preparations having been made, the necessary articles were packed
upon the horses, and these friends started. The equipments were few
and cheap. A heavy blanket, rifle, hatchet, knife, powder-horn and
powder, bullets, an extra gun-flint, a picker, a wallet well stored with
parched corn, some salt, and a tin cup.

Robertson "started with one horse, having no one to provide for but
himself." At some seasons of the year it was necessary to add to the
load upon the horse a bag of corn, for the supply of nourishment to that
invaluable animal. As a companion ever to be trusted, and costing the
hunter little for his support, there was the watchful dog.

The departure of Boone and Robertson was a noticeable event. They
foresaw not the great results of their present movement; they anticipated
not the grand designs of Providence, of which their migration was but
the initiative. They went, scarcely knowing whither they went, or for
what intent. There was vastly more in it and to result from it, than had
ever entered into "their philosophy." As John Rains said, and always
insisted upon the expressive word, they were going into the " *Wil-derado*
or *Well-dorado*: he never liked the Spanish spelling or pronunciation,
El-Dorado."

Whether Boone and Robertson travelled in company, it matters not to
inquire: they were together on the Watauga and the Holston, examining
the lands, and yet they were little in company: Boone loved solitude,
Robertson delighted in society. They were representative men, but
types of quite opposite classes of men. They each sought freedom from
oppression; but whilst the one became the celebrated hunter, explorer,
and pioneer—always seeking to be in advance of all other white men into
the remotest wilderness—the other was actuated by an ambition to lead
out and settle colonies, establish permanent homes, and reclaim this same
wilderness from the occupancy of wild beasts and savage men.

They both examined the lands on the Holston river. Boone's natural
disposition was indulged in penetrating farther into the then Western
wilds. Robertson visited the few settlers on the Watauga: he was pleased
with the country, and he remained to make a crop there in this year.

He always mentioned with praise the kind hospitality with which he was received and entertained by one Honeycut, who had built there his hut, and cheerfully supplied Robertson with provisions. A small stock of corn, and an abundance of fresh and dried venison and bear-meat, "with a fat turkey to fill up the chinks in the stomach," constituted the staff of life for those pioneer settlers. Honeycut had a good supply, was happy to entertain emigrants and to furnish them liberally "of such as he had."

In Robertson's attempt to recross the mountains through the dense and trackless forests, he was for some time lost. Entangled in thickets upon the mountain-top, wearied and exhausted, yet determined upon the direction he should take, he was arrested by a precipice down which it was impossible to lead his horse. There was he under the necessity of turning his trusty animal at large, to take care of himself, whilst his luckless owner should now trudge his lonely, wearisome way as best he could on foot, depending upon his faithful rifle, his yet unyielding resolution, and a kind *Providence*. He had been drenched with rain. His powder was wet and so damaged that he could not use it. He resorted to various devices to dry it. He attempted this by the warmth of his body, but it was so soaked and spoiled that he could not make his gun fire to kill any game. With the small supply of food in his knap-sack, and the still more scanty stock of nutritious berries he could gather, he wandered for *fourteen days*, till he was so reduced and weakened that he began to despair of ever reaching his home. When the sun shone out, he could take the direction which he was sure was right; but when the frequent clouds obscured the heavens, he was in-volved in perplexity and distress, so that both mind and body were nearly ready to fail utterly.

But as Judge Haywood says of this very exigency in which Robertson was placed, "there is a *Providence* which rules over the destinies of men, and preserves them to run the race which is appointed for them. Un-promising as were the expectations of James Robertson at that time—having neither learning, experience, property, nor friends to give him countenance—and with spirits drooping under the pressure of penury and a low estate, yet the God of nature had given him an elevated soul, and planted in it the seeds of virtue, which made him look forward, in the midst of discouraging circumstances, to better times."

His trust in Providence was not misplaced. Under the care and direction of that same kind Providence, two other hunters and explorers were in the same wild forest, and on horseback. The footsteps of all were so directed that "these three met in the nick of time," and far away from all human habitation. Characteristic of the hunters and pioneers of that day, these two horsemen insisted that Robertson should ride, and that they would accompany him on his way—making him to partake of their provisions prudently—until his strength was restored, and he returned so near to his house that he refused to allow them farther to go, or longer to be diverted from their hunting pursuits. We have not the names of these two friends in this time of need: it would give us pleasure to record them, for we might hope to find them again among those scenes in which Robertson acted so useful and distinguished a part; for, as the earliest historian of Tennessee remarks, "This is the man who, in the sequel of his history, figures so deservedly as the greatest benefactor of the first settlers of the country; the same person who will appear hereafter by his actions to have merited all the eulogiums, esteem, and affection which the most ardent of his admirers and most attached of his countrymen have ever bestowed upon him."

"Like almost all of those in America who have ascended to eminent celebrity, he had not a noble lineage to boast of, nor the escutcheoned armorials of a splendid ancestry. But he had what was far more valuable, a sound mind, an intrepid soul, and an emulous desire for honest fame."
—HAYWOOD.

1771. When he returned to his home in Wake county, he reported faithfully to his friends as to the difficulties to be encountered in passing through the forests and across the mountains, to the distant settlements then begun, or rather contemplated, upon the Watauga and the Holston, or Hogohegee. His mind was already made up to remove to the Watauga; and if he had been as yet undecided, the events which transpired in the fore part of this year settled that question for him, as they did for some others. He found the excitement among his fellow-citizens had not abated during his absence, and understood from them that there was no removal or even diminution of causes of offence and uneasiness. The Governor threatened resort to arms: the parties were arrayed, and the conflict occurred at the Great Alamance on the 16th May. The citizens were defeated, and for the time dispersed. We have no authority for asserting that Robertson took part with the citizens or Regulators. He certainly had many neighbors and friends among them, and, from the fact that he openly denounced the extortions and oppressions which had so aroused the people, we have little hesitation in assigning him a place at this critical and eventful moment.

Soon after this occurrence he was on his way, with his wife and child, for the "great West" of that day, never more to claim the right or act as a citizen of the old and settled portion of the State. He had entered upon his great career, and upon an extensive theatre for a patriot and a good man.

Without more than the common incidents of travel through the forest, he arrived at the Watauga, and was again welcomed by the hospitable Honeycut. He found Boone there again, not with intention to remain, but "bent on seeing the regions beyond."

> He roamed, and loved to roam
> "Far from the haunts of men;"
> And with the wild beasts, society,
> And in the forests, home
> He found.

Boone concurred in the propriety of adopting a form of government in this new and distant settlement. The laws of the State were not in operation here, there were no magistrates or executive officers, and they hoped the oppressive tax-gatherers and "Bums and Bumpkins of Tryon" "might never show their faces or processes among them." They determined to elect their own officers, and it would never have been safe for a minion of the royal governor to have attempted to exert authority in these new settlements.

After much consultation among the few heads of families who were there, it was decided to have written articles of agreement, by which all matters of controversy, all questions of right to property, should be speedily and quietly adjusted. They had found, as they hoped, a safe retreat from petty exactions under the show of legal process, and a quiet home in the wilderness; but they too well knew the necessity of law and officers, to believe there could be safety or advantage in discarding either. As their small community was on the increase by fresh arrivals, they delayed a full organization for some months.

When Robertson was a man of more extended observation, thoughtful experience, and calm reflection, he remarked: "Tyranny, by his servant Tryon, drove the people mad down there, drove them into the woods out here, made them just mad enough to be ready to fight for their rights; set them to thinking, talking, consulting, acting: then he fled, and was in good trim to pursue the same course and accomplish the like good results in New York; over which colony he was placed as governor, whilst Martin, a far better man, succeeded him in Carolina."

All these proud and exacting agents of the royal government were accomplishing a great deliverance for the American people. "They meant it not so," but a wiser and better power did. The hand of God was in it.

1772. As we have intimated, the prudence and good sense of Robertson, and the dawning of one of the excellent traits of his character, now
became more evident.   He took an active part in uniting the pioneer
settlers in the adoption of written articles for self-government.

Their safety and interests were to be promoted and secured only by
harmony and mutual confidence.   They must enter into a compact or
reliable organization.   And, as one of the earliest instances of record
among the pioneers over the mountains, Robertson and his sixteen adventurers did, upon the Watauga, enter into covenant and agreement
with each other to abide by certain rules for their own government and
intercourse, and for their dealings with the Indians.   They contemplated
at this early day to make regular purchases of land from the savages,
rather than to seize upon choice localities in despite of all opposition and
perils.   They determined to negotiate and pay reasonable considerations
for the homes they desired.

And this "beginning of compacts and covenants," which Boone communicated to Richard Henderson, (who subsequently became so worthily
known as the "Treaty-maker,") was the type, and furnished the rudiments
of those organizations and companies under Henderson, the incidents of
which form most interesting and instructive chapters in the histories of
Tennessee and Kentucky.

1772. May.   In the spring of this year the two Robertsons, James
and Charles, John Sevier, John Carter, and nine others, were chosen by
the settlers to convene at Robertson's Station, there to consult and to
adopt some form of government for the maintenance of defences against
the savages, for the preservation of order, and the administration of civil
justice among themselves.

From these thirteen delegates, a selection or choice of five was made,
who were intrusted with the authority of magistrates, having a clerk and
executive officer of their own appointment.

The existence of the Watauga government was three years prior to
that adopted "under the great elm tree, outside the fort at Boonesboro',
in Kentucky, on the thick sward of the fragrant clover," so highly yet
justly spoken of by the learned and careful historian, Bancroft,* (in the
seventh volume, just from the press, 1858.)

This is the earliest compact for civil government adopted anywhere
west of the mountains.   Four of the prominent officers in it removed to
the Cumberland, and three of them became active officers in the similar
government there: they were James Robertson, Lucas, Tatum, and Isbell.

---

* Vol. vii., pp. 365–367.

These early woodmen were. highly pleased with the lands and their location on the Watauga. Probably they had no thought that they could be tempted to encounter further privations and difficulties, and go yet deeper into the wilderness. Although little was known of the extent and richness of the great West of that day, it must be admitted that some of the leading spirits had bright visions, and anticipated the time when there would be settlements, farms, and towns where then were plains and valleys unmarked by the white man's foot or untouched by implements of husbandry. They saw not the part they would be called upon to act in that future.

> "Heaven from all creatures hides the book of fate,
> All but the page prescribed—their *present state*."

Here, as in all our advanced and border settlements, there came some persons of abandoned character, destitute of moral principles as they were destitute of property, and thus were the cares and labors of more worthy men multiplied.

In speaking of the commixture of good and evil spirits in such early settlements, we have heard the authority of Pope (and of *the* pope,) quoted in justification and explanation :

> "All nature is but art unknown to thee ;
> All chance, direction which thou canst not see ;
> All discord, harmony not understood ;
> All partial evil, universal good," etc.

Like as by the driving wind preceding the genial shower, the dust and malaria are swept away, that health and life and fruitfulness may follow, so here. The fierce, the wild, the reckless, the desperate, rush from the order and law and police of established society, and crowd upon the range of the aborigines. "Afraid of their own government, and of the rewards due to their demerits, unwilling to trust themselves entirely with the savages, for fear of the punishment for offences like those which had driven them from the bosom of civilization," they sometimes herded together in the wilderness, and involuntarily rendered to their country a beneficial service, which in no other way could have been extracted from them.

> " They leave society, for society's good."

" They formed a barrier on the frontiers between the savages and the industrious cultivators of the soil." Such is the sentence of Judge Haywood when these " refugees from justice, absconding debtors, and horse-thieves," were beyond the pale of law, and in no danger of arrest and arraignment before any legal tribunal or officer, who, like himself, would not connive at wrong and encourage the hope that any breach of law could escape detection and punishment. Not unfrequently did it appear that this "barrier," this protection, was

"Such as vultures give to lambs."

If these desperadoes could not succeed and thrive by depredations upon the Indians, they resisted not the temptation to steal from the whites; and when most successful in their forays among the savages, then were the innocent settlers yet more alarmed and in peril of life and property, for the Indians would not often make a discrimination between the marauders and the peaceful inhabitants, but wreak their vengeance upon all or any of the "Virginians," as they called the early settlers in Tennessee and Kentucky.

Many protestations and remonstrances were made by the well-behaved and well-disposed whites against the misconduct of these vagabonds. Often had they to send some of their most important members, at great inconvenience and peril of their lives, into the Indian territories, with presents and assurances that the conduct of these men was as obnoxious to all good men among them, as it was injurious to any of the aborigines. Yet they could not safely counsel or approve the acts of revenge taken by the Indians upon any of the whites ; for, had these desperadoes ascertained that such advice was given against them, then would they turn more fiercely upon their fellow-emigrants, and rob and steal from them to trade with the savages, or elsewhere.

The leading men in these early settlements certainly encountered great perplexities and troubles. They had to deal with caution and delicacy, with suspicious and wary red men, and yet had often to connive at the misconduct of some persons who seemed to belong to their own community. The theory of revenge, the law of retaliation among savages, did not restrain the avenger to the actual transgressor, or the really guilty party; therefore were the innocent not unfrequently made to suffer for the misconduct of others, whom they would gladly have restrained.

But we do not hereby intend to admit that the bloody deeds done by the Indians always, or generally, had the real or seeming justification of retribution. Their chiefs admitted to General Sevier, to General Robertson, and to others, that they had "bad man in their nations, who, like natural brute beasts, loved horses and would steal them," and that for . the scalps of their enemies their warrior spirit thirsted.

In the prosecution of our present history, we shall have to record many proofs of this "attachment of horses"—according to legal phraseology—

and of this "wounding the head of enemies and the hairy scalp of tres-
passers," in the language of Scripture. There were instances of white
men deeming it not reproachful for them to learn *ab hostes,* and boastfully to exhibit the "crown imperial" of a dead Indian.

The division line between the States of Virginia and North Carolina
had been run and established by Fry and Jefferson as far as Steep Rock
Creek, about three hundred and thirty miles west of Currituck Inlet.
The same line should have been extended to the Mississippi, but, as between regions of country which now constitute the States of Tennessee
and Kentucky, there was but the unmarked geographical line, which
caused doubts and disputes, legislation and litigation, for many years,
Commissioners were appointed by each of these parent States to run this
line, and in September, 1779, they met, and after due observations agreed
upon the point from which the line should be continued. After running
the line to Carter's Valley, some forty-five miles, they disagreed. The commissioners from North Carolina insisted upon running the line two miles
farther north than was approved by those from Virginia; therefore they
ran two lines parallel, and at that distance apart. The southern line was
run by a surveyor by the name of Walker, and has ever been known as
"the Walker line;" the northern one was run by Richard Henderson,
the great land-speculator and Indian treaty-maker, already mentioned.
The disputed boundary was not adjusted until 1820, when the Walker
line was fully recognized. It is true that Col. Anthony Bledsoe, afterward most favorably known and usefully identified with the earliest
settlements and perils on the Cumberland, had, as early as 1771, examined
this question of boundary; and, being a practical surveyor, in whom
much confidence was always deservedly reposed, he had extended the
Walker line some distance west, and thereby enabled many of the settlers
to decide for themselves whether they owed allegiance to Virginia or
North Carolina. Those upon the north side of this line claimed and
early enjoyed some of the benefits of the laws and some of the services
of officers of the State of Virginia; but "those who settled on the south
side of the Holston adhered to North Carolina, and lived without law or
protection, except by rules of *their own adoption.*"

The life and times of General Robertson will fully justify this assertion
of Judge Haywood, and prove how wise and prudent were the measures
and how beneficial the services he rendered during all his life, in rules
and regulations for several of the settlements, where the good "Old
North State" did not and could not grant "the salutary use of her protection, laws, and officers."

None of the documents relating to the Watauga government are in existence: that such is the case is cause of much regret; for, as the writer of the Annals of· Tennessee remarks, " It is believed that these Articles of Association formed the first written compact for civil government anywhere west of the Alleghanies; and could they be recovered, they would make a valuable and exceedingly interesting contribution to the historical literature of the Great West."

It was the good fortune of the writer of these notes singularly to discover and save from destruction the records of the similar association or compact of government established by some of these same wise and worthy men, upon the bluffs where is now the city of Nashville; and as James Robertson occupied a post of honor in each, and the necessities, objects, and interests of both were similar, we conclude it probable that the organizations were very much alike.

Tradition, as gathered up and recorded by Haywood and Ramsey, assures us that the settlers on the Watauga assembled in convention, and selected thirteen commissioners, representing, we presume, as at Nashborough, the various stations or settlements around their forts or blockhouses. From these thirteen, there were chosen *five*, who were to hear and adjudicate all matters of controversy, to adopt and direct measures for the peace, defence, safety, and well-being of the community. And if their authority had extended to military organizations and defences, the celebration of the rites of marriage, and the granting of administration upon estates of persons deceased among them, then should we find all the distinguishing features, and very notable ones, too, of the government of the Judges at Nashborough of 1st May, 1780.

The arbitrators, or court, at Watauga, consisted of John Carter, Charles Robertson, *James Robertson*, Zach. Isbell, and *John Sevier*.

We find these men and the other members of this Watauga government taking honorable positions, and rendering useful services to the State, when this incipient government had become no longer necessary.

1772. It was in the fall of this year that Daniel Boone, accompanied by his wife and children, and five other pioneers, with their wives and children, and with an escort of forty men, attempted to reach the interior of Kentucky. The party had left the Watauga stations in high hopes of reaching the new settlements in safety. They travelled on cheerfully—had passed over the greatest natural obstacles of the way; but as they marched down a narrow valley or gorge of the Cumberland mountain, (Sept. 25,) a sudden and fierce attack was made upon them by a large body of Indians. A son of Boone and five of the men were instantly killed.

Great fright and confusion was the result among the whites. A retreat seemed to offer the only hope of delivery from the close ambush into which the emigrants were entering. It was ordered.

The party returned in all haste to the Watauga and Holston settlements. There was "no renewal of the attempt to remove wives and children to Kentucky until after the close of Lord Dunmore's war, (Oct., 1774,) in which, though conducted at a great distance from these stationers, some of them, as we shall show, took an active and useful part. . . . In the mean time these families had temporarily established themselves on Clinch river."

1772. In this same year these settlers were assailed from another quarter, and by other men than the savages of the wilderness and the turbulent bad men in or near their own community. Although much had been done to conciliate the Indians, to establish order and good government for themselves, and this of necessity, and without imposing any responsibility or burden upon other people or communities at a distance beyond the mountains, they were not permitted quietly to enjoy their new homes or new government in these "ends of the earth."

By authority of Virginia, a treaty had been formed with the Cherokees, establishing a boundary to run west from the White Top Mountain, in latitude 36° 35'. And soon thereafter an agent of the Government of Great Britain, then resident among the Cherokees, ordered the settlers on Watauga *to depart the country.* Some of the Cherokees desired that this order should not be enforced; and many concurred in the consent for them to remain, if they would agree to make no further encroachments upon Indian territory.

Boone, Calloway, Harrod, and others had determined to persevere in their efforts to establish settlements in Kentucky. Henderson had commenced his negotiations with the Indians. He had learned from his agent, Boone, not only of the form of government which these pioneers to Holston and Watauga had adopted, but of the leases and purchases which Robertson, Brown, and Sevier had made of rich valley-lands. From these originated the grand conceptions which led to the famous treaty of March, 1775. These gave to Colonel Henderson the hope of a princely estate, (embracing most of Kentucky,) and of that initiative government at Boonesborough, from which two events, and his short connection with the first settlers on the Cumberland, he has for ever identified his name with western history.*

---

* Bancroft places the defeat of Boone (as we judge) several years too late. He says 25th May, 1775, whereas other authorities give 25th Sept., 1771, and 1773.

As to the inducements and determination to secure possession of the country purchased from the Cherokees at the Sycamore Shoals on Watauga, there can be no question; nor that the earlier claims to lands in the Kentucky limits were under royal grants and military warrants. The language of Boone, as given in Bancroft, conveyed the sentiment of most of the pioneers : " Now is the time to keep the country, while we are in it. If we give way now, it will ever be the case." Robertson and his friends had not long enjoyed their new homes before "one of the minions of a foreign prince" made his appearance among them. Cameron, the royal agent in the Cherokee nation, "must be bought up, or he would drive them off. They scorned his authority : they would not demean themselves by any attempts to conciliate. They defied him.

> " He ordered them *to depart*."

In after-life Robertson remarked, " this was the best thing ever done by the British Government. Never were threats so harmless, and yet so powerful : they were laughed to scorn. No man feared them out here, whatever they might have done in old Orange and in Wake."

" From a hatred to Tryon, and a contempt for the Indian agent, the people were easily conducted to the cherishing of both sentiments for the king, *their royal master*, as they called him : he was now no longer ours. These acts made a new set of Regulators, patriots, and soldiers out in the mountains ; and they were thus preparing to prove themselves such at ' King's Mountain,' and wherever else God, in his providence, or their country, in her need, should call them."

Some of the Cherokees desired that this order of the agent should not be enforced. Many declared their willingness for the whites to remain, upon condition that no further encroachments were made. The leases were extended, the contracts received further attention and confirmation, and the settlers did all they could to strengthen their title to these lands. In furtherance of this object, they deputed James Robertson and John Brown to negotiate with the Indians ; and for the sum of five or six thousand dollars in goods, some muskets, and other articles required by

---

If Boone and his friends, numbering eighty persons, were defeated on 25th May, 1775, and returned to the new Carolina settlements, none of them, by possibility, could have been present and participated in the organization of a government "under the great elm near the mouth of Otter Creek." That Convention met on the 23d, and the anomalous government was adopted on the 25th, the day of the defeat. Henderson's treaty-purchase was made March 23, 1775. There is a difficulty in settling these dates which it may be worth while to encounter at another time and connection.

the Indians, they obtained a lease of all the lands on the waters of Watauga, for eight years.

John Brown and the few settlers associated with him obtained a similar lease for an extensive tract of country upon the Nolichucky. About this same time the first settlement was made in Carter's Valley. These three settlements were sufficiently adjacent to give "aid and comfort" to each other; and they had been upon quite friendly terms with the Indians, until, at the treaty when the Watauga-lease was executed, some mischievous persons from the Wolf Hills in Virginia killed one of the Indians. The settlers were present in large numbers, and many Indians also. They were engaged in friendly contests at foot-races and other athletic exercises, when this unfortunate murder surprised them all, and gave alarm to white and red men. The very name of the persons who committed this deed was indicative of mischief; there were two or three of them, by the name of Crabtree. They had not participated in any of the sports or entertainments, but had lurked in the woods where the foot-races were run. Having committed this outrage, they returned, as was supposed, to the Wolf Hills, (now Abingdon,) and the citizens promptly consulted as to the proper measures to be adopted to prevent retaliation by the Indians, or, at least, that innocent persons should not be made to suffer for this wrong. Upon due consideration it was deemed advisable to do something more than denounce the act in the presence of Indians who were then on the ground, (and who were making haste to depart.) Some measure must be adopted to convince the nation that all such outrages were discountenanced and condemned by the settlers; therefore they deputed James Robertson to visit the nation, to do all he could to pacify and conciliate them.

It was evident from the haste with which the Indians had departed from the play-grounds, and distinct indications, by words and gesticulations, that they were highly excited and contemplated revenge. The mission of Robertson was therefore one of peril. The chief citizen was about to place his life in the hands of excited and revengeful savages, in very questionable hope of allaying their indignation and anger, so justly aroused. But he had at heart so much the interests of his neighbors, and was so conscious that in all his intercourse and dealings with these red men of the mountains he had given proofs of kindness and good-will toward them, that he had no fear of personal harm. And he well knew that to show to them such intrepidity and fearlessness, and at the same time such respect and confidence as would be manifested by his visit into the nation, was the most certain way to attain the ends

3

he desired. He quickly prepared for the embassy, taking a few presents with him, as was customary. He visited the Cherokee towns, and stated to the chiefs and people that the settlers upon the Watauga had a sincere desire to be at peace, to enjoy their friendship, and to trade with them; that this murder was universally condemned by them; that the perpetrators did not belong to their community, or come under the rules and regulations which they had enacted for their own good behavior; and that if the offender should come into their hands, he should be dealt with as his crime deserved. He remained several days with the chiefs.*

The Indians were gratified at this respect shown their nation, and by the assurances thus given of the friendly disposition of the whites; and they began to conceive a high regard for Robertson, who had conducted himself with so great propriety, dignity, and kindness among them. The skill and success with which he had effected the purposes of his dangerous mission, elevated him in the regard of his fellow-adventurers. From this time he was granted the post of honor; the cares and responsibilities of a leader, in civil and military affairs, were devolved upon him, and to the close of his life he found them to be many and weighty, and with small remuneration in a pecuniary point of view. Indeed, the men who labored most in those days for the service of their fellow-citizens had small desire, hope, or prospect of such reward for their toils and peril. To be credited for "deeds of noble daring," to know that they had done their country some service, that they had relieved or succored the distressed, defended the weak, avenged the wronged, and that these acts were properly appreciated, seemed to be "glory enough," and all the reward they desired. However much of this was due to them, and gratefully and graciously bestowed in their lifetime, the debt is not yet fully discharged; there remains a large accumulation, with compound interest, for their posterity to pay. We are all their debtors, and should delight to do honor to their memories.

---

* During Robertson's visit to the chiefs, he ascertained that the Indians had several prisoners in their nation. Application was made to the Governor to adopt measures to obtain the release of the captives. A demand was made upon the Cherokees for a redress of wrongs and a surrender of prisoners, but the Indians "so shifted the accusation from one tribe to other, that it was without effect."

It has been said that the Crabtrees had lost a brother in the attack on Boone's party, and that this shooting of an Indian at the ball-play was an act of retaliation. "This was the first Indian blood shed by a white man since the treaty of Bouquet."

It was not until the fall of 1774 [Collins' Kentucky] that Mrs. Boone became "the first lady in Kentucky." Boone was then in the employ of Col. Henderson.

" What can we pay for such noble usage,
But grateful praise ? so Heaven itself is paid."

"A grateful mind
By owing owes not, but still pays; at once
Indebted and discharged."

1773. In this year these settlers enjoyed their new homes in quiet: they received many accessions to their numbers, and they were mostly such persons as could be heartily welcomed.

CHAPTER II.

1774—1777.

1774. IN this year many parties of surveyors, with their guards, were sent out by the authority of Virginia, to select and locate royal grants and military warrants in Kentucky ; and as some of these parties passed through the Watauga settlements, they created " quite a sensation," and received there some accession to their numbers. Large tracts of land were selected in the south-western portion of Kentucky, and upon the borders of Tennessee. The settlers on the south side of the division-line noticed some of these surveys with interest, but not with jealousy or dislike. They knew that whosoever should occupy them must be identified with themselves, and that in the peace and prosperity of such settlements, whether north or south of this as yet unestablished boundary-line, all were concerned alike.

The Indians were alarmed at the advances. The claims and acts of these surveyors and woodmen, by word and deed, gave it to be understood that the country was owned by the whites. The Indians saw that they intended ere long to establish themselves therein, and thus occupy the great " stock-farm"—the hunting-grounds between the Tennessee and Ohio rivers. It was the great park for game. There were no Indian towns or settlements between the Ohio and Tennessee. It was open, neutral, vacant pasture-land.

The Shawnees had commenced hostilities by the attack upon the party of Boone. The destruction of the family of Logan, who had previously been the steadfast friend of the whites, aroused that bold warrior to deeds of daring, and he failed not promptly to use his influence among the Shawnees and other tribes to attempt the destruction of " the pale faces," the Virginians.

> " With wings as swift
> As meditation, or the thoughts of love,
> He swept to his revenge."

An alliance was soon formed between the northern and western tribes, and the work of havoc and destruction commenced along the entire Virginia frontier.

The settlers in Carolina upon that frontier could not be unconcerned at these massacres: they might well conclude that, if the settlements in Kentucky were destroyed, their own safety was endangered. They must be involved in the war; and if this should be at a later day, it would probably be under accumulated aggravations and disadvantages, therefore were they concerned to take a decided part at once.

Lord Dunmore, the Governor, was preparing to meet the exigences of the occasion with proper vigor, and to inflict such a blow as would at once terminate or greatly diminish these marauding and murderous incursions. He directed General Andrew Lewis to raise four regiments of militia and volunteers from the south-western counties, to assemble at Camp Union, and march down the Kanawha to the Ohio river.

General Lewis assembled his forces on the Greenbrier river, and there awaited the arrival of other troops, which he knew were organizing in the border-settlements of North Carolina. A company of fifty men was raised and equipped in what are now Sullivan and Carter counties in East Tennessee. This company was under the command of Captain Evan Shelby, and joined the regiment under Colonel Christian in the latter part of August, on New river; thence they proceeded and joined the forces of General Lewis, and the whole army took up the line of march about the first of September, and by slow and difficult advances arrived at the mouth of the Kanawha on the 6th day of October. For four days the army was encamped here, and without apprehension of danger.

1774. Very early in the morning of the 10th October, James Robertson and Valentine Sevier (who were officers in Shelby's company) were beyond the encampment, looking for deer or other game, and came suddenly upon the Indians, who had then advanced to within half a mile of General Lewis's camp. They were approaching in very regular order, and by a line extending from the banks of the Ohio back to the hills, and across the point towards the Kanawha river, evidently intending to confine the Americans to their position on the point between the rivers. Robertson and Sevier were within ten steps of the advancing foe: they fired at the advancing column. It was yet too dark to "take sight" or deliberate aim, but this fire was so unexpected that the Indians came to a general halt, thus affording Robertson and Sevier time to run into the camp, give the alarm, and arouse every man to arms. Instantly was Colonel Charles Lewis ordered to advance with one hundred and fifty men towards the hills and near the Kanawha river. The like force, under Colonel William Fleming, was directed to the right, up the banks of the Ohio. These forces had scarcely passed the line of sentinels, when they were met by the enemy, and a hot and deadly conflict commenced. In a short time the entire forces on each side were fiercely engaged, and the battle continued during most of the day. Many feats of daring and individual contests took place under and along the banks of the rivers, and the dead Americans and Indians were scattered from the waters of the one river to the waters of the other. Before the close of day the savages had retreated, the firing ceased, and the dead and wounded were hunted up and properly attended to.

"Of the Americans, one hundred and sixty were killed and wounded, and about the same number of the savage enemy."*—HAYWOOD.

The celebrated Cornstalk, a Shawnee chief, commanded the united forces of Shawnees, Delawares, Mingoes, and others, throughout the day. It is admitted that "he performed prodigies of valor, and that in whatever direction his voice was heard, from thence immediately issued a thick and deadly fire."

Not alone have the writers of the Annals of Tennessee, and of the biographies of her sons, given great praise to those who marched from East Tennessee and participated in this important battle, but all American historians applaud their conduct. All the provincial officers acknowledge their indebtedness to the two Tennesseeans who so providentially discovered the lurking foe, and fought so bravely throughout the day. It was by many admitted that, but for this timely discovery and alarm, the whole American force would in all probability have been routed and destroyed, upon the land or in the waters of the two rivers. The plan, the advance, and the attack throughout, evinced much judgment and bravery. The frequency with which the Shawnee chief was enabled to renew the assault from point to point, proved his extraordinary influence over his forces, and his readiness to make this a field of blood. He evidently hoped to be able to break the lines and drive the provincials into the rivers. Had he but succeeded in his struggle to penetrate the lines, he doubtless would have made the havoc and destruction much greater.

---

* Commissioned officers killed or wounded,   -   -   12
  Non-commissioned officers and privates killed,   -   -   75
  Wounded,   -   -   -   -   -   -   -   -   141
                Total,   -   -   -   -   -   -   -   228

—Monette.

It certainly is worthy of note that when this battle was fought, the first Provincial Congress was in session at Philadelphia; that in the "backwoods of America" a thousand men could be promptly called into service, equipped, and marched through dense forests, over the mountains and down the valleys, and, under brave and skillful officers, contend with any enemy that might be presented; that they had given the combined forces of the most warlike Indians such a reception and repulse that they did not in force renew their attacks upon the whites until they were assured the whites were at war among themselves, after the Declaration of American Independence.

During the absence of so many heads of families and brave men from the settlements in East Tennessee, we have no record of any alarm or disturbance to those settlements by the neighboring Indians, although it is not doubted that they had information of much of the preparation making for the deadly conflict, whether by the red men or the whites. Enjoying possession of their lands under the several leases and the incipient treaty made by Henderson in 1774, the earliest settlers, and the many who had more recently moved in, had as much land as they then needed; and, with an abundance of game and good crops, they had cause to be thankful and quiet.

1775. Under the compact of government adopted by Robertson and his associates, the affairs of the little community were well conducted. They enjoyed quiet generally, their "clearings in the forest" were extended, log-houses were substituted for tents and "half-faced camps." Their improvements were becoming too valuable and their homes too pleasant to be endangered by the termination of an "eight years' lease." An indefinite extension or renewal on long time began to be talked of as important. There was a general willingness to contribute means in order to secure such a result. Some of the Indian chiefs had manifested a friendly inclination to such desires. In the previous year consultations had taken place, and a scheme been projected among some very enterprising men, to make, not a *lease*, as Robertson and Brown had done, but a *purchase*, of "any extent of country which the Indians would sell." The people on Watauga were too poor to buy more than the territory they had already secured by leases, and with this they were well content, for it was rich and healthy.

Robertson however informed Boone (an agent for persons who contemplated the grand acquisition) that the chiefs and head men of the Cherokees "were becoming fond of gay clothing, of ear and nose-jewels, and of tinkling ornaments." They wished to indulge in some of the white man's tastes and habits. He believed they would trade—would sell.

The Transylvania Land Company was then organized. Colonel Richard Henderson and his associates had, in the year 1774, sent agents among the Cherokees, "to sound the chiefs in regard to a sale of their right and claim to the Kentucky country," of the richness of which Boone and others had given most glowing accounts. These agents said to the Cherokees: "You have no towns there; other Indian hunters kill the game there whenever they please, and probably more of it than do you. None of you have towns in that wilderness. . . . We will pay you for your claim. Come to the Sycamore Shoals, and have a talk with your friends."

Under such persuasions a number of the chiefs, head men, and warriors, made their appearance at the time and place appointed, to meet Colonel Henderson and others. The presence of Robertson was deemed important: he was personally acquainted with several of the influential chiefs: he had learned to converse in the Cherokee language. The Indians had much confidence in him, and it was true, as it was said, "He had winning ways, and made no fuss."

March 17th. "Upon this occasion," says Haywood, "and before the Indians had concluded to make the cession, Oconnostota, a Cherokee orator, called also Chief Warrior and First Representative, as also head prince of the Cherokee nation, (and the same person whose elegant 'Indian-Treaty pitcher' was presented to the Tennessee Historical Society by Mrs. President Polk,) delivered a very animated and pathetic speech" in opposition to any sale of lands; but, in despite of his eloquence and arguments and predictions, the cession was made. "The country which we and our forefathers have so long occupied [to quote the words of the orator] has been called for, and the small remnant of the nation, once so great and powerful, has become almost extinct." His opposition was unavailing, the treaty was made, and the Cherokee claim to Kentucky extinguished.

So much having been granted to Henderson and his associates, the Watauga settlers renewed their application for a change of their lease into a deed; and on the second day after the Henderson Treaty, a conveyance was made to Charles Robertson of a large tract of land, including the settlements upon the Watauga and Holston. Robertson executed regular deeds to the settlers, whose titles were confirmed ultimately by patents.

The deed to Robertson concludes: "The said Charles Robertson, his heirs and assigns, shall and may, peaceably and quietly, have, hold, possess, and enjoy said premises, without let, trouble, hindrance, or molestation, interruption, and denial of them, the said Oconnostota and the rest, or any of the said nation.

Signed in presence of

John Sevier,	Oconnostota,	his X mark.	[Seal.]
Wm. Bailey Smith,			
Jesse Benton,	Attacullecully,	X	[Seal.]
Tillman Dixon,	Tennesy Warrior,	X	[Seal.]
William Blevins,	Willinawaugh.	X	[Seal.]
Thos. Price.			

Jas. Vann, *Linguister.*

Six days later, Jacob Brown obtained a similar deed, for a large and choice body of lands on the *"Nonachucky,"* (now called Nolichucky,) which at this day are the rich and valuable lands in the counties of Greene and Washington.

These purchases were very fairly and honestly made, and were intrinsically of more worth than many a treaty made with greatest formality. And although they were by the State recognized as inchoate titles, (the sanction of the State being required in confirmation,) there was, in fact, no further consideration paid to the Indian grantors. Consequently it is reasonable and just to claim for these early *lessees* and *grantees* from the Indian chiefs, the credit and honor of fair dealings and the true initiative of future treaty-titles.

The Indians never charged Robertson, Sevier, or Brown, with having defrauded them; they never said that these men had deceived them; they never said to either of them, as one chief did to Colonel Henderson, "You, Carolina Dick, are a great rascal: you make believe we sold you more lands than we ever claimed or hunted on."

1774–5. But now our attention is called from the consideration of Indian disturbances to these few settlements, and of the measures which were adopted to secure peace and happy homes. Transactions of a far more solemn character aroused the energies and diffused the spirit of *independence* throughout the Colonies of North America. The measures which had for some time been pursued by the British Government towards these Colonies were moving "the great deep"—the inmost soul of the people—and impelling them to resistance, and ultimately to independence. This tendency was plain.

As early as April 5, 1774, suggestions had been made and measures

proposed for the assembling of a Provincial Congress, to consult and
coöperate with similar bodies in other Colonies as to suitable remonstrances
and opposition to the infringement of their rights. Delegates were
chosen to assemble at Newbern, North Carolina, in August, 1774. The
conclusion of their deliberations was, "resistance to all unconstitutional
encroachments whatsoever."

In the Annals of Tennessee it is happily remarked that though "the
infant settlements west of the mountains do not appear to have been
represented at Newbern, these western pioneers were laying the foundation of society, and her brave soldiery had volunteered in an expedition,
distant, toilsome, dangerous, patriotic, against the inroads of a savage
enemy: thus serving an apprenticeship in self-government and self-
defence, which events transpiring on the Atlantic side of the mountain
soon after rendered necessary and important."

> "Thoughts that frown upon our mirth
> Will smile upon our sorrow,
> And many dark fears of to-day
> May be bright hopes to-morrow."

And thus the patriots of that day thought, trusted, hoped, persevered,
and realized.

We have seen that the settlers on Watauga had early defied the orders
of haughty emissaries of the British Government, to depart from the
homes they had selected in the wilderness, preferring to trust to their
"rights by possession" and confirmations by the Indians. The truth is,
they had no fear of or love for a king who sat upon a throne thousands
of miles distant from them, and the consciousness of whose claims to
authority over them was only felt in the petty annoyances and arrogant
pretensions of strangers, with parchment-roll of high but contemned and
"brief authority."

Governor Martin denied the right of any individuals to enter into
contracts or treaties with the Indians, and claimed for the Colonial Government (or himself) the sole prerogative of sovereignty, and therefore
pronounced the purchases recently made to be illegal; and this he
announced by proclamation, so that the Indian chiefs themselves and
their people might hear of it, and believe that they had been imposed
upon, and consequently unite with the agents of the Governor in annoy-
ing the settlers, and in measures ultimately to drive them away. But he
greatly misjudged the character of these people, and the influence of his
acts and those of his agents. Indeed, we regard the measures and
speeches of men in power at that time, in England and among the

Colonies, as wisely and purposely ordained of Heaven to alienate the Americans, and force them to self-reliance and to independence.

"The second Provincial Congress assembled at Newbern, 3d April, 1775, being the same time and place appointed for the meeting of the Provincial Legislature. The members elected by the people to the one were generally the same elected to the other.

"As the Provincial Assembly, with few exceptions, consisted of the delegates to the Congress, and as the Speaker of the former was also the Moderator of the latter body, their proceedings are a little mixed and farcical. The Congress would be in session when the Governor's secretary would arrive, and then Mr. Moderator Harvey would turn himself into Mr. Speaker Harvey, and proceed to the despatch of public business. The Assembly too would occasionally forget its duty, and trespass upon the business of the Congress."

The Governor had, by proclamation and otherwise, denounced and endeavored to prevent the meetings of Congress: these were met by a counter proclamation, and by the enthusiasm of the people. The result was, "On the 8th April, 1775, the Assembly was dissolved by the Governor's proclamation, and thus ceased for ever all legislative action in North Carolina under the royal government." It was your own act; you cannot say "we did it."

One month later, or on 20th May, was signed and published the "Mecklenburg Declaration of Independence."

There are many proofs that the spirit of independence pervaded a large portion of the people of this State or Colony at that day. If they did not meditate a separation from the mother country, there was a decided spirit of resistance to acts of arbitrary power, and to all attempts at taxation without representation, and to the mode of appointing officers.

In August the Provincial Congress met at Hillsborough. At this time the haughty Governor had fled from his elegant home, and taken refuge on board his Majesty's, King George's, ship "Cruiser," in Cape Fear river. Thence he issued sundry proclamations and orders, the chief and best effect of which was to give the people a "merrier heart, brighter face, and many a jibe, joke, and jollification." They resolved to support the Continental Congress, and this "with an oath," and heartily.

A "Committee of Safety," empowered to preserve peace, order, and good government, was now appointed by the Hillsborough Congress; and it is justly said, "This was the most important committee ever yet appointed by popular authority, and it achieved one of the most difficult and trying ends of the Revolution. It substituted a regular government, resting entirely on popular authority, for that of the royal government, and annihilated every vestige of the power of Jo. Martin. Nothing but the idle and vain 'theory' of allegiance to the throne was left to remind the people of the recent origin of their power."*

We feel confident that the settlers with Robertson, Brown, and Carter, fully participated in the sentiments announced, and heartily concurred in the resolutions of their fellow-citizens, who were more immediately represented in the Congress and popular conventions and committees.

1776. The Congress of North Carolina met again, April 4, 1776, and this body passed "the first resolve, recommending a Declaration of Independence by the Continental Congress." This resolution was passed unanimously, and was presented to the Continental Congress, May 27, 1776, nearly six weeks prior to the Declaration, July 4.

It was ascertained that the measures of the refugee governor, and other royal agents, were brewing mischief in the Indian nations. Orders also from the British War Department were received by John Stuart, Superintendent, and by him widely circulated, to excite the native Indians to acts of violence and blood. The agent, Cameron, who resided among the Cherokees, was active in exertions to arouse the fury of the savages, and he might have had the "infamous reputation of success," had not a "half-breed" woman, known as Nancy Ward, communicated to the people of Holston, Carter's Valley, and Watauga, the preparations making by the Indians for an invasion and war. This intelligence was conveyed to the Committee of Safety in Virginia, and as, at the same time, information was given that some of the people at Brown's station or settlement, were *Tories*, Carter was advised to take prompt measures to " commit them to the 'good cause,' or place them under such surveillance" and care, that no harm should be done by them. A body of men proceeded to Brown's settlement, and called the inhabitants together, not letting them know for what purpose until they convened, and then an oath was administered to be faithful to the cause of American liberties. For further security, Brown's people were united with those on Watauga, with an agreement to elect officers to act for and over all as one settlement. Brown and Carter were elected Colonels, and Wommack, Major, and *James Robertson*, Commandant of the Watauga Fort. Here is the Regulator in appropriate position. These united settlements chose four delegates or representatives to attend the Convention or Congress at Halifax, and they took part in the proceedings and in the act to establish their distant region into a District, to be called Washington; thus, perhaps,

---

* Jones.

being the first to do honor to themselves and the cause of liberty, by selecting the name of the true representative of honor and liberty.

The history of the Watauga government will never be written with entire satisfaction. Complete justice to all the parties, governors and governed, cannot be done. It was simple in its form, democratic in principle, and popular in its administration. The persons who acted at various times as clerk, were men of worth; and the posts of honor and usefulness which they filled in this little community were but initiatory to degrees of greater honor, and to spheres of far more extensive usefulness. Felix Walker, Thomas Gomley, William Tatum, and John Sevier, served their apprenticeship here as clerks.

By the painstaking researches of the worthy annalist of Tennessee, the most interesting document relative to this government which has yet come down to our day, was discovered in the State archives at Raleigh. It is a Petition and Remonstrance of the citizens at Watauga; among other things, praying to be ANNEXED to North Carolina. It is in the handwriting of John Sevier, and is believed to have been composed by him. It will do credit to him who subsequently became Governor of the State of Franklin, and the first Governor of Tennessee. As it belongs also to the history of James Robertson, and is of great interest in its historical statements, we quote it entire :

"*To the Honorable the Provincial Council of North Carolina.*

"The humble petition of the inhabitants of Washington District, including the river Wataugah, Nonachuckie, etc., in Committee assembled, humbly showeth, that about six years ago, Colonel Donelson, in behalf of the Colony of Virginia, held a treaty with the Cherokee Indians, in order to purchase the lands of the Western Frontier; in consequence of which treaty many of your petitioners settled on the lands of the Wataugah, etc., expecting to be within the Virginia line, and consequently hold their lands by their improvements as first settlers; but to their great disappointment, when the line was run, they were (contrary to their expectations) left out; finding themselves thus disappointed, and being too inconveniently situated to remove back, and feeling an unwillingness to lose the labor bestowed on their plantations, they applied to the Cherokee Indians, and leased the land for the term of ten years : before the expiration of which term, it appeared that many persons of distinction were actually making purchases for ever; thus yielding a precedent, (supposing many of them, who were gentlemen of the law, to be better judges of the Constitution than we were,) and, considering the bad consequences it must be attended with, should the reversion be purchased out of our hands, we next proceeded to make a purchase of the lands, reserving those in our possession in sufficient tracts for our own use, and resolving to dispose of the remainder for the good of the community.

"This purchase was made, and the lands acknowledged to us and our heirs for ever, in an open treaty, in Wataugah Old Fields, a deed being obtained from the chiefs of said Cherokee nation, for themselves and their whole nation, conveying a fee-simple right to the said lands, to us and our heirs for ever, which deed was for and in consideration of the sum of two thousand pounds sterling, (paid to them in goods,) for which consideration they acknowledged themselves fully satisfied, contented, and paid, and agreed, for themselves, their whole nation, their heirs, etc., for ever to resign, warrant, and defend the said lands to us and our heirs, etc., against themselves, their heirs, etc.

" The purchase was no sooner made than we were alarmed by the reports of the present unhappy differences between Great Britain and America, on which report (taking the now united colonies for our guide) we proceeded to choose a Committee, which was done unanimously by consent of the people. This committee (willing to become a party in the present unhappy contest) resolved (which is now on our record) to adhere strictly to the rules and orders of the Continental Congress, and in open Committee acknowledged themselves indebted to the United Colonies their full proportion of the Continental expense.

" Finding ourselves on the frontiers, and being apprehensive that, for the want of a proper Legislature, we might become a shelter for such as endeavored to defraud their creditors, considering also the necessity of recording deeds, wills, and doing other public business, we, by consent of the people, formed a Court for the purposes above mentioned, taking (by desire of our constituents) the Virginia laws for our guide, so near as the situation of affairs would admit; this was intended for ourselves, and was done by the consent of every individual; but wherever we had to deal with people out of our district, we have ruled them to bail to abide by our determination; (which was, in fact, leaving the matter to reference;) otherwise we dismissed their suit, lest we should trespass on the Legislature of the Colonies. In short, we have endeavored so strictly to do justice on accounts, etc., from the Colonies, without pretending a right to require the Colony seal.

" We therefore trust we shall be considered, as we deserve, and not as we have (no doubt) been many times represented, as a lawless mob. It is for this reason, we can assure you, that we petition. We now again repeat it, that it is for want of proper authority to try and punish felons, we can only mention to you murderers, horse-thieves, and robbers, and are sorry to say that some of them have escaped us for want of proper authority. We trust, however, this will not long be the case; and we again and again repeat it, that it is for this reason that we petition to this honorable Assembly.

"Above we have given you an extract of our proceedings since our settling on Wataugah, Nonachuckie, etc., in regard to our civil affairs. We have shown you the causes of our first settling, and the disappointments we have met with, the reason of our lease and of our purchase, the manner in which we purchased, and how we hold of the Indians in fee-simple, the causes of our forming a Committee, and the legality of its election, the same of our court and its proceedings, and our reasons for petitioning in regard to our Legislature.

" We will now proceed to give you some account of our military establishments, which were chosen agreeable to the rules established by convention and officers appointed by the Committee. This being done, we thought it proper to raise a company on the District service, as our proportion, to act in the common cause on the sea-shore. A company of fine riflemen were accordingly enlisted, and put under *Captain James Robertson*, and were actually embodied, when we received sundry letters and depositions: (copies of which we now enclose you:) you will then readily judge that there was occasion for them in another place, where we daily expected an attack. We therefore thought proper to station them on our frontiers, in defence of the common cause, at the expense and *risque* of our own private fortunes, till farther public orders, which we flatter ourselves will give no offence. We have enclosed you sundry proceedings at the station where our men now remain.

" We shall now submit the whole to your candid and impartial judgment. We pray your mature and deliberate consideration in our behalf, that you may *annex* us to your province (whether as county, district, or other division) in such manner as may enable us to share in the glorious cause of Liberty, enforce our laws under authority, and in every respect become the best members of society; and for ourselves and constituents we hope we may venture to assure you that we shall adhere strictly to your determinations, and that nothing will be lacking, or any thing neglected, that may add weight (in the civil or military establishments) to the glorious cause in which we are now struggling, or contribute to the welfare of our own or ages yet to come.

" That you may strictly examine every part of this our petition, and delay no time in annexing us to your province, in such a manner as your wisdom shall direct, is the hearty prayer of those who, for themselves and constituents, as in duty bound, shall ever pray.

John Carter, Ch'man,	John Sevier,	John Jones,
Charles Robertson,	Jas. Smith,	George Rusel,
James Robertson,	Jacob Brown,	Jacob Womack,
Zach. Isbell,	Wm. Been,	Robert Lucas.

The above signers are the members in Committee assembled.

WM. TATHAM, Clerk, P. T.

Jacob Womack,	Jos. Brown,	William Newberry,
Joseph Dunham,	Job Bumper,	Adam Sherrell,
Bill Durroon,	Isaac Wilson,	Samuel Sherrell, jun.,
Edward Hopson,	Richard Norton,	Ossa Rose,
Lew. Bowyer, D. Atty.,	George Hutson,	Henry Bates, jun.,
Joseph Butler,	Thomas Simpson,	Jos. Grimes,
Andw. Greear,	Valentine Sevier,	Ch'r Cunningham, sen.
Joab X Mitchell, (his mark.)	Jonathan Tipton,	Joshua Barten, sen.,
	Robert Sevier,	Jond. Bostin, sen.,
Gideon Morris,	Drury Goodan,	Henry Bates, jun.,
William Crocket,	Richard Fletcher,	Will'm Dod,
Thos. Dedmon,	Ellexander Greear,	Groves Morris,
David Hickey,	Jos. Greear,	Wm. Bates,
Mark Mitchell,	Andrew Greear, jun.,	Robt. Mosely,
Hugh Blair,	Teeler Nave,	Geo. Hartt,
Elias Pebeer,	Lewis Jones,	Isaac Wilson,
Jos. Brown,	John J. Cox,	Jno. Waddell,
John Neave,	John Cox, jun.,	Jarret Williams,
John Robinson,	Abraham Cox,	Oldham Hightower,
Christ. Cunningham,	Emanuel Shote,	Abednego Hix,
Jas. Easley,	Tho. Houghton,	Charles McCartney,
Ambrose Hodge,	Jos. Luske,	Frederick Vaughn,
Danl. Morris,	Wm. Reeves,	Jos. McCartney,
Wm. Cox,	David Hughes,	Mark Robertson,
James Easley,	Landon Carter,	Joseph Calvit,
John Haile,	John McCormick,	Joshua Houghton,
Elijah Robertson,	David Crocket,	John Chukinbeard,
William Clark,	Edw'd Cox,	James Cooper,
John X Dunham, (his mark.)	Thos. Hughes,	William Brokees,
	William Roberson,	Julius Robertson,
Wm. Overall,	Henry Siler,	John King,
Matt. Hawkins,	Frederick Calvit,	Michael Hider,
John Brown,	John Moore,	John Davis,
	John Barley.	

This document is without date, but is indorsed, " Received August 22, 1776," and had probably been drawn up in the early part of that year.

It is presumed that the name " *Washington* District" was assumed by the people petitioning, at the suggestion of John Sevier, who had probably been acquainted with Colonel George Washington, now the Commander-in-chief of the American army; for Sevier was a native of Virginia, and had resided at and near Williamsburg. This was a most suitable tribute of respect to the character and patriotism of Washington. Were not these pioneer settlers and patriots of Tennessee *the first* thus to do honor to the Father of his country ?

Although there is left no record of the act granting the especial prayer of this petition for *annexation*, yet subsequent proceedings ɪ rove that such must have been the fact, as the people of this new district were represented in the Provincial Congress at Halifax, in November, 1776, at which the Bill of Rights and State Constitution were adopted. In the roll of members may be found, from " Washington District, Watauga Settlement," Charles Robertson, John Carter, John Haile, John Sevier, and Jacob Womack ; the last named did not attend.

We regard this as one of the most remarkable documents issued by the patriotic men of that day ; it is worthy of the careful study of the scholar and statesman, and the historians of the country.

The *residence* of James Robertson was on the north side of the river, at the upper end of the island ; Colonel Carter's was half a mile north of Elizabethton ; the hospitable *Honeycut's* was near the junction of Roane Creek and Watauga.

The " Watauga Fort" was erected upon a knoll in the bottom-lands, about one mile north-east of the mouth of Gap creek, and is at this day easily identified by the large locust tree and a few graves, on the right of the road to Elizabethton. In this fort the courts of the Watauga Association, or government, were held, and the affairs of administration conducted. There were erected here, of logs and poles, a court-house and jail, the former of which was, in 1782, converted into a stable. Several other forts were erected at convenient points.

The forts erected by these pioneer settlers, were usually made of pieces of timber firmly set in the ground and sharpened at the upper ends, and these surrounded the cabins and a necessary quantity of ground. Loghouses, or block-houses, as they were usually called, with port-holes, commanded the sides of the fort. These block-houses were, in some instances, surrounded by a ditch ; some of them were built with the logs

4

of the second story projecting several feet over the body of the building below, with look-out stations and port-holes at suitable points. The convenience of access to water and wood, and security from positions in which an enemy could find near and secure hiding places from whence to give annoyance, decided the location of these forts and stations. Such defences continued to be necessary for the retreat and protection of all settlements in East and Middle Tennessee down to near the close of the century.

About the middle of March the Watauga Committee received information of a contemplated invasion by the Indians, instigated, as we have seen, by British influence.

The residence of Charles Robertson was on Sinking Creek, near Watauga River, and information was brought to him, and promptly communicated to the Committee, "that the Indians are determined on war. The Cherokees have received a letter from Cameron (the British agent) that the Creeks, Chickasaws, and Choctaws are to join against Georgia, South Carolina, North Carolina, and Virginia; also, that Captain Stuart had gone up the Mississippi with goods, ammunition, etc., for the northern nations, to cause them to fall on the people of the frontier."

This was the savage policy of England against the people of this country. General Gage had said in a letter to Lord Dartmouth, dated Boston, June 12, 1775, "We need not be tender of calling on the savages!" England was no more "tender" *thirty-seven* years later.

The effect of this intelligence and such threats was, to produce a closer union among the settlers and very decided opposition to British influence and rule, as also to cause these woodmen to organize and drill for defensive and offensive war. These men of vigorous arm, of upright and buoyant heart, driven from the homes of their childhood, chiefly by the vexatious and tyrannous acts of a distant government, that had no sympathy in their sufferings, no thanks for their services, and no care for their welfare, were hidden in the fastnesses of the mountains, to be trained by hardships and skilfully prepared for important service and deeds of glory, in the hour of their country's greatest need. Divine Providence kept them as a *corps de reserve*, the body guard of Liberty, the concealed minute-men of Washington, to come forth to Musgrove's Mill and King's Mountain, and turn the tide of battle for their country's relief and safety. . . . .
The purposes of wicked rulers, who would have enslaved them or sold them to savage cruelty, were overruled for the wisest and best of ends.

After the trials were ended, the victory won, and independence acknowledged, these, and thousands of other rejoicing free hearts in America, could say to their brethren of England, as Joseph to his in Egypt : "As for you, ye thought evil against us ; but God meant it unto good, to bring to pass as it is this day, to save much people alive."

> " King though he be,
> And king in England too, he may be weak (and was)
> And vain enough to be ambitious still;
> May exercise amiss his proper powers,
> Or covet more than freemen choose to grant :
> Beyond that mark is treason."

The threat of Indian invasion had, as we have remarked, a most happy effect upon the people at Carter's, Brown's, and Watauga settlements— uniting them to resist the attack, and to denounce the cruel and wicked designs of Britain. They increased their defences.

The fort at Watauga was sometimes called " Fort Lee," and such is the name as given by Sevier, who was in command there.

The following letter from Sevier to the officers of Fincastle county, giving information of the approach of the enemy in large force, is brief indeed, without one word of the little fort having but a force of forty men ; no sign of fear, no solicitation of aid in so great peril. He knew it was enough to say to these patriotic men, " The enemy, six hundred strong, are coming, with the avowed intention to exterminate or drive us away.   .   .   .   *That's all*—let them come. We know you will also come, and so will others ; and we will discuss that matter with them, face to face, with our trusty weapons in our hands, and always ready in defence of our homes, our wives and children, and sacred rights :"

"FORT LEE, July 11, 1776.

" DEAR GENTLEMEN : Isaac Thomas, Wm. Falling, Jarot Williams, and one more, have this moment come in by making their escape from the Indians, and say six hundred Indians and whites were to start for this fort, and intend to drive the country up to New River before they return.   JOHN SEVIER."

July 20th, 1776.—The threatened invasion took place. The Indians, to the number of seven hundred, under chosen leaders, made their appearance near Eaton's Station, which is situated some five or six miles above the junction of the north fork with the main Holston river, and between these two streams. Troops had arrived at this station from the other forts and settlements in the neighborhood, and some small companies from Virginia and the more distant settlements of North Carolina.

Early in the morning of July 20th a force of one hundred and seventy men marched from this station in search of the enemy; discovered, attacked them, killed thirteen or more, and chased the others to some distance. When returning, they were themselves pursued and attacked with great fury and daring. The Indians, attempting to surround the whites, were again defeated, their commander was wounded, and several of the "chief warriors" were killed. The entire number of killed, as far as the Americans ascertained, was forty; this includes some who died of their wounds. "A great day's work in the woods," said Sevier.

The result of this battle was yet more favorable to the settlers than the destruction of some of their savage foes and the abating or checking of the hostile spirit of the Cherokees. It added still more to the determination and union of resolution to resist the cruel purposes of the British Government. It increased the confidence in and esteem for each other; attracted the attention and favor of the new Commonwealth; inspired military ideas and a contempt of danger from Indians; so that afterwards, as Judge Haywood says, "The inquiry, when in search of Indians, was not, 'How many of them are there?' but 'Where are they to be found?'"

July 21. On the next day a party of Cherokees, under the command of "Old Abraham," of Chilhowee, attacked the Watauga Station or Fort Lee, in which were James Robertson, who commanded, Captain John Sevier, and others, forty in all. They were repulsed with some loss.*

---

* It was at this time and place that Captain Sevier received to his arms, as she fled from pursuing savages, Miss Catharine Sherril, who subsequently became his wife. During the winter of 1776–7 Captain Robertson was at Wake county, North Carolina, to settle his private affairs, and to receive from Colonel Michael Rogers, guardian of his brother Mark, the legacies and personal estate to which he was entitled under the will of his father.

CHAPTER III.

1777—1780.

PARTIES of Indians still continued to lurk around the settlements, stealing or killing the cattle, if they could not capture or kill the inhabitants. These annoyances were so frequent and dangerous, that it became manifest that more active measures, upon a large scale, must be adopted to put an end to them. For this purpose it was deemed necessary to carry the war into the Nation. The Indians had too often and for too long a time seen the whites shut up in their forts and taking shelter in their stations; it was high time to prove to them that there were towns and homes in the "Nation," and men, women, and children there, liable to be attacked and destroyed.

With this end in view, the government of Virginia gave orders to Colonel Christian to raise a force and march to the very heart of the Cherokee settlements. "The place of rendezvous was the Great Island of Holston." A number of the Watauga people engaged in this expedition. Robertson accompanied it in command of a small company. He found little occasion for display of warlike spirit in the campaign.

Colonel Christian met with no opposing foe; the Indians, under the counsel of an influential trader among them, named Starr, panic-stricken, fled before the invaders. Christian destroyed several of their towns, and, with some difficulty, induced a few chiefs to meet him to consult on terms of peace. A general council was agreed to be held at Long Island the next May. The army then returned to Long Island and were disbanded. A small force was retained in service, and erected Fort Henry, so named in honor of the patriotic Governor of Virginia.

In the march through the Indian country, the officers and soldiers were surprised to see so rich a body of lands, abundantly watered, attractive, and, in the opinion of all white men, "requiring settlement and cultivation." Many of them, during their march or encampments, made selections for their *future homes;* not counting the cost or consequences to themselves or others.

Intelligence was rapidly communicated to the people upon the Roanoke, in Virginia, and the Yadkin, in Carolina, as to the character of this new country and its adaptation to the purposes of agriculture. The consequence was, the tide of emigration set heavily toward these Indian borders. Under the impression that the settlements were within the limits of Virginia, the military command of the country was committed to Colonel Arthur Campbell, of Washington county, Virginia. He ordered Captain Robertson to keep the people of Watauga assembled at two places, for mutual protection and safety. A force of four hundred men was ordered to be stationed on the south-western frontiers, to protect the inhabitants. This force was divided and placed under the command of Colonel Evan Shelby and Major Anthony Bledsoe. They were fully committed to the war of the Revolution.

These active measures had decided influence in favor of the quiet of all the settlements. A few murders were, however, committed. On the 10th of July, Frederick Calvit was shot and scalped. Captain Robertson pursued the Indians with a small force of nine men, killed one Indian, and retook ten horses. On his return in the evening, he was attacked by a party of Creeks and Cherokees, who wounded two of his men; Robertson returned the fire very bravely, but was obliged to retreat on account of the superior numbers of the enemy, some of whom were at least wounded. It was with much difficulty he " fought his way out." The Indians had surrounded his little party, but yet kept at quite a respectful distance. They appeared in large numbers before him, but gave way as the whites approached, so that the men escaped being wounded, and the entire loads of baggage were saved. Some of the horses were wounded.

Upon his return he aroused the people to further preparations, not merely for defence, but invasion. He had learned that the warlike Indians were probably in the minority. The "peace-party," he believed, would be strengthened by such show of warlike preparations. In this he did not misjudge. Ere long they entered into two treaties, one with commissioners on the part of South Carolina and Georgia, and the other with those appointed on the part of North Carolina and Virginia.

The Cherokees excused themselves for breach of good faith, ascribing the recent outrages to the Chickamaugas, a tribe settled upon a creek of that name, whose chieftain, Dragging Canoe, refused the terms of peace offered by Colonel Christian.

Captain James Robertson was appointed temporary agent for North Carolina, and instructed to repair to Chota, " the beloved town," in company with the warriors returning from the treaty, there to reside until otherwise ordered by the Governor. He was directed to make diligent search into the disposition of all the Indians, to discover persons disaffected to the American cause, have them brought before some proper officer to take the oath of fidelity to the United States, and, in case of refusal, to deal "as the law directs."

This agency and mission, thus intrusted to Robertson, reminds us of that with which Washington was charged by Governor Dinwiddie eight years before. Both youthful men, who had studied the wiles and artifices of the red men; alike watchful and distrustful of the agents and influences at work among them for annoyance and mischief; each having some experience in Indian warfare; known to be calm, prudent, patient, firm, and patriotic. Washington went forth, crossing mountains and rivers, and through the dense forests, to watch and warn and treat with savages, who were acted upon by jealous and unfriendly French Canadians. He was exposed to hardships and perils. He acted prudently and well, and his life was spared for many years of greater trials and service.

Robertson was commissioned to go among Indians whose friendship was no less to be distrusted; through forests and mountain-passes, equally difficult and unbroken, and where the perilous duty of his appointment required him to search out, denounce, arrest, and transport white men, *Tories*, crafty, treacherous, embittered, desperate men; refugees, "enemies of all righteousness" and of their country's cause. But none of these things troubled him; neither counted he his life too dear to be perilled for his country's good.

Wisely and well did he execute the trust, and a kind Providence preserved his life, that he might devote many years to hard, important, and unremitted labor for the establishment of society and government in the then far-off wilderness.

Washington was the patient, persevering, and successful Commander-in-chief; the first great and good President of these United States, happily and providentially raised up and sustained to organize our excellent form of government and set its wheels in motion. Robertson was called of the same wise and kind Providence to the endurance of hardships, to the exercise of patience, perseverance, fortitude, to military command, and to the various duties of civil office. It was ordained of Heaven that they should live and toil for the service of man; that end being accomplished, they did not live in vain. They acted well their parts, and in all of these there was glory and honor.

He rendered himself quite popular among the red men, and accomplished some valuable services for his fellow-citizens. He used to say, in after life: "Without inquiring how, I was restored to citizenship and invested with office in my native State: we lived and fought as neighbors for each other and our united country. Whether we were Virginians or Carolinians we asked and cared not; we were all for the General Congress and for Washington."* From this remark we presume he had reference to the request of the Virginia Commissioners that he would exert his good influence for their State as well as for Carolina, or that his residence was so near the yet undefined boundary between the two States, that it was questionable to which he belonged. The truth is, citizenship rather concerned pioneer neighborhood settlements than State pride.

Another duty enjoined on Robertson in this embassy was, to obtain possession of horses, and all other property belonging to citizens of North Carolina, and have the same restored to the proper owners; he was to inform the government of all occurrences worthy of notice, to conduct himself with prudence, and secure the favor and confidence of the chiefs. In all matters with respect to which he was not particularly instructed, he was to exercise his own discretion, "always keeping in view the honor and interest of the United States in general, and of North Carolina in particular." These instructions were dated on the same day the treaty was signed, 20th July, 1777.†

Thus early and thus efficiently and wisely did the people of these Western wilds exhibit skill, prudence, and firmness in affairs of government. Thus and then did they prove to the world and to posterity that they deserved, as they had resolved, to be a free, sovereign, and independent nation. They needed not, heeded not, and no longer would endure, the dictation and rule of any man or set of men who derived not power and office from the people themselves. And we may fully approve the commendation of the writer of the "Annals of Tennessee" with regard to the character of the anomalous government of Watauga, in which it could be said of our hero, Robertson, *magna pars fuit.* He was ever ready to perform his part, and with only such fee and reward as noble and patriotic men of that day knew how to deserve and value, and their fellow-adventurers to confer.

"No frontier community had ever been better governed than the Watauga settlement. In war and in peace, without legislators or judicial

---

* Mrs. Robertson remembered to have once asked this question: "I wonder if they will make Washington a king?" and the answer was: "If they do, he will be the king of our own choice. We will change the *man,* but not the *name.* He will still be King *George,* by the will of the people and the grace of God.

† See Appendix to Haywood.

tribunals, except those adopted and provided by themselves, the settlers lived in uninterrupted harmony, acting justly to all, offering violence and injury to none."

But the necessity for further continuance of this primitive form of government is about to terminate. The prayer for "*annexation*" is about to be granted, and yet the cares and burdens of defence and government to remain upon the "broad shoulders" of these people.

1777. In November of this year, by act of the State of North Carolina, the District of Washington was formed into a county of the same name; and "lands which have accrued or may accrue to the State by treaty or *conquest*," were made subject to entry, etc., and at very low rates; a liberal allowance being also made for original settlers and heads of families. So favorable were these terms, and the quality of the land so good, that emigrants came in rapidly and in great numbers, and of the most desirable character. The "bone and sinew"—the working men and working women, and working boys. and girls—came. They all came to secure homes, and with hearty good-will and nerve *to work*, and they set about it in earnest, and without hesitation or delay. Such were the founders of society and government in Tennessee.

The people now hoped that they would enjoy peace, and could attend to the clearing and cultivating of their lands and the improvement of their homes; therefore most of the guards were dismissed. But it ere long became evident that this disbanding of the troops was premature, this hope to be "deferred" till yet many a life should be sacrificed, many "a heart made sick."

The question of American independence began to be urged upon every man. It was the policy of the Whigs to ascertain (and this beyond all doubt) who were still openly or covertly adhering to a foreign yoke, and who the decided and reliable friends of American liberty. Therefore Whig Committees of Vigilance and Safety were everywhere organized. They pressed home to every man this one question, and demanded the taking of an oath of fidelity to the good and common cause. There was no neutral ground, and no person could be allowed to be indifferent. Every man, woman, and child took sides; and nowhere was this more the state of feeling and condition of society than in North Carolina; and nowhere else was watchful vigilance more required to guard against domestic foes than among the border settlers of North Carolina. To that remote and mountain-region had many dangerous and maddened Tories fled; to this retreat had escaped outlaws of every name and character. Dreading to fall into the hands of civilized men, and by them to be punished for their crimes; knowing themselves to be deservedly watched and distrusted, because of such offences, as also because they joined not in the common cause, they were ready for any act of annoyance or mischief, and anxious to have the savages partake of their own wicked and revengeful spirit. Often would they charge the Indians with having committed robberies and murders which they themselves had done, personally or by instigation. As the Whigs in office, and Vigilance and Safety Committees, were in possession of the names of most of these men of doubtful or bad character, it was seldom that any of them, when arrested, were enabled to escape with impunity by accusing or implicating the Indians.

The Whigs of the Revolution could truly say, "Indian foes are bad enough, in all conscience, but Tories are white devils." Their numbers were so great about this period that they boasted of their supremacy, defied opposition, and the enforcement of the laws against them ; but ere long it was seen that virtue is strong, principle is irresistible, and liberty triumphant. The Whigs resolved to vindicate the majesty of the laws, to make the nest of these firebrands so hot as to consume them. They renewed their organization of Committees of Safety, who called out skillful marksmen and woodmen, and made it their duty to patrol the whole country, capture all persons who were of suspicious character, put to death such as refused submission, or failed to give good account of themselves, or security for good behavior. Against such as were not charged with gross offences, they were not so severe, but upon them inflicted some punishment believed to be adequate to their guilt. Captain Robertson was a member of one of these companies or committees. In the same company were Sevier, Bean, and other men of unquestionable bravery and attachment to the American cause ; men not to be "practiced with," not to be imposed upon, not easily to be eluded, "dead shots."

A number of these Tory horse-thieves and highwaymen were captured and hung, but the leader and others escaped until the glorious victory of King's Mountain, when this notorious captain of banditti, Grimes, was caught and hung, and some others with him.*

The victory at King's Mountain was therefore a double victory. It relieved the country of a combination of enemies. It turned the tide in the American war. This triumph in these Western wilds sent a thrill of joy to desponding patriotic hearts elsewhere to the Eastern shores. Captain Robertson, as we have remarked, was an active man in all measures for the promotion of the peace, safety, and interests of his patriotic fellow-citizens. His name is enrolled as officer of the militia,

---

* This was *not* "Grimes, that good old man."

member of Committee, and Justice of the Peace. In the records of the Court for Washington County, Feb. 23, 1778, his name is found with those of John Carter, John Sevier, John Shelby, Valentine Sevier, and others, at which a case is presented, as follows :

"THE STATE, *vs.* . . . . . IN TORYISM. } It is the opinion of the court that the defendant be imprisoned *during the present war with Great Britain*, and the Sheriff take the *whole of his estate* into custody, which must be valued by a jury at the next court ; one-half of said estate to be kept by said Sheriff for the use of the State, and the other half to be remitted to the family of defendant."

John Sevier was Clerk of this Court, and Valentine Sevier the Sheriff.

"At —— term of Washington County Court, on motion of E. Dunlap, State Attorney, that J. H., for his ill practices in harboring and abetting disorderly persons, who are prejudicial and inimical to the common cause of liberty, and frequently disturbing our tranquillity in general, be imprisoned for the term of one year.

" The Court, duly considering the allegations alleged and objected against the said J. H., are of opinion that, for his disorderly practices as aforesaid, from time to time, to prevent the further and future practices of the same pernicious nature, do order him to be imprisoned for the term of one year, and is accordingly ordered into the custody of the Sheriff."

In another instance (as copied into the *Annals*) from these County Court records, the court ordered fifteen hundred pounds, current money, to be attached in the hands of the debtor, and appointed John Sevier, Jesse Walton, and Zachariah Isbell, Esqs., commissioners, to take charge of the same.

A number of leaders of the horse-thieves were shot, others bound to appear before the Committee, who imposed fines or inflicted corporal punishment, as they considered the offences merited. By such measures, and the incessant watchfulness known to be maintained, the Tories and Tory horse-thieves were in less than two months driven from the settlement. They openly joined the enemy or sought refuge among the Indians, and encouraged them to deeds of blood and plunder.

Governor Caswell maintained correspondence with Captain Robertson, at this time as Superintendent of Indian Affairs. On the 16th October he transmitted written instructions to Robertson, as such agent, in which he acknowledged the receipt of a letter from Robertson, covering a Talk from old Savanuca, one of the Cherokee chiefs, with whom the agent was on most friendly terms. The Governor enclosed a Talk for the Savanuca, or Old Raven, to be delivered to him and the nation at Chota.   Robertson was informed that it was the wish of the Assembly that he should remain as Indian Agent in the nation, in which request the Governor earnestly concurred.   Thus had he a double authorization for his office and action.

These few—and they are only a few out of many—instances give abundant testimony as to the wisdom, energy, promptness, and perseverance with which these patriots acted in "times which tried men's *souls*," and would have soon wasted away their bodies, had they not possessed "iron frames and nerves of steel."   They had hearts as pure as the most fine gold tried in the furnace of afflictions.

The second term of this County Court was held at the house of Charles Robertson, May 25, 1778, when the three persons named entered into bond for the faithful performance of the duties of "Commissioners of Confiscated Estates."   In the best organized communities in "the States," such proceedings were not better regulated.

CHAPTER IV.

1779.

1779. In passing through the years in regular succession, and enumerating or glancing at current events in which Robertson actively participated, we must mention that in this year there were two expeditions by the Americans into the Indian territories, one under Colonel John Sevier, two hundred strong, who crossed the French Broad river, fought the battle of Boyd's Creek, in which twenty-eight Indians were killed, and not one of Sevier's troop even wounded; the other under Colonel Evan Shelby to the Chickawauga towns, with five hundred men. The Indians fled before him, and escaped. With a large stock of horses, cattle, and deer-skins, taken from the retreating foe, Shelby returned to the settlements on the Holston.

The extensive purchase made by the Henderson Associates, and the further reports made by hunters and agents of the large land company as to the country beyond the mountains, and the very favorable terms upon which large tracts—a thousand acres—would probably be granted, were attracting unusual attention. The Hendersons, Hart, and other members of the company were now causing it to be extensively known that they were making preparations to emigrate, and take possession of the country. A considerable number of families agreed to move out in the fall. Some were to go by land, with cattle and what could thus be packed, others to descend the Tennessee to the Muscle Shoals, and being there met by their immediate friends, travel across to the Cumberland and into Kentucky; or if it should be deemed easiest and best, this party, with women and children, should continue all the distance by water. Many families were coming from the older portion of Virginia, destined for "Kentucky County," others for "Illinois County." These Virginians had friends already at the towns in Illinois, and were disposed to join them.

Among the persons at Watauga and Holston there were many of the old "Regulators," who had escaped the hands of the royalists. The cause of American Independence in the Carolinas and Georgia was shrouded in gloom; but Virginia was making conquests in the Far West. On each side of the Ohio was she organizing governments and establishing settlements. These were attractive to her citizens, and now, in the very trying hour of the War of Independence, were many of her yeomanry moving into her distant and wilderness territory; and this with a certainty of encountering savage Indians, instigated and aided by the common enemy.

The business of "boat-building" was now commenced in earnest. In the construction of most of the "water-craft" to be used by the emigrants in the contemplated voyage, a single tree, generally a poplar, was selected, and by the axe and adze a canoe or perogue was fashioned. A few "scows" or flat-bottomed boats were made of sawed plank, boarded up at the sides, with a roof covering the entire or only half the length of the boat.

"The Adventure" was to be the "flag-ship." This was a "partnership concern," and was to be large enough and so arranged as to accommodate a dozen or twenty families. This was to be under the immediate command of Colonel John Donelson, from Virginia, whose aim was to reach the contemplated spot on the Cumberland, and, as he, in his notes of surveys, would say : "Beginning at the French Lick, thence east by the Barren river and Kentucky river to the Ohio, thence with its meanders down to its junction with the Mississippi, down that to Lower Chickasaw Bluff, thence south to where the line would cross the Big Tennessee, up that river to Muscle Shoals, and around and with the *Great Bend*, so as to include, for me and my heirs, as rich land *there* as Colonel Henderson and his heirs will obtain on the Kentucky."

The fact is, Colonel Donelson had his surveyor's eye upon the Bend of Tennessee, but had agreed to conduct the "Adventure" and her precious cargo to the French Lick, from whence he would go and locate the many military claims he owned or could purchase. Grants known as "cabin-rights" were in that day offered for sale, as land-scrip or warrants are in this. These were bestowed under an act of much liberality passed by the State of Virginia.

Washington and Lee and Madison had an ambition to be large landowners. Donelson, who was associated with General Washington and other capitalists of Virginia, in one land company, came out West with the purpose of "enlarging his possessions." Surveyors had an advantage over other persons in selecting lands.

General Sevier also had caught the "land-fever" in Old Virginia, but he was too fond of popularity and of Indian warfare to make any good or extensive selections, and to secure perfect titles. Robertson wished to own lands, and, in his day, did own a vast amount of land; but he, like his friend Sevier, "preferred to serve, survey, and save the people, than to blaze and block, chip and chop, lot and plot, the richest lands in Sumner county."

But none of these great men ever entertained so large an idea, a project so vast, as that of Colonel Henderson. He would extend "from centre to circumference;" he would "grasp in all the shore," and this by treaty.

Boone expressed the sentiment of all of these men and of thousands of others; and, though he little thought of it, he uttered the will of Heaven: "Now is the time to secure all this country: we've got it, let's keep it!"

Why else was it put into the mind of Washington to enter and buy lands above and below and between the mouths of the Great and Little Kanawha? Why, under Providence, did so many of Washington's neighbors and acquaintance become land-owners at such great distances from their actual homes? Why Madison at the Grand Gulf on the Mississippi, and Randolph not far off? And to go farther back, only a step in the preparatory measures of Providence: Why did Britain grant twenty thousand acres to General Putnam below the mouth of the Yazoo, the like quantity to General Schuyler below the Walnut Hills, and the same amount to Thaddeus Lyman on the Bayou Pierre, for services in the French war of 1756; and then refuse them patents because they were Whigs or rebels? Was it another instance, wisely ordered, to make *old soldiers* "just mad enough to fight?" And was it to cause native-born Americans to "spread themselves," become concerned by varied and strong interests in distant portions of the wild uninhabited continent, over which it was ordained the one great united people should bear rule?

Preparatory to this emigration, it was agreed that a number of men should go in the spring of this year and plant some corn upon the Cumberland, that bread might be prepared for the main body of emigrants upon their arrival in the fall. To reach this point they would have to travel over five hundred miles by land, taking the circuitous route of the hunters; by water, more than one thousand. Robertson selected his men or found suitable volunteers to go with him, experienced woodmen and able-bodied men. They knew the importance of such a mission: they were intimate friends, good men and true.

Other parties were about to adopt the same measures. That tireless hunter, Gasper Mansker, was about to escort a few persons to the same section of country. Mansker had announced the place he intended to occupy, having killed deer and buffalo at the Sulphur Spring. So it was with the Bledsoes, who would not, however, go in company with others, this spring.

Sacks of corn and other grain were provided, and Robertson was ready the last of February to set out.

It seems strange that such a man, with such capacities for usefulness, and with these properly appreciated by his fellow-citizens, after enduring so much to secure a home, and with the advantage and privilege almost of " first choice," should be willing to abandon all his prospects there— esteem his toils, privations, perils, and sufferings *not enough*, or so far short of that measure, that he must seek for more and greater! But such was the man—such were many of the men of that day. And the women —God bless them—were made of the same stuff, and exactly to match. If any man could stay with honor and be useful, it was he, but he felt impelled to "arise and go forward."

"What fates impose, that man must needs abide;
It boots not to resist both wind and tide."

Early in this year, Robertson, accompanied by George Freeland, William Neely, Edward Swanson, James Hanly, Mark Robertson, Zachariah Wells, and William Overhall, and one negro man, set out on this adventure, to examine and settle upon lands which were believed to be included within the purchase made by Richard Henderson and company, at the treaty of 1775. They continued their wanderings and explorations, often following buffalo-paths, which almost invariably led through the dense forests and cane-brakes from water to water, and, more distinctly trodden, from one salt or sulphur spring to another, until they finally arrived at the present site of Nashville, the capital of Tennessee. Soon after their arrival, another small party, under the guidance of Gasper Mansker, (often erroneously written Casper Mansco,) arrived. Mansker had been here several years previously, when on a hunting expedition. They all united in planting corn near the Sulphur Spring.

Having aided in the making of some rude fences, and in the planting of corn, as also in "jerking of meat," (an abundant stock,) Captain Robertson mounted his horse, and "struck out into the wilderness" toward the rising of the sun. It was agreed that some of these first of the pioneers should remain to guard and gather the crops; others might return to the Watauga and Holston to assist the families in setting out, and return with additional emigrants in the fall. But Robertson had agreed to go to the Illinois and purchase "cabin-rights" of General George Rogers Clarke, from whom some of the emigrants recently from

Virginia gave assurance that such land-claims could be procured for very small sums.

In pursuance of such promise he made the journey, visited General Clarke, and had an understanding with him, to be carried into execution upon subsequent application. Not having to expend his money for the land-claims, " Robertson invested in she asses, mares, and tough pony-horses," and having found two or three men who wished to return to " the settlements," "he offered them seats upon the choicest of his animals."

With this drove they made their way across rivers, through forests and barrens, and over the mountains to Watauga, and were in time to "join the caravan" and march back much of the way they had come, and then, diverging to the north-west, strike upon the large buffalo-trails, and so approach the place of destination.

Kasper Mansker, Abraham Bledsoe, John Rains, and a few others, were adventurous hunters and explorers upon the Cumberland, on the east side, in the year 1769–70. And again, in 1771, Mansker, accompanied by Isaac Bledsoe, Joseph Drake, and a few others, visited the country. Springs, licks, creeks, and other localities well known at this day, were discovered by some of these pioneers, and yet bear their names. They had not crossed to the west of the river. Mansker came again in 1775, but none of the party remained. Michael Stoner was hunting upon the east side of Cumberland river, and between that river and the one ever since known as Stone's river. Stoner was here at as early a day as any other white man, except De Monbreun, a Frenchman, who had a cabin and dépôt for deer and buffalo hides and tallow, at the mound on the north side of the Sulphur Spring branch, a short distance from the mouth thereof.

Having mentioned these worthy persons as predecessors—the very discoverers of the rich bottoms and choice springs upon and near the Cumberland river—we shall proceed with our main narrative and its principal personage; and at the same time we disclaim all willingness to be considered as arrogating for Robertson undue honor, or any commendation he does not fully deserve. It is not needed or proper to detract from the merits of any of the worthy men who cast in their lot with him in this hazardous enterprise, in order to exhibit him in all his just proportions as a citizen, or in his civil or military character.

> " Let none presume
> To wear an undeservèd dignity.
> Good actions crown themselves with lasting bays:
> Who well deserves, needs not another's praise."

During the summer of this year the arrangements were made by

5

several families to start for the Cumberland. One party of emigrants
was to take the land route, which was a difficult and circuitous one, and
with stations or localities known as Cumberland Gap, Kentucky Trace to
Whitley's Station on Dick's river, thence to Carpenter's Station on Green
river, thence to Robertson's Fork on the north side of that stream, down
the river to Pittman's Station, crossing and descending that river to Little
Barren river, crossing Barren at the Elk Lick, passing the Blue Spring
and Dripping Spring to Big Barren River, thence up Drake's Creek to a
bituminous spring, (yet known,) thence to the Maple Swamp, thence to
Red River at Kilgore's Station, thence to Mansker's Lick, and thence to
the French Lick or Bluffs. With the exception of the first and last two of
these places, they are all in Kentucky. Some parties, in reaching the
Cumberland from East Tennessee, travelled as far out of the way as to a
station where Lexington now is, thence by Harrod's Station, now Harrodsburg, and so "around and around about."

The season was remarkably inclement. The winter of 1779–80 has
ever been mentioned as "*the cold winter,*" one of extraordinary severity.
The cold commenced early, and the emigrants by land encountered much
difficulty in their route, yet they arrived at the place appointed for rendezvous in safety, no deaths having occurred among them, and without
any attack by the Indians. They reached the river in December, 1779,
and between the middle of that month and the 1st January crossed the
river to where Nashville is now situated. The ice in the river was sufficiently solid to allow Captain Rains's cattle to pass over upon it. It is believed that the first day they passed at the Lick was "Christmas day," 1779.

On their way the Robertson party was overtaken by the emigrants
under the supervision and direction of Mr. John Rains, designing to go
to Harrod's Station. They were persuaded to join the Robertson emigrants.* Some others were added to their numbers at various points, so
that when they were all assembled upon the Cumberland, there were more
than two hundred, and many of them young men without families. A
number determined to settle on the east side of the river, and selected a
station about one and a half miles below the Bluffs, which was called
Eaton's or Heaton's Station, as Amos Eaton was one of that party.
About the same time there arrived a party from South Carolina, in which
were the two Buchanans, John and Alexander, two Mulherrins, Sampson
Williams, and Thomas Thompson. Rains immediately selected his body

* Rains had examined both sections of country, and declared "he felt like the
man who wanted a wife, and knew of two beautiful women, either of whom would
suit, and 'he wanted them both.'"

of land, and built pens for his nineteen cows, two steers, and seventeen horses, near the spring on Brown's Creek, (now between the turnpike and railroad to Franklin,) about two and a half miles south of Nashville.

Mr. Rains is entitled to the credit of being the first man to introduce neat cattle and horses upon the west side of the Cumberland river and into Middle Tennessee. And of this act it may be said, it was good, wise, and provident, and the benefit of the example has not been lost upon his posterity.

Many of these adventurers were also prompt in making selections of locations, marking some of the trees, clearing small tracts, erecting small cabins, not " despising the day of small things."

It will be remembered that at Robertson's former visit to the Cumberland, it was thought advisable that he should go to Kaskaskia, Illinois, " to buy cabin-rights from General Clarke." Robertson was under the impression that this Cumberland region would, when the line should be run, belong to Virginia, and therefore he was willing to undertake another long and tedious journey for the advantage of himself and associates. In estimating the hazard and weariness of such a journey, we must remember that it was to be accomplished on foot, and through a trackless wilderness, encountering and escaping he knew not how many foes— beasts and men; encountering and overcoming he knew not how many obstacles; encountering and crossing he knew not how many rivers! It is a tedious journey in our day, with all the improvements of civilized society—a thousand cultivated farms, flourishing towns and cities, and macadamized and railroads, and steamboats. But Robertson encountered all the difficulties and perils fearlessly and cheerfully, and returned a second time by Harrod's Station, the Kentucky trace, and Cumberland Gap, to the Watauga settlements.

Whatever arrangement he may have made with General Clarke, we know not, but soon after the arrival of the emigrants in 1780, the opinion began to prevail that the correct dividing-line would leave the lands upon which they were about to settle within the jurisdiction of North Carolina, where the " cabin-rights" granted by Virginia would not entitle the holder to possession. Richard Henderson was now out with a surveying-party tracing the line, and was in the neighborhood of the French Lick, and of these newly arrived emigrants. He was expected to unite with them in measures for defence against the Indians and for the harmonious adjustment of locations for themselves, as also in the organization of a government similar to that which had existed at Watauga. It is true that his last Indian treaty did not include any land south or west of the Cumberland river, but it covered all between that river and the Ohio.

And quite a princely estate would the present State of Kentucky have been for any one man, or one thousand ; but in lieu of these millions of acres he finally obtained two hundred thousand acres in what is now Henderson county, on the Ohio river.

But as a number of these first adventurers and explorers returned for their wives and children, and to aid other parties of emigrants, so must we in our narrative return and accompany some of the friends and families of these first settlers on their " winding way" to this " land of promise."

We have mentioned that the emigrants by land, with Robertson and other leaders, passed through the wilderness and reached their destination without attack by the Indians, and without the loss of one person, or any property : the party of emigrants to whom it is our duty now to attend were far less favored. The wife of Captain Robertson, and five children, and the wives and children of several others, were in the party who were now to *adventure* the very long, hazardous, and unexplored route by water, down the Holston, down the Tennessee to its junction with the Ohio, then up the Ohio, and up the Cumberland to French Salt Spring. The buoyant, cheerful spirit of the women seemed never to fail, and they permitted not the men to do all the hard labor in the navigation, but often would not be denied the privilege of lending a helping hand.

> " They worked with paddle, pole, and oar :
> They worked when every hand was sore :
> They worked with cheerful heart, and more—
> They worked with paddle, pole, and oar,
> Until they need to work no more,
> Now landed at the wished-for shore."

Although the narrative or journal of this voyage has repeatedly been published, it makes such an important portion of the history of the first settlements upon the Cumberland, and is so connected with the life and times of James Robertson, that we hesitate not to introduce it entire into our narrative.*

---

* One of the visits made by Captain Robertson to Illinois was not by land, but by a still more laborious and dangerous route. He made it by water, in a skiff or canoe, accompanied by Mark Robertson and one other, descending the Cumberland and Ohio, and, with extreme toil, up the Mississippi. He purchased some Spanish or Indian mares, and with them made his way through Illinois, over the Ohio river, through Kentucky, and to Watauga. Some of those animals were afterward brought to the Cumberland. So says Dr. Felix Robertson, and we have noticed it as we understand it.

1779.—VOYAGE OF THE DONELSON PARTY.

"JOURNAL OF A VOYAGE, intended by God's permission, in the good boat Adventure, from Fort Patrick Henry, on Holston river, to the French Salt Springs on Cumberland river, kept by John Donelson.

"December 22, 1779.—Took our departure from the fort, and fell down the river to the mouth of Reedy creek, where we were stopped by the fall of water and most excessive hard frost; and after much delay, and many difficulties, we arrived at the mouth of Cloud's Creek on Sunday evening, the 20th February, 1780, where we lay by until Sunday, the 27th, when we took our departure with sundry other vessels bound for the same voyage, and on the same day struck the Poor-valley shoal, together with Mr. Boyd and Mr. Rounsifer, on which shoal we lay that afternoon and succeeding night in much distress.

" Monday, February 28th, 1780.—In the morning, the water rising, we got off the shoal, after landing thirty persons to lighten our boat. In attempting to land on an island, received some damage, and lost sundry articles, and came to camp on the south shore, where we joined sundry other vessels also bound down.

" Tuesday, 29th.—Proceeded down the river and encamped on the north shore, the afternoon and following day proving rainy.

" Wednesday, March 1st.—Proceeded on, and encamped on the north shore, nothing happening that day remarkable.

" March 2d.—Rain about half the day; passed the mouth of French Broad river, and about twelve o'clock Mr. Henry's boat, being driven on the point of an island by the force of the current, was sunk, the whole cargo much damaged, and the crew's lives much endangered, which occasioned the whole fleet to put on shore, and go to their assistance, but with much difficulty baled her out and raised her, in order to take in her cargo again. The same afternoon Reuben Harrison went out a hunting, and did not return that night, though many guns were fired to fetch him in.

" Friday, 3d.—Early in the morning fired a four-pounder for the lost man, sent out sundry persons to search the woods for him, firing many guns that day and the succeeding night, but all without success, to the great grief of his parents and fellow-travellers.

" Saturday, 4th.—Proceeded on our voyage, leaving old Mr. Harrison, with some other vessels, to make further search for his lost son : about ten o'clock the same day found him a considerable distance down the river, where Mr. Ben. Below took him on board his boat. At three o'clock P.M., passed the mouth of Tennessee river, and camped on the south shore, about ten miles below the mouth of Tennessee.

"Sunday, 5th.—Cast off and got under way before sunrise; twelve o'clock, passed mouth of Clinch; at three o'clock P.M., came up with the Clinch River company, whom we joined, and camped, the evening proving rainy.

"Monday 6th.—Got under way before sunrise: the morning proving very foggy, many of the fleet were much bogged: about ten o'cock lay by for them; when collected, proceeded down: camped on the north shore, where Captain Hutching's negro man died, being much frosted in his feet and legs, of which he died.

"Tuesday, 7th.—Got under way very early: the day proving very windy, a S.S.W., and the river being wide, occasioned a high sea, insomuch that some of the smaller crafts were in danger, therefore came to at the uppermost Chickamauga town, which was then evacuated, where we lay by that afternoon and camped that night. The wife of Ephraim Peyton was here delivered of a child. Mr. Peyton has gone through by land with Captain Robertson.

"Wednesday, 8th.—Cast off at ten o'clock, and proceeded down to an Indian village, which was inhabited, on the south side of the river: they invited us to 'come ashore,' called us brothers, and showed other signs of friendship, insomuch that Mr. John Caffrey and my son, then on board, took a canoe which I had in tow, and were crossing over to them, the rest of the fleet having landed on the opposite shore. After they had gone some distance, a half-breed, who called himself Archy Coody, with several other Indians, jumped into a canoe, met them, and advised them to return to the boat, which they did, together with Coody, and several canoes, which left the shore and followed directly after him. They appeared to be friendly. After distributing some presents among them, with which they seemed much pleased, we observed a number of Indians on the other side embarking in their canoes, armed and painted with red and black. Coody immediately made signs to his companions, ordering them to quit the boat, which they did, himself and another Indian remaining with us, and telling us to move off instantly. We had not gone far before we discovered a number of Indians armed and painted, proceeding down the river, as it were to intercept us. Coody, the half-breed, and his companion sailed with us for some time, and telling us that we had passed all the towns, and were out of danger, left us. But we had not gone far until we come in sight of another town, situated likewise on the south side of the river, nearly opposite a small island. Here they again invited us to come on shore, called us brothers, and observing the boats standing off for the opposite channel, told us that 'their side of the river was better for boats to pass.' And here we must regret the unfortunate death of young Mr. Payne, on board Captain Blackemore's boat, who was mortally wounded by reason of the boat running too near the northern shore, opposite the town where some of the enemy lay concealed; and the more tragical misfortune of poor Stuart, his family and friends, to the number of twenty-eight persons. This man had embarked with us for the Western country, but his family being diseased with the small-pox, it was agreed upon between him and the company that he should keep at some distance in the rear, for fear of the infection spreading; and he was warned each night when the encampment should take place by the sound of a horn. After we had passed the town, the Indians having now collected to a considerable number, observing his helpless situation, singled off from the rest of the fleet, intercepted him, killed and took prisoners the whole crew, to the great grief of the whole company, uncertain how soon they might share the same fate: their cries were distinctly heard by those boats in the rear. We still perceived them marching down the river in considerable bodies, keeping pace with us until the Cumberland Mountain withdrew them from our sight, when we were in hopes we had escaped them. We are now arrived at the place called Whirl, or Suck, where the river is compressed within less than half its common width above, by the Cumberland Mountain, which juts in on both sides. In passing through the upper part of these narrows, at a place described by Coody, which he termed the 'boiling pot,' a trivial accident had nearly ruined the expedition. One of the company, John Cotton, who was moving down in a large canoe, had attached it to Robert Cartwright's boat, into which he and his family had gone for safety. The canoe was here overturned, and the little cargo lost. The company, pitying his distress, concluded to halt and assist him in recovering his property. They had landed on the northern shore, at a level spot, and were going up to the place, when the Indians, to our astonishment, appeared immediately over us on the opposite cliffs, and commenced firing down upon us, which occasioned a precipitate retreat to the boats. We immediately moved off. The Indians, lining the bluffs along, continued their fire from the heights on our boats below, without doing any other injury than wounding four slightly. Jennings's boat is missing.

"We have now passed through the Whirl. The river widens with a placid and gentle current, and all the company appear to be in safety, except the family of Jonathan Jennings, whose boat ran on a large rock projecting out from the northern shore, and partly immersed in water, immediately at the Whirl, where we were compelled to leave them, per-

haps to be slaughtered by their merciless enemies. Continued to sail on
that day, and floated throughout the following night.

"Thursday, 9th.—Proceeded on our journey, nothing happening worthy
of attention to-day; floated until about midnight, and encamped on the
northern shore.

"Friday, 10th.—This morning about four o'clock we were surprised
by the cries of 'Help poor Jennings,' at some distance in the rear. He
had discovered us by our fires, and came up in the most wretched condition. He states, that as soon as the Indians had discovered his situation, they turned their whole attention to him, and kept up a most
galling fire on his boat. He ordered his wife, a son nearly grown, a
young man who accompanied them, and his two negroes, to throw all his
goods into the river, to lighten their boat for the purpose of getting her
off; himself returning their fire as well as he could, being a good soldier
and an excellent marksman. But before they had accomplished their
object, his son, the young man, and the negro man jumped out of the
boat and left them: he thinks the young man and the negro were wounded.
Before they left the boat, Mrs. Jennings, however, and the negro woman
succeeded in unloading the boat, but chiefly by the exertions of Mrs.
Jennings, who got out of the boat and shoved her off; but was near falling a victim to her own intrepidity, on account of the boat starting so
suddenly as soon as loosened from the rocks. Upon examination he
appears to have made a wonderful escape, for his boat is pierced in
numberless places with bullets. It is to be remarked that Mrs. Peyton,
who was the night before delivered of an infant, which was unfortunately
killed in the hurry and confusion consequent upon such a disaster,
assisted them, being frequently exposed to wet and cold then and afterwards, and that her health appears to be good at this time, and I think
and hope she will do well. Their clothes were very much cut with
bullets, especially Mrs. Jennings's.

"Saturday, 11th.—Got under way after having distributed the family
of Mrs. Jennings in the other boats. Rowed on quietly that day, and
encamped for the night on the northern shore.

"Sunday, 12th.—Set out, and after a few hours' sailing we heard the
crowing of cocks, and soon came within view of the town: here they
fired on us again without doing any injury. After running until about
ten o'clock, came in sight of the Muscle Shoals. Halted on the northern
shore at the upper end of the shoals, in order to search for the signs
Captain James Robertson was to make for us at that place. He set out
from Holston early in the fall of 1779, and was to proceed by the way of
Kentucky to the Big Salt Lick on Cumberland river, with several others

in company, was to come across from the Big Salt Lick to the upper end of the shoals, there to make such signs that we might know he had been there, and that it was practicable for us to go across by land. But to our great mortification we can find none, from which we conclude that it would not be prudent to make the attempt; and are determined, knowing ourselves to be in such imminent danger, to pursue our journey down the river. After trimming our boats in the best manner possible, we ran through the shoals before night. When we approached them they had a dreadful appearance to those who had never seen them before. The water being high made a terrible roaring, which could be heard at some distance among the drift-wood heaped frightfully upon the points of the islands, the current running in every possible direction. Here we did not know how soon we should be dashed to pieces, and all our troubles ended at once. Our boats frequently dragged on the bottom, and appeared constantly in danger of striking: they warped as much as in a rough sea. But, by the hand of Providence, we are now preserved from this danger also. I know not the length of this wonderful shoal: it had been represented to me to be twenty-five or thirty miles; if so, we must have descended very rapidly, as indeed we did, for we passed it in about three hours. Came to, and encamped on the northern shore, not far below the shoals, for the night.

" Monday, 13th.—Got under way early in the morning, and made a good run that day.

" Tuesday, 14th.—Set out early. On this day two boats, approaching too near the shore, were fired on by the Indians; five of the crew were wounded, but not dangerously. Came to camp at night near the mouth of a creek. After kindling fires and preparing for rest, the company were alarmed on account of the incessant barking our dogs kept up; taking it for granted the Indians were attempting to surprise us, we retreated precipitately to the boats, fell down the river about a mile, and encamped on the other shore. In the morning I prevailed on Mr. Caffrey and my son to cross below in a canoe, and return to the place; which they did, and found an African negro we had left in the hurry, asleep by one of the fires. The voyagers then returned and collected their utensils which had been left.

" Wednesday, 15th.—Got under way, and moved on peaceably on the five following days, when we arrived at the mouth of the Tennessee on Monday the 20th, and landed on the lower point, immediately on the bank of the Ohio. Our situation here is truly disagreeable. The river is very high and the current rapid, our boats not constructed for the purpose of stemming a rapid stream, our provision exhausted, the crews

almost worn down with hunger and fatigue, and know not what distance
we have to go, or what time it will take us to our place of destination.
The scene is rendered still more melancholy, as several boats will not
attempt to ascend the rapid current. Some intend to descend the
Mississippi to Natchez; others are bound for the Illinois—among the
rest my son-in-law and daughter. We now part, perhaps to meet no
more, for I am determined to pursue my course, happen what will.

"Tuesday, 21st.—Set out, and on this day labored very hard, and got
but a little way : camped on the south bank of the Ohio. Passed the
two following days as the former, suffering much from hunger and
fatigue.

"Friday, 24th.—About three o'clock came to the mouth of a river
which I thought was the Cumberland. Some of the company declared it
could not be, it was so much smaller than was expected. But I never
heard of any river running in between the Cumberland and Tennessee.
It appeared to flow with a gentle current. We determined, however, to
make the trial, pushed up some distance, and encamped for the night.

"Saturday, 25th.—To-day we are much encouraged ; the river grows
wider; the current is very gentle : we are now convinced it is the Cumberland. I have derived great assistance from a small square sail, which
was fixed up on the day we left the mouth of the river ; and to prevent
any ill effects from sudden flaws of wind, a man was stationed at each of
the lower corners of the sheet, with directions to give way whenever it
was necessary.

"Sunday, 26th.—Got under way early ; procured some buffalo meat :
though poor, it was palatable.

"Monday, 27th.—Set out again ; killed a swan, which was very
delicious.

"Tuesday, 28th.—Set out very early this morning ; killed some buffalo.

"Wednesday, 29th.—Proceeded up the river ; gathered some herbs
on the bottoms of Cumberland, which some of the company called
' Shawanee salad.'*

"Thursday, 30th.—Proceeded on our voyage. This day we killed
some more buffalo.

---

* This "Shawanee salad" has given name and distinction to this locality. The
Rev. Dr. Green, of Nashville, in his Reminiscences of Missionary Services, and
of Fishing Excursions, tells a very good story to arrive at the origin of the name
of this place, " Pat's *Ingun* Patch." We think that neither an Irishman nor an Irishman's name had any thing to do with it ; but that, in honor of Col. Donelson's old negro
cook, "*Patsy*"—but always called "*Pats, for short*"—who gathered and cooked and
recommended " *the greens*," the place was named " Pat's Ingun or Onion Patch."

" Friday, 31st.—Set out this day, and, after running some distance, met with Col. Richard Henderson, who was running the line between Virginia and North Carolina. At this meeting we were much rejoiced. He gave us every information we wished, and further informed us that he had purchased a quantity of corn in Kentucky, to be shipped at the Falls of Ohio, for the use of the Cumberland settlement. We are now without bread, and are compelled to hunt the buffalo to preserve life. Worn out with fatigue, our progress at present is slow. Camped at night near the mouth of a little river, at which place, and below, there is a handsome bottom of rich land. Here we found a pair of hand mill-stones, set up for grinding, but appeared not to have been used for a great length of time. Proceeded on quietly until the 12th of April, at which time we came to the mouth of a little river running in on the north side, by Moses Renfroe and his company called ' Red River,' up which they intended to settle. Here they took leave of us. We proceeded up Cumberland, nothing happening material until the 23d, when we reached the first settlement on the north side of the river, one mile and a half below the Big Salt Lick, and called Eaton's Station, after a man of that name, who, with several other families, came through Kentucky and settled there.

" Monday, April 24th.—This day we arrived at our journey's end at the Big Salt Lick, where we have the pleasure of finding Capt. Robertson and his company. It is a source of satisfaction to us to be enabled to restore to him and others their families and friends, who were intrusted to our care, and who, some time since, perhaps, despaired of ever meeting again. Though our prospects at present are dreary, we have found a few log-cabins which have been built on a cedar bluff above the Lick by Capt. Robertson and his company."

The names of the persons who came in this company are given by Capt. Donelson as follows :

John Donelson, Sr.,	Jonathan Jennings,	Frank Armstrong,
Thomas Hutchings,	Benjamin Belew,	Hugh Rogan,
John Caffrey,	Peter Looney,	Daniel Chambers,
John Donelson, Jr.,	Capt. Jno. Blackemore,	Robert Cartwright,
James Robertson's	Moses Renfroe,	—— Stuart,
lady and children,	Wm. Crutchfield,	David Gwinn,
Mrs. Purnell,	Mr. — Johns,	John Boyd,
M. Rounsifer,	Hugh Henry, Sr.,	Reuben Harrison,
James Cain,	Benjamin Porter,	Frank Haney,
Isaac Neely,	Mrs. Henry, (widow,)	—— Maxwell,

John Montgomery,   Thomas Henry,   John White,
John Cotton,   Mr. Cockrell,   Solomon White,
—— Payne, (killed.)

There were other names not put down, women, children, and servants.

"Mrs. Peyton, whose infant was killed in the confusion of unloading the boat of Jonathan Jennings, during the attack upon it by the Indians, was the daughter of Jennings, and mother of Hon. Bailey Peyton. Her husband, Ephraim Peyton, had accompanied Captain Robertson with stock by land. The two young men who, with the negro man, jumped out of the boat to swim ashore, seized a canoe, pushed down the river, leaving the women (Mrs. Jennings and Mrs. Peyton and a negro woman) to their fate. The negro man lost his life in the water. The young men were intercepted in their canoe by the Indians; were captured, taken to the town of Chickamauga, where they *killed and burned the young man.* Young Jennings was about to share the same fate, when a trader, named Rogers, paid a handsome ransom for him, and saved his life; and the next morning his cry of ' Help poor Jennings' was heard by his friends in the fleet, who took him on board."

This narration is given by Mr. John Carr, of Sumner county. He is a most worthy man, a devoted Christian, and his statement of facts, within his knowledge, never questioned; but in this instance, evidently his memory of what he had heard and read is at fault.

The "Journal of Col. Donelson" is more authentic. Col. Donelson states that on "Friday morning, the 10th, about four o'clock in the morning, we were surprised by cries of ' Help poor Jennings,' at some distance *in the rear.* [That is, as he came down the river in his canoe.] He had discovered us by our fires, and came up in the most wretched condition." Col. Donelson's party was "encamped on the northern shore."

The time specified in the narrative of Mr. Carr is too limited. The transactions he recounts could not have transpired at the " Chickamauga town," and "young Jennings have reached the fleet the next morning." Young Jennings never did return to the boats, nor overtake them. It was his father's cry for help which was heard "the next morning about four o'clock." Young Jennings may have been ransomed by Mr. Rogers, and afterwards restored to his parents. And it may be true that the " Indians burned the young man." This, and one other, are the only instances we remember to have read of these Indians burning prisoners.

Such cruelty and crime have not been clearly proven against them. They usually spared the lives of young persons. There were, in the fifteen years of war which they waged against the whites subsequent to this attack upon the boats, very many children and young girls and boys captured by the Indians, and it is evident they spared their lives and retained them as prisoners, unless there was or seemed to be some pressing necessity to dispatch them by death. Towards men, and especially *spies*, there was much less indulgence and kindness or humanity. Perhaps, could they have taken a spy *alive*, they might have tortured him to death in the fire; but we have no unquestioned statement of such a tragedy and burning. Haywood, we doubt not, is Mr. Carr's authority for the statement, and upon what testimony the historian asserts it we cannot ascertain.

The southern, as well as the northern and northwestern Indians, were anxious to obtain the scalps of their enemies, old or young, unless there was a prospect of making them prisoners. They desired to have young men and young women as prisoners that they might make them slaves. It is unquestionably true that they often "cut, chopped, and mutilated the dead bodies of men whom they conquered after a hard fight." But young persons did not often make such resistance or cause them such labor and peril as to enrage them to this revenge.

The party of emigrants who joined Colonel Donelson at the mouth of Clinch was under the direction and command of Captain John Blackmore : they started from Fort Blackmore on Clinch river. From the statements of Captain Blackmore, Cartwright, and others, we are justified in stating that there were some thirty or forty boats (flats, dug-outs, and canoes) in the united fleet, and none of them with less than two families, and their goods, on board. Few of these "crafts" were constructed to stem the current, but rather to float down with the current. In Cartwright's boat there were three families.

As the result of the capture of Stuart's boat and crew, in which were the cases of small-pox, Mr. Carr has stated, and others have affirmed the same, that "great mortality" prevailed in the Cherokee nation afterwards. Without doubt the wretches paid dearly for their booty. In the "Narrative of Colonel Joseph Brown" this mortality is well considered as "a judgment on the Indians." It was said that when they were attacked with the small-pox, and the fever was upon them, they took a heavy sweat in their houses, and then leaped into the river, and died by scores. A large majority destroyed themselves, or died with the disease. This, and other diseases and vices, raged among them, and so increased that the nation was hastening to extinction.

It will be noticed in the journal of Colonel Donelson, under date March 12th, that there was an agreement that some of the land party under

Robertson should continue the journey from the Cumberland across to the
"upper end of the Muscle Shoals," there to meet the voyagers under
Donelson, or if they should not remain there for their friends in the
boats, they should mark trees, and leave evidences of having been there,
"and that it was practicable for the river party to go across to Cumberland or the Big Salt Lick by land."

"Robertson did not comply with this agreement, nor did any of his
party; nor is there any proof that he or they attempted compliance."
This remark has been made, and seemingly in terms and manner to censure General Robertson.

Our reply is, first, by a consideration of the persons and incumbrances
of the Donelson party. There were women and children who could not
have endured such a journey and exposure. The distance is about one
hundred and twenty miles in a direct line; by the present public high-
ways it is at least one hundred and forty miles; and by the meandering
course which would then have been pursued, in all probability, would not
have been less than two hundred miles. Three fourths of that distance
would have been through *dense cane-brakes,* and all of it through an
unbroken forest, never traversed by a white man.

Had Robertson been able to reach the "upper end of the Muscle Shoals,
and to have made marks and signs of having been there," and had Donelson been influenced by those signs to abandon the river route, he had no
conveyances for women and children. He would have been under the
necessity of abandoning goods, household stuff, and provisions of much
value; and some would have perished on the way, even had the Indians
not attacked them. But even with pack-horses they would in all probability have perished in the wilderness, or have been pursued by the
savages and destroyed. That cold winter "broke up" with extraordinary
rains. The Tennessee has not been known to be higher than in that
spring. The rivers and creeks to be crossed by such a party would have
been more perilous than the navigation of the Tennessee. It was well
they found no "signs" there.

1779–80. But we reply in the second place, that the Robertson party
arrived at the Great Salt Lick, or Bluffs, at the very end of the year
1779, after a long and tedious journey, with their horses much reduced
in flesh; that there was nothing upon which they could feed but the wild
cane; that the severity of the weather was such as had never been experienced in this country; that a first duty was to erect some shelters for
themselves and property, and block-houses with palisades for protection,
to make some preparation for the comfort and support of these friends
who were to come by water, (should they ever arrive;) that in January

and February it was as much as the Robertson party could do to sustain life by bear and buffalo meat; that the heavy rains commenced in February, and that their long continuance and consequent high waters forbade the attempt to search out a route to the Muscle Shoals; that had a party undertaken the journey, the probability seemed to be that the voyagers would have passed down the river before such friends could have arrived to meet them, or " make signs of having been there;" that every man and beast, with all the muscular powers they had, were needed in the work to be done here; that trees were to be cut down and prepared for houses, split for rails, for pickets, for floors, for doors, roofs, and chimneys, to clear land, and be in readiness for the planting season.

The impression prevailed among the Robertson party that their friends and families had not started, or would abandon the voyage until the winter was past, and that then the number of emigrants by water (going to " the Illinois and the Natchez") would be so increased that the party under Colonel Donelson " would enjoy the protection and company of a fleet of boats, and of a strong escort;" which was the case.

The presence of Colonel Robertson was required with these earliest emigrants. Articles of government were to be prepared, and a system of rules adopted. Had he gone to the Shoals, he could have taken but a meagre force, and at least three months would have been wasted in the opening a way and returning, and then after throwing away essential household goods, and all at the utmost peril to all.

NOTE.—"On the 21st July, 1821, Mr. Earle, aided by a number of hands, opened the mound which was on the west side of the Cumberland and north side of French Lick Creek, about seventy yards from each. This is the mound on which Monsieur Charleville, a French trader, had his store in 1714, when the Shawnees were driven from the Cumberland by the (Cherokees and) *Chickasaws*. Some broken pottery, and pieces of metal of oval form, with indented representation of the head of a woman on one side, were all that were discovered. This piece of silver was probably part of a watch-seal."

CHAPTER V.

1779, 1780.

In the "Adventure" there were about thirty families, as stated by Haywood; thirty or more men to manage and propel the boat, and to defend the party. The wife of Captain Robertson with her five children were of the number, and it is supposed the entire party must have amounted to one hundred and sixty.

They had been more than four months in accomplishing this voyage, and this during a winter of extraordinary coldness. A family can now leave the State of Maine and travel to California with less exposure and in one-fourth the time. The "adventurers" must have lived in close quarters on board their little vessel; but their safety, their hopes, their lives were all embarked in this one boat. A spirit of accommodation pervaded the party. The remembrance of the trials they had endured together, and the acts and words of comfort and kindness done and spoken to each other during this long voyage, were ever after pleasant memories, and served to unite them in strong and enduring friendships.

Their descendants should cherish the like sentiments. The names of many of these "adventurers," as also of others who at an early day were here, have become unknown, or have disappeared from the roll of citizens at the present day. But of many others it can be truly said, they have descendants, here and elsewhere, who do credit to their parentage; citizens of integrity, of industry, of intelligence, and virtue; useful, patriotic, benevolent; men •of worth, women of loveliness; young men of promise; girls the very pinks of perfection, ornaments of society, pride of creation, fit partners of worthy men.

What the plain, frugal, industrious, and happy parents of those days would think or say of some manners and customs, of the fashion and parade, love of money and love of dress, of discontent, whether with or without excess of this world's goods, in this our day, we will not venture to insert in "this present writing;" but we would modestly commend the matter "to every one's conscience in the sight of God."

Can Churchill's sentiment to any be applied?

> "Appearances to save, their only care;
> So dress seems right, no matter what they are."

We hope not, and that Will Shakespeare's remark about some young gentleman in olden time may not be applicable to any in our day or place—

> " The fashion
> Wears out more apparel than the *man !*"

This, however, only " by the way," an incidental remark.

The early settlers here certainly were a plain, economical, industrious people, "given to hospitality," "speaking the truth in love," recognizing " Divine Providence," and sincere in devotion to the cause of American Independence. They had avowed, sworn, and proven their attachment to the great cause for the success of which patriotic men in all the Colonies (or States, as they were generally called) were now fervently praying and heroically contending.

Although, by their removal across the mountains, they were the more distant from the very " battle-fields of the Revolution," their hearts were in the work; they, as wisely and as well as any other men in that eventful day and struggle, were ordained and trained, sent and stationed, where the invaluable services, which only such men could perform, would be most needed. And they acted well their part. They foiled the schemes of diplomacy, they secured the best part of this continent, " they kept the faith and the country."

The account they gave of the appearance of the bluffs and Salt Lick, when the companies arrived in the winter and spring of 1780, is, that although there was "open ground," there was no evidence that it had ever been in cultivation. The open space around and near the Sulphur or Salt Spring, instead of being an " old field," as had been supposed by Mr. Mansker at his visit here in 1769, was thus freed from trees and underbrush by the innumerable herds of buffalo and deer and elk that came to these waters. The place was the resort of these wild animals, among which also came bears, panthers, wolves, and foxes. Trails, or buffalo-paths, were deeply worn in the earth from this to other springs. Much of the country was covered with a thick growth of cane, from ten to twenty feet high. (Upon the banks of our rivers and creeks and on many plantations in Middle Tennessee, the cane has not yet been entirely destroyed.) Like the wild beasts who formerly found in its denseness their places of rest and concealment, like the Indians who,

6

" from the beginning," hunted the beasts, and traversed these well-stocked parks, and called them all their own ; so savage beasts and savage men have had to retire before the race of white men, and before settlements and agriculture. And so, too, the native, the original grasses, and the nutritious cane-brakes, which in all past time served for pasturage to countless herds of wild animals, have been or will be compelled to give way and disappear, to be succeeded by a Heaven-ordered, higher state in food, in men, and in animals.

> "Man, in society, is like a flower
> Blown in its native bud. 'T is there alone
> His faculties, expanded in full bloom,
> Shine out, there only reach their proper use."

These pioneers were " huddled in the few rude huts" which had been, as they remarked, " thrown together in a hurry, as men throw the brush in clearings, and pitch up a pen to keep the calf from the cow." " Wood was plenty, but it was cold work chopping wood."

And wild game was abundant, but very poor. " Many deer were found to have died of hunger and the cold." The settlers and hunters in Kentucky have recorded the same fact, attributing it to the long and intense cold.

There were some women and children with the Rains, Eaton, and Mansker companies of emigrants, but none, as we can learn, with the Robertson. Their " better halves" and " olive plants" "were to come with the household stuff, by the river route."

" Bear's oil was the only substitute we had for butter, lard, or gravy, and we learned to prefer it to either." Hunters have often said that bear's oil, when fresh, made them feel warm and strong. They became very fond of it.

Some of the men who had been in pursuit of game, and making explorations through the woods, were much surprised to discover the tracks of a large party of Indians. These were known by their tracks. All wore moccasins, and none of them turned their toes *outward*, as do white people. There were other unmistakable evidences of these being Indians, and in quite a formidable body. The news was promptly communicated to all the pioneers, and they were advised to " keep a sharp look-out."

It was considered proper to ascertain from them whether they came with professions of friendship, and could be confided in, or were to be watched as covert or avowed enemies. As they had encamped upon a branch of the creek, since known as Mill Creek, and a few miles south of the Robertson station, a visit was made to them, and, as far as could be understood by signs and intelligible words, the whites were assured "they had come only to hunt." They remained upon that branch of Mill Creek and hunted until summer weather commenced. Their encampment gave to that branch, or small stream, the name of "Indian Creek." They are believed to have been the first to molest the settlers.

These were Delaware Indians, and had come hundreds of miles to hunt upon lands to which they had no right. We have remarked that John Rains was one of the emigrants who earliest selected his tract of land and commenced improvements. It included much of the seventy acres, ("Waverley Place,") the residence of the writer of these sketches, and other places "beautiful for situation," the homes of taste and refinement. These lands are now in danger of being grasped by the outstretching arms of the city, where the cry of the "city fathers" is, as that of the horse-leech, *Give*, give, and seems never likely to say, Hold! It is enough!

Well, "as it was in the beginning, is now," so will it be hereafter: by some human being, by some Providence, by some improvement, by some change, (and whether for good or ill, the Lord only knows, but we maintain 'tis well and wisely ordered,) none of us can be permitted to find upon the earth an unchanged and unchangeable home. The experience of John Rains has been the experience of John Doe and Richard Roe, and of all the steady or changeful men, with monosyllabic or polysyllabic names, before and since his day. But among these pioneers, as he was the first to make his marks, and drive his stakes, to designate his location; so was he the first to "pull up stakes and make tracks" into the fort on the bluff. And many persons at the present day, with nothing like the inducements or necessity which impelled Mr. Rains, will hasten to the city; (and thus towns and cities are made.)

> "God made the country,
> Man made the towns."

But "to the point." Mr. Rains made a timely escape. The propriety and necessity of removal soon became evident. He had occupied his home three months and three days, when he learned that the Indians had killed John Milliken, on Richland Creek, and Joseph Hay, near the Sulphur Spring, and were very much disposed to make attacks upon all persons who were not under the immediate protection of the fort. "Mr. Rains moved to the bluff," says Haywood, or, as we would now say, *he moved to town*, "and continued there four years, before he again settled in the country." When he did so "return to the country," he found another excellent spring in his tract of land, (one thousand acres,) near which he was permitted to have a home during the remainder of his days, and they were many and pleasant, and usefully employed.

By the spring, the waters of which run through the Horticultural Garden, in what is now known as McGavock's Addition to Nashville, there was a fort or station erected, under the management of George Freeland, and called "Freeland's Station." The beautiful ground between that station and the Sulphur Spring was then covered by an almost impenetrable cane-brake, with a few buffalo-paths through it. Within a day or two after Hay was killed, old Mr. Bernard and young Milliken (son of the Milliken who was killed on Richland) were shot down near this station, and "their heads cut off." "The beginning of sorrows," said old Mrs. Neelly.

The people who had sought their separate homes "in the country" no longer "laughed to scorn" those who had "croaked of danger," but with one general consent took shelter at the block-houses and stations. For years thereafter, when they would attempt the cultivation of any crop, they resorted to the wise counsel of the "croakers." They took the crows, or ravens, for their teachers. They always placed some good marksman, with quick eye, upon an eminence, or perched in a tree-top, to "pick off" (as the term was) any prowling Indian, or give timely alarm of approaching danger.

The people began to see, also, that they must resort to some uniform, active, and reliable measures for defence and self-government. They were in danger, not only from foes without, but there was (or was likely to be) some disputes and trouble among themselves. As in communities, even from olden time, so in some of these there were turbulent spirits, busy-bodies, murmurers, men seeking more than their own, and a few with the ambition of Diotrephes, "looking to have the preëminence."

There were, however, wise men who had known the necessity, and enjoyed the advantages, of a form of government originating directly from the people, and had participated in the organization and administration of such when at Watauga: they resolved upon the adoption of a similar compact here. As Richard Henderson, and other members of the "Transylvania Land Company," were here at this juncture, he was foremost in urging the adoption of some form of government: he and his surveying-party had "come in," having run the line to the Tennessee River. Henderson also offered to sell lands under the treaty-purchase by the Transylvania Company, postponing payment until the Company's title should be duly confirmed. Therefore the compact, or form of government, known as the government of the "General Arbitrators," Triers, or Judges, or, more appropriately, the "*Government of the Notables*," was agreed upon, written out in fair hand, and all settlers who were disposed to observe and maintain good order and fair dealings were ready to subscribe these articles of compact. The original, together with many loose sheets of paper covered with writing, and of deep interest connected with the men and transactions of that day, were discovered by the writer of these sketches in the year 1846, in an old trunk which had evidently belonged to Colonel Robert Barton, who, as will be seen, was a useful citizen, one of the Notables of that day, and lost not his character for usefulness while he lived.

We shall insert these articles, and the proceedings of this government, entire in the Appendix, fearlessly asserting that the whole is worthy of careful consideration ; evincing much intelligence, prudent foresight, firmness, and patriotism. We shall have, however, to precede the written record with a running commentary, in order to preserve the memory of some occurrences not to be otherwise learned ; and thus, with the administrative and judicial proceedings, as presented "on the records," bring to light and perpetuate the events which transpired throughout the settlements on the Cumberland during these eventful times, when "the light was as darkness, as darkness itself," and some of even these "men's hearts failed them for fear, and for the things that were coming upon them."

We should, however, mention that although there was among the emigrants a great desire to penetrate the woods and discover the fatness of the land, whilst some followed out every trace made by the wild beasts, others "broke into the wild woods," where there was no pathway or track of animals, and were early convinced that it was indeed a goodly land, and well deserved to be possessed. Many began to erect their separate cabin for their individual home. They did not wholly neglect the construction of some defensive posts and places of refuge. None of these, however, were at first so finished as not to require to be improved and strengthened, and soon to be incessantly guarded.

When the people arrived upon the Cumberland they saw no Indians, and they knew of no tribe that was settled between its waters and those of the Tennessee, nor of any Indian towns north of them and south of the Ohio. Here seemed to be a vast extent of woodland, barrens, and prairies, inviting human settlement and the improvements of civilization. The Delawares, who had appeared on the head-waters of Mill Creek, and professed to have come only to hunt, had travelled a long distance. The Creeks and Cherokees claimed no lands within the limits of these new settlements, therefore it is not surprising that some of the people were reluctant to give much of their time and labor to the erection of forts and stations, when all wanted homes; and some had made haste to select the choicest places, thus creating discontent with others.

But the desire and temptation to mark, and blaze, and scatter abroad, and *locate* as soon as they learned a little of the richness of the country, was repressed by the experienced and prudent among them, sufficiently to "agree to give a portion of their time and labor to the erection of a few 'strong-holds' and defences, as also for the deposit of provisions, arms, and ammunition."

It was agreed that the fort at the Bluffs, or Nashborough, should be the principal one, and the head-quarters. Others were commenced about the same time, at the spring in North Nashville, as we have mentioned, and was called Freelands; one on the east side of the river, upon the first highland at "the river bank, called Eaton's;" others at or near the sulphur spring, ten miles north, called Gasper's, where is now the town of Goodlettsville; one on Station Camp Creek, about three miles from Galla-tin, on the bluff, and by the edge of the turnpike, called Asher's; one near the sulphur spring, eight miles from Gallatin, called Bledsoe's; one at the low lands on Stone's River, where the pike passes, called " Stone's River," or Donelson's, (in our day known as Clover Bottom;) and one at "Fort Union," at the bend of the river, above the bluffs, about six miles distant: here was once the town of Haysborough.

The fort at Nashborough was erected upon the bluff, between the south-east corner of the Square and Spring street, so as to include a bold spring which then issued from that point, the water of which dashed down the precipice, giving much interest and charm to the location.

This place of defence, like all the forts erected at other stations, was a log building, two stories high, with port-holes and look-out station : other log houses were near it, and the whole were enclosed with palisades or pickets firmly set in the earth, having the upper ends sharpened. There was one large entrance or gateway, with a look-out station thereon for the guard. The top of the fort afforded an elevated view of the country around. This view, however, was much obstructed to the west and south-west by a thick forest of cedar trees, beneath which, especially to the south-west (say toward Broad Street and Wilson's Spring) there was a dense growth of privet bushes. Upon lands with deeper soil and less rock, instead of cedar and privet, there were forest trees of large growth, and thick cane-brakes. The rich bottom-lands were covered with cane measuring ten to twenty feet in height. The ancient forest trees upon the rich lands in this region were of a most majestic growth ; all the ele-ments of nature seem to have combined to make them what they were ; and yet, although many of the loveliest sites for country residences have been hastily and unwisely stripped of their chief ornament and charm, and *civilized* man has speedily destroyed, by thousands in a year, such monarchs of the forest as a thousand years may not again produce, there remain, here and there, some lovely spots and glorious oaks not wholly dishonored or abased by the woodman's axe. There are a few, and but a few, of such native woods and magnificent trees remaining in the vicinity of the capital of Tennessee; but from the depth of our heart we cry,

"Woodmen, spare those trees!"

If once cut down, you nor our posterity will ever "see the like again."

As we have remarked, it was agreed to adopt the post on the Bluffs as the head-quarters—the place for general meetings—and the name of *Nashborough* selected, by which it should thereafter be known. This was in honor of *Francis Nash*, of North Carolina, a Brigadier-General in the Continental army, and who was mortally wounded at the battle of Germantown, October 4th, 1777.

At this place the delegates, chosen by the people at the different stations, assembled and adopted the Compact of government; and here were held the meetings of Notables, and the records kept, from which we shall freely quote, first premising, as a gentle hint to the cheerful hearts of old age and to the lively hearts of youth, that when this important measure was adopted, these forests and lands and the fresh air were rich, beautiful, and fragrant with wild flowers. It was *May-day!* the day for bouquets of sweet flowers, enriched with heaven's brightest tints: it is the time for gay assemblages " upon the green,"

"And 'neath umbrageous trees."

Henceforth let green old age and buoyant youth and laughing child-hood commemorate the day, and call to mind that the noble band of pioneer settlers on the Cumberland made this day for ever memorable, by initiating a form of government on popular representative principles.

> "Hail to the joyous day! With purple clouds
> The whole horizon glows. The breezy Spring
> Stands loosely floating on the mountain top,
> And deals her sweets around. The Sun, too, seems
> As conscious of the joy, with brighter beams
> To gild the happy world."

The 13th day of May hath its claim to remembrance as that on which "additional resolutions and further association were entered into at Nashborough," to regulate entries and locations of land; to protect and provide for the children and widows of those who should die or be killed by the Indians; regulating the military defences; calling into service men from each station; impressing horses; imposing, collecting, and appropriating fines, etc. And thus was initiated the "Government of the Judges," "General Arbitrators, or Triers," "chosen by the Freemen of the different stations" on the Cumberland.

As the names of Richard Henderson, Nathaniel Hart, and some others who were members of the great " Transylvania Land Company," are first in the roll of worthy signers to these articles, it is proper to repeat here that there was a lingering hope—in some a strong confidence—that the purchase made of the Indians in 1775 would, in some way, be of service to the early settlers. All felt confident that by that purchase the Indian title was fairly and fully extinguished; that, even should it be against good policy for the State to recognize treaties between the Indians and private citizens, and that the same policy would discountenance the absorbing by a few individuals of territory extensive enough for States, yet they hoped that by a multiplication of the parties interested, and by a partition of the lands among many, as also by reason of the consideration paid, and the great toils and perils endured, and positive advantages to the State accruing from the settlements, a liberal and equally sound policy would justify the confirmation to a good extent of titles to these settlers.

Col. Henderson was a sound lawyer, a man of thorough education, an accomplished gentleman, an honorable and patriotic man, and sought and took no advantage of the confidence placed in him. Sales were made, but payment conditioned on a confirmation. By the experimental line he had run, he concluded that the true line between North Carolina and Virginia would be some twenty miles north of the principal settlements then making on the Cumberland, therefore he and others ere long determined to establish themselves nearer the Ohio river. Henderson had a house in the fort at Boonsborough, on Kentucky River.

But this treaty-maker is entitled to the honor of having extinguished Indian claims to some of the richest lands in America, and of having assisted in the adoption of a written constitution of government for three distinct Colonies, embracing territory enough to have formed three instead of two great States. It is a notable fact that he, or the company, at the very earliest day, contemplated and desired to form a State similar to "the thirteen." They applied to the Continental Congress at Philadelphia in 1775, " to unite with them in the same great cause of liberty and mankind," and to be admitted into the Confederacy, with the name of *Transylvania*.

Col. Henderson had assisted in the erection of the station at Boones-borough, and in the organization of a government, or "Rules and Regulations," there, some years prior to the part which he acted here. He ·had his own house within the fort, or as forming a part of the enclosure. The same course pursued there, in the settling of lands by the company, was adopted here. The policy was liberal—far more so than that which was subsequently adopted by the State.

The State of Virginia, as did North Carolina, annulled his title, or refused to recognize sales under the company. Each State, however, granted to the proprietors two hundred thousand acres, and then appropriated to public uses the benefits of the treaty made with the Cherokees in 1775. The two hundred thousand acres granted by Virginia were on the Ohio river, in what is known as Henderson county. The State of North Carolina made a similar grant, and thus the lands on the Cumberland became exempt from the claim of the Transylvania Company. Purchasers here were never urged to make any payments on contracts into which they had entered. Old settlers ever retained for Henderson a very high regard as a gentleman and patriot.

Soon after the arrival of Captain James Robertson, the people at Nashborough, Freeland, and Eaton's Stations, chose him to be a *Colonel.* Here was office conferred by the people, the highest authority; and it was by unanimous voice. He had already earned this distinction, and well did his conduct prove, ever after, that it was wisely bestowed. He now became the leading spirit in all the settlements in the Cumberland district, Commander-in-Chief of the military forces, and "Chairman or President" of the Bench of Judges or Committee of Notables, down to the period when these, sometimes called Triers or Judges, descended from these primitive seats of distinction and usefulness, to be dignified as "*Justices,*" under commissions from the Governor of North Carolina.

Two hundred and fifty-six names are subscribed to the Constitution or Compact of government; and it is exceedingly creditable and well worthy of notice, that the most of them wrote their own names, genuine autographs. These original signatures, like those to other Declarations and Constitutions, deserve to be lithographed and studied. The private and public history of many of them can be given, (and, indeed, should be introduced or added, in order to render these sketches complete.) Many descendants of those original signers are yet living in this State, in Mississippi, and Kentucky.

As we have already stated, there were eight stations established and settlements commenced in 1780, and the inhabitants or settlers there entitled to "representatives in the Tribunal of Notables" or "General Arbitrators," as follows :

" From Nashborough, 3."

" From Gasper's, 2."   (Gasper Mansker's Lick.)

" From Bledsoe's, 1."   (Now Castilian Springs.)

" From Asher's, 1."   (Station Camp Creek.)

" From Freeland's, 1."   (Dr. M'Gavock's or Horticultural Garden.)

" From Eaton's, 2."   (Now Brooklyn, east side of the river.)

" From Fort Union, 1."   (Where Haysborough was.)

" Which said persons, or a majority of them, after being bound by the solemnity of an oath to do equal and impartial justice between all contending parties," etc., shall be empowered and competent to settle all controversies relative to locations and improvements of lands; all other matters and questions of dispute among the settlers; protecting the reasonable claims of those who may have returned for their families; providing implements of husbandry and food for such as might arrive without such necessaries ; making especial provision for *widows* and *orphans,* whose husbands or fathers may die or be killed by the savages; guaranteeing equal rights, mutual protection, and impartial justice; "pledging themselves most solemnly and sacredly" to promote the peace, happiness, and well-being of the community; to suppress vice and punish crime.   This is a summary of what they resolved and ordained.

What a right beginning for a great State ! Well may we feel proud to acknowledge indebtedness to pioneers who had such a thorough knowledge of all the elements essential to good government; that, as a people, they understood the "rights of the people," well knowing the inherent and inalienable prerogatives which belonged to them : being men of foresight, principle, virtue, and patriotism, they could at once pronounce and enact what was appropriate and best : cheerful and prompt in obedience themselves, vigilant and resolute to detect, condemn, and punish encroachments and violations.

" Knowledge is power," and the Whigs of the American Revolution possessed knowledge and used power knowingly, wisely, and well.

Having aided in a good work east of the mountain, and left it in capable and efficient hands there, they renewed their patriotic plans on the banks of the Cumberland.

Westward the star of empire took its flight.

The "solemn pledges" then made were truly regarded as sacred, and were faithfully observed. Acts then determined, decisions then made, boundaries then settled, have never been repudiated, unsettled, or re-

versed. Questions of title were then considered, cases were then adjudicated, which at this day affect millions of dollars' worth of property.
There was never any defiance of the supreme authority; no resistance to
the arbitrament of the Judges or Committee of Notables. All acknowledged and felt the necessity of authority and law—all resolved to maintain the dignity and integrity of their enactments. The Judges did not
abuse their trust, and the people had few difficulties to settle, few complaints to make of each other. The actual settlers were of industrious
habits and quiet disposition, sober and moral, intent to do well for themselves and for their children after them.

Roving adventurers, refugees from justice, absconding debtors and
mischief-makers, will find their way to new and retired settlements; and
it requires firm and united remonstrance and opposition on the part of
citizens, who will not allow any lawless intermeddling with themselves or
their own rights, nor defiance of the laws by which all rights are secured,
to hold such outlaws in check. A few men of known decision of character can accomplish a great deal for the peace of society and the rebuke
of offenders. The Committees of Safety, which were numerous throughout the Colonies during the War of Revolution, constituted an excellent
police; and through their watchfulness and exertions, Tories, horse-
thieves, and other offenders, were detected, exposed, brought to punishment, or, if they fled, information was given and passed from Committee
to Committee, and so from State to State. These lawless fellows sometimes became a terror to themselves, verifying the declaration of Scripture,
"The wicked flee when no man pursueth."

One of the best elements of our free, popular government, was expressly
set forth in the Compact of government at Nashborough, namely: the
authority of the people; a power *reserved* to the people at the various
stations, to *remove* their Judge or Judges and other officers, for unfaith-
fulness or misconduct, and to elect others to fill such vacancies.

This tribunal exercised the prerogatives of government in their fullest
extent, with the single specified exception of infliction of capital punishment. They called out the militia of the stations, "to repel or pursue
the enemy," impressed horses for such service as public exigency might
demand, levied fines, payable in money or provisions, adjudicated causes,
entered up judgments and awarded executions, granted letters of administration upon estates of deceased persons, taking bonds, "payable to
Colonel James Robertson, Chairman of Committee," etc.

The following paragraphs will certainly be read with much interest
and proud approbation. Among all the eloquent declarations of rights,

preambles, or recital of causes impelling to or justifying popular proceedings, which distinguish the American era, we know of none to
which we would sooner challenge attention than to these, *toutes les cir-
constances et dépendances bien considerées.*

"That as this settlement is in its infancy, unknown to government,
and not included within any county in North Carolina, the State to which
it belongs, so as to derive the advantages of those wholesome and salutary
laws for the protection and benefit of its citizens, we find ourselves
constrained, from necessity, to adopt this temporary method of restraining
the licentious, and supplying, by *unanimous consent,* the blessings flowing
from a just and equitable government; declaring and promising that no
action or complaint shall be hereafter instituted or lodged in any court
of record within this State or elsewhere, for any thing done, or to be done,
in consequence of the proceedings of the said Judges or General Arbitrators, so to be chosen and established by this our *Association.*

"That as the well-being of this country depends, under *Divine Providence,* on unanimity of sentiment, and concurrence in measures; and as
clashing and various interests and opinions, without being under some
restraint, will most certainly produce confusion, discord, and almost ruin,
so we think it our duty to associate, and hereby form ourselves into one
society, for the benefit of present and future settlers, and until the full
and proper exercise of the laws of our country can be in use, and the
powers of government exerted among us.

"We do most solemnly and sacredly declare, and promise each other,
that we will faithfully and punctually adhere to, perform, and abide by,
this our Association, and at all times, if need be, compel, by our united
force, a due obedience to these our rules and regulations.

"In testimony whereof, we have hereunto subscribed our names, in
token of our *entire approbation* of the measures adopted."

Such is the eloquent, beautiful, patriotic conclusion of the Articles of
Association of May 1, 1780.

Let our statesmen consider well this summary; and especially let the
young men of Tennessee (a State in which they are called at an earlier
age than in other States to study and discuss political questions, and enter
upon the arena where are debated state and national matters, the science
of government taught and eloquence displayed) study these words, imbibe
these sentiments, expatiate upon these doctrines: they will find ample
store here, and in these records, for a thousand *Fourth of July orations,*
and for as many May-day, pic-nic declamations.

On the 13th of the same month, "the additional resolutions and

further association were entered into," of which we have already given
the substance, and at the close of which are the two hundred and fifty-
six signatures.

Much has been said and written of the "anomalous government of
Franklin," (not Frank-*land*, as Haywood and others have called it,)
which was organized in East Tennessee, and the account of which
forms one of the most interesting chapters in the annals of Tennessee.
Much has been justly said in praise of its noble Governor, General Sevier,
of whom "the truth of history" requires us to say, he was in labors
more abundant, in sacrifices more liberal, in perils more frequent than any
and all other men, for the service of that people, and yet vilified by
rivals, outlawed by the State of North Carolina, seized and "spirited
away" as a criminal, pursued and recaptured by his friends, chasing and
subduing the Indians, triumphing over enmity, rivalry, and persecution,
elevated to the highest office in the gift of the people, made again and
again, and yet again, the Governor of the State of Tennessee, an honored
and useful Senator in Congress, and, finally, at the urgent solicitation of
the President of the United States, an ambassador, or commissioner, to
establish peace and determine boundaries with the warlike Indians, and
there to sicken and to die, and "no stone to tell his resting-place !"

We say that much has been written and published relative to that
"*imperium in imperio*," the State of Frank-lin and its distinguished
founder and Governor ; but here we recover the history of a State, in
every respect and aspect as peculiar as that—six years earlier in date—in
active existence for several years—the President or Chairman of which
was ever the friend of Sevier—they *par nobile fratrum*—but of which
the historians of Tennessee have had but a very limited knowledge.
Judge Haywood alludes to it on page 126, and others have only copied
what he there says, and thus the most interesting incidents in Middle
Tennessee history have hitherto remained unknown and unpublished.

It soon became manifest that there was much need for this government,
that it would have much to engage its attention, both in civil and military
departments. The people at the various stations were urged by their
sense of duty and some apprehension of mischief from the Indians, to
elect the number of Notables to which they were entitled, that the contemplated government might be put promptly into operation, and suitable
directions given for the election of military officers and the equipment
of "spies and sharp-shooters."

The alarm-cry was, "Indians about!" In this very month of May
they approached the strong defences at Eaton's Station, and within sight,
and open day, shot down Mr. Porter and James Mayfield. Shortly there-

after they killed Jennings, opposite the first island above Nashborough, and near the same time and place they killed Ned. Carver, whose wife and two children narrowly escaped, and reached the Bluffs.   In a day or two thereafter, they killed William Neelly and captured his daughter.

Although we have mentioned in this chapter the several early deaths caused by the Indians, we have omitted some particulars attending those occurrences, which will be noticed in the next chapter.   We have alluded to them here, that the reader might bear in mind the dangers by which these stationers were surrounded when they adopted their form of government, which is here added.

ARTICLES OF AGREEMENT, or Compact of Government, entered into by settlers on the Cumberland river, 1st May, 1780.

The first page is lost, and the second torn and defaced, but we can read distinctly as follows, supplying *in brackets* lost words:

"   .   .   .   .   property of right shall be determined as soon [as] conveniently may be, in the following manner : The free men of this country over the age [of twenty] one years shall immediately, or as soon as may [be convenient,] proceed to elect or choose *twelve* conscientious and [deserving] persons from or out of the different stations, that is [to] say: From Nashborough, *three;* Gasper's, *two;* Bledsoe's, *one;* Asher's, *one;* Stone's River, *one;* Freeland's, *one;* Eaton's, *two;* Fort Union, *one.* Which said persons, or a majority of them, after being bound by the solemnity of an oath to do equal and impartial justice between all contending parties, according to the best of their skill and judgment, having due re[gard] to the regulations of the Land Office herein established, shall be competent judges of the matter, and   .   .   .   .   hearing the allegations of both parties, and [their] witnesses, as to the facts alleged, or otherwise   .   .   .   .   as to the truth of the case, shall have [power] to decide the controversie, and determine who is of right entitled to an entry for such land so in dispute, when said determination or decision shall be for ever bind[ing] and conclusive against the future claim of the party against whom such judgment [shall be rendered.]   And the Entry Taker shall make a [record thereof] in his book accordingly, and the entry   .   .   .   .   tending party so cast shall be   .   .   .   .   if it had never been made, and the land in dispute   .   .   .   .   to the person in whose favor such judgment shall   .   .   .   .

"   .   .   .   .   in case of the death, removal, or absence of any of the judges so to be chosen, or their refusing to act, the station to which such person or persons belong, or was chosen from, shall proceed to elect another or others in his or their stead ; which person or persons so chosen, after being sworn, as aforesaid, to do equal and impartial justice, shall have full power and authority to proceed to business and act in all disputes respecting the premises, as if they had been originally chosen at the first election.

" That the entry book shall be kept fair and open by . . person . to be appointed by said Richard Henderson . . . chose, and every entry for land numbered and dated, and . . . order without leaving any blank leaves or spaces, ... to the inspection of the said twelve judges, or . . of them, at all times.

" That whereas many persons have come to this country without implements of husbandry, and from other circumstances are obliged to return without making a crop, and [intend] removing out this fall, or early next spring, and it . . . . reason . . such should have the preëmp-[tion] . . . . of such places as they may have chosen . . the purpose of residence, therefore it is . . . . be taken for all such, for as much land as they are entitled to from their head-rights, which said lands shall be reserved for the particular person in whose name they shall be entered, or their heirs; provided such persons shall remove to this country and take possession of the respective place or piece of land so chosen or entered, or shall send a laborer or laborers, and a white person in his or her stead, to perform the same, on or before the first day of May, in the year one thousand seven hundred and eighty-one; and also provided such land so chosen and entered for is not entered and claimed by some person who is an inhabitant, and shall raise a crop of corn the present year at some station or place convenient to the general settlement in this country. But it is fully to be understood that those who are actually at this time inhabitants of this country shall not be debarred of their choice or claim on account of the right of any such absent or returning person or persons. It is further proposed and agreed that no claim or title to any lands whatsoever shall be set up by any person in consequence of any mark, or former improvement, unless the same be entered with the Entry Taker within twenty days from the date of this association and agreement; and that when any person hereafter shall mark or improve land or lands for himself, such mark or improvement shall not avail him or be deemed an evidence of prior right unless the same be entered with the Entry Taker in thirty days . . from the time of such mark or improvement; but no other person shall be entitled to such lands so as aforesaid to be reserved . . consequence of any purchase, gift, or otherwise.

" That if the Entry Taker to be appointed shall neglect or refuse to perform his duty, or be found by the said Judges, or a majority of them, to have acted fraudulently, to the prejudice of any person whatsoever, such Entry Taker shall be immediately removed from his office, and the book taken out of his possession by the said Judges, until another shall be appointed to act in his room.

"That as often as the people in general are dissatisfied with the doings of the Judges or Triers so to be chosen, they may call a new election at any of the said stations, and elect others in their stead, having due respect to the number now agreed to be elected at each station, which persons so to be chosen shall have the same power with those in whose room or place they shall or may be chosen to act.

"That as no consideration-money for the lands on Cumberland River, within the claim of the said Richard Henderson and Company, and which is the subject of this Association, is demanded or expected by the said Company, until a satisfactory and indisputable title can be made, so we think it reasonable and just that the twenty-six pounds thirteen shillings and four pence, current money, per hundred acres, the price proposed by the said Richard Henderson, shall be paid according to the value of money on the first day of January last, being the time when the price was made public [and] settlement encouraged thereon by said Henderson, and the said Richard Henderson on his part does hereby agree that in case of the rise or appreciation of money from that . . . an abatement shall be made in the sum according to its raised or appreciated value.

"That where any person shall remove to this country with intent to become an inhabitant, and depart this life, either by violence or in the natural way, before he shall have performed the requisites necessary to obtain lands, the child or children of such deceased person shall be entitled, in his or her room, to such quantity of land as such person would have been entitled to in case he or she had have lived to obtain a grant in their own name; and if such death be occasioned by the Indians, the said Henderson doth promise and agree that the child or children shall have as much as amounts to their head-rights gratis, surveyor's and other incidental fees excepted.

"And whereas, from our remote situation and want of proper offices for the administration of justice, no regular proceedings at law can be had, for the punishment of offences and attainment of right, it is therefore agreed, that until we can be relieved by government from the many evils and inconveniences arising therefrom, the judges or triers to be appointed as before directed, when qualified, shall be and are hereby declared a *proper court* or jurisdiction for the recovery of any debt or damages; or where the cause of action or complaint has arisen, or hereafter shall commence, for any thing done or to be done, among ourselves, within this our settlement on Cumberland aforesaid, or in our passage hither, where the laws of our country could not be executed, or damages repaired in any other way; that is to say, in all cases where the debt or damages or demand does or shall not exceed one hundred dollars, any three of the said Judges or Triers shall be competent to make a Court, and finally decide the matter in controversy; but if for a larger sum, and either party shall be dissatisfied with the judgment or decision of such Court, they may have an appeal to the whole twelve Judges or Triers, in which case nine members shall be deemed a full Court, whose decision, if seven agree in one opinion, the matter in dispute shall be final, and their judgment carried into execution in such manner, and by such person or persons, as they may appoint; and the said Courts, respectively, shall have full power to tax such costs as they may think just and reasonable, to be levied and collected with the debt or damages so to be awarded.

"And it is further agreed, that a majority of the said Judges, Triers, or General Arbitrators, shall have power to punish in their discretion, having respect to the laws of our country, all offences against the peace, misdemeanors, and those criminal, or of a capital nature, provided such Court does not proceed with execution so far as to affect life or member; and in case any should be brought before them whose crime is or shall be dangerous to the State, or for which the benefit of clergy is taken away by law, and sufficient evidence or proof of the fact or facts can probably be made, such Court, or a majority of the members, shall and may order and direct him, her, or them to be safely bound and sent under a strong guard to the place where the offence was or shall be committed, or where legal trial of such offence can be had, which shall accordingly be done, and the reasonable expense attending the discharge of this duty ascertained by the Court, and paid by the inhabitants in such proportion as shall be hereafter agreed on for that purpose.

" That as this settlement is in its infancy, unknown to government, and not included within any county within North Carolina, the State to which it belongs, so as to derive the advantages of those wholesome and salutary laws for the protection and benefit of its citizens, *we find ourselves* constrained from necessity to adopt this temporary method of restraining the licentious, and supplying, by unanimous consent, the blessings flowing from a just and equitable government, declaring and promising that no action or complaint shall be hereafter instituted or lodged in any Court of Record within this State, or elsewhere, for any thing done or to be done in consequence of the proceedings of the said

7

Judges or General Arbitrators so to be chosen and established by this our association.

"That the well-being of this country entirely depends, under Divine Providence, on unanimity of sentiment and concurrence in measures, and as clashing interests and opinions, without being under some restraint, will most certainly produce confusion, discord, and almost certain ruin, so we think it our duty to associate, and hereby form ourselves into one society for the benefit of present and future settlers, and until the full and proper exercise of the laws of our country can be in use, and the powers of government exerted among us: *we do most solemnly and sacredly declare* and promise each other, that we will faithfully and punctually adhere to, perform, and abide by this our Association, and at all times, if need be, compel, by our united force, a due obedience to these our rules and regulations. In testimony whereof, we have hereunto subscribed our names in token of our entire approbation of the measures adopted."

The following or additional resolutions, and further association, were also entered into at Nashborough, this 13th day of May, 1780, to wit:

"That all young men over the age of sixteen years, and able to perform militia duty, shall be considered as having a full right to enter for and obtain lands in their own names, as if they were of full age; and in that case not be reckoned in the family of his father, mother, or master, so as to avail them of any land on their account.

"That where any person shall mark or improve land or lands, with intent to set up a claim thereto, such person shall write or mark in legible characters the initial letters of his name at least, together with the day of the month and year on which he marked or improved the same, at the spring or most notorious part of the land, on some convenient tree or other durable substance, in order to notify his intentions to all such as may inquire or examine, and in case of dispute with respect to priority of right, proof of such transaction shall be made by the oath of some indifferent witness, or no advantage or benefit shall be derived from such mark or improvement; and in all cases where priority of mark or occupancy cannot be ascertained according to the regulations and prescriptions herein proposed and agreed to, the oldest or first entry in the office to be opened in consequence of this Association shall have the preference, and the lands granted accordingly.

"It is further proposed and agreed that the Entry Office shall be opened at Nashborough, on Friday, the 19th of May, instant, and kept from thenceforward at the same place, unless otherwise directed by any future Convention of the people in general, or their representatives.

"That the Entry Taker shall and may demand and receive twelve dollars for each entry to be made in his book, in manner before directed, and shall give a certificate thereof, if required; and also may take the same fees for every *caveat* or counter-claim to any lands before entered; and in all cases where a caveat is to be tried in manner before directed, the Entry Book shall be laid before the said Committee of Judges, Triers, or General Arbitrators, for their inspection and information, and their judgment upon the matter in dispute fairly entered as before directed; which said Court or Committee is also to keep a fair and distinct journal or minutes of all their proceedings, as well with respect to lands as other matters which may come before them in consequence of these our resolutions.

"It is also firmly agreed and resolved that no person shall be admitted to make an entry for any lands with the said Entry Taker, or permitted to hold the same, unless such person shall subscribe his name and conform to this our Association, Confederacy, and General Government, unless it be for persons who have returned home, and are permitted to have lands reserved for their use until the first day of May next, in which case entries may be made for such absent persons, according to the true meaning of this writing, without their personal presence, but shall become utterly void, if the particular person or persons for whom such entry shall be made should refuse or neglect to perform the same as soon as conveniently may be after their return, and before the said first day of May in the year 1781.

"Whereas the frequent and dangerous incursions of the Indians, and almost daily massacre of some of our inhabitants, renders it absolutely necessary, for our safety and defence, that due obedience be paid to our respective officers elected and to be elected at the several stations or settlements, to take command of the men or militia at such fort or station;

"It is further agreed and resolved that when it shall be adjudged necessary and expedient by such commanding officer to draw out the militia of any fort or station to pursue or repulse the enemy, the said officer shall have power to call out such and so many of his men as he may judge necessary, and in case of disobedience may inflict such fine as he in his discretion shall think just and reasonable; and also may impress the horse or horses of any person or persons whomsoever, which, if lost or damaged in such service, shall be paid for by the inhabitants of such fort or station in such manner and such proportion as the Committee hereby appointed, or a majority of them, shall direct and order; but if any person shall be aggrieved, or think himself unjustly vexed and injured by the fine or fines so imposed by his officer or officers, such person may appeal to the said Judges or Committee of General Arbitrators, who, or a majority of them, shall have power to examine the matter fully, and make such order therein as they may think just and reasonable, which decision shall be conclusive on the party complaining, as well as the officer or officers inflicting such fine; and the money arising from such fines shall be carefully applied for the benefit of such fort or station, in such manner as the said Arbitrators shall hereafter direct.

"It is lastly agreed and firmly resolved that a dutiful and humble address or petition be presented, by some person or persons to be chosen by the inhabitants, to the General Assembly, giving the fullest assurance of the fidelity and attachment to the interest of our country, and obedience to the laws and Constitution thereof. Setting forth that we are confident our settlement is not within the boundaries of any nation or tribe of Indians, as some of us know and all believe that they have fairly sold and received satisfaction for the land or territories whereon we reside, and therefore we hope we may not be considered as acting against the laws of our country or the mandates of government.

"That we do not desire to be exempt from the rateable share of the public expense of the present war, or other contingent charges of government. That we are, from our remote situation, utterly destitute of the benefit of the laws of our country, and exposed to the depredations of the Indians, without any justifiable or effectual means of embodying our militia, or defending ourselves against the hostile attempts of our enemy; praying and imploring the immediate aid and protection of government, by erecting a county to include our settlements, appointing proper officers for the discharge of public duty, taking into consideration our distressed situation with respect to the Indians, and granting such relief and assistance as in wisdom, justice, and humanity may be thought reasonable.

"Nashborough, 13th May, 1780."

Richard Henderson,	Samuel Deson,	David Shelton,
Nathaniel Hart,	Samuel Marten,	Spill Coleman,
Wm. H. Moore,	James Buchanan,	Samuel McMurray,
Samuel Phariss,	Solomon Turpin,	P. Henderson,
John Donelson, C.,	Isaac Rentfro,	Edward Bradley,
Gasper Mansker,	Robert Cartwright,	Edward Bradley, Jr.,
John Caffery,	Hugh Rogan,	James Bradley,
John Blakemore, Sr.,	Joseph Morton,	Michael Stoner,
John Blakemore, Jr.,	William Woods,	Joseph Mosely,
James Shaw,	David Mitchell,	Henry Guthrie,

Francis Armstrong,
Robert Lucas,
James Robertson,
George Freland,
James Freland,
John Tucker,
Peter Catron,
Philip Catron,
Francis Catron,
John Dunham,
Isaac Johnson,
Adam Kelar,
Thomas Burgess,
William Burgess,
William Green,
Moses Webb,
Absalom Thomson,
John McVay,
James Thomson,
Charles Thomson,
Robert Thomson,
Martin Hardin,
Elijah Thomson,
Andrew Thomson,
William Seaton,
Edward Thomelu,
Isaac Drake,
Jonathan Jenings,
Zachariah Green,
Andrew Lucas,

James $\times$ Patrick,
^{his} ... _{mark}

Richard Gross,
John Drake,
Daniel Turner,
Timothy Feret,
Isaac Lefever,
Thomas Fletcher,
Samuel Barton,
James Ray,
Thomas Denton,

Thomas Hendricks,
John Holladay,
Frederick Stump, (in
   Dutch,)
William Hood,
John Boyd,
Jacob Stump,
Henry Hardin,
Richard Stanton,
Sampson Sawyers,
John Hobson,
Ralph Wilson,
James Givens,
James Harrod,
James Buchanan, Sr.,
William Geioch,
Samuel Shelton,
John Gibson,
Robert Espey,
George Espey,
William Gowen,
John Wilfort,
James Espey,
Michael Kimberlin,
John Cowan,
Francis Hodge,
William Fleming,
James Leeper,
George Leeper,
Daniel Mungle,
Patrick McCutchen,
Samuel McCutchen,
William Price,
Henry Kerbey,
Joseph Jackson,
Daniel Ragsdil,
Michael Shaver,
Samuel Willson,
John Reid,
Joseph Dougherty,
Charles Cameron,

W. Russell, **Jr.**,
Hugh Simpson,
Samuel Moore,
Joseph Denton,
Arthur McAdoo,
James McAdoo,
Nathaniel Henderson,
John Evans,
Wm. Bailey Smith,
Peter Luney,
John Luncy,
James Cain,
Daniel Johnson,
Daniel Jarrot,
Jesse Maxey,
Noah Hawthorn,
Charles McCartney,
John Anderson,
Matthew Anderson,
Wm. McWhirter,
Barnet Hainey,
Richard Sims,
Titus Murray,
James Hamilton,
Henry Dougherty,
Zach. White,
Burgess White,
William Calley,
James Ray,
William Ray,
Perley Grimes,
Samuel White,
Daniel Hogan,
Thomas Hines,
Robert Goodloe,
Thomas W. Alston,
William Barret,
Thomas Shannon,
James Moore,
Richard Moore,
Samuel Moore,

Elijah Moore,
John Moore,
Andrew Ewin,
Ebenezer Titus,
Mark Robertson,
John Montgomery,
Charles Campbell,
William Overall,
John Turner,
Nathaniel Overall,
Patrick Quigley,
Josias Gamble,
Samuel Newell,
Joseph Read,
David Maxwell,
Thomas Jefriss,
Joseph Dunnagin,
John Phelps,
Andrew Bushoney,
Daniel Ragsdell,
John McMurty,
D'd. Williams,
John McAdames,
Samson Williams,
Thomas Thompson,
Martin King,
William Logan,
John Alstead,
Nicholas Counrod,
Evin Evins,
Jonathan Evins,
John Thomas,
Joshua Thomas,
David Rounsavall,

Isaac Rounsavall,
James Crocket,
Andrew Crocket,
Russell Gower,
John Shannon,
David Shannon,
Jonathan Drake,
Benjamin Drake,
John Drake,
Mereday Rains,
Richard Dodge,
James Green,
James Cooke,
Daniel Johnston,
George Miner,
George Green,
William More,
Jacob Cimberlin,
Robert Dockerty,
John Crow,
William Summers,
Lesois Frize (?) (some
    name in Dutch hie-
    roglyphics,)   ·
Amb's. Mauldin,
Morton Mauldin,
John Dunham,
Archelaus Allaway,
Samuel Hayes,
Isaac Johnson,
Thomas Edmeston,
Ezekiel Norris,
William Purnell,
William McMurray,

John Cordry,
Nicholas Tramal,
Haydon Wells,
Daniel Ratletf,
John Callaway,
John Pleake,
Willis Pope,
Silas Harlan,
Hugh Leeper,
Harmon Consellea,
Humphrey Hogan,
James Foster,
William Morris,
Nathaniel Bidlack,
A. Tatom,
William Hinson,
Edmund Newton,
Jonathan Green,
John Phillips,
George Flynn,
Daniel Jarrott,
John Owens,
James Freland,
Thomas Molloy,
Isaac Lindsay,
Isaac Bledsoe,
Jacob Castleman,
George Power,
James Lynn,
Thomas Cox,
Edward Lucas,
Philip Alston,
James Russell,

REMARKS.

After the adoption of the "Articles of Agreement," Col. Henderson proceeded to make sales of land under the Watauga purchase of 1775. He allowed each settler to buy one thousand acres at the price of *ten dollars*, and issued to the purchaser a certificate of such purchase, with a clause providing for further proceedings to confirm the title when a land-office should be more regularly established.

Col. Henderson had two brothers with him, whose names may be seen among the foregoing signatures, Nathaniel and Pleasant Henderson. They commenced a station at an early day upon Stone's River, not far from the place where Col. Donelson began his first settlement. They had done little more than erect what were called "half-faced camps," cut and burned off some cane, before the depredations of the Indians caused the abandonment of each of these enterprises.

The Hendersons were natives of Hanover county, Virginia, but removed to Orange, North Carolina, after the treaty purchase in 1775. Pleasant and Nathaniel, in 1776, made a visit to Boonesborough, and in their return endured extreme sufferings and many perils passing through the wilderness. The reports made by these intelligent and reliable men, as to the richness of the country over which they had travelled, and of the "countless, incredible numbers of buffalo, deer, and bear, and wild Indians enough to give a little variety and attractiveness to the hunter's life," confirmed the marvelous stories of "the Long Hunters," and of others, insomuch that the spirit of adventure and love of pioneer life was awaked afresh among those who were then already far beyond the organized jurisdiction of the State, and the quiet of settled, civilized society. Men who had already incurred a thousand dangers, and were enduring a thousand hardships in the far-off mountain fastnesses, began to consider it for their happiness, the good of themselves and their posterity, to seek new lodgments, where only wild woods, wild Indians, and wild beasts were to be seen.

It was a strange passion which actuated these huntsmen pioneers—a strange Providence which ordered and ruled the hearts and lives of this class of men. They all abhorred tyranny, they had ever breathed the free air of heaven, and roamed at will through the boundless forests and prairies, which seemed prepared expressly to engage their attention and await their subduing toil. It was their duty and their destiny.

CHAPTER VI.

1780—1781.

AMONG these earliest pioneers there was much anxiety to explore the country. The denseness of the cane-brakes rendered this a laborious work. All the rich lands were covered with cane: through these there were paths made by the buffalo and other wild animals. The largest of these roads passed from one sulphur spring to another. There is common salt in all these waters. The emigrants or stationers soon passed along these trails, and sought out places whereon to begin their improvements.

Allthough the winter had been one of such remarkable severity, and the spring rainy, these researches had been prosecuted with great earnestness and cheerfulness. Buffalo, deer, turkeys and other game had been so abundant, (though lean,) that none then apprehended the early arrival of a day of destitution and almost starvation. But ere the close of this year their sufferings commenced: they had no corn, no bread; "jerked" or dried meat was the substitute. And the procuring of meat, ere long, was attended with much exposure and peril.

February. The Indians made their appearance in the neighborhood of the stations; and although they did not immediately manifest a direct hostile spirit by attacking the whites, they were evidently watching them, and intent upon giving so much annoyance and alarm to the game as to disperse the buffalo and deer from their old haunts near the French Lick.

The Indian policy of dispersing the wild game, which seems to have commenced in the spring, was prosecuted earnestly towards the fall of this year. During the two succeeding years it was practiced with such success, that the stationers were under necessity of adventuring to distances and places afar off, and thus exposing themselves to any wily savage.

We may here, in general terms, so anticipate the events of the three first years of the stationers on the Cumberland as to say, they were years of privation, losses, and gloom. Remote and separate improvements had to be abandoned. The people were driven in, and under necessity of congregating at the Bluff or French Lick Station, and at Eaton's. Some continued at Freeland's. At Mansker's they lingered to the close of this year. (But more of these events in proper order.)

They all had kindred or friends at other advanced stations; some in Kentucky, some who had gone to "the Illinois" and to "the Natchez." At those places it was imagined that there was greater safety, and such strength of numbers and supplies, that fields and gardens could be cultivated without the laborers being shot down or tomahawked when at their work.

Some began to regret that they had not gone with their friends who had parted their company at the mouth of the Tennessee; others wished the boats had not been broken up to make but indifferent cabins among the cedars. "Shall we flee the country?" was the question. "Better," said some, "to leave while we may, than remain and die of hunger, or be massacred by the savages." "No," said a few resolute men, "No!" And there were some brave-hearted women who said "No." "This is the place for which we set out. We sought this for our home in the wilderness; we have a right to settle here; it is a goodly land; none of us are sick; we can live on fresh and dried meat. A good Providence protected us, women, and children, in our five months' voyage; and this through perils and sufferings and hardships, more and greater than we have seen here. We are content to abide where we are." So said Mrs. Cartwright and Mrs. Neelly, "mothers in Israel." And so said Mrs. Robertson, Donelson, Caffrey, Purnell, Jennings, and Blackemore, and the wives of the Bledsoes, who afterwards came by the long land route. Nearly every one of these held the same religious sentiments, and often comforted themselves and others by their "trust in Providence."

It is an interesting fact, worthy of record, that all of these women were well educated in the doctrines of revealed religion; they brought their Bibles with them, they offered the first prayers in this then far-off wilderness, and said not, "How shall we sing the Lord's song in a strange land?" for here they did often sing the songs of Zion; not only to quiet and lull to sleep their children, but to cheer their own hearts and nourish the graces there.

If "Paul and Silas could pray and sing praises to God at midnight and in prison," so there were some here to whose faith and prayers there were granted "the cloud by day and the pillar of fire by night." They were of that class of wives, mothers, and Christians, who sought for the path of duty, who had faith in God, and devoutly asked Him for direction and protection. Such women could well assist to hold up the hands of stoutest and bravest men.

These men and women were inured to toil and exposure. They were willing to "endure hardships as good soldiers." Hitherto a faint heart had been unknown among them. Desperate must have been their condition, when such a people were almost ready to confess themselves defeated, and so soon.

Perhaps the chief cause of apprehension was their very limited supply of powder and lead. Indeed, it is truly astonishing how they ever obtained such a quantity of these indispensable equipments for support and defence.

When they emigrated, they brought with them a good supply. At first, and for months, they had little apprehension of trouble from "savage men," who were seldom seen; but being constantly tempted to shoot the wild game, that in countless droves was ever in sight, they wasted their ammunition heedlessly and needlessly. The stock was therefore greatly reduced by the end of the first year. When this was noticed, the question of sending hundreds of miles to the settlements in Virginia or Carolina (proper,) to purchase and pack powder and lead to these settlements, was beset with difficulties.

"Who shall go for us?" This was the important yet delicate question. It was pondered in the hearts of many who did not ask it audibly. Who shall leave wife and children here, now exposed to death from two sources, famine and the savages; leave them for months, perhaps never to return, or, if permitted to escape all the perils of the journey and again to reach the Cumberland, probably to find all dead—famished by hunger, killed by the Indians, or devoured by the wild beasts!

And in the minds of any was there distrust, jealousy, or cavilling, for fear that in the absence of brave and generous men upon such a mission, those who remained should make yet more favorable selections of land? Far from it.

Robertson, with one of his sons and some other good woodmen, in company, we think, with one of the Bledsoes and persons from that station, went on this mission late in the fall. Robertson returned, as he had at first determined, after visiting Harrod's, Boone's and Briant's Stations in Kentucky. The Bledsoe party continued to Watauga, and came back with some accession of numbers—wives and children.

But these "thoughts of woe," and the shadows of coming events, have drawn us a little in advance of true chronology; we will therefore gather up some of the sad occurrences to the close of the year 1780, and somewhat in the order of time in which they transpired.

In the spring of this year, and at a time when the stationers were generally felicitating themselves upon the quiet they enjoyed, the goodly land to which they had been conducted, and the happy homes they were soon to have; when the magnificent forest charmed their eyes with its deep, rich verdure, the air was fragrant with the sweet perfume of the wild grape and of jasmine flowers, in the stillness of eventide, a gun was heard, whose report was not familiar, yet at the time attracted little remark or notice.

Men who had no wives or families here, did not always lodge in the same station. After the labor or hunt of the day, such persons would sometimes stop and remain all night at a station with whose population they were not regularly numbered. At a social visit, or to partake of a good supper, they might tarry all night, and their absence from their "home station" caused no alarm. Married men, or men with children requiring attention, were always expected to "be at home at night," to provide for and protect their own. And yet they all were given to a generous hospitality and to a reliable friendship. The apostle's injunction had been read within the hearing of every one many a time and oft: "Look not every man on his own things, [exclusively,] but every man also on the things of others."

But what of the report of that strange gun? Who has killed another buffalo or deer or bear? Who tarries till night to secure his game? To which of the encampments has he gone? Who is missing? Some of these questions were asked, but not until the next evening was the startling fact made known, that "a man had been shot and scalped!" The first emigrant had been killed; the savages had begun here the work of bloodshed. They had all looked upon the dead; few, if any, had gazed upon the victims of the scalping-knife and tomahawk. There was some curiosity to see the body of Joseph Hay. He had been shot through the body, hacked with the "small battle-axe" of the Indian, and the scalp cut and torn from the upper part of his head. Some attempt had been made to sever the head from the body. His clothes were not stripped off, but were saturated with blood. His gun, shot-pouch, horn, and hunting-knife were gone. He was interred in the open ground upon the point of land east of the "French Salt Lick," now usually called the Sulphur Spring.*

---

* Judge Haywood says, "Milliken was killed on Richland Creek, five miles west of Nashville, and was the first white man killed by the Indians." Whether John Milliken or Joseph Hay was the first cannot now be investigated, and is immaterial. This, however, is certain, that the body of Joseph Hay was the first which was gazed upon by the people at the stations in such a mangled condition, and

The news of this event was promptly communicated to all the emigrants, and request made that the settlers at each station should hasten the erection and completion of suitable defences; that officers, civil and military, should be chosen; that spies should be sent out, and sentinels placed to give alarm of danger.

There was some excitement for the time. It served a good purpose. Until this time there had been very little apprehension of danger. Some of the emigrants continued to camp beneath trees in the open woods, and maintained no watch by day or by night. Now the cry was, not "Every man to his tent," but, Every man with his axe, wedge, and hand-spike! It was, "Down with the trees; cleave them asunder; haul them together; roll up the logs; build up the strong-hold; drive down the palisades; keep a sharp look-out!" This warning was needed, for "the signs of Indians about" were discovered at various places near the stations.*

About midsummer two men, by the names of Goin and Kennedy, were at work between Eaton's and Mansker's Stations; they were killed and scalped. The injunction or caution had been given for one of them to watch while the other worked, but it seemed that both were at work, and were shot down as they, in their labor, came near a brush-heap "and thicket." Near this same time D. Larimer was killed at a short distance from Freeland's Station. He was scalped and beheaded. Close upon this followed the death of Isaac Lefevre. He was shot down, scalped, and butchered on the river bluff where Line street terminates. About the same time, Solomon Philips was shot near the spot where is now the High School building, corner of Spruce and Broad. He escaped to the Bluff Station, but lived only a few days. Solomon Murray, who was with Philips, was killed on the spot, and scalped. At this same place Robert Aspey was also killed. Benjamin Renfroe, John Maxwell, and John Kennedy were fishing near the mouth of the French Lick branch.

which they interred in that "first cemetery of the first settlers." We believe that Milliken's body was buried where it was found, on Richland Creek.

* In May, 1780, the Assembly of North Carolina had passed a resolution to grant to officers and soldiers of the Continental line a bounty or compensation for military services, payable in lands in the Western country—Tennessee west of the mountains. The Spanish agents heard of this, and saw at once that the Western population would thus be rapidly increased, and by a class of men to whom war would have no terrors, and with whom there could be no trifling. They dreaded these neighbors. They invited Chickasaws and Choctaws to a conference in the Chickasaw nation, and there artfully engaged some to attack the early settlers on the Cumberland, and this at a time when she was our professed ally in war against England. Thus a secret enemy in concert with England.

Indians crept stealthily upon them, tomahawked and scalped Renfroe, who fought desperately, and made prisoners of the two others.

As Col. Donelson and his voyagers ascended the Cumberland, some of the emigrants were attracted by the appearance of good lands and eligible sites for settlements at and near the mouth of Red River. A few of them determined to make their "locations" there. The Renfroe and Turpin families (connected by marriage) were of this number. And that brave scout, wakeful soldier, and early companion of Robertson, Valentine Sevier, with a few of his family connections, soon united with others to settle at the Point, and where is now the flourishing town of Clarksville. In June or July, Nathan Turpin and one other person were killed and scalped there.

These murders becoming now so frequent, and this settlement being so distant from Robertson's, Freeland's, Eaton's, and others, and there being indeed so few men at these Red River locations, it was deemed proper to remove. The Turpins were intimate friends or relatives of the Freelands, and they sought to reach Freeland's Station, while some others determined to stop at Eaton's, on the east side of the river. All, however, hastily determined to leave. After concealing, as best they could, some of their goods, they started together. Having travelled as far as they could through the cane, brush, and dense forest, and over a very uneven country, at dusk they encamped. Here, after a short consultation, a few of the men, and several of the women, reproached themselves for their hasty flight, and for having left so much of their movable property. They determined to return for it. That night they cautiously approached their deserted cabins, and, by break of day, had gathered what they preferred this time not to leave behind them. They resumed their march for the upper settlements, and at night encamped about two miles north of Sycamore Creek, upon the edge of a small stream. In the night they were attacked by the Indians. The firing was sudden and destructive. About twenty persons were killed at this encampment. Of the number were Joseph Renfroe, Mr. Johns, and his numerous family. It is believed that several persons who were with those who had encamped on the way the night previous, had awaited the return of the party with the recovered goods; and thus were their children and youth slaughtered at this sudden and furious onset. The havoc was awful.

A Mrs. Jones was the only person who escaped to rehearse the sad tale of woe. It was by following the tracks of the first party of fugitives that this frightened and lone woman was enabled to reach Eaton's. Her clothes were nearly torn into shreds, as she ran through the bushes for twenty miles.

Those of the first party who renewed their flight the second day reached the upper station in safety.

This was a horrible affair. The impression prevailed that the party of Indians must be large and well armed, yet the stationers promptly determined to visit the place of slaughter, to recover any who might by possibility survive, and to bury the dead.

"The Indians had made off with the horses, and such property as suited them; chopped, broke, and scattered such as they cared not to take away."

The small stream upon the bank of which this slaughter took place has been ever since known as "Battle Creek." It is in truth a misnomer, for, as far as we have ever read or heard, there was no battle; the shooting, and killing, and scalping were all done by the savages, and this so suddenly and hastily that little or no resistance was made by the whites.

As was ascertained soon after, these savages were Choctaws and Chickasaws, who had no provocation or cause of quarrel with these pioneer settlers. The Choctaws never pretended to have any claim even to hunt upon these waters. As far as any roaming savages—whose nearest wigwams were two hundred miles distant—had a right to these lands, and the wild beasts thereon, the Chickasaws could make out the best pretence of title, next to the Sewanees or Shawnees, whom their ancestors had driven from this country a century ago. And yet this conquering tribe (the Chickasaws) had not dared to build towns, plant fields, or light their council-fires in all this region. What provocation had they received? What could induce or justify this attack?

The war for American Independence was in its middle, and near its most critical period. British emissaries had been busily at work with these south-western Indians, as they had with the northern and those between the Ohio and the lakes. That noted agent and plotter of conspiracies, Doctor Conolly, had been at work for years among the Shawnees east of the Ohio, and had now extended his operations to these otherwise peaceable tribes at the south.

They were instructed to "drive back these Virginians, or make wolf-bait of their carcasses." In compliance with such injunction and agreement, and to secure "such bait," this party of Choctaws and Chickasaws had invaded this country, prowled around the settlements, and "shot or chopped down whomsoever they could." They were very successful in this summer's incursion, and themselves escaped with wonderful impunity.

There was no "good feeling" between these two Indian nations east of the Mississippi and the fugitive Shawnees, who had found a miserable living near the junction of the Ohio and Mississippi, upon the low lands west.

The thought occurred to Robertson and others to conciliate these neighboring savages, to withdraw them from British alliance, and gain them as friends to these American settlements.

It was also known to Colonel Henderson, Robertson, and others, that there were some disputes and ill-feelings between the Cherokees (under cover of purchase from whom these pioneers in part set up their right to settle here) and the Chickasaws. Neither of these tribes dared to brave all dangers and occupy the hunting-grounds between the Tennessee and the Cumberland, or between the Cumberland and Ohio. Colonel Donelson gave some information as to this enmity between these nations which was useful.

Some of each nation were willing to see "the white man" interposed. And yet both, and especially the Cherokees, dreaded such an advance of "the Virginians," and the destruction of game which always ensued. With them also British agents had been tampering, and had found some of that nation, as they found many of the Creeks and Seminoles, ready to war for "the King."

Among the Choctaws and Chickasaws, only a small number were engaged to make war upon the Americans; and the parties who had commenced depredations at the mouth of Red River, probably enrolled all who could be enlisted for such hellish purposes in those tribes.

Robertson sought to communicate to them the peaceable and friendly disposition of the settlers upon the Cumberland; but in the initiation and conducting of such measures as might be productive of desired results there were many difficulties apparent, and there might be others yet greater which could not be even imagined.

Here were these thirty unprovoked murders—"brothers' blood crying from the ground!" What could atone for these? Would it be politic, even if it were possible, to enter into covenants of peace, and these deaths unavenged? Would not these and other savages regard the whites as contemptible cowards, and fit for naught else than "wolf-bait?"

But, on the other hand, could all of the settlers be restrained from retaliation? Robertson insisted upon "seeking peace and pursuing it." No one objected to the determination to kill any and every Indian against whom there was good reason to allege complicity in these outrages.

Through the agency of old Monsieur De Monbreun, some Cherokees of friendly and reliable character had commenced a small traffic with the whites. But when these murders were committed, the trading Indians became alarmed, kept at a distance, or perhaps returned to their own nation. Although some were regarded with suspicion, yet there was never any positive testimony to convict such traders of participating in what had been done. It was well, however, that they "made themselves scarce and invisible," as Ewin said, for the murders were continued in various parts of the settlements. Having broken up those which had been commenced near the mouth of Red River, the Indians seemed determined to wage a war of total destruction.

They next appeared near Colonel Donelson's first encampment on Stone's river, where they caught a negro man named Jim, who was a body-servant and cook belonging to Col. Henderson. After the adoption of the Articles of Agreement and Compact of Government on first of May, Col. Henderson went to the Kentucky stations, leaving this servant Jim and a young man who assisted in surveying, in charge of some small amount of property, to await his return. This black man and the chain-carrier made a visit to Clover Bottom, or Donelson's first station, and as they were descending the river the Indians intercepted and killed them. Col. Henderson had an improvement near Donelson's, a half camp.

And whether at the same time, and as of the same party, we know not, but near to the same time and place they killed and wounded several others. James Randolph Robertson, second son of Colonel James Robertson, was killed by the same Indians. This was a young man of much promise.

Some cavillers asked, "What does the Colonel now think of pacific measures? What will he say now about abandoning this Aceldama, this field of blood?" "Kill them, yes, kill them!" said the Colonel, "'making a difference:' spare the innocent!" "Yes," said George Freeland, "*if* there are innocent ones hunting around here, notify them by powder and shot that they are too far from home; so far that a good rifle-shot will help them to a *short cut.*"

Rains and others were for giving quick and hot pursuit in every instance. A more vigorous system of police and espionage was demanded and adopted.

The enemy became very bold. A party was repeatedly known to approach the two stations on the west side of the river, and to lie in wait between the Bluff and Freeland's.

At the place now occupied by the Verandah Hotel, corner of Cedar and Cherry Streets, which was then a low, wet spot, covered with thick-set undergrowth, Philip Catron was badly wounded in the chest. He was on horseback, returning from Freeland's Station. He sustained himself upon his horse, and was thus carried to the gate of the Bluff Station, (east end of Spring Street.) He continued to spit blood for months, but finally recovered.

John Caffrey and Daniel Williams had fastened their canoe to the shore, and were ascending the steep bluff near the station, when they were fired upon and both wounded in the legs. Captain Rains was providentially near with two or three others; they rushed to the rescue. A sharp contest ensued near the sulphur spring. Raines saved Williams from death and scalping.

Old Mr. Bernard had commenced "a clearing" near Denton's Lick, (now known as "Buena Vista Springs,") and was busily at work when the Indians killed him, cut off and carried away his head. The two young Dunhams were working near by; they escaped to Freeland's Station; but another young man, son of John Milliken, was shot down, beheaded, and his head taken away.

The Indians who committed outrages on the west side of the river were Creeks and Cherokees, and some few Delawares or Shawnees. The Creeks manifested a bloodthirsty spirit. The bodies of the unfortunate victims who fell on this side of the river were often shamefully mutilated. Here only were heads cut off. Of those who fell beneath the Indian tomahawk near the Bluff Station during the autumn of this year, we may mention Jonathan Jennings, who had commenced an improvement opposite the point of the first island above Nashville. A rude dissection was made of his body, proving conclusively that his murderers were not skilled in anatomy or surgery. Parts of his body, or that of some other victim, they hung upon the bushes.

On the east side of the river some persons were killed at various places—James Mayfield and a man named Porter, near Eaton's; the latter in midday and in view of persons at the station. They made safe their retreat, though pursued by the whites, "yelling like Indians!"

Ned Carven was killed at his "clearing," four miles east of Nashville, (where William Williams, Esq., now lives,) and his wife, with her two small children, hid themselves in the thick cane until the next day, when they safely reached Eaton's. John Shockley and Jesse Balestine were killed not far from the same place.

"In this summer Robert Gilkie sickened and died; he was the first man of the settlers that died a natural death. Philip Coonrod or Conrad was killed by a tree falling on him," near where is the junction of Cherry and De Monbreun Streets. A servant of Mrs. Gilkie's was dangerously wounded by a gun-shot, when attending to the cows, near the west side of the Public Square. "A lot of children ran and screamed, and the Indians ran and screamed the other way."

8

The Stumps had commenced improvements north of Eaton's Station, on White's Creek; Jacob and Frederick were there at work, or "prospecting," when the Indians fired upon them, killing Jacob and giving chase to "old man Frederick." It was a close race for three miles to Eaton's, up hill and down dale, through privet and through cane, and into the cedars near the station, where it was stoop here, shy there, fleeing from his pursuers. They were very close upon him several times; so near as to strike at him with the hatchet, which one of them finally threw with such violence and accuracy that, "passing near his head with a whiz, it fell in the bushes twenty feet before him." He supposed the Indian stopped to hunt for it, and followed no farther. He used to say, "Py sure, I tid run dat time!" He not only "Stumped it, but heeled it," as Williams said.

1780. The same party of Indians proceeded on the east side of the river up to Bledsoe's Lick and Station, and killed two persons, names not recorded; and at a short distance from the station they surrounded William Johnson, killed and scalped him. They shot some cattle; and this was a serious loss, as only a few were yet in the country. They burned some buildings and fences.

That giant man with "the big feet," Thomas Sharp Spencer, was returning from a hunting-excursion, with several horses laden with meat and skins; and when only a few miles southeast of Bledsoe's, was encountered by a party of Indians, who fired at him, wounding him and capturing his horses, but not him. He saw "they were too many for him," and therefore he made good use of his "seven-league boots" and "made tracks;" no doubt as large as those which (according to Haywood) frightened away all the Frenchmen except old Mr. De Monbreun, years before. "Spencer grieved mightily about his horses and the meat," and men, women and children sympathized in these losses. It was not long, however, before he went forth again, and then returned "bringing spoils with him." He was remarkably fond of *bear-meat,* and could find and kill more bears and fatter ones than any other two hunters. He had no appetite for *bread,* other than *dried* meat. If he had meat in his stomach and meat in his sack or pouch, he was a contented man. "He greased his meals with a pint of bear's oil, and felt the better for it." Other hunters had been with Spencer on this excursion, but he was alone with the pack-horses when they fired on him.

Another party of hunters, about this time, was attacked near Asher's Station, on Station Camp Creek, and with the same result as with Spencer, "the loss of horses and game." (The particulars not known.) There was a cabin in a thicket near this station, in which a family lodged; the Indians fired between the logs, killing one person and wounding another. They then proceeded towards Bledsoe's again, and were met by Alexander Buchanan, who, with a party of men, was searching for these murderers and horse-thieves. Buchanan was at the head of his men, following mostly the buffalo-path, and he suddenly met the Indians. He shot down their leader, and the next one being wounded, the others fled, leaving the horses and packs to the whites.

Soon after this, Colonel Robertson, together with this same Buchanan and eighteen others, pursued a party of Indians from Freeland's Station, forty or fifty miles, to Duck River, killed and wounded several, and recovered considerable property. These Indians had killed the cows of the stationers. The destruction of a cow was a sad grievance. The remark is not extravagant nor the statement incredible, that "the killing of a milch cow was next to that of husband or child—a wife or mother could shed tears for *either*."

The Indians would not shoot a horse, if they thought there was any prospect of capturing the animal; but oxen, cows and hogs they killed, because they could not drive them to their own country, and because by so doing they inflicted injury upon the whites. In many instances the cattle would be found with deep gashes in various parts of their bodies, made by the tomahawk, or with arrows sticking in their sides.

In the fall of this year the Indians came very near to the fort on the bluff, and fired upon several persons who were at work at the gate and palisades. They fired and ran, as was their custom, concealing like wolves and foxes in the cane or underbrush. In this instance Mr. Taylor was badly wounded, but not mortally. Pursuit was made to a short distance, but Colonel Robertson and some others dissuaded, fearing an ambush. Indeed, to pursue such a creeping foe into the privet and cane was almost in all instances attended with fatality to the pursuers. One of the spies, however, wounded an Indian and obtained his hatchet and gun.

Near Eaton's Station the savages again and again appeared and committed outrages. Indeed, the havoc which they had already committed, and the manifestation of hostility and danger, was such that the stationers at the outposts were urged to come in. Even that experienced and fearless hunter and pioneer, Gasper Mansker, acknowledged that it would be best to convene at fewer places, strengthen them as strongholds, clear away all the trees and underbrush from around the stations to a distance too great for the ordinary range of Indian guns, and the load they usually put in. This was good advice, but he and some of his immediate associates did not hasten to desert "Mansker's Station." They lingered there: some tarried too long.

About this time Captain Leiper, in command of fifteen men, pursued Indians to Harpeth River. The Indians heard the whites as they came "with a rush through the cane," and for some time "attempted to escape with the horses and plunder," but the pursuit was becoming too close and earnest. The horses were burdened with the various articles stolen from the whites, insomuch that they were often entangled and stopped by the bushes and cane. The savages did not take the time and precaution to cut the ropes and thongs by which the loads were fastened upon the animals. At the first fire of a gun from Leiper, every Indian fled to the bush, abandoning all the horses and whatever was on them.

Leiper was certain he wounded the Indian at whom he fired; "the fellow dropped his gun and ran." "The red-skin imp, I made him limp," said the captain, a few nights after, when rehearsing the incidents of the expedition at *his wedding*.

This marriage of Captain Leiper formed an era in the history of the stationers. This was the *first wedding* on the Cumberland. As a preliminary measure, and next to the birth of the first child at the Bluff, it has been duly recorded by the first historian, (Haywood.) Upon consultation with his Associate Judges of the "Notable Tribunal," Colonel Robertson, as head of the government, deemed himself authorized to celebrate the rites of marriage; and he performed his part of the ceremony with suitable dignity. The result was a happy union, and some worthy posterity. This was the first marriage west of the mountains.

"There was pretty much of a feast at this wedding," and a most cheerful company. They had no wine or ardent spirits, they had no wheat or corn-bread, no cakes or confectionaries, but they did have "any quantity of fresh and dried meat, buffalo tongue, bear meat, venison saddle and venison ham, broiled, stewed, and fried," and "jerked;" and as a great delicacy for the ladies, some "roasting-ears," or ears of green corn roasted or boiled, or made into *succotash*. Before and after supper they enjoyed the *dance*, not "upon the green," but upon the puncheon floor.

After this initiative ceremony, Colonel Robertson and other "Judges or Triers" at various stations deemed it suitable, right and needful to unite other parties as man and wife. Several of these marriages are mentioned in Haywood. They have all been regarded as legal and valid, as much so as those performed since the year 1783, after the laws of North Carolina were extended over these settlements.

The Choctaws and Chickasaws, who were among the earliest to attack the stationers, to kill the whites and capture their horses, did not long remain near the settlements. It is presumed that they (as tribes or nations) had not entered fully into the measures for a "Confederacy" proposed between the northern and southern Indians. The first hunters and explorers of this Cumberland and Tennessee wilderness had occasionally met with Chickasaws, and without doing each other personal injury. The messages and small presents sent to some of them, at an early day, by these stationers, probably gave some satisfaction.

The cause of offence alleged by them, and because of which they justified this invasion of the Cumberland settlement, was, that General George Rogers Clarke had erected "Fort Jefferson" within the Chickasaw country, about eighteen miles below the mouth of the Ohio. This was a "fillibustering expedition," with which the pioneers on Cumberland had nothing to do—no connection whatever.

Let us continue our narrative of Indian "fillibustering expeditions" into these settlements. A small station had been established on Station Camp Creek, and was called "Asher's," and was entitled to a judge among the Notables. In the summer of this year it was abandoned, and the people took refuge at Mansker's. At this last-named place no Indians had as yet been seen, nor their trails discovered through the woods near by, therefore the hunters ventured to greater distances, and an undue confidence of exemption from danger was entertained. This was no place of safety, as was soon to be acknowledged.

An attempt to make salt at Mansker's Sulphur Spring had terminated in disappointment. Other water was sought for, and it was determined to make the experiment at Neelly's Lick in Neelly's Bend. Here William Neelly, the early hunter and companion of Mansker and Robertson, prepared to make salt. In this he was assisted by several of the stationers at Mansker's. They obtained some salt after tedious boiling of the water.

Mr. Neelly had put up his temporary camp at a short distance from the spring, where he had one of his daughters with him to perform the duties of cooking for the men who were cutting wood, filling the kettles, and "tending the fires." Mr. Neelly hunted and killed deer and buffalo for the people thus at work, and had returned to the camp from a successful hunt, bringing with him a fat buck. Being much fatigued when he reached the camp, he threw down the deer and lay himself down to rest, while his daughter undertook the preparation of venison steak from one of the hams which she had skinned. The dogs had gone with the laborers at the Lick, Neelly had fallen asleep, and his daughter was busily engaged in preparation of the supper for her weary father and the men, whom she expected by the dusk of evening. She was passing out and in the tent, unconscious of danger, "singing one of the songs of Zion," for "her parents were professors of religion, and trained their children in religious duties."

Suddenly guns were fired near by the camp; her father raised himself half up, and with a groan fell back dead; Indians sprang upon and tied her, seized her father's gun and powder-horn, and led her away captive. They made very great haste, a stout Indian holding her on either side, compelling her to run, until, when she was so exhausted as to falter and be ready to sink, one or both—not rudely—supported her. And so they hastened away with her during nearly all that night. She was conducted to a Creek encampment, and thence to the distant Creek nation.

When the men came from the Lick to the camp, they found Mr. Neely killed and scalped, and the daughter absent. It was too dark to discover the number of the Indians, or any evidences of a struggle by the daughter for life or under captivity. They came to a quick conclusion not to tarry at the camp, lest they might be shot down; and as to pursuit, they could not decide which way to go. They hastened to Mansker's, at which they arrived before daylight, causing much alarm and distress by the sad news they related.

In the morning, a few men sought the trail of the Indians who had Miss Neely in captivity. They discovered the trail, and decided that she was alive, and that other parties of Indians were in the same woods.

The advice of Mansker, concurred in by Miss Neely's friends, was, "not to pursue, lest the captors should take her life." Her life was spared. After several years' captivity, she was released—exchanged—married reputably in Kentucky, made a good and exemplary wife and Christian mother.

This, and several other occurrences of alarming character, the shooting of all the cattle and hogs, etc., belonging to the Mansker Station, induced the abandonment of the place wholly after the Clover Bottom defeat.

The account of the attack upon and defeat of the whites near "Clover Bottom," as given by Judge Haywood, is, in several particulars, inaccurate, (as we are assured by surviving members of the family, and upon a careful examination of records and papers.)

It was not *Colonel* but *Captain* John Donelson who was there with his servants and a few friends, from Mansker's Station, and Captain Gower and son, and John Randoph Robertson, (brother of Col. Robertson,) and several men and servants from the Bluff Station.

Col. Donelson was an aged man, and remained at Mansker's. As the owner of the field of corn at Clover Bottom, he had proposed to the people at the Bluff to go there with boats, and "gather the corn on the shares," (that meant to divide it equally,) thus giving to the stationers at the Bluff the one half of the field.

The agreement was to "go at the same time, stick by each other, fill both boats with the corn, and come out of Stone's River in company." Then Captain Gower might descend the Cumberland to the Bluff, and Captain Donelson land his boat on the east side, or take it up to the mouth of Mansker's Creek, and pack his corn to Mansker's Station.

Upon the "set day" the parties and boats entered Stone's River and ascended to the corn-field, (in the bottom-land where the Lebanon pike passes through it, and the bridge is across the river.) A small patch of cotton had been planted on the east side of Stone's River, a few rods below the bridge. It was while Captain Donelson and party were gathering some of this cotton, in the morning, that Captain Gower and party determined to start down the river, in despite of the remonstrances of Donelson, saying, "It will take us all day to reach the Bluff; we will risk it," and pushed off from shore.

As Gower's boat was passing the narrow channel on the west side of the small island at Clover Bottom, not more than six hundred yards below the place where he had loaded, a large body of Indians, who were well hidden in the bushes on the west bank of the river, fired and killed all but one white man and two negroes. The white man and one of the negroes jumped out of the boat into shallow water and escaped into the cane, and, after wandering through the woods until midnight the next day, they reached the Bluff Station, and forced their way between the pickets and to the door of the block-house before they were discovered or had awakened any person within.

The other negro or mulatto was a free man, known as *Jack Civil.* He surrendered to the Indians, went with them to the Chickamauga towns, near Lookout Mountain, and then with the pirates and outlaws who settled the place on the Tennessee river, which hath acquired notoriety as *Nicka-Jack*, or *Nigger-Jack*, unquestionably so named after this mulatto.

Jack visited the settlements on Cumberland after the long Indians wars were over. He admitted to Captain Donelson and to others that he was with several of the parties of Indians from Nicka-Jack and Running-Water towns when they stole the horses of the stationers, but denied that *he* had ever killed or shot at a white person. It was generally believed *he lied.*

Gower's boat, loaded with corn, and having in it three dead bodies, and several of the dogs which the party had taken with them, came in sight of the people at the Bluff in the forenoon of the day after the slaughter, and was brought to shore where is now the upper Steamboat Landing, or east end of Broad street. The dead (whose faces were gnawed by the dogs) were buried, and the corn taken in sacks and baskets and by a cart to the Station.

The escape of Captain Donelson and party is related in our biographical sketch of Colonel John Donelson. Suffice it to say here, that it was only after much difficulty they passed through the cane to near the mouth of Drake's Creek, crossed the river, and reached Mansker's Station on the next day at night.

A runner had been sent from the Bluff to Mansker's the morning after the white man and negro had reached the Bluff, to give notice of the death of Captain Gower and others, and to ascertain if Captain Donelson and party had escaped. They had not then arrived, and the runner returned before any of them came in, so that the impression at the Bluff, at Freeland's and Eaton's Stations, was, for nearly a week, that Donelson and those with him had all been destroyed. They, however, all escaped.

Many of the clearings in which corn was planted this year were in the rich bottoms of the river and creeks, and a high tide of the river in July covered most of the fields and destroyed the corn. This made it more necessary to procure and dry the different kinds of meats. "The white and black walnut, and smooth and shell-bark hickory-nuts, furnished a valuable addition to their stock of edibles." Large quantities were gathered in the fall.

At a distance of twenty or thirty miles from the Bluff there were buffalo, bear, deer, and other wild game in abundance. The inventory of one hunting-party which had been out a few days on Caney Fork, shows enough to account for the love these pioneers had for the wild woods and its sports :

We should all turn Nimrods, or perhaps try to excel that "mighty hunter," and attempt to rival Boone, Spencer, and the "Long Hunters" of Tennessee and Kentucky, if we could do our part of a five days' work with success like this "five days' hunt on Caney's:" "Bears, 105; buffaloes, 75; deer, 87; total, 267." Returning from this episode, this hunting-party and drive, we must examine into the situation of the "old folks at home."

The enumeration of disasters which we have given for the last nine months must have prepared the reader to see once more the question of abandoning the settlements renewed. The record is: "At length they began to be disheartened; and a considerable part of them went this year to Kentucky and Illinois." And the conclusion of the record is:

" In the winter this emigration was stopped by the want of horses, and all the inhabitants were collected in two stations."

These two stations were Robertson's at the Bluff, and Eaton's, (two and a half miles distant,) on the east side of the river, on the first bluff below. Freeland's was not wholly abandoned at any time. The loss of horses was much lamented, and these thefts greatly incensed the owners; yet "there was no help for it, seldom recovery, and no compensation." It cannot be doubted that, had there been more horses, more of the stationers would have departed; and thus the perils of the few who were determined to remain and hold on "at all hazards and to the last extremity," would have been greatly increased. As it was, the paucity of numbers, feebleness of defences, and destitution of ammunition and provisions, may well have been conjectured by their wily foes, and "the imps of the evil one who egged them on," (to use one of their expressive phrases;) and they hoped to "burn them out, shoot them down, and use them up."

The conclusion to which the pent-up few arrived, was both logical and thological: " Providence has so ordered it that we can't get away; some of us would not if we could, no more of us could if they would !" Colonel Robertson and his brother had more horses stolen than any half dozen other pioneers; but, like Ewin, Rains, and Buchanan, the Robertsons "came to stay."

There were no reproaches cast at those who deemed it wisest and best to depart. It is true that every argument was used to dissuade any from going, but all arguments and persuasions failing, that old fellow, David Hood, "the said Hood," with his usual aptness of Scripture quotation, remarked, "If a wife or husband or our friends will depart, let them depart! They are not under bondage in such a case !"

Of the number of those who did depart we must mention all the Donelsons, with their families and some of their connections. Some called this "a desertion of friends, and a giving them up to the tomahawk and scalping-knife." It certainly had some effect upon others from whose presence so much had not been expected, and it saddened the prospects and hearts of the little band who "came to stay." But there was a wise providence in all this, as we have clearly shown in our sketch of Colonel Donelson and his family.

We may here remark that he had a large family, many negroes, women, and children, most of whom could have contributed nothing to their own support, or to the defences of the stations; they would have been "consumers and not producers" of provisions. To have shut them up in the fort at the Bluff would have caused some embarrassment, and perhaps dissatisfaction. At one of the stations in Kentucky, these negroes could more safely work in the fields, and thus raise provisions for their own sustenance and that of others.

We cannot doubt, that had Colonel Donelson's family remained at Mansker's—a place with extensive cane-brakes on every side, and easily assailable—they would have been utterly destroyed or captured. They could not, as at Robertson's and Eaton's, cast their lines into the river and thence draw some supply for their tables ; and when besieged or assailed, no prompt aid or relief could be afforded from either Robertson's or Eaton's.

Captain Rains removed his family and negroes to Kentucky. Leaving his wife and children there, he, in company with Mr. Stull, started from Carpenter's Station to return to the Cumberland. This station was in the "Knobs of Green River." They had several horses packed with various articles for their friends at Eaton's and the Bluff. Before they had reached Muldrow's Hill, coming towards the head-waters of Red River, they encountered a large party of Indians. Stull was in advance, "in the lead, Rains in the rear." Stull exclaimed to Rains, "See what a company of people coming!" Rains discovered instantly that they were Indians, and replied : "Indians! turn quick!" Stull hesitated; kept gazing, unstrapped his gun, and brought it into rest. The Indians were upon him in a body, many guns were fired; Stull fell from his horse, pierced no doubt with many balls. Rains fled, was pursued, but escaped ; two bullet-holes through his clothes and slight wound to his horse. He wandered through the woods, was out in the great "sleet;" with much difficulty he reached Carpenter's Station. While now tarrying there, Colonel Robertson arrived from a visit to other Kentucky stations. In a week or two they were joined by four other persons, and they came safely to the Bluff. Rains was "a mighty hunter." In one winter he killed *thirty-two bears* within seven miles of the Bluff, mostly in Harpeth Knobs, south of Nashville. His " Betsy was a gun that never missed."

"So many having departed," as Mr. Ewin says, it is suitable and proper for us, in this narration, to pause and contemplate acts and results up to this time, the end of the year 1780.

The settlements had extended from the mouth of Red River (indeed there was a "beginning" at one place below the mouth) to Bledsoe's Lick, a distance of one hundred miles, (by the river,) and at various points intermediate ; particularly near the Bluffs, Eaton's, and Bledsoe's. Eight or ten forts or block-houses had been erected, and to some extent palisaded.

Companies of spies had been organized, and good hunters risked their lives daily to procure the daily food. But when ammunition was exhausted, "the caisson empty," what service could either hunters or spies render ?

There remained a few who were desponding, a smaller number who manifested a murmuring and rebellious spirit. No one believed their position to be safe. They had no expectation of being permitted to enjoy quiet, or that it would do to intermit their watchfulness. Their lives depended on ceaseless vigilance.

At a very critical time Colonel Robertson was absent. Indians were committing ravages in all parts of the settlements. Colonel Robertson had gone to the stations in Kentucky for various purposes. He desired to ascertain their strength, concert some measures for support and defence, to learn the "prospects of the American cause," what aid General Clarke could render in this direction, and how best to conciliate the Chickasaws to whom Clarke had given offence. He failed not to obtain some powder and lead, with which he returned to the Cumberland.

His escape from the savages as he came through the open prairies or barrens of Kentucky, and through the cane-brakes of Tennessee, passing across the Indian trails, and by their half-extinguished camp-fires in several instances, was regarded by himself and others as remarkable. He met with no interruption either going or returning. But his arrival here was yet most opportune.

He crossed the river at the Bluff on the 15th of January, 1781. Leaving his pack-horse at that station, and learning that his wife and children were at Freeland's Station, he hastened to greet them, and to rejoice with them that they and he were yet alive. The news of his arrival at the Bluff had reached his family in advance of his own appearance before them; for some one who saw him as he was being ferried across the river, had gone to Freeland's to communicate the joyful news. As he approached, he was welcomed, not only by his family but by every one, as he had been at the Bluff. While he asked and answered questions, he allowed "his powder-horn to be handed round, as generous lovers of Maccaboy are pleased to see their snuff-box serve the company." He had a few bullets to spare in his shot-pouch, and the destitute helped themselves economically. The main stock of powder and lead was at the other station.

He replied to inquiries relative to the stations in Kentucky, and as to the recent emigrants from the Cumberland to Kentucky. Having a late supper, the company did not retire at an early hour, but when all had laid down to sleep, and perhaps were having pleasant dreams, Colonel Robertson was wakeful and watchful.

It was near midnight : the quick ear of Colonel Robertson heard movements at the gate, which were to him suspicious. He listened, raised himself up, seized his gun, uttered the terrific cry, "*Indians! Indians!*" His voice awakened every individual at the station. All knew it could be no false alarm, and instantly every one was up, to seize some weapon of defence. There was one "log-house or pen which had not been completely chinked or daubed—there were large openings between the logs" —in this Major Lucas and a negro man belonging to Colonel Robertson, and others, were lodged. When the alarm was given, Major Lucas rushed out of the cabin, and was shot down, mortally wounded. The Indians fired a great many times into this building, wounding several, and killing the negro man of Colonel Robertson.

Judge Haywood says, "These were the only fatal shots, although *not less than five hundred* were fired into the houses!" We have no right to question the truth of this statement.

"Non nostrum inter vos tantes componere lites."

We can fully credit the assertion of one of the women : "The Indians yelled like a *thousand* devils!" and Hood said "There certainly was a *legion*." The Indians continued long enough around the fort to enable Colonel Robertson, and four or five other persons, to load and fire near half a dozen times. He gave directions "not to fire at random;" "keep from before the port-holes;" "darken the flash;" "watch the doors." He was the only person who was sure that he " nicked the red," and saw the Indian he shot at, fall. He saw him plainly, and aimed at his head.

So great was the uproar from the firing and yelling of the Indians, that the stationers at Eaton's and the Bluff were aroused, and the small swivel at the latter place was fired. The savages had much dread of a cannon. They knew that the whites were fully awake, and that relief might be expected for the besieged. They found the logs of these stations too new and green to burn, and they could not effect an entrance ; daylight was approaching, and they "made themselves scarce," as Captain Rains said, for "he came from the Bluff with a few trusty gunmen, a good supply of powder and ball, and earnest looking for the rascals," but "the rascals" were gone. Rains always called Indians "rascals." The one whom Colonel Robertson shot was found partially covered in a piece of low ground, a mile distant to the west, shot in the head, as was believed at the time. From the traces of blood, and evidences of some having been carried upon the backs of others, it was evident that a number had been wounded, and perhaps killed.

It is stated that the moon was shining at the time of this attack; that the Indians very seldom stood still, but kept up an incessant running, and jumping, whooping, and yelling. The party of Indians who had made this attack was certainly strong, numbering from fifty to "one hundred;" some said "hundreds." Having failed in their intention to capture this station, and "a certain Robertson," the savages were determined to do all the mischief they could. They continued to make circuitous marches, at safe distances, around the stations, with the purpose of "frightening away the buffalo, deer, and bear," thus rendering the procuring of supplies difficult and dangerous. In this they were quite successful.

Having received a reinforcement of Cherokees, "they burned every thing before them; immense quantities of corn and other produce, as well as the houses, fences, and even the stations of the whites."* These stationers were matter-of-fact people, accustomed to deal with realities— not timid, dreamy alarmists.

The summary we have given—the roll of the killed and wounded— afford cause enough for all the anxiety and terror which existed. But our enumeration is incomplete. Instances of murders at various points have been omitted, as some of the names of persons, the times when and places where they suffered, cannot now be determined with certainty. But we will continue the sad recital of woes, which it seemed could only end when we should record the extermination of the last white man. The names of those who thus early came here and were massacred, deserve to be perpetuated, as well as the names of others who, by a kind and protecting Providence, endured and survived the trials and horrors of the times. We would not stigmatize the names or memories of those who saved their lives by flight. Indeed, some of them departed as though "called" to "fight and suffer" at other posts.

We have not the intention to determine and announce by which course the greatest good would have resulted, "either this or that." We certainly believe that these pioneers were "foreordained," "predestined" (very strong and expressive words) to be the "forerunners," and "to prepare

---

* This "immense quantity of corn and other produce" must have been in some subsequent year. In this first year the clearings were small, hastily made, and much shaded. The "fences," such as they had, were of newly split timber, and green, with *brush*. The *brush* would burn rapidly. As we have stated, the July freshet destroyed much, wild animals more, and wild Indians not a little. They helped themselves to the green corn for roasting, and to the dry for hominy and bread. And thus we conclude that "immense quantities of corn and other produce" were not *burned* in the winter of 1780–81. The Indians destroyed whatever they could, no doubt.

the way before," and for the great people which should come after them. In the commencement and furtherance of this grand design and important event, they were called to endure conflicts; indeed, they had a love for such adventures and exposures. Here is "a notable fact"—none were *anxious* or willing to *retrace their steps.* At every remove they penetrated farther into the western wilderness:

> "They took no steps backwards!"

> "Their way is o'er the mountain heights,
> Their home is in these western wilds."

The word of command by Robertson, at the very outset, was, "Are you all ready? Forward, march!" If there was no truce to the warfare by the Indians, there was no abandonment of the purpose, both to conquer the Indians and subdue the country. If they sometimes advanced rashly, and with numbers too small, and equipments inadequate, so that prudence or necessity induced a change, or a concentration of forces, there was always cherished the determination *yet to triumph.*

"*Io triumphe!*" says Horace, but our perverse fellow, Hood, would use it thus: "Jo and I try—um,—p, he! Chero-ke-he!"

Patience, fortitude, and perseverance were ultimately to succeed. "Jupiter helps those who put the shoulder to the wheel."

CHAPTER VII.

1781.

AND now, although there was such evident danger, and the outer or feebler stations were abandoned, some of the people would linger around these new homes, or make occasional visits to them; and thus were a number exposed to the hidden foe, and slain. Among the loiterers near Mansker's were David Goin and Patrick Quigly. They were "caught napping." The Indians gave them "a nap that knows no waking." The sylvan poet, Clark, used to repeat some poor doggerel relative to this event, thus rendering a little aid to traditionary history. He certainly was no exception to the saying of the Latins,

"Poeta nascitur non fit."

He was neither born nor educated to be a poet, and yet "he filled up his measure with his metre."

Their bodies were found together in the house, and in such a position as proved that they had been killed "outright when asleep." They felt not when their scalps were taken. But in the history of these settlements we have to record a number of cases where persons were scalped, and lived to good old age thereafter. An instance must be mentioned at this very time.

The Dunhams had settled at their "location," that body of land which is now beautifully improved and embellished, well known as "Belle Meade," the residence of General William G. Harding.* They had

---

* We take pleasure in recording that at Belle Meade, or Dunham's Station, several hundred acres of beautiful woodland are preserved in an undefaced condition, and in that lovely park visitors may enjoy a sight somewhat like that which the early pioneers enjoyed. They may behold two hundred deer, twenty buffaloes, and half a dozen elk. This park and that of Colonel Hart, (a descendant of him whose name appears on the roll next to that of Colonel Richard Hen-

erected a log-house, and made considerable advances in the construction of "Dunham's Station," but were now, like others, compelled to seek safety in a better strong-hold, therefore they moved to the Bluff—"moved to town." A few days thereafter, Mrs. Dunham directed her little daughter to go to the place where some wood was cut, and bring her an armful of sticks and chips. The pile of wood, recently cut, was not more than three or four hundred yards from the Fort, somewhere near the junction of Spring and College Streets. The tops of trees which had been cut down were imprudently left as they fell among the small cedars and privet bushes, which grew thickly all over the ground south of the Square to the branch. In or near this wood and tree-tops, Indians were concealed. As the little girl approached to gather wood, "the savages gathered her."

Of course she screamed at the top of her voice, and the mother, without a moment's reflection or hesitation, ran out to her relief. The men, who were at dinner, did the same. The mother, being in advance, was shot by the Indians, and quite dangerously wounded.

Judge Haywood says, "Mrs. Dunham lived many years, but not having perfectly recovered her health, she afterwards died."

But where is the child? What was done with the little girl? The Indians had caught her by the hair, held her in terror, by her cries to attract persons from the fort. They were cutting off her scalp as the mother ran towards them and was shot down. At the sight of the men rushing from the fort, armed to attack them, the Indians fled into the thickets. They had cut and pulled off the skin from the top of her head, with an irregular circular cut, having a diameter of about six inches. Judge Haywood adds, "They did not kill her, for she is still alive." And yet it devolves upon us to say that, like her mother, "she afterwards died."

Pursuit was made of the enemy for a short distance without harming them. This was a warning to leave no brush-heaps, and to keep a constant lookout for danger. This occurrence was spoken of by some of the stationers as "a sad but needful warning." It is very probable that, after dinner, the men would have returned in an unsuspicious manner to their work, and have been shot by the Indians in ambush.

Perhaps it was upon this occasion that Rains and Castleman agreed upon "a still hunt—just a little expedition—a sort of private affair." Following the trail of two or three Indians, who had killed or scalped a little girl, "they came quietly upon the heels of the rascals, and,

derson,) near Paris, Kentucky, are the only ones known to us where there is such preservation of the "antient order of things." We honor men of such taste.

somehow, 'Betsy' and 'Sister' were both pointing at the Indians. If you had been within a reasonable distance, you might have heard a gun fire. We heard it. Something hit one of those Indians, for he fell, and did not run off with the others. . . . This old rusty gun and butcher-knife, we think, belonged to that Indian, and *this scalp to the little girl*."

It was kind in them to offer this "crown-piece," but it was no longer of any use.

"Do but think,
How severe a thing it is to wear a crown!
A sceptre may be broken
In strongest hand,
And fairest brow may drop
A jewelled diadem."

At a later date, when the number of these cases was multiplied, "the said Hood," with his imperturbable humor, would select a position by the side of others who had suffered loss like himself, and do this with intention of making some reference to "his select company." Besides the soubriquet by which he was usually known, he was often called "Opossum." Little Miss Dunham always called him "Possum." But nothing offended him—he could not get mad. He never swore or threatened upon any provocation. Indeed, we may presume he prayed for the savages who tried and failed to kill him.

There were other occurrences which proved that the savages were daily in the neighborhood, but we pass to the account of the engagement of the 2d of April, 1781, commonly called the "Battle of the Bluff." We condense from Haywood:

During the night of the 1st of April a numerous party of Cherokees came and lay in ambush near the fort. In the morning three of them approached the fort, fired, and ran off, yet not out of sight, for they were seen reloading their guns, and occasionally waving their hand to attract notice. This was evidently a banter and defiance; it was so regarded by the whites. They could not endure to be thus "bearded," and, although there was some talk of the danger of an ambush, the men resolved to "go forth to battle."

A party of more than twenty mounted their horses and rode forth the gate. They dashed down the descending ground (towards Broad Street and the branch) in pursuit of the retreating foe. The few Indians who had kept themselves in sight, and tempted the whites to come on, made a stand near the bank of the creek. The position is near the junction of College and Demumbrane streets. The men dismounted at Broad

9

to give battle. A considerable body of Indians was concealed in the bed of the creek and among the thick bushes, and suddenly fired upon the horsemen as they dismounted. The fire was returned with alacrity, and with some effect. The horses fled up the hill towards the fort. At this moment another party of the savages raised the yell and war-whoop, and dashed forth from their hiding-places on the side of the hill, (near Cherry Street.) They attempted to "head and catch the horses" which fled towards the French Lick. Quite a number of Indians pursued the horses. Some of the horses ran by the fort, but, finding the gate closed, continued towards the spring.

At this juncture, and while the fight was continued in the bottom, the larger body of Indians had arisen from their covert, and commenced a movement towards the fort, not only to cut off the retreat of the small number of whites at the creek, but to attack and enter the fort. The horses passed through their line, and drew after them many who preferred the capture of such a prize to any respect for discipline and command of chiefs. At this moment, also, "the dogs in the fort, seeing the confusion, and hearing the firing, ran towards the branch or low grounds, and came upon the yet unbroken line of the enemy. These dogs were trained to hostility to savages, and they made a most furious onset, and kept the Indians busily employed in self-defence.

The pursuit of the horses and the contest with the dogs so occupied the Indians, and withdrew them from their position and aim to intercept the party at the branch, or attack the fort, that a way was opened for escape or retreat to the fort, and for some aid to advance from the fort. Had these Indians maintained their position, or extended their line towards the river, not a man could have returned to the fort. They were in great peril at all times. The savages with whom they were immediately engaged greatly outnumbered them, and a much larger force was interposed between them and their friends at the fort. Five of their number had been killed, and two disabled by wounds.

They resolved to attempt an escape to the fort. Taking with them their two wounded companions, they commenced to run, and were pursued by their enemies. There was no time to reload their guns: to have stopped would have been to encounter an overwhelming force. And it would have been an easy matter for the main body of the enemy to have swept across to the river's bank, and thus have completely enclosed the disabled and now almost disarmed whites. That they did not thus intercept and capture or destroy them, can only be accounted for as was done in the exclamation of some of the pious mothers: "Thanks be to God, that he gave Indians a fear of dogs and a love for horses!"

In this retreat Isaac Lucas was shot down, his thigh broken. His comrades could not stop to ascertain whether he was mortally wounded, nor to render him assistance. They perhaps had passed him in the race before he fell. As he fell, he turned his face towards the advancing foe, determined to make some fight. While he was retreating, he, like the others, was hastily reloading his gun, and had succeeded in driving home the charge at the instant he was shot down. "He did not lose his presence of mind, but quickly primed his gun, took deliberate aim at the stout Indian who was in the lead of the pursuers, and shot him dead in his tracks."

The people in the fort saw him fall, and that he was alive, but in danger of being killed and scalped. He lay within the range of the guns of the men at the fort, as was evident by an Indian being wounded by a shot from that distance. The foe, seeing the danger and manifestation of relief to the retreating party, made a halt, and did not reach Lucas, who moved himself to a short distance to escape their aim. He was afterward brought into the fort, laid upon his back a few weeks, and then got up with little suffering or lameness. It is due to him to state that after he had killed the nearest foe and crawled to a more secure place, he was prompt to reload his rifle and look to the position of his hatchet and butcher-knife. He was anxious to secure the warlike implements of the warrior he had killed, for he thought he was not removed; but in this he was disappointed. This and other warriors were buried along the creek banks.

There was one contest "almost under the walls of the fort." Edward Swanson was one of the retreating party. He was pursued and overtaken by a "big Indian" within twenty yards of the fort. The Indian gained upon Swanson, and struck him with his gun upon the shoulder, causing Swanson to drop his gun. Swanson turned upon his pursuer and seized hold of the Indian's gun. Then "commenced a life or death-struggle for its possession." From the effects of the blow he had received, the want of a firm hold upon the gun, or the superior strength of the Indian, "he wrested it from Swanson, and knocked him down on all-fours." The gunmen at the fort could not venture to fire at the Indian, lest they should shoot their friend.

At this critical moment, John Buchanan, the elder, rushed out of the gate to Swanson's relief. He did it effectually. He killed the "big Indian on the spot where they had contended." And he preserved the Indian's gun as long as he lived. (That gun and the one with which Buchanan killed this and other Indians, and hundreds of wild animals in these primeval forests, would be treasures in our State armory, as choice relics of the early and perilous times here.)

This terminated the day's work on the part of the whites. Thus ended the Battle of the Bluff.

The Indians continued their efforts to secure the frightened horses, but with little success. The animals were so much frightened by the yelling of the Indians, the firing of guns, and the barking of dogs, that few of them suffered themselves to be caught; most of them came to the entrance of the fort and were gladly admitted.

The Indians stripped and scalped such of the whites as they had slain, and slightly covered up their own dead. They gained five good guns also.

At night, seeming to have some accessions to their numbers, they appeared before the station and fired repeatedly at it, doing no harm.

The stationers discovered "quite a knot of Indians a few hundred yards distant, west of the station, and they determined to load and fire the swivel at them." To this there was some remonstrance; those objecting saying, "There are too many trees in the way, and we have not the powder to waste." Of cannon-balls they had none.

The gun was loaded, several of the men contributing powder, pieces of lead, pieces of horse-shoes and other pieces of iron. The little cannon was placed in position and fired : being in the stillness of evening, the report was indeed "like the booming of a cannon!" It seemed like a signal-gun, and was soon answered by another from Eaton's Station.

It unquestionably startled the savages, for they fired not another gun, but departed.

A party soon arrived from Eaton's, upon the bank opposite the Bluff Station, and made the signal-call for boats to be sent over for them. The boats were fastened at the bluff bank, under protection of the watch in the station. Two men quietly passed the boat to the other shore, and ferried over their friends, who were admitted into the station, and kept watch till break of day.

In the morning spies went forth to examine the woods, trace the steps of the enemy, and search for the bodies of the whites who had been slain. They soon reported that the Indians had departed beyond Richland creek. There were evidences that some of the slugs fired from the swivel had reached "the knot of Indians," for the bushes were "cut and split and rent," and the Indians must at least have been frightened, for they left there several articles which otherwise they would have retained.

The incidents of this battle were ever fresh in the mind of Mrs. General Robertson, and she rehearsed them to attentive listeners a thousand times, for she lived many years thereafter, and her mind was clear and memory distinct.

She said she stood by the sentry at the gate as the horsemen passed out and dashed down the hill through the cedars and bushes. She had a glimpse of the Indians upon whom the whites made the attack, heard the crack of every gun, saw some of the movements of the Indians who were in ambush; and then "her heart began to fail, for fear that every man who had gone out would be killed, and the station probably fall into the hands of the murderers."

She, as did some others at the fort, saw the large party of Indians moving from their lair and advancing with evident intention to cut off the retreat of the horsemen, and perhaps attempt an entrance into the fort. She and other women had a gun or axe in hand, resolved to die at the gate rather than admit an enemy there.

She saw the horses fleeing—the Indians turning in pursuit—and supposed that every man who had gone out was killed or captured. Presently she discovered some of the whites attempting to escape to the fort, hotly pursued, and in utmost peril from the pursuers and from those of the ambushed party who had not joined in the chase for the horses.

There was terrible excitement in the fort. She advanced to the position nearest to the retreating party, to fire upon their pursuers. The pack of fifty dogs was raving to join in the melée and hubbub, and—probably at her own suggestion—the sentry "let slip the dogs of war." They never made such music before; they out-yelled the savages; they ran "like mad," and fiercely attacked the advancing Indians.

She saw how greatly the savages were surprised. They could not pursue the whites, and firing at the dogs wasted the loads they needed to shoot at the white people. These Indians joined in the hunt for the horses.

And "she patted every dog as he came in at the gate, and thanked God it was no worse." "What a deliverance!" said she.

A few days prior to this battle, Col. Samuel Barton had been wounded by a rifle-ball in the wrist of his left hand, and could not go forth to participate in the contest. He had been in search of his cattle down by the branch where the horsemen dismounted, when several guns were fired at him. The wound in the wrist was the only one he received in his person—one other passed through his clothes—and he escaped, being on horseback.

The two brothers, John and Alexander Buchanan, were out also in search of beef at the same time. When they heard the firing, they were near the ground now occupied by the Hume High School Building. They knew the firing was by Indians, and, making their retreat west and north of Capitol Hill, they reached the fort in safety, Colonel Barton being there before them.

The Buchanans said, " We did not like this way of fleeing like wolves to their den, or frightened rabbits to their burrow, but we did it, and are now ready to go forth to meet the foe."

> " The foe," however, had fled,
> And the whites did not pursue.

The stationers often said what was true, that the Indians would always *fire and run ;* and that when fired at by the whites, they would flee, although they might presume or know that the guns of the white men were empty and harmless. It is truth to say, the whites sometimes did the same. It was true wisdom, *ab hostes docere.* The art of dodging was well understood and scientifically practiced by both parties. To tread on dry leaves and not crush them ; to move, even by the windward, and not be heard or scented ; to see quicker, tree quicker, aim, fire, and hide quicker, than other spies or hunters, were accomplishments giving notoriety and honor.

And it is worthy of record that pioneers here, as is the case with experienced hunters generally, "knew the crack of every gun owned by the whites, as certainly as they distinguished the voices of friends from foes." The Indians' guns were often indifferent, and they usually put in small loads.

A few days after the events which have been enumerated, William Hood (a brother of the hard-headed old fellow, " the said" David Hood) was killed just on the outside of Freeland's Station. This was soon followed by the death of Peter Renfroe, killed between that station and the Sulphur Spring, (or French Lick, as it was then called.) From appearances of the cane and path where Renfroe was killed, it was evident that he contended long and stoutly with three Indians, who finally overcame him, scalped and disfigured his dead body in a most horrible manner. The fight seems to have been conducted with knives and hatchets, and Renfroe must have cut some gashes in his assailants before they cut him down, "and almost cut him up." His body was interred at the grave-yard south-east of the spring.

Shortly after this, four brave and valuable men were killed on Richland Creek, south of the Bluff and Freeland's Stations. They were hunting in the cane, anxious to return with a supply for the families in the stations. They were good hunters and marksmen; but " it is supposed they approached the Deer Lick with intention of watching for game, which would come at their usual time of resort for water, and that the Indians were waiting in ambush, and killed them almost at the first fire. It is probable that some of them were in the act of slaking their thirst at the spring when the Indians fired upon them. Here were six most trusty men, and good spies too, killed in a few days. It did seem as though they would soon all be destroyed.

It was perilous to be here in any place whatsoever, in the house or at the door, in the woods or in the field, in the night or in the day. Hood well said, "It is all comprehended in this saying, namely: 'perils in the wilderness.'" To pass from station to station, though so near to each other that the report of a rifle could be heard the distance, was to "run the *guantlet*" with peril of life. And yet these people made almost daily visits to each other. As to what was transpiring "in the regions beyond," they could have no knowledge, except at most uncertain periods.

Distressing as were these "beginnings of sorrows," the events of the first two years were to be repeated through a long series of years; thus recording the founding of civilized society in Middle Tennessee in deep furrows of distress, such as should cause the rich, happy, and prosperous citizens who now quietly enjoy abundant fruits from trees of such pioneer planting, to revere their memories and imitate their virtues. Here we witness "the beginning of an end so bright and glorious." Hood once heard Colonel Robertson say to Mr. Ewin: "It is sweet to die for one's country," and replied, as all other brave men and patriots would do, "It is much sweeter and more agreeable to *live* for it."

These were "troublous times" to the settlers on the Watauga, Nolichucky, and French Broad; there was no end or diminution of Indian outrages there. The pioneer settlers in all parts of that country knew there was one man among them who never wearied in watching, toil, or fighting for their safety and happiness. The "Argus-eyed, Briarean" patriot, John Sevier, seemed almost to possess the power of ubiquity; ready to distribute liberally of his provisions, with a strong arm to defend or deliver, and with hosts of trusty men to go where duty called or he dared to lead. He headed many a scouting and avenging party; he made repeated and effectual invasions of the Cherokee country; he gave deserved chastisement to their warriors, and brought home to their towns and habitations the bitterness of war; he held many "talks," and entered into many treaties with their chiefs; he spared their women and children; he treated all prisoners with kindness. The Indians honored him as a brave, loved him for his truth and humanity. They delighted to designate him as "Chucky Jack," and he approved the soubriquet. The war which he waged, the chastisements he inflicted, and his threatenings and councils—so far as they operated to restrain those savages—resulted to some extent in favor of settlers on the Cumberland and in parts of Kentucky. There was, however, a portion of Cherokees against whom none of his measures were directed, and upon whom none of his acts or admonitions had effect. These were the pirates and robbers of Chickamauga and adjacent towns on the Tennessee.

In a "talk" to the Cherokees on 4th January, 1781, he used this language:

" We have killed many of your young men and destroyed your towns. You know you began the war by listening to the bad counsels of the King of England, and the falsehoods of his agents. We are now satisfied. If you desire peace, we, out of compassion to your women and children, are disposed to treat with you on that subject."

The measures of Sevier on that side of the mountains were looked to to arrest some of the mischief aimed at settlers on this; but neither there nor here were the counsels of peace to prevail. These matters were subjects of frequent conversation among the Cumberland stationers.

The saying of David Hood has often been repeated : "Gifts from England and instigations from Tophet kept old Sevier on the *ki-ve.*" These mischievous influences were yet to work out fearful suffering and havoc both there and here.

But amidst the alarms and perils of life among these Cumberland stationers, the duties, decencies, and amenities of civilized society were never pretermitted. As in olden time, when the Deluge was about to whelm the world, people "married and were given in marriage," so here. The marriage of Captain Lieper has been mentioned. And now the " Chairman of the Committee" of the Provisional Government performs the like pleasant ceremony, by which Edward Swanson was made the "lawful husband," and widow Carvin the truly wedded wife ; and "enjoined to live together as such lovingly." Then came the turn of James Freeland and widow Maxwell, Cornelius Riddle to Jane Mulherrin, and John Tucker to Jenny Herrod or Harod.

Hood used to amuse *himself* (if he did not others) by an odd play upon these names and unions, particularly by his jumble and jingle of " Riddle and Mull—Mull-Herrin."

> "Not for the summer hour alone,
> When skies resplendent shine,
> And youth and pleasure fill the throne,
> Our hearts and hands we twine;

> But for those stern and wintry days
> Of peril, pain, and fear,
> When Heaven's wise discipline doth make
> This earthly journey drear."

And thus were these early marriages celebrated; some to be early and sadly ended, others lovingly to continue for many years the "journey drear" through the gloom, until brighter days did dawn; cheerful and peaceful at the close for some who had spent years of "wearisome days and more wearisome nights," to plant this garden in the wilderness.

> "Thus doth the ever-changing course of things
> Run a perpetual circle—ever turning."

We have a parchment roll, "written within and without." We have been presenting the list of deaths. We have now to turn the other side, with a few names of earliest births.

Chised Donelson, son of Capt. John Donelson and Mary Purnell, his wife—born in a half-faced or open camp near Clover Bottom, June 22, 1780. Died in infancy.

John Saunders, born at Mansker's Station. He became sheriff of Montgomery county. He was the first *male* child born on the Cumberland, who grew up to manhood.

Anna Wells, born near same time. She lived to be grown, to marry, and be a mother. Haywood says she was the first female child born in these settlements.

The first male child born at the Bluff, or Nashville, was *Felix Robertson*, the sixth child of Col. *James Robertson*. Born January 11, 1781.

This first-born of our city yet lives. The infant of January, 1781, is now the venerable and venerated patriarch of 1858.

He has lived to see the grand results of his father's toils and sufferings, of his mother's faith and patience; the countless and incalculable benefits accruing from the bravery and patriotism and wisdom of the associates of Robertson at the Cumberland Stations.

The first *living* monument erected, he remains to us the representative man of the worthies of another age and century.

"There is a time to be born and a time to die," and to babes there is no option; time, place, and parentage, rest with others. To be born at all is an event, an era in every one's history. To be born in a quiet, happy home, is cause of gratulation and rejoicing; to become a "babe in the woods" is to begin as an infant imitator of Him who, more than eighteen centuries ago, "cried in the wilderness."

But to come into the world in a canebrake, "where no shelter is," exposed to the pelting of the "pitiless storms," to chilling frosts or burning heat; to enter the struggles of life in the midst of the conflicts of war; to begin, not as "The Child of the Regiment," but of parents whose ears are stunned with savage war-whoops, and when at every moment their lives are exposed to the Indian's tomahawk and scalping-knife, this is indeed to be "born unto troubles," and into "a world of troubles."

In such contingencies were these earliest children born. In such an eventful period was our venerable friend, Doctor Felix Robertson, presented to his parents and to the view of the beleaguered stationers at the Bluff, where is now the city of Nashville and capital of Tennessee.

Much as we have found gratification in our historical researches, and highly as we have been pleased and interested in tracing the incidents in the life of General James Robertson, the father, we have been rather induced to prepare and present these sketches by our regard to the wishes of Dr. Robertson, the son. We desire that he may give to them his approval, before it may be too late to secure such a sanction.

But it is not the "Life of General Robertson" alone that we attempt to write. "The times" in which he lived, were pregnant with great events. His connection with those events and the men of those times makes it necessary, as it will be both a duty and a pleasure, to speak of many other men of distinguished merit, and whose names and services are identified with the early history of Middle Tennessee.

We find satisfaction also in the thought that there are lessons in the lives of these early settlers worthy the study and imitation of all who may come after them. They planted in hope, though in the midst of dangers and hardships seldom endured. We have peacefully and prosperously entered into their labors.

To all our young men we say:

"Look up, my young American!
Stand firmly on the earth,
Where noble deeds and mental power
Give title over birth."

CHAPTER VIII.

1782.

As the winter of 1781–2 approached with rains, snow, and sleet, the apprehension of destitution and suffering among the stationers was very great. They had endured much in the two years of settlement, or imprisonment and siege, as their condition may more properly be called. They had seen the majority of original adventurers depart; they had seen yet sadder and more discouraging sights than such desertion — a large proportion of their small band stricken down and savagely mangled by enemies still lurking around and far outnumbering the whites. They had been enabled to cultivate, gather, and house but a small supply of provender for their cattle, or food for themselves.

Can they be cheerful and hopeful under such circumstances? Can they deem it probable they will be enabled to hold out against the enemy? Indeed, can they endure, survive the hardships of another winter? There were no accessions to their numbers. Many of their strong men had already fallen beneath the shot of the rifle and the blow of the tomahawk. Could a more gloomy prospect be presented? Why did they not depart?

There was in all these pioneers a strange contempt of hardships and exposures, a fearlessness, love of adventure, and determined perseverance which constituted them "a peculiar class of people."

The more than Spartan band which now remained could have no expectation of other emigrants, unless there should occur some decidedly favorable event in the progress of the American Revolution; some conciliation of savage enmity, or the proof they should give of ability to sustain themselves in position, despite of all surrounding obstacles and assaults, and all the feebleness and destitution within.

They determined to try it yet longer. They had, in an abundant measure, the gift of *perseverance*. Many are the evidences we have found of a prevailing confidence in an *all-pervading Providence;* and that there must have been in their minds, perhaps unconsciously to them-

selves, the impression that they were "destined to such hardships," and
to "abide in their lot" was duty and wisdom. Certainly all men have
not such faith, resignation and endurance.

As we have intimated, the severities and perils of another winter were
now to be endured or tried. What few cattle the stationers had remaining were not in the best condition to resist cold weather, snow, and rain;
and the only shelter, or the best, they found beneath the cedars. True,
some of these afforded very good protection, the thick branches hanging
down to the ground on every side.

"A *sleet*" (during the fall or in the winter) was of astonishing magnificence. It gave the forests a brilliancy and beauty such as none of these
people had ever before witnessed. They gazed upon it with wonder and
admiration. They had seen the earth, trees, shrubs, and plants covered
with ice elsewhere, but such a glory as this they had never beheld.

There were leaves lingering on the trees of the forest to an unusually
late season, seemingly with the purpose of contributing to the grandeur
of this display. The cedars were rich in green, and many a vine rejoiced
in graceful curves and festoons through the branches and to the lofty
tree-tops. All, all were encased in ice, as in the most transparent glass.

There was a weight of glory, beneath which the beautiful forest gracefully, if not thankfully, bent to the very earth. Limbs of tall forest trees
turned themselves downward, that the beholders might see what riches
they bore on every arm—jewelled were they all.

When the sun arose in its brightness, and without a cloud, casting its
beams upon the scene, the beholder exclaimed: "How beautiful! How
surpassingly grand!" The brow of that central elevation was more
resplendent than any crown sparkling with jewels. It was there all
brilliancies were in rivalry. From the mighty forest east of the river,
from the north and the south, there were contributions of loveliness,
until on that Capitol Hill the brightest of heavenly radiance concentred,
as though beauty in natural scenery had gone "from glory to glory," and
was piled up to the heights of celestial splendor.

> "The eastern horizon is radiant and bright,
> And the hill-tops are bathed in a halo of light."

On every limb, sprig, leaf, there were diamonds, (and all of *purest
water*.) There were gems of richest hues pendent on every vine. Millions and millions of jewels sparkled and trembled in this world of light—
a corruscant lustre on every side. The brightness of the heaven of
heavens seemed to enrich the earth; miniature stars were set in this
earthly crown; they trembled with their burning light. It was a flame,

a sea, a flood, a heaven of light, lustre, and loveliness spread out and over all, to

> "Shine forth its Maker's praise.
> A glorious mirror, where the Almighty's form
> Glasses itself in jewelled light!"

"Come and see the works of God, who maketh the outgoings of the morning and evening to rejoice."

But, after such a display of beauty, such a lavish profusion of brightness, could there come darkness and desolation? Even so. The south wind blew, the dark storm-clouds gathered, the beating rains came down, and the splendor of the morning was gone; the forest nymphs were robbed of their jewels. "The glory had departed." The perfumed Naiad of the South had hastened to bedeck herself with diamonds; she breathed upon them, they melted, and were absorbed in her own bosom of essences.

But anon old Boreas, "blustering railer," the storm-king of the north, came down; bitterness was in his breath, rigidity in his features, and he put forth his ice-cold hands to clasp and chill whatsoever had warmth and freshness in it. His rule began; he triumphed now.

Winter maintained its rule, and with small relaxation. "In dead earnest" it "held on to the bitter end." Within the forts the people were in safety and with warmth enough; but they were under necessity often to go forth into the forests to hunt, and no peril could be so imminent as wholly to deter them from killing wild game. Their mode of hunting was not the chase, but the still hunt, or by watching at the licks; dangerous both.

The attacks upon the settlements had been so frequent during the past year, and such destruction committed by the Indians and wild beasts, that the supply of provisions was small indeed. A most anxious concern was expressed by heads of families. They resolved to guard most sedulously against all waste. It required little time or examination to ascertain the extent of their stores, and to pronounce them inadequate, unless used with economy. Resort continued to be had to the river for fish and to the forests for game, but to obtain either was alike attended with danger. There might be a murderous Indian in ambush near.

The people were in crowded quarters; their spirits chafed at this confinement. They were at peace among themselves, but the fire burned in the bosoms of many towards the beings who caused them so much anxiety, privation, and suffering. Some were anxious to go forth and hunt Indians or buffaloes, they cared not which, though we believe they would have preferred the biped to the quadruped. The warlike spirit would have been allowed its gratification had there been ammunition to supply those willing to go on such excursions, and yet have a supply in reserve at the stations.

Wolf and turkey-pens were built, and snares and dead-falls for rabbits and squirrels. Sometimes a life was lost in visiting these traps.

A colloquy has been related, the substance of which we will use.

Frequent remarks were made about these early stations being deserted; the departure of so many of "the original adventurers;" queries whether they "went farther and fared better;" and whether many of them would not, ere long, gladly return. In their pent-up condition, all such topics were frequently introduced into the evening's conversation. Again and again they asked each other the question, "Are we strong enough to maintain our position?" The conclusion was, "Better able to stay than to depart." "Our strength is to sit still," said Hood, quoting (as he asserted) Scripture.

"No," said Ewin, "move as if you had the legs of a centipede, and as many hands as legs, and as many eyes as legs and hands together."

The idea was to make a show of being numerous and strong, active and watchful.

"Why are we here? Is there any purpose in it, other than to eat bear-meat, buffalo, and venison, or to give ourselves, our wives and children, a sacrifice to a savage foe?"

The answer was, "We are the advance-guard of American civilization; we are no longer the slaves of foreign despotism. We were compelled to flee from tyranny, and have found liberty in the wilderness which God had prepared for the strong, the brave, and the free. No Tryon can domineer over us here. King's Mountain is an offset to Alamance. Who knows but we are to be the 'forlorn hope' of the great army of patriots, 'set for the rising or falling of many?'" said our theological commentator, "the said Hood," as Andrew Ewin named him.

The result of all these discussions, however often renewed, was, that "this land was to be subdued, these solitary places to be made glad, and this desert, ere long, blossom as the rose."

"If we fail," was the remark of some one, "it must never be from cowardice," and this sentiment was in every heart. Bledsoe often said, "If we perish here, others will be sure to come, either to avenge our death or to accomplish what we have begun. If they find not our graves or our scattered bones, they may revere our memories, and publish to the ages to come that we deserved a better fate."

Robertson always insisted that "these rich and beautiful lands were not designed to be given up to savages and wild beasts. The God of creation and providence had nobler purposes in view."

The two Dutchmen, Mansker and Stump, united in the avowal, "Pe sure we comes to stay." Eaton swore that his station was on the right side of the Cumberland. Virginians can't back out.* They had all "followed in the footsteps of that illustrious predecessor," Thomas Sharp Spencer, the discovery of whose "enormous tracks, near where Eaton built his station," so much astonished and alarmed the French hunters, as related by Haywood.

Spencer was of that class of adventurers who "take no steps backward." It was not therefore the fear of an enemy that restrained these men from "military expeditions, (in a *small* way,)—from extended hunting excursions—or that could make them discuss the question of "holding on or giving up." The meagre stock of powder and lead was an item in every debate and decision. The less there were of these, the more were they considered. The caution of every man, and woman too, was, to those who went forth with gun in hand, "Take sure aim; don't fire unless you can kill. Make every load bring down an Indian or a buck."

Colonel Robertson made a careful examination into the supplies. The necessity of strictest economy was evident, and all were disposed to accept the caution of Colonel Robertson and others of the "Committee of Government."

Ample time was now allowed for the dressing of buffalo, deer, and bear-skins. Peltries had accumulated until it could truly be said "they had not where to bestow their goods" of this sort. There was an odd remark of "the said Hood," which we may give in this connection, though little worth, except to show the mind of the man, and the license taken in his commentaries, only adding, they were generally kindly received, coming from "such an odd fellow."

He remarked, "I am better dressed than that man who 'cried in the wilderness before me;' he had but 'a leathern girdle,' I am doubly skinned all over."

In the operation of "dressing skins," the *brains* of the animal were an almost indispensable emollient. Its mucilaginous nature is still regarded by hunters as superior to any other appliance for such purpose. It gives a pleasant, pliable texture to the skin, so that they may have "a velvety feeling," and be "agreeable to the person when made into dresses." And many of the deer-skins thus dressed were made into vests, pants, and even shirts, to be worn next to the person, as well as into the common

---

* Eaton considered the settlers west of the river as in Carolina.

"hunting-shirts," as outside covering. These "hunting-shirts," with "leggins" and "*mockasons*," (as the pioneers always spelled that "covering for the feet" which is now known by the word "*moccasin*,") and the cap of coon-skin, fox, or hare, constituted the entire and ample wardrobe of many a stationer, and ancestor of persons who now-a-day "dress in purple and fine linen," and "fare sumptuously" every day, *giving no thanks*, and forgetful of their forefathers, "who lived on *chipped* venison and *bar-meat*," "asking a blessing and returning of thanks."

"The said Hood remarked one day to some fellows who were 'kicking up a fuss, that they had nothing to eat,' how unlike they were to Jeshurun, who did n't kick until he was full and waxed fat."

"He was a *lean fellow* himself, and with his two, or 'double skins,' made an awkward figure in person, as he was otherwise odd. He wore a long 'hunting-shirt, all ruffled down before,' and with strips of leather as fringes all around the borders."

For moccasins, buffalo-skin was preferred. The dressed buffalo-hides were highly prized as substitutes for woollen blankets. With such a wrapping, several persons could lie together upon the ground and keep warm in winter, and keep dry in the rain. When *parties* went out to hunt, they usually took with them some "pack-horses," and on these one or more buffalo-robes, according to the number of hunters in company. They asked no other covering or shelter ; and then,

> "To tread on the dry leaf,
>   And not crush it ;
> To handle the rifle,
>   And not rust it ;
> Preserve safe your powder,
>   And not damp it ;
> To pierce with the eye,
>   And not wink it :
> Shoot at the bounding deer,
>   And not miss it,"

this was the hunter's art and hunter's pride. We should be suspected of "wild romancing" were we to relate the hundredth "hunters' yarn" which we have heard. A single specimen may suffice : it is of Castleman, one of the best marksmen and spies, where all were eminent in this science and practice.

"Castleman fired, girdled a white oak, nicked the epidermis of an Indian's back, knocked over a catamount, brought down a flock of turkeys from the tree-tops, laid out a buffalo, blazed a section of land, split enough boards to cover a shanty;" and, said he, "if I fired more than once, you may say I wasted time and ammunition, and am now wasting breath."

Stump used to add, that "he was on the other side of the hill, and hid himself, knowing Castleman could shoot all round it."

It seems strange to us, but the old stationers who passed through these perilous scenes of Indian warfare have often declared that "they enjoyed themselves well, and had many amusements, notwithstanding what were or are called privations and sufferings." Sufficient explorations had been made to satisfy them that the country was rich and very desirable for permanent homes. They preferred it to the Watauga and the Holston.

"The Colonies have cast off fear of the king, and restrained all further prayer to him," said "the said Hood," "and Robertson is in George's stead."

They could not assign the limits to the war for Independence, but here they had no thought that a king would ever again rule over them; their warfare was only with Indians and wild beasts in the boundless forests of America. Here they felt, talked, and acted as freemen: they could be nothing else, they would be nothing less. Whenever they could avail themselves of any channel of communication with friends in Carolina or Virginia, they sent to them the most favorable accounts of the country. They gave glowing descriptions of its soil and forests, and of the droves of buffalo, herds of deer and other game — reasoning well, that where there were such inducements, the certainty of trouble from the Indians would not deter all from coming. They had learned that by resolution of the Assembly of North Carolina, liberal grants of "bounty-lands to officers and soldiers of the Continental line" had been made, and were confident that many of those grants would be located here; therefore they looked for emigrants. The State of Virginia also had made similar grants. Surveyors, and land-hunters, and game-hunters entertained most favorable opinions of the country near the mouths of the Cumberland, Tennessee, and Ohio; and in those regions large bodies of land were taken up by military land-warrants.

This was used as an argument by leading men at these Cumberland Stations, to encourage themselves and their associates in the resolution to hold possession here to the last extremity. They would not always be the advanced-post and the farthest off from civilization. There were, indeed, some who had already gone to the "regions beyond." Some of their own friends and early adventurers had gone to "the Natchez" and "the Illinois." Now let us send back across the mountains the cry, "Come over and help us!"

"Buffalo-tongues and bear meat, saddles of venison and fat turkeys,

10

will tempt them to come." Better men, however, were needed than such as were actuated by the cravings of the gourmand.

The result of the battle of King's Mountain was, in many respects, encouraging and beneficial to the American cause. Those by whom it was gained were the acquaintances and personal friends of many of the leading men here, and there were no more hearty rejoicings in all the Confederacy than there were among these "beleaguered and bedevilled pioneers." If there was any growing indifference among the western adventurers for the success of the great American cause, this victory over Ferguson and the Tories changed that into a burning patriotism.

"If they can whip the British and Tories there, we can whip the Indians here. We are greatly enfeebled by the departure of so many of our associates, but they may be called to a better service elsewhere; but stay some of us will."

Such expressive phrases as these: "our country," instead of "the King's country;" "we, the people," and not "the subjects of his Majesty;" "our Constitutions, rights, and liberties," instead of the "Acts of Parliament," had now become household-words in the stations on the Cumberland. And the power of England arrayed against these back-woodsmen alone could not have conquered and made them loyal subjects again.

Some did go to Kaskaskia and Vincennes, but to aid or sustain the victory of Clarke over Hamilton, and to magnify the honors of the "Old Dominion." Some did proceed to Natchez, but "they rose against the Spaniards," they adhered to the Americans. And when their *liberties* were threatened, they traversed the Indian wilderness, and returned to the Cumberland to encourage the hearts and strengthen the hands of patriots here. Thus came Hines and Turnbull and Alston and others, who again found homes and service and honors and resting graves in Mississippi.

When, late in the fall or winter, there was a renewal, by a few, of the suggestion to *depart*, the matter was soon ended by the condition of the waters, and the want of conveyances either by water or by land.

As Colonel Robertson had succeeded in a treaty of peace with the Chickasaws this year, the danger of interruption from the tribe of Indians by whose acknowledged territory emigrants by water must pass, was now removed. But the heavens had not furnished water.

CHAPTER IX.

1782.

THE heart of Colonel Robertson and the hearts of these patriotic "outsiders" were made glad by the news they received of the victory gained by their friends and acquaintances, Mayhew, Sevier, and Shelby, at Monk's Corner. They rejoiced in the defeat of the Hessians and Tories there, though it would certainly increase the troubles upon these borders, by driving desperate men into the Indian nations, whence they themselves would make forays, or excite the savages to do so, upon the weak and exposed stations.

Ere long these stationers heard of the battle of Eutaw, and of the surrender of Cornwallis. And they were informed that the Tories were covered with dismay, and many of them driven to desperation. The names of Tories were published and transmitted from one Vigilance Committee to another, and from State to State. The Whigs were confident of triumph, and perhaps were somewhat harsh and severe in treatment of those of their fellow-citizens who had acted with the enemy. As it was, "great numbers of them took shelter among the Cherokees, and threatened to avenge themselves for real or imaginary wrongs whenever opportunities should offer."

It was at this time that "Colonel Pickens requested Colonel Sevier *to make the Indians drive them out of the country.*" Sevier had a very willing mind for any such a service, and in several of his incursions into the Indian country he captured some of these refugees and desperadoes, and "discharged them from the limbs of white-oaks and chincapins." But the horrors of border warfare were greatly aggravated by the successes of the disciplined troops within the States.

A few persons known to have been Tories, or of very equivocal character, came to the Cumberland settlements, depressed in spirits, truly desirous of exemption from further suspicion, and further participation in strife and warfare. They knew that to create division and contention among the few settlers here would have exposed them all to destruction by the savages. Therefore they expressed a willingness, and in some instances an anxiety, to be permitted to act with the Americans and to become good citizens. Perhaps most of those who came here had intended to pass on down the Cumberland, and find a retreat in a yet more distant wilderness. The difficulties and dangers attending the farther progress by land or water arrested some here, at least for a time. Some took the oath of abjuration and fidelity.

As we intimated at the close of the previous chapter, the river was too low for floats or rafts; and such slow navigation would have been attended with the greatest peril. The winter had set in; the season was unfavorable to emigration by water or by land. Stay, therefore, they must, until "a more convenient season." Some remained, with secret or avowed intention to depart in the spring. "Relatives and friends had preceded them, and in dreams they were beckoned to follow," said some to Colonel Robertson. "They have, then, probably gone to that 'bourne whence no traveller returns.'" Dreams continued to disturb the sleep of some of the good women whose near relatives and friends were afar off; and it cannot be denied that some "stout-hearted men" could be influenced by their wives and their dreams.

Colonel Robertson was accustomed to call this "our promised land," and his wife would sometimes add, "the promised land ought to insure rest to its inhabitants." Mrs. Jennings would patiently say, "Our rest will be in the grave: not here, but hereafter; not upon earth, only in heaven." There were here some women of faith and prayer; they greatly cheered and comforted their husbands and others in sorest trials. Many and marvellous were the instances of wisdom, endurance, and bravery exhibited by these "pioneer women of the West." We could name many a man who, in those desperate times and most destitute circumstances, could truly quote Shakspeare, (as they learned it from Sampson Williams, or some one else,) when speaking of his wife, "my woman,"—

> "She is mine own;
> And I as rich in having such a jewel,
> As twenty seas, if all their sand were pearl,
> The water nectar, and the rocks pure gold."

It will be our duty and pleasure to "pay our respects" to some of these worthy women, either in the progress or at the end of our more immediate narration.

The "families" of the Bledsoes, Shelbys, and of some others of the pioneers of 1779–80, were not yet here. As Mrs. Brown wisely and wittily remarked, "Husbands and sweethearts sometimes endeavored to hide themselves in the wilderness, but they were sure to 'blaze the way' for us to follow. They knew that such solitary places could not be glad, nor such deserts blossom, *without the roses.*"

> "The world was sad, the garden was a wild,
> And" these hunters "sighed till woman smiled."

"Very few females were here in 1781," says Haywood. Perhaps it would be more just to say, the proportion of females was large. It was more toilsome and perilous for them, with their "olive-plants," to be transported and transplanted into such a distant wilderness than can well be conceived by persons at the present day. But, as Ewin used to say, "those who were here were like rays of sunshine through a cloudy sky." "We need such ministering angels," said Robertson, to which we imagine Sampson Williams would have replied, had Walter Scott published Marmion "as soon as he was born," by quoting—

> "O Woman, in our hours of ease
> Uncertain, coy, and hard to please;
> When pain and anguish wring the brow,
> A ministering angel thou."

But, being somewhat in trouble and querulous, some one quoted and interpolated from an older and more sublime poet:

> "Angels, contented with their *joys* in heaven,
> Seek *not to toil with men.*"

And we must add our comment upon this quotation: if this assertion of the poet is true, then one of the virtues in "Paradise Lost" was here "regained." The women claimed it as their right to aid the men; their prerogative to care for the sick and the wounded; their happiness to cheer the husbands and "nurse their babies;" and this they did "through wearisome days and more wearisome nights" for long, long years. For this they then were entitled to and did receive the praise of men; for this they are entitled to lasting "fame." If Milton's angels would not have "done likewise," our pioneer women were "better than they:" they had aptness for every good work.

Instances have been mentioned where such women participated, not only in all the outdoor labor of the men, but shouldered their musket, stood guard, pounded the *hominy*, cooked the victuals, washed dishes, cleaned house, and "went a-visiting," with an infant sitting on the hip, or strapped to the shoulders, after the fashion of the squaws with their pappooses.

If God made the angels to enjoy their happiness in heaven, he made women to find their happiness in trials, toils, duties, and sufferings on earth, and therefore may they be exalted a little higher than the angels in the world to come. Faith, that works by love for the weal of others, must purify the heart of the believer and worker. For these there are crowns of glory laid up—kept in reserve : we hear of none such "in store" for any other angels.

Some of these were women of prayer, and would gladly have taught the heathen the way of peace and newness of life, in obedience to Emmanuel. They did "remember the Sabbath-day," but they would not claim to have kept it holy ; they did read and love the Bible, but they wished for the living ministry. It is recorded to the credit of all, both men and women, that they recognized a Divine and superintending Providence, and the religion of the Bible—the Protestant religion.

There were sinners among them, profane swearers, wicked and ungodly men ; and there came, in an "undue time," "fallen angels." As elsewhere, so here : in the motions and commotions of society, scum and dregs will appear. "Sic—sick," said the moralist upon one occasion. Sic, thus it has been with other communities—sick, diseased members in them—and here.*

There was, however, a pervading religious sentiment, a consciousness that all men are sinners, that a change of heart and life was needed by all, and that to effect such a change, a power superior to what any one could bring to bear upon himself, or on others, was needed. But, as a general sentiment, they dreaded rather than desired to feel that power. Strangely they wished, yet hated, to undergo the change.

There was a feverish state of mind in all these pioneer settlements, a nervousness of spirit and body, originating, no doubt, from their long-continued and peculiar circumstances, which, in after years, became intense and uncontrollable. In the long Indian wars, their perils, the uncertainty of their condition, with eyes and ears strained, and ever wide awake for the sight or cry of "Indians," the whole system, physical and mental, was kept at greatest tension. Working together with this there was a consciousness, a moral conviction, that "all was not well" with them in concerns of infinite and everlasting importance. In the time of "the Great Revival," some persons who had passed through the long Indian wars acknowledged that they had for years more dread of being

---

* Not the wise, but the otherwise.

brought under the converting influence of the Spirit of God than they would have had if suddenly aroused from midnight slumbers by the yell of savages within their cabins.

We have alluded to one very considerable supply of food which the settlers had gathered from the forests. In all the woods near the various stations there were many black and white walnut trees, hickory-nut trees, of the large and small kind, and upon the ridges or highlands chestnuts. These nuts were usually found in great abundance; they were gathered, not only in baskets and sacks, but even by cart-loads, and taken to the forts to be "hulled," housed, and dried. In the long winter evenings there was "a general cracking of nuts" and cracking of jokes around the rousing fires.

During this winter, of 1781–2, the "stationers," as they called themselves, enjoyed, comparatively, a quiet time. They were indeed a little band, and avoided exposure, insomuch that few were fired on by the Indians. In fact, there is reason to believe that if hostile Indians came into the Cumberland region during the entire winter, they were not in such force as to venture an attack upon the forts in which the whites were assembled. The spies, however, knew that there were Indians skulking in the neighborhood, and they kept the "stationers" duly advised of dangers. The supplying of the cattle with food caused no little anxiety and hazard. Green cane was cut down, and packed in places where it could be conveniently and safely fed out to the cows and calves. Although in the act of cutting and hauling cane there was much noise made, and consequently exposure to a lurking foe, yet some of the owners preferred to risk their own lives in this way to the hazard of having their cattle killed or driven off by the Indians, or die of hunger.

As the winter was passing away, the people adventured out, and to greater distances. In these excursions they discovered many signs of Indians. Whites and Indians had fired at each other through the cane.

1782. In February, as John Tucker and Joseph Hendricks were returning by the path from Freeland's Station to the Bluff, they were fired upon when near the Sulphur Spring, and each of them had an arm broken. The Indians attempted to "head them," and it was with difficulty, and after a close race, that the wounded men reached the Bluff Station in advance of their pursuers. These men had inexcusably, or from some reason unrecorded, gone without their guns.

Here was unmistakable proof of enemies near at hand, ambushed at a very important point, midway between these two stations. The swivel or alarm-gun was fired to warn the stationers at Freeland's and Eaton's.

The dry, hard, rough humor of Sampson Williams was indulged upon this occasion as upon most other instances. We cannot, however, quote his sayings; they might be deemed apocryphal. He possessed a most retentive memory, knew the corner-trees of every early location of land upon the Cumberland, and in "the regions beyond." There was a strange commixture in his composition—ardent in his friendships, bitter and unforgiving in his enmities. In the bestowment of public office and political favor, he ever boldly advocated the preference of his old and tried companions, the pioneers.

There were other men of distinctive traits of character, men whose peculiarities could not have been fully developed, whose capacities could not have been fully tested, except in such times and circumstances as these. The places were here for them to occupy. A wise Providence had raised them up for those positions. The training they needed and received was not in schools of learning. *Roughness and toughness, blunt and brave,* sums up their character. Of this class of men were Buchanan, Castleman, and Rains: many others should be honorably mentioned with them. Indeed, there was no place here for timid men or idle women; courage and energy were required in all. The ordination of Heaven had provided for such exigences; the pieces were made to fit, to match. Such was their own judgment of themselves, and they acted up to this impression.

A favorite expression of Colonel Robertson was, "Man proposes, but God disposes." His quiet, thoughtful appearance induced some to regard him as phlegmatic in temperament and insensible to warmth of feelings. Such opinions were unjust. Calm and self-possessed, he restrained himself from sudden outbursts of anger or of love. He was never highly elated, never deeply depressed. His temper, his language, his deportment, were without flash, polish, or display; he put on no airs, had no disguises.

There was no educated surgeon at any of the stations; but there was no fear and hesitation to attend to broken limbs or gunshot wounds. Men and women were prompt to do all they could in such cases. And the success with which these operations were usually attended is astonishing.

The two wounded men had their broken arms splintered and supported by straps across the shoulder, and were in a very short time perfectly recovered. Colonel Robertson repeatedly dressed wounds. Such surgical operations he had performed before, and he had occasion to practice not only upon others but upon himself, as we shall see hereafter.

There was "a search after the enemy," but they had departed. So it was thought. But some ten days afterward another person was shot, yet nearer to the principal station on the Bluff. The unfortunate person was "the said David Hood." It is an extraordinary case, and deserves to be related as Judge Haywood has told it:

"They shot him down, scalped, and stamped him; then ran in pursuit of others towards the fort, but did not capture them. Hood, supposing the Indians gone, got up softly and began to walk towards the fort on the Bluff, when, to his horror or 'mortification,' he saw the same Indians making sport of such a dead man, blind and bloody, attempting to walk. They then fell upon him again, and having given him several new wounds, apparently mortal, they keeled him over and left him. He fell into a brush-heap in the snow, and next morning was tracked and found by his blood, and was placed as a dead man in one of the out-houses, and left alone. After some time he recovered, and lived many years."

This was truly a marvellous recovery. "Shot down, scalped, kicked, and stamped; then pummelled again, wounded more and more, pitched over into a brush-heap in the snow, left there all night, searched for and found the next morning, borne to the fort and placed as a dead man in an out-house or shed, and left alone until needed preparations should be completed for his interment!" The facts of this case are well authenticated. The witnesses were many, and Hood "did recover and live for many years."

After Hood had been placed in the out-house as a dead man, there was a desire on the part of some of the women to see the corpse, and they crowded around and over the body. They insisted that there were such signs of life as made it inexcusable to leave him in that situation. At their solicitation he was removed to better quarters, his wounds dressed, and cordials administered. As warmth was diffused through his benumbed and half-frozen body, the blood started afresh from the many wounds; lints and bandages were ready, and tendered by more than one of the sympathizing females. Ere long he was enabled to speak and encourage all to believe he could survive. He was committed to the nursing of the women. The rapidity with which his wounds healed astonished every person: he was soon walking about, and before the hot weather of the summer, was recovered and able to go to work at his occupation of coopering.

He was ever looked upon with curiosity and interest, as a man raised from the dead. Hood had some humor about him, and as a recital was sometimes requested of his recollection of the transactions, he did not refuse to gratify the curiosity of inquirers. During these wars there were a number of men, women, and children who survived after having been scalped. They were reluctant to talk about it, and few of them would untie their head-handkerchief, or remove the skull-cap, and subject their pates to manipulation and inspection. Hood, however, was an exception; he could take and give jokes upon his name, his acting the "opossum," his being frozen and thawed out, and "what an ado the women made over him."*

In the narrative of John Rains, the account of "the said Hood," or David Hood, " the Possum," is stated thus :

" One of the most interesting incidents connected with the early history of Tennessee, is one in which a man named David Hood figured. He was coming up from 'Freeland's Station,' below the Sulphur Spring adjoining Nashville, when several Indians gave chase to him, firing upon him as he ran. He, thinking there was no other chance for his life, concluded to try '*possuming it*,' and so fell flat upon his face in the weeds, *as if dead*. The Indians ran up and gathered around him, and one of them very deliberately twisted his fingers into his hair, to scalp him. His knife being very dull, he let go, took a better hold, and sawed away, until he could pull it off, poor Hood bearing it meanwhile without a groan or show of life.

"After the deed was done, they stood around a little while, reloaded their guns, and started on towards town, (or the Bluff Fort.) One of the Indians gave him a few stamps in the back as they started away. After a while, Hood raised his head cautiously, peeped out under his arms, and at last, finding the coast clear, got up and started towards town.

" Mounting the ridge above the Spring, what was his dismay to find himself once more in the presence of the whole gang ! Again he started, but again they fired upon him as he ran. One of their bullets cut him deeply across the breast, but finally, after getting so close as to pull off one of the skirts of his coat, the Indians abandoned him. When quite spent, he dropped behind a log in the corn-field near by, after facing around to get one fire at them, and was rescued by some whites who came out at the sound of the firing. He was placed in an out-house, none thinking he could possibly recover; but the next morning, some one

---

*"All that is very likely," Ewin used to say; "very often they make the greatest ado about *nothing*. That accounts for their fuss over you."

" None of them would like to lose their *hood*," was his reply : "that's me !"

"No, not though 'twere like Mrs. Hogan's, made of coon-skin," replied the Clerk.

" You would make a mighty fuss to lose your crown-piece," said Hood.

" Yes he would," interposed Mrs. Hogan; "no man more."

going in there, finding him still alive, asked him whether he '*wasn't dead?*' '*No!*' he said in a feeble voice; and he 'thought he could live, if he could only have *half a chance!*' They took his case in hand, and he became a sound man, and lived many years to glory in his successful instance of '*possuming.*' I often saw General Robertson making up rolls of lint for his wounds."

This account is substantially the same as that given by Judge Haywood and others who knew "the said Hood" well. He used to joke freely of the manner in which he yielded up *his hood*, or skull-cap. "They got it," said he, "but still, after all, I *hoodwinked* them, and saved my *life*. I think my life worth more than that crown-piece; and I have this advantage of the rest of you, the savages can't jerk me by the hair of the head, nor get another trophy. You may thank me for teaching you how to play sham and dummy. I owe the opossum many thanks."

The assertion that he turned and "fired at the Indians" is unquestionably incorrect. If he had a gun, the Indians would assuredly have taken it when he lay as a dead man in their power. Such remarks "creep into" narratives very easily, when written many years after the events. At this instant there was a report of several guns. Promptly the sentinels were at the look-out stations : women and children were speering in every direction. It was soon, however, ascertained that the firing was at a flock of turkeys, and the men were coming in with nearly a dozen of these large and beautiful wild fowls.

Flocks, *droves* of a hundred turkeys, would sometimes march within fifty yards of a cabin; and the first settlers thus easily obtained a rich supply of this choice wild game. By the aid of a dog, the turkeys were readily made to "tree," and when thus upon the limbs of the trees, their attention was almost exclusively given to the dog as he ran around and kept up a continual barking. Thus the hunter could approach, select his gobbler or hen, and down with them, load and shoot again. There is no more choice eating than a well-stuffed and well-cooked wild turkey. Our mothers and grandmothers "could not be beat" in this part of housewifery. And in all the world there were no cooks to be "named in the same day" with them, when the cooking of buffalo-tongue, bear-meat, and venison is mentioned. Such was the opinion, not only of Colonel Robertson, but of every man with a well "cultivated taste." The art is not lost, however. There is science, true science, in the preparation of a saddle of venison, buffalo, or venison steak, roast, baked, or boiled bear-meats—the perfection of science in the making of bread. Only one in a thousand knows how to make good coffee, or rich and delicious soup.

Fried chicken, bacon and eggs, and spice-wood tea, a thousand and one can prepare these. The good housewife in those days rightfully gloried in the baking of the hoe-cake, ash-cake, and johnny-cake. And then, after frost, "when pawpaws and 'simmons were ripe," if they had a fat opossum and sweet potatoes, and any one mentioned "good eating," the universal exclamation was, "Oh, ho; don't talk!" "There's no getting sick on that, nor on bear's meat and bear's oil."

Many a hunter would swallow half a pint of bear's oil as he would so much pure water. No one ever sickened with this meat or the oil, when not tainted or rancid. Few and simple were the utensils and condiments in the practice or art of cookery. The appliance of salt was usually enough, without other "seasoning." "Salt was precious, and precious scarse, and had not lost its savor."—(Saying of "the said Hood.") Few were the diseases to which they were subject. Pneumonia and neuralgia were unknown. Captain Rains's remark is apropos :

"We used to think we had the devil to pay (and a heavy debt, too, running on long instalments) before the doctors and the lawyers came; but the doctors introduced diseases, and the lawyers instituted suits, and now we have all to pay. Good health and harmony had prevailed until they came."[*]

Several adventurous persons had erected a fort on the head-waters of Red River, near the Cross Plains, in Robertson County. The principal men were the Mauldins and Kilgores ; and the settlement was known as Mauldin's or Kilgore's Station. These "stationers" considered themselves so remote from the usual hunting-range of the Indians, that they rather rejoiced in the security. "All such rejoicing was vain." The savages were sure to find them out. They did so, and in one day killed two of their number, Mason and Hoskins. At the same time and place Sam Martin was captured. Sam was a quarrelsome person, and of bad character. There were no tears shed because Sam was a prisoner. All the women said, "Naught is never in danger," and the men concurred in sentiment, "A happy riddance! Hope he will do them as much harm as he did us." Isaac Johnston was captured by the same party of Indians, and taken into the "Nation." He sought opportunity to escape, and happily succeeded. He returned to the Cumberland in safety, and reported that Sam was perfectly "at home" among the red men.

---

* Captain Rains, after protracted and costly litigation, lost a few acres of his choice body of land. The statute of limitation, through his indulgence, operated in bar. This embittered him against lawyers and his successful litigant.

After these two men were made prisoners, the party of Indians lingered in the neighborhood stealing horses. In this they were so successful that they secured almost every animal belonging to these stationers. And although they had thus obtained valuable booty, and greatly distressed the whites, they resolved to attack the station itself, or approach it nearer than they had hitherto done, in hopes of gaining possession of another horse.

It is probable the Indians noticed the arrival at the station of a party of white men, with their horses. John and Ephraim Peyton had started from near Bledsoe's, to go to the settlements in Kentucky. They arrived at Kilgore's, or Mauldin's, in the evening. At about the same moment of their entering the enclosure, or stockade, the two young Masons (who belonged to the station) and some others came in, bringing the scalps of two Indians, whom they had shot when watching for deer near a lick.

These young men had been at the lick by themselves, and as two Indians approached, they shot them. But, fearing there might be others in the woods near by, they returned to the fort and reported what they had done. Several persons returned with them to the lick, where they found the Indians dead. They were thus avenged for the death of a brother, and had scalped the fallen enemy.

All were confident that there were many Indians lurking near, and that cautious watchfulness was important to their safety. And sure enough, in that very night the Indians approached to the very gate and picketing. They had succeeded in stealing the horses of the Peytons also. In truth, every horse was gone: they had not one left. With such success the thieves must have greatly rejoiced. They moved off leisurely, and were joined by other Indians with other horses. The loss of the Peytons' horses was discovered at daybreak, and they, with as many men as could safely be spared, started in immediate pursuit. They overtook the Indians at what is ever since known as Peyton's Creek, where they were resting and eating. The whites fired and killed one Indian; the others fled, and the horses were recovered. The white men were so fatigued with their march on foot, and withal becoming confused as to the course they should take, concluded to encamp for the night.

During the night the Indians made a circuitous route, and were enabled to take a position in ambush between the station and the tired party. As the whites came leisurely along, the Indians fired and fled with all haste. One of the young Masons and Josiah Haskins were mortally wounded. The situation of these men prevented any pursuit of Indians. The dead were taken to the fort and buried, and the place abandoned. They moved to the station at the Bluff. The Peytons came with them, and

soon thereafter returned to Bledsoe's.   They finally secured a rich tract
of land within a few miles of Gallatin.

It is probable that a portion of this party of thieving Indians made
an attack upon George Aspey and Thomas Sharp Spencer on Drake's
Creek.   Aspey was killed and Spencer wounded   No braver men ever
lived than these.   Spencer saw that his companion was dead, and, having
a shattered arm, it was folly for him to "stand his ground;" therefore he
made long strides and his usual "big tracks" for the station.

Sampson Williams called that "Spencer's retreat with the seven-
leagued boots."

"That's the time he *made tracks*," said Andrew Ewin.

"Humph!" said Rains, "he's done that all his life."

"Enough of this: let's talk about something more important," was the
remark of Col. Robertson.   "A general retreat has been *again* proposed.
Last fall and winter you all united against it.   Some are determined to
go, and there seems to be a desire with a great many to have a general
consultation.   That is but fair, though I am utterly opposed to breaking
up.   I shall be the last to leave."

A consultation was agreed to be held, Ewin to write the resolution in
favor of staying; and each of these men pledged themselves to "hold
on."

The spies and hunters reported "signs of Indians" almost daily.   The
horses had been stolen, and the cattle and hogs at every station driven off
or killed.   They had no teams wherewith to break up ground for planting.

The season seemed favorable for emigration.   Some wished to follow
friends down the Mississippi, others talked of the Illinois, but the
majority of those who were at all disposed to depart were in favor of
Kentucky.   Could boats have been built, that voyage was practicable,
though dangerous.   To go to the stations in Kentucky would now be
attended with more toil and exposure than to have undertaken it during
the last fall or winter; for they had neither horses or oxen sufficient "to
pack or haul the stuff," or whereon any of the enfeebled women and
children could ride.   And their stock of powder was much reduced.

A council of the inhabitants was called; the "proposition was introduced to break up these settlements and go off."   In behalf of this
measure it was urged, that at every point at which settlements had been
attempted, beyond the immediate protection of the forts at the Bluff
and Eaton's, the people had been attacked and driven from their clearings; that there was no safety for the life of any one outside of the
forts, and, with the small supplies, very little within; that from the infor-

mation derived through the French hunters and a few friendly Indians, and from many indications, there could be no doubt that a fierce and murderous war was to be waged. The parties of Indians are now known to be small, but they may soon be increased, and the scenes of havoc of the preceding year renewed.

"See how we are now standing : from habit, induced by prudence and necessity, standing back to back, all *facing out*, like a covey of partridges watching for a creeping enemy.

"More than two years have now passed, and we are fewer in numbers and occupy much less ground than we did a year ago; we have diminished means of all kinds for defence or expansion; we are now hemmed and hungered, hunted and herded, buffeted and badgered, worse than at the first."

Such might have been, and probably was, the argument by the advocates of removal.

To this it was replied by Col. Robertson, as truly reported by Judge Haywood : "Robertson pertinaciously resisted the proposition. 'It is impossible to get to Kentucky; the Indians are in force upon all the roads and passages which lead thither. For the same reason it is impossible to remove to the settlements on the Holston. No other means of escape remain but that of going down the river in boats, and making good our retreat to the Illinois, (where we might find a few of our friends, or going down to the French and Spaniards on the lower Mississippi.) To this plan insuperable obstacles are opposed. With such boats as we have, a few may get away, risking the dangers of the navigation, and of being shot by savages on the bluffs and all along the shores.

"'But how can we obtain wood with which to make the boats that are needed? It cannot be procured. The Indians are every day in the skirts of the woods all along the bluff; we look for them under every shrub and privet and cedar, and behind every tree; they are ready to inflict death upon whoever shall attempt to fell a tree for a canoe, or to saw it for lumber.'

"These difficulties were all stated by Col. Robertson," says Haywood, and there was no exaggeration; everybody knew the facts to be as he had stated. He did not speak with indifference or contempt of the sufferings they had already endured, or of the dangers which then surrounded them. He did not deny or doubt that the probabilities were that the Indians would attempt to drive them away or utterly destroy them. 'There is danger attendant on the attempt to stay, as there is in the effort to go, and in the attempt to do either we may by destroyed. Every one must decide for himself: do as you please : you all know that my mind is made up; I have never thought of leaving; I am determined not to leave. There are others who have never entertained the idea of departing; we know each other. We hope there are others who, though they have talked of going, may yet conclude to stay. We have a right to stay. If we do not stay, who and when will others come? Who will stay? When we came, the whole country was in possession only of the buffalo, bear, deer, and all wild animals; there were no Indians living within hundreds of miles of our settlements.

"'Here is the extensive rich country; we shall find no better. And if there is another spot equal or comparable to this, it is altogether probable we should not be allowed to possess it with any less peril and suffering than attend our staying here. By a careful observance of our rules of economy and watchfulness, I believe we can do better and be safer here than we are likely to do or be by flight. And we all have some friends who are anxious to join us here: we have sent them glowing descriptions of the country. Many of us have reported it as superior to any other on the continent, and some of them no doubt have disposed of their old and comfortable homes for the very purpose of coming here: we are sure that some may be on the way at this very moment. When they are coming, shall we fly from their approach?

"'We have reason also to believe that the Revolutionary War will not last much longer, and that it will terminate in favor of our liberty and independence. Then we may rely upon large accessions of population. Officers and soldiers will come to select and settle their bounty-lands.'"

Such is the substance of the speeches of Colonel Robertson and of those who concurred with him, and had resolved to remain "at all hazards and to the last extremity."

The noble band were instinctively drawn together at this conference; and when Colonel Robertson added to his former remarks, "We have to fight it out here, or fight our way out from here," Rains caught up the sententious remark, and he and others continued to repeat it, and they adopted the first part of it as their motto and resolution,

"FIGHT IT OUT HERE!"

That Robertson was entitled to the credit here given to him, and that his remonstrances and arguments had much influence in preventing the contemplated abandonment, we are well satisfied; but there were other men whose arguments and weight of character were happily combined with his. There is abundant evidence in the papers to which we have referred, and presented by us to the Tennessee Historical Society, to prove that there was one person with Robertson "from the beginning," wise in counsel, excellent in working, a scholar, a penman, reliable as a friend, determined as a patriot—the man to whom we are indebted for more information of those interesting and eventful times than to any other; and yet whose very name is not so much as mentioned in The History of Tennessee by Haywood, or others who have copied from this earliest history. We name him with respect also as the father and ancestor of worthy, intelligent, business men, who, by his example and the *copy* he set from which he taught his sons to write, (and which copy we found among his papers,) successfully enforced the lesson of industry,

"IDLENESS IS A MISCHIEVOUS VICE."

Such was the sentiment of *Andrew Ewin*, who, at a later date, adds a *g* to his name.* He did much of the writing for his fellow-emigrants; he kept all the records of the government of Judges or Notables, and remained Clerk for the Sessions Court to the day of his death. His peculiar handwriting is easily distinguished from all others: his style of composition, as will hereafter be shown, was sententious, nervous, and appropriate.

But, as resolutely associated with Robertson and Ewin, should be named Anthony and Isaac Bledsoe, Isaac Lindsay, Thomas Molloy, George Freeland, Samuel Barton, Daniel Smith, and others whom we have already mentioned, or whose names will be found upon these records; and though now there are but few among us who bear such paternal names, yet should the living hold their memories worthy of all honor.

"Good actions crown themselves with lasting bays :
Who well deserves, needs not another's praise."

The "Remonstrance" to breaking up the settlements is in the hand-writing of Andrew Ewin; and from some imperfect drafts and the completed copy, we infer that there was much deliberation in that "council of the stationers." In our researches we have become satisfied, however, that many of the pioneers had departed, and that now others followed in this and the two years following. Such worthy and reliable men as the Freelands, the Turpins, Lindsays, Shaws, Alstons, after securing their preëmptions, sold them and descended the rivers Cumberland, Ohio, and Mississippi, and reëstablished themselves upon the rich and broken cane lands from the Walnut Hills to Natchez. They were a valuable class of citizens wherever they lived, and their presence and influence in the Mississippi Territory and State were ever conducive to the peace and

---

* In Haywood, "Andrew *Erlin*" and " Mr. Ewing" are mentioned.

11

improvement of the country. Others whom we could name passed through these Cumberland settlements—making here but a short continuance—and cast in their lot with the early American settlers in that same cotton country. But we here anticipate events, and go beyond our proper territory. The presence of some of these persons will be recognized in the records of the Notables and in the narrative of events on the Cumberland in 1782–3.

In despite of the dangers from Indians, there were persons who were continually out in the woods, hunting deer or searching for choice tracts of land. In the fall of this year, Daniel Smith, William McMurry, and two or three others were on Bledsoe's Creek in prosecution of these objects. As they were crossing the creek, (at the place where James Winchester afterwards erected a small mill,) the Indians fired upon them and killed William McMurry. Smith was wounded, dropped his gun, but caught it up again, and turned with his companions to "make fight." The enemy found it not at all difficult to escape in the cane.*

In April of this year the Legislature of North Carolina passed an act allowing to the settlers on Cumberland *rights of preëmption.* By this

---

* This was the same person subsequently and most reputably known as General Smith, Secretary of the Territorial Government, (and, for a short time, acting Governor,) and the successor of Andrew Jackson as Senator in the Congress of the United States. He also filled many offices of inferior grade, but in all positions he acted well a useful part. General Smith was a man of classical education, an accurate surveyor, and accomplished gentleman. He married ——— Donelson, a daughter of Colonel John Donelson. He selected one of the richest bodies of land in Sumner county, near the mouth of Drake's Creek. As early as 178- he commenced the erection of stone buildings near a noble spring upon that tract of land. He finished there a large dwelling and some out-houses of the hard blue limestone. and gave his place the appropriate name of "Rock Castle," by which it is known at this day. The present owner is *Harry Smith*, a grandson, who manages his large estate of nearly three thousand acres with prudence and agricultural skill. The identical *rifle* used by General Smith during the Indian wars, is now in possession of his grandson, and is relied upon as much as any gun of modern make, to hit the mark or kill at a reasonable distance.

General Smith was associated with "Dr. Thomas Walker" in running the line between Virginia and North Carolina; and as commissioners for such purpose on the part of Virginia, they met Colonel Henderson and William B. Smith, Commissioners in behalf of North Carolina, at Steep Rock Creek, on 6th September, 1779; where due observations were taken, and "the point fixed to the satisfaction of all parties," as the *beginning* whence the division-line should be run. After running forty-five miles to Carter's Valley the Commissioners disagreed. In consequence of such disagreement, the two lines were run, and the disagreement not settled until 2d February, 1820, when the accuracy of Walker and Smith was sustained.

act there was granted to each head of a family six hundred and forty acres; to single or unmarried men, over twenty-one years of age, a tract to include their improvements, provided they had been here on or before the 1st of June, 1780. Salt-springs and licks were reserved from such preëmptions, together with six hundred and forty acres of land adjoining and including the spring or lick.

"In this year also the Legislature of North Carolina, after a great deal of uncommendable tergiversation, established courts of equity in all the districts of the State."

We shall have abundant reason and opportunity to show that Judge Haywood has not used terms too harsh or unwarranted in the foregoing paragraph; and in so doing, we shall not "travel out of the record," but confine our remarks to these early settlements and people on the Cumberland. The Old North State had her cares and burdens more immediately at home, and at this early day had virtually said to emigrants, "If you will rush into that distant wilderness, you must take care of yourselves: establish your strongholds and defend them yourselves."

On the 19th April General Washington issued his proclamation for the cessation of hostilities, and recommending the offering of thanks to Almighty God for the many blessings conferred upon the American people.

Whether the stationed pioneers on the Cumberland received intelligence of this suspension of active warfare before the fall of the year, we know not, but in December they were assured that the Revolutionary War was actually ended on the 30th of November. "When they heard this, they rejoiced." We need not doubt this. Andrew Ewin raised himself up to his full height, whenever, in after-days, the reception of this news was mentioned, and he said that "Robertson, and all the rest of us, felt a foot taller, and straightened from the bend of a dog's hind-leg to an erect figure."

For a time this event seems to have influenced the conduct of the Indians. If they came near the settlements, they were in pursuit of game. Indirect messages were sent and received, expressive of a friendly disposition, and suggestions were made to them by Col. Robertson, that if some of their chiefs would make known such a wish, the States might appoint some persons to hold talks and conferences with them. He wished to explain to them the character of his settlement on the Cumberland; that he and all others came here, not for war, but peace; not to disturb the red men, but to enjoy quiet homes and cultivate their fields; that they had "treated for these lands and paid for them."

The stationers communicated to their waiting friends the news of the

It would have been difficult for any inquirer, even at that day, to have ascertained satisfactorily the motives by which savage tribes were actuated in their various movements. And if we should attempt to explain the schemes and conduct of leading chiefs, as avowed in talks, or seemingly developed at later days, we might greatly err. There is a Providence, a certain overruling Providence, directing or affecting this heathen people, which the Christian student may well regard with interest. We sometimes think we could offer some instructive or plausible suggestions upon this mysterious dealing, but then, again, we distrust our own wisdom, and forbear. We leave to others to take hold of prominent events, as we record them ; and if they can see where and how all the links in the great and lesser chains connect, they will not have studied in vain or unprofitably. If "an undevout astronomer is mad," the student of history who denies a superintending Providence is a fool. When these Indians deserted their towns on the Chickamauga, some of them returned to their old haunts, but most of them moved some forty miles farther down the river, and built what were subsequently known as "the Five Towns," or " Five Lower Towns." Here were soon concentrated the most warlike portion of the nation. The principal part of the population was here.

At these towns they were nearer to the Cumberland settlements, and to the great park of buffalo and deer. They could not resist the temptation to hunt, where game was so abundant. They became envious of these white settlers ; they felt disposed to contend, not only for the wild animals, but for the wilderness itself. Perhaps we shall discover some other and a covert influence operating, and which continued to work upon the weak and murderous spirit of these savages for many years, and to the great distress of the stationers on the Cumberland.

These Indians had no right, did not even set up a claim, to these lands, either before or during the American Revolution. So far as Indian titles were recognized, these wild unoccupied lands belonged to the Chickasaws. Prior to the Revolution the Chickasaws held considerable possessions, for towns and fields, on the north side of the Tennessee. The "Chickasaw Old Fields," above Muscle Shoals, are well known : they had some small towns in the same section, and yet this nation was concentrating its population upon and near the Bluffs of the great Father of Waters. These highlands thus obtained the name of the Chickasaw Bluffs.

In respect of Indian titles to lands on the Cumberland, we may remark in the way of summary, that by an early treaty the northern tribes had ceded the lands to Great Britain ; that at the Long Island of Holston, a Cherokee chief remarked to Colonel Richard Henderson : "You, Carolina Dick, have deceived your people: you told them that we sold you the Cumberland lands, when you know we only sold you our *claim.* They belong to our brothers, the Chickasaws, as far as the head-waters of Duck and Elk Rivers." The Chickasaws ceded these lands at the treaty held on the spot where Nashville now stands, in June, 1783, under the authority of Virginia. This was the Donelson and Martin Treaty, which, being authorized only by one of the States of the Confederacy, does not appear among the treaties made under sanction of the United States. They confirmed this at Hopewell, as did also the Cherokees. At the conference held in Nashville, or at Colonel Robertson's, the Chickasaws repeated these declarations in the presence of the Cherokees, who approved of what was said, or did not contradict. At a subsequent council the Cherokees admitted the declaration of the Chickasaws was correct. Thus the "stationers" were not intruders upon lands of any Indians, and assuredly not upon any rights of Indians of the Five Towns. These Cherokees had no rights here.

The people at Eaton's Station determined to construct, "in a small way," a *corn-mill* and *hominy-pounder.* For these purposes they made a dam across the small creek which empties into the Cumberland at the foot of the high land on which the station was erected. By the construction of a race, or ditch, by the side of the branch, sufficient fall of water was obtained to turn a pair of rudely cut stones, and thus "to do some grinding by a slow process." But the *hominy-pounder* was the "*chef d'œuvre,*" the masterpiece of original and aboriginal machinery.

To beat corn and make hominy by the use of the hand-pestle and the spring-pole was no novelty. The "living creature" was always there: when that moved, it moved, not otherwise. But here is a device by which, "while water runs, *the thing* will keep *thumping,* and crack the corn." A trough was made some twelve feet long, and placed upon a pivot, or balance, and was so dug out that by letting the water run in at one end of the trough, it would fill up so as to overcome the equipoise, when one end would descend, and the water rushing out, the trough, or log, would return to its equilibrium, coming down at the other end with considerable force, where a pestle, or hammer, was made to strike with force sufficient to crack the grains of corn.

This was an *awfully slow process.* But of old, "necessity has been the mother of invention." So another millwright, or rather wheelwright, who was Mr. Cartwright, constructed a wheel, upon the rim of which he fastened a number of cows' horns, in such position that as each horn was filled by water from the little stream, its weight turned the wheel so that the next horn presented its opened empty mouth to receive its supply of water-weight, and thus keep the wheel in constant revolution. To a crank was attached the apparatus for "corn-cracking." And so the water descended, filled the horns, served its turn in turning the wheel, was emptied out as it passed its apex, and many little blows (or "*chug, chugs,*" as the miller called them) were made upon the quart of corn which was deposited in the mortar; and so that worked. Heyden and James Wells were the owners of this mill-seat, water-wheel, trough, and hominy-block. They rank as the earliest millers in Middle Tennessee.

Their "successful experiment" was soon "bruited abroad," and "scared up" rival establishments in the Cumberland settlements. Gasper and his brother George Mansker "commenced their little fixings for making meal, not a mile from Mansker's Station, and succeeded as well as they expected; that is to say, not *overly* well." But the "master-millers" were Frederick Stump and John Buchanan. "Captain Stump had a real good dam, and real good mill, and made right-down good corn meal, at his mill on White's Creek. And he had a distillery *too.*" "*Two,* too, too, too, 'till the Indians burned it up, or burned it down. And then he built much larger, or else 'twas Johny Wright, the Englishman." (So says Overton and his chum.)

Mr. Rouncevall also erected a mill on a branch of White's Creek, and "the dam it washed away, and then he give it up." Major Buchanan had *the mill* on Mill Creek, two miles south of Nashville, and "the road passed from the Bluff (Nashville) to Buchanan's mill across the academy (college) land."

CHAPTER X.

1783.

JANUARY 1st. In all parts of the Confederacy there were congratulations among the people on this first day of a new year. Seven years had come and gone, in which little of cheerfulness and the giving of gifts had commemorated the incoming year.

Peace had been proclaimed, independence acknowledged, and the hearts of the people were indeed glad. This joy spread all over the land; its waves were not delayed upon the mountains—the tidings were hastened to the settlements on the Cumberland; and, having a little powder left, they could not refrain from appropriating a portion for a *feu de joie*, to which they added an unlimited amount of *hurrahs*, jubilations, and congratulations. It was "Hurrah for Washington, hurrah for Congress, hurrah for Carolina, and *hurrah for us!*" Great as was the joy elsewhere, there was no small amount of it here. A common exclamation with the mothers and grandmothers was, "Bless the Lord! Bless the Lord!"

And now let us quote from the records of the Court and Government of Notables.

"North Carolina, Cumberland River, January 7th, 1783.

"The manifold sufferings and distresses that the settlers here have from time to time undergone, even almost from our first settling, with the desertion of the greater number of the first adventurers, being so discouraging to the remaining few, that all administration of justice seemed to cease from amongst us; which, however weak, whether in Constitution, administration, or execution, yet has been construed in our favor, against those whose malice or interest would insinuate us a people fled to a hiding-place from justice, and the revival of them again earnestly recommended; and now, having a little respite granted, and numbers returning to us; it appears highly necessary that, for the common weal of the whole, the securing of peace, the performance of contract between man and man, together with the suppression of vice, again to *revive our former manner of proceedings*, pursuant to the plan agreed upon at our first settling here; and to proceed accordingly, until such times as it shall please the Legislature to grant us the salutary benefit of the law duly administered amongst (*us*) by their authority.

" To this end, previous notice having been given to the several stationers to elect twelve men of their several stations, whom they thought most proper for the business, and being elected to meet at Nashborough on the 7th day of January, 1783,

"Accordingly there met at the time and place aforesaid,

Colonel James Robertson,	Heydon Wells,
Captain George Freeland,	James Maulding,
Thomas Molloy,	Ebenezer Titus,
Isaac Linsey,	Samuel Barton,
David Rounsevall,	Andrew Ewin,

Constituting themselves into a Committee for purposes aforesaid, by voluntarily taking the following oath, viz.:

" ' I, A. B., do solemnly swear that, as a member of Committee, I will do equal right and justice, according to the best of my skill and judgment, in the decisions of all causes that shall be laid before me, without fear, favor, or partiality. So help me God !'

" The Committee so constituted proceeded to elect Andrew Ewin to be their Clerk, John Montgomery to be Sheriff of the district, and Colonel James Robertson to be their *Chair-man*. And to fix the Clerk's fees."

In Haywood's history, Robertson bears the title of *Captain* down to the year 1784, whereas it is evident from these records and many papers, that he had been honored by his fellow-citizens with the higher rank and title of "Colonel." And this he bore for many years, and until he received from General Washington the commission of Major-General.

Military titles were not so common and cheap in those days as they have become since our war of 1812 with England and with Mexico. The rank of Colonel or General implied some memory of service rendered, or a pledge of readiness to "dare and do or die" in defence of the country. Neither words nor ammunition were wasted then.

After the organization of the primitive government on May-day, 1780, down to January, 1783, we have no records, not even a fugitive scrap or sheet, of which that ready Clerk, Andrew Ewin, was usually so careful. The people were so greatly exposed and kept in such constant alarm, some leaving, and many agitating the propriety or possibility of remaining; all admitting that their perils were imminent, and were likely so to continue for an indefinite period, that we may presume there were no regular meetings of the Judges, and no regular minutes made. In all probability there were no consultations, decisions, or acts requiring a record. Indeed, there could have been little else attended to than the procuring of meat from the woods and the maintenance of their defences. Their numbers were reduced to seventy men.

From our researches we conclude that, immediately after the adoption of the "Articles," an election was held at the stations; and that then Robertson was chosen Colonel; Donelson, Lieutenant-Colonel; Lucas, Major; and George Freeland, Mauldin, Bledsoe, and Blackemore, Captains. After the "fright, fight, and flight," or the "dispersion," there was (as we have shown) a "revival" and "election," and who were then "the chosen" appears upon the records, under date of 15th March, 1783.

When such a man as Colonel John Donelson deemed it best to take his departure, and did remove with his family to Kentucky, who would censure others for going? How many braver and hardier pioneers could be found, *who would remain; stay,* happen what might?

Often would these encaged pioneers have repeated among them the gloomy adage, "The darkest hour is just before the break of day." They had already seen so many dark hours, that some doubted whether day would ever dawn. The least opening of the clouds and faintest streak of light was gazed at, and awakened some expectations in strong and in faint hearts. They could not—none could—lift up the veil and penetrate the *future.* The clouds shut down too near and densely around. The noise and confusion of war with England was said to have passed away upon the other side of the mountains, and that the sweet influences of peace were there, whilst here the conflict seemed but begun, or continued under the revengeful spirit of England, our late enemy, the jealousy of France, and cunning of Spain, our late allies, and all working with the same instruments, the savages upon our borders. *Malum per se, malum nascens per alios.*

As some of the Spanish officers had entered into correspondence at this time with Colonel Robertson, we shall notice it, and some other matters, in our "*comments*" at the end of this chapter.

In the spring of this year information was received by the stationers that the State of Virginia had appointed, or was about to appoint "plenipotentiaries, with full powers" to enter into negotiations with Indian nations upon or adjacent to her western borders. In a short time it was understood that Colonels Donelson and Martin had received such appointments, and that they desired to invite the Cherokees and Chickasaws to meet them at one of the Cumberland stations.*

* See Chapter X.

They were also in expectation of the arrival of a company of surveyors, and, as was supposed, fully authorized by the State of North Carolina to run out tracts of land, to which the stationers were entitled, and a large tract donated to Major-General Greene for his military services. This was much spoken of among the settlers, who now hoped that, under the sanction of the State, quiet homes would be acquired, that the population would be so increased, they need have not much fear of Indian hostilities, and that a regular government would soon exist.

Within a few days after this meeting of the Committee of *Twelve*, or of ten out of the twelve, the people had the pleasure to receive a visit from Commissioners appointed by the State to lay off lands for the satisfaction of services rendered by officers and soldiers of the *regular* army, and also to examine the claims to preëmption rights by settlers on Cumberland, prior to June, 1780; also to lay off twenty-five thousand acres of land given by the Assembly of North Carolina to General Greene, "as a mark of the high sense entertained of his extraordinary services in the war of the Revolution."

The Commissioners, Absalom Tatom, Isaac Shelby, and Anthony Bledsoe, were accompanied by a guard of one hundred soldiers, as also by several families of emigrants. This, indeed, seemed a most fortunate juncture, and well calculated to inspire hope and confidence; but they soon had to say, "these hopes were not without the counterpoise of savage persecution."

Roger Top, one of the guard who came with the Commissioners, was killed, and Roger Glass badly wounded, and this within a few days after they had arrived. (The place at which these two men were attacked by the Indians, is believed to be the spring near the residence of the writer of these sketches, two miles south of the Public Square in Nashville.) Two nights thereafter the Indians killed a man near Wilson's Spring, now in the city.

These were daring acts, for the savages must have known of the fresh numbers arrived, and of the military escort. The Commissioners were in session at the fort on the bluff when these outrages were committed; but the guard was so strong, and so many of the people (anxious to see the country on Duck River) accompanied the Commissioners when they proceeded to run out the lands for General Greene, that no disturbances were made by the Indians to the surveyors. A few surveys were made for various persons, in different directions from the bluff; and when the Indians discovered explorers, or surveyors, unprotected, they were very ready to seek their destruction. Thus they found and killed Ireson and Barnet soon after the return of the large party from Duck River. They also killed William and Joseph Dunham, on Richland Creek, and Daniel Dunham, not far distant, and another near Mr. Castleman's, south of Dunham's. They also shot and killed Betsey Williams, who was riding on the same horse behind Patsey Rains: then Joseph Noland, and a son of Thomas Noland; and some time later in the year they killed the father himself; and then the father of Betsey Williams above mentioned. They also killed William Mulherrin, Samuel Buchanan, and three others, who were guarding Buchanan's Station, which was erected about five miles from the Bluff. William Overall and Joshua Thomas were killed; "and so the Indians kept on killing," carefully avoiding an open conflict. Yet we must, at this date, mention an instance of their coming into an open field to fight. The Indians in numbers came to the settlements at the Bluffs, stole all the horses they could find, and started south with the best speed they could make. A party of twenty white men, under the command of Captain Pruett, pursued, overtook, fired upon, and dispersed the Indians, recaptured the horses, and recrossing Duck River, they encamped for the night. At daylight the Indians attacked the whites, and killed Moses Brown. The whites escaped out of the cane-brake into open ground, halted, and formed in line of battle; the Indians advanced in good order, and commencing the attack, shot down Daniel Pruett and Daniel Johnson, wounded Morris Shine and others. The Indians had numbers sufficient to overpower the whites, so that the latter abandoned the horses which they had recovered, and made the best of their retreat to the Bluff; indeed, losing some additional horses and several valuable lives. It was really a sad defeat of the whites, over which the savages greatly rejoiced.

Captain Pruett contemned the practice of fighting from behind trees, in which real "Indian hunters" acquired great advantages. The Pruetts had but recently arrived, and were unpracticed in Indian warfare.

The condition of the stationers improved very much this year. There were accessions to their numbers, and these of most respectable character, and many improvements in progress in various directions. It was cheering to the people here to learn that yet much larger numbers were added to the settlements in Kentucky. The year was distinguished by the increase in Kentucky.

The mode of reaching those settlements was not encompassed with so many difficulties as had been encountered by emigrants to the Cumberland. The great channel was the Ohio River and its tributaries; and the boats used varied in construction and in name from the lumber-raft, flats, arks, barges, keels, perogue, canoe, skiff.

Some goods were brought by the same conveyances, but for the establishment of the *first dry*-goods store in the new country, the stock was packed from Philadelphia to the Falls upon horses. This was the store of Daniel Broadhead. The second store was at Lexington, and was opened by Colonel (afterwards General) James Wilkinson.

Small supplies for the Cumberland settlers were purchased at Wilkinson's store, and thus a knowledge obtained by some of these stationers of a man who was already forming schemes which he deemed of vast importance to the interests of the great valley of the West in all coming time : schemes mysterious at the time, and never fully exposed : schemes in which the Cumberland people were craftily sought to be implicated through a few of the prominent citizens.

It was several years later than this when a small dry-goods store was opened at the little town in the cedars at the Bluff. And then salt was of more value than silks and broadcloths.

The name of "Lardner Clark, Merchant and Ordinary Keeper," may be placed at the head of the list of dealers in dry-goods, thimbles, and pins for ladies, dinners and liquor for men, and provender for horses.

The merchant-princes of our city, and the landlords of our hotels, need not be ashamed to be called "successors of Hon'ble Lardner Clark," for he was Justice of the Peace also. Ten horses, packed with goods from Philadelphia, travelling by slow stages through the length of Virginia, and arriving at the Bluff in the fall of the year 1786, was a sight worth looking at, and proves that Nashville was not then "a one-horse town."

We doubt if the Honorable Lardner Clark, in the half-dozen years in which he was in business, imported or sold a single dress of silk or satin. Cheap, plain chintzes and calicoes, and unbleached linens and coarse woollens, constituted the choice of the stock.

For his imported goods the merchant was glad to receive peltries : skins of all sorts and sizes, from the buffalo bull's, the monster bear's, down to the spotted fawn's and soft, fine velvet of the beaver and hare.

We know not who was first adorned with an elegant, stiff brocade petticoat; (but there were several among our grandmothers before the close of the last century;) that was a distinction among ladies who had little of pride and envy. This, however, we may assert of each and all of those who were here in this year of our Lord 1783 : (and for several years thereafter :) they were very glad to wear moccasins and leather aprons through the day, and to sleep wrapped up in a buffalo-robe and bear-skin at night.

Almost every man acquired some knowledge of the *modus operandi* usually practiced in the dressing of skins. It is true that there were a few persons who possessed superior science in this matter : some who could give a deer-skin "the softness of velvet," the beauty of "Canton crape silk."

Every kind of garment for the wear of men and boys was made of dressed skins. We do not assert that they all wore such, and " nothing else." What we do mean, however, is, that no man was ashamed to wear leather breeches or a leather hunting-shirt or fur cap. Most of them were very well contented to be thus clothed. Some were satisfied, or under necessity, of wholly dispensing with every article made of wool, cotton, or flax. Like "the said Hood," they could say that "from the skin out" they were dressed in skin—moccasins, pants, shirts, cap, and gloves all of dressed or undressed skins. Almost out of the world, but "in the fashion."

In a rainy day, or an evening's recreation, the men assisted in "cutting out, in spinning the thread, and in sewing up garments." The process of making the thread or leather strings was often skilfully managed, in cutting a delicate thread or a stouter "*whang.*" A shoemaker's awl was "the needle of that day." Men were useful sewing-machines, and "the women loved to have it so." And thus men and women helped each other, clothed themselves comfortably and genteelly in the fashion, and were as useful and happy as happy could be. *In rebus sic stantibus.*

This "matter of dress" has occupied much of the attention of the human family from the days of our first parents, when they saw that they had "nothing to wear," down to this our day of extravagance, when a lady in whose wardrobe are twenty-five dresses will assert that she is in the condition of Grandmother Eve, and has "nothing to wear."

In the year of our narrative, 1783, there was a contest carried on between the "highe nobilitie" in England and France as to the invention of "*knitte hosen,*" and "suche liken gearwain." The company of stock-ing-knitters in Paris gave the credit to the son of a Scotch king, thus dignifying the art with *royalty.* In England this was questioned. In "Actes, anno 3 and 6, Ed. VI., cap. 7," there is a clause "limitinge the tymes for buicing and selling of wolles, chamblettes, wolsteade, stamine, *knitte hosen,* knitte peticote, knitte gloves, sleives, hattes, cappes, tapis-sery, coverlectes," etc.

We know of no notable discoveries or inventions by the early settlers on the Cumberland, unless it was of the labor-saving kind at the "hominy-mortar," or primitive mill, turned by cow's horns.

This we will say, and say it proudly: With neat simplicity, and leather dress, they had a noble bearing. No royal son of Scottish king, or heir-apparent to England's throne, no dutchess born or queenly maid, could face the king of day or King of Heaven with nobler step, a clearer eye, a better heart, or more heavenly hopes than some who walked on the free soil and among the mighty monarchs of these forests wide.

"To dress or not to dress," and "wherewithal shall we be clothed?" were questions asked and discussed, and *decided*, too, among these pioneer stationers. But the same questions are agitated now by their posterity, as if as wise and worthy persons as ever lived had never given the matter consideration or adjustment.

The Indian, with his "tie-round," is dressed: the king, in his purple and fine linen, is no more. What is taste and fashion? "Nothing to wear," or "*wrapped as a mummy?*" To *all future* generations we willingly submit all these and such like questions.

This reminds us of a controversy waged during the last year (1857) between the daughter of a clergyman and the son of a late United States Attorney-General, as to the authorship of a poem, entitled "Nothing to Wear."

Miss Flora McFlimsy had been invited to the "Stuckup's party," and her indulgent lover wished her to go, knowing she had a dozen fine dresses.

> "The fair Flora looked up with a pitiful air,
>   And answered quite promptly, 'Why, Harry, *mon cher*,
> I should like above all things to go with you there,
> But, really and truly, I've nothing to wear.'

> "'Nothing to wear! go just as you are:
> Wear the dress you have on, and you'll be by far,
> I engage, the most bright and particular star.'
> .   .   .   .

> "For bonnets, mantillas, capes, collars, and shawls;
> Dresses for breakfasts, and dinners, and balls;
> Dresses to sit in, and stand in, and walk in;
> Dresses to dance in, and flirt in, and talk in;
> Dresses in which to do nothing at all;
> Dresses for winter, spring, summer, and fall."

Jefferson has been suspected of plagiarizing from the North Carolina Mecklenburg Declaration; other great men have exposed themselves to the like suspicion; when the simple truth may be, and is, that each age, or era, has its own peculiar train of thought and expression, and this, as a vein of sentiment and turn of representation in language, is not exclusive and individual, but more or less pervading and general.

Mental as well as physical idiosyncrasies are traceable to a wide extent. Thus is distinguished one nation from another nation. Now we have no idea that either of the parties contending for authorship of the poem on ornamented or dressed nakedness—"Nothing to Wear"—ever read any portion of the "Kick-a-poo's song." We vouch not for its age or authorship, but give only the lines which we deem original and suggestive.

It seems that a young chief, Octo-killa-bucka, had procured a yard of calico, which he offered to his Kate-eo-kah, or wife, as a girdle for her waist : she objects to hiding any of her well-formed person, or hampering the freedom of her limbs, and says to him :

"Go add it to the eagle's wing,
  Go try it on the on-to-dok, [wild turkey,]
  Go wrap it round the crane's straight legs,
  Go fold it on the swan's fair breast,
  Go scarf it round the wild gazelle,
  Go bind therewith the bounding doe,
  Go hide therein the sun's bright beam ;
  Then ask if they are beautified ;
  Then ask if, with the flying cloud,
  If to the tops of tallest trees,
  If o'er the sands or on the waves,
  If through the brakes, or in the air—
  They pass with ease, with more of grace,
  Than when unbound and undisguised
  They run, or swim, or chase, or fly,
        Hook-foot-a-ree !"

That is absolutely "with nothing to wear," no other covering than *hook-foot*, or their own *skin*.

The Commissioners from North Carolina, with their guard and surveyors, accomplished no very important service for the stationers. They proceeded first to Elk River, and by observations ascertained the thirty-fifth degree of north latitude, at an eminence since called "Latitude Hill." Starting from that point, they ran what was called the "Continental line." It passed the Harpeth River five or six miles above the town of Franklin.

Another duty intrusted to these Commissioners was, to examine claims of persons who considered themselves entitled to preëmption rights under the Act in favor of those who were settlers on the Cumberland prior to the first day of June, 1780. Some of these claims were presented, approved, and certificates issued. (We have never seen any records of the acts of these Commissioners. They would be interesting.)

In this connection we may as well state, that in the next year (1784) another line was run by General Rutherford, subsequently known as the "Commissioner's line," varying somewhat from that of 1783. This line was run in pursuance of an Act of Assembly, passed at the request of

12

officers who had served in the late war. The line "began on the Virginian line, where the Cumberland intersects it; thence south fifty-five miles; thence west to the Tennessee River; *down the river to the Virginia line;* and thence with that line east to the beginning." These boundaries included the land in the Great Bend of Tennessee—all lands on the east side of that river to the Virginia or Kentucky line.

Accessions to the Cumberland settlements came this year from an unexpected quarter. At the commencement of the settlements under Robertson, Bledsoe, Mansker, and Eaton, war was waging between Spanish and English forces for the possession of the Floridas. Spain was the nominal ally of the Colonies in the War of Independence.

In May, 1781, the Spanish forces prevailed, and by the final treaty of 1783, the last foothold of Great Britain upon the lower Mississippi was removed—her possessions yielded up. The student of American history will notice here a singular occurrence in behalf of the great cause of Independence and its advocates.

At the time when the British forces laid siege to Pensacola, in the spring of 1781, there was strong confidence among the English subjects near Natchez, that the Spaniards would be overwhelmed and the Floridas be restored to Great Britain. Large grants had been made to officers who had served in the Canadian or French war of 1756, as to Generals Putnam, Schuyler, and Lyman; and they had located their respective claims of twenty thousand acres each, between the mouths of the Yazoo and Bayou Pierre. Lyman alone remained to occupy his tract on the waters of the Lusa Chitta and Bayou Pierre. He was a decided *royalist, opposed* to separation from England. Putnam and Schuyler returned to their homes, the one in Connecticut, the other in New York, at the posts where Providence and the necessities of an embryo nation should most need their presence and services. They were *Whigs, ready* for the *Revolution.*

Lyman found at Natchez and in the surrounding new settlements, British subjects who were willing to unite with him in an effort to overthrow the Spanish authorities in that quarter. They concerted measures, laid siege to Fort Panmure, on the bluff at Natchez, captured it, and deemed themselves good and loyal subjects of King George. Engaged in this little rebellion and successful uprising against Spain, were a few persons who had sympathized with the "Regulators" in North Carolina, and had fled thence to avoid British petty tyranny; and were now found, strangely, fighting for the restoration of British rule, when they knew how bravely some of their most intimate and dear friends were contending to throw off that same power, and to establish the Independence of the United Colonies. With such patriots at heart they sympathized.

Rather be the loyal subjects of the King of England, however, than the compulsory slaves of the King of Spain.

They had triumphed; but it was only for a few days. News arrived that an overwhelming force was ascending the river, and that the Spaniards were coming in such an enraged temper that the lives of no rebels would be spared, and that, "at least, all their property would be confiscated." They resolved to save their lives by timely flight, and with them some of their property. Lyman, the royalist, with a few others of the like sentiments, fled; and, after a toilsome march, reached Savannah and Charleston, then in possession of the British.

Some who had taken no part in the recent acts of resistance to overthrow of Spanish rule, trusted in their innocency, and remained to recognize the power which should establish the supremacy. But others, who had an infusion of independence and of the leaven which was working in the great heart of the American people, ("of, or akin to, 'the original Regulators,'") determined that they should never be the subjects of the King of Great Britain or of the King of Spain. They must "return to their brethren." The Spanish authorities denounced these men as rebels, and, "being such and refugees," whatsoever property they had left was "confiscated."

Of those whose names may be seen here, we may particularize Philip Alston, John Turnbull, James Drumgold, (or Drumgoole,) James Cole, John Turner, Thomas James, Philip Mulkey, Thomas Hines. They remained at the Cumberland settlements several years, aided in the defences against the Indians, rejoiced with their friends in the acknowledged independence of their country, had their patriotic sentiments greatly strengthened, received much insight into Spanish hypocrisy and instigation of Indian depredations upon their friends here, and a strong desire to return to the Mississippi, avenge themselves, expel the Spaniards, recover their property, and secure their homes and the territory as rightful portions of the United States.

Providence had "forbidden the banns" between these Americans and the Spaniards; had separated them from the royalists who fled to the British ships at Charleston and Savannah; had compelled them to return for a little season to their friends; and there, in due time, opened the way for their reëstablishment upon the lower Mississippi—there to carry forward the American settlements, the great cause of civil freedom, improvement in agriculture, and of Protestant Christianity.

"Some of the prominent rebels were made prisoners and taken to New Orleans, where they were imprisoned, threatened, but their lives spared."

Those who had come from North Carolina and Virginia, and had rela-

tives and friends yet there engaged in the cause of freedom, or at some
of the stations in Kentucky and on the Cumberland, contending with
British and Indian opponents, now commenced their hasty retreat. They
packed what they could upon their horses, and travelled through "the
wilderness," as it was called for forty years thereafter, and reached the
stations on the Cumberland in this year, 1783. A few of the number
who set out on this journey were attacked by some Cherokees, and lost
their lives. Of the others, several of their names may be seen among
the two hundred and fifty-six signatures to the Articles of Government,
near the close of the list.

"The Wilderness" was an extent of forest and prairie country, of more
than three hundred miles, forty miles above Natchez, through the Choctaw nation, (crossing the Tombigbee and Tennessee and other rivers,) to
the settlements on the Cumberland.

When these "refugees" returned, there went with them other "good
men and true," the Turpins, Freelands, Greens, Shaws, forming the
nuclei of excellent neighborhoods, and known as such to the present day.

Mr. Mulkey was the only enthusiastic religionist among them. Shaw,
though not yielding to the "new light," "no creed, creed," was well
established, rooted, and grounded in the faith. They were decided and
intelligent Protestants, though not all members of any religious denomination : one, perhaps, a scoffer at all religion.

Many of them filled offices of trust and profit in the Territory and
State. General Hines distinguished himself at the battle of New
Orleans, in command of the light-horse. He had known General Jackson at Cumberland, cherished with him a hatred of the English and the
Spanish, aided in his victories over Indians and Spaniards, and in the
final glorious triumph of 8th January, 1815, and lived to hail his friend
and chieftain "PRESIDENT OF THE UNITED STATES."

Upon the early records of the Sessions Court at Nashville may be seen
evidences of the "trading character" of John Turnbull and Philip
Alston. And though the "Superior Court of Quarter Sessions" in
Davidson county, Tennessee, may have considered its decision final and
conclusive, yet we know the matter was for years thereafter litigated
in Mississippi, involving much research into transactions of that early
period.

This reference to the courts and to judicial proceedings serves properly
to introduce some of the adjudications of the day, as presented upon the
records of our government of Judges or Notables. These records,
under date 7th January, 1783, present sundry cases of interest. It will
be noticed that this tribunal exercised extensive powers, and was the

watchful guardian of the interests of the people, and had authority to attend to civil and military affairs.

They had an eye upon "new-comers," were ever ready to impart to persons of good deportment information as to valuable tracts of land, and to unite with others in aiding to erect cabins and clear up a new field. No act of neighborly kindness was more common or cheerfully rendered than that of house-raising and log-rolling. These improvements required aid, and the strong men, and enough of them, were never wanting upon such occasions.

CHAPTER XI.

1783.

"JANUARY 7th. John Thomas produced in Committee a note of hand against John Sadler, for the payment of two good cows, or heifer w^t calf, on the 1st of November, in the year 1780: proved his accompt: desired the Committee to award the damages sustained, obtaining at the same time an attachment against the estate of s^d Sadler on entering into Bond in the sum of one hundred and twenty pounds, payable to Col. James Robertson, Chairman of Committee, or his successors, conditioned for the prosecuting of his suit to effect; and if cast, to pay all costs and charges incident thereto: Issuing at the same time a Summons for Gasper Mansker, as garnishee of s^d Sadler, to appear at our next Committee on the 5th day of February.

"James Hollis appeared in Committee and declared on oath that Joshua and Eneas Thomas threatened the taking away of his life, whereby he is hindered in the pursuit of his lawful calling: on which a writ issued for apprehending s^d Thomases; and Isaac Linsey, Heydon Wells, and David Rounsevall, ordered to take recognizance of them for their good behaviour in the mean time and their appearance at our next Committee, on the 5th of February.

"Wm. Steward appeared in Committee and proved an account against the estate of James Lumsday, deceased, of £22 9s.

"Committee adjourned to the 5th day of February next."

"North Carolina, Cumberland District, January 18th, 1783.

"At a Committee called at ye desire of ye inhabitants for the offering of an Address to ye States Commissioners, in behalf of some *minors* and heads of families, the first of which was deprived by their minority, and the others by not arriving here by the time prescribed by ye Act of Assembly for obtaining of lands; and that they would represent their case to the Assembly in hopes of their indulgence toward them: and that the Commissioners would, in the mean time, be pleased to receive their locations for their improvements; to the intent that they might be generally known, in hopes that others would not interfere therewith:—To which the Commissioners were pleased to return an Ans' that, to the first, they would do every [thing] in their power for them : But to receiving their locations, it did [not] come w'in the line of their duty, etc.

"The members then present were Colonel James Robertson, Captain George Freeland, Thomas Molloy, Isaac Linsey, Heydon Wells, David Rounsevall, Ebenezer Titus, Samuel Barton: Likewise Captain Isaac Bledsoe and Captain J. J. Blackemore appeared and qualified for members of Committee, and after discussing of the above business, the same Com^tee on motion made by James McCain, proceeded to take the deposition of Isaac Neelly, viz.: that he, the s^d Isaac Neelly, was witness to a Bill of Sale, ye contents of which, he believes, was a Bed purchased of Jourdan Gibson by ye s^d McCain—and further ye deponent s^d not.

"The Com^tee proceeded no further to business, but referred to their former adjournment, and so dismissed."

"North Carolina, Cumberland District, February 5th, 1783.

"Committee met according to adjournment. Members present, Captain George Freeland, Isaac Linsey, Heydon Wells, David Rounsevall, Ebenezer Titus, and James Shaw elected for Nashborough, appeared and qualified for a member of Com^tee.

"The Com^tee then proceeded and swore in John Montgomery, to be Sheriff of ye District, and Andrew Ewin, for Clerk to ye Com^tee.

"On motion made, ye Com^tee granted administration of the Estate of John Turner, dec'd, to Mr. John Marney, s^d Marney entering into bond w^t Heydon Wells and John Dunham, securities, for the sum of one thousand pounds, proclamation-money, payable to Colonel James Robertson and his successors, as chairman of Com^tee or their assigns, and also qualified as by law required. And there not being a majority of members present, they proceeded no further, but adjourned until the first Tuesday in March, 1783."

As this page of the Records of "ye Com^tee" there are several papers stitched in, and, as being interesting to legal gentlemen, we will copy.

"N. C. The Committee to the Sheriff of Cumberland District, Greeting :

"We command you that you take the body of Jn°. Sasseed, and him safely keep, so y^t y^o have his body before our Com^tee the first day of March next ensuing, there to satisfy Jn°. Fisher the sum of twenty pounds, which lately in our s^d Com^tee the s^d Tucker recovered against the s^d Sasseed; as well for damages, by reason of the non-performance of

certain promises by yᵉ sᵈ Sasseed, before yᵗ time made, as for 10s. costs
and charges by the sᵈ Fisher in the sᵈ suit in that behalf expended;
Whereof the sᵈ Sasseed is convicted and liable, as to us appears of
record, besides our fees for this service. Herein fail not, and have them
there this our Writ. Witness Andrew Ewin, Clerk of our Comᵗᵉᵉ, at
office the 10th day of Feby. 1783."

   "N. Carolina }   To the Sheriff of Cumberland District,
                                            Greeting :

"We command you that of the goods and chattels, lands and tenements of Jon. Morgan, you cause to be made the sum of twenty pounds,
which lately Jnᵒ. Owens in our Comᵗᵉᵉ recovered against the sᵈ Morgan,
as well for damages by reason of non-performance of certain promises by
yᵉ sᵈ Morgan before yᵗ time made, as for costs and charges in the sᵈ suit
in yᵗ behalf expended; whereof the said Morgan is convicted and liable,
as to us appears of record, and have the sᵈ monies before our sᵈ Comᵗᵉᵉ on
the 1st Tuesday of March next, to render to the sᵈ John Owens his
damages, cost, and charges aforesᵈ. And have then there this writ.
Witness Andrew Ewin, Clerk of our sᵈ Comᵗᵉᵉ, at office this 10th day of
Feby., 1783."

These writs prove that there were records kept prior to 1783, and
probably from the first organization in May, 1780, with interruptions
by the Indian war, but we have found none of them. This is also shown
by the language in the preamble, "We think it highly necessary to *revive*
our *former* mode of proceeding."

"We, the subscribers, do hereby promise to deliver to the Committee
for the inhabitants, such horse or horses as they shall think proper to
commit to my care, at any time they may order; and for the true performance of this, we do bind ourselves in the penal sum of twenty pounds
specie. As witness our hands and seals this 1st day of March, 1783.

William $\times$ Loggans,   [L. s.]

(his mark.)

James $\times$ Hollis,   [L. s.]

Julius $\times$ Sanders,   [L. s.]

Jonathan Drake,   [L. s.]

William $\times$ Pruit.   [L. s.]

                                       "N. C., March 4th, 1783.

"Committee met, according to adjournment. Members present, Col.
James Robertson, Geo. Freeland, Thos. Molloy, Isaac Linsey, David
Rounsevall, Eben. Titus, Saml. Barton, and James Shaw.

"The Committee then proceeded to take under consideration an Address offered to them relative to the inhabitants of the Cumberland, giving of their assurance of Fidelity to the government of the State in which they reside; which unanimously was approved of by Com^{tee}, and agreed that it should be done as soon as opportunity would serve."

Letters of administration on several estates granted and sundry suits continued, one against John Dunham, for "detaining of a bed," (a rare comfort in those days.) Here is one worthy of quotation:

"Danl. Hogan and wife vs. James Todd; Parties appeared: And ye Com^{tee} recommended it to the parties to adjust matters themselves."

It is not possible for the inhabitants of the present day fully to understand all the various trials endured by the first settlers: Read the following quotation from these Records, and then seek to render proper homage to these pioneers.

"Nashborough, March 4th, 1783.

"The following address offered to the Committee as Guardians of this Infant Settlement:

"Gentlemen:—Considering that ye safety and welfare of this our country does, under Divine Providence, depend on ye unanimous and joint concurrence of ye settlers: That our remote situation, and the want of officers legally authorized for ye administration of justice amongst us; being such y^t no regular proceedings at law can be had to punish offenders against the same.

"And whereas, our present circumstances seem to declare it our wisdom and interest to endeavor the cultivating of peace and friendship w^t ye savages around us; and y^t ye interests of such already in alliance and amity w^t ye States, whether Indians or others, remain sacred and inviolate: And seeing our circumstances are such; Least any persons should be encouraged thereby to ye contrary practices, from a presumption of escaping with impunity: That this Com^{tee} would strictly forbid all and every person or persons here residing to form or prosecute any measures or proceedings that may in any wise be prejudicial to ye lives or properties of ye afores^d allies; or any practices ye consequences of which may in any wise be prejudicial to ye peace and welfare of this our infant settlement, under pain of information and prosecution hereafter to be had.

And whereas, we are frequently traduced as unworthy of the care or protection of the State; Being a People inimical to the cause of Liberty, and as such, fled to a hiding-place from justice: and being willing, as far as in us lies, to give all possible satisfaction to ye contrary, by giving such assurances of our fidelity to ye government of the State in which we live, (and whose protection we humbly implore and hope to enjoy,) as by ye Laws thereof are prescribed :

"Acknowledging it our bounden duty so to do.

"And if these Hints meet w^t y^r approbation : Let it be then agreed upon by this Com^tee that each member thereof first take ye oath of abjuration and Fidelity as by ye law of this State prescribed, or give proper assurance of having taken it heretofore, and have at no time since been engaged in the interests of the enemies of ye United States :

"And that after the rising of this Com^tee, the s^d oath shall be administered to every male inhabitant above ye age of sixteen, of every Fort or Station on ye waters of Cumberland : Except such as shall give the assurance of having taken it heretofore as above specified : And that the residence of one week shall constitute a person an inhabitant.

"The above rec'd the approbation of Committee.

" Test, Andrew Ewin, Clk. of Com^tee."

"At a Committee called March 15th, 1783.

" Members present, Col. James Robertson, (and seven others.)   When on motion made, the Committee agree that an address be sent to the Assembly, acknowledging our grateful sense of their late favor in granting us lands : praying them to grant us the salutary benefit of government in all its various branches : and that a land-office may be opened on such a plan as may encourage the settling the country; that the protection of it may be less burthensome.

"And that Col. James Robertson present the same, being elected thereto by the people.

" On motion, agreed that six spies be kept out to discover the motions of the Enemy, so long as we shall be able to pay them : Each to receive seventy-five bushels of Indian corn p^r month, (to be under the direction of Col. Robertson and Capt. Bledsoe.)   The subscription of Nashborough, Freeland's, and Mansker's Stations, filed w^t ye Clerk Com^tee.

" The Deputation of Thomas Fletcher to ye Sheriffalty of ye district, by John Montgomery, *disannulled* : and the Com^tee elect the said Fletcher themselves, who was sworn Sheriff of ye district of Cumberland.*

" It being thought necessary for our better defence, in these times of danger, that officers be chosen in each respective station to embody the

---

* John Montgomery was suspected of being engaged "with Colbert's gang," in "piratical" and fillibustering operations.   He arrogated authority to appoint a friend to fill the office conferred upon himself, "without consulting Com^tee" or the people.   Montgomery was gone, and Tom Fletcher being a clever fellow, "Com^tee themselves elected and swore him in."   That's a case in point.

inhabitants for their greater safety : Accordingly there was made choice of, at Nashborough, William Pruit for Captain ; Samuel Martin and John Buchanan, 1st and 2d Lieutenants ; and Wm. Overall, Ensign.

"At Freeland's Station, Joshua Howard, Captain ; James Donelson, Lieutenant ; and John Dunham, Ensign.

"At Heatonsburg, Josiah Ramsey, Captain ; James Hollis, Lieutenant ; Joshua Thomas, Ensign.

"At Mansker's, Isaac Bledsoe, Captain ; Gasper Mansker, Lieutenant ; James Linn, Ensign.

"At Maulding's, Francis Prince, Captain ; Ambrose Maulding, Lieutenant.

"April 1st, 1783.

" Committee met according to adjournment. And proceeded to consider of the following Address, which unanimously rec'd their approbation :

"An Address to Committee, April 1st, 1783.

" Gentlemen :—Whereas the purchasing of Liquors brought from foreign parts, and sold to the inhabitants here at exorbitant rates ; and carrying away the money out of the country, will greatly tend to the impoverishing of this infant settlement :

" For remedying of which evil—Let it be resolved and agreed on by this Committee, that from and after the first day of April, any person bringing liquors here from foreign parts, shall, before they expose the same or any part thereof to sale, enter into bond before some member of Com[tee], with two sufficient securities, in the penal sum of two hundred pounds specie, payable to the chairman of our Committee and his successors as such, that they will not ask, take, or receive, directly or indirectly, any more than one silver dollar, or the value thereof in produce, for one quart of good, sound, merchantable liquor ; and so in proportion for a greater or less quantity : And any member of Com[tee] before whom such bond is given, shall grant certificate thereof to the giver :

"And any person selling or exposing to sale any liquor brought from foreign parts, not having entered into such bond as afores[d], the same shall be liable to be seized by warrant granted by any member of Com[tee], which they are hereby empowered and required to issue ; and so seized to secure and deliver the same, until they shall enter into such bond as afores[d], or otherwise oblige themselves to transport their liquor again out of this settlement. Provided always that if neither shall be done within twenty days ; after such seizure the same shall be deemed and held forfeited, and shall be sold, and the money arising thereby shall be applied to the use of the Public at the discretion of the Committee.

"And if any person upon giving bond in either of the premises as afores[d], shall afterwards make default therein, and on information and prosecution, be convicted thereof by sufficient witness before our Committee, their Bond shall be deemed and held forfeited, and judgment be awarded against them accordingly : And on refusal or delay to satisfy such judgment, the same shall be levied on their goods and chattels by distress, and the money arising thereby applied as afores[d], under direction of Committee.—Provided always that such prosecution shall commence within six months after default made.

"Approved, resolved, and agreed by Com[tee].

"Test, Andrew Ewin, Clerk.

"On motion, ordered that Wm. Overall administer on the estate of Patrick Quigley, dec[d].   Bond fifty pounds specie, payable to Col. James Robertson, Chairman of our Com[tee], etc.

"On motion, ordered that a *Road* be opened from Nashborough to Mansker's Station, ...   and another from Heatonsburg to Mansker's.*   Overseers appointed and direction to call out hands to work on the same.   .   .   .   .   The Com[tee] then proceeded to the causes on Docket.   .   .   .   .   In attachment,   .   .   .   Gasper Mansker, garnishee, ...   informed Com[tee] he had received two mares, etc."

"In a trial of Humphrey Hogan *vs.* John Brown, Isaac Mayfield, and his mother, for detaining of a kettle, [same as given in the second chapter of the history of Nashville, where] Com[tee] find for plff. his kettle, and that John Brown and his mother-*in-law* pay the costs of suit."

---

* The fort or station which Mansker and his associates built in 1780 having been abandoned and destroyed, he erected another, either in fall of 1782 or spring of 1783.   This last station was built on the creek, and about a mile farther up the creek.   It was here he had his experimental mill.   He always insisted that "it vas a coot mill-seat, only it hadn't much vater."

A few years after this date, Mansker was elected a Lieutenant-Colonel of the militia, and "donned a neat fitting suit of regimentals."   He commanded several expeditions against or in pursuit of the Indians ; but he never marched by the side of his men.   He would rather, by such a wave and motion of the hand as sportsmen use to repress the ardor of their pack or setters, caution his troops to "follow him softly and at a little distance."   He never allowed any one in the woods to go in advance, or, as he said, to "take away the *scent* from him."

He had a very "coot olt *vrouw:*" she survived him but a few months.   They left no child to perpetuate his name.   The *place* should inherit the name.   "Let no other name *intrude!*"

About this time Elmore Douglas, James Franklin, James McKain, Charles Carter and others settled on the west side of "Big Station Camp" Creek, where the upper Nashville road to Gallatin passes.

The next suit is between Mrs. *Olive Shaw* and *Fred. Stump*, concerning a piece of land which Wm. Rentfro cleared near Heatonsburg. The parties, at recommendation of Com^{tee}, and in their presence, settle the dispute, and Stump agrees to pay the rent in corn next fall—" Conditioned that y^e *Plff.* pay costs of suit."

O, Shaw! how much did you get from that Stump?

Suits about a canoe, a heifer, a bed, and other articles are disposed of, "And Com^{tee} adjourn to 1st Tuesday of May."

"May 6th, 1783.

"Committee met according to adjournment. Members present, Col. Robertson, Molloy, Freeland, Barton, Rounsevall, Linsey, Titus, Shaw, and Capt. Isaac Bledsoe. . . . When Thomas Molloy informed Com^{tee} that he had, since the last sitting, at ye request of some of ye members, sent letters to ye Agent for ye State of Virginia, residing at ye Illinois, and likewise to ye Spanish Governor, informing them that some of our people had gone down ye river this spring upon pretence of trading w^t ye Chickasaw Indians; But, by the report of some lately come from ye Illinois who met w^t y^m in their way here, We are afraid that their design was to assist in plundering of some of the Trading Boats : and that if any such thing should be committed or effected by or w^t ye assistance of any belonging to us,—That it was contrary to ye principles and intentions of ye generality of people here : as we detest and abhor such practices ; and that we would endeavor for ye future to prevent any such proceedings :

"Which information and conduct of Mr. Molloy was unanimously approved of and acceded to by ye Com^{tee}.

"On motion made, Resolved, and agreed on by this Com^{tee}, That from and after this 6th day of May, 1783, No person or inhabitant of this Settlement shall trade, traffick, or barter w^t any Indians, nor resort unto them on ye other side of ye Ohio or of ye dividing ridge between *Tenasse* and Cumberland waters, nor go down these western waters upon pretence of trading to the Illinois or elsewhere,—*without permission* first had and obtained of the Committee : and likewise giving bond, w^t approved security in any sum at the discretion of the Com^{tee}, payable to ye Chairman thereof and his successors as such, conditioning that their conduct shall not directly nor indirectly in any wise prejudice the interests of this Settlement.

"On motion made, Such of the members of the Committee as had not heretofore taken the oath of abjuration and fidelity in this State, proceeded to take it; which was first administered to their Clerk by Col. James Robertson, and afterwards by Clerk in Com^{tee} to the members as afores⁴, and the rest of yᵉ members made oath of having taken it heretofore in this State, and had at no time since been engaged in yᵉ interests of Enemies of yᵉ United States."

Then follows upon the records the "slander suit" between Hogan and Ray, in which the two girls, who were witnesses, extinguished Mr. Hogan's hopes of damages. On the next page of the record there are nine cases disposed of, among others a hog case, a horse used in hunting, "a piece of cleared grounds," "cattle won at cards," dismissed as illegal; and for "a clevis lent" and delayed to be returned. On next page are various interesting questions settled, and the one last entered is compromised, "and the Clerk and Sheriff give up their fees !"

"After which the Committee adjourned to yᵉ 1st Tuesday in June.
                              "Andrew Ewin, Clerk."

                                                          " June 3d, 1783.

"Committee met according to adjournment. [Nine members present, who are named.]

"When, on motion made by Major John Reid, relative to assembling of the Southern tribes of Indians at the French Lick, on Cumberland River, for holding a Treaty with the Commissioners appointed by the State of Virginia: When the Committee, considering how difficult it will be for a handful of people reduced to poverty and distress by a continued scene of Indian barbarity, to furnish any large body of Indians with provisions, and how prejudicial it may be to our infant settlement should they not be furnished wᵗ provisions, or otherwise dissatisfied, disaffected wᵗ the terms of the Treaty: On which considerations the Committee refer it to unanimous suffrages of yᵉ people of this settlement, whether the Treaty shall be held here with their consent or no : And that the suffrages of yᵉ several Stations be delivered to yᵉ Clerk of Committee by Thursday evening the 5th inst. At which time the suffrages of Freeland Station, Heatonsburg, and Nashborough, were given in, and are as follows :

"Freeland's Station, no Treaty here, 32 votes.

"Nashborough, no Treaty here, 26 votes.

"Heatonsburg, no Treaty here, 1 vote=59.

"Heatonsburg, Treaty here, 54 votes.

"Nashborough, for a Treaty here, 30 votes=84.

"The other stations of Gasper Mansco's and Maulding's, failing to return their votes.

"Committee then proceeded to the causes on the Docket."

The first relates to "detaining a bed :" whether it was of feathers, shucks, straw, or leaves, we know not; how wide or how long it was, we know not, but by contract, deft. was to "extend" it. And either the "detention was too long" or the "bed too short," and the Com^{tee} gave judg^t against Dunham, without decreeing an extension to suit David Gwin's long legs.

The last entry under this date is as follows:

"The Committee resolves as follows: That if any person shall bring spirituous liquors here, and expose the same to sale to any person during the time of the ensuing Treaty w^t ye Indians, or of their continuing here, That the same shall be forfeited to all intents; and the money arising by the sale of such liquors be applied to ye use of publick, under direction of Com^{tee}.

"Adjourned to 1st Tuesday of July."

"July 1st, 1783.

"Committee met according to adjournment. Present," the nine Judges as usual.

A suit "concerning cattle," a "case of slander and defamation," etc., disposed of. Then are the following entries:

"In a trial between Geo. Freeland and Sam Deson, [testimony taken and recorded,] Peter Sides deposed that he saw ye Deft. whip a negro then in possession of the Plff., another witness acceeded to the aff^{sd} on oath. The witnesses for ye deft. being called and sworn, James Harris said he saw the afores^d negro *throw a clod* at a child of ye s^d Desan. Sarah Lucas, that she saw y^e *mark* of a stroke on a little girl of s^d Desan, which ye s^d negro had given her; and that the s^d negro had insulted herself w^t very abusive language. Likewise Jenny Tucker deposed that the s^d negro had treated her w^t very abusive language; on which Com^{tee} found for ye Plff. damages 6d. and costs of suit."

"*Resolved* by Committee that two men be sent to ye Illinois with Letter to ye Agent for ye State of Virginia, and by him to be transmitted to ye Spanish Governor; In order to extricate ourselves of any suspicion they may have of our countenancing or assisting of a certain *James Colbert*, on ye Mississippi, in his piratical proceedings. And that y^t sum of £20 be given ye s^d men for their services."

To persons who can gather up the items of cotemporaneous history, the foregoing brief record will be very interesting and suggestive.

"*Resolved*, That from and after this present Committee, no person who shall not subscribe to our Association, shall be entitled to any benefit of commencing or prosecuting of any suit or ye recovery of any debt in this Settlement.

"Com^{tee} adjourned to ye 1st Tuesday of August."

"August 5th, 1783.

" Committee met," etc.   Present ten Judges, "James Maulding" being one. We copy the following :

" In a trial of Frederick Stump *vs.* Isaac Rentfro, brought by attachment against ye Estate of s^d Renfro.—James Hollis, witness for ye plff. being called, sworn, and heard, and likewise the deposition of Isaac Mayfield, by which it appeared to the Committee that ye s^d Isaac Rentfro did hide in a certain place at Red River old station, a quantity of iron as his property: which he afterwards disposed of to ye afores^d Stump ; and likewise, that James Rentfro did afterwards fetch away a quantity of such like iron from ye identical place ye s^d Isaac had hid that iron which he s^d was his property : and David Rounsevall, summoned as garnishee, (the afores^d iron being lodged in his custody by James Rentfro,) declined making defence ; for which the Committee considered that ye Plff. of ye iron lodged by James Rentfro in custody of the afores^d Rounsevall, shall have sufficient to satisfy his debt of £31 12s. and costs of suit."

Several other cases disposed of, and then these records conclude thus :

" *Resolved* on by this present Committee, that from and after the rising hereof, no foreigner bringing any Liquors from foreign parts, shall ask, take, or receive for ye same, directly or indirectly, any more than one silver dollar p^r. gallon, or ye value thereof in produce : Giving bond and security, or be liable to ye same forfeiture as by the Resolve of the 1st April, 1783.

" Test, Andrew Ewin, Clk."

" Conclusion of the Committee."

1783. Having thus given the greater portion of proceedings under this primitive government, it is proper to add some remarks, by way of commentary.

In the first place, we commend them to the perusal and study of all classes of persons, as containing much that is interesting, amusing, and instructive. They deserve the examination of the historian and politician. They merit the commendation of patriots and freemen. They should awaken gratitude in all, and highest praise, that whatsoever these Notables designed or performed, was really for the best interests of the early settlers and of those who have come after them. They made no decisions, pursued no course, adopted no measures, which have resulted in injustice or wrong, or that we could wish reversed.

Men of lawless and dangerous character are sure to resort to new and retired settlements. Some such came to the Cumberland. Their conduct was observed, and though their presence in the settlements was not desirable, there was no resort to harsh and lynching measures to drive them away. The moral influence of good citizens combined, was deemed the essential element in all salutary laws and beneficial administration. If the enlightened will and distinct voice of the people sustained or condemned any measure, there was sure to be energy enough to carry that will into execution. And there could be no necessity for sudden and frenzied assemblages, which, under the blinding heat of passion, should arrogate to themselves the administration of laws that had been intelligently and calmly intrusted to others

With very few exceptions, the early settlers were intelligent, industrious, moral, peaceable men. They surmounted difficulties to arrive here; they endured privations, toils, perils, to stay here; they desired homes in this new country; they carefully sought them out; their main business was to occupy and improve. Each one of this class found enough to engage mind and hand : their time and talents best employed in attending to their own business.

It certainly is true that among the settlers here, as was the case at the earliest settlements in Kentucky and Ohio, the majority were men of energy, of sound judgment, and of moral worth. And such men were accompanied by wives of equal merit—suited for such men. They were fitted and foreordained for the great work they performed, laying the foundations of society and government. In the aims and deeds of such persons, in their toils and sufferings, in their frugality and plainness, in their log-huts and simple fare, there is nothing of which any wise man or virtuous woman should be ashamed. They possessed neither proud extravagance nor mean selfishness, and would have been ashamed of the transmission of such vices to their posterity. They who possess them now have greatly degenerated, and must have baser blood puddling in their veins.

We claim not such nobility for all the pioneers. The base-born, the foul, the vicious, as rotten, half-sunken drift upon the tides of our great rivers is found in the way or in the wake of the beautiful and peopled steamer, came, and sometimes, as if in wanton mischief or heedless recklessness, endangered all with which they came in contact. They are destined to sink, some in the channel, others near the shore. Wisdom counsels their avoidance in either position.

The march of an army, great or small, stirs up the dregs of society. There are always in such parades some persons to whom "dirt will stick." Accompanying or following the military guard which arrived with the Commissioners of North Carolina, in 1783, were a few emigrants having no merits to commend them to good society.

13

Judge Haywood mentions the treaty with the Chickasaws, "held on the spot where Nashville now stands, in 1782, under the authority of Virginia, by Donelson and Martin." P. 361.

Monette, in his Valley of the Mississippi, vol. ii., p. 216, says, "The State of North Carolina obtained from the Chickasaws, in a treaty held by Colonels Donelson and Martin, *near* the present site of Nashville, in the *autumn* of 1783, the relinquishment of a large district of country upon the Cumberland, extending southward to the sources of Duck River. This territory was subsequently comprised in the district of Mero, and the jurisdiction of North Carolina was subsequently extended upon the valley of the Cumberland River;" and refers to American State Papers, Indian Affairs, vol. i., p. 15, folio edition.

Then again, Monette, same vol., p. 268, says, "The Indians were assembled *early* in the year 1783 in the *vicinity* of Robertson's Station, where a treaty was concluded. In this treaty the Chickasaws, for and in consideration of certain amounts to them paid, agreed to cede and relinquish to the State of North Carolina an extensive region of country, extending nearly forty miles south of the Cumberland River, to the dividing ridge between the tributaries of that river and those of Duck and Elk Rivers. This cession, subsequently confirmed by the treaty of Hopewell, in the year 1785, was formed into a land district," etc.

Dr. Ramsey, in Annals of Tennessee, p. 459, makes the above quotation from Monette, p. 268. Then on p. 489 he says, "The Chickasaws claimed and ceded the Cumberland lands, at the treaty held by Donelson and Martin, in 1782 or 1783," and adds, " *Where* this treaty was held, its exact date," etc., he "has not been able to ascertain." See Governor Blount's letter of Jan. 14, 1793, to the Secretary of War, American State Papers, V., 432, etc.

The original records of the anomalous government at Nashborough, under date June 3, 1783, together with other old papers recovered by us, and deposited in the State Historical Society, will settle some of these uncertain and disputed points.

The State of *Virginia* had appointed Colonels Donelson and Martin to visit these settlements and hold a treaty with the "Southern tribes of Indians," not the Chickasaws only, but the Cherokees and others. To assemble these Indians in a settlement which they had endeavored and had almost succeeded to destroy, to bring these enemies to the people where they had committed so many murders and cruelties, to partake of hospitality from those whose cattle they had driven away, and whose fields they had wasted, was regarded as imprudent and dangerous.

The eye of some injured husband, father, son, or brother, might pierce into the guilt of the savage murderer, and the spirit of revenge nerve the arm to strike the murderer down.

And why should the State of Virginia assemble the Indians here upon the territory of North Carolina? These questions were warmly debated at the stations, of which there were then five, (counting Mansker's and Mauldin's, which had been virtually deserted.)

There is no portion of these records in which we take much more pride than in what relates to the votes and conduct of inhabitants here, upon matters so hazardous to their peace and safety. The small numbers of the inhabitants were to be exposed, their seven stations, in the first year, now reduced to three, (for the people were but recently returning to the vicinity of the deserted posts at Mansker, Bledsoe, and Asher;) and then, the most doubtful and troublesome matter of all, to furnish a satisfactory amount of provisions for, perhaps, some of the very Indians who had destroyed the corn, killed the cattle, stolen the horses, and massacreed the relatives or friends *of surviving stationers!* But these items being discussed, as wise men and freemen associated upon the one great principle, that "the *majority shall decide and rule*," it was agreed to submit the main question, "Treaty," or "No Treaty," here to the people of the stations.

It appears that of the people on the Nashborough side of the river, where it was proposed to hold the treaty, two to one were *opposed;* but they were out-voted by those at Eaton's, on the east side of the river. The names of the persons voting, and the votes they gave, are preserved on scraps of paper, and correspond with the entries on the records.

It certainly is worthy of mention, that Colonel Robertson, who resided at Freeland's Station, voted "No Treaty here," as did every other man there. At Nashborough the vote was twenty-six to thirty, the majority voting for the treaty. But the *controlling* vote was at Eaton's, *eighty-four to one.*

And now take notice of the noble spirit of these *Eatonians!* It is worthy of highest commendation. Their settlement was upon the east side of the river, and had always been less exposed to the attacks of the Indians than those on the west; but having carried the question over the heads of their neighbors, and thereby exposed them to dangers which they wished to avoid, the Eatonians promptly passed "Resolutions that, on the days of the treaty," they would attend and "assist with person and property;" and fifty-four voters signed the resolutions. Well done, Eatonians! And we doubt not that every man was at the treaty-ground "with person and property." With person, to watch and defend against all mischief from white or red man; with property—provisions to feed these questionable guests, that they might not suffer hunger, and that the inhabitants on the west side of the river should not be overburdened.

The Commissioners were appointed by the State of Virginia. They had been among these settlers for some weeks, awaiting the assembling of the Indians. Colonel Donelson, it will be remembered, had retired with his family to Davis's Station, in Kentucky. His friend, (and, if not then, in after days, family connection,) Colonel Martin, was associated with him in this Commission.

During their leisure time, waiting for the arrival of the chiefs, these friends visited the rich lands above the mouth of Stone's River, around the Hermitage, and where Colonel Donelson had his second station and selection of an unsurpassed body of land.

The Indians were invited to assemble at the large Sulphur Spring, about four miles north-west of Nashville, on the east side, and a few hundred yards from the Charlotte Pike. The beautiful location had been selected by Colonel Robertson for his own station and home. There he afterwards erected the brick dwelling, which yet remains in good preservation: that was, until within a few years past, the place of the "Nashville Camp-ground."

The treaty began and was concluded in the month of June, 1783. Green corn was not then sufficiently advanced to yield roasting-ears. There being no "fire-water" administered, wherewith to pervert the hearts and madden the brains of the many persons there assembled, the meeting and deliberations were conducted quietly, and concluded amicably. A few ball-plays and foot-races, contests at "high and long jump," constituted the sum of the amusements on the occasion.

The Indians were treated hospitably, and were dismissed with such presents as could then be bestowed. These Indians were highly pleased with Colonel Robertson and the stationers generally.

This treaty being made under authority of one of the States, and not of the Confederated States, was exposed to an objection similar to that which Virginia and North Carolina had made to the treaty of Colonel Henderson, and is not to be seen in the published volumes of Indian Treaties. Its provisions and boundaries were, however, subsequently confirmed, or renewed and settled, by the Treaty of Hopewell, in 1785.

The acquaintance with some of these Indians, formed upon this occasion, was serviceable to the Cumberland settlers in after-years. Some information was obtained relative to Spanish efforts to excite these Indians to enmity and warfare against the settlers. Colonel Robertson deemed it proper, during this year, to address a letter to the Baron de Carondelet, to contradict reports which the Spaniards had heard, or pretended to have heard, of designs entertained by the people of Cumberland to make a descent upon the Spanish possessions on the Mississippi.

A correspondence had also been commenced between Don Estevan Mero, another prominent Spanish officer, and Colonel Robertson, which we may have occasion to allude to more *in extenso*. It will be further noticed that these people had to defray the expenses of embassies to foreign courts. The government of the Notables was no contemptible *parvum imperium in imperio potentiæ*. It was the wisest, the best organized, and the best managed state, government, or community west of the mountains, in that day. Such form of government, such rules and regulations as they had adopted, emanated from themselves; and the officers were of themselves, and chosen by and for themselves.

Independent, self-relying, self-sustaining, and self-defending, as they were, "cribbed, cabined, and confined," as they were, and distant—then so far distant—from the mother State, and the Confederated States, there was a readiness, and, indeed, anxiety to "declare, *by oath*, their fidelity to the government of the State." The Notables were not of that class of men who would "lay burdens upon other men's shoulders," and stand themselves aloof and exempt. They "stood always in their lot." If they took responsibility, they did it with a hearty and a good will. As, in log-rolling and house-raising, the best men took the *but-ends*, so in clearing away rubbish, laying the foundation and erecting the fabric of government, the same class of men put their own shoulders to the work, and *then* they "called upon Jupiter."

The Notables had approved "the Address" of March 4th, in which, among other proposals, the members of Committee were *first* to take the oath of abjuration and fidelity, and afterwards proceed to have all others take the same. This address was followed by another, adopted at a called meeting on the 15th March, for the opening of a land office under the laws of North Carolina, and that Colonel Robertson, being elected a Representative to the Assembly, should go and attend to these and other interests of his fellow-citizens and his devoted constituents on the Cumberland. The records say that he was "elected by the people." He had been elected Colonel, Commander-in-chief of the Militia, Chairman of Committee of Notables, President Judge to whom penal bonds and forfeitures were made payable, and now he is duly elected the first Delegate and Representative to the General Assembly of North Carolina, from the free and independent citizens at the Cumberland Stations.

He attended—we presume travelling about seven hundred miles at his own expense, to reach the seat of government—and we shall see hereafter some of the good results of his presence in the Assembly.

We call attention to the next entry upon the records, the employment of "*six spies*, to be kept out so long as we shall be able to pay them, to *discover* the motions of the enemy. Each to receive seventy-five bushels of Indian corn per month; to be under command of Colonel Robertson and Captain Bledsoe."

"Six spies were to be kept out," and to be paid four hundred and fifty bushels of corn per month! We have no information and no scale by which to estimate the value of corn among these settlers, other than in this instance, and in the price for wolf-scalps at a later date. We know that it is recorded in the history of early settlements in Kentucky, say in the year of destitution here, 1781, that corn sold as high as one hundred and seventy-five dollars per bushel. To get it at fifty dollars a bushel was buying it on most favored terms. We cannot discredit what we have heard, that as high a price or higher would have been given here, if it could have been obtained at that. But these spies performed a most perilous duty: many of them lost their lives; and when the Indians killed or captured a spy, they tortured him while living and mangled his body when dead. It seems "the enemy was about," and that besides the six spies thus employed, new officers were elected at the five stations.

The Commissioners and their guard had "come and gone"—marched into the country, and so marched out again; leaving the Cumberlanders to their fate—that is, to the care of themselves and "tender mercies" of savages. But they made the entry upon their records, "the enemy is about," no doubt having reference mainly to prowling Indians. And yet, as a fact which we consider worthy of some comment, after the election of captains, lieutenants, and ensigns at the stations, the next entry, under date "April 1st, 1783," gives us the first knowledge of another enemy: "*Liquors* brought from foreign parts, and sold to the inhabitants here at exorbitant rates."

The first question which suggests itself is, Whence came this liquor? Who brought it, and how? We know that in a subsequent year there is recorded an interesting case relative to "a *cask* of liquor from Kaskaskia," Illinois, and which has suggested the origin or definition of the name of that ancient town: we do not suppose that this "liquor from foreign parts" came by water and from that direction, but, like some other importations, had safe conduct under the guard. There were, however, a few trading boats in those days. The Committee resolve that importers shall enter into bond, in the sum of two hundred pounds specie, that they will not ask, take, or receive more than one silver dollar, or the value thereof, for one quart of *good*, *sound*, merchantable liquor.

We commend to the notice of our readers the day on which this "Address" was presented and adopted—"*April* 1st!"

Locksmiths are a very wise and useful class of mechanics, but there is an old adage that "even fools laugh at these." As it was then, has been, is now, so we fear it will be hereafter, that sumptuary laws and laws regulating eating and drinking, laws condescending to the minutiæ of "buieing and sellynge," as in the instance of "*knitte hozen*," will be evaded, or stir up a fuss. We believe that it is just as wise, and no wiser, to attempt to legislate a people into religion, as it is to legislate them into frugality in living, cheapness in dress, or into temperance and morality. The rudiments of such an education, the principles and essential elements for holiness in heart, and moderation and chastity in life, are of higher origin than the laws of Assemblies or of Legislatures. The fountain and the code are Divine. Acquaint the people with these, impress upon them the dignity and Divine authority, the salutary influence ever to result from obedience to these; give them the Bible, and an education such as it inculcates; let the principles of religion, morality, temperance, be imbedded *in the heart*, and human legislation, with such Divine sanction, may well come to the aid of the "higher law," and rightfully punish open transgressions. We do not reject the laws of the State, we do not contemn the wisdom of the Legislature, we do not despise human institutions, or scoff at moral associations or temperance societies—we approve of them as ancillary helps, not as substitutes for the Church or the word of God. The first settlers upon the Cumberland brought with them their "family Bibles," and forgot not the commandments, doctrines, or precepts. They had not for several years the living ministry among them.

Pirates and highway robbers were upon the rivers and by-traces or pathways, and in this year had commenced the plundering of boats upon the Mississippi. The Spaniards and French carried on considerable trade in skins, furs, and tallow, from the upper Mississippi to New Orleans, returning with loads of dry-goods, groceries, and specie. Armed bodies of desperadoes whose presence had been spurned in the settlements, where the moral atmosphere was too ethereal for their lungs, had congregated at various points on these channels of commerce or near the paths through the wilderness. Some such lawless fellows had left the Cumberland settlements and gone down the river; which led to the interesting entry upon the records of May 6th, 1783, the sending of a letter to the Agent of Virginia in Illinois, and also to the Spanish Governor. This is followed by some resolves regulating trade with the Indians, and the taking of the oath of abjuration and fidelity.

We find that they had some card-playing and gambling in those days as well as in ours, and that Committee pronounced contracts having such origin or consideration, null. Persons familiar with the history of the South-west in early times, will recognize the name of Colbert as a leader of notoriety, and whose name is to this day affixed to a certain locality on the Tennessee River.

The Committee at this date, July 1st, 1783, resolved to make all the settlers "toe the mark"—subscribe the Articles of Association : Read the resolution. Next follows some litigation as to right of certain property, hidden at the breaking up of the Red River Station. And finally Committee conclude their labors and the record, by fixing the price of liquors from foreign parts at one silver dollar per gallon instead of one dollar per quart. *Query:* Was the importation so abundant, or did the water leak into the casks ? *Kas-kas-kia.*

EXTENSION OF STATE AUTHORITY AND ORGANIZATION OF FIRST COURT IN DAVIDSON* COUNTY.

1783. Oct. 6th. Under an Act of Assembly of North Carolina, the Governor issued commissions to four of the citizens on the Cumberland,

---

* CHARACTER OF GENERAL DAVIDSON, from Haywood and Annals.—This county, like the other three west of the Apalachian Mountains, received its name from an officer of the army of the Revolution, General William Davidson, of Mecklenburg county, North Carolina. He was a native of that part of the State which had early exhibited an enthusiastic devotion to independence and freedom. He sought and obtained a command, though of inferior grade, in the Continental army. In that service he was considered a gallant officer, and acquired reputation.

When the enemy overran South Carolina, he left the regular service, and was immediately appointed General in the North Carolina militia. In this new sphere of duty he manifested great zeal and public spirit. It was he whom Colonel McDowell sought, to invite him to take the chief command of the troops at King's Mountain. He was constantly on the alert to disperse the Tories and annoy Lord Cornwallis, while his head-quarters were at Charlotte.

After the battle of Cowpens, Morgan, in removing the prisoners for safe keeping to Virginia, was pursued by the British army. General Davidson having under his command some active militia men, hastily collected in his neighborhood, endeavored to retard the pursuers, and at every river and creek caused them some delay; and thus contributed essentially to the escape of the American army and

to wit: Isaac Bledsoe, Samuel Barton, Francis Prince, and Isaac Linsey, to organize an "Inferior Court of Pleas and Quarter Sessions," at Nashborough. This "Inferior Court" was, by the Act, invested with extraordinary powers; not unlike or much inferior to those which the Committee government or Notables had exercised for years previous. This newly erected State tribunal was, indeed, clothed with legislative, military, and judicial powers, as may be seen by an examination of the Acts of Assembly. And to men so well skilled and accustomed to the exercise of such high prerogatives, the continuance of powers and functions under a new name caused no inconvenience. They had, indeed, been Judges before, but now they were Justices; they had been "members of Com^tee," but now were members of Quarter Sessions; they had been Notables in the administration of all the affairs of the Cumberlanders, whereas now they had become Magistrates of Common Pleas; from holding the reins of government, they descended to holding an inferior court. But they did all things well.

The members of the court being present and qualifying, they elected, "as a matter of course," and "as in duty bound" as well, because "they could do no better," *Andrew Ewin*, Clerk. He had not been required to give bond during his years of service previously, but now bond is required in the sum of £2000; and he adds another letter to his name, Ewi*ng*. And so ever after he writes it with a *g*.

"The court fixed on a place for building the court-house and prison, agreeing that, in the present situation of the settlement, they be at Nashborough; to be built at the public expense, of hewed logs. The court-house to be *eighteen feet square!* with a leanto (or shed) of twelve feet on one side of the house, with benches, bar, and table, for the use of the court. The prison to be of square hewed logs, a foot square; both with loft floor, except the same shall be built on *a rock*."

---

the prisoners which encumbered its march. In this service General Davidson lost his life. On the 1st February, 1781, the British army, accompanied by loyalists who knew the roads and crossing-places, came to the Catawba River at Cowan's Ford and began to cross. Davidson rode to the river to reconnoitre, with the hope of devising some plan to keep them back, at least for a time. A Tory who knew him, and who was in advance piloting the enemy, was near the bank, and shot him. Knowing he was mortally wounded, he rode back hastily to his men, gave some orders, and soon expired.

An intrepid soldier, a true patriot; never did man love his country with more ardent affection. His name should be ever dear to the people of North Carolina and Tennessee.

The contract for erecting these magnificent buildings was let *a vendue*, 14th October, 1783, to the lowest bidder. These houses for the administration of justice being thus provided for, these four Justices signed the records.

And henceforth the place is no more Nashborough, but Nash-*ville*— the city. This change of name took place July, 1784.

CHAPTER XII.

1783.

As insinuations have been thrown out and questions asked in regard to the motives and influences under which the name of a prominent Spanish officer was given to these settlements upon the Cumberland, we deem it proper to give our opinion also. The question is, Why was this portion of the State called "*Mero* District?" Was there any intention to separate from the Atlantic States, and unite with the Spaniards? At the division of *Washington* District, *Mero* was formed. These are representative names: they are indicative of two forms of government, of opposite principles, and of people who have a separate history—distinct in their entire career as nations, variant in manners and customs, in religion and politics; who have never coalesced and harmonized by intermarriages, or in any great effort for the world's improvement or elevation of the masses. How happened it that names so antagonistic could be chosen, and possibly at the suggestion of the same persons?

It will be remembered that when Robertson and others of these pioneers were living on the Wautauga, at the very commencement of our Revolutionary War, and in the opening of that grand and glorious career which placed Washington upon the heights of fame, his name was selected for the district of country constituting the State of Tennessee. This is supposed to be the first instance in which his name was so selected and applied to any place or section of country, and the suggestion or selection has been attributed to General Sevier, then and always the intimate friend of General Robertson. They were equally and uniformly the admirers of that greatest and best of men. They both hated tyrants and tyranny; they both loved and contended for the rights of man, for the liberty of speech, and the freedom of conscience. Had Robertson now abandoned his principles and his friends; had he now ceased to admire Washington and to love his country? Was he now to part with his friend Sevier and all true Americans? Could he expatriate himself, abjure his religion, acknowledge the supremacy of the Pope, and swear allegiance to the King of Spain? *No, never.*

The District of Mero included the entire region of country north-west of the mountains, the Cumberland region. It was so called after *Don Estepan Mero,* a Brigadier-General in the armies of the King of Spain, Governor and Intendant of the Provinces of Louisiana and West Florida. Spain had been a cautious, calculating, and dilatory ally of the Colonies in the War of Revolution ; not that she loved our cause or approved the principles for which we contended, but rather that she hated England. This was well understood by the great men who stood in the fore-front of that great contest. General Robertson was not ignorant of Spanish character, principles, or craftiness. He could not falsify the sentiments of his heart, or repudiate and stigmatize the faith in which he had been educated, and the associations with freemen, hitherto cherished by him "as dear life itself." It will not be difficult to make these positions plain and satisfactory. If General Robertson ever disguised his real sentiments, it was only when he had to contend with the "cunning craftiness" of learned and practiced intriguers of the Spanish government.

These Spanish officers and agents had used many expressions of friendship towards the early settlers on the Cumberland and in Kentucky. They resorted to various artifices and offers to draw the western settlers into alliance and under the influence of their government. When they could not flatter and bribe, then they resorted to annoyance and savage warfare. It may with perfect truth be asserted, that these early settlers endured as much for the sake of liberty as any other people. Their love for American Independence was manifested by as patient endurance, and by as firm resistance of foreign and domestic enticements, as were ever brought to bear upon any portion of the American people. Sufficient credit has never been given, justice has never been done to them. Suspicions have been cherished, insinuations have been thrown out, as to the integrity of these people; which should be repulsed, and, indeed, might better be cast down at the threshold of other communities.

We believe the correspondence between this Spanish General and Commandant and Colonel Robertson commenced in 1782. It was of a decidedly pacific character, and marked with unquestionable and earnest expressions of a desire on the part of his fellow-adventurers and settlers on the Cumberland to make no encroachment upon Spanish rights—to do no act which might give offence to that people. He had heard that they were, or pretended to be, apprehensive of a descent or invasion by these western emigrants. Governor Mero well knew the feebleness of the settlement on the Cumberland—that it was exposed to attack by the various Indian tribes, and that the Indians outnumbered its population as a thousand to one. And he well knew that the Spaniards exercised an influence over most of these tribes which the few pioneers, struggling for existence in their pent-up quarters, could not countervail. But he also knew the resolute character of such Americans; that where they once planted their foot and drove down the stakes for their tents and blazed the trees for their "donation" or "preëmption," they were sure to hold on until other settlers should be securely located around.

Governor Mero was well aware that the Americans had not encroached upon the territory of Spain, but were settled within the acknowledged treaty limits of the United States; yet he and all the Spanish officers and population on the Mississippi were alarmed and jealous.

General Robertson having learned that they were apprehensive of an invasion by these few adventurous pioneers, thought proper to write to Governor Mero, under date of January 29, 1788, assuring him of the friendly disposition of the Cumberland settlers: that such reports as had reached the Governor's ears of a hostile disposition were false; and he concluded with expressions of friendship on his own part, and in behalf of the stationers.

By reference to the proceedings of the Committee of Notables, 6th May, 1783, it will be perceived that the Committee were willing to and did take decided measures to arrest and hold to bail such persons belonging to their community as were disposed to "plunder the trading boats" on the Mississippi.

There were marauders, or "pirates," on the Mississippi, Tennessee, and Ohio, no doubt, but these robbers made no discrimination between Spanish, French, or American boats, goods, or owners: they went for the plunder. Therefore the Committee, at the same time they addressed Governor Mero, sent a letter "to the Agent of the State of Virginia residing at the Illinois." In those letters they declared that they "detested and abhorred all such practices;" and they spoke the truth.

The Committee imposed restrictions on the trade with the Chickasaws, and required all traders to enter into bond not to disturb the peace, or infringe the rights of person or property of others, whether Indians, Spaniards, or Americans.

No better disposition could be manifested by any state or government towards a coterminous government, than was professed and shown by the government of the Notables towards the Spaniards.

When this little government in the wilderness, by necessity compelled to act independently, seized the violators of the laws of neutrality and good neighborhood, and held them to bail, it acted wisely and well.

When Montgomery and others were arrested, it proved its "detestation and abhorrence" of all fillibustering expeditions.

Governor Mero replied, 20th April, 1783, thanking Colonel Robertson for his friendly communication, and for the assurances of friendship it contained, promising to write to McGillivray, the Creek Chief, and to the Spanish Commandants above the Walnut Hills, to use their exertions with the Creeks and Cherokees to restrain them from any incursions into or interference with the American settlements. He admits that he had granted the Cherokees permission to settle on the west side of the Mississippi, and concludes with an invitation to Colonel Robertson to do likewise; adding promises of indulgence as to religion, exemption from taxes, and certain worldly prosperity.

Colonel Robertson was in possession of information as to the country about "the Natchez." He could foresee the consequences of American settlements upon the banks of the Mississippi. He predicted the day as near at hand when the settlers west of the mountains must have the use of that river in conveying their produce to market : he well knew the importance of quiet to the settlers, and that, if they could remain undisturbed but a few years longer, they would be in sufficient strength to defy the Indians, and the Spaniards also. And knowing the intimacy existing between those parties, he could not doubt as to the best policy of the settlers. It was to attend to their own affairs, encourage emigration, "strengthen their own hands," preserve the friendship of the Spaniards, and gain that of all the savage tribes.

If he distrusted the sincerity and disinterestedness of the Spaniards, as many persons did, he had the wisdom and prudence to retain such sentiments unuttered. Leading men in North Carolina participated in all the anxiety of the leading men upon the Cumberland. When this correspondence commenced, the war of American Revolution was in progress, its end uncertain, its results *in nubibus*. These settlements had been made and sustained without military aid from the American Confederacy, or even from Carolina or Virginia.

They had found the difficulties of emigration across the mountains so many and great, that they could not hope for early and rich advantages to result from commerce, through such forests and mountain-passes. As the tide of emigration set westward, so they concluded must the interests of trade be found in the same channel and direction. But the Spanish authorities have posts upon those rivers; they control the mouth of the Mississippi; their friendship may be secured; we cannot clearly see what may transpire hereafter—what may be the relations or the interests between us; here is a distinguished and influential officer; we are about to select a name for this district of country; it may convince him and others of our friendly disposition, and he may like the compliment; let us take his name—therefore *Mero* it shall be.

But that these Americans, that Colonel Robertson ever intended to become a willing subject of his Catholic Majesty; that, when seeking to throw off the rule of the King of England, he was ever inclined to come under that of the King of Spain, is an assertion utterly preposterous and false. Whatever else may have been contemplated here or in Kentucky in 1783, or during the succeeding years of exposure, anxiety, and privations, down to 1789, it cannot, with truth, be said that these pioneers, for one moment, entertained the thought of yielding up the principle of self-government, the inherent right of the people to rule. Having denied the arrogant pretensions of royalty in England; having claimed and exercised the prerogative of choosing their own officers, enacting their own laws, and imposing their own taxes, they never could have been made the willing, or the unwilling, subjects of such a government as that of Spain.

As the war for independence was approaching a happy and certain triumph, there was manifested by France and Spain much anxiety and opposition to the extent and the settlement of our western boundaries. Each of these, our allies in the war, had great possessions upon the Mississippi and its tributary rivers, and they had seen enough of the American character and *penchant* to excite jealousy and distrust of all accumulation of strength and advances by these settlers west of the mountains.

We shall have occasion to notice the Creek Chief, McGillivray, who is mentioned in this letter of Governor Mero, and to prove that the promises in this letter were made to deceive: that instead of advice or commands to maintain peaceable and friendly relations with these settlements, this very chief of the Creeks, and other chiefs of the Cherokees, were instigated and aided in robbing and murdering these settlers. The decree had gone forth, "Give them no rest."

England, France, and Spain concurred in the treaty for American Independence, but each commenced a system of annoyance and depredation upon our settlements and our commerce, which, with the first, led to war, and, with the two last, worked a forfeiture of all claims of gratitude for any services rendered in the War of Revolution.

England held possession of forts which, by treaty, she should have surrendered, and incited and armed the savages for massacre: France, in the frenzy of her Revolution, and in the madness of her "Age of Reason" and irreligion, insulted us within our borders, and, like England, seized and confiscated our property upon the high seas. Spain, unchanged and unimproved in disposition and habit, continued her practices with the

Indians, and sought, by bribery and the inhibition of our inland commerce, to absorb or annihilate the western settlements.

No "pent-up Utica" was ever more annoyed than the small settlement upon the Cumberland. Its remote inland position exempted it from much of the malign influence of the emissaries of England and France, but its exposure to Spanish and Indian jealousy and hatred combined, was greater than any other portion of our country. Had the three hundred pioneers who came to Cumberland in the winter and spring of 1780, crossed the Atlantic and selected their homes in the denseness of a forest among wild beasts and hostile savages, two to four hundred miles from other small settlements of civilized men, there to endure hardships, there to lay the foundations of a great State, the voyage, the enterprise, its men, measures, and the results, would interest the historian, the orator, and the poet. It was a great work which these emigrants undertook ; they endured more than the dangers of the sea—they suffered a thousand-fold more than they anticipated ; and great and penetrating as may have been their gaze into the *future*, and extensive and glorious as may have been the hopes of improvement and power to result from what they did, they could not have conceived of one ten-thousandth part of what even some of their children now see and enjoy.

At the same time that Mero was lavish in professions of amity, and did actually manifest kindness and hospitality to visitors and traders from these settlements to New Orleans, and spread wide his net with alluring promises and invitations, he engaged his traders and agents in exciting the Indians to commit all sorts of depredations upon the settlements, with the view of *driving* them from their new home upon the Cumberland, proffering better ones farther down on the Mississippi. Spain knew not what she did. She saw not far into the future. There was no necessity to coax or drive : an overruling Providence had *fixed this matter wisely.* "The destiny" of the people of these United States was written like as of old, "Behold, the land is before you : go ye in and possess it."

The tide was set in that direction, and all the artifice and power of Spain could not arrest its onward progress, nor change these "native republicans" into subjects of a distant monarchy—these Protestants to Papists—or contravene the wiser, better purposes of Heaven.

The jealousy of the Spaniards continued to work : they kindled fires in the forests and prairies of the South; but the prevailing "American winds" set so constantly in that direction, and towards the west, that the incendiaries and their agents were, ere long, themselves destroyed or forced to flee the country.

The Americans were not slow to learn the art of "fighting fire with fire ;" and for many years this was made the veritable "Terra del Fuego" between the Americans and the Indians, by the instigation of the Spaniards. Indians were employed to fight Indians. The annual recurrence of the smoky atmosphere occurring in the months of October and November, known as "Indian Summer," was calculated to keep alive the watchful care of the settlers. They looked "*abroad*" for enemies. Weighty cares devolved upon the Notables in this little government on the Cumberland.

The Spanish policy continued its work, and we shall have occasion hereafter to notice it and its results.

14

CHAPTER XIII.

1784.

IN the early part of this year, Commissioners again arrived from North Carolina to survey and lay off military bounty-lands. They came, accompanied by a guard, as in the previous visit. The records of their proceedings show that, in pursuance of the request of officers, the point at which the surveys should begin "upon the Kentucky line" had been adopted; and now, being accompanied by their guard and a number of citizens, they commenced at the State line, and "ran south fifty-five miles to Mount *Pisgah;* then forming themselves into two parties, one ran to the Tennessee, and the other to the Caney Fork." This is known as the "Commissioners'," in contradistinction to the "Continental line."

The Providence of God seemed that day to say, in the words of another memorable occasion: "Get thee up into the top of Pisgah, and lift up thine eyes westward, and northward, and southward, and eastward, and behold"* the goodly land! "Your wives, and your little ones, and your cattle shall abide in your cities, (or stations,) until the Lord have given rest unto your brethren, as well as unto you."

There was an earnest searching through the woods by all the company for choice places for themselves or friends, and the lands east of the Cumberland (now Sumner county) were pronounced "the richest we have yet seen; good for corn, wheat, tobacco, every farming purpose." And so they have proved to be.

The Inferior Court of Pleas and Quarter Sessions was convened in January. The four Justices, Isaac Bledsoe, Samuel Barton, Francis Prince, and Isaac Linsey, who had organized the court on sixth of October in the previous year, were now assisted by the four others who had been commissioned at the same time, namely, James Robertson, Thomas Molloy, Anthony Bledsoe, and Daniel Smith, and, being qualified, proceeded to business.

---

* Deuteronomy iii.

To show the spirit and character of this tribunal, their determination to maintain a good reputation and friendly intercourse with their neighbors, we quote the following from the proceedings at this first session, after being fully organized. We doubt not it has reference to some transactions of the "Colbert party."

"January 6th.—On motion made to court concerning allegations against James Montgomery, as an aider and abettor in the treasonable piratical proceedings carried on in the Mississippi against the Spaniards, it is the opinion of the Court that the said Montgomery be holden in security in the sum of £150 for his appearance at our next court, on which Elijah Robertson and Stephen Ray became securities for his appearance."*

---

* As far as we have been enabled to learn the character of "Colbert's piratical proceedings," they were a kind of "forced dealing," or levying of "black mail," distinguished by a less or greater amount of extortion and violence, according to the respective forces of the parties. These Algerines arrested boats ascending and descending the Tennessee and Ohio. They usually offered to trade, giving buffalo, bear, and deer skins, and peltries of various kinds, buffalo tongues and venison hams, in exchange for such articles as they discovered on board the emigrating or trading boats.

Whiskey, rum, taffia, sugar, coffee, and salt, powder and lead, calico, stroud, and blankets, beads and knives, guns and hatchets, were articles invariably sought for, purchased, or seized and taken away without leave or compensation. In the attempt to trade, it was an easy process from chaffering to disputing, from angry words to blows, from robbery to murder. It may indeed be true that in the securing of such contributions "they did not commit murder, nor deprive the owners of all provision and clothing." We must, however, entertain doubts of the truth of such a statement, or discredit the success of "the pirates."

The men who were usually found at that day upon the Western and Southern waters—and, indeed, so long as the navigation was conducted by pole and oar—were generally of that class which "neither feared God nor regarded man"—a rough and hardy set. Few of them, we believe, would have submitted quietly but to an overwhelming force; and to an equal one never without resistance.

Therefore, we conclude that whatsoever of success the "Colbert gang" attained in the acquisition of property by intercepting boats upon these rivers, was rather by artifice and barter than by actual robbery.

There is another construction to be placed upon what these early records indicate, and we prefer to adopt it. It is that the reports as made by the Spaniards were greatly exaggerated, and that the government of "the Notables" and the first Quarter Sessions Court (the members of each of which tribunals were the same men in person or spirit) were not only opposed to all fraud and robbery, but exceedingly anxious to establish and perpetuate friendly intercourse with the Spaniards and the savages.

The pioneer settlers here and in Kentucky agreed fully with "the said Hood" and the Scripture when he quoted it, "Salt is good." Laborious and tedious efforts were made to boil down the water of the various sulphur licks, but to our "Sulphur Spring" in Nashville alone have we found the expressive and distinguishing terms, "the Salt Works," applied.

We believe the records do *not* show that Montgomery "appeared and stood his trial," but *fled*, or "*kept dark*" for a time. Reports were in circulation to the prejudice of another person as having been concerned in these transactions. He denied the soft impeachment, procured a number of "letters from Virginia, which being read and considered by the Court," the opinion is given that such reports ought not to be credited, and that he should be allowed to settle and "*become a good citizen.*"

Upon these early records there are many orders, rules, and proceedings which clearly evince the upright principles, the independent character and resolution of the Court to prevent or punish vice, maintain order, and advance the good reputation and improvement of the country.

At this court a person is presented for disregarding the law authorizing and requiring the marriage relation, and the court imposed the "fine of twenty-five shillings, *proclamation-money*, upon *each* of them," under the ninth and tenth sections of the Act of March, 1741, "For the better observance of the Sabbath, and the suppression of vice and immorality."*

All officers were required not only to take the "oath of office," but the "oath of abjuration, and subscribe the Test." These oaths were administered to

Anthony Bledsoe, 1st Colonel.
Isaac Bledsoe, 1st Major.
Samuel Barton, 2d Major.

Kettles of various shapes and sizes were brought from the Holston settlements, and a furnace was erected in the low grounds near these favorite waters. Lardner Clark, merchant, and J. C. Mountflorence, gentleman, originated this experiment. In June, 1790, they leased these "Salt Works" to a most worthy man, Captain Anthony Hart. By it Captain Hart promised "the full quantity of six hundred pounds' weight of good dry salt for four weeks' use of the works, provided that if furnaces burn down or the arches break," he was not to pay or deliver that full quantity.

He certainly made salt there, or obtained it elsewhere, for on the 27th of the month the contract is "credited by 150 pounds for the rent of the kettles the first week;" other quantities are endorsed as credits upon the lease.

Mountflorence, we believe, was here in the years 1788, 1789, and 1790, dealing in lands, lots, and peltries, giving entertainments, and practicing law.

Among other old scraps of paper in the historical collection, is one of which we here give a copy:

"DEAR SIR:—Please to account with Captain Anthony Hart for the little venture of *swan skins* which you were so obliging as to take down to the Natchez for me.

"Dear Sir, your obedient servant,

"J. C. MOUNTFLORENCE.

"ANDREW JACKSON, Esq."

* The reply of Evan S. was, "There is so much danger from Indians, it is no wonder people are afraid to sleep alone."

Casper Mansker, 1st Captain.

George Freeland, 2d   "

John Buchanan, 3d   "

James Ford, 4th   "

William Ramsey, Jonathan Drake, Ambrose Maulding, and Peter Sides, Lieutenants.

William Collins and Elmore Douglas, Ensigns.

Daniel Smith was appointed Surveyor.

The residence of nearly every one of these persons is easily recognized at the present day.

The April term of the court was "opened at the house where Jonathan Drake lately lived, and adjourned to meet immediately in the house in Nashborough where Israel Harman lately lived."

By Acts of the Assembly of North Carolina passed in April and May, a town was established at the Bluff to be called *Nashville*, in memory of the brave and patriotic Colonel *Nash*, who was killed in the battle of Germantown.*

The Commissioners for the town of Nashville were directed to lay off

---

* Francis Nash was early engaged in resistance to acts of tyranny in North Carolina. In the year 1771, he was a Captain in the band of Regulators, or the "Regulation War." By the Congress of North Carolina he was appointed on 24th August, 1775, as one of the Committee to prepare a plan for the regulation, peace, order, and safety of the province. Governor Martin having fled from his costly palace, had taken refuge on board an armed vessel, whence he was issuing his angry and inflammatory orders, insulting to the people, and by them generally despised. The province was thus deserted of its chief magistrate. Upon this Committee consequently devolved the duty of proposing a system of government which should meet the exigencies of the occasion. This Committee appointed sub-committees throughout the province, whose duties were to watch the acts of all the agents and emissaries of the "refugee Governor," and all persons of whose attachment to the rights of the people there were doubts and distrust. This Committee determined the qualifications of electors, and exercised "every other civil power necessary in order to relieve the province in the present unhappy state to which the administration had reduced it."

On the 1st September, 1775, the Congress of North Carolina conferred the rank of Lieutenant-Colonel upon Mr. Nash, in the First regiment of the Continental Line. At the battle of Germantown he commanded as Brigadier-General, and, at the head of his brigade, fell, bravely fighting for independence.

Davidson and Nash were from the same State, held the same rank, both fell in engagements that were unsuccessful to the American arms, but in a cause dear to all freemen and patriots, and which, finally, had a most glorious triumph. Their names are worthily associated in the metropolitan county and metropolis of Tennessee.

two hundred acres of land at the Bluff, (near to, but not to include, the French Lick,) in lots of *one acre* each, with *convenient* streets, *lanes,* and *alleys;* reserving *four* acres for the purpose of public buildings. A provision was made to allot to citizen subscribers such number as they should draw, for which they were to receive deeds; in which deeds there should be inserted the condition, that within *three years* the grantees should make certain specified improvements upon their lot or lots.

Samuel Barton, Thomas Molloy, and James Shaw were the "Directors and Trustees" appointed in the Act, and deeds executed by them are among the first titles recorded in Davidson county. They recite the "consideration, *four pounds,* lawful money, and the proviso and condition that the purchaser should build or finish within three years on the lot, one well-framed, log, brick, or stone house, *sixteen feet square* at least, eight feet clear in the *pitch."*

Talk about "a lodge in the wilderness!" Boast of architectural beauty! Inquire for the spacious mansions of the first citizens! Here are buildings erected *secundem artem et legales. Sixteen feet square,* with *eight feet pitch!* Only two feet less than the Court-house and Jail; and "Who needs more room?" was the contented exclamation of several of the mothers who came round in the "Adventure."

The deeds executed by these Directors and Trustees bear date 8th April, 1785, generally, but it is probable that few if any were executed earlier than the dates of their acknowledgment and record in 1788.*

It is due to our honorable Justices and to a fair exhibition of society in that day, (in which were the very elements in existence and operative throughout human society the world over,) that we make further reference to some of their proceedings to enforce an observance of the duties of religion and of all the proprieties of life. Under the old act of 1741, already referred to, this Court repeatedly entered prompt proceedings against offenders. The evidence or testimony is usually made part of the record. The preamble to the act recites that, "Whereas, in well-regulated governments, effectual care is always taken that the day set apart for public worship be observed and kept holy," "all persons are enjoined carefully to apply themselves to the duties of religion and piety —to abstain from labor in ordinary callings. All violations to be punished by fine of 10s. *proclamation money."*

---

* 1801. The town was placed under an *Intendant* and six Commissioners.

1804. The population was four hundred.

1806. Town incorporated, Mayor and six Aldermen. Joseph Coleman, first Mayor.

Profane swearing, intemperance, lewdness, and other vices and improprieties, also to be punished. And the breaches of this law were as promptly punished in 1784 as they are in 1858—though they had but "the stocks, the chunk of a jail, and the sham of a Court-house eighteen feet square." David Wallace was imprisoned and held to bail to answer at the next term of the Court for *abusing* an *Indian*.

There was another act under which some fines were imposed. The character of the offenders and offence may be understood from this preamble: "Whereas, wicked men, too lazy to get their living by honest labor, ... make it their business to ride in the woods and steal cattle and hogs, alter and deface marks and brands," etc. When convicted, as some were, they were

> " ' Fined and confined,'
> And scorched with a brand
> In the left hand,
> As you may see,
> With big letter T."

A *ferry* was established, by order of Court, across the Cumberland River, at a point above the mouth of Sulphur Lick Branch. The description of boats mentioned in the statutes and licenses were ferry-flats, canoes, and pettiaguas or perogues. As emigration increased and trade and travel through the land advanced, ferries were very profitable. It may be seen that General Robertson and Colonel Weakley, and other men of distinction, owned or leased ferries, and had their ferry-house and ferry-boats. The Court fixed the rates of ferriage; and in this year directed two or three roads to be opened.

There is one other matter of general history to which it is proper here to refer, as there was some "feeling apropos to Tories, fierce and revengeful." We have rehearsed the measures which were adopted by the government of the Notables to enforce the taking of oaths of allegiance and abjuration. But as some of the old Tories became rather impudent and arrogant, even *seeking for offices*, it was "Enacted, that such persons shall hold *no office or consent to be candidates for office.*" Penalty £50.

"Owing to previous hasty and imperfect legislation, the oath of allegiance and abjuration needs to be changed;" it is now required of all persons to "take the oath of *fidelity* to the *Independent State* of North Carolina;" and "to reveal to the legislative and executive powers all treasons and treasonable conspiracies," etc.

The penalty upon Tories for holding office was soon hereafter increased to £500. These penalties and disabilities were only slowly and reluctantly removed after the State of Tennessee had been established.

Some of these Tories came at various times into the Cumberland settlements, but being "spotted," viewed with some dislike, and finding doubtful "rest for the *sole* of their foot or the *soul* within them," they "passed on to the land of the heathen and the rivers thereof." Some seemed almost compelled to become Ishmaelites, "their hands against every man and every man's hand against them."

During the summer and fall of this year, there came various reports to these settlements as to outrages committed by "*Colbert* and his gang of pirates." Several barges passing to and from Orleans and St. Louis with goods had been robbed, and as some of the participators in these acts were believed to have been, at least for a time, in the Cumberland settlements, and might possibly implicate innocent persons and create distrust and prejudice against these stationers, it was deemed advisable to protect their reputation. Upon consultation it was thought proper for Colonel Robertson to address the Commandant at St. Louis, exculpating the stationers from all participation with or countenance of any of those "pirates and brigands," as they were termed. (See Chap. ix., "Further Proceedings," etc.)

Colonel Robertson wrote a very suitable letter to Mr. Francis Cruzat, of St. Louis, in compliance with this wish of his fellow-citizens, which was forwarded by "express canoe." To this letter Colonel Robertson received a very friendly reply, dated "4th Nov., 1785," in French. As it is interesting, and furnishes the only information as to the character of Colonel Robertson's letter, to which it is in answer, we give below the translation.*

---

* SIR:

I have had the honor to receive your letter by which you convince me of the pain you experience from the hostility and robberies which Colbert and his people have committed upon the Spaniards on the Mississippi; and that you were in possession of certain proofs by which the slaves and other property could be identified, and that you would endeavor, if possible, to have them returned, and that you would seize them as property justly to be restored to your allies. Such a proceeding on your part, so analogous to the just idea which the Spaniards have always had of the equity of the American States, proves to me, sir, that not only the people of Cumberland have not coöperated with those brigands, but that they are very sensible to all that humanity has suffered from the evils which we have sustained from those vagabonds.

In consequence, I thank you, sir, for the information which you have had the complaisance to give me, that two negroes—the one taken at Mattattok and the other on the Arkansas—are with the Chickasaws in the hands of whites; and

This correspondence will remind the reader of the similar one commenced by Mr. Molloy in the previous year, which he reported to the Notables, and received their high sanction. Colonel Robertson had already secured the confidence and esteem of some of the Chickasaw chiefs and warriors, therefore could he give assurance that his efforts to recover from persons in that nation property which had been stolen and secreted there would not be ineffectual.

When he received the letter from Mons. Cruzat, he was on the eve of starting on the long journey to the Assembly of North Carolina; but before his departure he engaged some persons to make inquiry about the negroes which were said to have been stolen by "Colbert's gang," or such as were reported to be in possession of white men who had taken refuge in the Chickasaw nation.

The journey to the seat of government and return to the settlements—in all not less than twelve or thirteen hundred miles—together with attention to public business before the Assembly, must have occupied several weeks. He returned home near the end of the year, and was again busily engaged in attention to the interests of his fellow-citizens and the adjustment of his private affairs, that he might be ready to recross the mountains as a representative to the next Assembly; for he was reëlected for the year 1785. The business of friends was also greatly accumulating on his hands. Many were the inquiries which were made of him as to the lands in this "far-off wilderness," and "the danger from the Indians."

One of the earliest measures to which Colonel Robertson gave atten-

---

that if you knew their masters, you would undertake to withdraw them from the Indians. But it is impossible for me to procure for you the proof, because Colbert and his people are scattered into several bands, and are carrying on a war by robbery and pillage everywhere; and has so large a number of persons, that the verification of the property would multiply contest between those who have been the victims of his rascalities.

Very grateful, sir, for the thanks which you and the people of Cumberland present to me, for my reply to the Indians who had come to ask of us land whereon to settle; I assure you, sir, as in this occasion so in all others, we act so as to maintain the friendship, the union, the good correspondence established between our two nations; that we shall listen to no plans which would injure my honor, my duty, or the pacific intentions of my sovereign. And if in the country under my command I can be useful to you and to those who may merit your recommendation, I declare to you that I shall exert myself to convince you of the gratitude and high consideration in which I have the honor to be, sir, your very humble and very obedient servant,

FRANCIS CRUZAT.

St. Louis in Illinois, 4th Nov., 1784.

tion in the Assembly, was to have an Act passed providing for the cases of minors and other persons who had failed to obtain from the Commissioners, in 1783, certificates of their preëmption rights. This was one of the duties enjoined upon him, "being elected thereto by the people" in the spring of 1783. Events which occurred after the Act in favor of preëmption rights in 1782, naturally formed preëmptioners into classes more or less meritorious. Some had gone off when the public distress was very great and disheartening, and lived for a time at stations in Kentucky; some had remained and defended the country through all perils and sufferings; others had done the same, but were minors and not included in the Act of 1782 ; and yet others had come to the stations subsequently to June 1st, 1780, had remained and bravely assisted in defending the settlements; some were killed and had left widows and young children. These were classifications.

This Act of 1784 left persons of the first description to claim their preëmption, but to pay the price required in the Acts of 1782 and 1783. Those who had remained to preserve possession of the country in despite of all hardships, and were yet living, were to have their lands without any price to be paid to the State. These the Act particularly names. Colonel Robertson furnished this list to be inserted in the Act, placing his own name *last*. Cicero says, "Modesty is the science of decorum as to time and place of action:" "Modestia scientia est opportunitatis idoneorum ad aliquid agendum, temporum."

Although Colonel Robertson had no knowledge of the "classics," no acquaintance with the Latins, he was a "born-gentleman," and always knew how, and never failed, to conduct himself *comme il faut*. Old Monsieur De Monbreun used to say of Colonel Robertson, "He alway know savoir faire, vat to do, and he do him."

In this catalogue of steadfast, worthy men mentioned in the Act, Robertson fulfils the scripture, "The first shall be last," but in this position he is dignified and honored. At the same time that he is "the chiefest citizen," he is the servant of all—the honored representative, but their obedient agent.

There were *seventy* persons entitled to be placed in the first class. Then the Act provides for sixty-four who had been killed, giving to their heirs lands, as to those who had survived. The quantity of land given to each of these was six hundred and forty acres, or one mile square, or in such form as to include their improvements, if they had made any. Then the other cases are provided for to the number of nineteen ; among these last were Robert Thompson and Sampson Williams. Lest it should be inferred that there were but *seventy* persons who remained here through all the dangers and privations, we must state that there were a few, and but a few, who, having made their entries and paid the specified price for their lands, were therefore not named in the Acts.*

Another matter to which Colonel Robertson was requested to give attention, and in which he was successful, was to have a Land Office opened in the district. The business of entering and surveying lands commenced in earnest. Emigrants were arriving; the sound of the woodsman's axe was heard from many places in the forests; log-cabins and worm fences were to be seen in all directions; the noble forest trees were "girdled" or cut down; men, women, and children were busily engaged in "the burning of the brush," clearing off the ground, and opening the virgin soil for the various seeds and grain, from which they confidently anticipated an abundant harvest, to be gathered in the joy and quiet of autumn.

The toil-worn stationers indeed thought their "brighter day had dawned;" that, at length, they would enjoy peace and plenty.

But, alas, it was not so. It was not so "written in the book of fate." "Through much tribulation," was the frequent quotation of Mrs. Robertson and Mrs. Cartwright.

"The said Hood" always availed himself of such an occasion or remark by others, and especially when furnished by the good old ladies, to repeat the same scripture or quote a passage of similar import. But he did this with such a tone and manner, that it was impossible to determine whether he was really reverential or in jest.

He was, however, a great favorite with the women and children. He had the "science" of being always present to respond to a call for a bucket of water from the spring, a turn of wood, a call or hunt for the children. In these services he made himself useful, and would not suffer the children to quarrel and fight.

As far as we have ever read or heard, William Hood was the only man who ever saved his life by the artifice to which he resorted—designedly acting in imitation of that remarkable animal, the *opossum*.

That he did this, and quite successfully, we have elsewhere shown. He asserted it at the time, always persisted in the assertion, and was a man of such strange peculiarities and endurance, that his assertion was never doubted by those who knew him and witnessed his recovery.

Could the fugitives who had returned, or the recently arrived settlers,

---

* Some of those who had thus secured an *inchoate* right to land, retired for a season, and when the wars were ended or dangers diminished, returned and perfected their titles by *settlement*.

have been enabled to lift up the veil of the future, we doubt much if they would have all now been here. They could not see the gathering clouds, nor hear the muttering thunders.

It is certain that the expectation was that the settlers would seldom be annoyed by the Indians, and that if wicked men from their own people, or who had gone hence, did not provoke the Indian tribes, peace would be preserved. At this day there seemed to be no very great apprehension of evil to result to these stationers from the jealousy or sinister aims of England or France. or even Spain. The pages in the "black book" of diplomacy were closed—had not yet been opened; the letters which spelled out the deep designs were not yet legible. The letters were there—traced in invisible ink, which *exposure to the fire* would bring out in distinctness.

As these cheering prospects were brightening and numbers increasing, there passed light clouds across the horizon.

The Spaniards manifested jealousy, sullenness, and opposition. They set up a claim to territory far to the north of any line which had hitherto been urged by them. They knew that the American Confederacy was not wholly approved, not working in harmony and advantageously, or giving satisfaction.

We were then in the childhood of independence. The Spaniards had not heartily rejoiced at our freedom and independence. They did not like the *union* of the States; and least of all were they gratified to see the emigration into these western wilds. As the tide rose over the mountain-tops and swept down from the head-waters all along and upon the shores of the beautiful rivers which empty from the south and east into the "Father of Waters," they could not conceal their anxiety or suppress their murmurs. They pretended great concern for the poor Indians!

If they could not roll back these waves, they determined to impede and disturb their onward flow; they should not sweep o'er all the valleys.

The settlements were extending and strengthening much more east of the mountains, upon the Tennessee and Holston, south of the Nollachuka and upon French Broad, than upon the Cumberland; but as some of these advances were into Indian territory—or territory which they now denied having yielded by proper treaties—there was an increasing irritability among them, wrought up and made use of evidently by more designing parties than savages.

This fact should be borne in mind throughout the history of early settlements upon the Cumberland, that the Indians who attempted the destruction of the Americans here were living within the acknowledged limits of the United States, and therefore had no right to treat with any foreign power, nor could any foreign government treat with them, or claim a *protectorate* right and obligation over them; and to instigate them to war upon any of our population was an offence—*casus belli*—which would have justified an open declaration of hostilities by the Confederacy or the Union against the prime instigators. It would not be endured at the present day. England, France, and Spain had recognized the boundaries of the United States; and for either of them to instigate the Indians to war, or to furnish the incentives and weapons for such a purpose, was a breach of good faith, a violation of international comity.

Clearly did Spain thus act toward the State of Georgia, and more covertly, but no less wickedly, did she excite and aid in hostile measures against the "small estates on Cumberland."

The treaty made at Pensacola, June 1, 1784, between the three Spanish Governors and McGillivray, the influential Creek Chief, was an implied agreement to "drive off the settlers upon the Cumberland, or *to destroy them utterly.*" (This wish and purpose were subsequently avowed in correspondence between the parties.)

The compact at Pensacola was only the *initiative* of many other crafty measures developed in future years. We shall have many occasions to refer to Spanish intrigues, agents, and instruments, and to speak of the deeds and character of the chief of the Creeks.

The persistence of Spain in some of her pretensions and practices was somewhat instigated and sustained by France, whose influence was weighty in this country at that day and for many years thereafter. In deference to the views and solicitations of this our early and recognized ally, our government did lend a listening ear to the pretences, the excuses, and arguments of Spain, and judged not hastily or harshly of the conduct of many of her offending officers.

The administration of Washington saw that without some concession, flattering to the vanity of Spain, the Indian wars would be continued, and a happy conclusion to the negotiations as to "navigation and boundaries" would be interminably delayed.

The policy of our government was, in truth, wise and best; but required a great amount of *forbearance. By temporarily yielding, we gained all.*

The relinquishment or retrocession of extensive tracts of country to the Indians, which they had by repeated treaties granted, and on which many American families had settled, may have gratified the haughty *dons*, but did not wholly terminate their mischief-making nor fill to surfeiting the appetites of the savages. In some respects this concession seems to

And wounded Phil. Mason, not badly, 'tis clear,
For he fled, with Nic. Trammel, half-way to the station,
While Nic. hastened on to 'rouse the whole nation.
Phil. tied up his wound, looked sharp for the foe,
And for his friend Trammel and others, who'd go,
And fight to the utmost for the fat doe.

Trammel had made all haste to Eaton's Station, and procured assistance and a fresh supply of powder and ball. With his few friends he came to where Mason was, and found him able to join them, and anxious for the rencounter. They had discovered that the party of Indians was strong in numbers, but they hastened on to where the deer had been killed. The Indians and the deer were gone—all the Indians and the best of the deer.

The whites followed their trail, but in the haste of pursuit of those who evidently had the deer and deer's skin, (as they could easily see from the repeated instances of the skin and meat having been struck against the bushes and trees,) they did not notice that the number of persons whose trail they were following had greatly diminished. The most of the Indians had turned, perhaps one at a time, to either side, that the whites, if they pursued for recapture of the venison, and to be avenged on the *robbers*, might fall into ambush.

When Trammel and Mason, and their four friends, who were on horseback, had overtaken the foe, they hastily dismounted, rushed upon them, and killed two Indians. The whites were making sure, as they thought, of the "bone and meat of contention." In the meantime the other Indians had gotten possession of the horses, and each party of Indians fired. The whites had not primed their guns when they were fired upon. At this firing Mason was mortally wounded, and the four friends, seeing their situation was most perilous, concluded to escape. The Indians now had the game and the *horses*, which they prized even above a white man's scalp.

Trammel and his friends were separated in their flight, but he had not gone far in the woods before he discovered other white men, whom he induced to return with him to the contest. Indeed, Trammel was opposed to the retreat and the desertion of Mason, but the others did not tarry for such a certain "surrounding." "They said the contest was too unequal." Now Trammel had found "the man in the woods" whom he knew to be "braver than Julius Cæsar," and a better rifleman. This was Josiah Hoskins. These two took the lead. There were again six in the party. They found the Indians, and renewed the fight; *killed* three Indians, and, as Judge Haywood says, "fought till both parties were tired." The Indians were *treed*, and kept their position, each party firing as they saw an opponent expose his body. This was continued so long, that "Trammel and Hoskins, who were enthusiastically courageous, and bent upon making their enemy yield the palm of victory, precipitated themselves into the midst of the Indians," a portion of whom they saw retreating, as was imagined. The result was, these rash men "received the fruit of their temerity :"

"They fell by the hands of the foe,
All fighting fiercely for the doe."

"The rest of the white men maintained their ground until both parties were willing to *respire* from their martial labors." A drawn battle !

Cook had read the "Battle of the Kegs," but he could not begin to tell of this "Battle for the Doe," on White's Creek, in any such short metre.

But there was another fight a short time thereafter, and not many miles distant, which is thus told :

"Aspie, together with Andrew Lucas, Thomas Sharp Spencer, and one Johnston, had left the Bluff on horseback, to go on a hunting tour to the head waters of Drake's Creek. In crossing the creek their horses stopped to drink, when the Indians fired upon them, shooting Lucas through the neck and through the mouth. He, however, dismounted, but in attempting to fire, the blood gushed out of his mouth and wet his priming. Perceiving this, he crawled into a bunch of briers. Aspie, as he alighted from his horse, received a wound which broke his thigh, but still he fought *heroically*. Johnston and Spencer acquitted themselves with *incomparable gallantry*, but were obliged to give way, and leave Aspie to his fate, though he entreated them *earnestly* not to forsake him. The Indians killed and scalped Aspie, but did not find Lucas, who shortly after returned to his friends. The whole family of the Aspies were *superlatively* brave."

We have given this name as Haywood has it, though the correct spelling is *Espey*, as upon the records and among the signatures of the "Compact of Government" in 1780.

Another death should be mentioned, that of Cornelius Riddle. He had killed two turkeys and hung them up on a tree, and was in pursuit of others. The Indians, hearing the report of his gun, came to the place, lay in ambush, and on Riddle's coming for his turkeys, they fired and killed him. His companion fled. The Indians thus obtained one scalp

15

and two turkeys.   This was between Buchanan's Station and Stone's River.

In this year "Colonel Isaac Bledsoe built a fort at Bledsoe's Lick. (The land is now owned by Mr. Jerry Belote.) During this same year also, Colonel Anthony Bledsoe built a fort at 'Greenfield,' about two and a half miles north of Bledsoe's Lick, on a beautiful eminence, and in the heart of one of the richest bodies of land in Sumner county. (The place is now, 1857, owned by David Chenault.)"

Such is the statement of Mr. John Carr, upon whose authority we here anticipate the construction of several other forts in Sumner county:

"In 1786, Esquire John Morgan built a fort on the west side of Bledsoe's Creek, near the mouth of the 'Dry Fork,' about two and a half miles north-west of Greenfield. This fort also was on a beautiful eminence, in the midst of a very fertile country. (The land is now owned by William Baskerville.)

"In 1788 I helped to build a fort at the head of Drake's Creek, on the top of the ridge, about five or six miles north of Shackle Island.

" In 1790 or '91 Major James White built a fort about three and a half miles north-east of Gallatin, on the waters of Desha's Creek. About the same time Colonel Saunders built a fort on the west side of Desha's Creek, about two and a half miles from White's Station.

" In one of these years Jacob Zigler built a fort about a mile and a half north of Cairo, on the western branch of Bledsoe's Creek. This fort was taken in 1792 by the Indians. There were four killed, four wounded, and thirteen prisoners carried to the nation. I was one of the men who followed them.

"About the same time Captain Joseph Wilson built a fort about three miles south-east of Gallatin. It was called 'Walnut-field' Station.

" It is not to be understood that these stations were all continued till the close of the Indian war in 1795. The three upper stations, Morgan, Greenfield, and the Lick, I believe were kept up till the close of war.

"JOHN CARR."

The following extracts from the records furnish information as to some of the manners and customs and transactions of that day, which may be interesting to a few in our day. They not only show to us what matters of fact often engaged the attention of the Worshipful Court, but to what ingenious tricks for abbreviating his entries the old Clerk, Andrew Ewen, was driven. It made him an original stenographer:

"Wm. Hamilton
Wm. Fletcher. } Ass. & Batt.

"And^w. Wickerham b'ng sworn, sayth y^t he saw Wm. Hamilton go to turn ye Deft. out of his house, on which ye s^d Deft. resisted; & they laid hold on one another and fell, ye plff. uppermost: And when they were parted, he saw y^t ye s^d plff'. *nose was bit*, but saw no blows pass.

"Jas. Buchanan and Wm. Simpson corroborated w^t y^e ab've."

"J. Archer
J. Lynn. } tressp-case. Jury &c.

"Jas. McCain sworn, says, Jno. Duff employed him to sell *a little mare* for h^m at Public Sale, which y^e Deft. bought. Jury returnd—find for y^e plff. ass^s dam. on y^e occasion to $20. 'Tis therefore cons^{dr} by y^e C^t y^t y^e plf. recov^r y^e Deft. y^e sum af^d and costs suit."

The next entry is: "Ordrd y^t Sam. Henry be fin^d 10*ss*. for profanely swearing y^e pres^{nce} of y^e C^t."

The following entry has arrested attention, as it is believed the "Jno. Civil" mentioned is the free mulatto man who was captured by, or fled to, the Indians, in the attack upon Captain Gower's boat near Clover Bottom; the same "Jack Civil" whose negro blood and mono-syllabic name originated that of Nigger Jack—Nick-a-Jack. It seems that General Robertson had not included Jack's name in the roll of worthies mentioned in the Act of Assembly as being entitled to a grant of land; but the effort was made to secure a *preëmption* claim in his name. It would be a matter of historic interest to see the papers which it is said "Col. Jos. Martin" had, transferring Jack's right; but "the bad-ness of the weather" spoiled the papers, and—the claim.

"Elijah Robertson being sworn, sayeth that he had ord^{rs} from Col. Jo's Martin w^t a number papers impowering him to enter in the name of s^d Martin the preëmption right of a certain John Civil which papers he lost by the *badness of the weather*, and y^t in ye s^d papers he saw a n^o of Depositions proving a legal purchase and transfer of s^d land from s^d Civil.

"ELIJAH ROBERTSON."

This entry is not in the Clerk's hand, but wholly in the bold handwriting of Elijah Robertson himself, and by him signed. It reminds us of the other entry of the fighting and biting between Pillows and Denton.

On these early records there is frequent mention of *Taffey* and *Whiskey*, (sometimes with the qualifying adjectives "*good* and *sound.*") *Red Wine* must have been a delicacy. How it was introduced here, whence it came, why and where concealed on the river's bank, what excitement and litigation it caused, may perhaps be satisfactorily learned by perusal of the records and papers in the case in Court involving the question of ownership of "A Cask of Red Wine," shipped from "*Cas-kas-kia* on the Ilenois," "concealed in the river and thereafter brought to Nashville."

"Everybody wished to taste it." Many feared the Mississippi river had faded its redness and reduced its quality; they were, however, perfectly willing "to taste it, free, gratis, for nothing." "Some offered a deer skin for a pint or a quart of it." The honorable Lardner Clarke, merchant, Sam Martin, (of course,) *Mr. Wycuff, Mr. Truckey,* (both proper men,) John East, and John Sigvault, were prominent litigants, or "*concarned!*" "The *Batteau*" in which the cask was conveyed from port to port is an object of interest. "The Battle of the Kegs" was fought again here. We discover now the real name of that town in Illinois, which, though sometimes spelled *Cus-cus-ca*, at others *Caskaskia*, Caskcaskia, Cuskcuskia, still preserves the signification, the *Cask* and the *Cus.*

It is not at all surprising to find the following entry upon the records soon after those relative to "the cask of red wine." Ezekiel Smith was certainly the "ablest single-handed Judge Lynch" of whom "the Bench and Bar of Tennessee" can boast.

"Ezekiel Smith of s⁴ county was summoned to ansʳ unto Joel Stearns, a compᵗ of assault and battery, to damage of £200. Whereas yᵉ s⁴ Stearns saith that he was abused by s⁴ Smith, having of him tied, whipped him with switches on his naked skin—likewise took yᵉ s⁴ Stearns, fastened him with a cord round his neck, raised him up to a limb of a tree, till he felt all the pains that he would have felt in death. The first thing that he knew after that, he yᵉ s⁴ Stearns, was lying on yᵉ ground, that yᵉ s⁴ Smith bid him rise—and that he has made no satisfaction to yᵉ s⁴ Stearns."

There are other cases not unlike the foregoing in which various persons are implicated. Several of these had their origin "away, down in old Virginia," and others as far back as the times of the "Regulators at the

Alamance," and in some of the transactions of the *Tories* during the Revolutionary War. Very few of the old Tories were ever allowed to find a home on the Cumberland.

1784. At this period our old acquaintance, Philip Alston, (whom we saw when we were young,) occupies much of the time and attention of the Court. He had sold a tract of land, a mill, etc., near the Bayou Pierre in the Mississippi Territory or Florida, as then claimed by England and Spain. As we have elsewhere intimated, Alston engaged in an overt treason against the Spanish government, and fled to "the Robertson stations." His property on the Bayou Pierre was declared forfeited and confiscated to the crown. This was the defence set up by the person who had purchased the property, he alleging that it was by Alston's own wrong that the property was condemned, so that the purchaser could not possess and enjoy it. The truth is, the purchaser from Alston was as much implicated in the treason as the seller. Both fled together and came and registered their names for protection and citizenship here. They, a few years thereafter, returned to their chosen inheritance, "renewed the contest there," and lived not long enough to see all the difficulties settled, but left them to heirs and sons-in-law. It is a singular fact in the history of Philip Alston, that, although he had engaged in the overthrow of the Spanish authorities at Natchez, failed and fled, was denounced as a traitor, his estates condemned and sold as forfeited by reason of his treason, yet he returned, recovered that property, and removed to Mexico, ingratiated himself with the Spanish authorities, became an Empressario with an ample annuity, and died holding such Spanish commission.

April 6th, 1784. "Appeared Humphrey Hogan bound in recognizance at suit of John Kitts—for good behavior, &c. . . . John Barrow sworn: Sayeth, Hogan threatened he will kill Kitts' hogs, if he did not keep them from his door, and also *whip himself.*" . . . "To make friends, Kitts agreed to dismiss recognizance and pay the costs;" leaving it at Hogan's discretion, we presume, whether to "whip himself," or not.

In a suit between Wm. Hamilton and John Childers, about a horse bought with a "gambling note" given by Childers to Abraham Taylor, proven that "Taylor said he would *pull off his hat* and thank Childers, if he would forgive him the abuse of the horse; give him what *meat* he had, and a receipt against the note." And "they agreed to play *quits,* against which there was no law." "The opossum," who was in Court at the time, said, "That beats me!" Taylor was a little afraid of consequences

mentioned.   The elevation to the top of the chief mound is two and a
half poles; its diameter two poles.   The declivity is an angle of about
forty-five degrees.   .   .   .   .   .

"An entrenchment and circumvallation enclosing forty acres encircles
this mound and others of lesser size.   There is a circumvallatory parapet
five feet high.   On this parapet are small tumuli, like towers, about
ninety-five feet apart.

"Other mounds, entrenchments, and elevations are to be seen in various
directions."

CHAPTER XV.

1786—1787.

"In this year the boundaries of the settlements remained stationary, but the number of inhabitants increased." The settlers were encouraged to expect an entire exemption from depredations by the Cherokees; but in this they were destined to disappointment, as we shall see. "The Creeks were waging a deadly war against the Georgians." This they had prosecuted for the past five or six years, and their vengeful and marauding disposition could not be wholly restrained to their side of the Tennessee River; nor from crossing the territory of the Cherokees in order to reach the settlers on each side of the Cumberland Mountain.

But the earliest acts of hostility experienced this year by the citizens of Cumberland, were from the Cherokees themselves. These were the killing of Peter Barnet at a place below Clarksville, on the waters of Blooming Grove; and the killing of David Steele and wounding of William Crutcher, in that same region. The Indians had left Crutcher badly wounded, and doubtless as they supposed mortally, with an old hunting-knife sticking in his body; but he revived, reached one of the stations, and lived to a good old age. "Crutcher kept that knife many years." We suppose the Indian did the same with his, which he took in exchange.* These acts were done within the recently acknowledged

---

* It was of this occurrence that Captain Prince said to Crutcher, "I suppose, William, the Indians went upon the principle that a fair exchange is no robbery." "I am glad," said Crutcher, "he used his old dull knife instead of my long sharp one. I would not object to the exchange, if he would let me stick my knife in him!" Crutcher had received two gunshot wounds also, one in his side, the other in his thigh; from which he fell, and the Indians rushed upon him. It is to be noticed that they did not scalp him or Mr. Steele. As long as Crutcher lived he scrutinized the appearance of every Indian he met, and glanced his eye upon every hunting-knife. But he never recognized his man, or saw his "long sharp knife" again.

The Indians often called the pioneers, "Long Knives."

treaty limits—proving how little confidence was to be placed in these treaties and concessions. How salutary the measures of the Commissioners!

The history of the next attack upon any of these settlers, we condense from Haywood, from the narratives of John Peyton* himself, and from John Carr.† This was an attack made by a large party of Cherokees upon John Peyton, a surveyor, Ephraim and Thomas Peyton, his brothers, Thomas Pugh, John Frazer, and Esquire Grant, in the month of February of this year.

The party of white men having killed much game, had camped for the night on a small island just above the mouth of a creek which empties into the Cumberland River on the north side, near the line of Smith and Jackson counties, between Carthage and Williamsburg. The Indians were sixty in number, under the Cherokee chief, Hanging Maw. The party of hunters or surveyors were fatigued, and were lying upon the ground around their fire, their horses being fastened near by. It was Sunday night; they had given some part of the evening to playing cards, (for they had an old greasy pack, says Carr.) Their dogs and horses gave some intimation of danger; but the tired hunters concluded that wild animals—wolves—were attracted by the meat in the camp, and that there could be no other enemy near. Therefore they "chunked up their fire" and laid themselves down again, John Peyton leaning on his elbow near the fire, hissing on the dogs. Suddenly the Indians fired a volley upon them, wounding four of the six white men.

As John Peyton jumped to his feet, he had the wisdom to throw his blanket over the fire, thus to give himself and party some chance to escape in the darkness; and O, how great was that darkness! The whole party fled, escaping through the Indian lines. They cast their blankets from them, and each pursued his own way through the woods, bare-headed and without shoes. They were seventy miles from Bledsoe's Station, the ground was covered with snow, and yet each of these men, after several days' wandering, arrived at the station and recovered of their wounds and exposure. John Peyton was shot through the arm and shoulder; Thomas Peyton, through the thigh; Frazier, through the leg; and Grant, through the knee. Thus four of the six were wounded. It is strange they were not all killed outright; marvellous that they ever reached home; and yet more that they all recovered, and were often

---

* John Peyton died, at his residence on Station Camp Creek, in Sumner county, in 1833, at the age of seventy-eight.

† John Carr was living in the same county in 1857; died in the fall of the year.

engaged in other Indian skirmishes. Ephraim Peyton and Pugh escaped without a wound; but Peyton, by jumping down the bank to cross the creek, sprained his ankle very badly, and lay for some time in agony. Crawling along on the ground, he found a stick which answered the purpose of a staff to support and aid him in hobbling along. He was several days thus suffering and laboring to reach the white settlement— the last one to come in. All the others had arrived, one at a time; each reporting all the others killed.

John Peyton sent a message the next year to the Indian chief that he might retain the horses, blankets, saddles, guns, and other articles, "if he would return the *compass* and chain." In reply the chief sent this: "You, John Peyton, ran away like a coward, and left all your property; and as for your *land-stealer*," (the compass,) "I have broken that against a tree!"

The stream of water where these occurrences took place has ever since been known as "Defeated Creek." These men did not "give it up so." In a few years, they with others completed their surveys and established locations there.

It becomes our duty to record here the sad and awful death of Colonel *John Donelson*, which occurred in the month of January of this year. After the attack made upon Gower's boat and Captain Donelson's friends in Stone's river, near the "Clover Bottom," in the fall of 1780, Colonel Donelson removed with his family to Davis's Station (near Harrod's) in Kentucky. A number of the earliest stationers on the Cumberland moved away at the same time. During his residence there in the five succeeding years he was much engaged in locating Virginia land-claims for himself and his many acquaintances in Virginia; and it is stated that he entered large tracts of the rich and beautiful land in the immediate vicinity of Lexington. He was a practical surveyor of well-established reputation before he removed to this part of the country. Such was the estimation in which his integrity and capacity were held in Virginia, that he had been often called to the discharge of important trusts. He was at one time engaged in running the boundary line between Virginia and North Carolina. He was present at the treaty near the Long Island of Holston, April, 1777.

The information which he there obtained in regard to the lands in the Great Bend of Tennessee, operated strongly, in connection with other inducements and influences, to his expedition, or "Adventure," as he calls it, from Holston down the Tennessee. For further information as to his character and public services, we refer to the sketch of the "Donelson Family" at the close of this chapter.

We mentioned the arrival at the settlements, during the last year, of a physician.

We now notice that gentlemen of the green-bag are here also : Edward Douglas and Thomas Molloy announced that "they would practice law" —*in all* the courts—*in Davidson county*. Real saddle-bag lawyers, riding the circuit. These gentlemen anticipated an increase of the courts—and doubtless of business; for the Act authorizing the organizing of the county of Sumner was now to be put in force.

"Neither of these gentlemen had studied law as a science; but, being of sound practical sense, and possessed of good business talents and of the gift of the gab—good talkers—they soon had clients. A few pamphlet laws of North Carolina were all the law-books which were in the country for many years."

The families of these and some others, being now here, added much to " good society and sociability !" that is to say, " the lawyers' *wives* did this.

Colonel Robertson had freely expressed his disapprobation, yea, indignation, at the treaty of Hopewell, and the deafness and indifference of the State and nation to the cries of suffering from these western people. When at the Assembly in November and December last, he procured the passage of an act authorizing the *court* in Davidson county to call into service a company of men for the defence of the settlements. He said he had summed up in the *Preamble* all the arguments he intended to urge in behalf of its passage, and to leave the members of Assembly without excuse for their unconcern and inaction.

The act was passed, reciting "the frequent acts of hostility and cruelty committed by the Indians on the inhabitants of Davidson county, and that necessity required the taking of some measures for their protection." Three hundred men were authorized to be raised, equipped, supported and employed, in that county, and in opening a road for emigrants and guarding them from Clinch to Nashville. As Haywood says, " *the indispensable clause*" was inserted, that the "*State Treasury* should be taxed with none of the expenses."

Davidson county was looked upon by the old counties in the light of distant foreign territory, not entitled even to the benefit of a *protectorate*. The several acts of Assembly which Colonel Robertson and Colonel Bledsoe at various times procured to be passed, virtually constituted the County Court the head of government west of the mountains. It was a province, rather than a county. There was a commingling of legislative and executive power intrusted to the justices. It was no new authority for these men; they had, from necessity and before the sanction of the State had been asked or given, assumed and exercised equal prerogatives; and the people had no distrust of such men. They were identified in every measure.

As one act of this Quarter Sessions Court, we quote from their records the following:

"*Whereas,* The frequent acts of hostility committed by the Indians upon the inhabitants of this county for a considerable time past, render it necessary that measures should be taken for their protection:

"1. *Be it resolved,* That 210 men shall be enlisted and formed into a military body, for the protection of said inhabitants, to rendezvous at the lower end of Clinch Mountain.

"2. Every able-bodied man who shall enlist and *furnish himself* with a good rifle or smooth-bored gun, one good *picker,* shot-bag, powderhorn, twelve good *flints,* 1 lb. good powder, 2 lbs. lead-bullets or suitable shot, shall be entitled to receive each year, for his services, one blanket, one good woollen or fur hat of middle size, one pair of *buckskin breeches,* and *waistcoat, lined!*"

Then a tax is imposed upon the inhabitants of Davidson, *payable in specifics:* such as *corn, pork, beef,* or other provisions.

These were solely for the use of the troops. Places were designated as suitable for depots, and a *money tax* was also levied, to defray expenses of delivery of provisions at the stations for the troops.

Officers were allowed the same clothing as the soldiers. The *Paymaster* could draw on the *sheriff* of Davidson for money to buy powder and lead.

"Leather breeches, full of stitches;
Leather breeches, buttoned on!"

On the 10th of January, three of the United States Commissioners, Hawkins, Pickens, and Martin, concluded a treaty with Representatives of the Chickasaw nation—Piomingo, head-warrior and minister; Mingatuska, one of the great chiefs, and Lato-poia, the beloved man. These Chickasaws had gone to Hopewell, in South Carolina, at the solicitation of the United States Government, made through Colonel Robertson and others who enjoyed an influence among that nation.

At this treaty the Chickasaws accepted boundaries, as limits, for homes and hunting, which, so far as these settlements are concerned, are well represented in the Cherokee Map; they extended down the Ohio and Mississippi to the Choctaw line. Land was reserved to the United States for a trading-post at the mouth of the Ocochappo, where it empties into the Tennessee below the Muscle Shoals.

This treaty was a confirmation of that which had been made at Nashville in 1783, by Donelson and Martin, as Commissioners on the part of Virginia.

In this year the fort erected by Esquire John Morgan on the west side of Bledsoe's Creek, near the mouth of "Dry Fork," and Greenfield Station, both upon beautiful eminences, about two and a half miles apart—Greenfield at the south-east—were greatly extended and strengthened.

The position of self-reliance, self-defence, and independence which the people of Cumberland were authorized by the legislation of the State to assume, and which, from their natural and relative position, was a necessity, has been mentioned. They were not afraid to avow their sentiments, to claim their rights, or to exercise their powers, when occasion required. The spirit of rebellion or resistance to lawful authority was never cherished or cultivated here, although it may be seen throughout the history of these early settlements that there were many and urgent causes of discontent, and for a general uprising of the people.

The attributes of sovereignty were conferred upon them to a great extent by the Legislature of the State, (if they needed that sanction.)

The magistrates were authorized to levy, collect, and disburse the revenues, to raise, equip, and sustain troops—an army—to attend to "domestic and foreign relations," and to many other matters which, of right and necessity, belong to a sovereign and independent people. Here there were no political party divisions, no jealousies and contentions among aspirants to office. No office had a salary which could tempt cupidity. No man "shirked or cowed" when danger threatened or duty urged. "To your tents, O Israel!" "To your stations, and to arms!" were proclamations which of that day, or of a day more ancient, aroused the hosts to arm and to the defences. The men in office, and the people around them, professed a recognition of the rightful supremacy of the State. They were, however, beyond the annoyance of strangers sent among them as officers "to lord it over them." The sentiment of independence had full play, with strongest incentives for cultivation. Acts of tyranny aided in planting this colony. Emissaries of foreign governments continued their annoyances, and ingrained the principle of self-government.

Between these stationers and the parent State intervened extensive regions of mountainous and unbroken forests; and the settlements of their brethren on Clinch, Holston, French Broad, and Nolachucka. There they had been driven by the exigencies of their situation, and a consciousness of right, to organize an independent government; and, in honor of "the man of letters and of science," call their new political association "The State of Franklin." The convention which adopted a

Constitution for this new State in August, 1785, was the result of meetings and consultations had in the fore-part of that year and in the fall of 1784. In the present year, 1786, there was presented the exercise of powers which utterly repudiated and defied the authority of the parent State. Judges commissioned by the State of Franklin held Courts twice a year at Jonesborough, and Judges holding like judicial powers from North Carolina opened their Courts at Buffalo, ten miles distant.

This conflict of authority and the conflict of persons, arising from political and individual preferences, belong to the history of men and times on that, rather than on this side of the mountain. Yet it seemed proper to refer to these events occurring at this date, as they affected very many of the friends of the Cumberlanders; and evidently so engrossed the attention of the State, that less care or concern were felt for these more distant pioneers. There was here a strong sympathy with the "Franklinites." Sevier and Robertson were never divided.

His Indian wars kept at bay the savages, or were fought for the relief of these settlers, as well as for his more immediate neighbors. He and his adherents had avowed and shown a sympathy and service for these western people, more decided and beneficial than any which had ever been manifested by the State itself. And there was not one man or family on the Cumberland who would not have appealed sooner to General Sevier and the authorities of Franklin, than to any of the powers of North Carolina. If, in East Tennessee, General Sevier was pursued by "a man of Belial, the son of Bichri," stealing the hearts of the people by plausible excuses, they, like Israel, returned to their first love and loyalty; and rejoiced to make "Chucka Jack" First Governor and Chief Ruler of Tennessee. General Robertson encountered difficulties, had his opponents, and a few secret revilers, but never any strong array of bitter enmity, or jealous, interested aspiration. We cannot believe the fiercest foe or most rabid reviler of either of these men ever suspected them of a towering ambition for the sake of the salaries they received. They unquestionably expended a thousand-fold more than they received. A year's pay then was much short of a quarter's salary now, and the labors less divided. Who now could pay house-rent with Governor Sevier's salary?

In August of this year the first meeting was held to organize a Board of Trustees for "Davidson Academy." The Trustees resolved at once to put a subscription paper in circulation, to obtain means wherewith to erect a building and to endow the institution. They adopted a form of subscription with a special clause for donations *in lands*. And thus the Academy, College, and University of Nashville received several tracts, in addition to the two hundred and forty acres now included within the corporate limits of the city of Nashville.

By Act of Assembly passed this year the county of Davidson was divided, and the county of Sumner authorized to be organized. This name was given as a testimony of respect for Brigadier-General Jethro Sumner, of the North Carolina line during the Revolutionary war. There are rich lands, highly improved farms, elegant dwellings, intelligent, hospitable, thrifty farmers, and choice society, in this county. Very great attention has been given to stock-raising. The reputation of the county for superior horses, mules, and neat cattle, has extended far and wide. Here the first crops of tobacco planted on the Cumberland were secured. "A Tobacco Inspection" was early established at Cairo, in this county, and large shipments have been made from that "Landing." Gallatin, the county seat, is situated on a branch of Station Camp Creek, having a pleasant, gently undulating surface, with streets of good width, a handsome Court-house, several convenient churches, and other public buildings. The surrounding country is rich and beautiful.*

---

* EXTRACTS FROM FIRST RECORDS.—1787. Eight Justices met 10th April; appointed David Shelby Clerk, Martin Hardin Junior Sheriff.

October. Ordered that corn be received for taxes at two shillings and eight-pence per bushel; good fat bear meat, if delivered where troops are stationed, four-pence per pound; prime buffalo beef, three-pence; good venison, if delivered as aforesaid, nine-pence; bacon, nine-pence; dried beef, six-pence; salt, two shillings four-pence per pound.

"Our army swore terribly in Flanders!" Judging from the number of fines imposed for profanity and Sabbath-breaking, some Flemish soldiers were here.

"State ⎱ For stealing a pair of *leather leggins*. Proof taken: judg-
vs. ⎰ ment passed that he be *reprimanded*, and acquitted on paying
Bazil Fry. ⎰ costs."

"The Grand Jurors present Joshua Baldwin for *altering his name* to Joshua Campbell, and Ephraim Peyton, for taking away, *by force*, a mare from Joshua."

Tavern Rates established by Court: One half-pint of whiskey, such as will *sink tallow*, two shillings; bowl of toddy, made with loaf-sugar and whiskey, three shillings and six-pence; one quart bowl punch, with fruit, ten shillings; dinner and grog, four shillings and six-pence.

Jan. 12, 1789: Andrew Jackson admitted attorney-at-law.

When General Jackson became candidate for President, it was published to the world that he spelled *all correct* "*Oll Korrect*," and the *O. K.* are familiar to everybody.

We were startled to read the following record:

Wednesday, 6th Oct., 1790: Court met according to adjournment. Andrew Jackson, Esq., proved a bill of sale from Hugh McGary to Gasper Mansker for a negro man. which was O. K." These are the exact capital letters. We find another instance of this abbreviation, and two where the letters seem to be O. R.

GALLATIN

CHAPTER XVI.

1787.

WE have mentioned that a new county was authorized to be established on the east side of the river in the year past. It is bounded north by Kentucky, east by Smith county, south by Wilson county, the south bank of the Cumberland River, and west by Robertson and Davidson. It was reduced to these limits in 1799. The lands are rich and fertile. The principal streams are Goose, Bledsoe, Station Camp, Drake, and Mansker. Celebrated springs : Tyree and Bledsoe or Castalian.

On the second Monday in April of this year, the persons who were appointed as Magistrates assembled at the house of John Hamilton to organize a County Court. They were "General Daniel Smith, Major David Wilson, Major George Winchester, Isaac Lindsey, William Hall, John Hardin, and Joseph Keykendall, Esqrs." The Clerkship was conferred upon David Shelby, who continued in office to the day of his death; a good clerk and worthy man. To this already highly respectable tribunal there were soon added Colonels Isaac Bledsoe and Edward Douglas. And thus there were associated in this Court, men of education, sound judgment, good morals, and of great influence in the community. The commendation bestowed upon these gentlemen was, that most of them could worthily fill the office of Governor or Chief Justice ; " fit for a Lord Chief Justice or the Governor-General." In those days no man held an office as a mere sinecure, nor solely for sake of the pay.

Each of these persons is entitled to some more extended notice or memoir than we can now bestow. They were connected with the civil and military affairs of the Cumberland settlements, but intimately with those of the county of Sumner, and deserve most honorable mention in the history of our " Early Times."

With men of such capacity and character at the head of affairs in Sumner and Davidson, the people seemed reasonably to have expected quiet and prosperity. Inasmuch as these men could promote and secure such results, they were attained. The hearts of the people were with them. They were worthy of all confidence and esteem. But there were hearts and hands which none of them could influence or control: hearts full of all mischief; hands holding the deadly rifle, the hatchet, and the knife, and which spared neither men, women, nor children.

"And now the thickened sky
Like a dark ceiling stood."

The remark with which Judge Haywood opens his record of the events of this year, is worthy of quotation as an introduction. It is the third time he has used it, and justifies our appropriation of it. "In this year the settlements were not extended, but continued as they had been for some time, except towards Red River, where they considerably expanded."

This expansion of settlements consisted chiefly of emigrants who had recently arrived. They selected lands, and commenced with great earnestness and vigor to deaden the trees, clear their lands, and erect their log-houses. They were advised by the earlier "stationers" not to delay the construction of a fort at some suitable central point.

The expectation which some may have indulged, that by reason of their remote position upon Red River, being out of the usual range of the savages, their new settlement would not be discovered or be disturbed, was soon to be disappointed. They were not long hidden or secure. The cup of bitterness of which others had tasted was to be commended to their lips; they were to share in the afflictions of their brethren. As these new settlers sought homes here, and hoped to enjoy the quiet of their homes, under the shelter or in union with the older stations and settlements, they were required, and readily assented, to enroll themselves as "fellow-citizens and fellow-soldiers."

Much of the time and means of the people of Cumberland was required in providing provisions and forage for "the troops." But the defences at the various stations demanded strengthening; and yet, such was the anxiety of each individual to "locate" and establish for himself and family a home, that there was often manifested a reluctance to "spare the time" which was asked by public officers to enlarge the enclosures, erect palisades, and clear away the trees and undergrowth near the forts. New emigrants could not at first appreciate the importance of removing trees, stumps, and brush from around their fort and huts. The Indian guns seldom harmed any one at "long shot," but where they could avail themselves of any shelter, they would go "upon all-fours," *pedibus et manibus*, or like the snake, and thus approach near enough to wound or kill.

The troops and the volunteers had much to do in the course of this year, pursuing and chastising the enemy. The largest and best organized forces for such purposes were now assembled and armed which had ever been called into service in these settlements. All "able-bodied men" were regarded as soldiers, liable to be called into service at a moment's warning. And few, indeed, were the aged or crippled who were desirous or willing to be "exempt." Several warlike expeditions were undertaken, and others contemplated, but not prosecuted, during this year.

The Cumberlanders hitherto had been ably represented in the Legislature of North Carolina. Colonel Robertson and Colonel Bledsoe were the worthy and well-qualified representatives, but in the fall of this year David Hays is sent in place of Colonel Bledsoe. A journey from Nashborough to Tarborough in those days was like the crossing of the continent:

> "It was through the woods most all the way,
> Midst perils at night and perils by day,
> And 'over the hills and far away.'
> They went on bravely, but not to stay;
> They spoke out plainly what they had to say,
> Then hastened back the same wild way,
> Right 'over the hills and far away.'"

The delegates from Davidson (Robertson and Hays) made a solemn statement of the sufferings of their constituents, which they presented to the General Assembly at Tarborough. They say:

"The inhabitants of the western country are greatly distressed by a constant war that is carried on against them by parties of Creeks and Cherokees, and some of the western Indians; that some of their horses were daily carried off secretly or by force, and that their own lives are in danger whenever they lose sight of a station or stockade; that in the course of the present year *thirty-three* of their fellow-citizens had been killed by those Indians, (a list of whose names they annex,) and as many more had been wounded; that by original letters or talks from the *Chickasaw Nation*, which they submitted to the Assembly, it appeared that they were uneasy or jealous lest encroachments should be made on their hunting-grounds; and that unless some assurances were given them that *their* lands should not be *located*, there was reason to apprehend that they shortly would be as hostile as the Creeks and Cherokees; that these counties have been settled at great expense and personal danger to the memorialists and their constituents, and that by such settlements the adjacent lands were increased in value, by which means the public has been enabled to sink a considerable part of the domestic debt.

"They and their constituents" (say these worthy representatives) "have cheerfully endured the almost unconquerable difficulties in settling the western country, in full confidence that they should be enabled to send their *produce to market* through the rivers which water the country; but now we have the mortification not only to be excluded from that channel of commerce by a foreign nation, but the Indians are rendered more hostile, *through the influence of that very nation,*" (Spain,) "with a view to drive them from the country, as they claim the whole of the soil !

" We call upon the humanity and justice of the State to prevent any further massacres and depredations of ourselves and our constituents; and we claim from the Legislature that protection of life and property which is due to every citizen, and recommend, as the most safe and convenient means of relief, the adoption of the Resolves of Congress, of 26th October last;" (that the States which owned western lands cede them to the United States.)

This was a well-considered paper. In the preparation of it William Blount, Esq., assisted. The plain allusion to *Spanish influence* is worthy of notice, and proves that these men were not afraid to place on record in a formal public document a bold assertion, charging Spain with the instigation of these cruel murders, whilst the high officers of State and Commissioners in correspondence and negotiation with Spain seemed to ignore these deeds of cruelty, and some even of them to charge all the provocation and wrong-doing upon the western settlers.

Colonel Hays, by marriage, was connected with the family of Colonel Donelson. He was an admirer of Washington, the personal and political friend of Generals Sevier and Robertson, and an unswerving advocate for the Union of the States. He erected his station on the east bank of the Cumberland River, and called it "Fort Union." The stationers there were entitled to one member in the tribunal of Notables. The town of Haysboro' had a very limited existence, but the name and merits of Col. Hays should not be lightly esteemed by any persons who consider the worth and services of pioneer settlers.

We must make mention of some of these Indian outrages, and of the acts of retaliation by the whites. We condense from Haywood :

"They killed old man Price and his wife, and *chopped the children.*" These are the Judge's expressive and descriptive words. This was at Hendrick's Station, on Station Camp Creek. The savages seemed to take pleasure in mangling the bodies of their victims. Near the same time and place they killed a boy named Baird, and "split and scalped him." At a short distance above Bledsoe's Lick they killed William Hall and his son, and another person. The mangled and bloody bodies of these men were brought into Bledsoe's Station, and laid upon the floor in the presence of three pregnant women, whose after-born children were *marked,* one as if a bullet had been shot through the head, and the two others upon the backs of their necks with red streaks, as of blood streaming down from "scalped heads."

At a few miles to the north, John Allen was attacked, shot through the body, but escaped, and recovered. He "tucked a portion of his shirt in the wound, and thus staunched the blood." The next victims were old Mr. Morgan and Montgomery's son, on Drake's Creek.

Two companies started in immediate search and pursuit of the Indians. Captain George Winchester was in command of one, and William Martin of the other. As these two parties were hunting for the enemy, and skulking through the cane, they suddenly approached each other, when some of Captain Winchester's men fired, and killed young Ridley, in Martin's company. This was done under the belief that Ridley was an Indian. This sad event induced the men of both parties to abandon the pursuit of the savages. Seldom, indeed, did a troop of white men successfully search out a solitary Indian, or a half-dozen of them, in canebrakes. These children of the forest had learned the noiseless tread of the wild-cat, and the art of concealment of the fox.

In May they came close to the residence of Colonel Robertson, on Richland Creek, and shot Mark Robertson, a brother of the Colonel. From the broken cane and blood upon the bushes, it was evident that Robertson had contended long and fiercely with his foes, ere he yielded to their tomahawks and knives. The Indians who had committed the late outrages were believed to have come from the west side of Tennessee, and below the Muscle Shoals.

THE TOKA OR COLD WATER EXPEDITION.

The settlers determined to endure these cruelties no longer. The war must be carried into the enemy's country. So many of the murders which had been committed could be traced to Indians living near the Muscle Shoals, that Colonel Robertson sought information as to the location of their town, its number of people, and the best route by which an invasion and an attack could be made. There was no white man among the stationers who had ever traversed the intervening forest for half the distance. But two friendly Chickasaws, one known by the name of *Toka,* soon came to Colonel Robertson, furnished the desired information, and offered themselves as guides. Their services were readily accepted, and preparations were made for the march. Men were mustered, guns examined, powder-horns filled, and bullets run. "Jerked venison" and

17

other dried meats, and parched and pounded corn, were in the knapsacks for food. A few floats or boats of raw hides were constructed for the transportation of arms and indifferent swimmers across the Tennessee River. Such were the preparations for the expedition by land. Colonel Robertson was in command of these troops. Lieutenant-Colonel Robert Hays and Lieutenant-Colonel James Ford acted under Colonel Robertson. This force consisted of one hundred and twenty men, well chosen and well armed for that day. The Chickasaws had given information that there were usually to be found canoes belonging to the Indians, some of which would probably be found near the point to which they designed to conduct "the army."

But it was also deemed advisable to send some boats around with a supply of provisions. These boats were to ascend at least to a "crossing-place" belonging to the Chickasaws, (well known to this day as Colbert's Ferry.) If the land force found too great difficulty in crossing the river where they should reach its banks, they could march down to this cross-ing-place, and there be ferried over by their own boats. And if in any attack upon the Indians some of the whites should be disabled so that they could not march, the boats would be used to transport them back to the settlements. This river expedition was placed under the command of David Hay as principal officer. Moses Shelby was in command of one of the boats. These boats were well manned; good oars and poles were supplied, so that by rowing and punting it was calculated that they could reach the point of destination, by the long water route, as soon as the land force could make its way through the cane-brakes.

The "Fleet," under command of "Commodore Hay," consisted of three vessels. "Admiral Hay," as Rains used to call him, hoisted his flagstaff upon the good ship bearing the Spanish name of "Piragua," commonly and familiarly called "The Pirogue." The two other vessels were of less magnificent proportions, and bore Indian names, the "canoes."

Having seen the naval armament depart, Colonel Robertson was ready to march. Most of the troops had been mustered into service at the residence of Colonel Robertson, and thence marched into town or to the Bluff, where the "formidable body made a grand display." Such a military parade had never been witnessed upon the banks of the Cumber-land. The women and children from Eaton and Freeland were there. A great shaking of hands took place; brief *farewells* were uttered; fathers and husbands leaving a parting blessing and injunction: "Take care of yourselves and of the cattle: keep a sharp look-out till we re-turn!" "Eyes right, quick is the word," said Colonel Robertson, and they were soon out of sight.

"Peace is despaired,
For who can think submission!
War, then, war,
Open or understood, must be resolved!"

The march of this "army" is described by Haywood. The route pursued was, necessarily, very circuitous : "By the mouth of Little Harpeth; mouth of Turnbull's Creek; thence up the same to its head; thence to Lick Creek of Duck River, down Lick Creek eight or ten miles, leaving the creek to the right hand; thence to an *old lick as large as a cornfield!* thence to the head of Swan Creek; thence to Blue Water Creek, which empties into the Tennessee a mile and a half above the lower end of the Muscle Shoals."

Truly, as Parson Craighead said about the soldiers of the cross, these soldiers "were led in a way they knew not, and by paths they had not known." Indeed, it was the instruction to the guides to avoid the usual routes of the Indians. And thus had they safely arrived near the mouth of Blue Water, and in hearing of the rapids of the Tennessee.

They encamped some miles distant, but within sound of the falls or shoals, in the evening. Most of the men were very anxious to have a view of these rapids, of which they had heard some marvellous accounts. As they were sitting around their camp-fires, many inquiries were made of some of the men who descended the Tennessee and crossed over these shoals with Colonel Donelson and his party of emigrants, on Sunday, 12th March, 1780. The story of the good ship "Adventure" was rehearsed, commencing with the departure from the Long Island of Holston to the arrival at the French Salt Lick. The various perils, sufferings, and escapes, the firing of the Indians upon them, and the misery and deaths caused by the savages, were recounted without the least abatement. They were fired upon when near these shoals, and probably by some of the very Indians who lived at the town which the army designed to attack. These navigators declared that the descent of the fleet across these long rapids was a most perilous "running of the gauntlet," and one of the most marvellous escapes that had ever been known. The savages were shooting at them from the shores; it was cruel death to land on either shore; the awful rapids were before them; they must go forward, trusting in Providence to preserve them. The waters were at an unusually high tide, and they passed in safety. "No thanks to the Indians," said Cartwright; "with much cause to thank Providence."

The Chickasaw guides had described the situation of the Indian town near the great Cave Spring, the Indian name for which signified "Cold Water." The citizens of the beautiful town of Tuscumbia, Alabama, now obtain their supplies of pure, fresh, and cold water from this spring It flows from beneath a bluff of limestone—a beautiful little river as it gushes forth.

The Indian village was on the west side, at a short distance from this glorious fountain of cold water. The country is level or gently undulating; the lands are rich, and were covered with heavy cane. It is a lovely portion of the charming valley of the great Tennessee. Creeks and Cherokees occupied the wilds upon that side of this broad river. The Indians who resided at this town were mostly Creeks. Adventurous Frenchmen kept up some traffic here. From these traders the savages received their supplies of "fire-water," of arms, and ammunition; and there had been intimations, through the Chickasaws, that these very traders encouraged the depredations upon the Cumberland settlements. This was the town and these the enemies which "the army" had thus far marched with intention to destroy.

The question of difficulty now was, how to cross the river. They must do so, and not cause alarm; they must do so, and keep their powder dry; they must do so with their horses. Various plans were adopted or had in contemplation. The floats of hide were unpacked, and anxiety expressed for the morning's dawn. Before the break of day they learned that it would require hours of travel through the cane before they could reach the river. Toka had given intimation that one or more canoes would probably be discovered "at a certain out-of-the-way place."

By information from one of the parties of scouts which returned to camp at midnight, it was ascertained that the river was at too great a distance for them to reach it and return before the break of day. The Indian guide now declared that the encampment must be eight or ten miles from the shoals; and yet they said that the roaring of the falls was distinctly heard, the night was so very calm, with a cool air and clear starlight.

At earliest dawn the troops were mounted and on the march. The same course was pursued as on the day previous. At midday they came to the banks of the river. Here they sought concealment during the remainder of the day. Such was the position of the main body. A few experienced spies were sent to examine a plain path, which Toka said led to a crossing-place not far off. They were ordered to watch both banks of the river, and discover whether the enemy were alarmed, or making preparations to obstruct a passage of the river.

This party discovered some Indians on the opposite bank, apparently looking for the approach of the army. These spies "lay close." They

had found a secure hiding-place in the cane and bush, and from this concealment they narrowly watched the path, the crossing, and the enemy.
These Indians were spies; such, at least, was the conclusion of the whites,
who noticed that in approaching the river they advanced with great
caution, slowly, with stooping posture, and from tree to tree.   At length
they waded across to an island, which was near their side of the river.
After having continued their cautious movements for some time, they
entered into an old canoe, pushed it from the shore, and near to the
middle of the river.

The whites had resolved not to fire upon them, unless they should land
so near their ambush as to make it necessary to kill them in self-defence,
or to avoid exposure.   When the Indians ceased to propel their canoe
any farther, they plunged into the water, washed and amused themselves
for some time as swimmers, and then paddled the canoe back to its
former landing, and soon disappeared.

The white men had discovered some cabins on the southern bank, but
saw no person, or animal, or fowl, anywhere around them; they were,
therefore, satisfied that they had been deserted.   And now whether this
abandonment of these cabins was caused by information or apprehension
of an invasion was an inquiry of some importance.   If they knew that
Colonel Robertson was approaching, or now encamped near this crossing-
place, would they not attack him and his men as they should attempt to
land; or would they not abandon their town, and thus disappoint the
invaders of any achievement worthy of so long, tedious, and expensive a
march?

Colonel Robertson had ordered his favorite scout, Captain Rains, with
a squad of fifteen men, to go up the river.   If he discovered an Indian,
he must capture him alive, if possible.   If they found any canoes or a
crossing-place, immediate report must be made to head-quarters.   The
utmost caution was enjoined.   Captain Rains moved towards the mouth
of the Blue Water, but had made no discoveries.   He had not seen an
animal, or heard even the crowing of a cock, or the barking of a dog.
There could be no Indian settlements in that direction.   About sunset
Captain Rains received orders to hasten back to the main body.

From the report of the six or seven spies who had watched on the
river's brink, and who had observed the Indians bathing, Colonel Robertson was resolved to attempt to cross the river at that point, or near it.
Those spies proposed to swim the river and bring over the same canoe
which had been used by the Indians.   They pledged themselves to furnish that boat to aid in conveying the troops across.   Every man was
convinced that their presence could not be kept from the knowledge of

the Indians another day. Colonel Robertson issued orders for every man to be in readiness to move as soon as the light of day had departed. He wished to cross, under cover of the night, and attack the town at break of day. Officers and soldiers heard the orders with great satisfaction. They marched from the upland into the low-bottom, upon the margin of the river.

The men who had engaged to furnish the enemy's canoe, swam the river, and presented it to Colonel Robertson. They had been directed to visit and examine the deserted cabins. They had performed this duty also, and reported that "no living creature was there." It was evident that the enemy was not apprehensive of an invasion. Into this large canoe forty men, with their firearms, were speedily packed, or permitted to hold on to its sides, and, by swimming, aid in the "ferrying over."

A large crack in the bottom of the boat had been stuffed and corked with the clothes of some of the men; those in the boat placed their feet firmly upon the clothes to prevent the water from rushing in to fill and sink the boat. They had not proceeded far when the water rushed in with such violence, they were compelled to return to the place whence they had started. A number of the men who were in the canoe handed their guns and powder to some of their companions, and promptly leaped into the water, with the view of lightening and aiding in propelling her to the shore.

"In these operations some noise had been made," and before the boat could be baled out and the hole securely stopped, day had dawned. A forlorn hope—a brave company of about forty men—were safely passed over, and took possession of the opposite bank. They were posted in the most advantageous positions as sentinels, and for defence. As soon as it was seen that this party had safely crossed, and had taken positions, the remainder of the troops, too impatient to await the return of the boat, plunged into the water, some upon and others swimming by the side of their horses. The leather boat, laden with guns and ammunition, was passed over by swimmers. And thus, as Captain Rains used to say or sing, in the words of the familiar old play,

"The fox and the geese, they all swam over,
Firebrands in their teeth."

"All but the geese," said Denton. "Don't slander my foxes," said Sampson Williams. There were some amusing incidents during the passing of the troops, but the injunction to observe silence was regarded as far as possible. The river was at a low stage, so that although they were in the water for a distance of three-fourths of a mile, they could wade most of the distance. The exhibition upon the southern shore was truly ridiculous. With the exception of those who had passed over in the boat, most of them were there with their clothes perfectly wet. Some had put their clothes in their hats or tied them around their heads and hats, hoping thus to keep them dry. But during the time allowed for the horses to eat some corn, and for the men to take a breakfast of jerked venison and parched corn, "the wet clothes were hung upon the bushes to dry."

An army *en deshabille!* Real *sans culottes.* An invading army, within six miles of the enemy's stronghold, and on the enemy's side of that broad river! They themselves described their whole appearance as most laughable. The sun had shone out brightly, and then there came clouds and a sudden summer shower. The deserted cabins and large forest trees afforded shelter and dressing-rooms, for the order had been given for every man to "prepare to mount."

"They donned their duds in less than no time," and were mounted, awaiting marching orders. They were "allowed no further time for chat." Having ascended the bank, and proceeded a short distance, they entered the Barrens, and discovered a plain path, with a westerly direction. Toka informed Colonel Robertson that the path led to the corn-fields near the town. They kept this path for about five or six miles, and came to the fields; thence, by a slight change of their course, and at a distance of less than two miles, they came to the Cold Water Creek. There was a gradual descent towards the creek. The town was on the opposite side.

The Chickasaws had accurately described the position of the town, and predicted that the warriors would run to their boats at the mouth of the creek. Colonel Robertson had given orders to Captain Rains, with a few of his "right hand men," to take one of the guides and be ready to intercept the enemy, or fall upon them at the bank of the river. The distance to the mouth of the creek was farther than to the town, and upon the east side there was no path.

The main body having arrived to where the ground descended towards the creek, the example of the commander was followed by every one; and they struck into a sweeping trot, crossed the stream, finding but a narrow pathway up the western bank. They rushed into the town. The Indians had discovered the approach, and were already in precipitate flight. The most of them made for the river, as had been anticipated. Many had reached the edge of the water, and were in the act of "shoving off" their canoes, when Captain Rains arrived and commenced the work of revenge and slaughter.   A portion of Colonel Robertson's force followed the fugitives down the creek, and united with Rains.

Twenty-six Indians were killed in the boats and in the river.   There were also three French traders and one white woman killed in the boats. The principal French trader and six other Frenchmen, or French half-breeds, were taken prisoners.   But one or two Indian women were captured.   It was supposed that the women and children had been sent away, from some intimation the Indians had received of the contemplated invasion by the whites; but this, to us, seems improbable.   The wily savages were certainly taken by surprise.   They fled in great haste, leaving all their property; some of them did not take gun or tomahawk. They did not tarry to fire upon the invaders.   Women and children could conceal themselves in the cane and high grass by which the town was surrounded.   But the truth is, that Indians of the character and habits of these, seldom had wives or children.   They associated as out-laws, as a company of thieves, as robbers and murderers.   It was so here; it was the same at Nickajack and Running Water.

After this dispersion and destruction of these Indians, the huts were examined, and all that was valuable secured; and then every cabin was burned and the place made desolate.

CHAPTER XVII.

1787.

A LARGE stock of goods belonging to the French traders was taken and packed to the river at the mouth of the creek, and placed in the canoes which had belonged to the Indians. These articles were "tafia, (a French rum,) sugar, coffee, clothes of various kinds, blankets, handkerchiefs, beads, paints, knives, tomahawks, tobacco, powder, and lead, and other articles suitable for Indian commerce."

All the personal property found in the Indian huts (a miserable inventory and outfit, indeed) was thrown out of doors before the fire was applied; so that, if there were women and children concealed in the thickets, "they could take what was left."

The army encamped near the ruins; a guard was stationed at the landing to prevent the boats being stolen in the night. The next morning the loading of the boats was completed. There were three very good canoes into which the goods were packed. The command of these was given to Jonathan Denton, Benjamin Drake, and John and Moses Eskridge. The Eskridges had a smaller canoe tied to the side of their larger one. The five Frenchmen, a child and a squaw, (the wife of one of the Frenchmen,) being all the prisoners, were placed in the boats. This fleet being thus ready, pushed from the shore and descended the river. They were ordered to move slowly down, and be in readiness to aid in the transportation of the troops across the river. The Cherokees had informed Colonel Robertson of a suitable crossing-place some distance down the river, from which the troops could march more directly and easily back to the Cumberland, than by the route pursued in coming to the Muscle Shoals; and the officers resolved to adopt that course.

Toka and his companion were furnished each with a good horse, saddle and bridle, and as many goods as they could pack. They were highly satisfied with the allowances made to them. They accompanied or guided the army this day. The course pursued was necessarily a very circuitous one. They made a march through the hills, passing through some pine woods, and came to the river at the place known to this day as Colbert's Ferry. The boats arrived about the same time. Here a safe passage was effected. And now it was resolved to release the prisoners. The light canoe was given to them; their trunks and clothing were restored to them; they were furnished abundantly with sugar, coffee, salt, and provisions. These supplies were placed in the boat, and they were directed to take possession and return *up the river*. They made no delay, but were soon under way, every one, men and women, seeming to rejoice at such a deliverance.

The boats were thus relieved of considerable encumbrance, and the men of care and risk with prisoners. They set sail cheerfully down the river, bantering the horsemen for a race to Nashville. Colonel Robertson here received reports that all his men were safe. Judge Haywood says that "when the troops had recrossed the Tennessee, they found that not a man had been lost, not one wounded."*

After giving the prisoners an outfit and seeing them make haste away, the remaining stock of sugar and coffee was equally divided among all the troops. The dry-goods and other articles were more securely stowed away in the boats, and directions given to land and store them at Eaton's Station, to be there sold or divided. Colonel Robertson with the main body took up the line of march, and arrived at his residence without any serious obstacle; and the men hastened to their respective stations and families. They had been absent precisely nineteen days, under marching orders every day but one. Every man had behaved well; and every man could give a good account of himself and of his companions. Each one was required to rehearse to their friends and families the various incidents of the march, battle and river passages. "They had seen some very rich and beautiful country, and some very rough and miserably poor, near the Big Tennessee; that was the broadest river they had ever seen. Upon the whole, they were better satisfied with their homes on the Cumberland, since they had now seen so much of the world!"

Some of the men remarked, "It is well sometimes to go from home." "It is far more agreeable and better to return and stay at home," replied Colonel Robertson. This, however, was a pleasure not long allowed to him at any one time.

We must inquire after our "naval expedition to Cold Water," under the command of "Rear-Admiral Hay and Commodore Shelby and—

---

* There may be seen among the old papers we have deposited in the Tennessee Historical Society, a "certificate *for wine furnished the wounded*" in this expedition.. It may be possible that this relates to the wounded in Shelby's boat—"the naval expedition."

(another, whose name is not preserved in the Navy Department, or memory of any of the surviving stationers on Cumberland.) It is much to be regretted that the Homer of this wild country, in his "Miscellanies in Prose and Verse," did not write, rehearse, and sing of the "Toka and Hay expedition," as he did of "Nickajack." We cannot make up for this omission of Clarke in prose or verse, but will "tell the tale as others told it." Haywood must be our chief authority for the history of this voyage.

The three boats had descended the Cumberland and Ohio to the mouth of the Tennessee with great ease and rapidity, though the waters were low. In ascending the Tennessee they made no use of sails, as the weather was very calm. The boats were propelled up the river by the use of oars, paddles, and poles. They had proceeded without any molestation, and with very few objects to attract attention, until they came near the mouth of Duck River. At this time Commander Shelby discovered a canoe at the shore within the mouth of that stream. His curiosity was excited, and he turned his vessel and came alongside the strange craft, when a heavy fire of muskets was opened upon him by Indians who were concealed in the bushes at only a few yards' distance. By this first fire, one man was killed and three wounded on board the boat. Josiah Renfroe was killed by a musket-ball through the head, John Top and Hugh Roquering were dangerously and Edward Hogan slightly wounded. There were twenty men, besides officers, in the three boats. With much difficulty was Shelby now able to remove his boat beyond the reach of another fire from the concealed enemy. He, however, succeeded, and no further damage was sustained.

During the time occupied in attending to the wounded men, the boats were brought together, or "alongside," in the middle of the Tennessee, and a short consultation held. The conclusion was to abandon the voyage and "return to the place whence they had sailed." They returned and cast anchor at Eaton's Station, where the wounded men were duly cared for, and the stores secured to await the general distribution among the "land and naval forces."

Colonel Robertson thought it advisable to write a justification of this destruction of the Indian town and warriors, and to forward it to "a person of note at Illinois." This was done that he might make known to the French people there the cause and manner of death of the Indian French traders. If those men had not instigated the savages to commit their deeds of cruelty and plunder, that they might share in or profit by the spoils, they certainly had furnished them with powder and lead and "fire-water," without which they would have done "no ill to their neighbors" on the Cumberland. We presume that the "person of note at the Illinois" to whom Colonel Robertson addressed his explanatory letter was Mons. Cruzat, from whom a letter may be read as bound near the beginning of the first volume of his manuscript letters, in the Library of the University of Nashville.

Colonel Robertson states that, "for some years past, a trade has been carried on by some Frenchmen from the Wabash with the Indians on Tennessee. The trade had formerly been managed by a Mr. Veiz, and whilst under his management the Indians were peaceable towards us; but for two or three years past these Indians have been extremely inimical at all seasons—killing our men, women, and children, and stealing our horses. He had sufficient evidence also that these Indians were excited to war against us by the suggestions and instigations of these traders, who both advised them to war and gave them goods and means to carry it on. The Chickasaws had told him that *they* had been offered goods by those traders if they would go to war with us. A Creek fellow had been seen and conversed with, who wore a set of silver armbands above his elbows; which ornaments, he said, were given to him by the French traders for going to war against us.

"Their incursions upon us this spring have been more severe than usual, and I determined to distress them. For this purpose I took a part of the militia of Davidson county—followed the wayward track of one of their scalping parties who had just been doing murder here. This led us to a town on the Tennessee at the mouth of Cold Water. We destroyed the town, killed a number of warriors, and, as we suppose, about thirty of them. Some few of the French imprudently put themselves in the action and fell with the savages. They were in very bad company. If they were of any better disposition or character than the Indians, they gave us no evidence of it, but the contrary. Therefore they suffered. The prisoners, however guilty, were released, and with proper supplies.

"From that place I sent a party of men by water around to Cumberland. As this party descended the Tennessee, they met five other Frenchmen with boats, having goods to trade with those very Indians. The commander of the party took the boats with the five men, and brought them around to the Cumberland River. He then gave them their choice, to come up to the settlements and stand trial for what they had done and could be proved against them, and thereby try to regain their goods and liberty; or else be discharged then and there. If they wished they could go home, but without their goods. They chose the latter, and departed.

"The taking of these boats was without my knowledge or approbation. I am now endeavoring to collect the property that was in them; and I desire you to notify the owners, that if they can make it appear that they were not guilty of a breach of the laws, and did not intend to furnish our enemies with powder, lead, and other goods for our destruction, they may, upon application here at Nashville, have their property restored to them. Ammunition and firearms certainly are contraband. We make no objection to a peaceful commerce and a lawful trade. If those Indians would be peaceable, we should never attempt to deprive them of any trade they can procure; but whilst they continue at war, any traders who furnish them with arms and ammunition will render themselves very, very insecure."

Thus the case was ably argued, the acts of the Cumberlanders fully justified, the views of international law and of articles contraband of war correctly and well presented. We can again commend our little inchoate republic, its officers, and people, for their wisdom, bravery, and good behavior. The French traders never demanded a restoration of their goods. They virtually ceased their intermeddling; and the Spaniards became their successors, and exceeded them in mischief.

The Indians were greatly mortified and irritated by this daring invasion of their country. For a very short time the stationers were exempt from annoyance. They probably expected too much from what had been done, and that the dread of other incursions would restrain them from murders and thefts. Such seemed to be the result for a month, and not longer. Small bodies invaded the settlements, and by a renewal of the deeds of carnage at many points gave evidence of increased hostility. Captain Shannon, in command of a few men, pursued one of these parties, and discovered them at the bank or shore of the Tennessee. Some of the Indians were eating, others making preparations to cross the river. Shannon and his little corps approached those who were eating, fired, and rushed upon them. Here ensued a fierce hand-to-hand fight. Castleman and Pillow each killed his antagonist. The Indians, who were out of the camp, were commanded by "Big Foot," a very determined and brave warrior. They hastened to mingle in the fray. The parties were equal in numbers, or so nearly so, that every man could encounter his foe. The conflict was a doubtful one for some time. Castleman and Pillow having relieved themselves of their immediate enemies, sought to encounter others or to aid their friends. Pillow discovered Luke Anderson in a struggle with an Indian of superior strength, both having hold of Anderson's gun, and the Indian about to wrest it from its owner. Pillow made a sudden spring upon the savage, and at one blow with his tomahawk divided his skull at the very moment when Anderson's grasp upon the gun was broken. This proved to be the leader, whose "footprints" were "as extensive as those of Thomas Sharp Spencer." Both were called Big Foot.* Castleman said this was the stoutest, fattest Indian he had ever seen; and Pillow added,

> "When he lived, he lived in clover,
> When he died, he died all over."

Anderson said, "He never kicked. I thought myself *a goner*, and my gun too: I felt sad at that thought: Pillow saved us both."

"The Indians finding themselves *worsted* and their leader fallen, raised a yell and took to the bushes." "*Scalps* and other *property* were recovered, which the whites recognized as rightfully belonging to the people on the Cumberland."

In July, information was communicated to Colonel Robertson that two hundred Creeks had crossed the Tennessee with the avowed intention to attack the whites on the Cumberland. This information was received from Mr. Perrault, a trader, by whom Colonel Robertson had written to the Chiefs and Headmen of the Nation, expressing a willingness to be at peace with them. He also stated the necessity of his recent invasion of their country. His acts had only been retaliatory; they were confined to that town whence issued the horse-thieves and murderers who caused so much distress and irritation among the people living on the Cumberland.

Mr. Perrault said he had fully explained the language of the letter and all these matters to them in the most satisfactory manner he was capable of doing. He assured Colonel Robertson that he had endeavored to dissuade them from war and further depredations. They, however, declared their purpose to proceed into the settlements. "They wanted horses, and there is the place to get them. If we cannot get the horses without killing some of the people, we shall risk the worst to obtain the horses. We will not do *much harm this time;* but if the whites again venture into Indian country with an army, then they may expect a merciless war. We know their strength, their positions, and how and where best to worry and waste them."

Such was the report as made by this French trader. What he said as to the declarations of the Indians was believed to be correct. What he said of his own efforts to pacify them, and turn them from their purposes

---

* *Oo-la-se-la-na.*

of war and plunder, was received with "many grains of allowance." The friendship of Perrault was problematical. Colonel Robertson was further informed that the Indians intimated that they were *backed* by the Spaniards, but that they would fight without such encouragement or help.*

The information thus received from Perrault and others was certainly very plain and threatening. Being "forewarned," the settlers ought to be "forearmed." The Indians justified their course by the law of retaliation for the three warriors whom the North Carolina people had killed some eighteen miles below Chota, and they thought it safer and more convenient to avenge themselves in the Cumberland settlements than elsewhere. And so this army of two hundred invaded the Cumberland settlements, and dispersed itself in parties to steal and to kill.

Colonel Robertson hastened the supplies for the battalion which was authorized to be raised for the protection of Davidson county, and Captain Evans was appointed to its command, with the rank of Major. These troops were assembled at Clinch, and under their escort, in several detachments, there came to Cumberland a number of emigrants, most of whom proceeded to the lower or most northern settlements of Cumberland, near Clarksville.

Under the authority and direction of Colonel Robertson some of these recent emigrants were called into service, and directed to act as patrols, or spies. Their duties were to traverse the woods on the frontiers of the settlements, to watch the Indian or buffalo traces, to conceal themselves near the crossings of the rivers and creeks, and thus waylay the enemy; to follow their tracks or trails; to kill or capture as best they could. Although they were *men*, they were instructed to renew the play of their *childhood*—"hide and seek." · The hunting of turkeys and deer was an agreeable and safe amusement; the chase of bear and buffalo was more rough and hazardous, but in the hunt and chase of Indians there was required not only the noiseless tread, the cautious advance, the quick sight, and the sure aim, but the *first fire.* Deer and turkeys always fled from their pursuers; buffaloes and bears, when wounded, would sometimes turn upon the hunter; but as often were the Indians themselves the *hunters* as the *hunted.*

"At that time the canes, weeds, and small bushes grew up so spon-

---

* At this period there were several transactions of public interest engaging attention. Representatives were to be chosen to the Legislature: the closing session of General Sevier's *"State of Franklin:"* organization of a party in East Tennessee to invade the Spanish colonies of Louisiana: discussion of the new Constitution adopted by the Convention at Philadelphia, and now submitted to the people: Spanish intrigues in Kentucky, and here.

taneously and luxuriantly in all parts of the country, that two or three men, even without horses, could not pass through without leaving a trace discernible, without any uncertainty, and which might be followed without danger of mistake."

And yet it frequently happened that persons, with unpracticed eyes, crossed again and again, without detection, the trails of Indians which Rains, Castleman, and other woodsmen would detect "when on a running trot." And they would take the track and follow it "like their own trusty hounds." Their horses, as well as their dogs, would "snuff an Indian, or an Indian's footprint."

Although the Indians gained their living by their guns, they often missed, or only wounded : their guns were usually of an inferior quality, and they loaded with an inadequate quantity of powder and ball. This accounts for the fact that they seldom killed any of the whites at over fifty yards' distance; and that when they fired at the stations, or blockhouses, the whites often taunted them about firing "squibs." They needed their ammunition to secure the game for their daily meat; and their supplies were usually so stinted that they would seldom load with a full or heavy charge. "Many of their guns would *kick* with a full load," and "this the savages greatly dreaded, not only that it threw their guns off of sight of the object aimed at, but bruised their faces, and threw them over, or knocked them down."

The whites were careful not to *waste* either powder or lead; and how either party had even their scanty supplies, is more than we can satisfactorily explain.

We believe that thousands of wild animals were allowed to pass unharmed, and that many human beings escaped a deadly wound, because of the scarcity of powder and ball. Who should wish the supply had been greater or more abundant? Wolves and turkeys could be and were caught in pens, but to obtain other game, the "old-fashioned smoothbore must be made to talk," as was the term in that day.

In boasting, many a backswoodman gave in the inventory of his wealth as follows :

> "The best shooting gun,
> The fleetest nag,
> The prettiest sister, and
> The most fruitful wife."

And Jones says, "The wife often had good reason to be jealous of her husband's attachment to the gun and horse." And "a good Providence, and the abundance of humanity there is in mankind," did not permit "the prettiest sister" long to remain without her attachment also. And then "the brother and father transferred the prerogative of boasting to his own sons, who gloried in it, and often fought to maintain preëminence." "Good boys, who love their sisters, will claim for them this distinction, and will fight for it, *until* they fall in love with some *other girl;*" so it is said; but these "grown-up children in the woods" claimed the distinction of beauty and loveliness for a sister, until she obtained a husband; then they were ready to boast of or fight for any other virgin.

"The contra-dance and the jig were the very common evening's exercise and entertainment at the stations." It was regarded as a healthful exercise and pleasant recreation. It was much practiced at all the early settlements west of the mountains. We have been told by persons now living (1857) that they have participated in these amusements upon "a *puncheon*, or split-log floor," with moccasins upon their feet, pants patched at the knees and "elsewhere," with greatest glee, without a thought of sin or emotion that should disturb a saint.

We know not why this may not have been. (Our own parents did the same, and if any one can boast of excellent parents, "we more," as Paul saith.)

Excitement was the essence of the happiness allowed to people in their situation. The hunters and spies found enjoyment in their fatigues and perils through the woods. The people engaged some men as constant scouts; others acted as such "on their own hook."

So true is it that the exigencies of the times bring out, from their coverts, men of extraordinary traits and qualifications, who otherwise would never have risen into distinction. With all their eccentricities, they usually had some very excellent qualities: they were the real "knights-errant" of that day; they were the "watch-dogs of the settlements," as one of the Indian chiefs called them, "who never bark, but were sure to bite." Their science was sometimes at fault. Cunning and caution did not always secure success or enable them to escape unharmed. Many artifices were resorted to by Indians and the hunters of Indians. A very usual one was the imitation of wild animals. They could bleat like the deer, bark like the wolf, gobble like the turkey. These simulated voices were used to attract the wished-for game, whether animal or man. To "gobble up turkeys" was not very difficult; to imitate the whoop and chatter of owls was easy and common. The prudent hunter studied all these cries and calls, and became acquainted with the habits and haunts of animals and fowls. They knew when and where a wolf would *not* bark, when and where an owl would *not* woo-hoo, when and where a turkey should be expected to keep silence.

The anxious pioneer, with ear unpracticed, listened, and was sometimes

18

attracted to his ruin. The game of deception is always dangerous. Mr. Beale Bosley (living within view of the Capital) was in this year anxious to kill a turkey. He commenced the call upon his "turkey-bone," (the large bone of the wing.) He heard the reply, and pushed his way through the woods and cane. He was "gobbled up" to where there was an open space around the cave spring, a short distance from his present residence. He expected there to get a shot at the gobbler. He approached the edge of the cane which surrounded the open space, when he heard a quick "*hist* and *whistle*." "I knew that turkeys did not whistle, and I jumped back into the thick cane only in time to avoid the shot of the *Indian* gobbler."

Castleman's experience, or "luck," as he called it, was different He heard "a fellow who evidently wished to test the truth of the doctrine of *metempsychosis*, to be passed into a big whooping owl," and he concluded to gratify his longing. "It was in the dusk of the evening. The imitation of this large bird of night was very perfect, yet I was suspicious. The *woo-hoo* call and the woo-hoo answer were not well timed and toned, and the babel-chatter was a failure; and more than this, I am sure they are on the *ground*, and that won't begin to do. I'll see you, says I to myself, and as I approached I saw something of the height of a *stump*, standing between a forked tree which divided near the ground. Well, I know there can be no stump there; I put 'Betsy' to my face—that stump was once *a live Indian*, and he lay at the roots of those forked chestnuts. And if he was ever buried, it was not far off! That stump of Indian was."

Old Mr. Mansker was once "gobbled up" by an Indian. Before he was within shooting distance, he was certain it was an Indian's simulation. He thought two could play at that game, but that his was the most dangerous part, being the "moving object." He had "eyes which could see and ears which could hear;" he could see almost entirely around himself with his peculiar keen eyes. He approached so cautiously that he designated the tree behind which was his adversary. The human gobbler was there, certain. Art was now to make him "uncover." So, keeping his left eye upon that tree, and the muzzle of "Nancy" in the same direction, he moved along. ("I can see on pote side and pehind too," said he.) The distance was greater than an Indian would be likely to fire, but just right for "Nancy." And "she wished to 'speak to him.'" He was sure the Indian had seen him, therefore he feigned to pass to the right. His device was successful. The Indian began to "slip slyly along" to another tree somewhat in advance of Mansker. Though moving slow and low, that left eye was on him through the bushes and wild grass. "'Nancy' spoke to him," *bang!* The fellow fell upon his face with a "*yah!*" "I took his old gun, and there she is," (pointing to the rack for guns. These racks or supports for guns were two small forked sticks nailed to a log of the cabin, or stuck in auger holes. Such were the gun-racks in every cabin.)

The recital of such adventures had a wonderful charm. They always told the tales in great earnestness, and each man had his marked peculiarity. They had "a fund of humor," real dry humor—their jokes actually "cracked." As to these artifices, the imitation of the calls of animals and wild fowls, we could enumerate others, of the truth of which we have no question. During the protracted Indian wars upon the Cumberland stationers, there were many instances in which it was believed that the whites were thus deceived and slain ; as there were also many experiences of "hair-breadth escapes." Castleman could relate at least half a dozen cases in his own experience as a hunter and spy. He certainly killed two Indians who attempted to practice this "animal magnetism" on him. One we have mentioned ; the other was the instance of "the fawn calling for its mamma," a device very common among deer-hunters everywhere. Castleman heard the "mà-à!" and "instantly two guns were fired!" One of them was "Betsy," the same that had killed the Indian owl or stump ; the other was an Indian's gun, the ball from which cut off some of the fringe from Castleman's leather hunting-shirt. "I knew I had fetched him," said Castleman ; "he lay upon his face, and never said 'mà-à!' again."

The best service rendered by Major Evans and the cavalry was in conducting families of emigrants from the Clinch to the Cumberland. The militia of the counties were called also to perform similar duty. Kirkpatrick, Mansker, Rains, and other captains, were sometimes in discharge of such duties. To those who performed such service "Guard Certificates" were granted, signed by these officers. These certificates constituted a safe paper currency, and were used in all ordinary business transactions among the settlers.*

Captain John Rains was, with Colonel Robertson, always a favorite officer ; and, therefore, often selected to go on scouting and dangerous expeditions. In one of these excursions they came upon a party of Indians which had been doing mischief in the settlements ; some of the Indians were killed, and the others took to flight. "A fine young fellow was noticed : John Rains, Jr., and Robert Evans, determined to capture him.

---

* The writer has deposited a bundle of these "Guard Certificates" with the Historical Society at the Capital of Tennessee.

The Indian was very fleet, and they had a tight race, but young Rains caught him. This Indian youth was committed to the care of Captain Shannon. He remained for some time in his family. He took the name of *John Rains*, by which he was ever after known. He was sent to Washington (city,) where he remained two years; then he was brought back to Nashville, and soon thereafter restored to his nation. At his departure he was supplied with clothes, a horse, and gun and ammunition. We have no further knowledge of him, only that a wild young girl had fallen desperately in love with him."*

As a number of the privates in Major Evans's battalion were enlisted in East Tennessee, or east of the mountain, they had no particular local interest upon the Cumberland; therefore they were employed in "scouring the woods," as the military term then was. They did not accomplish much in the hunting and killing of Indians. "A half-dozen old spies would have accomplished more of that kind of business." The troops, however, rendered good service in the encouragement and protection they gave to emigrants; at one time, twenty families came under their escort. We regret that there is no registry of the names of those and other emigrants of this year.

The Indians were now committing so many acts of cruelty, that the people demanded other and active invasions of the Indian country. They were convinced that these Indians were from the towns on the Tennessee. Those who had been in the Toka expedition, were ready to enrol themselves and destroy the Chickamauga towns, from whence came some of the savages who had shamefully mangled the persons who unfortunately fell under their guns and hatchets.

Colonel Robertson headed a company and marched for several days toward those upper towns, when he was met by a deputation from the Chickamaugas, offering assurances of friendship, and asking him to abstain from acts of hostility at this time. He was induced to confide in these professions, and to credit the insinuations thrown out, that the wrongdoers lived at towns lower down the Tennessee. With such assurances and impressions he abandoned any further march, but sent them in return a friendly answer.

Robertson and Bledsoe, as the Representatives to the Legislature from Davidson and Sumner, had a right to speak out, and they did speak plainly of what they knew and felt. They denounced the course pursued towards the stationers on Cumberland, as a reproach to any State

---

* Captain John used to say, "The Rains shall never cease; they shall descend as long as there is any necessity for seed-time and harvest."

or people who had any feelings of humanity, any sympathy for sufferings, any self-respect, any patriotism, any State pride. The effect of these appeals was, that they were fully authorized to take care of themselves. By an Act of Assembly the Courts of Davidson and Sumner were authorized—to do almost every thing they pleased, "Provided always" that no call was made upon the State Treasury—no additional burden thrown upon the eastern or old counties. All the money and all the troops which could be raised in Davidson and Sumner were at the discretion and use of the people for their defence.

Such power and means were not misplaced. During the session of the Legislature of North Carolina, (at the beginning of the year,) Colonels Robertson and Bledsoe became acquainted with General James Wilkinson, from Lexington, Kentucky. He was regarded as a wealthy merchant, whose intercourse and influence with prominent men in Kentucky, and down to New Orleans, whose intelligence and manners, and *whose opinions*, made him an object of attraction. He sedulously cultivated the friendship of the two Cumberland members. Wilkinson's projects (whatever they were) found advocates in the Legislature not a few. Many persons in Washington District were deeply implicated; and measures in progress for a descent of the Tennessee, and to the Spanish towns, even to New Orleans.

How far Robertson and Bledsoe countenanced or opposed such schemes, we are unable to declare with full confidence. This, however, we can say, they never intended to become Spaniards, anti-republicans, or anti-Washingtonians.

We shall have occasion to discuss the so-called "Spanish Conspiracy," and to introduce to our readers a person of education, craft, and influence, a chief of extraordinary authority among the Indians of the south, the noted Creek Chief, Alexander McGillivray, who sought "the expulsion or destruction," he cared not which, of all the settlers upon the Cumberland. Of these matters more anon.

Here it is proper to insert the following letter from Colonels Robertson and Bledsoe to Governor Caswell :

"CUMBERLAND, June 12, 1787.

"DEAR SIR :—Nothing but the distress of a bleeding country could induce us to trouble you on so disagreeable a subject. We enclose you a list of the killed in this quarter since our departure from this country to the Assembly. This, with the numbers wounded, the vast number of horses stolen from the inhabitants, has, in a degree, flagged the spirits of the people. A report is now here, and has prevailed throughout this country, and we are induced to *believe it,* that the *Spaniards* are doing all they can to encourage the several savage tribes to war against the Americans.

"It is certain, as the Chickasaws inform us, that the Spanish traders *offer rewards for scalps* of the *Americans.*

"A disorderly set of French and Spanish traders are continually on the Tennessee, and we actually fear are a great means of encouraging the Indians to do us much mischief.

"We should wish to take some measures to remove these disorderly traders from the Tennessee, and wish your Excellency's advice in the matter."

To this it would seem the Governor could only reply in expressions of sympathy and regret for the afflictions of the people, and to conclude :

"It will give me pleasure to render you all the aid in my power." He had the will, but not "the power."

Under date of July 2d, Colonel Robertson again addressed the Governor from Nashville, giving an account of the Toka Expedition, and destruction of the town at the mouth of Cold Water.

He describes the excessive sufferings of the people—that they are beyond endurance. Something must be done to stop or diminish these outrages.

In this letter he alludes to the expedition he had commenced against the Chickamauga towns, and under what assurances and inducements he had abandoned its prosecution. That he had requested them to send a deputation to his house, and that, in compliance with that request, a party visited him under a flag of truce, were hospitably entertained, and gave assurances of friendship ; but in these assurances no confidence could be placed, "as several persons were killed during their stay, and one man *at my house,* and *in their sight !*"

"They impute the mischief to the Creeks. They hope to deceive us by their pretensions to be very good Cherokees, good Indians, white man's friends, and such other lying flatteries. The constant incursions of the Indians oblige me to keep the militia continually in service as guards, scouts, etc., for our situation at present is truly deplorable."

The following entry upon the records of Davidson county is deserving of insertion here :

"OCTOBER TERM, 1787.

"*Resolved,* That for the better furnishing of the troops now coming to the country under command of Major Evans, with provisions, etc., that *one-fourth* of the *tax* of this county be paid in *corn, two-fourths* in beef, pork, bear-meat, and venison; *one-eighth* in salt, an eighth in money, to defray expenses of removing provisions," (to places specified.)

The prices of these *specifics* is fixed thus :

" Corn, 4s. per bushel, (equal to fifty cents.)

" Beef, $5 per 100 lbs.

" Pork, $8 per 100 lbs.

" Good bear-meat, without bones, $8 per 100 lbs.

" Venison, 10s. per 100 lbs.

" Salt, $16 per bushel !"

They were a hungry set, and fond of meat; never thought that one dish was enough ; roast, fried, broiled, boiled, and stewed, were none too much. They also hungered for the "bread of life," the word of God. And from this time forth they enjoyed the living ministry—a preached gospel.

" Craighead, the learned Presbyterian, was beautiful, but cold and unimpressive, as a speaker." So said that excellent man, John Carr.

" Ogden, Haw, Massy, Williamson, Lee, McHenry, and O'Cull, mostly Methodists, were full of zeal, and preached with great unction and success," says the same good man.

> " Words are the motes of thought, and nothing more ;
> Words are like sea-shells upon the shore—
> They show where the mind ends,"
> Nothing more :
> Its depths
> You cannot all explore.

Expressions of friendship came from Creeks, Cherokees, and Spaniards, and none of them were entitled to be believed.

> "They paltered in a double sense."

" Is it well with thee, my brother ?" was asked with an uplifted knife or hatchet, or with the loaded musket, or application of "fire-water."

Colonel Robertson had been informed that some of the Delaware Indians had been invited by the Spaniards to settle near the Shawnees on the Mississippi; and he was apprehensive that then erelong might come in contact with "our friends, the Chickasaws," and then with the people of Cumberland. He desired to bespeak their good will and friendly intercourse. With this in view he addressed a "talk" to them, and forwarded it by two trusty carriers on board the slim canoe, the "Rundown."

The peace of these settlements had been endangered, time and again, by white men who sought to carry on trade and traffic with Indians. Many of these traders were rogues who needed to be watched as attentively as the savages themselves. It will be remembered that "the Notables" had to give attention to this matter, and that under that anomalous and inceptive government some persons were arrested and held in bail for their good behavior. This watchfulness had continued down to the present time, and was not abated for some years later.

A law had been enacted which prohibited all persons from going into the Indian nations, without a permit or *pass*. These permits were to be signed by an officer of the United States government, the Governor of North Carolina, or some military officer of Davidson or Sumner counties. Citizens of these counties were subject to heavy penalties for wickedly provoking, plundering, wounding, or killing friendly Indians.

(One or two original passes may be seen among the old papers in the Tennessee Historical Society, deposited by the writer of these sketches.)

Colonels Robertson and Bledsoe were again in attendance as representatives to the Legislature. It was a long, tedious, and perilous journey which these western members had to perform, but they never failed in this or other duty required by their fellow-citizens.

During their present attendance the same sad tale had to be repeated of savage warfare, of deaths, wounds, and robberies, caused to their constituents. On the 11th of December they presented to the Assembly a well-written address, rehearsing these sufferings, showing the very exposed condition of the pioneers, the importance of the position they occupied, the difficulties with which they had to contend, and the combination of powers to drive or seduce them away, or utterly to destroy them.

In this address they enumerated *thirty-five* deaths caused by the Indians this year, prior to their departure from the settlements. And before the discussions upon the address were terminated, they added the names of five or six more victims to the awful catalogue.

It would have been in the order of time to have mentioned a journey which Col. Robertson and Col. Bledsoe made to the stations in Kentucky in the month of July, this year. Their main object was to consult with the Kentuckians about an invasion of the Creek nation.

As we have stated, there seemed no other means by which quiet to these settlements could be secured, but the destruction of the towns of their enemies. The upper and lower towns on the Tennessee were regarded as "hornet-nests," which must be burned.

At this visit to Kentucky, Robertson and Bledsoe received promises of assistance to be given in the fall of the year after the crops should be gathered. This promised aid was thankfully received, though the impatience of the Cumberland stationers could not well endure the delay.

It has been imagined that these gentlemen had another inducement or purpose in visiting Kentucky: that their acquaintance with General Wilkinson, his polite attentions at Tarborough down in the old North State, and his proffered hospitalities in Kentucky, had some influence in their undertaking this journey.

We know of no evidence that they met with men who were believed to be actually engaged in the then much-talked-of "Spanish Conspiracy." It cannot be doubted that the subject was presented to their consideration; that strong arguments could be urged of prospective commercial advantages.

But some of the agitators were advocates for a separation from the States upon the other side of the mountains, and of alliance with the Spaniards. To each of which measures the Cumberland people were decidedly opposed. Fortunately—we may say, certainly—these stationers had no reason to love the Spaniards, none whatever except the Divine injunction, "Love your enemies."

So difficult a precept was not likely to make traitors and royalists of these hardy Americans, enclosed in what was aptly called a "*slaughter-pen*."

It is an honor for any man to advocate the cause of religion. The knowledge of things Divine in their origin, sanctifying in their influence, and saving in their results, is the acme of all possible attainments for the human intellect. To be the advocate and the teacher, is but the one office filled and dignified in its highest calling. The office and the service of the ministry should ever be sacred, pure, and ennobling. No man should rashly and presumptuously enter into it. The calling and the appointment are of God. The best, if not the only evidences of such a separation and consecration, are the manifest favors of Heaven, the good fruits of their labors.

Our study and story is, "Pioneer life," and, as a part of our learning and recital, the preachers and the preaching of the gospel are deserving of honorable mention.

There is a class of ministers which is entitled to the distinction of "Pioneer heralds of the Cross." These are the ministers of the Methodist Episcopal Church. The system itself has features most happily adapted for such a service. The spirit which animates the body, impels to labor not only in the pleasant fold where the flock is securely housed, but to follow, search out, and save the far-off wanderer. And thus, in the history of early settlements west of the Alleghany and Cumberland Mountains, to and beyond the Rocky Mountains, have these men lifted

up "a voice in the wilderness." Such devotion can never lack the favor
of Heaven, or fail of good and grand results.   There is an apostolic zeal,
a consecration and a self-denial in such a service, which may well be pronounced "heaven-born," Christ-like.   The inferior honor which comes
from men could not induce, much less sustain and reward, such devotion
and toil.

We would never knowingly "rob Peter, to enrich Paul;" we would un-
dervalue no man's services in the groves of the academy, in the laborato-
ries of art, in the fields of agriculture, or in that field where the harvest
is whitened and ripened for the laborers chosen and sent of Heaven to
gather it in.

It is an important act to lay a good foundation, but no less to build
suitably and well thereon.   The forest, the underbrush and useless stones
must needs be removed, before the temple or the city can appear.   There
is a diversity of gifts, duties, spheres, structures, there is a diversity in
attainments, knowledge and qualifications, but there is only that "wisdom
which is from above," that is "first pure, then peaceable, gentle, easy to
be entreated, full of mercy and good fruits, without partiality, and without hypocrisy."   Where the Banner of the Cross is displayed, it can
only legitimately be in the cause of truth and righteousness, and held up
"of them who make peace."

"Giving honor to whom honor is due," we record the arrival of the
Reverend Benjamin Ogden as the first minister of the Methodist Episcopal Church who made his appearance to labor in the Cumberland settlements for the year 1786.   At the close of his year's labors in the
Cumberland Circuit, he reported sixty-three members, four of whom were
colored persons.   "This was the beginning of Methodism in Tennessee,
west of the mountains."

"Mr. Ogden was a plain, strong, effective preacher, and did much in
planting Methodism in the western wilds.   He was much beloved by the
people, a few of whom still remain, cherishing the memory of the venerable man."

In the year 1788, Combs and McHenry were appointed to the Cumberland Circuit.   These were good men, faithful and laborious.   Barna-
bas McHenry acquired distinction for moral and intellectual strength.

In 1789, the Presiding Elder was Francis Poythress, and Thomas
Williamson and Joshua Hartley were appointed to the charges on Cumberland.

"In 1812, the Western Conference extended its borders so as to embrace Tennessee, Kentucky, Ohio, Indiana, Illinois, Missouri, Mississippi,
and Louisiana.   Only a few points, however, of such a vast territory

were occupied by the ministry, because of the sparseness of the settlements. The membership was at that time over thirty thousand."

It is truly said, "the pioneers of Methodism in the West and South-west were of untiring zeal and great ability. Indeed, there were, giants in those days. Many of their names are familiar; they are household words. The memory of Ogden, McHenry, Poythress, Lee, Birchett, Massie, Crane, Burke, Gwin, and hundreds more, is a sweet savor to the Church."

As we have recorded the beginning of the settlements upon the Cumberland, the foundation of civil society, and shall leave to the present and to future generations to behold, admire, and enjoy the grand results of worldly prosperity, so have we shown with what instrumentalities the gospel was introduced, and the cause of learning, of truth and righteousness were advocated here in early times, yielding to others to speak of the triumphs of the present day, and of the glories which shall be hereafter.

We have stated that "the beginning of Methodism west of the mountains was here;" so was it with Presbyterianism. The advocates and representatives of the peculiar religious sentiments of these denominations, Ogden and Craighead, have been mentioned. Without "unchurching" each other, or using bitter denunciations of person or labor or aim, they found an ample scope and urgent demand for all that they could say and do to reclaim the vicious, instruct the ignorant, comfort the afflicted, and save the lost.

To contend earnestly for the truth, for the truth's sake, is ever a duty. To do so without pride, and with the spirit of meekness, is a rare qualification and attainment.

"The truth of history" has not recorded—and never will—that any one age, or generation, or denomination—Protestant or Papal—was possessed of all the wisdom, all the virtue, or all the grace, attainable by or vouchsafed to man. They who are thus wise in their own conceit, certainly have little of the wisdom or spirit of the apostle who pronounced himself "a fool in glorying." They are so, with none of his excuse. Perhaps to the end of time, and the end of earthly opportunities, there will remain some of the class who are "ever learning, and never able to come to the knowledge of the truth." And yet the truth alone can make one free. No one questions the piety or zeal of these pioneers: doubtless it was not all according to knowledge—estimating knowledge by modern standards. "Are we better than they?" is a question well worthy the consideration of some persons; as, also, how much it would result to the benefit of the world, if more men in our day had more of the zeal and wisdom of these pioneers. These men claimed to have "blazed the way" for the new settlements. They made their "marks" wherever they went; their "trails" are not yet effaced. The good they did, lives after them. Others are honored, treading in their footsteps. Ministers of other denominations were here before the close of the century, and here to witness the astonishing scenes of the years of the Great Revival. But other traces are to be made, other highways to be cast up.

A road was opened in this year from Bledsoe's Station or Lick, across to the main emigrant road from Clinch to Nashville. Where this road crossed the Cumberland, Fort Blount was established; and most of the emigrants found sufficient inducements to settle upon the rich lands in Sumner. The population of this new county was soon to exceed that of Davidson, and other roads were opened in the settlements there. So also in Davidson, orders were passed for similar neighborhood convenience.

An enumeration of the inhabitants was ordered and carefully made. The males over twenty-one years of age amounted to 477. Negroes, male and female, over twelve and under sixty, amounted to 105.

About one hundred and sixty-five thousand acres of land were taxed. Nearly one-fifth of this was in the name of Colonel Robertson. Town lots in Nashville, twenty-six. Colonel Robertson was agent for many land-owners, and it is probable that it was in this character that he gave in so large a number of acres of land for taxes.

Whether to be mentioned as an improvement or acquisition or not, we have to record among the "erections at Nashville" in this year, the noted one designated the "Red Heifer." This was a primitive or pioneer distillery, at which "raw corn whiskey" was made. It became a place of great resort by some of the men of Cumberland. It belonged to John Boyd. Whenever "a run" or the hot alcohol was ready, the custom was to "blow a horn." At the sound of the horn all the "thirsty souls" hastened to the "Red Heifer." This distillery was erected upon the bluff at the "Spout Spring," which poured forth its then flush stream at the eastern end of "Spring street." At that day a good stream of pure limestone water gushed forth at that place and formed quite a cascade over the bluff. In this day, that spring has nearly ceased to send forth its waters. Boyd's Red Heifer continued for several years, and then it "dried up entirely," "incontinently," as one of the habitués used sorrowfully to say. May we not claim for the Red Heifer the origin of the familiar invitation, "Come, let us take a HORN?" It should be mentioned that a buffalo's horn, neatly scraped, was the common "drinking-cup." Cow's horns were often used, but the horn of a buffalo was always preferred. A person could not take a drink at the "Red Heifer" unless he "took a horn;" so our conclusion is not "far-fetched," that

this western provincialism had its origin in one of the facts here mentioned—from the "blowing" or the "drinking-horn." The blast of the
horn was as fatal to some men, as the call with the "turkey-bone" or
"bleat of the fawn." The Red Heifer and the crouched Indian were
both enemies in disguise—they called men into danger and to death.

It was true in those days, as it is in ours, that the habitual lovers of ardent
spirits would "pay any price rather than go without it." And whether
it was with the vain hope to check this ruinous appetite, or to prevent
extortion by manufacturers and retailers, the County Court endeavored
to "fix the selling price of drinkables and eatables :"

"Whiskey per quart, one dollar, and so in proportion.

"Dinner, two shillings, [or, twenty-five cents.]

"Suppers and breakfasts, one and six."

We are sure that at such rates we should not touch our lips with the
"vile drinkables." We could, however, put in a bill of fare of "eatables"
at those prices.

But let us now examine the letters to which we have referred. The
State of *Franklin* had maintained its fitful existence for several years.
It originated from circumstances which well justified those who advocated it or held offices to maintain it. We glory in the anomalous
government of the Notables upon the Cumberland; and we are proud of
Sevier and others who stood by him in the Franklin government. The
history of the State of Franklin belongs to East Tennessee, and we only
here allude to it and to its approaching euthanasy, for the purpose of
adding two letters which were addressed to "Governor John Sevier,
Mount Pleasant, Franklin," from steadfast friends.

"NASHVILLE, August 1st, 1787.

"SIR :—By accounts from the Chickasaws, we are informed that at a
grand council held by the Creeks, it was determined, by that whole
nation, to do their utmost this fall to *cut off this country;* and we expect
the Cherokees have joined them, as they were to have come in some time
ago to make peace, which, however, they have not done. Every circumstance seems to confirm this.

"The 5th day of July, a party of Creeks killed Captain Davenport,
Agent for Georgia, and three men in the Chickasaw nation, wounded
three and took one prisoner; which the Chickasaws are not able to resent
for want of ammunition. The people are drawing together in large stations,
and doing every thing necessary for their defence. But I fear, without
some timely assistance, we shall chiefly fall a sacrifice. Ammunition is

very scarce; and a Chickasaw now here tells us, they imagine they will reduce our station by *killing all our cattle*, etc., and *starving us out.*

"We expect, from every account, they are now on their way to this country, to the number of a thousand. I beg you to use your influence in that country to relieve us; which I think might be done by fixing a station near the mouth of Elk, if possible, or by marching a body of men into the Cherokee nation. Relieve us in any manner you may judge beneficial. We hope our brethren in that country will not suffer us to be *massacred* by the savages, without giving us any assistance; and I candidly assure you that never was there a time in which I imagined ourselves in more danger.

"Kentucky being nearest, we have applied there for some assistance, but fear we shall find none in time. Could you now give us any? I am convinced it would have the greatest tendency to unite our counties; as the people will never forget those who are their friends in a time of such imminent danger. . . . . I have written to General Shelby on this subject, and hope that no division [diversion?] will prevent you from endeavoring to give us relief, which will be ever gratefully remembered by the inhabitants of Cumberland,

"And your most obedient humble servant,

"JAMES ROBERTSON."

"SUMNER COUNTY, August 5th, 1787.

"DEAR SIR:—When I had last the pleasure of seeing your Excellency, I think you were kind enough to propose, that in case the perfidious Chickamaugas should infest this country, to notify your Excellency, and you would send a campaign against them without delay. The period has arrived that they, as I have good reason to believe, in combination with the Creeks, have done this country very great spoil by murdering numbers of our peaceful inhabitants, stealing our horses, killing our cattle and hogs, and burning our buildings through wantonness, cutting down our corn, etc., etc.

"I am well assured that the distress of the Chickamauga towns is the only way this defenceless country will have rest; the militia being very few, and the whole country a frontier, its inhabitants all shut up in stations—and they, in general, so weakly manned, that in case of an invasion one is scarcely able to aid another—and the enemy in our country daily committing ravages of one kind or another, and that of the most savage kind. Poor Major Hall and his eldest son fell a sacrifice to their savage cruelty two days ago, near Bledsoe's Lick. They have killed about twenty-four persons in this country in a few months, besides numbers of others in settlements near it.

"Our dependence is much that your Excellency will revenge the blood thus wantonly shed.

"Your obedient servant,

"ANTH'Y BLEDSOE."

These two letters afford a view of the sufferings of these stationers—their exposed situation and approaching perils, not as well understood from any other source. The resolution taken by the Indians (under Spanish influence) was, "to starve them out," "burn them out," "kill them *out and out.*" They came very near accomplishing such a nefarious, murderous purpose. And well might they apply to their personal and political friend, General, or, as they recognized and respectfully addressed him, His Excellency, Governor Sevier. He had often in times past given the savages so many chastisements for their acts of cruelty, and so distressed them by invasions, that the Cumberland settlements derived some advantages therefrom. The Indians could not venture to leave their nation in large numbers to prosecute a distant expedition, for if they did, "Chucky Jack would destroy everybody, and all their towns at home."

In the very last days of the Franklin government, the State of Georgia had entered into an engagement with Sevier to invade the Creek nation, and punish those savages for their horrible murders of the white people. General or Governor Sevier at all times had sufficient influence and means to bring into the field a respectable force. He supplied arms, ammunition, and provisions for many of his expeditions from his own resources. He was, in November, 1787, informed by Governor Matthews, of Georgia, that "provision had been made by that State to invade the Creek nation in the spring, and to accept the services of fifteen hundred men from the patriotic State of Franklin."

In the spring, (April, 1788,) when the State of Franklin had virtually "ceased to be," and he was hunted by the authorities of the old State, "as a partridge in the mountains," he could assure Governor Matthews and other friends in Georgia, and in like manner Colonels Robertson and Bledsoe and the suffering people on Cumberland, that, "Let matters occur as they may here, (in Franklin,) if I am spared I purpose joining the Georgia army with a considerable number of volunteers, to act in concert against the Creeks; though many of our enemies are making use of every diabolical plan in their power, in order to destroy our laudable intention."

The appointment made in October, 1787, by Congress, of three Commissioners, one from Georgia, one from North and one from South Carolina, to enter into negotiations with the Indians, induced the Governor of Georgia to postpone the contemplated expedition into the Creek nation. This left Sevier to act at home as the exigencies of the times might demand. He knew that his friends on Cumberland were in most imminent danger, and he could not turn a deaf ear to the entreaties of such men as Robertson and Bledsoe. And besides the outrages done there, (on Cumberland,) similar ones were committed among Sevier's very neighbors.

He therefore invaded the Cherokee country, (whence these murderers chiefly came,) encountered their warriors, and defeated them in several battles, escaping marvellously, without the death of one man.

The Creeks and Cherokees (mostly from Chickamauga and Lower Towns) continued their murders on Cumberland.

The Indians were greatly perplexed, worked upon, tampered with, and by various parties. There were agents among them from the Spanish Kentucky Association, promotive of Spanish views, as has often been charged.

" General Bowles was active among the Creeks and Cherokees, as likewise were the partisans of Governor Blount, for the purpose of exciting them to commence hostilities against the subjects of Spain in the Floridas and Louisiana.

"The emissaries of Genet were equally busy, but with contrary views."—Western World, Sept., 1806.

The remark above made about "the partisans of Governor Blount," no doubt was made in the spirit of condemnation, in accordance with the sentiment of the predominant party, and of the administration by which he was expelled from the Senate of the United States.

Viewing his motives and conduct from the position we are enabled to occupy at this day, we must applaud instead of condemn. To divert the Indians and Spaniards from their wasting and bloody warfare upon the territory of which he was Governor, was laudable; to make them devour each other, or to have invaded Indian and Spanish territories to punish and subdue them, would have been wise and just. Such measures would only have anticipated events a few years. The laurels won in the Creek, Seminole, and Florida campaigns would have decked other brows.

But "the man" was all this time among the Cumberland settlers to whom was reserved the glory of achieving the purposes of pioneer great men, who foresaw and foretold great and coming events: men whose fault it was to be anxious to pluck fruit before it was fully ripe. The American government and people could not blink these questions, nor be reluctant to recognize the necessity of terminating foreign intermeddling and savage cruelties.

Our narrative furnishes but a tithe of the aggravations and insults to the American people, provoking to invasion and retaliation. The offences accumulated until they were past endurance, and the drama closed with the entire expulsion of Spaniards and Indians, and the peaceable occupancy of all the country to the Gulf and to the Pacific. Only one act remains as a small afterpiece, the receiving into the American embrace all the territory which Spain ever possessed on or near these United States.

A settlement was commenced in this year upon Station Camp Creek. It was known as Hendrick's. Mr. Price and his family were interested in the locations and the buildings, and were lodged in one of the houses. An hour before daybreak the Indians made an attack by firing into the house, and then breaking open the door. They rushed in and commenced a general slaughter. Mr. and Mrs. Price were killed, and several of the children were either killed or severely wounded. The Indians did not tarry long enough to scalp all the dead and wounded, but fled and concealed themselves in the cane, whence they again issued to commit other outrages.

1787. April 7th.—"The Grand Jurors of the State aforesaid present Jesse Cain for refusing the currency of the State!"

Here was a notable controversy. The State was afflicted with a worthless currency, and Jesse Cain, like his illustrious predecessor, felt it to be "too grievous to be borne," and that he should, by the receiving of it, be made a beggar and a vagabond all the days of his life; therefore he refused it. The State thought itself able to punish him for this refractory spirit, and determined to "give him Jesse," but failed. So it was again true that "Cain killed Abel!"

19

CHAPTER XVIII.

1788.

WE shall open the leaves of our history of early times on the Cumberland for this year with the appropriate language of Judge Haywood : " The gates of this year were. unfolded under circumstances less propitious than in olden times usually accompanied the like ceremony at the temple of Janus. The settlers experienced a *mixture* of *prosperity* and *distress.*"

We have so long dwelt upon the dark shades of this canvas, that we will now gladly search out the sunny spots and the fringes of light. First, then, the "prosperity," and afterwards the "distress;" and, finally, make some investigation into, or decomposition of, this "mixture," that we may show how it was compounded and stirred up by the infusion of poisonous foreign ingredients.

We may premise that the proportion of "prosperity" was very small, really *homœopathic*, or, according to legal phraseology, "two grains of allowance," one in agriculture and one of population.

The quantity of "distress" will have to be estimated as the pound avoirdupois to the two grains infinitesimal. This mixture certainly had an over-proportion of *bitter* in it; and yet Judge Haywood asserts that the whole composition furnished "a foretaste of a final triumph over the calamities by which the settlers had been so long oppressed."

There was a small increase of population. These emigrants were of excellent character, and they brought with them very valuable stocks of cattle and other property of much worth in a new country. And the few earlier settlers now rejoiced in the hope and assurance that these new adventurers would attract yet others. The hearts and hands of all were united and strengthened. They felt strong confidence of success—that the settlements could and would be maintained; and that the country was most happily adapted to agricultural purposes, and the raising of cattle.

The experiments already made in the cultivation of cotton and tobacco attracted much attention, and aroused the ambition of farmers. All this was hopeful and cheering. But they were not to taste an unmingled cup. "They were still to be disturbed by the implacable enmity of the savages."

It would really seem that as these settlements grew strong, and gave the greater attention to the peaceful arts of agriculture and domestic comforts, the fiercer was the warfare waged against them.

At this period there were several questions agitating the minds of the people at all these transmontane settlements. Among stationers on the Cumberland the one engrossing subject for years had been how best to defend themselves against the murderous Indians. Questions of politics had not as yet caused excitement, or arrayed these few neighbors into political party organizations. That day was coming: those topics were now to be presented and discussed.

The "Confederacy of States" was everywhere felt and acknowledged to be "rickety," and inadequate for the protection and promotion of the welfare of the American people. The settlers on Cumberland had experienced benefits to a most insignificant extent from either the State or Confederacy. The citizens of North Carolina, under various influences, and with hopes and proffers of advantages, were induced to keep aloof from the proposed closer and stronger union of the States. Such were the pervading sentiments in North Carolina. These matters had been under consideration, warmly debated in the Atlantic and interior counties, but now awakened attention among these remote woodsmen, politely called "outside barbarians."

Very few *facts* could be adduced from which weighty arguments might be addressed to these border settlers, to convince them that the newly proposed "Constitution for the United States" would be *beneficial* to them. The question was, however, to be presented. A convention was to be held. The proposed Constitution was submitted, and, by an almost unanimous vote, *rejected.* Robertson and Bledsoe voted against it *at this time.*

It was adopted by ten States. They constituted then "The United States." North Carolina stood as a separate, independent State. Between these distant, feeble, and exposed settlements struggling for existence, and the united eastern States now organizing the "Federal Union," there was an extensive, unsettled country, and then the strong opposition of their friends in the Atlantic counties of the Old North State. But, besides all this, there were offers, exigencies, and arguments of almost irresistible power urged, and patent to the mind of every settler on the

when the heavens showered down their diamonds, and jewelled every tree-top and limb and leaf, would be fresh in mind, and he would say, "The forests are gone : there is no beauty or loveliness here."

But we must hasten back just three-score and ten years, and into the woods, which then, in February, 1788, were "here and there, and every-where;" and here and there, and almost everywhere, were the savages "on murderous deeds intent." Their tracks were seen very near to the town; they were certainly concealed in the cane. The people were warned to be on the look-out, and to avoid exposure. "Caution" was the word at the stations, in the fields, and to all passing to and fro.

The Indians had stolen corn from almost every crib. The *wolf-trap* set to catch an Indian had never taken and secured a prisoner. Many such traps were stolen or missing, whether by the prowling wolf or the prowling savage, none could tell.

In an out-house or crib near Eaton's Station there were several casks of beans, from which it was suspected the Indians helped themselves at night, by inserting an arm through the space between the logs. Wolf or beaver traps were set in the beans, and chained to the logs inside. And sure enough one of the traps was sprung, and a man was standing close to the outer wall, with his arm through the crack, and could not withdraw it.

A generous negro had forced open the door, and was hard at work to unlock the jaws of the grim iron monster. It took the aid of yet another person to make it "let go." And then that broken arm required splints and bandages. That poor lazy *white man* did not remain many months thereafter in the Cumberland settlements.

They never caught an Indian, but lost several traps in the attempts.

At this date the Indians (Creeks) cautiously approached Bledsoe's Station in the night, and, shooting between the logs, wounded George Hamilton. They also wounded Jesse Maxey, who was at a short distance from Asher's Station. He could not escape his savage foe; he fell, and they scalped him, and then, as he lay upon the ground, they thrust a butcher-knife into his body, and departed. He was all the time conscious of what occurred. He said they used him very roughly in jerking off his scalp. He thought the knife-wound must prove mortal, and he offered up his final prayer, as he supposed. In this helpless and bleeding con-dition he was found, was taken to the station, and recovered.

William Montgomery had built his house and commenced improve-ments on Drake's Creek in a previous year. One of his sons was wounded there in the last year. Now the Indians killed this same young man and two of his brothers, when at the spring, not more than one hundred yards from the house. This was a horrible sight: the three interesting boys scalped, mangled, and dead—fallen together as though they had contended for each other. These earliest murders this year were on the east side of the river, but outrages were not limited to that section.

Early in March, the Indians approached the "Sugar Camp," near the residence or station of Colonel Robertson, where young Peyton Robertson, John Johnston, and some other boys were engaged in gathering the "sap" and taking it to the camp, where it was to be boiled down to molasses and sugar—"the deliciously sweet maple molasses and sugar!" These boys saw the Indians rushing in to cut off the retreat to the camp and house: they fled in different directions. Peyton was killed, probably after he was captured; Johnston was made a prisoner, and remained such for several years in the "nation."

Robert Jones was killed near the house of David Wilson. He had been cautioned "not to be so noisy wherever he went," thus giving notice of his whereabouts to the Indians. The hunter's admonition of that day has become the political apothegm of this: "Never to halloo until you are out of the woods." Jones was killed in the day-time; so was Ben Williams about the same time, near the head of Station Camp Creek.

The widow Neelly, a pious and excellent woman, was killed near Neelly's Lick, in Neelly's Bend of Cumberland; and Robert Edmonson had his arm broken by a bullet at the same time and place, but hid and escaped.

In the month of October of this year, two men of the names of Dunham and Astill were killed, at a few miles west from Nashville. They were "scalped" and "chopped," as had become quite common. Dunham's station was thus destroyed. Southerland Mayfield had a station upon the west fork of Mill Creek, a mile above Brown's. A company of ten or twelve Indians made their appearance near the buildings, but did not attempt to enter any of them. Had they made such attack they could have destroyed women and children, for the men were at a considerable distance from the fort, engaged in building and baiting wolf-pens. The party of Indians approached cautiously the place where Mayfield and his two sons and Mr. Jocelyn were busily engaged on their rude structure. They had a soldier placed on the look-out, or who should have been on the "sharp look-out," but who had inexcusably left his post, where the guns and other articles of the party were deposited. "The Indians got between the white men and their guns." Mr. Mayfield and one of his sons and the soldier were killed. The other son of Mr. Mayfield, named George, was captured, and remained a prisoner ten or twelve years in the Creek nation, (to which this party of Indians belonged.) Mr. Jocelyn (afterwards a Colonel in Militia) had a close race and narrow escape. The place was abandoned—survivors removed to Rains's Station.

Brown's Station was attacked fiercely, and several persons killed. The names of such as have been recorded, are James Haggard, —— Adams, and four boys, two of them sons of Mr. Stowball or Stovall; one, a son of Mr. Brown, and the other of Mr. Denton, whose father had a station north of Nashville. In consequence of these murders and the great perils at these outposts, this and others recently commenced were deserted. The people from Browns also retired to Rains's Station. The hunters, men and boys, would, however, in contempt of the peril, occasionally visit their wolf and turkey pens. And thus some were captured or killed of whom no trace could be found.

Bears and wolves were found in great numbers for half-a-dozen years after the first settlement, in the Harpeth Hills, ten or twelve miles south of Nashville. Although the "bear hunt" was laborious and dangerous, yet man and dogs were exceedingly fond of it, and few dogs would leave the trail of a bear to scent that of an Indian. Yet one of the Castlemans had such a dog. "Red-gill never failed to open upon an Indian's track, if leave was given;" that is, the slut would indicate silently the nearness of Indians, and then at the signal or word—leaving bear, buffalo, elk, or deer—pursue the savage, always leading some others of the pack with her. Indians disliked to be thus pursued by dogs; they were in great perplexity when so pursued. If they fired at them they seldom killed them, and if they failed to kill, or only wounded, the pack was often the more fierce, and allowed no time to reload; and then was the time for the white hunter to rush into the thickest of the fray. Several Indians were overtaken and killed in just such contingencies as these. Several instances could be mentioned in which hunters rushed upon Bruin to relieve their dogs, and were in great peril of their own lives. Rains and Buchanan had such a contest with a bear and her whelps, and they said they would prefer to encounter half-a-dozen Indians.

Consultations were held among the "head-men of the settlements." Measures were proposed for retaliation. Men were ready to volunteer for such a service and go at a moment's warning. Some doubts were expressed as to the towns whence these murderers came; the general belief, sustained by much proof, was, that they were Creeks. And what just cause had they to wage such a warfare? If it was to be avenged for the deaths of the few men of their nation who were slain at Cold Water, they had already taken the lives of at least two for one, and property a thousand times more valuable. Colonel Robertson and Colonel Bledsoe, as the authorized representatives, civil, military, and political, of the two counties, Davidson and Sumner, were considered to be the proper persons to attend to the interests of their constituents—to give their opinions, and to direct such measures as they might deem proper. They "believed that his Satanic majesty instigated the Spaniards, and he and the Spaniards in partnership instigated the Creeks; and that, in all probability, the biggest devil in human form was the Creek chief."

These gentlemen addressed a joint letter to this chief, Alexander McGillivray, and in the early part of March forwarded it by the hands of Messrs. Hoggatt and Ewing, who in fact volunteered to undertake the long journey and mission. They proceeded to Little Tallassee, the residence of McGillivray; were politely received, hospitably entertained, and thence returning, brought a reply dated April 4th, 1788. To this correspondence, the character and conduct of this crafty and influential chief, we must devote a chapter at some later date. Hoggatt and Ewing expected some good influence to result from the visit they had made, and their interviews with McGillivray. He made professions and promises, but he was speaking and acting falsely, or else could not exert an authority which should exempt the Cumberland settlers from depredations by his people. To which of these conclusions we must arrive will be determined by future developments.

During the spring and summer many improvements were made in the vicinity of Bledsoe and Greenfield Stations. The Bledsoes were regarded by their fellow-citizens as being in a fair way to enjoy the homes they had selected at so early a day, and for which they had endured so many perils and so much suffering. But now falls a heavy blow upon that settlement and upon the entire Cumberland community. On the 20th of July, in the evening, Colonel Anthony Bledsoe heard his cattle running past the door of his house and the dogs barking. He stepped out of his room into an open passage between his double log-house, and was instantly fired upon and mortally wound. He lived long enough in full possession of his senses to give directions about his worldly affairs, make his will, and leave some last words of comfort to his afflicted family. "A young man named Campbell was killed at the same time."

The heart of Colonel Robertson had been pierced again and again: this death was an almost crushing blow to him. With the Bledsoes he had long been intimate; they had taken counsel together, they had toiled and travelled together. From early life they had associated in the management of private and public affairs; they were steadfast friends, and by their office as Representatives to the Legislature, and in the recent measures to discover, and, if possible, abate or remove the causes of enmity on the part of the Creeks, they fervently hoped to render united and lasting service.

But now this earliest of pioneers, this upright man, reliable friend and valuable citizen, is suddenly cut down, savagely murdered in his own house and in the presence of his family. There was lamentation throughout the settlements, and had there been any intermission to the duty of watchfulness and defence, public demonstrations of sad respect would have attended his funeral. Armed men came to bury him : hardy woodsmen were there : every man came, and marched in the solemn procession with his rifle upon his shoulder and deep grief within his heart ; and there they buried him.*

Shortly after Col. Bledsoe was killed, the Indians killed, scalped, and hacked a man by the name of Waters. He was fishing "in a deep hole" in the creek a short distance from Cragfont, the residence of Col. Winchester.

Ten or a dozen new "clearings" were commenced in Sumner county in the fall of this year. These emigrants came under the escort of the guard commanded by Colonel Mansker and Major Kirkpatrick. Other families came at the same time and settled near other stations. In all there were twenty-two families, or about one hundred and forty persons, white and black. They brought with them an unusual amount of house-

---

* This sad event, as related by one of the family some ten years since, is thus :

On the night of 20th July, 1788, a number of Indians approached and placed themselves in ambush about forty yards in front of a passage dividing the log-houses occupied by the two families of Anthony and Isaac Bledsoe. To draw the men out, they then sent some of their party to cause an alarm, by riding rapidly through the lane in front. Roused by the noise, Col. Anthony Bledsoe rose and went to the gate. As he opened it, he was shot down ; the same shot killing an Irish servant, named Campbell, who had long been attached to him. The Colonel did not expire immediately, but was carried into the house, while preparations were made for defence by Gen. Wm. Hall, and the port-holes manned till break of day. The wife of Isaac Bledsoe suggested to her husband, and then to her brother-in-law, in view of the near approach of death, that he should, by will, make provision for his seven daughters. He had surveyed large tracts of land and secured grants for several thousand acres. The law of North Carolina then gave all lands to the sons, to the exclusion of daughters.

Mr. Clendening wrote the will ; Col. Isaac Bledsoe supported his dying brother while he affixed his signature, and thus were all his children left to share in his landed estate.

But the devoted wife, whose name this providence had changed to "widow," had yet to suffer from savage cruelty.

hold stuff, and a good variety and large stock of cattle, and "some of the best game-chickens and stallions." "They had more iron kettles, pewter plates, iron spoons, and crockery ware, than had ever been seen in these regions before."

"They were a fore-handed people, well off and likely to do well, and everybody was glad to see them."

"Bees" for log-rolling and house-raising were more numerous this fall and winter than they had ever before been known.

TENNESSEE COUNTY.*

In this year a new county was authorized to be organized, taken from the northern portion of Davidson, and to be called *Tennessee*, extending from the Kentucky line westwardly and across the Cumberland, and embracing a large extent of territory.

Although an act was passed for the erection of such a county, and some measures were taken in the next year for such a purpose, yet a complete organization did not take place until January, 1791, under the Territorial Government. We state this as the impression of some aged citizens, who seem to be confirmed in their recollections when informed that there are *no records* to be found of a date earlier than 1791.

The existing records begin on Monday, 17th January, 1791, as follows:

"TENNESSEE COUNTY, 3d Monday in Jan., 1791.

"Present, the Worshipful Benj'n Menees.

"The Court was called, and adjourned till to-morrow."

"TUESDAY, 18th Jan., 1791.

"The Worshipful Benj'n Menees called Court, and produced a Commission as a Justice of the Peace for the County of Tennessee under the hand and seal of his Excellency William Blount, Governor of the Territory of the United States south of the River Ohio, bearing date 15th Dec., 1790.

"Proclamation being made of the Justices appointed, George Bell, Esq., John Philips, Esq., and Martin Duncan, Esq., commissioned as aforesaid, took the oath of office, etc.

"Anthony Crutcher, Esq., produced a commission from his Excellency as Clerk of this Court, upon which the said Anthony Crutcher, *being appointed by the Court*, took the oath and entered into bond in $5000.

"James Boyd, appointed Sheriff till July term next. Hopkins Lacy and Bennett Searcy, Esqs., Attorneys at Law."

* For Tobacco Statistics, see Chapter XX.

At the April Term, John Montgomery, Esq., produced the Governor's commission, and took the oath and his seat as a Justice.

But an examination of the records of 1791 furnishes us the evidence of business transacted by the Justices of the county in April, 1790, relating to the year 1789.

Under date of " October 18th, 1791," is the following entry :

" Ordered that the Auditors appointed at the April Term in *the last year, for the year* 1789, be appointed for the year 1790, and that they act accordingly."

It was customary with the Court of Pleas and Quarter Sessions to appoint, in each year, Commissioners to audit and allow claims against the county which had originated in the *previous* year. In 1788, '89, '90, these were almost exclusively " certificates to persons who had served as soldiers in the Guards, to escort emigrants from Holston to Cumberland."

We are enabled to give one of these Guard Certificates, or a complete Roll of a Guard Company of Tennessee County, "sworn to before Benjamin Menees, Esq.," who was the first " Worshipful " of the county :

"TENNESSEE COUNTY, Nov. 8th, 1790.

" these are to Certify that agreeable to General orders Capt. William Glass served on Guard to Holston and back as Captain and the following is a true Return of the privates,

" Robt. Prince
" Benjamin Hudson
" John French   Who Served 36 Days
" David Walace
" Isaac Henry   WILLIAM GLASS"
" Richard Martin

On the back is this certificate :

" Jenevery ye 28 this day Captain W^m glass maid oath that this is a true and just return

          " Sworn to before me

                    " BENJAMIN MENEES

                              " Esqr."

In further proof of a county organization of an earlier date, we quote the following entry, under date of 19th April, 1791 :

" Joseph Nevill, as *former Sheriff*, is allowed £12 for his Ex-Officio services for the term of *nine months* in the year 1790."

The Court gave attention to "the streets and Public Lot" in the town of Clarksville, appointing overseers and "the hands to work on and clear them out."

We cull from these old records a few items somewhat curious and of a tell-tale character. Nicholas Coonrod (who is one of the worthies whose signature may be seen on the roll of names to the Compact of Government, 1st May, 1780) sued out an attachment against *thirty-nine* individuals whom he supposed might be indebted to one Samuel Stout, against whom he held a small judgment. Of the thirty-nine, twenty-nine swear "they owe him nothing," nine owe for "a *point* of whiskey," or "a dinner and a *point* of whiskey;" and "William Reasons owes nothing, but has a *Bible* in his hand which he has reason to think belongs to defendant, and therefore delivers it." We care nothing about the whiskey, but we think we know somebody who would rejoice to see that "old Bible."

Of all places of notoriety mentioned in these old records, the one which enjoyed preëminence was "Patton's Still-House." We have not learned its whereabouts in the county, but the frequent orders for "viewing, laying off, and clearing out" roads "to it," "from it," and "by it," induce the opinion that it was "a favorite watering-place in its day," and a rival to the town. There was one very significant name in the same direction and neighborhood, that of "Jacob *Wine-Miller.*" Jacob was appointed on the first jury to view and lay off a road from Clarksville by Brantley's Ferry to the Still-House; and he had associated with him eleven very worthy men, such as John Montgomery, Hugh Bell, and Philip Hornbarger; but, in the dozen or more orders, all the jurors are directed to select and take "the nearest and best route to Patton's Still-House!" Jacob must have moved away, or "settled on his lees" right there, for several of the last orders are, "to clear the track by Wine-Miller's *old field* to Patton's Still-House."

1792. The tax levied in this year was 3s. on each poll, and 1s. on each hundred acres of land, and 3s. on every hundred pounds' worth of property, for contingent charges. Double these sums to discharge arrearages due the different guards sent to escort families from Holston, payable in certificates or cash.

We find upon these old records the name of that ubiquitous and mysterious person, James C. Mountflorence, and here again he appears and disappears *in character :*

"Wm. Crutcher ⎱ Garnishees sworn.
    vs. ⎰ (In Attachment.)
James C. Mountflorence

"Anth'y Crutcher has *a tumbler, 3 chairs and a Bowl.*"

Several persons answer that they "owe him nothing, but that *their wives* have some articles which they purchased of *Mrs. Sanders!*" Such is the record.

Here are the footprints of "an elegant gentleman." The man who could pry into the secrets of Talleyrand, the Directory, and of Napoleon, must needs be a man of etiquette and shrewdness and versatility. He who could grace an assembly, and flirt with the belles of Paris, could sit on a stool or dance with the pioneer women on a dirt floor in log-cabins on the Cumberland. To ladies dressed in silks and satins at the Tuileries, and to those who appeared in homespun and moccasins, he could be alike graceful and polite. If he dined with the nobility in Europe, he drank red-wine and relished buffalo tongue and bear-meat with their peers on our Sewanee. At Nashville and Clarksville he was the same astute observer, and polished, fascinating gentleman that he had been at Paris and Versailles; and which he continued to be when again there in 1799, with Marshall and Ellsworth and Davie.

But those "three chairs, that Bowl and tumbler," had they tongues, "could tales unfold and secrets tell."

Close upon the heels of this "case of Attachment," comes the following entry, which we copy *verbatim et literatim*, under date of April, 1793:

"I, John Irwin, of my free will and accord, do *hearby* acknowledge and certify, the *Raskelly* and *Scandoullous* Report that I have Raised and Reported *Conccarned* Miss Polly Mcfadin, is *faulse* and Groundless, and that I had no Right, Reason or Cause to Believe the same. Given under my hand this 26. March 1793.

"Test   "(Signed) JOHN IRWIN.
    "Francis Prince,
    "Robert Ashley.
"Also proven by the oath of Francis Prince."

If any of our readers should be vexed with an unsatisfied, unenlightened curiosity to know what this "Raskelly and Scandoullous Report" was, we must leave them where John Irwin said he was—"*in the dark!*"

This Honorable Court, consisting of "The Worshipful Francis Prince, John Philips, Isaac Philips, and John Montgomery, Esqrs.," on the 16th July, 1793, regarded itself as invested with some high prerogatives, and, like that in Davidson county, was not afraid to record its opinions and decrees, even to the annulling of the laws enacted by the legislative power. The record is worthy of notice, and we copy it:

"Anth'y Crutcher, Esq., Clerk of Tennessee County, came into Court and offered James Adams, Hugh McCollum and Julius Sanders, his securities for his collecting fines and taxes on Writs, &c., agreeable to a Law passed by Governor Blount and two of the Judges, (to wit, Anderson and Campbell:) the Court refused to have any security from the Clerk, as they did consider that law was made without any authority: And they would pay no attention to it—and directed the Clerk not to receive any of the taxes agreeable to that law: Also Hugh Lewis, Register for the County aforesaid, tendered sec'y. for the receiving Taxes on Deeds, &c., but the Court also refused as above, and directed him not to receive any taxes on Deeds, &c.''

Perhaps this law of the Legislative Council raked over the coals which had been left in the fire kindled by the old British "Stamp Act." The question was debated for a few months, and at a subsequent term the Court reversed its decision, and received the securities.

Whether it had been customary for the jurors to squat tailor-fashion or toad-fashion down on the ground in the presence of the Worshipful Court, or, being taken from the by-*standers*, were to remain standing during the trial of causes, we know not; but in the fall of 1793, the Court "ordered James Adams to make seats for the jurors to sit on."

As Nashville had its "Black Bobb" and "Black Bobb's Tavern," so Clarksville enjoyed a like advantage and reputation in "Cæsar, a servant of Captain Prince." "And the Court passed a resolution that Cæsar be permitted to build a house in one corner or side of the *Public Lott*, for the purpose of selling cakes and beer, etc., so long as he conducts himself in an orderly manner and has permission from his master." Persons are now living who bought "cakes and beer," and "bread and meat," from Cæsar at his house in one corner of the "Public Lott," and say, "He had just as good as anybody in those days."

In the next year licenses were granted to several persons to keep "ordinaries," or taverns. At the same time that "Boyd's Red Heifer" was yielding her poisonous stuff at Nashville, "Patton's Buffalo Bull" was "horning" the people around Clarksville.

We have mentioned the death of Colonel Evan Shelby, and the loss of his goods upon the Cumberland. A negro woman belonging to him had escaped, and found a home and a husband among the Chickasaws, and there were difficulties interposed to her recovery. At least, the representations made to the Court induced it to pass an order authorizing Moses Shelby, the administrator, to sell her as a runaway for what he could get. The administrator thereupon gives a Power of Attorney to David Smith to sell her, and "Smith reports that he sold her for the a----

of $160, payable in an order on Captain Stone, of Knoxville, Attorney for *John Pitchlyn, Lincaster* of the Choctaw nation, and also two horses." Interpreters were usually called *"Linguisters:"* here it is yet further corrupted to *Lincaster.*

In 1796, "Dr. Morgan Brown was authorized to establish a ferry across the Cumberland, at Blountsborough ; and to build a mill, a floating mill, on either side on the main Cumberland River, opposite Deson's Island, on either side or on both sides, as he may see cause." And an acre of ground on each side was condemned for the benefit of the mill. Edmondson's mill, and others in various parts of the county, had, for years before this, cracked corn and made meal for the inhabitants of this county. Several floating mills were put in operation at the various rapids on this river. Some of them were continued for a dozen or twenty years. Some families got their bread by these mills, but no man ever made his fortune by a "floating mill," so said "Jo. Miller" and "Doctor Brown," both of them famous as corn-crackers and crackers of jokes.

NARRATIVE OF THE CAPTIVITY OF COLONEL JOSEPH BROWN, OF
MAURY COUNTY, TENNESSEE.

The following narrative we have heard from the venerable man himself, at his own hospitable residence. But in the form now presented, we are permitted to copy it from Wales' South-Western Monthly, of January, 1852 :

"I was born in North Carolina, 2d August, 1772. My father was an active man in the struggle for Independence during the Revolutionary War with Great Britain, and served as a guide to Colonel Washington's and Colonel Lee's troops of horse, when they were in Guilford county, North Carolina, at the time of the battle at that place, 15th March, 1781. For this service he received a certificate, paid afterwards in land, when the office was opened at Hillsborough, in 1783. He entered several tracts of land on Duck River, and on the waters of Cumberland and Tennessee; and he was endeavoring to get to them when his boat was taken by the Creeks and Cherokees, as there was no road to Nashville, only a pathway, and that by Kentucky. . . . Others had taken the river route, and my father was resolved to pursue the same course.

"In April, 1788, we set sail, or commenced our descent of the Tennessee. When we were passing the Chickamauga towns, the Indians sent runners across from Chattanooga to Running Water and Nickajack towns below, giving notice of our approach.

"There was a half-breed Indian there, named John Vann, who spoke English plainly. As we came nearly opposite Running-Water town, we saw a number of canoes ascending the river, evidently prepared to encounter and arrest us. They had flags unfurled. They came alongside of our boat, when my father remarked, 'There are too many of you at one time.' He had been hailed by Vann, and found that there was at least one who could speak and understand English; therefore he objected to their crowding around our boat in such numbers; and we discovered the Indians were taking up their guns and hatchets from the bottoms of their canoes, where they had them covered by their blankets.

"Vann replied to my father, 'It is time of peace; we keep the Hopewell and Holston treaties. We only want to see where you are going, and to trade with you, if you have any thing to trade on.'

"By this stratagem they got on board of our boat. There were four of their canoes which had thus boarded ours, but there were many others coming, or along the shore. They forced our boat to the shore, at the mouth of the creek in front of Nickajack.

"Vann kept up conversation with my father, for the purpose of deceiving him; talked of the danger of the Muscle Shoals, and that one of their number would accompany us.

"Very soon after we reached the shore, an Indian really drunk, or pretending to be so, was flourishing a sword in a careless or threatening manner. He caught me by the arm, and pulled me to one side, as if to do me harm. My father took hold of the Indian, told him I was his little boy, and he must not touch me. He let me go, but as soon as my father turned his back, he struck my father with utmost fury across the back of the neck, cutting his head nearly off, as I noticed when my father fell overboard into the river.

"I then ran forward to the bow of the boat. The Creeks had taken my mother, little brother, and three sisters out of our boat into their canoes, and landed at a short distance off. There they all went ashore, and the Creeks started away with their prisoners. My oldest and youngest sisters were brought back the next morning to Nickajack.

"When I had reached the shore and gone upon the bank, I was committed to the charge of an old white man, who told me I must go home with him, about a mile distant. Many of the Indians were engaged and had been busy in searching our boat, and knocking open boxes and barrels.

"The white man and myself walked away, and I soon heard a number of guns fired. I thought it might be that the Indians had shot off the guns they had taken from our men. I did not then think of their killing any more than my father; and the Indian who had done that deed was a drunkard.

20

"The old man in whose care I was, told me, before we reached his house, that he expected all the white men from our boat were killed, and that was the occasion of the firing and great noise. The wife of this, my conductor, was of French descent, as she and the old man, her husband, told me. She was a French girl who had been captured near Mobile when she was very young. Her husband, the old man, looked much like a half-breed, though he claimed to be English or American. His name was Tunbridge, and he had a son a noted warrior and a head-man, whose Indian name was *Chia-chatt-alla*. Among white people he was called *Tom Tunbridge*. His mother was a full-blood Indian. The old French woman was his step-mother.

"It was this Chia-chatt-alla, or Tom Tunbridge, who claimed me as his prisoner, and had committed me to the charge of his father. He intended I should make corn for the old people, and serve them as a son. After I had arrived at the cabin, there came in an old fat squaw, who began an angry conversation with 'my old Miss. and Mass.,' and often turned to me with a most threatening countenance. They afterwards told me that she complained of their attempt to save my life, for that 'I was large enough to notice every thing, and would escape, and some day *pilot* an army there, and destroy them all!' I did not then consider this prophetic, or ever likely to come to pass; but it did.

"The old fat squaw said her son would come and kill me. His name was *Cutte-atoy*. He was head-man of the town of Tuscagee, a small town opposite to Chattanooga. When he came to Tunbridge's hut, he asked for me, and declared his intention to kill me. He drew his knife, approached me with such purpose, when the wife of Tunbridge interposed. 'I should not be killed in her house.' He caught hold of me and jerked me out of the door. There I saw ten or a dozen Indians with guns pointed at me, and tomahawks raised to chop me into mince-meat. The old French woman followed me out and begged for my life. They spurned her away. She then said they should not spill my blood there, nor in the path to the spring. (This she explained to me afterwards.)

"They then pulled me to one side and began to strip off my clothes, that they might not be blooded at my slaughter. The old woman continued her entreaties. Finally she happened to use the proper argument. She asked Cutte-atoy if he took any of the white men prisoners. He could not say he did. She replied, 'This is none of your prisoner. He belongs to my son Chia-chatt-alla. He will avenge the death.'

"Some of the Indians who had come with *Cutte* said, 'Cutte-atoy captured a negro woman, and has sent her up to Tuscagee already.' This aroused the foster-mother, who commenced more vehemently to reproach him, and then to threaten that if he killed me, her step-son, Chia-chatt-alla, would kill the negro woman. 'He had better go along home to his negro woman.'

"The other Indians by this time joined with the woman, saying that Chia-chatt-alla would be sure to do as she had said. And to this opinion Cutte-atoy very soon arrived. My pantaloons had been restored to me. I drew them on, for I felt rather uncomfortable, *in every way*, 'just at that particular time.' I was permitted to return into the cabin. Old Tunbridge told me I was one of his family: I must call him ' Uncle,' and young Tom Tunbridge ' Brother.' The hair was shaved from my head, leaving only a small scalp-lock on top, in which to tie a bunch of feathers. I was also deprived of my pantaloons and supplied with a strip of cloth, or piece of stroud, 'like other boys of my age.' I worked in the corn, and at whatsoever I was required to do. They treated me kindly. . .

"Some of the Creek Indians threatened repeatedly to kill me, and came near doing so twice. I have the mark from a blow given me by one of the Creeks.

"During the winter of '89 I suffered very much from the cold, and my exposure in cutting wood and taking care of a few cattle and horses. I had to hunt after them in the cane and wood, and over the rough and steep hills, almost mountains. I heard that General Sevier, old Chucky-Jack, as the Indians called him, was fighting the Indians and destroying their towns at a terrible rate. The Indians had a great reverence for, and yet a great dread of him and his mode of warfare.

"After the defeat of Colonel Martin near Chattanooga, and the taking of Gillespie's Station, we heard that the 'old General' surprised the Indians on Coosa River, killed a large number of warriors, and captured forty or fifty of their women and children. Thereupon the Indians proposed an exchange of prisoners. Here was my chance for deliverance. They, however, opposed my exchange, on the score of my coming from North Carolina. They said the East Tennesseans, or Franklinites, had no right to demand me. But the head-man of the Indians said that Governor Sevier was 'so contrary that he could do nothing with him: that he, the Governor, had possession of his daughter, and therefore I must be released.'

"This settled it, and my exchange followed, as well as that of my two sisters. I was indebted to Gov. Sevier for my liberty, as also were my two sisters for theirs. We got back to the residence of an uncle in Pendleton county, South Carolina, after a captivity of eleven months and fifteen days.

"My mother and other sister were released after seventeen months' imprisonment or captivity.

" My little brother was detained five years down among the Creeks. He was the youngest of the children, and had forgotten the English words he used to know.

"After our release, we moved—*by land this time*—to Cumberland, and settled on the east side of the river, about three miles below Nashville.

" I heard of the approach of Indians, and of their attack upon Buchanan's Station in 1792, and hastened to Nashville, and then with others to Buchanan's. The Indians had disappeared; but I, at once, recognized my old *chum*, 'Chatt;' Tom Tunbridge, my 'Brother.' There he lay dead, pierced with balls, shot down into his body as he was blowing the coals to set fire to the fort.

" I was in several skirmishes with the Indians. . . . I was with Col. Hays; was with Ross, the post-rider, and Col. Friley, when Ross was killed and Friley and myself were wounded; was out under Captain Gordon and Captain Rains, and so of others. . .

"At the request of Col. Robertson, I searched out a route through the forests to the towns of Nickajack and Running Water; and acted as one of the guides to the army in that expedition. We called it 'The Burnt-Corn Expedition,' because of the quantity of corn the men had parched to take with them for food.

" I served in the war of 1812, under General Jackson. Through his agency, in a great measure, the negroes and their increase—fifteen in all—were restored to me.

" I was out afterward for four months with General Jackson in the Creek war, and was at the battles of Tallahatchee and Talladega. Gen. Jackson sent to me, on learning that I was elected Colonel of the Twenty-seventh Regiment, wishing me to take command of the Cherokees, as I was the only officer who spoke their language. But the East Tennesseans kept them back, and so they were not brought under my orders.

"On the morning of the battle of Talladega, *Gen. Robertson* came to me, desiring me to act as aide-de-camp; the men having faith in my experience as an Indian fighter. I consented to do so, in case I had no new order from Gen. Jackson.

"I went with Major Conn's column of eighty men; and, by some mistake, we were thrown obliquely to the right, and in contact with some five hundred Indians in one body, when we had a severe battle. Here about seventy Indians fell. They fled—such as could flee—and fairly ran the gauntlet between the two lines; our men following them several miles. . . . This was my last battle with the Indians."

Colonel Brown has within a few months past, (April, 1858,) furnished an interesting narrative and reminiscence of Indian times, addressed to the present writer, and deposited in the Tennessee Historical Society. It contains several items of information new, or less accurately stated by others. We may make use of what it contains suitable, in our narration. His object is to show "the judgment of Heaven which fell upon the Indians" for their cruel treatment of his father's family—that the small-pox destroyed hundreds of them.

By the attack which the Indians made upon the boat of Jonathan Jennings in 1780, "they caught the small-pox ;" it spread among them, and thus "the judgment of Heaven," as Col. Brown pronounces it, fell upon them eight years prior to the events narrated by Col. Jos. Brown. Col. B. is now eighty-six years old.

"Among other emigrants from North Carolina to Cumberland, was the father of Colonel William Pillow, of Maury county; (from whom may be seen a communication to the President of the Tennessee Historical Society at the State Capitol, written in 1858, when in his eighty-sixth year.) This brave old man, and his dashing, daring, fearless son, Col. Wm. Pillow, yet living, came to Cumberland with other emigrants under the escort of the Guard, commanded by Capt. Elijah Robertson, and settled at Brown's Station, four miles south of Nashville.

" The present Col. William Pillow was in most of the Indian expeditions from the time of his arrival to the termination of the war. He was under Captain Rains in the Elk River expedition, and in other pursuits. He was also out under the command of Captain Gordon; also under Captain Murray in chase of the Indians who killed John Helen at Jonathan Robertson's Station. When in this pursuit, he with others of the party crossed the Duck River, about five miles below where is now the beautiful town of Columbia, and continued their march day and night with utmost speed, until, on the hills near the Tennessee River, the Indians' camp-fire was discovered. Captain Murray ordered his men to charge to the right and left, obliquely, and thus enclose them at their encampment on the bank of the river.

" William Pillow was with the part of the company recognized as spies. They fired first upon the Indians, killing at least one by the camp-fire; the others ran down the river's bank, and were arrested by Captain Murray. They then jumped into the river, and were there easily shot.

" Mr. Maclin shot one before he got into the water.* Pillow hearing a gun fired at a place which he had just passed, pushed his horse up the

---

* The headstone which used to stand at the grave of Col. John Maclin, now lies in the pavement, near the lamp-post, corner of Broad and McLemore street.

steep second bank of the river, and discovered his friend John Davis, pursued by four Indians. Pillow dashed forward, and the Indians darted into the woods and thick cane; but he pursued one of the Indians till he shot him down.

"At that moment Captain Murray, Thomas Cox, Robert Evans, Luke Anderson, and William Ewing rode up, and Pillow pointed out to them the direction one of the Indians had taken. They pursued, saw the Indian attempting to mount Pillow's horse, (which Pillow had abandoned in his pursuit of *his* Indian.) The fellow mounted, was pursued, overtaken, and after a contest was killed. Pursuit was made by Andrew Castleman, and others, of the two other Indians whom Pillow had turned back from pursuing Davis. Castleman discovered them immersed in the water under the Bluff, their heads only out of the water. They were killed; and, at a short distance off, others were found and shot. Thus eleven warriors were certainly slain, and several squaws were taken prisoners."—Narratives of Pillow and Davis, *and Ramsey's Annals.*

Colonel Pillow's services were in demand, and he never failed to respond to calls thus made on him. He was very active in the Nickajack campaign, as will be mentioned in proper place. He served also in the later Indian wars under Gen. Jackson.

Pillow and Brown, Charles and Beale Bosley, and a very few others, survive as worthy monuments of a race of men who should never be forgotten by people occupying the Cumberland valley. Although not of the number of "earliest stationers," they were here to render good service in trying times.

Colonel Robertson inserted in the "State Gazette" of North Carolina a "Notice to Emigrants," that the road was opened from Campbell's Station to Nashville; that many families had gone out under the protection of the Guard, and that the Guard would be ready to escort others about the 1st of October.

General Davidson and the newly appointed Judge, John McNairy, and others, had come under escort of the Guard.

General Robertson had traversed this route alone, in company, and with a guard. He made fourteen visits to North Carolina, in most instances wholly to attend to the interests of his fellow-citizens on the Cumberland. Besides these long journeys to North Carolina, he made several trips to Kentucky, for like purposes, and one or two to Illinois.

The "Fourth of July" was not a national day here, but their "toasts" were, "Our Settlement: the Salamander, which lives in the fire!" "The Phœnix: which lives in solitude, and revives from its ashes!" "The

Bed of Pansy or Heart's-ease: trodden upon, yet spreads and perfumes the air."

"All, to reflourish, fades;
As, in a wheel, all sinks, to reäscend:
Emblems of man, who passes, not expires."

The ministers of the gospel often availed themselves of the trials and condition of this people, and of passing events and incidents in their history, to illustrate and enforce the Divine teachings and the lessons of Providence.

By Craighead, the scholarly Presbyterian, and by several of the zealous Methodists, real Boanerges, none of these resources for illustration or argument were neglected. This settlement was of "the Lord's planting," "the outpost," "the advanced guard," "the nucleus," "the germ," "the seed-bed," of civil and religious liberty. It must be cultivated, guarded; it would flourish, and

" O'er all the land prevail."

These men prayed and labored for the advance and triumph of civil and religious liberty. They were a self-denying and godly set of men. They gloried, actually " gloried in the Cross of Christ;" and were never " ashamed of it."

A day of religious frenzy was approaching. It came, with its physical and mental contortions, the true "iliac passion" in individuals and camp-meetings. A strange and anomalous condition. But it passed away—passed away as the storm passeth:

" Like broken wrecks along the shore,
And others sank, to rise no more,"

there may yet be discovered sad evidences of deeds and doctrines which at one time may have been regarded as the best proofs of "zeal for the Lord," guarantees of lasting fame to the prominent actors, and teachings never to be forgotten by a grateful posterity.

Better so, a thousand times better so, than heartless infidelity, or to have yielded to any debasing idolatry or hurtful superstition. In the very excess of the strange emotions, there was an awe and reverence for felt and present Deity. The being of God was recognized, dared not to be denied. An invisible and mighty Spirit was known to exist and to be able to operate upon the *minds* of men, and thus to show a power irresistible and subduing.

The *results* were reformation and improvement. There was a careful study of the word of God, much of exhortation and of prayer, and consequently an advance in useful knowledge and good morals.

There was a tornado : it overthrew many a tall Anakim, it cast down some of the haughty ones, and exalted too highly some men of low degree. A few mighty oaks were topped or prostrated, and gave space for sun and air and genial rains. A thousand blooming shrubs and the thick waving harvest, and doubtless some rank weeds, have found room to flourish. It was a strange work ; but it was one of the ways of Providence.

A vast majority of those who then made a profession of religion, were consistent Christians in all after-life, and silenced scoffing infidelity.

CHAPTER XIX.

1789.

AGAIN we quote from Judge Haywood : "The year 1789, as it rolled into view, brought with it some ordinary and some extraordinary events." The honorable historian, however, in his narration, makes no particular distinction or classification of these events. The usual or ordinary events were murders and thefts by the Indians. "They kept up hostilities during the whole summer, and killed a number of persons whose names are not remembered." Although such is the summing up by the learned historian, he yet has furnished a list of between twenty and thirty persons who were killed, four severely wounded, several captured, and thefts of horses and cattle untold.

The proofs of Spanish jealousy and hostility accumulated during this year. Her officers and emissaries, Spanish (and American?) were becoming more confident and more presumptuous, and probably possessed of more money.

The evidences of British aims upon these western settlements have never been so fully brought to light as have the proofs against Spain. Enough, however, has been developed at various times to satisfy us that *much has been concealed.* At this time Lord Dorchester, Governor of Canada, had an emissary passing through the settlements in Kentucky; a man who had the rank of Colonel in the British army, by the name of Conolly, whom the Federalists or "Washingtonians" made to flee in haste from the territory and escape to Canada. When he arrived in Canada, he found the great "director of the affairs of the Creeks," General Bowles, *there,* partaking of the hospitality of Lord Dorchester, at Montreal. As Colonel, or Doctor, Conolly, "with his celebrated and influential *squaw,*" dared not to return to these settlements, the conclusion to which he and his Lordship arrived was, that *Bowles* should go as the British emissary. He could afford the conspirators much information as to the disposition of the Creeks and Cherokees. Therefore, under the assumed name of Drummond, he came to Kentucky in the fall of 1789, and remained for several weeks in Lexington and Louisville. Thence he proceeded down the river and passed over into the Cherokee and Creek nations, in order to withdraw their attachment from the Spanish government, and engage them in the interest of Great Britain. Having formed acquaintances with some of the chiefs, and partially developed his British scheme, he found some ten or eleven of the chiefs ready to embark with him to England. He had the money or the authority from some high source to command passages on board an English vessel, and, with his chiefs, sailed to London, in 1790. They remained there about six months. Bowles had conferences with officers of State.

During that visit Bowles became acquainted with another conspirator, General *Miranda*, a discontented Spanish Don or aspirant to power, whom both England and France encouraged in some of his projects.

Bowles returned with commission and epaulettes as a *"General,"** and the extraordinary title of "Director," and "cast McGillivray in the shade."

The State had been divided into four Congressional Districts. Washington District included all the territory now constituting the State of Tennessee. The election of a Representative was to take place in March, and the returns to be made to the Clerk of the Superior Court of the District, at Knoxville. By common consent, General Sevier (who had so recently escaped the troubles of his position as Governor of the State of Franklin) was the candidate. The people were determined to manifest their confidence in him, and gratitude to him for his many and incalculable services. General Robertson, and other leading men on the Cumberland, at once avowed their preference for Sevier, and he consequently received here an almost unanimous vote.†

---

* (1858.) "Billy Bowlegs," who has within a month past surrendered, has "cut a pretty wide swath" in those everglades and hammocks; but Billy Bowles, "General and Director of the affairs of the Creek nation," wore English epaulettes, swelled, and exploded.

† General Robertson had not entertained a doubt of his friend's election. He greatly rejoiced at this better method to "soothe wounded feelings," than that practiced by Colonels Tipton and Roddy in the Assembly, when, in discussing the motion to remove from Sevier the offensive charge of treason and restore to him the rights of citizenship, they seized each other by the throat, while the member from Hawkins (one of Sevier's firm friends) cried out, "Soothe him, Colonel, soothe him!" which exclamation was reported in not very equivocal but equivalent language, "Smooth him, Colonel, smooth him!" that is, "Lay him on the floor!" They were separated; a challenge ensued, but mortal combat was prevented. But the "Tipton and Sevier parties," political divisions of long standing, were continued during the lives of these energetic men, and infused some elements into

And thus this devoted patriot and soldier, from whom the Assembly of North Carolina had but recently removed the charge of treason and disqualification to hold any office of trust or profit, (because of his active conduct as head of the Franklin government,) became "the first Member of Congress from the great Valley of the Mississippi."

On 20th January the Indians killed Captain Hunter in front of Johnson's Station, and dangerously wounded Hugh F. Bell. A party of white men collected hastily and pursued the Indians with utmost speed. At the distance of an hour's ride, as they were passing through the thick woods, the Indians fired upon them and killed Major Kirkpatrick and wounded Foster and Brown. The whites had imprudently rushed into an ambuscade, from which they escaped only with such a loss.

It was in May that Judge McNairy, accompanied by a number of friends or emigrants, set out for Cumberland. They had crossed the Clinch River and travelled until night, when they encamped. They had fed "their horses, cooked their breakfasts, and were about to renew their journey, when a large party of Indians fired upon them. The whites were thrown into great confusion, and fled to the woods. The horses, saddles, saddle-bags, and most of their clothing and blankets, were thus abandoned to their assailants." They acknowledged that "they did not stand fire" upon that occasion. They saved their lives, that was all. Taking the back-track, they swam across the Clinch, and reassembled upon the east side of the river. Three persons were killed in the McNairy party : a man named Stanley, a friendly Chickasaw chief and his son, who were returning from a visit at Knoxville to their own nation. The Judge had been out in the previous year. Judge McNairy soon after came to the Cumberland and entered upon the duties of his office and the accumulation of a fortune. In the summer of this year Miss McGaugh was killed, near Hickman's Station, but a short distance from Nashville.

Several of the stationers had gone to Kentucky to procure salt and ammunition. As they were on the return trip, and were approaching Bledsoe's Station, they were attacked, and Hugh Webb was killed. "The man who had married Jane Hendricks," was killed near Winchester's Mills; and Henry Ramsey, who had n't married anybody, was

---

parties after the leaders had disappeared from among the living. So difficult is it to "soothe or to smooth" the common minds where "the anger is inappeasable among the gods." Sevier and Tipton were never reconciled. Sevier was always *for Washington* and his measures and administration. As much could not be said of his opponents.

shot "through and through," as he was passing from Greenfield to Bledsoe's Station. He was one of the "seventy," a favorite of General Robertson.

General Robertson, with several hands, was at work in a field not half a mile distant from his house, having placed one man as a watchman to detect the approach of Indians, and, if need be, to give the alarm. At about eleven o'clock the man on the "look-out" became suspicious that Indians were in the cane not far off. He sought to keep between the people at work and that part of the woods from which he expected the creeping foe. General Robertson's attention was called to the same causes of suspicion, and he attempted to take a searching look into the woods, when several guns were fired at him and others in the field. The Indians fired at "long shot," and fled. General Robertson received a wound in the foot; the ball passed through without breaking a bone. No other person was wounded.*

Colonel Robertson issued orders for pursuit of the foe. About sixty men promptly turned out under command of Lieutenant-Colonel Elijah Robertson. Andrew Jackson was one of the troop in this pursuit. The wound prevented Colonel Robertson from riding on horseback, and his brother, Elijah, was providentially detained. The command was devolved upon Sampson Williams, Esq., with the rank of Captain. Having hastily convened at Colonel Robertson's, they marched soon in the morning, taking the trace or trail of the Indians, which led up West Harpeth to the ridge of highlands at Duck River; here they became convinced that the Indians were out-travelling them, and that so large a force would probably not overtake the retreating foe. Captain Williams here selected twenty men with best horses, and determined to rush forward and overtake them. This was a first thought; but these chosen men declared they could sooner overhaul and more safely approach the Indians on foot than on horseback. "No sooner said than done:" they dismounted, committed their horses to others, and set off in "a regular jog-trot." They kept the trail, went up the river a mile and a half, crossed in the night, turned down the river bank, and kept on until they were so involved in the thick cane and darkness, that they could go no farther with satisfaction. They lay upon their arms and on the ground

---

* It was at this time that Colonel Robertson exclaimed, "If I only had old Captain Rains and Billy here!" uttering a wish that this favorite scout, John Rains, and his brother William, were present to pursue these savages. But he found a very ready and efficient leader for a party to go in pursuit, in the person of Sampson Williams.

till break of day. As soon as it was light enough to see and determine the course they should take, they hastened on. To their own and the Indians' surprise, the pursuers and the pursued were but a few hundred yards apart. Each party had slept on the ground in the dense undergrowth, with only a narrow ridge intervening.

Captain Williams was at the head of his little company, and was the first to discover the Indians. They were mending up their fire, evidently preparing to roast some meat and bake a little meal into the form of a pone. There seemed to be about thirty Indians; and they had not discovered Williams's party. The white men rushed like furies down upon the Indians, many of whom were yet lying stretched upon the ground. When within fifty or sixty yards of them, the whites fired; the Indians fled, leaving one dead upon the ground, and five or six wounded. The wounded were seen to be helped off by their companions; they crossed the river on the north side, and disappeared before another shot could be fired at them. The place were they were attacked was a hollow or drain at the river's edge. The Indians in their flight left on the ground sixteen guns, nineteen shot-pouches, and all their baggage, consisting of blankets, moccasins, leggins, skins, and other articles. They did not fire a gun at the whites.

Captain Williams with his men recrossed the river at the same ford where the Indians had now passed over, but did not pursue them farther. They struck upon the path or trail which they had followed when in the pursuit, and soon met their friends with the horses, and so returned to Nashville.

In this instance the whites had fired their guns when at too great a distance, and fired through the cane, which intercepted or broke the force of most of the balls. The purpose was to so astonish the Indians that they should hastily flee and leave their guns. This was the result; and Williams acknowledged that this sight afforded him much pleasure and relief, for had they not fled, but seized their guns, (which probably were loaded,) they might have returned the fire with fatal effect. The whites were upon ground elevated above the Indians, and thus in position to have been more certainly hit; whereas, in shooting down hill, the Williams party "over-shot." The truth is, the whites did not act with all wisdom in this instance; at least, they admitted they might have "done better," that is, killed more, had some of them reserved their fire or have caught up the Indians' guns and used them upon the foe retreating across the river.

But such is the history of this "first Indian campaign and Indian fight," wherein the "Great Captain" in after-days, *Andrew Jackson*, is known to have been engaged. He was a private here, but "bold, dashing, fearless, and *mad upon his enemies*," as Sampson Williams said. Ever after this hot pursuit and "sudden lighting down" upon the Indians, Sampson Williams and Andrew Jackson were "fast friends," and "had a great ambition for encounters with the savages." This passion they were permitted to indulge to their hearts' content, until the private soldier, here, became the "conquering hero," the General in Chief, commander of armies and navies.

It has been said that these early settlers were not only a daring but a reckless set of people; that they placed very little value upon life, whether their own or the Indians'; that they prized a horse and rifle beyond all other property; that they could amuse themselves with the violin and the dance, while the Indian war-whoop was heard around their station, and their guns firing into the port-holes. "That in the midst of all their trials and suffering, they enjoyed themselves, in their way, as much as other people in the piping time of peace and plenty." Truly they had a good stock of bravery, fortitude, and cheerfulness. Had they been timid, irresolute, and desponding, they never would have come here; or, having thus far exposed themselves, would have sought and embraced an early opportunity to have escaped.

True it is, they usually welcomed new emigrants with "a dance in the evening." It was a mark of respect to the newly arrived, it was a time of cheerfulness and gratulation among the old stationers; and policy dictated the maintenance and exhibition of a good heart and unswerving perseverance. Their dances were all conducted with decorum, wholly exempt from any movement or posture that would excite immodest thoughts or desires.

"Honi soit qui mal y pense !"

We confess that they did play cards and draughts; that they did run foot-races and pitch quoits; they did waste many an idle hour in idle chat, and would have wasted much powder and lead in target-shooting or other sport, but they had them not for such indulgence. The character of these settlers for intelligence and morality would compare favorably with that of any other pioneers in these United States. They certainly do not deserve to be classed as an ignorant or an immoral people; unquestionably they were a brave, hardy, industrious, kind-hearted, and hospitable people.

However satirical, we might say pharisaical, were the remarks of the proud Churchman, Hugh Jones, "Chaplain of the Honorable Assembly of Virginia, and minister of James Town," we shall quote them for the

COLUMBIA

amusement of our readers. He gives this classification in his little book which was published about the year 1750. His summary reminds us of the soubriquets of our own day, "corn-crackers," "tucka-hoes," "buck-eyes," "hoosiers," "woolverines," "suckers," and "pukes."

"If New England be called a receptacle of Dissenters and an Amsterdam of religion, Pennsylvania the nursery of Quakers, Maryland the retirement of Roman Catholics, North Carolina the refuge of *Runaways*, and South Carolina the delight of *Buccaneers* and *Pyrates*, Virginia may justly be esteemed the happy retreat of true Britons, and true Churchmen for the most part: neither soaring too high nor dropping too low; consequently, should merit the greater esteem and encouragement."

We are tempted to add this concise commentary: "Let another praise thee, and not thine own mouth."

Few new settlements in the wild woods of America have been wholly exempt from obnoxious persons. They have been "the refuge of runaways," a hiding-place for absconding debtors and fugitives from justice. But our readers will remember the indignant denial of such a character by the "Notables," and will admit that their lives disproved such slander.

There may be seen in the first volume of General Robertson's manuscript letters, (in the Nashville University library,) a "General Order," under date, April 5th, 1789, calling upon the militia officers to be ready with their men to march, at a moment's warning, in pursuit of every Indian foe; to find their trail, follow, overtake, and punish them. Their outrages are so many and so great as not to be endured.

Thus in the midst of all their cares and labors, in building for themselves unhewed log-huts, clearing and fencing their lands, ploughing and hoeing, or gathering their crops, at midday or at midnight, every man was liable to be called upon to "bestir himself," and pursue a savage foe. Whoever dallied when summoned, could not "hold up his head" among honest and brave men. The call of the trumpeter, the word sent by a man, woman, child, or servant, could not be disregarded. As with that noble class of citizens, the firemen of our city, at the tap of the fire-bell, it is a race to the engine and a race to the flames; so with these pioneers, it was a contest who should be "first in the chase" and "in at the death." "Good excuses" were often reported and accepted. "Feigned or false ones" were sometimes made. Brave men, minute men, patriotic, public-spirited, reliable men; men whom "it would do to tie to," (as became the expressive term,) these constituted *a class*, and a large class of the early settlers. "The *slack-twisted*," and men who would "*shirk*," were known and understood as persons who "could not *come it*." The thumb at the nose, with open extended palm, was expressive of utter contempt in that day, as now.

There was an encouraging accession to the population during this year. These emigrants were well supplied with horses, neat cattle, and "a few pigs." The amount of silver and gold was very small. Horses and cows, axes and cow-bells, constituted the ready "circulating medium." To this indispensable yet variable currency was added the "military warrants" for land, and, as small change, the Guard certificates.* Peltries and buffalo hides served very well to supply the demand for "foreign exchange," or rather Eastern and Southern purchases. Small supplies of salt, sugar, and coffee, came from Orleans; usually by the way of the *Illinois!* and Kentucky! The necessity of axes and cow-bells, and the high value set upon them by the pioneer settlers, may be understood, when we reflect that the cattle were "turned into the brakes to browse," and "must be belled that they might be found;" and "axes were indispensable in clearing lands, felling trees, making fences, and building houses."

And, as was remarked, "the bell had a herding, taming influence upon cattle, even so much so that wild animals have been known to be attracted by its sound, and to come up to the pen with the oxen and cows."

We have in mind the case of a little boy, to whose neck his mother tied a small bell, that he might be traced should he go outside the picketing; and that he was actually searched for and found, occasionally *tinkling* his bell, and then amusing himself by picking up pebbles and throwing them into the river. That little fellow was in danger of being caught by the Indians. Little boys who disobey their mothers, and stray from home, are sure to run into danger. They need to be "held and bell'd," as Omnibus says to Birchrod, though he puts *two l's* in each word, "for emphasis."

The cow-boys were often in danger of being ambushed and captured

---

* Persons now living (1858) remember to have heard, in trade, the expressions "two-twenty" and "six-forty," "I will give or take a 640." These amounts indicated so many acres of land. There is a 640 very near the city of Nashville, on the Lebanon Pike, which was once sold for "three axes and two cow-bells," as we have been credibly informed. "A faithful rifle and a clear-toned bell" were traded for another tract. Each of these pieces of land is now worth many thousands of dollars. One of the most valuable farms in Maury was lost and won at a game to us unknown, and is to this day called by the name of the game, "*Rattle and Snap.*"

by the Indians. Some were caught, scalped, and killed, others taken as prisoners into the Indian nations. Hunters and spies had some peculiar methods of communicating intelligence, asking for help or supplies, appointing time and place for meeting, giving intimation of danger, or directing to relief.

They adopted some very expressive emblematic signs or figures, which to the initiated, or the learned in hieroglyphics and "spy-craft," were of great importance, and readily interpreted. We have heard many of these explained, but can venture to rehearse only one example:

"A family of five persons were killed: a tall man, a short fat woman, and three children, at some place to the north. Five sticks were cut of various lengths; the longest, being forked or split, indicated the man, the thick short one the woman, and three of smaller sizes and lengths the children. They were all scalped, as is shown by the peeling of the bark. There were thirteen Indians, as we are informed by the stick with stripes and thirteen notches; and they have fled south with two prisoners, as we judge from the pointer and little strips of bark, seemingly tied together."

Sometimes all the intimations would be upon one stick, or a piece of bark. A spy finding, at places well known, some of these mysterious articles, would bring them to the station, where a consultation would be held, and conclusions drawn as to the meaning. A spy or hunter would intimate to his friend his want of powder or lead, or other want, and the place at which he would look for supplies.

In the narrative of Captain John Davis, he mentions the placing a pone of corn-bread in a forked dog-wood, and hinting to his lost companion, by some bent and broken twigs, where to look for something of importance; and by attention to which the wanderer, almost ready to perish, discovered the food, and his life was saved.

As several persons had been killed, and others scalped by the Indians at the crossing of the Sulphur Spring Branch between Nashville and Freeland's Station, it was resolved to destroy the cane upon the intervening lands, and construct a bridge over the ravine. The cane was repeatedly set on fire, and much of it destroyed. And the Justices of the Quarter Sessions imposed a tax for this year, payable in *specifics* and money, "for the support of the guard, and to build a bridge across the French Lick Branch, below the town of Nashville."

The people at these two stations (now within the city limits) experienced interruption to their intercourse by high water. In such times they had to use canoes and ferry-boats, or go west, and, by a very circuitous route through cane-brakes, "head the back-waters." Some persons

21

had been shot at and wounded in that route. Large trees had been felled across this branch at several places below the spring, and served as "foot-bridges," or "logs to cross on," until the high waters should remove them.

These inconveniences and interruptions induced the court to levy a tax for a bridge. But such was the necessity of increased service from the guard, that the appropriation was subsequently withdrawn, and the entire tax applied to military and emigrant purposes. A bridge was at a subsequent period erected across this branch near its mouth, and so weighed down with stones that it could be flooded, and not floated away. When the river was low, and no back-water interrupted the crossing, the path usually taken between these stations was by the Sulphur Spring.

The place first, and for many years, used for the burial of the dead, was the point of land in the bend of the creek, and south-east of the Sulphur Spring. Several graves may yet be seen there. That spot, and to a considerable extent the ground around, was quite open, and exempt from cane and trees, when the emigrants arrived here in 1779. It was the spot where the first corn was planted.*

A register's office had been established in Davidson county. After the division of Davidson and the organization of Tennessee county, the question was much debated, "whether the office of register was not vacated," he residing in the new county; whereupon the Honorable Justices quieted public anxiety and settled the question by an *obiter dictum*, and thus the matter became *res adjudicata*, though *coram non judice*, by this resolve :

"The Court is of opinion that the register's *place* is not vacated by the division of the county, and by his being *thrown* into the county of Tennessee, provided he still keep a *deputy* in Davidson."

Sampson Williams, Esq., and two or three others, took notice of this opinion of the Court, and were a little hypercritical in their comments. And the Court—*reversed* their former decision !

Ministers of the gospel, gentlemen of the green bag, and the sons of Esculapius, with small saddle-bags, now made their appearance, and became identified with society. The cause of education, the matters of litigation, and the necessities of medication, now had their advocates and promoters. Representatives of the learned professions appear.

Throughout this year General Robertson continued his inquiries to ascertain the connection, by treaty or otherwise, existing between the

* Corn was also planted at the mound near the river, and north of the Sulphur Spring Branch : there the cane had been destroyed.

Spaniards and the several Indian tribes. He became not only the more supicious, but, indeed, convinced that the protracted Indian war against these settlements had much of Spanish craft and hatred in it. He was already engaged in diplomacy. He knew something of the purposes of the Spanish officers, and of the instrumentalities by which they hoped to attain their ends.

In the feeble and exposed condition of the settlements, great wisdom and prudence were requisite in conducting correspondence and inter-course with the Spaniards, lest matters should be yet more complicated and troublesome.

Letters had passed between General Robertson, Governor Mero, and other Spanish officers, as also between him and McGillivray, the Creek chief, (an active agent in the mischief.) That correspondence is now continued through the night of gloom which covered all the western settlements. At this time we find General Daniel Smith engaged with General Robertson in conducting the correspondence.

General Smith's residence was Rock Castle, in Sumner. He was a man well educated, an accomplished gentleman, and a soldier. He acted as Secretary of State in the Territorial Government, Senator in Congress from the State, as successor of Andrew Jackson, who had resigned.

The great question of the day was the adoption or rejection of the Constitution of the United States. It had been presented and rejected by a very large majority. The Confederacy had been tried. In all the States it had been discarded : the necessity of other form and union of government was everywhere admitted. What shall it be? How can it be? These were important questions, and the difficulties and objections to the proposed union, as presented in the Federal Constitution, seemed so many and so mighty to the people of Carolina, on the Atlantic side of the mountain, that they had rejected it by an almost unanimous vote. To the people on this side of the mountain, the doubts and objections were more and stronger.

That great range of mountains, forbidding much of social intercourse, and all of business, (as it then seemed,) was a natural barrier to any firm and profitable union. It suggested the idea of an eastern and a western government. The impossibility for these settlements to exist without the free navigation of the great natural channels and outlets to the Gulf, the importance of which few persons indeed, in the Eastern States, could understand, or cared to consider — these matters were suggested and urged, and greatly perplexed the minds of many of these stationers.

But the arguments and the influences in favor of a closer union with the other States and the patriotic republican friends in those States, and an unbounded admiration for Washington and abiding confidence in his Heaven-directed mission, prevailed.

The second Convention met: the Constitution was presented, discussed, and, by a vote of more than two to one, was ratified.

This result gave great satisfaction. Men who had been indifferent or opposed, now congratulated the warm advocates upon the adoption.

The State had stood aloof: it was the separate and independent State of North Carolina. But could she claim to have gained that separation and independence without aid or sympathy from her sister States? No, no; it was a united Declaration of Independence, a common war, a conjoint triumph. All must be Federalists, all must be Republicans. Few indeed were they who refused the sentiment to Washington—

"First in war, first in peace, and first in the hearts of his countrymen."

And now the good Old North State is one of the United States. She is no longer *out*, but *within* the *Union*.

The acceptance and adoption date from the 13th day of November, 1789.

The administration of General Washington had experienced much anxiety and embarrassment in the intricate negotiations with Spain, and in all measures proposed or efforts made to adjust difficulties with the Southern Indians, from the "outside position" maintained by North Carolina. Hopes were now encouraged and entertained that all these perplexing questions would speedily be settled, and peace and prosperity result.

These western people now expected more from the United States than they had ever received from the parent State or the Confederacy. They believed they had already endured too much; they thought they had long and cruelly suffered from the parsimony of the State; and they gave free expression to all their feelings. The desire for separation was diffusing, and was cherished by the people of Cumberland. They had been accustomed to legislate, to adjudicate and to act for themselves. It would be no new position for them to occupy; no duties, no cares, no burdens would be devolved upon them which would take them unawares, or to which they would be found unequal.

By repeated acts of legislation, the people of the Atlantic counties had indicated a determination not to defray one dollar of the expenses, or to share in the burdens of the distant settlements over the mountains and on the Cumberland River.

Some politicians in the Eastern States soon after this began to say, "Let us secure the Fisheries: what matters it to us, if the navigation of the Mississippi is yielded for five and twenty years, or for ever?" Not much less selfish, and indifferent to the welfare and prosperity of these settlements, was the spirit of some petty demagogues in the Old North State.

All men are not blessed with that clear vision which discerns objects afar off. Some think they can " see men, as trees walking," but never pray for the removal of the film, that they may " see plainly."

The great facts in American destiny, although they cast their shadows plainly in advance of their coming, could not be discerned or credited until they stood forth in all their magnificence to the common sense of every man.

In Washington District, (or East Tennessee,) the alienation of the people from the State had gone so far as to produce a separate organization. They deliberately threw off the authority of the State. They set up for themselves.

" The *State of Franklin*" had its day; and so had the "Government of the Notables." Men of intelligence and patriotism were concerned in each of these anomalous States and transient organizations. They were a necessity of the times and interests of the people. They accomplished a good service; and that was glory enough. Though they are ended as distinct organizations, their good results are not yet terminated or inoperative.

But the worth and the services of the prominent actors could not thus soon be ended. There was much more for them to do and to suffer. Sevier and Robertson, and other noble spirits, were trained to "endure hardships, as good soldiers."

In the spring of 1784, the Legislature of North Carolina had passed an Act of Cession : plainly evincing a desire to be relieved of her "mountaineers" and "children in the woods." But when she saw them so willing to set up for themselves, there came "a second thought," and in October the Cession Act was repealed. Disappointment and irritation resulted. The Franklin Government arose, conflicts ensued, and then the State of Franklin ceased by a euthanasia.

The satisfaction of officers and soldiers of the continental line, by liberal bounty-lands, must be made; and as the State foresaw the day, and that not distant, when her north-western and transmontane territory must be relinquished, it would do very well to satisfy all such obligations from these wild lands. The State would have so much the more left within her diminished boundaries when the separation should have been accomplished.

In December of this year, the Assembly, having in view this policy, passed an act to pay the officers and soldiers who had been engaged in

General Joseph Martin's fruitless expedition against the Chickamauga towns;* and, with offensive discrimination and niggardliness, exempted the treasury of the *State* from liability for one dollar, and made the whole payable out of the treasury of the District of Washington.

"The western people believed that the aim was to obtain from the sale of the lands more certificates of public debt;" and the opinion was entertained that North Carolina could expose them to the tomahawk and scalping-knife, without any sympathy for their sufferings, and without having the least inclination to prevent them.

"In the judgment of these mountain settlers, past experience had fully demonstrated the advantages which were to be expected from a renewal or continuance of their connection with North Carolina :" they were to fight for themselves, protect their own possessions, and pay all the taxes. If such taxes were not sufficient to defray expenses, they must increase them, or let the debts remain unsettled. "Let them see to it," and not call upon the State treasury. Many instances of such treatment were supposed to be scattered through the public annals of the country. The expenses of maintaining, protecting, and governing the settlements through various channels, had greatly accumulated. Every law was carefully worded, so as to restrict the burdens of payment to the Districts of Washington and Mero. The instances to the contrary were very few and inconsiderable. The great and inevitable exception was "the maintaining of the western members at the Assembly. These expenses were defrayed from the State treasury !" and amounted to about sixty dollars to each member !

The members from the Atlantic counties were ever on the alert, and complaining of the multiplicity and magnitude of western claims. The bickerings and contentions were on the increase between these Representatives. We doubt not that the western members did, as was said, "intimate the necessity of yet larger claims and appropriations—the present and growing circumstances would render these indispensable." But they were not unwilling to see the fears of the Atlantic people yet more aroused, that the separation might be hastened. They saw that nothing was to be gained from longer adherence to the State, and they hoped that, by an early separation, there would be the larger extent of unappropriated lands in the new State.

---

* And that very invasion of Indian towns caused those lawless savages, with their bad temper much imbittered, to move farther down the river, and finally to establish themselves at Nickajack and Running Water, whence they made their mischievous incursions into the Cumberland settlements.

The Atlantic counties had the power to dictate terms, and in the "Chickamauga Act" they manifested their determination to use this "power of the majority."

We need not deny that "the western people did not think it material by what means they could draw from a treasury replenished by the sales of lands which the unassisted valor of the western people had plucked from the hands of the savages, and which had also been rendered valuable by the settlements which the same valor had planted upon them. They may have judged, that to get into such a treasury through an unguarded avenue, which the proper owners or guardians had left open and forgotten, might not, in a court of conscience, be an unpardonable crime; especially if the court were created amongst the western people." "The learned say, that all consciences are not made in the same mould, nor of the same length; and it has been shrewdly suspected that, upon this subject, a North Carolina and a Tennessee conscience would be found to differ materially."

"About this time it was believed that the western people and their members were not deficient in the advancement of all their just claims, and lost no opportunity to present them whenever there was a hope of having them favorably passed on. And as their constituents were not opulent enough to make them neglect trifles, they claimed, it was thought, full measure for all their services and supplies, and omitted no claim from a motive of disinclination" to swell the account.

" Either by accident or design, the ungrateful creed was inculcated, that more expeditions against the Chickamaugas and other Indian tribes would soon become necessary."

" Upon its trail there followed the odious suggestion, that whenever the western people wanted money, they pretended that the Indians plundered and scalped their inhabitants; embodied the militia, and continued them in service till their pay amounted to the sums they wanted; that there were endless sources of expenditure, which would never cease to furnish claims and complaints for the unwilling ears of the Atlantic members, who had nearly as much complacency about this time for the *yell of the savage* as for the *claims* and *complaints* of the *western Representatives!*"

" These rumors did not fail of their effect. Each party ran with joy to the formation of articles which were to sever them for ever."*

The Representatives from the counties on the Cumberland actively participated in all the discussions in the Assembly.

---

* Haywood.

An act was passed, which authorized and required the Senators in Congress to execute a deed or deeds conveying to the United States of America all right, title, and claim which North Carolina had to the sovereignty and territory of the lands situated within the chartered limits of North Carolina, and west of the line beginning on the extreme height of the Stone Mountain, where the Virginia line intersects it, etc.

On the 25th day of February, 1790, Samuel Johnston and Benjamin Hawkins, the Senators from North Carolina, executed a deed in conformity with the cession act; and on the second of April of the same year, Congress in behalf of the United States accepted the grant. And thus the authority of the Old North State ceased. She was relieved of her many inquietudes, and the western people greatly rejoiced in their deliverance, and "began to open for themselves the paths to prosperity and glory."

The "first, second, and third conditions" in the Deed of Cession have peculiar marks of the unkind and selfish feelings by which the majority in the North Carolina Assembly were tinctured. But we will not comment upon them. They were sufficiently criticised and condemned by western members at the time, and by their constituents generally.

There were some savage murders in this year, which should be mentioned before we close this chapter.

Colonel Isaac Tittsworth and his brother John had arrived at the Cumberland settlements in safety, under the protection of the Guard. After a short delay at Bledsoe's and Mansker's, they proceeded with their wives and children, and several servants, and commenced their settlements near the mouth of the Sulphur Fork of Red River, in Tennessee county. Here they were attacked by the Indians, and, as was reported and believed, "their wives and children were killed; *not one escaped.*" [*]

A hunting-party, consisting of Colonel Tenen, Evan Shelby, Jun., Abednego Lewellen, and Hugh F. Bell, were in pursuit of game, and fell into an ambush, when the Indians fired and killed Shelby and Lewellen. Tenen and Bell made a narrow escape, being pursued for many miles.

In September, a party of Indians approached the spring at Buchanan's Station. They discovered John Blackburn and fired upon him—at least a dozen fired at him at the same time; he was riddled with bullets, was scalped, and a spear left sticking in his body.

"Colonel George Winchester was out with a scouting-party, and upon Smith's Fork he came upon a fresh trail of Indians. He pursued them down the creek, on a buffalo-path; and, no doubt, the Indians

---

* Haywood, p. 244.

were apprised that they were after them, and accordingly selected their ground for battle. The path led through an open forest to the crossing of the creek, and immediately a heavy cane-brake set in.

"The spies were a little in front. They were Major Joseph McElrath and Captain John Hickerson, two very brave men.

"Just as the spies entered the green cane only a short distance, the Indians, lying in ambush, fired upon them. Hickerson was instantly killed; McElrath escaped unhurt. Winchester was close behind, rushing up. Both parties commenced firing, and kept it up for some time. Frank Heany was wounded; and the Indians having greatly the advantage, Winchester thought proper to retreat. By retreating he hoped he could draw them out of the cane into more open ground. In this he did not succeed.

"There is no doubt that Captain James McCann killed a celebrated warrior, whose Indian name, Ne-ussee, signifies 'The Moon.' He was a hare-lipped man, of large size, and the only one in the nation thus marked. No doubt this Indian shot down and scalped Captain Charles Morgan, a year or two before. Morgan lived several days, and stated that it was a hare-lipped Indian who shot and scalped him.

"One of my brothers was in this expedition. The Indians, after the establishment of peace, said 'the Moon' was killed. The Indians reproached us with having a fool warrior along. There were two Dutchmen in the party by the name of Harpool, John and Martin.

"The Indians were under a second bank of the creek in the cane. . . . . John Harpool told his brother Martin to 'run down and drive them up, while he killed one,' as they practiced in deer-drives. Martin rushed in and raised a great whoop at the top of his voice, making the cane crack at a terrible rate, and the Indians broke and run. He was ever afterwards called the 'Fool Warrior.' I knew them both well; they were good soldiers." *

By an act of Assembly passed near the close of the session, at the instance probably of the Representatives from Davidson, Sumner, and Tennessee counties, the County Courts of those counties were "enjoined, at their next April term, (1790,) to make a list, to be signed by the Chairman, of all licks fit for the manufacture of salt, including Eaton's, Denton's, Neely's, Casper's, Madison's, Drake's, Stoner's, and Bledsoe's, which were to be sold. All others were declared vacant, and subject to location and entry."

Commissioners were to cause to be surveyed the several licks and

* John Carr.

springs fit for the manufacturing of salt, with six hundred and forty acres of land adjoining; advertise and sell the same within twelve months. Two of the reserved licks, with adjoining land, were to be retained for the use of Davidson Academy, for which commissioners were ordered to execute deeds to the trustees. The moneys arising from such sales were to be appropriated to the use of the District of Mero, as should thereafter by law be appointed.

A "Tobacco Inspection" was provided for at Clarksville, in Tennessee county. Subsequently, there was one established at Cairo, in Sumner county. Clarksville has maintained her distinction and preëminence as "the first point" for the shipment of tobacco.

For interesting information as to this article of commerce, we refer to Chapter XX.

Provision was made for persons wounded by the Indians in the District of Mero. By this act, the County Courts of the three counties were authorized to pass the accounts of physicians, surgeons, and nurses for attendance upon persons so wounded and disabled, and accounts for provisions and maintenance.   These being certified and authenticated, as required, were to be receivable for taxes and other public dues in the District. Accounts thus passed were redeemable in the District—not elsewhere. The State would have nothing to do with them. Hitherto she had not made provision for such obligations out of her treasury, and it was not now expected that such sufferers should look for aid or sympathy beyond their county and this District.

In anticipation of the business which surgeons and physicians were about to have—arising from Indian wars—and the gratuitous services which it was presumed they would render the poor and afflicted in their need, an exemption was granted to them from all militia duties.

Equity powers, and—a more liberal salary, were granted to the Judge of the Superior Court for Mero District.

The year 1789 was regarded as quite a prosperous one for the Cumberland people. It was, in after-years, sometimes mentioned as a year of comparative peace—only thirty persons killed, a few scalped and otherwise wounded, and one half only of the horses belonging to the people stolen.*

But this sentiment was prevalent: We shall be able to maintain our ground. We shall expect aid and protection from the United States

---

* The number of horses stolen by the Indians from these settlements was now estimated at one thousand. General Robertson and his brother Elijah had lost ninety-three, and his immediate neighbors seventy-five.

Government, to whose jurisdiction and care we shall soon be transferred. The administration of Washington will "defend us from all the
assaults of our enemies." They spoke of him as "the man appointed of
Heaven to deliver them out of the hand of their enemies."

General Robertson, and other influential men, honestly and zealously
inculcated these sentiments. The majority of the people were admirers
of Washington, placed unlimited confidence in him, and, perhaps, had
unreasonable expectations from the government to the Presidency of
which he was so earnestly called and unanimously elected.

However, not every man was even "*for Washington.*" "Such greatness and such goodness were indeed overpowering; to be admired—but
also dreaded!"

We will not record the name of the author of this expression.

There was one transaction at this period in Georgia, with which some
of the early stationers on Cumberland were connected, that merits a passing notice.

On the 21st December, 1789, the Legislature of Georgia passed an act
granting to Zachariah Cox and his associates, in consideration of $46,875,
three million five hundred thousand acres of land in the Great Bend of
Tennessee.

General Sevier, and other prominent men in East Tennessee, Colonel
Donelson, and perhaps one or two others here, or who had been here,
were interested, either by advances and as original partners, or by gratuities. General Sevier had ten or twenty thousand acres at the mouth
of the Blue Water Creek, which empties into the Tennessee, near the
head of the Muscle Shoals, the right to which he relinquished to the
United States, for the privilege of entering five thousand acres of other
unappropriated public lands. Colonel Donelson had been an original pro-
jector of a settlement there.

The impression was made upon the Cumberland settlers that the successful establishment of white settlements there upon the border of Indian
territory, would have a most happy influence in restraining savage incursions into the Cumberland settlements; therefore these stationers felt much
concern when they learned that the general government, or administration of Washington, had given orders to prevent or break up the entire
project. It was denounced as illegal, fraudulent, and corrupt, contrary to
treaty stipulations, and to the "non-committal, non-aggressive policy" of
the government.

As a legal question, there can be little doubt that the State of Georgia
had a right to sell lands, prior to the union; that these lands were within
her boundaries; and although the nomad tribes, the wild Cherokees, or

some of the Chickasaws, may have continued to set up a claim, their best title had been purchased once and again, by contracts, the resulting benefit of which accrued to the State ; therefore the purchase of the State by the great Tennessee Land Company was good and valid.

On 2d September, 1790, the agents of this company issued public notices to the proprietors, that on the 10th January, 1791, they, and whosoever would join them, would embark from the confluence of Holston and French Broad Rivers, for the purpose of forming settlements near the Muscle Shoals.

They were forbidden to depart on any such expedition, and threatened with a warfare by the savages, to check the horrors of which, aid should not be granted, either by the Confederacy or the State. The Indians were to be "let loose upon them, without bit or bridle, with knife, gun, hatchet, and fagot."

Most of the proprietors, or associates, were deterred, and desisted; abandoning one of the most lawful, well-devised, and well-designed *"filli-bustering expeditions"* known in the early history of the great West and South.

Following close upon the denunciation and defeat of settlements in the Great Bend of Tennessee, came the Treaty of Holston, on the 2d July, 1791, by which the whole country east of the Tennessee River (including the three million five hundred thousand acres) to the Cumberland River, forty miles above Nashville, and thence with the dividing ridge between Cumberland and Duck, to a point whence a south-west line would strike the mouth of Duck River and Tennessee, was restored—given to the Cherokees ! " Civilization craw-fishing !" exclaimed "the said Hood."

We believe that the Cherokee nation had not a town or settlement on the east side of the Tennessee River, unless we admit the few bark camps and insignificant shanties opposite the site of Chattanooga to be the exception. That they had no ownership in all this forest region will be fully proven hereafter. The Chickasaws had yielded their pretensions to the country south of this line drawn from the Cumberland above Nash-ville to the mouth of Duck River, even the " Chickasaw old fields," near Muscle Shoals, "leaving it to the white people to keep it as hunting-ground, make it a battle-ground, or clear it for corn-ground."

The news from the Kentucky settlements was very disheartening to settlers here. For years the Kentuckians had desired independence— separation from Virginia, and admission into the Confederacy. An election of delegates to their *seventh* Convention had taken place. This Convention met at Danville, in July, 1789, when they found that, instead of the way having been opened for the attainment of their desired object, new obstacles were thrown in the way. Another Convention must be called for the next year, and then another, nine in all, before Kentucky could be enrolled as a State.

"If such are the difficulties and delays there, what may they not be for us?" said some here.

Some numbers of Bradford's Kentucky Gazette, and publications in other forms, had reached Cumberland settlements, with just, yet bitter complaints of the proposed surrender of the navigation of the Mississippi. These stationers were "troubled on every side: without were fightings, within were fears."

CHAPTER XX.

1790.

THE act of cession having been accepted by the Congress of the United States, it became its duty to provide a territorial government. An act for this purpose was passed on 25th of May, for the government of the "territory south of the Ohio River." It constitutes this territory into one district, for the purposes of a temporary government.

The privileges, benefits, and advantages to be enjoyed here, are such as had been granted and guaranteed to the people in the territory northwest of the Ohio River, by Act of Congress, passed in July, 1787, except so far as is otherwise provided for in the conditions set forth in the Act of Congress accepting the cession made by North Carolina. One of these conditions is, that no regulations made or to be made by Congress shall tend to emancipate slaves. Congress is hereby expressly forbidden and precluded from all intermeddling with the institution of slavery in this territory.

The duty now devolves upon President Washington to nominate the officers for this territorial government. Who shall be Governor? The Representatives to the Assembly of North Carolina from Washington and Mero Districts had repeatedly met with a gentleman in the Assembly who was of graceful and accomplished manners, kind and sociable in disposition, of business habits, extensive information in Indian affairs, and who had given many proofs of sympathy and interest for the pioneer settlers. This gentleman was *William Blount:* with some faults, a man of eminent worth and abilities. He was a favorite with these acquaintances, and doubtless received their hearty recommendation. He was nominated, the nomination confirmed, and received his commission, dated 7th August, 1790. The Territorial Judges were Joseph Anderson and David Campbell.

Governor Blount arrived in the territory on the 10th October, and took up his residence at Mr. Cobb's, near Washington Court-house, between Holston and French Broad Rivers. Some of the Governor's letters to General Robertson were dated at "Cobb's," as may be seen in Robertson's manuscript letters. He entered upon the discharge of the duties of his office with much earnestness, and persevered with untiring energy; a little vacillating in sore perplexities.

The character given to him for eminent talents, familiarity with Indian affairs at the South, and the reputation he had acquired in public life, insured him a cordial welcome among the people on this western river. It is due to Governor Blount to say that in the Assembly of North Carolina, and the Congress of the United States, he had appeared as the champion, the decided and eloquent friend and defender of the interests and characters of these pioneers. The people of Tennessee owe much to the early counsels and measures of Governor Blount. All may not deserve the highest commendation, yet there is enough to entitle his name to enrolment among the intelligent and useful public officers of Tennessee.

His political sun was obscured in its setting. But if his complicity in projects (ever involved in *mystification*) was *without criminality*, and if he was made a *sacrifice to State policy* and *diplomatic craft*, the time has come when the State of Tennessee should desire to relieve his name from reproach, and herself from the stigma as the first State dishonored by the expulsion from the Senate of the United States of a citizen and Senator, upon whose private and public life, until then, high eulogiums had been bestowed.

We must say that the indifference manifested in this State for the fair fame of its early great men—of which class of patriots no State in the Union ever possessed more worthy ones—is inexcusable. The names of these worthy citizens are, indeed, perpetuated upon the statute-book and in the map and geography of the State, and perhaps these are as suitable monuments as could then have been afforded. But the time has arrived when full records of the acts and public services of such men should be embodied and published ; and hereafter monuments and statues be erected which should attract the admiration and awaken the inquiry of all of the present and future generations in the State. We have counties named in honor of Blount, Sevier, Robertson, Shelby, Bledsoe, Jackson, Polk, and Grundy. This is all very well, commendable; but we need, for our schools, biographies and historical narratives neatly prepared and for common use.

The names of one or two excellent women are likewise perpetuated. We have good authority for the following anecdote: When the county of Blount was to be organized or the act to pass, in 1795, and the seat of justice to be named, 1796, Blount, then Governor of the Territory, humorously remarked, that as the Territorial Legislature was disposed to attach his name to the county, they ought to place the name of his wife there, as she was to him the centre of attraction and inseparable.   Therefore the county-seat was called *Maryville*, in honor of his wife, Mary Blount, formerly *Mary Grainger*.   Whereupon the Honorable M. Carter, whose own name was about to be distinguished in the same way, by *Carter county*, requested that the seat of justice should be called *Elizabeth*ton, for which there was just as good reason as that urged by Governor Blount, and thus the name of Elizabeth Carter has its locality. (Perhaps her paternal name may be found in some of the old manuscripts deposited in Tennessee Historical Society, with letters from Willie Blount, as it was furnished to us with those letters.)

Abundance of documents remain, and are readily accessible, for the preparation of an interesting life of Governor William Blount.

The Governor commissioned the necessary civil and military officers for the counties.   Daniel Smith was appointed Secretary of the Territorial Government: of him we must speak hereafter.   The appointment of the military officer for each district was reserved to the President. John Sevier was nominated and received the office of Major-General for the District of Washington, and James Robertson for the District of Mero.   These commissions were issued in February, 1791.

Governor Blount made most happy appointments to office in the counties.   The early pioneers he regarded, as of right, entitled to the honors and emoluments of such offices as were to be held among them; and there were enough of honest and qualified men to fill all these offices. They were not overlooked; and thus we find the few survivors of the inchoate government at *Nashborough* of 1780–83 continued in power. It is with pleasure we also find that one of the very earliest settlers and worthiest of men, *Captain John Donelson*, received and accepted a commission, a copy of which we give below.*   The oath of office was taken the same day before Judge McNairy.

---

* The commissions were written by Governor Blount in his excellent, large hand :

"William Blount, Governor in and over the Territory of the United States of America, south of the River Ohio.

"To all who shall see these Presents, Greeting :

"Know ye that I do appoint John Donelson, Esq., of the county of Davidson in the said Territory, a Justice of the Peace for the said County, and do authorize and empower him to execute and fulfil the duties of that office according to Law, and to have and to hold the said office during his good Behavior, or during the

The people here had been for so long a time without a thoroughly organized government with sufficient officers, that they now indulged in perhaps extravagant anticipations of benefits speedily to result from the new administration. The officers in each county were identified with the interests and prosperity of the country; and they were men to dignify the office they held, by the faithful discharge of its duties.

The commission from General Washington to General Robertson was regarded as a certificate of merit and distinction from the very fountain of honor, and worthily bestowed upon the very chief citizen here. General Robertson could not fail to appreciate this mark of confidence, and we shall have occasion to present indubitable evidence of his high regard for General Washington.

For ten years a savage war had been waged against these feeble settlements. The most numerous and warlike of the southern tribes of Indians were their enemies. They were enemies, in violation of professions and treaties of peace; they were enemies against stationers, whose aim was to pursue only the peaceful arts of agriculture; they were enemies, departing from their own to trespass upon territory they had never possessed— the questionable pretensions of right to which they had relinquished for considerations once and again paid to them. They were enemies by the machinations and instigations of a nation recently associated with us in the contest for freedom and independence; a nation having high pretensions to religion and all the refinements of civilization; a nation under solemn treaty obligations not to disturb our peace. The Spaniards, by artful persuasions and corrupting presents, ensnared and inflamed these savages to robbery and murder; "therefore they had the greater sin."

Let us take a survey of our progress. Commencing with emigrants to the number of about three hundred, in the cold winter and wet spring of 1780, organized into seven companies, which commenced settlements and erected defences, we see them soon so greatly harassed and slaughtered that but a third of their number remains, and a majority of these settlements and stations had to be abandoned. With difficulty could a foothold be maintained at the three forts first constructed. Then again with some accession of numbers to the settlements, with other

---

existence of the Temporary Government of said Territory, with all the powers, authorities, and privileges to the same of right appertaining.

"Given under my hand and seal in the said Territory, this 15th day of December, in the year of our Lord 1790.

"By the Governor: WM. BLOUNT.

    "DANL. SMITH."

22

treaties, with other boundaries, with other largesses to the Indians, with changes of jurisdiction, with some change of officers, and with a novel change in the form of government—the settlements are now expanded further than at any previous date.   But it is a matter of curious inquiry, to what extent had this struggle for ten years given possession of the country to the stationers ?

Here has been the *post of danger;* here the "Banner Troop" of civilization and republicanism; here that "covetous eye peeping narrowly into the rich and boundless unknown wilderness," that eye which the Spanish Don said "must be put out," the keen gaze of which irritated and alarmed the proud Castilian and the aboriginal American.   But let us quote the good authority of Governor Blount as to the extent of the settlements.

EXTENT OF CUMBERLAND SETTLEMENTS.

1792. In one of Governor Blount's letters to the Secretary of War, he says : "I will give you a description of Mero District.   The settlements extend up and down the Cumberland River, from east to west, about eighty-five miles, and the extreme width from north to south does not exceed twenty-five miles, and its general width does not exceed half that distance ; and not only the country surrounding the extreme frontier, but the interior part, (which is to be found only by comparison with the more exposed part,) is covered generally with thick and high cane, and a heavy growth of large timber, and where there happens to be no cane, with thick underwood, which afford the Indians an opportunity of lying days and weeks in any and every part of the district in wait near the houses, and of doing injuries to the inhabitants, when they themselves are so hid or secured that they have no apprehensions of injuries being done in return ; and they escape from pursuit, even though it is immediate.   This district has an extreme frontier of at least two hundred miles."

Freeland's Station was less than a mile from the Bluff, the French Lick branch intervening, and much heavy cane.   Eaton's Station was on the east side of the river, distant and below the Bluff two miles, being at the first high land.   The forests intercepted the view of the one fort from the other.   During a number of years the small improvements that were made extended but four or five miles from these stations.   And thus it is easily perceived that the territory occupied, and so partially occupied, was very limited indeed ; and including Asher's and Bledsoe's to the east, and Mauldin's and Sevier's to the north of the Bluff, they were all within a radius of less than forty miles.

Taking the station at the Bluff or Nashville as our stand-point, and casting our eye around, we see where there are or have been *stations* and *clearings*.

Directly to the *north*, the first is Freeland's, then Denton's.

North-west is another Freeland's or Bosley's, then the two Robertsons' and Joslin's.

West is Cockrill's, Hodge's, Johnson's, Dunham's.

South-west, Brown's, Mayfield's, Castleman's, (on west fork of Mill Creek.)

South, Thompson's.

South-east, Rains', Buchanan's, Caffrey's; Clover Bottom: Hays', Donelson's, (Jackson's.)

East of Cumberland: Hickman's, Hays', Drake's, Rock Castle or General Smith's, Asher's, Bledsoe's, Greenfield's, Hall's, Zeigler's, (Blackemore's, McMurray's,) Mansker's, (Donelson's again.)

North-east, Neelly's.

North-north-east, Eaton's, Stump's, Rounceval's.

The number of emigrants who arrived in the fall of 1789, and during the present year, was such, that inquiries were made as to the population of the District. The estimate was "about seven thousand." This included men, women, and children; white and black. The number of men able to bear arms was stated to be little under one thousand.

The strength of the southern tribes of Indians, from data furnished by Indian agents, was "fifty thousand men." The Creeks and Cherokees were the most numerous of these tribes. (We think the number of warriors exaggerated.)

In many respects the prospects for the settlers on the Cumberland seemed bright indeed, and cheering. The few surviving stationers concluded "that the worst was past;" they encouraged their recently arrived friends in the belief that they would not have to suffer the horrors and cruelties of savage warfare, as others had, during long years of feebleness and exposure. And yet these "old citizens" failed not to advise their friends "not to be too adventurous, or adventure-*some*," as is the truly expressive word, used by one entitled to speak. The savages were not to be trusted; they knew nothing of the sentiment of real love for the white man; and the machinations of the Spaniards were deep, mischievous, and yet operative.

General Robertson, and others in his council and confidence, had information as to the aims and practices of the Spanish officers, and Creek and Cherokee chiefs, which kept alive the spirit of watchfulness and distrust, though the feeling generally pervading was, that little danger of being shot by the Indians need to be feared. The chief care and guardianship should be given to their horses. These, the Indians *would* steal—" they could not refrain from it"—and in the accomplishment of these thefts, they were exceedingly cunning and successful; they caught them " in the range," they unharnessed them from the wagon or the plough, they led them away from the stables; and this when the owners or drivers were at but a few rods distant. They could tread upon dry leaves as noiselessly as a cat, and were careful not to break a limb or turn a branch of a bush with its leaves out of its *natural position*. Old hunters and cautious spies cultivated to the utmost acuteness their own eyes and ears. They could discover the misplacement of a bush or a leaf, and prudence required that attention should be given to such proofs of man or animal having been there. Their dogs taught them much; and the dogs likewise became astonishingly wise under the training of their owners, and from observation of the cautious steps and listening attitude of their masters. The pioneers had "troops," "large packs of watchful and faithful dogs." "The number of dogs exceeded the number of people." These trusty and wakeful guardians often gave the first alarm of "Indians about." Cattle also snuffed the presence of savages, and gave signs of fear. Next to the dogs, the horses seemed to have the quickest eye, the keenest scent, and ears pricked up to catch the sound of step or breathing of living creature near by. When a hunter paused, held his breath, and listened, the dog or the horse would do the same. They would squat and crouch to the ground, as if possessed of the very thoughts of their master, or awaiting to hear or see the foe or the game.

In hundreds of instances the spies and hunters gave credit to their dogs and horses for timely alarm and safe deliverance from the insidious Indian. They took great pride in telling of these escapes, and in praising the faithful animal. In talking of these events—whilst they patted the dog on the head, or smoothed down the mane of the horse—it seemed indisputable that the listening, devoted creatures actually understood the language, and appreciated the compliments. We regret that we cannot rehearse these tales as the hunters told them. At each station, the women had some most marvellous story of this kind, and these made up a portion of the interesting reminiscences of travel or settlement in the wilderness, or of passing events. The early settlers never complained of the " troops of dogs" and the " music of the hounds." They were the playmates of the children, the companions of the men, the guardians of all.

In this year the Indians manifested a desire to trade; they brought in venison and skins to exchange for powder and lead, for blankets, stroud, and calico, for tomahawks, beads, and vermilion.

In this friendly disposition the settlers were disposed to indulge them. There were certain Indians, long known to the settlers, in whom confidence could be placed; but others came, always with the introduction, "White man's friend!" who needed to be watched. The keen eye and discerning mind of old pioneers, men or women, would detect a treacherous look or gesture of these "enemies in disguise." The women were sometimes far more watchful and successful in detecting than the men. The dogs could scent out and indicate an enemy in disguise. The deceitful foe would shrink at the snuffing and scrutiny of the faithful friend of the white man. The dog would notice an Indian's countenance, the objects upon which he gazed, and watch him at every step. He would stand between him and the white person, or by the side of his own protectors and protégés. He would do so, to guard the horse. Invaluable to the early settlers was the faithful cur and the persevering hound! Although they discriminated, they never became entirely friendly to the Indians. Those who came to barter were warned not to irritate the dogs.

This opportunity for trading was made use of by some of the savages to steal horses. The Indians—all Indians—had a passion for horses. "They desired them, that they and their squaws might straddle, and pack, and travel upon his back, though so poor that every bone in his body might be counted."

Licenses to enter and trade in the Indian nations had been granted to various persons. Some of these "Indian traders" proved to be unworthy of trust. They were charged by the Indians with fraud in trading, they were suspected to have encouraged the thefts of horses, that they might share in the profits of resale to the Spanish agents or in the barter for skins in the nation. There was proof that some of the traders had grossly cheated the Indians, and given cause of offence. Of this the savages did not hesitate to avail themselves in excuse for some of their own acts. The law of compensation, or retaliation, is universal among Indians.

As these occurrences were producing irritation, ill-will, and danger, to white and red men, amendments to the License Law were suggested, but not immediately acted on; and the thefts continued.

The new emigrants, to whom the horses generally belonged, were greatly irritated: they became belligerent and anxious to fight. They had never endured perils and hardships like the earlier settlers; they had not fought for the lands they were about to possess and cultivate; they had no "hair-breadth 'scapes" of which to tell; no contests with or victories over the savages of which to boast. They were not of that distinguished class of which Captain Rains spoke, who "fit, bled, and died," for this rich country. There was wanting in their experience and personal history the most interesting chapter of incidents, such as others took pride in relating, and all in hearing.

General Robertson had much difficulty to quiet some of these pugnacious spirits. He assured them it was wiser to endure the ills they suffered, than rashly aggravate and fly to others they knew not of. He and the older settlers had endured a thousand-fold more of hardships, sufferings, and loss, than any which had befallen the newly arrived : they advised to patience, to avoid threatening or rashness; that they were about to endanger their own lives and the peace and lives of others; they would aggravate every trouble; they were unacquainted with the traces, defences, and lurking-places of the Indians; they ought not to set the example of contempt to the authorities, to the wisdom and experience of the earliest stationers.

With such arguments, scarce restrained they the *headstrong*, that they had not rushed furiously into conflict, indiscriminately, with every Indian.

The first attempt of General Washington to form a treaty with the Creeks was a failure. Exertions were renewed through sundry persons, and especially by the embassy of Colonel Willett. By these attentions and solicitations the dominant chief, McGillivray, was prevailed upon to travel to New York, to enter into negotiations with the administration. The Government had furnished ample funds for the travelling expenses. This politic chief determined to make an impression. He prepared for a display; taking with him eight and twenty of the principal chiefs and warriors, armed, painted, and plumed, with silver bands on their arms and rings in their noses, with blanket and breech-clout, with moccasin and leggins, and tinkling ornaments: they were, indeed, the "cynosure of all eyes."

The administration had been advised of the coming of the chiefs, and prepared to give them a hearty welcome, comfortable accommodations, and liberal entertainment. McGillivray was highly complimented, and his friendship and that of his people solicited as one of the " nations of the earth."

The *"Tammany Society"*—then but recently organized—made great preparations in Indian dresses and ornaments for this occasion. They came out with all their " savage paraphernalia," painted and dressed as Indians, with hatchets, war-clubs, bows and arrows, with nodding plumes of horse-tails, and hip-bands, red and blue. They, doubtless, thought themselves worthy of the envy of the *"Simon-pures."*

The *Grand Sachem* of the Tammanites was most " savagely arrayed." He was very rude, and nude indeed, for—*a sham.*

The Creeks received these attentions with stolid indifference, or with the *grunt*, which, whether it signifies little or much, they alone can tell.

The result was the treaty of August 17th, 1790; a treaty unsatisfactory to the Creek nation, and certainly not less so to the stationers on the Cumberland. By it a large territory was ceded—or "restored?"— to the Creeks; presents given and annuities engaged. By a private article, McGillivray received a hundred thousand dollars, in satisfaction of his demands for losses of property. This treaty gave great offence to the people of Washington District. The "restoration" of an extensive wilderness, which the savages needed not—which these Indians had never dared to occupy—their *claim* to which they had parted with by several treaties, for considerations paid to them, and in the execution of which great inconvenience and loss must ensue to white settlers—this article in the treaty was condemned, and the administration charged with ignorance, partiality, and truckling—ignorance or contempt of former treaties—of the rights of purchase and settlement—partiality to the Indians, and of obsequiousness to Spanish, French, and English artifice and flattery.

A treaty having thus been made with the Creeks, the Cherokees were informed, through agents, of the desire or willingness to hold a treaty with them. Major King, of Knoxville, was commissioned by Governor Blount to visit the chiefs of that nation, inform them of the New York treaty with the Creeks, and urge upon them the duty and advantages of engaging in a treaty for permanent peace and boundaries, exchange of prisoners, and compensation for property stolen.

The Cherokees were then divided into Upper and Lower, or Northern and Southern parties. The Hanging-Maw was the leader of the North, and Little Turkey, of the South.

Upon Major King's return, he reported that the Indians professed great willingness to enter into a treaty, and that they should come prepared to take their white brethren by the hand and smoke the pipe of peace.

Governor Blount had been made acquainted with the views of the Administration in contemplated intercourse with the Indians; "a course of forbearance and conciliation," to "wean and win" them from the Spaniards. In pursuing this line of conduct, the Governor encountered many difficulties—was perplexed, embarrassed, vexed; was catechized, criticised, and chastised. Closing his gubernatorial term after unwearied watchfulness and labor, he received a highly complimentary address from the Legislature, and the confirmation and enhancement of

These lands were within the boundaries of the State of North Carolina, as acknowledged by civilized man; they were within the limits of the United States, as recognized by recent treaties between the chief powers of earth. These thousands of peaceable and industrious farmers had entered upon the lands, only after considerations had been paid to the roving savages "to quiet their claim of title," and purchase their good-will. They had received grants from the State of North Carolina, to which the sovereignty and domain of right did appertain; they asked the privilege to stay and have granted unto them the rights of preëmption. They were willing to buy again, and pay a second time. They insisted that they should not be violently thrust out as *wrongdoers*, to gratify the vanity, or in the vain hope to secure the friendship, of savages who would not, and could not, worthily occupy these improvements. They believed the measures for their expulsion resulted from the artifices and inter-meddling of a nation whose emissaries were among these savages in dero-gation of right, of treaty, and the comity of nations.

We have thus presented, in condensed form, our views of the vexed questions to which Governor Blount had to turn his attention: questions more learnedly discussed in these log-stations, than by cabinets and heads of departments elsewhere.

There was one offshoot of advancing civilization, or settlement, which the Governor had *orders* to arrest and extirpate, either by the military power of the government, or to advise the Creeks and Cherokees that they would be *permitted* to accomplish it "in their own way:" this was the contemplated settlement of the rich lands in the Great Bend of the Tennessee and around the Muscle Shoals, under the grant of three mil-lions and a half of acres by the State of Georgia to the Tennessee Land Company, composed of Cox and his associates, of which we have already taken some notice.

Influential men, and personal friends of Governor Blount, were inte-rested, directly or *indirectly*, in this large grant of valuable lands. The lands in Greene and Hawkins counties, entered in John Armstrong's entry-office, amounted also to the large number of three and a half mil-lions of acres, or not much less. Here were formidable interests against which the new Governor was called to contend. But to these was added Spanish jealousy and intrigue.

Spain had given countenance, but not much aid, to our War of Inde-pendence. She wished us success, that thereby the greatness of England might be diminished. But she lost not sight of her own interests at any moment of her inefficient participation in the struggle. Neither France nor Spain desired to see the States of the Confederacy grasping territory upon the western waters; and they expressed opinions quite unfavorable to the boundaries which we demanded in the negotiations for peace and independence.

The uneasiness of Spain, arising from a view of the extension of our western settlements, was early apprehended by our government. It was well understood that the principles of the two governments were antagonistic; the character, sentiments, pursuits, and habits of the two races so distinct, that they could never coalesce and prosper in union.

Spain exerted herself to accomplish three or four objects : First, to prevent these western settlements; second, to entice the settlers within her own acknowledged territory; third, to destroy them by savage warfare; and we may add, fourthly, to alienate and separate them from the people of the United States east of the mountains.

Beginning in the year 1785, the American Government has continued negotiations, or sought to negotiate with Spain for a more satisfactory adjustment of boundaries, and for the establishment of amicable relations upon the water and the land. Procrastination is the especial prerogative of Spanish diplomacy, therefore we at the present date are only *in medias res*. Five years more of tedious, prevaricating, and vexatious negotiations have to be endured, and five years of wearisome, wasting, and vexatious warfare by the Indians, imbittered and sustained by agents of Spain.

In the first instance, Spain advised that we should accept boundaries less extensive towards the west, that we might not settle here. But seeing the parties of emigrants crossing the mountains, selecting homes and erecting stations for defence, she, in the next place, commenced her operations with the southern Indians. This tampering began in 1784, or immediately after the termination of the American Revolution. They had the hardihood to attempt to justify some of their offensive practices.

We may here state that, by the treaty of 1763, Great Britain secured the right to navigate the river Mississippi, in its *whole extent*, and by the treaty of 1783, acknowledging American Independence, transferred this right to the United States; and that it was *subsequent* to this cession to our government (and in which she was a participant) that Spain received the cession of Louisiana and the Floridas from England. As a consequence, our right to the navigation was prior to the possession by Spain of the French and English territories named.

And yet Spanish posts were pushed up the river above the thirty-first degree of north latitude, (the southern treaty-boundary of the United States,) and the Spanish authorities set up a claim to country far to the north of that degree. This pretence of right they based upon the fact, that Spanish troops had taken some few feeble stations from the British during the Revolutionary War, which places were within our boundaries. To this we replied, "You engaged in that war as *our ally*, to aid us in securing the country for *ourselves*, and not for you, or for France, our better ally and friend. We never contemplated a *partition*, nor will we ever agree to it."

Having acquired in this unwarranted and covert mode possession of several prominent positions upon the Mississippi, her artful officers endeavored to *entice* the early western settlers to desert their own country and their new homes, and accept liberal grants from Spain, free of all charge, with a guaranty of the free exercise of their religion, and the free navigation of the Mississippi. Having had little success by this artifice, the *third* measure, which, indeed, had at all times been hinted at, and partially in operation, was to "let slip the dogs of war"—excite the Indians to make havoc in these settlements; "drive them either back across the mountains, down into our swamps and dominion," or "kill them every one." "Drive us back, or to the devil!" said Captain Rains.

Having made little progress towards the attainment of these aims, she closed the mouth of the river. She denied our right to navigate it below the thirty-first degree, and even proceeded to dispute the right as far down as that degree of latitude, although the territory upon the east side was American territory.

We may understand the fears, the objects, the policy, and conduct of Spain, disguised as far as it was possible at the time, but fully made manifest in the end, acknowledged, indeed, without repentance, and with little sense of shame. This will be shown in due time.

"At some periods, when she had hopes of effecting a separation, her officers paid the most flattering attention to our leading men, and granted commercial privileges which none but themselves could grant.

"At other times, when that hope faltered, hosts of savages were sent upon our frontiers, supplied with all the munitions of war, and encouraged to 'bloody murder.'

"When afraid of the rumored invasion by the western people, they recommended to the Indians peace with their neighbors, the Americans. But as soon as difficulties appeared less formidable, they again excited them to war and mischief.

"Sometimes the leaders of our unprotected settlers, pretending esteem for their officers, and a wish to be under their government, would procure an abatement of the horrors of war. But *liberty* to these settlers was of more value than all the benefits the Spaniards had it in their power to bestow. And though leaders might, in calamitous times and circumstances, think proper to *temporize,* they never could entertain the serious wish to coalesce with them. All the wealth of the Spaniards could not bear comparison with the single article of liberty."*

The instructions from the American Government to all her officers in the South was, to treat the Spaniards with politeness, and " to act only on the *defensive* toward the Indians, for (or from) fear of offending the Spaniards, who had unjustifiably taken them under their protection."

The patience of the Administration was greatly tried by all these annoyances and artful practices of Spain. The patience of the settlers was worse tried, and at times exhausted.

The forbearance of our Government at that day was the first instance exhibited, and with happy results, of the political apothegm, "masterly inactivity."

The Indians occupied territory intermediate the Spanish and American settlements. The Spaniards had the ear of most of the chiefs and warriors; had long practiced "the giving of gifts;" had traded with them, and pledged the friendship and power of the king to protect them and their lands against the encroachments of the Americans. Spaniards did not require large tracts of land for cultivation, as did the Americans. "Indians and Spaniards could ride the same pony, and the Indian on before; but Americans would always be first, or, if they got on behind, they seized the reins, and managed all." And thus both Spaniards and Indians were jealous and afraid of their *own destiny,* and of that of the Americans; and these sentiments made them, for a time, "wondrous kind," and "to each other true."

The policy of our Government was to make them "love us more, and each other less;" "not to force them to a closer intimacy and union."

" The said Hood's" quotation is apropos here, though he applied it to another case : " Heap coals of fire on all their heads, and they'll soon burn up with vengeance toward each other."

The Spaniards were, in every view, in the wrong. But the impudent and inexcusable wrong was by entering American territory, establishing posts at the Walnut Hills and other places on the river, with the infamous aggravation of intermeddling with Indians and others living within the United States. But more of this elsewhere.

We will show most clearly the overruling Providence in all these affairs.

We advance to the fall of this year, and quote from the narrative of John Carr in the South-Western Monthly :

---

* Haywood.

"Benjamin Williams settled about two miles and a half from where Gallatin now stands, near where James House now resides. The Indians came in the night, killed him, his wife, and children, and I believe a negro or two. One boy ran up the chimney, and kept concealed until they left. *Philip*, the negro, is still living, and the only one of that family who escaped.

"Mr. Samuel Wilson had settled about one mile north-east from where Gallatin is, and was out the morning after the Indians had killed the Williams family. He had not heard of the murder, although it was not more than three miles off. He was looking for his stock in the cane, in the direction of where Williams' family had been killed. He heard some one riding toward him in the cane. He took to a tree, and immediately an Indian came in view, on horseback. Being a fine marksman, and having a good rifle, he fired and killed the Indian. He then hallooed at the top of his voice to "surround them, boys, surround them!" and ran for home. The Indians broke and ran likewise.

"I believe it was in this year the Indians killed John Edwards, at the place where Salem meeting-house now stands, four miles north-west of Gallatin."*

---

* We have no other authority for murders in 1790. Mr. Carr lived at the time in the vicinity of Gallatin, was personally acquainted with the persons killed, and his memory remarkably correct.

CHAPTER XXI.

1791.

IN February of this year, President Washington signed the commission appointing Robertson a Major-General of the United States for the District of Mero, in the territory south of the River Ohio. He accepted the commission, which superseded the one he had for some years held under North Carolina.

The office of District Attorney was intrusted to *Andrew Jackson,* Esq.*

During the past year, the Creeks seldom came to the settlements to trade. It was evident that the treaty of New York was not to be faithfully observed. That a part of the nation denounced it as soon as informed of its nature, was known to our Government. That the opposition party was encouraged, if not organized, under Spanish and British influence, there were some reasons to suspect. Additional presents and increased annuities were given to some of the chiefs, to increase and confirm their friendship, *if possible.* Our enemies were close observers of these measures; and, within our own territories, with our own Indian population, they had their traders and agents.

A *rival* to McGillivray had appeared. He was impudent, mean, and crafty; but as yet without any high military rank, or high-sounding title. He was regarded as "the imp of the Britishers," among the southern Indians. But he must "do some *great thing,*" or receive some magniloquent soubriquet, else he could not rule and shine among the Creeks.

He is advised "to travel;" so he sails for England. In due time, he will return.

---

* Gov. Blount entertained a very favorable opinion of "Mr. Jackson." In a letter to Gen. Robertson, subsequent to this date, in regard to infractions of the treaty of Holston by white persons, he writes: "Let the District Attorney, Mr. Jackson, be informed: he will be certain to do his duty, and the offenders will be prosecuted."

In his absence, the agents of mischief were at work. The influence and power of McGillivray were on the wane. The evidences of a hostile spirit were on the increase. Between the Creeks and the Georgians, the conflict had begun—or had not ceased. And past experience warned the people in this territory that the warfare would not be confined to that region or people, but that the Cherokees would be involved in it, and both Creeks and Cherokees would make invasions of the feeble and exposed settlements in this territory.

The Governor having had the friendly conference with the Chickasaws and Choctaws at Nashville, desired to assemble the Cherokees also, with a view of mutual explanation, and the hope of terminating the system of irritation and roving for plunder, which so often and so surely led to murder.

The Governor's wishes were communicated, through several friendly Indians, to the chiefs of the nation. By some of the traders he sent talks and presents. There were men in the nation—red and white—who were "black-hearted rascals." These, whether traders with licenses from our own Government, or traders and agents covertly of Spain or England, or savages who thirsted for blood, having heard of the contemplated conference, set themselves busily to work to defeat the meeting.

They endeavored to dissuade all the chiefs, head-men, and warriors, from visiting the Governor, and from holding any "talk" with him. The place proposed for the meeting was Knoxville.

The enemies of the conference were the enemies of peace. They industriously circulated a report that the purpose of Governor Blount and the advocates of the meeting was to assemble them on that side of the river, so that the soldiers and settlers might suddenly fall upon and destroy them. And even if the Governor and some other good and reliable white men might be disposed to treat the Indians kindly, and do them no harm, yet they could not restrain all others from taking revenge for injuries which had been done to the settlements there and upon the Cumberland.

Governor Blount, believing that many of the traders were, at least, not acting a friendly part for the Americans, issued a proclamation revoking their licenses and recalling them from the nation. Some hastened to "make use of the unrighteous mammon," before they left the nation. They asserted or intimated that they were recalled, because of their friendship for the Indians, and they greatly encouraged belief in the rumor of evil and treacherous designs at the proposed treaty.

To counteract the mischief likely to result from such falsehoods, it was important that some person of character should promptly visit the nation.

"Who shall go for us?" was again the question. Governor Blount answered his own question: "General Robertson must go." Others said the same: "General Robertson is the man." And General Robertson hastened his preparations for the embassy, and was ready to depart on the 8th of June.

In July, 1777, fourteen years prior to this date, he had undertaken a similar mission into this Indian country. He went then as Ambassador from Watauga, or the State of North Carolina. He goes now as the Representative of the Territory, a large portion of which had at that time never been visited by an American, but which Robertson and his associates had recently honored by their presence, and made known to the great powers of the earth as a place of loveliness and distinction; a place where the women should be praised for beauty and virtue, and where the men should be distinguished by knowledge and power. He goes from Nashville, to "the beloved town," Chota.

He visited the nation; was welcomed by the chiefs, many of whom became acquainted with him at his former visit. Others seemed gratified at the opportunity of forming his acquaintance. All knew him by reputation, as the head-man of the Cumberland settlements; that war had been waged against that settlement, and that his own life had been repeatedly in danger. He came, as "a Brave:" for this they honored him. He came as a Friend: for this they welcomed him. He came as an Honest Man: for this they trusted him.

He inquired for the slanderers, for the cheats, for the mischief-makers. He convinced the Indians that the licenses of the traders had been recalled, because they were men with false hearts and two faces. "General Washington, the great father of all our States and nations, has instructed Governor Blount to see that the Cherokees are not cheated. He wishes his red children to improve their homes, cultivate lands, have cattle, and live quietly by the side of the white people. The Cherokee country is all within the limits of the United States, and you must not open your ear to the words of agents from other countries. England and Spain and France are nations a great way off—on the other side of the big water. You cannot see their head-man or king: your principal chiefs can go and see Washington—he is the red man's friend; Governor Blount is your friend; I am your friend. None of you shall suffer harm at the treaty or by the way. If any of your young men act bad, you must punish them. If any of our people act wrong, we will punish them."

By his proper bearing, intercourse, and assurances, the purposes of his mission were so far successful that the Indians agreed to attend at the place appointed, about the present site of the city of Knoxville. They

23

came in considerable force. The entertainment was liberal; the interviews friendly. The result was the Treaty of Holston, of July 2d, 1791.

The treaty was forwarded to the President, by him submitted to the Senate, and confirmed November 11th, 1791. The President issued his proclamation commanding its faithful observance. With the Cherokees there seemed now reason to anticipate peace and good neighborhood. To the stationers upon the Cumberland the prospects were cheering. They hoped the Creeks would not come so far to indulge a mere passion for robbery and thirst for blood. They would probably be influenced to some good degree by the friendly disposition of the Cherokees, and by the fact that they could not easily make incursions into these settlements without such expeditions coming to the knowledge of the Cherokees. The stationers in fact began to regard the Cherokees as in positions to serve for them as a *cordon militaire*. "The said Hood" was not of this opinion: "Picketings sharpened at each end, and both ends pointing this way," said he.

The hostile spirit of the Creeks was, however, on the increase. Their depredations and bloody deeds were rather confined to Western Virginia, some few places in Kentucky. Mr. John Farris and his brother, of Lincoln county, were fired on by a small party of Creeks, who were returning from "a horse-thieving tour" into Kentucky. John Farris was wounded in the shoulder by one ball, and his arm broken by another.

Horses were stolen from the various settlements upon the Cumberland. These losses were regarded as very grievous, and the owners were greatly irritated. Some were of the impression that the thieves were Cherokees, and others believed the Cherokees received and secreted stolen horses. They saw no distinction between Cherokees and Creeks: they were all Indians, living in the same region, all along to the south of our settlements. Creeks were intermarried and mixed with Cherokees at the towns whence the thieves and murderers came. Several influential Cherokees were avowedly hostile. The excitement among the settlers was on the increase. The sentiment of Edmeston was, that "None of the Indians were to be trusted—they are all rascals; none of them can get a lick amiss."

Information had been received of the celebration, at Lookout and Chickamauga towns, of some captures made in Kentucky and at other places. The Creeks had returned there and held a scalp and a war dance. They paraded some scalps taken from Cumberland settlers. These events took place within a few days after the conclusion and signing of the treaty at Holston. Indeed, before the conference was concluded, information was received that the Creeks had in that very week killed the family of Mr. Miller, upon the Rolling Fork of Cumberland. In this one slaughter were Mr. Miller, his wife, and four or five children. John Thompson was killed when working in his corn-field, a few miles south of Nashville. This was in June. Within the present limits of Davidson and Sumner counties, thirteen persons were killed in the months of June and July.

A most savage and brutal inhumanity was manifested in many of these cases of murder. They had repeatedly cut off the heads of their victims, and inflicted many ghastly wounds; they always scalped when they could, repeatedly inflicting this mark of dishonor with so little danger to life, that in these settlements there were from fifteen to twenty persons who for years survived the rude and bloody treatment. But now there is a savage feeling manifested not hitherto indulged: they skin the entire head—they abuse and expose the bodies of females as they had never done before. Whenever they captured or killed a white man who was known to be a *spy*, they "wreaked vengeance upon him." As Judge Haywood says, they "chopped him," "they made mince-meat of him," "wolf-bait." Castleman said, "They will hack you with hatchets, riddle you with bullets, and stick arrows in you, till you look and feel like the 'fretted porcupine.'" This old hunter and quick-sighted spy would talk in this style, cheerfully or seriously, of the perils to which he and other adventurous pioneers exposed themselves. They did not dread extreme and protracted torture. They knew the Indians would not spare them as prisoners; they would certainly kill them, and this by many wounds; therefore, their teaching and resolution were, "avoid being taken alive, but if you cannot escape, sell your life dear; make them pay in advance."

Torture by fire, we believe, was not practiced: we have found only two instances *reported*. But the very savage spirit which was repeatedly indulged upon those who were killed this year, aroused the people to insist upon more efficient measures to prevent or punish the depredators. "We have been negotiating for peace. The Creeks entered into solemn treaty at New York, and the Cherokees at Holston, and yet not a week has passed without either a robbery or a murder at some place within the Territory! What have we gained by American Independence? What by our transfer from an appendage of Carolina to a Territory of the United States? What good has resulted from the treaties, and from all the presents thrown away upon these savages? 'Pearls thrown before swine, who have only turned to rend us.'" Such were the exclamations of the suffering settlers, uttered in grief and bitterness. They were asked to suffer in patience! Officers of the General Government were sometimes spoken of as having a jealous eye more constantly and keenly turned upon their fellow-citizens than upon the Indians. They were frequently

warning the people not to trespass even by hunting upon Indian territory! The restitution to the savages of such extensive wild woods was
a grief and vexation, not to be endured in patience and in silence, nor at
all. By this very recent treaty, July 2d—under the instructions or expressed wishes of the Administration—the Indian boundary was approached
to the very edge of the Cumberland settlements, "from the top of the
Cumberland Mountain, direct to the Cumberland River where the
Kentucky Road crosses, down said river to the ridge which divides the
Cumberland from Duck River, *forty miles above* Nashville. . . Thence
by a south-west line to mouth of Duck River."

This treaty was made under power reserved to the General Government. The States, as such, could no longer exercise the "treaty-making
power." The Territory could less pretend to any such prerogative. But
"it matters not by whom or what authority treaties were made, they
exercised little restraint upon lawless spirits;" they insured not perfect
friendship or peace. Among both red and white men, it must be
admitted, there were turbulent spirits—men of violent passions, who
would not yield to arguments, and regarded with indifference the gentle
persuasives to peace.

"They had a contempt for all cowards!" This was the speech uttered
by some white men, and echoed by some of the red men; and, as is often
the case, such are the persons to provoke difficulties, by which better
men may sometimes be involved, and the braggarts "shuffle out of harm's
way." "Sneaks like to see brave men fight." Here were men who were
"open-mouthed" and bitter in their denunciations of the Administration;
talking loudly of its imbecility at home, and of its obsequiousness to
foreign nations, and dread of Indian tribes within its own borders. And
yet, when the country called for soldiers, some of these bravado orators
could never meet that call but by "*hired substitutes.*" They were, however, few in number. We know whereof we affirm.

We acknowledge that the causes for discontent, real and apparent,
were many. It is not at all surprising that many prudent and really
brave men were much excited, and ready to go at a moment's notice
where duty called, or an enemy could be punished. Many had lost
relatives and friends or property—they had wrongs to avenge, but preferred to do it under the sanction of authority.

The interference of Spain and England with savages within our own
boundaries, was, indeed, insulting and mischievous; an infringement of
national rights, in violation of treaties, contrary to international law—a
gross indignity. Such conduct would not be endured now, "no, not for
an hour."

But we must remember that the government was but recently organized; was then examining its powers—only beginning to understand and put them forth.

Forbearance is an excellent virtue at all times. It was the grace of wisdom then. We were the advocates of new principles, new theories, and a novel experiment. The sovereignty of the people here was to startle the sovereignty of people and of rulers "by Divine right" in other lands.

Washington was wise and patient. He foresaw the day, not distant, when other nations might become our debtors in a long account of patience. The views of President Washington, which entirely disapproved all acts of retaliation upon the Indians, and all hostile incursions into their country, were communicated to Governor Blount, and through him to the officers of the territory.

The Governor earnestly besought General Robertson to use his influence with his fellow-citizens on the Cumberland, that the wishes of the President might be respected.

Doubtless, some of the intricacies and perplexities of the negotiations with Spain were suggested to the Governor, and to General Robertson. They were to observe the treaty, conciliate the Indians, not even "rail at the Spaniards;" withdraw the Indians from the Spaniards, and attach them to the United States.

General Robertson was directed to hold "talks" with them; make presents as he should judge advantageous; supply them with provisions, powder, and lead. His accounts, sustained by proper vouchers, would be paid by the United States.

General Robertson endeavored faithfully to carry out these instructions. But he had to encounter strong opposition from neighbors and friends.

The "pacific policy" was, by some, most fiercely condemned as "the counsel of the foolish shepherd to his unarmed sheep, when the wolves were devouring them—a fat wether, an old ewe, and a few small lambs: These will satisfy their thirst for blood. If they waste the wool in reaching the flesh, do not bleat; the *traps are set;* we'll catch them by and by."

Indeed, it is not strange that there were few among the settlers who could understand and approve this policy; and it was no difficult task to produce a strong prejudice against it; and, consequently, some distrust of the ability and friendship of the Administration for these outposts and persecuted settlers.

They said the policy could emanate only from persons at a distance, and unacquainted with the exigencies of the occasion, who had no conception of the sufferings of the people, and who indeed seemed determined not to believe the half that was told of Indian outrages. The opinion of General Knox, Secretary of War—that "the whites were almost invariably the aggressors, and the Indians the injured party"—was supposed by many to be the sentiment also of Washington. The knowledge of this sentiment was not withheld from the Indians and Spaniards. It was calculated greatly to countenance and encourage these parties, and to irritate or dishearten the settlers.

They had never known the quiet protection of a strong paternal government, and now the strong arm of the "regular army" was to be used to thrust American citizens—whole families—thousands of worthy people, from homes they had selected in the wilderness. The population upon the Cumberland was too limited in numbers (if there had been any disposition to do so) to have attempted settlements south or west of the recent treaty limits; but they sympathized with their friends on the east side of the Mountain, who were disturbed by the Indians and reproved by the Government.

By the treaty of Hopewell, the Creeks who resided within the boundaries of the United States were very properly taken under the protection of our Government. The Spaniards had the consummate folly to make this a matter of complaint. In diplomatic correspondence, it was alleged as sufficient cause of displeasure to His Catholic Majesty. And how or why? Because Spain, in some earlier treaty with the Creeks, had guaranteed to them the protection of Spain! This was characteristic of the insidious policy of that Government. Upon the very close of the great treaty by which England, France, Holland, Spain—the principal powers of earth—recognized the introduction of the United States into the "family of nations," this Spanish Government, well knowing the territorial limits and the denationalized state of these savages, in the year 1784 enters into a solemn treaty, the main purpose of which was to encourage them to the indulgence of much arrogance and pride, and to set at defiance the proper authority of the Government in which they lived.

The theory and practice of *protectorates* have undergone much discussion and improvement since that day. And so in regard to treaties of purchase and cession of territory. We have had occasion to mention several treaties which were made between *private citizens* and so-called chiefs, head-men, and warriors of Indian tribes. The States, and finally the General Government, overruled or revised these transactions, seized and confiscated the territory so acquired, claiming that the rights and benefits of such private treaties should inure to *the State*. This was well enough. But we cannot avoid the opinion that in these treaties the one party was no more pragmatic than the other; and that the rights of private citizens, (white men,) in possession of these lands, were more entitled to respect than any rights of *savage nomads*, (red men.)

But we are willing to leave this suggestion to political casuists, and turn our attention again to treaties entered into by "high contracting parties"—the Government of the United States, and Ocon-es-to-ta, Big-Paunch or Hanging-Maw, the Mad-dog, *and other dogs*.

Perhaps it was no more than "in duty bound;" but it was the pleasure and the effort of the Federal officers of the territory, and of the "talking friends" of the Administration or of the new Constitution, to inculcate the opinion or awaken the hope that there would be found far more dignity and weight in a treaty formed by Commissioners of the *United States*, than could attach to or result from one in which only a single State participated. They seemed to expect that some marvellous wonder-working virtue would go forth from a treaty thus sanctioned, which should heal all the infirmities and exorcise all the demons in all the bodies of all the Creeks and all the Cherokees. But these parchments were not composed of leaves from the tree sanctified to "the healing of the nations."

There were treaties of limits and boundaries, but still there were trespasses. There were treaties of amity and peace, and yet there was no end to the depredations and the murders.

President Washington promptly sought for information as to the causes of these protracted wars. His earnest wish was to discover, and, if possible, remove the grounds of offence. He well knew that Indian warfare was savage, cruel, remorseless. He knew it had been prosecuted here for—"lo, these many years." He desires to put an end to it. He seeks for information through the Indian agencies. He learns that the boundary lines in the State of Georgia are not to be run. The Commissioners on behalf of the Government were ready, but the hostile party threatened a forcible resistance. The Treaty of New York is openly denounced. The power and influence of McGillivray had to yield for the present to this opposition. His *rival* had been abroad, had visited England, enriched himself with goods and a *double title*, and now proclaims himself "*General Bowles, Director of the Affairs of the Creek Nation!*" The travelled monkey!

He boldly announces that he is clothed with full authority from the British Government to conclude a treaty for the Creek Nation. He would engage for a revocation of their treaty with the United States;

their lands should be restored; the lines should not be run. He used
" great swelling words;" he was the embodiment of power to do all these
things ! He made liberal distribution of goods, and was attracting much
attention, and increasing the hostile feelings of the nation. He denounced McGillivray—or everywhere declared that he had been imposed upon, cheated, if not bribed, at the Treaty of New York. On the
26th October he addressed a letter to the United States Commissioners
who were in waiting at Rocklanding; and, with impudence like that he had
shown among the Cherokees, *he* is ready to form a treaty with the United
States, but the former one should not be executed; and concludes with
an array of all his titles, "*General* and *Director.*"

McGillivray and some of the friendly chiefs insisted that Bowles had
never been chosen a chief by the nation. The Commissioners asserted
that he must be an impostor, a liar. Bowles said that McGillivray had
deceived the nation; but others suspected that he was the one attempting to practice a gross imposition.

It was, indeed, believed Spain had gone this length in her intermeddling
with Indian affairs; but " the American Commissioners discouraged the
idea that Bowles had assurances of support from the Government of
England." An incredulous set were they.

That Bowles had received some encouragement from a high source we
cannot wholly discredit. The British Government was certainly encouraging the northern Indians to war against us. Posts were withheld,
which by treaty should have been given up; and the information of a
contemplated league between northern and southern Indians to make war
against the United States, traced it to British counsels. If they would
do the greater, why not the less ?

The Administration was concerned at the complication of Indian wars.
The complicity of England and Spain was becoming more evident and
troublesome. The benefits which had been expected to result from the
interviews and engagements with McGillivray, seemed now to have vanished. His faithfulness and friendship were distrusted by many.

The Government was preparing an expedition against the northern
Indians. The exposed and suffering people here, complained a little that
their situation was not understood, or was disregarded by the Administration. They insisted that there was as hostile feeling rankling in the bosom
of the southern Indian, as in the northern. There were evidences of
this one sentiment being rapidly on the increase, in both sections. Emissaries passed from one quarter to the other, and measures seemed to be
contemplated for a general Indian war.

The aim and counsel of Washington was, by no means to aggravate the present difficulties on either hand : do nothing which would enable England or Spain to draw the Indians into closer intimacy; no act of which either of those Governments could avail itself to our prejudice.

He wished the settlements in Kentucky and on the Cumberland to become peaceful, neutral ground, and yet a barrier to intercourse between the savages north and south.   Persons of turbulent disposition must not go from the settlements into the nations.   All voluntary military expeditions against them must be broken up.

The friendship of the Chickasaws and Choctaws must be carefully preserved and strengthened.   These two tribes, although so removed from contact and intercourse with any of the then American settlements, had continued friendly.   The Chickasaws alone were in contact by treaty boundaries with our settlements, and they were much exposed to incursions and annoyance from the tribes who were unfriendly, and to the efforts of Spanish emissaries to turn them from us.

The Shawnees were settled on the west side of the Mississippi, and east of the Ohio; between them and the Chickasaws there was enmity which originated upon the banks of the Tennessee, was cultivated and increased by conflicts in the buffalo-paths and chase of game near the Cumberland or Shawnee River, and made traditional and perpetual by the naval or "canoe fight" upon the waters of that river, and the expulsion of the Shawnees from the southern country.

The Shawnees were more friendly with the Creeks and Cherokees than with the Chickasaws, and yet the usual route for intercourse between these remote tribes, whether by land or water, was through the Chickasaw country.   The friendship which the latter tribe maintained for the people of the United States, secured to them the hatred of other tribes and the unkind machinations of the Spaniards.

The warlike feeling was now predominant in all the Indian nations, and, under the influence and direction of England and Spain, was chiefly directed against the Western and South-western settlements in the United States.

A coalition was evidently suggested and discussed between tribes living many hundreds of miles apart, who were to be supplied with implements of war by sovereigns whose *provinces* were conterminous to ours.

The project was presented to the Administration to afford the Indian warriors an opportunity to indulge this their ambition—to offset the enemies' scheme.   Why should we not turn these same weapons against the instigators ?

The Government was preparing an expedition against the Indians in the Territory north-west of the Ohio, to be under the command of General St. Clair. The scheme proposed was, to offer inducements to the southern Indians to join the American army. "To set Indians to fight Indians;" "Greek to meet Greek." "Dog eat dog," said Rains, when he saw two "rascals" fighting.

If they chose to fight each other, well, if fight they would, and they seemed intent upon war somewhere and with somebody. If the southern tribes could be persuaded to unite with the regular army of the United States, so much the better. Such were the suggestions to the Administration. The humanity of this measure was condemned by at least one of the members of the Cabinet. Others contended for the right and propriety, and usage of nations, to seek or accept of *allies*. And as the Indians were ready to be used as instruments of wrong and cruelty, in the hands of our professed friends, but insidious foes, it was our privilege to wrest, if possible, such weapons from their hands, and turn them against the primary wrong-doers, or make them to "hack each other." If war is justifiable, we see not why the wisdom and morality of such a course should be condemned; why more than to set dogs and wolves to fight and kill each other, that thereby both may be prevented from falling upon and devouring the sheep. Their teeth were whetted for the carnage : make them to "gnaw their tongues for anger," and to bite and devour one another.

The Creeks and Cherokees were committed against us. Spanish craft outran American policy. Tecumseh and the Prophet, backed by gifts and promises, tempted the Creeks and Cherokees to war upon the United States, and to their expulsion and ultimate ruin. But the steps and process were marked with suffering and blood.

Consultations were held with *Piomingo*, the Mountain-Leader, or principal chief of the Chickasaw nation, about sending some warriors to join the army of the United States, north of the Ohio. He was informed that orders had been received from the War Department to enlist soldiers in this Territory, to be marched to Fort Washington or Cincinnati, and that it would be agreeable to the Department to have a company of Chickasaws marched to the same point, to act in concert with the United States troops. They should receive the same rations and pay as others in the service. Piomingo engaged to command a company of forty or fifty Chickasaw braves, to act as spies or render other service. He came with them to the residence of General Robertson, where they were more fully equipped, commanded, and instructed. Thence they marched to join General St. Clair.

The call upon the people of this exposed Territory to volunteer for such a distant service, did not meet with any enthusiastic response.

Strange it seemed, that settlements so feeble and so oppressed, now suffering, and threatened with greater suffering, should be called upon to send volunteers hundreds of miles to assist the "Regular Army" against a distant tribe of Indians, and at the same time be forbidden to chastise an enemy upon their own immediate borders, who had been engaged for near a dozen years in robbery and murder of this people! As might have been anticipated, there were but a few volunteers for such a service. Through the persuasions of Governor Blount and General Sevier, a small force was organized and marched. General Robertson raised no company here, but as Chickasaws agreed to go and were needed as spies, he promised to furnish some ammunition and other articles to those at home, for defence against their and our common enemies. "They should not be neglected during 'The Leader's' absence." Piomingo must have discovered such neglect of watchfulness, or want of discipline in the American army, as to give him and his warriors a disgust with the association or alliance, for on the 3d of November, only the day before the unfortunate battle, he and his few men withdrew, and were not in that sad defeat and bloody slaughter.

It is true, he had received intelligence that his country was threatened with an invasion, and he had already, with the approbation of the American commander, sent off twenty of his men, to hasten home for defence of their own families and nation.

The disastrous defeat of St. Clair occurred on the 4th day of November. He was completely routed, leaving six hundred slain, abandoning cannon and most of his baggage. It was a sad, sad affair. It greatly encouraged the warlike party North and South. The anxiety of the government, and of the settlers, was increased a thousand-fold.

Now it was seen that the efforts for a Northern and Southern *coalition* would be vigorously urged. If possible, it must be prevented, or its efficiency counteracted. The General Government now began to perceive more clearly the gathering storm-clouds.

This unfortunate affair was well calculated to give the Indians an extravagant opinion of their prowess. They had destroyed the regular army of the United States, commanded by a distinguished general of the Revolution. Hitherto Indians had been afraid of the "big guns," but now they had captured the whole park of artillery of the north-western army. With all their preparations and equipments, the whites were defeated, artillerymen, foot, and dragoons. If they could destroy such an army as that, what might they not do with the scattered settlements and their badly equipped militia?

These thoughts and questions were readily presented, and seemed likely now to obtain such replies as would favor the hostile parties, and the "grand coalition." The conduct of the Americans (as viewed by some) was not calculated to inspire dread or respect. Upon this recent battle-field the Americans were disgraced, the prestige of the regular army lost. So the Indians and some of their advisers thought, or wished to have it believed. The same counsellors and warriors now talked of the stationers with much contempt, real or feigned. "They have, for years, submitted to be robbed and murdered, and this they must have endured either from want of pluck or want of strength, and now they can be destroyed!"

At the Conference of Nashville, and Treaty of Holston, the Indians had learned much of the condition and resources of the settlements. They had reconnoitred some of the strong-holds. They knew how greatly exposed to attack were these pioneer settlers.

Why not now combine, North and South, and, with ample supplies promised, or to be obtained from British and Spanish agents, "wage an exterminating warfare upon these Virginians? The great King of the Spains has promised a restoration of our hunting-grounds. We can regain them, and expel these American intruders."

Many of the Indians lent a willing ear to these suggestions; they believed it could be done; that the settlers had wronged them—defrauded them; and so greatly wronged them as to enlist the sympathy and aid of such powerful and *disinterested* nations in their behalf. Now they must join the league—the confederacy. They prepared for an open declaration of war against the United States.

"They are a doomed race," said General Robertson to General Sevier. Captain Rains used his own peculiar phraseology to denounce Spaniards and Indians.

At the July session of the County Court of Davidson county, 1791, "John Rains is fined *five shillings*, paper money, for profane swearing," which sum he promptly paid, and it appears in the treasury accounts of the State.

General Robertson used to make excuses for "the *outspoken* blunders of Rains: he *would* call "a spade, a spade!" With him, Indians, whether dirty or painted, were "red rascals;" and Spaniards, "don'd rascals!" And on this occasion he told the court. "You may fine me, and confine me; I have no compliments to pay any *rascals*, whether Indian, Spaniard, or- *that* black-hearted one," (alluding to a personal enemy.) "A spade's a spade; a dog is a dog!" and then "he *let out*."

This blunt saying originated with Aristophanes, who lived in the fifth century before Christ. It is quoted by Scaliger and others. Scaliger ascribes it to Philip of Macedon. The entire phrase is in Latin : *"Ficum voco ficum, et ligonem, ligonem."* " I call a fig, a fig; a spade, a spade."

Measures were adopted this year to ascertain the population of Mero District. The returns made the whole amount to *seven thousand and forty-two.*

It becomes us to know something of the Indian nation commonly called *Shawnese,* or *Shawanese.* The earliest authority to which we can refer is *De Laet.* His work in Latin, *Novus Orbis,* or description of the West Indians, was published at Antwerp, in 1633. De Laet calls them Sawanos, and their language was pronounced Saw-wan-noo. They evidently came from the far south into Florida, into Georgia, across the Tennessee to the Cumberland, at each remove indicating their presence by their name affixed in the traditions of the country to some river or natural feature of the country traversed : Savanna, Savannehas, Sawana, Sewanne, and the like.

A branch of the nation passed on to Piqued, in Lancaster county, Pennsylvania, thence to Piqua on the Scioto, north of the Ohio, and was absorbed by the north-western tribes, or finally reunited with another portion of the original nation, which having been for a time associated with Creeks or Muscogees, came to the Tennessee above the Muscle Shoals. Thence they were driven by the Chickasaws, and for a time settled on the Sewanee, or Cumberland River, leaving tumeli and walls where they rested long enough to establish a town, or erect such earth or stone-work for defences.

The Chickasaws attacked them in their Cumberland settlements, and drove them across the Mississippi and the Ohio. At Shawnee town they had their principal settlement east of the Ohio, whence parties annually recrossed the river to hunt in the great park between the Ohio and Cumberland, and Tennessee.

At the time of the white settlements on Cumberland, 1780, some of the Shawnees were settled at Lance de Grace, or New Madrid, under Spanish protection.

Bartram and other writers say these Shawnees were taken as prisoners into Kentucky, and thence permitted to pass over the Mississippi. It is by the same authority stated that the "Sawanees" once possessed extensive territory, extending from the Kentucky River south-westward to the Mississippi; that the *Delawares,* or Leni-Lenaps, were united with the two branches of Sawanos, and occupied extensive hunting-grounds below the junction of the Ohio and the Mississippi.

They had been in the habit of crossing the rivers Mississippi and Ohio, to hunt in the vast prairies, or barrens and forests, between the Ohio and Cumberland, and Tennessee. And thus we find the Delawares camping on Indian Creek, (as we have stated,) a few miles south of Nashville, in 1780, the very first year of white settlements here. And a few years later we see them engaged in forming the Northern and Southern Confederacy, and in making war upon their old enemies, the Chickasaws.

Having, in their migrations, passed over so much of the continent, been in alliance or at war with so many tribes, they had acquired the language, or dialects, of various tribes and nations, and were thus better qualified to negotiate between distant nations, North and South.

Both of these tribes, Sawanees and Leni-Lenaps, were subjected and absorbed by the Five Nations. The Confederacy of the Five Nations consisted of Mohawks, Senecas, Tuscaroras or Onondagos, (as the three older tribes,) and of Cayugas and Oneidas, (as the younger.) The Delawares, or, as they called themselves, *Leni-Lenapes*, (*original people*,) exerted great influence over many other tribes, especially of the Northwest.

None but the Delawares and the Five Nations could call a *general council*. Wyandots and Hurons might call subordinate councils. Through the cunning policy of the Five Nations, (who have been called the *"Indian politicians,"*) the Delawares were involved in the League of the Six Nations, and claimed authority to sell lands to the whites. They urged the Confederacy between the Northern and Southern Indians. They were the first to come, camp near, and spy the whites on the Cumberland; perhaps active agents in the warfare waged against them, and in this attempted coalition. Thank God, they *failed*—failed in every way, and faded away.

CHAPTER XXII.

1792.

WE mean not to be charged with plagiarism by using the language of Judge Haywood as introductory to the chapter of 1792, when we say, "this year was distinguished by some ordinary and some extraordinary events." Ordinary events are such as occur to common observation and daily experience; extraordinary, such as are aside or beyond the usual line of order. Wars and rumors of war, however startling, were not acts or topics altogether novel to the stationers and farmers on the Cumberland. However frequently they had been aroused or painfully afflicted, their frequency had not engendered indifference. They could not say, "'Tis naught, 'tis naught!" There were men here who sometimes "*talked boastfully*," and endeavored to "laugh to scorn" those who spoke of dangers from an Indian war. These, however, are not known as having entitled themselves to be enrolled among "safe counsellors or brave soldiers." There is virtue in silence like unto the very excellency of wisdom; and, in charity to the reputation of some who are long since dead, we will ourselves practice this estimable grace, and record not how they "lived, to fight some *other* day." Our summary for the year is, "alarm, perplexity, havoc."

Omitting any enumeration of the many murders of the settlers in East Tennessee, (or Washington District,) we may give the aggregate of the killed in Mero as *sixty*; the wounded, many; captives, a few; and the loss or destruction of property, very great.

By reference to the map, the reader will be surprised to find so small a territory now partially occupied by the settlers. In the spring of 1780, with numbers less than four hundred, (counting every soul,) a few settlements and stations were commenced at the extreme positions indicated upon our sketch of the country. And now, after twelve years of contest, toil, and endurance, they have extended only in one direction different and farther than then; that was into Tennessee county upon the Red River, at Maulding's and vicinity. The number of improvements within the original distances and adjacent to the earliest stations, was of course increased. The population is now over seven thousand, and it is unquestionably true they had "room and verge enough," and needed not to go "to the regions beyond." A territory that supports its hundreds of thousands now, and can nourish richly its million, was no insignificant possession for that day and people. But they were a *representative* class. Each one considered himself very much like Robinson Crusoe,

"Monarch of all he *surveyed.*"

And, therefore, as the Kentucky line had been run on the east, and the broad river Tennessee was a natural boundary most suitable, to the west, they came very readily to the conclusion that an all-wise and kind Providence had called them here to homes for themselves, and to a rich inheritance for their posterity. They had come in to possess this goodly land. They found it the great park for wild beasts, and not the home of human beings. That God, to whom of right the forests and the prairies and the thousands and tens of thousands of cattle belonged, had kept it an open and inviting field for civilized man. *The heathen were not here*, but upon the other side of that long, broad, natural boundary, the big Tennessee; and now if they come here, "the children of Israel must drive them out." And they resolved to do it; but so great a domain and so rich, was not to be acquired and improved without a contest. We have seen "the beginning," but not "the end." The fierceness and bitterness of the strife is now to be felt and tasted. The *second war* is to be waged: its records, as of all wars, are stained with blood and scandalized by savage cruelty.

In the chapter of the preceding year, we have shown that the acts of hostility by the Creeks were continued acts of war and violations of solemn treaties; but now it becomes our duty to show how these were on the increase, and this by a more defiant and open avowal and declaration. War is to be proclaimed boldly, and prosecuted with rage.

In the outrages of the past year the Cherokees denied participation: in the earlier part of this year, the Creeks doubtless were the chief actors. The malign influence of foreign emissaries, *dona et arma ferentes*, acting upon the Indian love of crafty warfare, had so far urged forward the preparations by the hostile portion of the Creeks, that the few consistent advocates of the treaty of New York could not now induce them to lay aside the tomahawk and scalping-knife.

The power of McGillivray was greatly diminished: he sat in the shade of the great "Director," but not content to act a subordinate part. He could not deny that he had "feathered his nest" when the treaty was made; and the news began to leak out and run abroad that there was a private article added to the New York treaty, by which he had received the good round sum of *one hundred thousand dollars* and the rank of a *'Major-General.'* The result of this discontent among the treaty chiefs and warriors was, our Indian Department had to increase the gifts and annuities to the others. The fire has already burned as of a long time; its sweep, its fury, and destruction are on the increase. "The end is not by and by."

January 2d. In a letter from Governor Blount to General Robertson, he says: "I am glad to learn the good treatment you gave the Creek chief. . . . . I have heard that the Little Turkey chief has sent you a very friendly letter, and begs a supply of powder and lead; these things are trifles and had better be spared, if they can, than refused. But they are too much for an individual to give, therefore you ought to keep an account of all such expenditures."

The visit of this Creek chief had something of mystery about it. Of course he came with professions of friendship, and he was politely received and hospitably entertained by General Robertson. But his presence attracted attention, and awakened some suspicion. As an act of policy and prudence, the people were advised to attend to their usual avocations without any distraction or notice of his presence; while, as a matter of etiquette and espionage, Jonathan Robertson accompanied the chief very politely and observingly. If Robertson acted so well his part as not to allow the chief to detect the secret purpose of his companionship, the Chief conducted himself with so much propriety as not to utter a word or do an act to which exception could be taken. He came with professions of friendship to the settlers, was hospitably entertained, and departed as he came—*a spy.* This was Cot-ea-toy.

About the same time several Cherokees (whether head-men or not we cannot discover) came into the settlements; they likewise called upon General Robertson. They asked very respectfully "to be permitted to kill some game as they passed over the white man's lands," and thus enjoyed the privilege of spying out the strength and position of the settlers. These visits of Cherokees and of the Creek chief were made with sinister purposes.

Governor Blount had been practiced upon very artfully and very successfully in several instances; and we shall show, by extracts from his letters to General Robertson, that he continued to place confidence in the professions and treaties. General Sevier said, "The Governor is too confiding; he hopes against hope." The character of Watts was such as to have caused distrust of his sincerity; and the same might properly be

24

said of other chiefs who were so intimately associated with him.   At this period Governor Blount writes to General Robertson thus : "*January 5th.* . . . . Watts has sent me a *peace-talk* and a string of *white beads.* I believe he is in earnest," etc.

The Governor had a strange fancy in furnishing "trifles," and "accepting of trifles."   "Powder and lead" were the trifles, the bestowal of which upon the Indians he commended ; and, in return, the chiefs sent peace-talks and strings of white beads.   The General Government had done the same, and urged its own authoritative example to the observance of others.   Therefore we have no censure to bestow.   We cannot detract from the merits of Washington, and we would not set down aught to the prejudice of our Territorial Governor.

He seemed to yield to the sentiment of the Secretary of War, that the Administration was doing for these remote settlements "some great thing whereof they should be glad" and very thankful; inasmuch as a small troop of cavalry was sent across the mountains, to do nothing else than march through and around the settlements, and then come in and be quartered upon them.   In his letter of early date in January this year, after some remarks about the supply of arms, he adds, "The cavalry must find their own rations and forage, for which they will be paid."

Orders were issued by General Robertson for the organization of the militia in the three counties of Davidson, Sumner, and Tennessee.   The command of the General over the militia of the district did not, as may be seen by the Governor's orders to Major Sharpe, authoritatively and at all times include that troop of cavalry.   Sharpe's was a somewhat independent Government force.   The Major was directed to act in concert with the militia of the county in which duty might require him with his troop to be found.   The militia were distributed by General Robertson at the various stations in such numbers as could be afforded.   A force of five hundred men was reserved, and to be exempt from these special local duties at the stations, but subject to the "moment's call for any emergency."   Colonel Elijah Robertson was in command of this body of minute-men; Colonels Mansker and Winchester were subordinate officers. A separate command was given to General Robertson's favorite ranger, Captain Rains; he was stationed at his own house, about two miles south of Nashville, and near to Buchanan's Station.   He had two men always armed, and could call six or eight by the blast of his horn, and they were of that class of men who "were sure to come."

One of the earliest demonstrations of hostility upon these settlements this year, was at the extreme north-west, at the mouth of Red River, near the site of the collinated town of Clarksville.   .

Upon one of the small hills at the junction of Red and Cumberland Rivers, there had been settled for some years an early friend of General Robertson, and one whom we introduced to our readers eighteen years ago. By this time he ought to be recognized as an "old acquaintance." He had served throughout the War of Independence; he had fought with the Indians many a time and oft. He and his wife had escaped each with a slight wound. They were the happy parents of many children. They sought a home upon the very outskirts of the Cumberland settlements. They loved the pioneer and back-woods life. He had been a hunter from his youth; with a figure as erect as an Indian, spare of flesh, with a clear skin and bright blue eye, he was ever upon the watch. "Remarkably fond of his horse, of his wife, and gun, of his children, and his hounds," (for this is the inventory and the order of classification,) he retained his quick sight and hearing, which had detected the nightly approach of the enemy at the battle of Point Pleasant, in 1774. Here is *Valentine Sevier*, who had obtained the rank of Colonel, with his wife and children, and all his worldly wealth; he had erected houses for himself, his sons-in-law, and the families of Price and Snyder, (connections by marriage.)

The Indian outrages experienced in the District of Washington, and the chastisements sometimes inflicted upon the depredators by his brother, General Sevier, were communicated to Colonel Sevier. He was also quickly informed of the murders and thefts done in the settlements around Nashville. He had learned that these were on the increase, and that General Robertson was calling for volunteers, and especially with the view to select, or give advice in the selection of spies and rangers.

Colonel Sevier had in family five sons, and several sons-in-law. Three of his sons were of sufficient age to serve in the militia, and were ready to go where their father or their country called. Their father had occasionally met with General Robertson, after they had both selected their homes upon the Cumberland. When he heard of the call for "a turn-out of marksmen," he had but to say to his sons, "You have permission to go," and they hastened their preparations to ascend the river to Nashville. "Their mother parted with them with a smile and without a tear, sending messages to friends at the upper stations." Little thought had she that these three active young men, brave young soldiers, would never reach the stations to deliver her commands, nor ever return to receive her welcome, and comfort her in after-days. They had not a sufficient number of horses for the short journey of forty miles. The deficiency of provender for cattle was another inducement to them to determine to go in a canoe or pirogue, and to take with them a good supply of provisions.

On or about the 18th day of January, 1792, the three sons of Colonel Sevier, named Robert, William, and Valentine, accompanied by John Price and two or three others, "set sail," or, speaking according to fact and mode, began to ascend the river by the use of poles and paddles. To what point they had ascended, we have never ascertained. But the tradition in the Sevier family is this: that a party of Indians had discovered the ascending boat when at the lower side of one of those remarkable bends of the river, where it makes a sweep of ten or fifteen miles and comes around almost to the same place, leaving only a mile or two of high lands between; that the savages crossed the narrow isthmus, secreted themselves in bushes near the river's edge, where the boat would be run close to the shore; that here the first attack was made, in which the three Seviers were killed or mortally wounded; that the Indians having fired their every gun, and seeing all the party were not killed, hastened to reload, whilst Price, and whoever was with him, turned the boat out into the stream and by the opposite shore, and so "paddled down the river;" that the Indians then recrossed the isthmus, and intercepted the descending boat, which was now hastily abandoned. The Indians boarded it, scalped the young men, and carried away whatever they desired of the goods and provisions.

After a day or two passed in the woods and cane, Price discovered the hills on the east side of the river, (now Clarksville,) and, with much delay and the expenditure of breath in "hallooing," recrossed to Colonel Sevier's Station.

The news he delivered "came like a thunderbolt upon these aged and bereaved parents. It was the heaviest calamity which had ever befallen this branch of the family;" and very similar to that experienced by General Sevier's family at the Battle of King's Mountain.

Colonel Sevier communicated the sad intelligence to his brother in language expressive of deepest grief; but was not disposed to flee, or desert his post. He was resolved rather to strengthen his defences. In this work, he and Mr. Snyder, his fellow-stationer and friend, promptly engaged. Other friends assisted, and the like help was rendered by Sevier and Snyder to the half a dozen families who had built their log-cabins on the present site of Clarksville.

Much sympathy was expressed by the people in this bereavement of Colonel Sevier. Very great alarm spread through the settlements. But, as Captain Prince said, "Since they have commenced the game and given us the warning, we must attend to both. Fear has never killed any of us, but the Indians have. The deaths of the Seviers should be avenged."

Colonel Sevier's was the station nearest the mouth of the river. Some

small clearings had been commenced lower down the Cumberland, or north of Red River, but were now abandoned. The other settlements and stations in the county of Tennessee were on either bank of Red River, and toward the Kentucky line. Many horses had been stolen during the fall and winter from these settlements. To be deprived of these animals was distressing, and perhaps to some of the owners a cause of greater anger and irritation than would have been the loss of a relative. The latter event produced sorrow, deep sorrow; but the theft, a fury and madness.

The settlers in this county had early commenced the culture and cure of *tobacco*, and had succeeded most happily; but they were recently much concerned at the obstacles thrown in the way of trade, and the sale of this, their most valuable crop. The Spaniards threatened and coaxed, tempted them, tried them, "shut the mouth of the Mississippi, and forbade the Western people the navigation of its waters." If the tobacco-raisers upon Cumberland shipped their tobacco to Orleans, it was liable to seizure and confiscation. If sold at home, it must be to men who were smugglers or enjoyed some especial privilege from Spanish officers in selling again; and these privileged persons would "buy only at their own prices." They exercised the same option and chance for selling at exorbitant prices any groceries or goods which they saw proper to bring up the river and exhibit to the needy settlers. There were instances when the indispensable article of *salt* sold as high as *thirty dollars* per *bushel*. It was carefully dealt out by the tablespoon or teacup. Sugar and coffee were often measured in the same way.

AMOUNT OF TOBACCO SHIPPED FROM CLARKSVILLE.

(The following statistics have been kindly furnished us; are reliable and interesting :

The points from which the shipments are made are Clarksville proper, or the upper landing, and Trice's, or the lower landing. We include in the shipments from the lower landing, Red River and Linnwood. The commercial year begins and ends on the 1st of September.

From the 1st of September, 1857, to the 1st of August, 1858, thirteen thousand hogsheads of leaf have been received. By the 1st day of September, these receipts will be increased by one hundred hogsheads. But we state the quantity in round numbers as above:

13,000 hogsheads, a $150, ...	$1,950,000
2,200 hogsheads strips, a $200, . . .	440,000
Making a total of . .	$2,390,000

If any one should consider this estimate too large, it can be answered that the hogsheads usually shipped at these points are well known to average, net, 2000 to 2100 pounds of leaf and 1200 pounds of strips, and that the average price, during the season, for leaf has been 7 to 7½ cents.

It may indeed be said that the tobacco shipped from Clarksville yields to the business operations of the place about two and a half millions of dollars.)

On the 1st day of February a meeting of the committee for the county of Tennessee was held, of which Captain William Prince was chairman. A well-written address or petition was adopted and forwarded to General Robertson, to whom it is directed. It recites:

"That your petitioners, having convened together at the request of the distressed part of Tennessee county, in order to set forth their grievances and to pursue some method for their relief, beg leave to represent to you, sir, that they have much to dread from the Indians as the spring season approaches. The recent murders and ravages committed by them on our frontiers, too evidently prove their intentions on this quarter. We already feel the effects of the navigation of the river being shut up, by which means we shall be deprived of the very necessary article, salt; that article having already raised in its price. Immigration to this country by water must frequently cease. We also beg leave to assure you that the frontiers will break up unless some speedy method is taken to secure them from the inroads of the savages, which must be followed by the most fatal consequences. We are much afraid, sir, that Government has not vested their officers in this country with authority to carry an expedition against any nation or village of Indians. Yet we are confident that something must be done with the Indians that do the mischief on our frontiers. We are willing to pursue every lawful means to procure peace and tranquillity among us. Therefore, we beg leave to suggest to you the idea that an *express* be sent to the Commandant at New Madrid," (on the Mississippi,) "setting forth that it is his people that do the mischief in our country, and whatever else you may think proper. . . Make a full representation of our distressed situation and grievances, to Governor Blount. . . We have confidence you will do all in *your* power to relieve the distresses of the people under your command."

The situation of the people in Tennessee county exposed them to attacks by the Shawnees, rather than by any other unfriendly tribe; and these Indians were under the protection of the Spanish officers at New Madrid, or *Lance de Grace*.

We notice that, in anticipation of an increase of troubles from the Indians, a council of officers was held at which it was resolved to send out a party of about one hundred men to "scour the woods between this District of Mero and the Tennessee River." This was resolved upon about the 10th of March, and promptly communicated to the Governor, who, in a long letter of 1st of April to General Robertson, cavils and criticises the language of this resolution, fearing (and no doubt with reason) that the intention was to "scour the woods toward the Tennessee, '*beyond the ridge*,'" or more than some twenty miles from the Cumberland. He repeated his injunction to "observe the Treaty of Holston," and this at a time when these settlements were forewarned of threatened *invasion.*

The Governor, although much experienced in Indian craft and treachery, certainly had too much confidence in Watts and other chiefs. In this letter, the Governor says, "A peace-talk has been addressed by Little Turkey to the Lower Towns, and that he disapproves of their preparations for war. . . . Since this talk, John Watts, *whose friendship may be depended upon*, and his exertions too, in favor of peace," etc.

As a "P. S." to this long letter, the Governor says, "I have just received *another* message from Watts, who is coming to deliver one prisoner and forty stolen horses."

And in a few months Watts is badly wounded in both legs in the attack on Buchanan's Station.

After the attack upon the boat and the killing of the Seviers, the next appearance of the Indians was near Bledsoe's Station. They wounded Oliver Williams and Jason Thompson. Thompson lived a few miles south of Nashville.* He had been at home but a few days after he was wounded, before his house was attacked by some twenty or thirty Indians. In this attack, he was killed, as were his wife, one son, and one daughter. Another daughter was taken prisoner. Mrs. Caffrey and her son, and another small boy, (name not mentioned,) were also captured. These were taken to the Creek and Cherokee nations, and retained for years as slaves.

We have endeavored to ascertain the locality of the principal stations or improvements west of the Cumberland River, (at this date,) and to present them on the small map. Surrounding or near to these were other improvements, or small "clearings and deadenings," and hastily and rudely constructed log-houses. Attacks had been made upon these stations, persons had been killed or wounded at each of them; and, with

---

* The Tennessee and Alabama Railroad passes a little to the west of the place, four miles from Nashville, near a large spring, old buildings, etc.

exception of General Robertson's, Rains', and Buchanan's, they had to be abandoned.

"Johnson's Fort," consisting of a double log-house and a few small log-huts—partially picketed in—was upon the beautiful eminence where is now the large brick dwelling of Mr. Charles Bosley, only about six hundred yards north of the Pike. There is a spring, (and over it a stone building,) near the residence. At this spring the Indians killed two small children in open day, and wounded one slightly, and another dangerously. "They were all scalped, and laid upon each other: a heap of children, living and dead." One boy escaped with a broken arm: one little girl, with her brother and sister lying dead upon her, was found to be alive, and lived for twenty years thereafter.

Mr. Bosley has distinguished a spot in front of his residence by a cherry tree, which has grown to be very large, and yet flourishes there—at the very locality where Captain Hunter was killed and beheaded.

Colonel Kilpatrick pursued these Indians, and when on their trail, near Dunham's Station, was fired upon and killed—beheaded and mangled— as Captain Hunter had been. Mr. Bennet Searcy was of the company with Colonel Kilpatrick, and was dangerously wounded, as was also Hugh F. Bell. After wandering in the woods for two days, Mr. Searcy reached the Bluff or Nashville Station.*

John Cockrell had erected a house at the spring which bears his name to this day. He was much in the habit of watching for deer at the Sulphur Spring, over the ridge from Mr. Bosley's. When riding near that spring, he was fired upon by an Indian, without being wounded. But his horse fell and caught his foot beneath him. When in this position, and whilst the horse struggled, got up and ran off, Cockrell fired at the Indian, wounded him, and, as was believed, mortally. Having recovered his feet and upright position, he did not tarry to scalp his foe—for fear of others—but made his way across the ridge to Johnson's Fort. The bones and tomahawk and knife of an Indian were found some months thereafter, at about two miles distant.

At Brown's Station four boys were killed, scalped, and thrown in a heap, as the little girls and their brothers had been at Johnson's.

We have heretofore mentioned the deaths caused by the savages at Castleman's and Dunham's. The enemy, in small parties, was in all parts of the settlements. There was no safety for any one in passing

---

* Bennet Searcy filled several honorable and useful positions in Davidson county.

from any one station to another. There was yet sufficient cane over all the country to afford the Indians places of ambush or retreat.

On the 8th April, the house of Benjamin Williams, near Gallatin, was attacked at night, and himself and seven other persons were killed. A negro fellow (then young and active, and who was alive not long since) made his escape into the woods; and one little boy, who in his fright climbed up and supported himself for hours in the *chimney,* also escaped. All others in the house were murdered and scalped.

The next victims were in the same neighborhood. They were Mrs. McMurry, Mrs. Ratcliff, and her three children. Then two sons of Robert Desha, on Station Camp Creek.

In quick succession came the death of "Moses Kuykendall, and many others," whose names are not recorded. In the same neighborhood several persons were wounded. These were near Bledsoe's.

On 24th May, as General Robertson and his son Jonathan were sitting upon their horses at his spring, a party of Indians fired from behind the trees and cane, wounding both of them; the General in the arm and Jonathan in the hip. The shot caused the General to drop his gun. In attempting to recover it, (his horse being restive,) he fell to the ground, and the horse fled. The Indians were rushing up, with tomahawks lifted, to put an end to the "Head-man of the Stationers," when Jonathan Robertson, by a well-directed shot,* wounded, as was believed, the two savages who were advancing to secure the scalp. The Indians were thus arrested in their approach, and the Robertsons escaped. The ball passed through the arm of General Robertson from the wrist to near the elbow, shattering one of the bones. It was a running sore for years. These Indians continued prowling near the residence of General Robertson, and, on the next day, they killed a boy (name forgotten) within sight of the house. And the day following, they killed a little girl near Nashville.

On the 26th, an attack was made on Zigler's Station. This fort or station was erected in the fall of 1790, or spring of 1791, upon the west fork of Bledsoe's Creek, and about one mile and a half north of Cairo. The lands here were very rich, and well adapted for the growth of tobacco. There had been a great increase of population in this section, as there was near Bledsoe's.

As there were hostile parties in all directions through the settlements,

---

* Mrs. Robertson, Mrs. Neelly, and other pioneer women, were great sticklers for the word *providence,* instead of *chance.*

the duty of having sentinels properly stationed during the day, to guard the hands who were at work, was enjoined, and was generally attended to. And since the Indians had in so many instances recently surrounded, fired, and broken into houses, and slaughtered whole families, the advice of all officers, civil and military, was, by no confidence or hope of safety, to be induced to omit the keeping a guard at night; and, as additional safety, for as many as could well be accommodated, to assemble and pass the nights in one station. And thus it was at Zigler's. The people had worked and watched all day. But at night they pretermitted watchfulness, and sat down to eat and to play. Having worked hard and eaten heartily, they slept heavily. Whilst they slept, the enemy approached, surrounded the building, opened the door, rushed in, and commenced a terrible slaughter; and no doubt would have killed many more persons, had they not cried out for quarter. The Indians understood this cry, and spared the suppliants. Some resisted, and were killed or wounded. There were thirty or more persons in the house: five were killed, four wounded, eighteen taken prisoners, three or more escaped, after a long and hot pursuit. This was the largest number of settlers taken at any one station. It added fearfully to the gloom in all the settlements, and to the dissatisfaction with the heads of Government.

The Indians must have contemplated this attack for some time before it was made. By some agreement, the several small bands assembled on the night of the 26th to besiege and capture this station. They had succeeded, and, so far as has ever been reported, without the loss of a man or one wounded. They greatly rejoiced at their success. Indeed, they had sustained very little injury from the whites for months in which they had been so successfully engaged in slaughter and capture of the settlers, and in "spiriting away their horses."

These were injuries too grievous to be borne. Could we pause, as we must, in this sad narration, we would sit down: no, rather, we would hastily rise up, and call upon God to deliver us out of the hand of our enemies. What reflections can we in calmness make upon the frequent recurrence of these murderous deeds? Shall we say, We pity this distressed people; we sympathize with them in this time of deep affliction? or shall we cruelly intimate, with the Secretary of War, that they deserved it all?

No, rather, we partake of the feelings of the stationers. We look at General Robertson, and think and feel and are involuntarily ready to act as he did. He grieved and chafed under the restraint put upon him: he loved and honored Washington, he desired to exhibit respect and obedience to authority; but, at the same time, he admitted his hand was forbidden to "lay hold on vengeance." We do as he did, "*clench our fist and grit our teeth.*"

The fire was burning in that heart. He knew the opinion of General Sevier; they agreed, and had repeatedly expressed the conclusion at which they had long since arrived : "There would be no cessation of these murderous deeds, so long as a retreat and refuge was allowed to such savages, whether east or west of the broad Tennessee." The country they called their own must be invaded, and the towns made up of a savage set, the brigands and banditti of the nations, Creeks and Cherokees, "*must be destroyed.*" If there are yet the advocates of peace among them, they have lost or ceased to exert their influence for peace. The voice of all seems to be for war.

CHAPTER XXIII.

1792.

In this chapter we resume the history of events from the commencement of the year. We shall thus present some items of interest which we deem it best to exhibit in this connection.

The attention of the General Government had been called to the continuance of Indian outrages at the South, and to notice that "their warfare was in total disregard of treaties." It had reason also to be much concerned at the hostile movements of the Indians of the North-west. It had its troubles with the whiskey insurrection or rebellion in western Pennsylvania. This excise law, or tax on whiskey, entered into the politics of the day among the people of this Territory. In Washington District there were the Sevier party and the Tipton party: the first was the Administration, or law and order party; the latter, the party opposed to "extortion and the infringement of the rights of taste and conscience." There were questions and negotiations with England, and—as more concerning our narrative—questions with Spain, which gave the Administration much perplexity and uneasiness.

But by what causes are the Creeks and Cherokees so hostile to the western settlements? What instigates to such ceaseless warfare? Early in January, President Washington thought proper to refer these questions to the Secretary of War. On the 16th of that month he replied. His report could afford no satisfactory answer. Sufficient information, however, had been communicated to the War Department to satisfy any one who had not already prejudged the matter, that treaty engagements with savages would not be sacredly kept, when such strong temptations and corrupting influences were presented as had hitherto been brought to bear upon them. "Powder and lead, stroud and whiskey, me know him," said a sub-chief; "*Paper*, me don't know him." On some accounts the Indians deserved to be greatly pitied. Although naturally very watchful, suspicious, and without guile, yet they were often deceived and imposed upon by crafty white men; deceived by their assertions, and corrupted and enraged by their gifts and poisons.

Shall the civilization and Christianity of Americans yield to the savage law of retaliation? Can these savage acts be longer endured? Are they not on the increase because of the forbearance and endurance of the Americans? Shall we not arise and go forth in our might and in our fury, to avenge these many murders and exterminate these fiends? Or shall we await until another and a better spirit shall exorcise the demon? Thus the stationers interrogated each other. They derived very little consolation or encouragement from what had yet been done or promised by Government for them. And the successes of the arms of the so-called "disciplined troops" were so trivial and so questionable, that no lively hopes were cherished of deliverances or defences from their interposition.

There was one reliable friend among the red men, to whose friendship and conduct the Cumberland settlers justly had respect. This confidence was founded on years of intercourse, and a knowledge of his truthfulness and integrity. Although an Indian of the full blood, *Piomingo* had ever resisted all the persuasions of other tribes and of the Spaniards to turn him or the Chickasaws against the people of the United States. His faith was, at times, most sorely tried. The Spaniards, the Shawnees, and the Delawares on one side, the Cherokees and Creeks on the other, annoyed, threatened, coaxed, invaded and attacked his people, but he continued the friend of the Americans. We will not insist that his attachment for General Robertson alone secured the continuance of the friendship of his nation to these settlements, but it did as far as his influence could extend. He loved no other white man as he did General Robertson.

In March, General Robertson received information by a runner from Piomingo, that the settlers might apprehend some depredations from the Shawnees and Delawares. The stationers in Tennessee county had already sustained losses of lives and property by marauding parties, who were supposed to have come from the Spanish territory on the other side of the Mississippi. These injuries and the expectation of their continuance—aggravated by Spanish assumption of absolute control of the navigation of the great river—awakened much and earnest discussion among the settlers, and induced them to hold a public meeting. The result of that meeting, or the pervading sentiments, are embodied in the Address of the Committee of Safety, of 1st February, which was given in the last chapter.

Upon the reception of this address, General Robertson promptly wrote to Don Portell, the Spanish Commander at Lance de Grace. His letter was dated February 13th, 1792, and a copy is bound in vol. i. of his letters.

General Robertson was wise in counsel; he was no blusterer. His quiet, calm deportment induced some few persons to entertain the opinion that he was unsusceptible, void of tenderness, imperturbable, and indolent. We have heard this said, but by persons who certainly have not studied his life as we have. His whole life was one in which wisdom, courage, and energy were constantly demanded and exercised ; we do not say "consummate wisdom, unequalled bravery, and astonishing energy." It will do to say, however, he possessed enough and used enough to discharge the duties which devolved upon him—and them *well*. He wasted no talent, he abused no power and no person.

He desired for all his toils the triple reward—the approbation of God, of his own conscience, and of his fellow-men ; and we confidently trust he failed of neither. At this time he was complimented by his fellow-citizens, and he gracefully turned the sentiment to the chief officer in the Territory. "The thanks of the people of Mero District" were tendered to Governor Blount, which he acknowledged in a very handsome manner; concluding, in his letter to General Robertson, "I beg you and the District to believe that no man (non-resident) can participate in whatever affects them, more than I do."

In due time General Robertson received, by the return of his messenger, a reply from the Commandant of the Spanish post at New Madrid. We shall quote most of the first paragraph, and without extended comments upon it, or controverting it, (however much inclined to do the one or easy to do the other.)

"Your favor of 13th February indicates that which all good neighbors ought to preserve one with another, a strict union and sincere harmony ; which is the *genial system of my nation*, uniformly joined with the purest ties of humanity, to which only we are accustomed !"

He then relates that he had called in a Delaware Indian, Ka-la-yah, (known to the Americans as *Raccoon*,) and made sundry inquiries of him about mischief done on the Cumberland. He answered for himself, "as the very charm of innocence," and "charged the mischief to the *Great Capot*, who commanded the Delaware band in those incursions to Cumberland." "Nevertheless, I made him promise by the *name of His Catholic Majesty*, my master, that he shall live in friendship. I also ordered in two other chiefs, one a Shawnee, the other a *Cherokee*, . . who promised as Ka-la-yah had done." And then he adds, "But as an Indian is not to be depended on, it is necessary to be upon your guard !"

"Thank you, sir," said General Robertson, "there are two of you in that category."

The Don then mentions a gang of horse-thieves, "headed by a certain Mr. Morris," (an old Tory from Carolina,) and relates how sure retributive justice had been to overtake him. "He now tastes the fruits of his robberies, for he passed here last fall on his way *to New Orleans*, having lost the use of his right leg, owing to two wounds he received from the Indians."

"Yes, sir," said General Robertson to Captain Rains and others to whom he read the letter; "we knew the truth would some day leak out, that Morris was with the Spaniards—*his* friends and *our* enemies—and now has gone to *New Orleans* for a *safe retreat*. *Retributive justice!* Is it that of which you speak? Then consider and dread the just reward of your own deeds!"

General Robertson deemed this letter of "Don Portell, of *Lance de Grace*," well worth preserving. Colonel Daniel Smith pronounced it "the rarest specimen of impudence!" Talk to us of "a certain Mr. Morris!" a horse-thief, when they are riding the best horses we ever had in the settlements, stolen by this "same Mr. Morris and his gang of horse-thieves, Indians and Spaniards." They have also written to Government of "*a certain Robertson*." General Robertson laughed heartily at this. By the same messenger, another letter came from Don Portell to M. Andrew Fagot, who was residing at Nashville, in the equivocal character of a trader and gentleman of leisure. A copy was furnished General Robertson, in which are repeated the sentiments expressed in the other letter. We doubt not that Portell was desirous for peace and friendship, as was said, "inasmuch as it promoted the *genial system* of my nation"—and no farther.

We must note here that the Spaniards give a meaning to the word *genialis*, genial, pronounced *hay-ne-al*, somewhat of a more significant and active character than is attached to it by the English; with them, the "Sociedad ed propaganda Fide" is the very embodiment of their "genial system," though it be conducted by *auto da fé*, in fagots and in fire. It means *propagation, that which produces*. So that General Robertson and Colonel Smith spoke *learnedly* when they said "their genial system is that which produces thefts, murders, cruelties." Rains denounced them and their system, with an oath, or something very much like an imprecation: "He did n't believe the *don'd* rascals, no how."

Among Republicans, titles of royalty and nobility sound strangely, and are generally eschewed; sometimes they have been attached to persons

to commend them for great merit, as a queenly person, "the duchess."
In our own youthful days we often saw

"Old *King* Cole,
The jolly old soul."

And there are yet living, in Middle Tennessee, persons who in their
younger days saluted an early settler at the French Lick Station by the
soubriquet of "King"—"King Boyd," as he was by young and old designated and distinguished. For what personal merit, whether from figure,
gait, or mind, he acquired this distinction, we know not; but this we
know, ("from the papers,") that it is claimed for him, that "he kept the
first tavern or ordinary at Nashville," and that his merit and preëminence
in this matter is contested by a very distinguished African, known upon
the records, and by persons yet living, as *Black Bob*, or "Old Good
Behavior," (having his license *dum bene se gesserit.*) But there is none
to dispute or deny that "King Boyd" established the first distillery upon
the Cumberland, and that it acquired as much notoriety as "Black Bob's
Tavern." Neither of them was any great affair to be proud of, or to
boast of, or to write of. But John Boyd's "*Red Heifer*" *was notorious.*
At about this date a rival distillery was established by Stump, on White's
Creek, about five miles north of Nashville. The demand for whiskey
was on the increase. The "regular soldiers," as Colonel Sharpe's troop
was called, the militia at musters, and the spies in their excursions,
now required "rations of spirits." At this date Governor Blount
directed General Robertson to supply "our friends, the Chickasaws and
Choctaws, with whiskey." General Robertson had at sundry times
prior to this date furnished Indians with small quantities. The District
of Mero had borne considerable expense for the like purpose, but now
these supplies are to be at the charge of the General Government.

The town is on the increase : two taverns, one distillery, and a knap-
sack of chintz and calicoes for a dry-goods store, and twenty-one cabins
fenced in. A blacksmith's shop was established at the very start, upon
a stump. The girdled, deadened trees stand leafless all over the plain.

Governor Blount held several conferences with Creek chiefs during
the early part of this year. One at Coyatee, in the nation, at which
there were two thousand warriors marshalled in two lines, to receive the
Governor; professedly to do him great honor, but doubtless with equal
desire to make a display of their military strength and discipline. The
chiefs, Watts, Hanging Maw, and the Breath of Nickojack, renewed
professions of peace and friendship. The next meeting with chiefs was

at Nashville, or near General Robertson's Station, with Chickasaws and Choctaws; that conference ended on 10th August, with like professions of amity.

A liberal distribution of presents was made, a rifle to each chief. "Fifty good rifle guns were presented to the Mountain Leader, and those who joined General St. Clair's army, and some other chiefs." The stock of goods for distribution consisted of one thousand five hundred blankets; one hundred pieces blue strouds, calico, linsey; blue, red, and yellow binding; fifty suits of clothes and fifty hats for the chiefs; piece of scarlet cloth for leggins, ETC., *underscored ;* five hundred scalping-knives, etc. It is not probable that this entire stock was distributed at that time. The Cherokees were not invited to this conference, yet several of them attended. And there can be little doubt they came with sinister aims, to discover the strength of the settlements and the assailable points, and that some of these very Cherokees were engaged in the attack on Buchanan's Station, which was soon thereafter made.

On the 26th of May, Governor Blount gives General Robertson a most glowing description of his visit to Coyatee, of his reception by the thousands of Indians, the *feu-de-joie,* and of the cheering and acceptable expressions of friendship made by the savages—chiefs, warriors, and even squaws and pappooses. They must have heard of "the doings in New York," and resolved to imitate the display of the officers of the societies of Tammany and St. Patrick, Mayor and Aldermen of the city, and the officers of Government, at the reception of McGillivray and his chiefs. These two lines of warriors, "two thousand in number," the Governor says, must have presented a sight which would have delighted Hogarth fully as much as it did Governor Blount.

> When next they thus parade,
> "May we be there to see!"

The warriors were not equipped as American militia, with corn-stalks for guns; they had muskets, rifles, and shot-guns, bows and arrows, and blow-guns. The variety of head-dress was very great—horses' tails, cows' tails, coons' tails; but the plume feathers from roosters' tails were most numerous. Their faces and bodies were painted red and white. A goodly number flourished a "three-point blanket;" all wore "the shame-piece" of red, blue, or yellow "strouds." A large majority of them were well-formed men. Some of the officers were fully dressed "like white people," and made quite a flourish of their swords; were very proud of epaulettes and a sash; more than one had the epaulette fastened upon a bare shoulder, and a red sash tied round a naked body. They would not

25

suffer the blanket to hide these evidences of rank and dress. The
squaws sat at a distance, "fully or half squat upon the ground;" and
the children, many of them, as God made them, without bandage or adorn-
ment, *in puris naturalibus:*

> "Naked head and butt and knee,
> Before, behind, as nude can be;
> Like babies when they 're just set free
> From a hollow stump or hollow tree."

Such was the array and display before the Governor. He and his
escort were surprised, he was delighted: he never was indifferent to display himself. The speeches made upon the occasion are not reported,
nor how much buffalo and bear-meat and venison were eaten at the feasts,
nor what were the savory dishes which regaled his taste and smell; but
this they reported, "We had enough to eat and to spare." Now whether
this abundance consisted in the supply of provisions which the Governor
took with him, or of food furnished from the cuisine of Chull-culla and
other squaws, is a debatable question.

Hastening home from this scene, and before the enthusiasm and éclat
had passed away, the Governor sat down and addressed General Robertson. Well did he know the anxiety of General Robertson and the people
around him; and having derived so much pleasure from his visit and
the promises there made, he hastened to communicate his impressions to
those who so much needed comfort. In his letter (which was intended
for publicity) he scouts the idea of the citizens of Mero District being in
"a state of danger," and quite rebukes them for "despondency." "How
is it that your citizens alarm emigrants by their tales of danger and
suffering?" says he. "Your people may take *spirits,* for in a short
time all *must* be well!"

This seems strange language, after all that we have related of the
massacres and sufferings of these "citizens." It was not their custom
or their policy to magnify the dangers or to discourage emigrants; they
invariably manifested satisfaction at their arrival, extended to them a
hearty welcome, and cheerfully turned out to aid them in "log-rollings
and house-raisings." "The truth of history" will justify us in the statement, that the Governor's injunction to "take spirits" was coupled with
one from the Scriptures, to take "wine for the stomach's sake;" and
some of them practiced accordingly. That there was danger to the
settlers, we have shown; that there was danger to emigrants, was proclaimed by the fact that a guard was required to protect them from

Clinch to Cumberland. But thus they did come, and a goodly number of them, and worthy emigrants too.

Among the number we now find "General Rutherford, who had exchanged all his lands in North Carolina for lands in Cumberland;" Wm. G. Lewis, the Fords, Phillips, Dickersons, and others. Some of the McGavocks had made "locations" and purchases of lands; and they never made a bad one. They were men who added a 640 to a 640, and then made a profitable use of what they acquired. The family deserves, as do many others, to have a more extended notice than we can give. The earliest purchase by the McGavocks (probably) was the "six forty" of George Freeland—the founder of Freeland's Station—much of which is now the "McGavock Addition" to Nashville. The first year's crop of corn—a large one—made after this purchase, almost paid for the land. The corn was sold at from three to five dollars per bushel.

We have shown how incessantly General Robertson devoted himself to the discharge of the many duties and cares devolved upon him, and that in no year were his anxieties and labors greater than in the first half of this; and we shall see no diminution of calls or withholding of his services to the end. As we have intimated, he did not fully approve the restrictive orders from Government. He agreed with General Sevier, "the only successful warfare with savages is to be waged in their own country." His spirit chafed at the confinement "east of the ridges which divide the waters of Cumberland and Tennessee." Like his own noble warhorse, he champed the bit with foam and fury; gladly would he, at times, have let the reins fall loosely upon the arched neck of the proud animal, and, with his rifle at his saddle-bow and sword in hand, have led his best marksmen into the very heart of the enemy's country and the thickest of the fray. But he had taken the oath of office, and he designed, by his example, to teach the invaluable lesson of obedience to "the powers that be." Of this he spoke again and again.

Under these circumstances it was that certain "fire-eaters" determined to disregard the advice and authority of General Robertson, and to make an invasion of the Indian country whence had come so many of the savages who had murdered "our citizens and stolen our horses." A leader of one of these parties was Captain John Edmeston, a very good citizen, who could not resist the cries of the bereaved, and the demands of his neighbors for revenge. Edmeston took command of a volunteer company, and was about to invade the Indian country—and act somewhere, without and against the proper authority, and "on his own hook." General Robertson disapproved of the organization and its avowed purposes. Such a force departing would reduce the proper defences, or interfere with his own plans. It was too small, and unfit to go on a distant expedition. He, therefore, forbade Captain Edmeston and his volunteers to engage in any such project.

A few days thereafter the General received an anonymous letter, of which we give an exact copy, only premising that the preservation and filing of it with his regular correspondence, without a single remark or evidence of wounded feelings on his part, gives us an insight into another of the excellent traits of his character :

"Sir :—I was much surprised when I heard of your wishing to stop Capt. John Edmeston from going against the Indians with a volunteer company, in order to Retaliate for the damage they are daily doing us. But, hearing it generally reported in the country that it has Always been your Endeavor to stop all those that wish to do good to this country, and damage to the Indians, I must join with the rest of my Countrymen, and wish Edmeston Great Success, and you gone from hence, and A better in your Room.
"I am a Citizen of Mero District !
"July 10th, 1792."

The above is addressed : "Mr. James Robertson, Brigadier-General, Mero District," and sealed with red sealing-wax.

It would be a pleasure to us to enlarge upon this matter ; but the times, and the circumstances in which we have in our narrative left these "our countrymen," forbid the turning aside from our appropriate narrative.

In the early part of August there came to the residence of General Robertson a respectable number of Chickasaw chiefs and a small delegation of the Choctaws. They came by invitation, to meet Governor Blount and General Pickens, as representatives on the part of the United States Government. The Spanish agents had exerted themselves to dissuade these nations from attending the conference at Nashville ; and with the Choctaws they had so far succeeded that but a few came. These two nations were quite friendly towards the United States, and in their intercourse with each other. The Spaniards, the Creeks, and the Cherokees kept a close watch upon the Choctaws and Chickasaws, and used many artifices to alienate them from the United States, but without success. The former persevere in their wrong-doings. It is but fair to denounce the trio as enemies.

About the 1st of October, John Birkley and son were attacked near Bledsoe's. When one of the Indians was in the act of scalping the son, the father took deliberate aim and killed the Indian who had hold of the boy, and they escaped. Several other persons were shot, some killed, some wounded, in that same neighborhood. Samuel Wilson, of Sumner, pursued some Indians who had stolen horses from James Douglas. After a hot pursuit, he, and the three or four friends who were with him, came so near as to shoot down one of the Indians, when the others abandoned the horses and fled into the cane.

On the 8th October, Wm. Stewart was killed near Neelly's Station, on White's Creek; and in the night of the same day they burned *Stump's Distillery*, which was also on the same creek. Who was harmed or benefited by this? The same party of Indians proceeded to Sycamore and burned several houses and cribs of corn; thence to the settlements on Red River, pursuing the same career. They were pursued, overtaken, one killed, some wounded, and the horses regained.

These attacks continued in despite and contempt of the "cavalry" employed to defend Mero District. These Southern Indians had heard of " Harmar's defeat"—that " mounted men could be put to flight by Indians on foot." And the ignominious example set in Ohio was soon to be followed here—in a small way.

As Major Sharpe's troop, or two companies, were to serve for a limited period, and to terminate on 11th October, the Governor directed or authorized General Robertson to enlist others to take their places, and to be very careful to avoid heavy expenses; for example: " You may agree to pay an *express one dollar a day !*" A man who must ride with all speed, and at the peril of his life, must do it for a dollar a day! Money must indeed have been scarce in those days; but fortunately the daring expressmen were not intent on pay alone.

We have quoted the order of Governor Blount to Major Sharpe to discharge services in the counties of Sumner and Tennessee, and this, *independent* of the command of any other officer there. In that county, and in Tennessee, there were as good officers as Major Sharpe, who *outranked* him, and lived within the District. In the county of Sumner, Colonel Winchester was the officer of highest grade. His delicate sense of honor and view of military etiquette would not permit him to continue in service when thus treated, and he threw up his commission. Governor Blount was informed of this by General Robertson, and in reply regretted to part with his services; but contends that the order was perfectly proper, and meant no dishonor to Colonel Winchester. " I had shown it to you, and you, if there had been cause, had the *first right* to complain."

General Robertson certainly was entitled to command all the troops within the District, the Colonels in the three counties being next in command under him. We pretend not to be an arbiter in these questions of military etiquette.

Major Sharpe was ordered here from a distance, to assist in defence of Sumner and Tennessee counties, or of the District; and, when occasion required, to "act in concert" with the militia of the counties, and to pass from one county to the other on the lookout for or in pursuit of the enemy. In each of these counties there were Colonels and Lieutenant-Colonels, who outranked him, in the militia of their counties. And the view of Governor Blount and General Robertson seems to have been, that this was a troop emanating for the time being from the United States Government, through its representative, the Governor of the Territory, and, therefore, to be viewed somewhat in the light of "regular United States troops," and properly independent of the militia organizations of the District.

But as the term of service of Major Sharpe was soon to terminate, and no certain record is left of their having even seen an Indian whilst in service here, there was no expressed desire for their continuance. Prompt arrangements or enlistments were made by General Robertson to supply their places; and Colonel Winchester was willing to resume his proper rank.

At the treaty at Nashville, a Creek chief, *Coteatoy*, had been present, and carried home to his nation such a report of the speech made by General Robertson, as, to many of the warriors of that nation, seemed to justify the course they had for a long time pursued, and were very willing to continue. In a "talk" sent from the "Lookout Mountain, September 10th, 1792," from the Glass, he reports Coteatoy's version of the General's speech as follows: Colonel Robertson said, "There has been a great deal of blood spilt in our settlements, and I *will come* and sweep it clean with your blood." "And now take notice, that the first mischief that is done, I will come."

Coteatoy added, "It is certain that mischief will be done, and that some of the young Creeks who are daily going to that settlement may do mischief, and others be made to suffer for it—do it who may; they, therefore, concluded it would be as well to take the initiative." But, the Glass, John Watts, the Bloody Fellow, (or Eskaqua,) and some other head-men, give assurance to the Governor that they have diverted these warriors from their warlike purpose, and sent them to their homes. Such is the substance of these two "talks" from the Bloody Fellow and the Glass.

These "talks" were sent to the Governor for purposes of deception. Before they had reached him, *open war was declared*. The five Lower

Towns of Cherokees (in the population of which there was a mixture of Creeks) had held their war and scalp dance at the time Watts was concocting the peace-talks to be signed by the chiefs at Lookout.

Their declaration of war against the "United States," meant the settlements on the Cumberland, as these were nearest to them, and most exposed.

A friendly Indian hastened to communicate to Governor Blount the news of war, and that John Watts himself, in command of one hundred Creeks, was at one of those towns, (Nickojack,) awaiting the assembling of five hundred Cherokees, who were rapidly coming in; that they intended to invade the Cumberland settlements, and wage a war of extermination.

The Governor was deceived by the talks from Lookout Mountain. On the 14th September, he wrote to General Robertson:

"I heartily congratulate you and the District of Mero upon the happy change of affairs. I really had dreadful apprehensions for you."

And on this same day he orders General Robertson to "discharge such part of the Brigade of Mero District as may be in service under my order of the 12th instant"—only two days previous.

This system of orders and revocation was perplexing. The Governor was made to recognize dependence upon the War Department, and to make his subordinates share in the same feeling. The General had long complained of the restrictions placed upon him and the people here. They had endured so much and so long that there was no virtue in it— they were charged by the Indians with weakness and cowardice.

As soon as the Governor received information of the hostile preparations under Watts, and that a large body of Indians had crossed the Tennessee, he started an express to the Secretary of War, giving the information. He also immediately issued orders to General Sevier, in Washington District, and to General Robertson, in Mero District, to assemble their brigades and prepare for defence of the country.

"The danger is imminent; delay not an hour," says he to General Robertson.

How sudden this change! On the 14th it was, "I heartily congratulate you and the District upon the happy change!" And now, on the 16th, "The danger is imminent!"

Six hundred savages had then crossed the Tennessee to destroy the settlers in Mero and Kentucky! The militia, summoned by General Robertson, assembled at the places designated. The special order from the Governor to Major Sharpe is as follows:

" Major Sharpe, of Sumner county, who commands all the troops *in* *service*, for the protection of the frontiers, is to be considered as subject to the orders of no superior militia officer, *not in actual service*. But in case of any militia being turned out from either of the counties, by the commanding officer, to chastise the Indians for recent depredations, he will cordially coöperate with such part of his command as may be in that particular county.

"*No pursuit* is to be continued *beyond the ridge dividing* the waters of Cumberland and Duck Rivers. Patrols and reconnoitring parties to be kept out from the stations, in search of, and to prevent any further depredations by, the Indians; and in case any Indians should be found lurking or skulking about to the *northward of the ridge* aforesaid, in the woods, off any path, or fleeing, to be considered and treated as enemies, save only Chickasaws and Choctaws, women and children. . . . .

" Such men of Tennessee county on duty as are draughts, to be discharged on the arrival of the men under the command of Captain Lusk, and their places to be supplied by a part of his own men."

The force under Major Sharpe and Captain Lusk consisted of one hundred and ninety men, cavalry and infantry. This force was distributed to nine separate stations, " from Taylor's Spring, near Bledsoe's, down the east side of the Cumberland, down to the *Cave Spring*," near the junction of Red River and Cumberland.

Such was the extent of country, on the east side of the river, to be patrolled and defended. The extreme stations were at least seventy miles apart, with a wide interval of hills and dense forest, from Eaton's to Maulding's, and to Clarksville.

The apprehensions of danger, or the causes for distrusting the friendship of the Indians, were such, as to require the employment of *spies* as a distinct class of soldiers. These were generally engaged and paid by the people of a station ; in other instances, by the head of a family, or by two or three families settled near each other. The favorite spy of the settlements on the west side of Cumberland was Abraham Castleman. " He was fearless, with a quick sight, and a sure shot." " He made no noise or tramp as he walked ; and, with his body a little bent, he seemed ever looking for Indians, or marks on the trees." He had been " chain-carrier" in most of the surveys.

This trusty spy had taken a circuitous route through the woods extending as far as the Indian War-trace, fifty or sixty miles from Nashville. He passed around the present site of Murfreesboro'. Near that place he discovered the trail of many Indians. He hastened back to Nashville, coming by Buchanan's and Rains' settlements. He gave the alarm, and advised the settlers to leave their homes and take shelter in the strongest stations. This advice was generally accepted.

Upon reception of Castleman's report, General Robertson sent Captain Rains, and with him Abraham Kennedy, (an active young man,) to take one direction, and two other spies, Clayton and Gee, to take another direction, and so to pass from opposite courses around the Enolee, or Big Spring, and thus confirm or disprove the report of Castleman.

At the Spring, (around which is now the beautiful town of Murfrees-boro',) a friendly (?) Indian, with a few associate hunters, had fixed his camp. He was known to the settlers as the "Black Fox," or Enolee. Castleman stated that his camp was *deserted*, and construed this as an indication of danger. He was well acquainted with this "Old Fox," and had "spied him" for several months, during which he had camped there, and hunted through that rich section of country. He and his party, it is true, were camping and generally hunting upon lands recognized by the recent treaties as Indian territory, but they were daily resorting to the settlements to sell venison and skins. Castleman knew that the Indian hunt was not over at that season. Why, then, had he removed? And where is he and his party?

The congratulations from Governor Blount, the advice to "take spirits," and a slight suspicion that "*Abe* had—had seen no Indian, but had smelled at a cold track," prevented the implicit confidence in his report, which at all other times had been given. This induced the sending out of Rains and Kennedy, and of Clayton and Gee.

They made their semicircular routes. Clayton and Gee were ensnared by the enemy, and killed. Rains and Kennedy returned on the third day by Buchanan's, and reported to the pent-up people, "No traces of an Indian army are anywhere to be seen!"

Now several days had passed since Castleman had reported he had discovered the trail of two or three hundred Indians. His reputation was in danger. Some of the people were incensed at his conduct. They had "deserted their homes, their crops, their cattle, and fled like frightened sheep, because a watch-dog *thought* he smelled *something!*"

Castleman cleaned his gun, the faithful "*Betsy,*" he picked his flint, he filled his powder-horn afresh, and run an extra number of bullets, and said, "I'm going over to Buchanan's to see the enemy;" meaning his friends there who complained of the alarm and trouble he had occasioned.

The report of Captain Rains gave much satisfaction, and produced a momentary calm. The people were thrown off their guard; the troops which had been ordered to march to meet the invading hosts returned to

of hats," to induce the besiegers to believe the fort to be "strongly manned."*

The Indians some years after acknowledged that they were surprised at the number of guns fired from the fort; that the want of harmony among themselves, and the knowledge that their presence in the settlement had aroused the whites; that they had discovered where the troops had recently marched, and believed them yet *fully* organized at some point in the settlement, and preparing to *intercept* their return, and the failure to begin the attack until daylight, discouraged them. They deemed it best to retreat, and did very much as the "wicked do, when no man pursueth."

They left upon the ground, guns, swords, tomahawks, and articles of value fully sufficient to remunerate the besieged for their expenditure of powder and lead. The calmness of Mrs. Buchanan, the deliberation with which she gave directions and encouragement to others, and perfect coolness in firing her musket, were ever after the subject of remark and commendation. "She had killed buffalo and deer, but she would not boast of having killed an Indian, though she could not plead innocent of the *aim* and *intention.*"

This effort of the allied forces for the destruction of the settlements, seems to have exhausted their energies. For two months the settlers here were undisturbed; indeed, it seemed like a truce. "Strange lulling of the stormy waves!" sung "the said Hood." "They can't scalp me!"

And here we pause in our narration of wars and murders by the Indians. Occasionally a horse was stolen. "They can't help that; 'tis their nature too."

We should not leave the impression that the Indians had wholly abandoned the war: far from it; they were prosecuting it with fury in Washington District, in Western Virginia, and in Kentucky. And we doubt not that the invaders of Cumberland were greatly induced to return from this distant region to defend their own country, and to strengthen other

---

* The expression, "Show your hat!" was very common and significant in early times. Whether it originated from instances such as we have just related, or from the artifice practiced by spies when they sheltered themselves from a savage enemy behind trees, and exposed their "hats without heads in them," to draw fire from the enemy, and thus gain an advantage, we know not. Any cunning device, any artifice by which a person was thrown off his guard, or his attention diverted, or means or efforts wasted, was expressed by saying, "He was killed by a show of hats," "conquered by a show of hats," or such a man "triumphed by a show of hats."

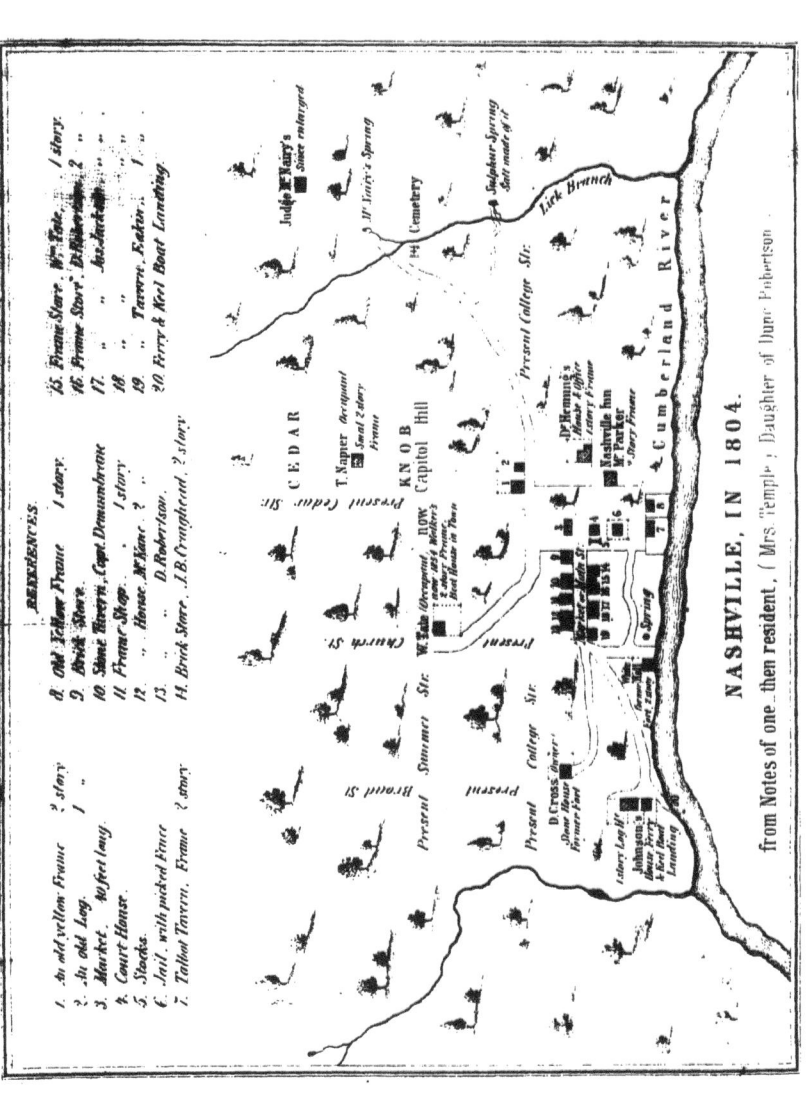

NASHVILLE, IN 1804.

from Notes of one then resident. (Mrs Temple; Daughter of Dun.r Robertson)

expeditions. They feared the threats of General Sevier. · He was now establishing his head-quarters at the junction of Clinch and Tennessee, or "South-west Point." From that position he could watch and command very extensive regions of country, and the very best crossings and traces of the Indians.

Another event is to be noted, which may have had some influence in favor of "our stationers." It was about this period that the fraud by which "General Bowles, the great Director of the Affairs of the Creeks," had for a time obtained distinction and power, was exposed, and the nation drove him forth as an impostor. This invading force had heard of this. McGillivray was reinstated in office.

Judge Haywood says, " The Indians, though they rioted in the excess of cruelty against the people of Cumberland and Holston, and were preparing to bring fresh and multiplied misfortunes upon them, were viewed by the Government of the Union with indifference, and not even with displeasure. The people of the United States turned a deaf ear to the tale of suffering anguish which the western people never ceased to utter. They were unwilling to incur the expenses of more Indian wars; and they held all that could be said upon the subject as a threadbare story, which they had no longer the patience to hear. And notwithstanding the great danger to which the people were hourly exposed, the Government was inclined to *disband* the militia which was stationed on the frontiers for their protection."

It seems that, in despite of all efforts to prevent it, the coalition between the Creeks, Cherokees, and Shawnees was pretty fully established. During this year Governor Blount had many communications with chiefs and head-men of the Cherokees. His desire was to induce them to join the United States against the Shawnees; but to all his messages, verbal and written, they manifested not only reluctance, but indignation. If his application had been to make war against the Chickasaws, their answer would have been different. They were influenced by the Spaniards and Shawnese emissaries. Proof was accumulating of the deceitful and unfriendly intermeddling of the Spaniards. We have stated that most of the mischief done to the Cumberland settlers, before and since the actual declaration of war, was by Creek Indians. This tribe of Indians had no cause of quarrel with these settlers. The distance was great between them. The Creeks never owned, indeed, never set up a claim to any land where these settlements were made. The war here was therefore unprovoked and without excuse.

The court-house, jail, and "stocks," were subject to "all sorts of uses and abuses;" insomuch that the Honorable Justices began to consider it needful for their own reputation, for the dignity of justice, and for "decency's sake," to put the "seat of justice in order." The "stocks" had its own fastenings, the jail its doors, bolts, and bars, but the court-house, "eighteen feet square—built by contract at the lowest bid at *vendue*"— had but the openings cut through the logs, for doors and windows.

The first settlers were always for "a clear show and a fair fight," and opposed to arguments and adjudications with "closed doors." And yet it was not proper that the court-house should become a stable. Therefore the Court

"Ord'ᵈ that David Hay repair the Court-house, by making two doors, well fixed and hung, with three window-shutters well hung; and the house well *chinked*, sweeped, washed and cleansed, and the benches repaired."

Such was the first, the primitive court-house, on the Public Square in Nashville. When saplings and swinging limbs of trees became inaccessible, "everybody hitched his horse" to the court-house, the jail, or the whipping-post.

The persons named in the following letter will justify its insertion entire, or so far as the individuals alluded to are concerned. It is addressed to General Robertson by Governor Blount:

"KNOXVILLE, October 28th, 1792.

"With pleasure I forward the commission for Major *Tatum*, and request you to use your interest with him to induce him to accept it. Public service requires that he should.

"Can't you contrive for *Hay* to resign, and I will promote *Donelson*, and appoint *Jackson* second Major."

Captain Donelson did become Colonel, and Jackson, ultimately, "Major" General, and "Commander-in-chief of the Army and Navy of the United States."

For a moment we turn away from military officers, to look after other affairs than Indian wars and ravages.

In this Cumberland region, what progress has been made in the way of improvements of farms in the country, or houses in the towns, or commerce on the river, or roads through the woods? Much had been done to burn off the cane and undergrowth; forest trees were "girdled and deadened," over hundreds of acres in all directions, and to distances varying from four to six miles around or near to the *original stations*. These were the beginnings of plantations and farms, which in time have become "cleared," fully opened, properly enclosed, and highly improved.

The crop of corn in 1792 was abundant and sold at a handsome profit. The emigrants who arrived this year, the troops and friendly Indians, created a lively demand.

General Robertson had authority to purchase for the troops and for friendly Indians, and to supply them, to a small extent, with what the Governor had pronounced to be "trifles," "powder and lead."

On 2d of December, he is requested by the Governor to "purchase the two thousand bushels of corn at McGavock's." This corn was cultivated and gathered upon the lands north of the French Lick Branch, (now town lots.)

It was required for "our friends, the Chickasaws," and General Robertson engaged to have it delivered to them at the Chickasaw Bluff, and he paid for its delivery there.

Upon being informed of this, the Governor, perhaps very properly, remonstrated, but in respectful terms:

"If they have corn given to them, surely they can afford to carry it down the river themselves. They will use much more than they otherwise would do. And besides all this, if we deliver corn at the doors of the Chickasaws, we shall be asked to do the same for Choctaws!

"Make out your accounts for such and other purchases, as 'Deputy Indian Agent,' and not in your character as 'General;' and hereafter have all corn you purchase for the Indians delivered at your own house."

The few families occupying the fort, and the less than a dozen log-houses, in the town of Nashville, (not enumerating open tents,) had their "patches of corn and vegetables" at various places convenient. The grinding of corn was done at Buchanan's Mill on Mill Creek, south of the town. The main road passing through the town, was from Freeland's Station, crossing the low grounds and branch, near the Sulphur Spring, and entering the Public Square at the north-west corner, thence diagonally toward the south-east corner, in front of the fort or station, on south about Market street, across the branch, over the "Academy lands," and to Buchanan's Mill. Another road was opened west to Johnson's, Dunham's, and the neighboring stations; another path led off south. And, so there were a number of paths to the various settlements and improvements. Indeed, with exception of the first named, they were "by-ways" instead of "high-ways."

The months of October and November were passed by the Cumberland settlers in somewhat an unusual exemption from Indian disturbances; but as the war was prosecuted upon other western settlements, it was not wise or prudent to intermit watchfulness or neglect the defences. But, as if to convince these settlers that they were not too far off or forgotten by the savage foe, a party of Indians entered the settlements about the first of December, and made a very bold attack upon a party of cavalry, which was ranging about eight miles from Nashville. They killed one of the troopers, and routed the entire party. The attack was sudden and fierce, and the whites did not "stand fire." In excuse they magnified the number of Indians to hundreds, whereas there were but a score. "Their yells," no doubt, "sounded like a thousand devils" to ears which had never heard such unearthly sounds before.

There was but one person killed or lost in this attack. His name was *John Hankins.* He was "a poor fellow, half-witted, who would never keep in time or in his place." In the retreat, "fool-like," he turned round and pointed an empty gun, as though he would shoot the whole of them. He was killed, scalped, and cut to pieces. The Indians made no further pursuit.

"Give him Hankins!" was a very common expression. In Kentucky it was, "Give him Goss!" These bywords were probably expressive of opposite characters and deeds.

In Kentucky, Goss was a very stout man, "who could whip his weight ten times over in wild-cats." Keep out of his way, behave yourself, or "you'll get Goss."

But Hankins was "not worth shucks;" as they throw tubs to whales, and meat to pursuing wolves, to stay their stomachs and their speed, so "give them Hankins," and we'll escape.

This little troop obtained some addition to their numbers; returned to the "battle-ground," as one of them unwittingly and unwittily called the place, where they never even faced their foe or stopped to return the fire. This small party of cavalry consisted mostly of "new emigrants," who had wished to enjoy the sport of an "Indian hunt!" If we were in possession of the muster-roll, and could name every individual in that party, we should prefer to commit it to the flames.

"*Sic transit gloria equitorium !*"

The horsemen fled on the 4th of November, 1791, though their commander, St. Clair, had the prestige of a revolutionary reputation. A little squad of horsemen followed their example on the 7th December, 1792, though they had for commander—*nominis umbra.*

During the month of December the Indians committed some murders in these settlements, and "stole many horses and much truck and luggage." Of the persons killed, we should mention John Haggard. He was killed about six miles from Nashville; and the savages, seemingly in wanton sport, or to wreak a terrible vengeance, shot *twelve balls* into his body, and then mutilated him. He had been a spy. His wife had been killed a few months previous, in the summer. We regard it as probable that Haggard had committed some acts to avenge his loss and bereavement; and now the Indians *riddled* him and *chopped* him.

These savages seldom marked their victims with peculiar evidences of brutality, unless there had been some real or supposed grievance and provocation. As to *spies*, they ever formed a distinct class of enemies; and, whenever they could, the Indians gave unmistakable tokens of hatred and vengeance towards them. Their expressive designation of spies was, "the eyes and the ears," and "the watch-dogs," of the settlements. Therefore they plucked out their eyes and cut off their ears, and sometimes, head and ears, arms and legs.

We cannot conclude this chapter without a few' remarks upon the seeming indifference of the United States Government to the sufferings of these remote and exposed settlements. Much of this apathy and deafness to the cries of these emigrants is to be attributed to the Secretary of War, (Knox,) and the statements made to him by Mr. Seagrove, United States Indian Agent among the Creeks. The interference, complaints, and misrepresentations of the Spaniards had also a very considerable influence. That the Administration of Washington was enabled to launch the great ship of state, when the waters were yet troubled—to unfurl the "Flag of the Union," court and secure the favoring gales which have since so prospered us in our national voyage—is cause of thankfulness to a kind and superintending Providence.

The deep policy of Spain, (aided much by the opinions of France in advocacy of her pretensions,) the ignorance of the true character and condition of western settlements, and an unjust prejudice against them, account, in a great measure, for the little credence given to their tales of woe, and for the little sympathy felt in their sufferings by the Government and the people of the Eastern States.

The reports made by Governor Blount, and the representations and petitions of the people in these remote settlements, were too much overlooked. As it had been under the State of North Carolina, so it continued to be, for some time, under the General Government.

These pioneers were regarded as a daring, self-willed set of adventurous land-pirates—ever ready to set up for themselves, to take all they could get, making a pastime of war, laughing at fear, mocking at calamities, reckless of life, and would be extravagant and reckless of money—if they

26

had it, or could make others foot the bills.   Therefore, as the Old North State had refused appropriations out of her treasury, so should the national treasury be safely guarded and exempted.

Governor Blount was called upon to vindicate their character and his own disbursements.   To this call he was prompt to respond; he felt himself competent for the task; he undertook it cheerfully, and well sustained himself and justified his constituents.

We might quote largely from his report.   It, however, more properly belongs to the " Life and Services of William Blount," which we hope may erelong be published.

" King Boyd" used to tell a very good story of one of Piomingo's mountain warriors.   Mingo Multubbe desired some " Bald Face," or raw whiskey.

" How much ?"

" Jug—you fill him—young warrior—snake bite him—die soon—whiskey cure him."

"A gallon is too much."

" No—snake very big," replied the Indian, as he marched off in triumph with the liquor.

They never killed that snake.

We could name several prominent citizens whom he was in the habit of biting in those early times; and thousands in our day are so completely " charmed," that they would " rather be bit than not bit."   " To be cured is not the question."

The satirical remark of " Lawyer Douglas" is said to have aroused the Justices of Davidson county to the adoption of an order to clean out the Court-house :

" May it please your Honors : It is a rule of equity, that every suitor shall come into Court with a clean shirt—narrative .

" Without unnecessary offence to the majesty of law, the ermine of the Judges, or purity of anybody, I defy suitor or advocate, much more the Honorable Court, to maintain pure thoughts and white linen in such a sheepfold and pig-sty !"

This " cleansing" was not let out at " Public Vendue," but David Hays was " ordered" to attend to it, and to see to it that batten doors and batten windows, " on their wooden hinges turning," should be " well fixed and hung."

Now, the man who, with his brother, could start a town but six miles off, and around it gather attractions which for years had well-nigh absorbed our rising city, must have felt himself a little embarrassed, perhaps indignant, at such an order.

But in "Haysboro" they never had a "court-house, a jail, or pair of stocks," although "many persons believed it the *fittenest* place, and most needed there, of any they had ever seen."

Since the construction of a Macadamized road and a railroad from Nashville to Gallatin, Colonel Hays' town has become a miserable *"Ilium fuit."*

CHAPTER XXIV.

1793.

THIS second Cherokee war now increases in fierceness and destruction. This is a year of havoc. The little republic upon Cumberland, though long accustomed to sufferings, blood, and carnage, and placed where she must contend with savage foes in warfare, has also to contend with civilized in diplomacy. The position so long occupied by these "small estates" on Cumberland, had accustomed General Robertson and others to many of the intrigues and artifices of "state craft," as well as to the cunning and cruelty of savage war.

As yet, no year of peace had been enjoyed. Longer than the siege of Troy, has already been the siege of Cumberland. Many as have been the murdered, and horrible as have been the scenes of blood, the appetite of the foe is not satisfied, the thirst for blood is ravening still.

It is under such circumstances, and the certainty of their increase this year, that "the Governor of Virginia," says Haywood, "must take it into his head to trouble Governor Blount" about a little tape-string of land, which that State claimed south of the Henderson line; "as if Governor Blount and this people were lying on *a bed of roses*—had abundant leisure on their hands, and could indulge in recreations."

Some years previous there was occasional leisure to plant roses, and a momentary but delusive hope that those who thus indulged their taste for embellishments and fragrance, might live to enjoy, in safety and leisure, some gratification for all their toils and care. The time had been when gayety, balls, and clubs were known, and the Indian war-whoop, arrow, tomahawk, and musket caused but slight emotion and interruption. Indian wars had long been intermingled in their labors and *divertisse-ments;* but now, the threatening and the preparations of the Indians announced an increase of the havoc, and with more and better guns than were usually found in the hands of savages. The Spaniards had given to Creeks and Cherokees fresh and large supplies of all the incentives and implements for havoc.

Before resuming our usual and sad narrative, we trust we may be excused from drawing in a small "hook and line," which was, some time since, thrown out. Perhaps there may be something on it.

The little town of Nashville, hitherto "fenced in" to keep out Indians, buffalo, and other wild beasts, receives some attention from the Honorable Quarter Sessions Court, which appointed "Genl. Danl. Smith, Thos. Molloy, and Jas. Mulherrin, or any two of them, to re-survey the land laid off for the town of Nashville, the Academy land, and the public land belonging to John McNairy, Esq., adjoining the French Lick."

The Academy had a' "two-forty" on the south of the town, and a "six-forty" at Gasper's Lick; the town had its "two-forty," but how many "John McNairy, Esq.," had, is none of our concern, any further than this, to admit that his Honor was a very good Judge—of lands. He has long since departed, a learned, diligent, and true-hearted Federalist, and Federal officer; his lands have descended to his children and children's children. And "the Judge's Spring," a fresh fountain of purest water in his day, flows undiminished for the use of the town, near the French Lick.

In East Tennessee they were favored with the circulation of that "signal" little sheet, "The Knoxville Gazette," now actually published in the town of Knoxville, and not, as it was at first, in the town of Rogersville. Besides the distinction of having *the* newspaper, Knoxville was the seat of Government, Governor Blount was there, and General Sevier just across the river; but the town, like ours, was in the woods. People here, as in olden time, received the word of the law and the word of news "at the mouth," by the living messenger.

The faithful Clerk of the County recorded many of the incidents of the day occurring in this region; and our little hook and line bring up the following:

"Whereas, in an affray that happened on the second day of September, 1793, between Wm. Pillows and Abram Denton, in fighting, the said Pillows *bit of the uper eend* of Denton's right *year*, upon which s^d Pillows come into open court together with Abram Denton, and the s^d Pillows *open* declared that he bit *of* his *year* aforesaid, *without any intention of injuring* s^d Denton."

That is the whole of the entry, and seems to have been placed there *in perpetuam rei memoriam*, and, therefore, by the historian is not to be overlooked. Under an old law of North Carolina, the act of maiming was a penal offence, for which Pillows might have been punished. But we judge that there was a greater desire to have this "affray" put on record, to save Denton from ever being charged as having been "*cropped*" for offences under another old law. These evidently were old citizens, old soldiers, and old friends; Denton had his "station" not far from town, and Pillows "circulated promiscuously." We presume they had been to the "Red Heifer" and "embraced this opportunity and each other," as many did in Western Pennsylvania in the whiskey insurrection the year following. But this was a small affair and easily adjusted, particularly as the records say there was "no intention to injure."

Governor Blount sometimes thought the Indians had "no intention to injure" *any more;* and the General Government ·had long since entertained the opinion that they never had injured the settlers very much. At least, such was the impression produced here by so long turning a deaf ear to their cries, and neglect to send them help and means of defence. As to the disposition of the Cherokees since their open declaration of war, the Governor certainly cherished strangely favorable sentiments.

On the 5th January he wrote to General Robertson, and enclosed an order for the discharge of Major Sharpe's troops : "You must keep down the expenses. This is the constant injunction from Philadelphia."

The people of Cumberland were used to such a cry, coming from a distance beyond the mountains. When a part of North Carolina, and their lives in danger at every step they took, if there was the least intimation of a demand upon the treasury, the reply was sure to come, "Don't call for money; you need not ask for any measure which will add further burden to the State. And so now : you have placed yourselves in a position of great danger, and you must fight it out. The treasury cannot be oppressed to help you!"

The Governor says, "To supply the place of Sharpe's brigade, you may organize *a company of infantry and eighteen horsemen !* but neither with nor without your orders must they pass the Indian boundary, unless in pursuit of Indians who have committed murders or stolen horses; and for such pursuits they must have your orders. And all your military orders must be in writing !" Take a *wide sweep,* as in a *circus !*

He says, indeed, that these restrictive orders are in conformity to those from *head-quarters;* and yet he hopes for peace, when there is only war.

On the 8th he writes, that in a few days he should have a meeting with the Indians at South-west Point, "after which he expected there would be *profound peace.*" And on the same day he informs General Robertson that he had discharged the troops in East Tennessee, "retaining only one company of infantry and twenty-five cavalry of General

Sevier's brigade, to be stationed at South-west Point." And thus the country was left in quite a defenceless condition.

There seemed a combination of influences within the United States against affording aid in men or money to these besieged settlements. The Treasury Department greatly dreaded expenditures here. The War Department was making preparations for another grand army in the North-western Territory. The Department of State watched with keenest eye our foreign and domestic affairs, and was exceedingly distrustful of and opposed to every appropriation and measure which might embarrass negotiations then pending, or accumulate difficulties in the way of such as it was desired to engage in at some not very distant day.

The Administration, it is true, had its purpose of not only securing the navigation of the Mississippi, but of the river itself, its thousands of miles of tributary streams, and of all the unexplored and unmeasured territories thereon. England yet encouraged the Indian warriors to disturb the settlements in Ohio and Kentucky, and Spain persisted in the same practices with the tribes at the South. The strength of those warlike nations was in the South, and they made it to be felt by the people of Cumberland. The Sovereigns examined the map of America to see the position of the "nest of Americans on Cumberland;" they wished to know if these were "refugees from justice or absconding debtors," "who had sought a hiding-place in the wilderness;" whether these men were truly attached to republican principles and democratic institutions; whether they could not be tampered with, dealt with, intrigued with; whether flattery would win them, gold would bribe them, lands elsewhere would suit them; whether threats would alarm them, and sufferings break their hearts.

There were emissaries in the settlements who found turbulent spirits, many real causes of complaint, and an abundance of material heated and ready for a flame; but it was easy to learn that in whatsoever explosion should occur, the prayer and purpose was that destruction might fall upon the Indians and the Spaniards towards the South, the English and the Indians towards the North.

Politicians, statesman, and chief executive officers inquired into the condition of this people, seven thousand in all, (men, women, children, and servants,) enduring the "conflict of ages," famine and bloody murder: nine-tenths of the earliest settlers destroyed in fierce protracted war; the noblest heroes shot down by secret murderers, and Robertson yet spared, around whom the new, the daring, and the true-hearted emigrants cluster, to beseech him to lead them forth to hunt and destroy the foe. He let them know that in his heart there was sadness and sorrow for the dead, there was sympathy for the bereaved and the afflicted, and a deep sentiment of gratitude to all these new emigrants. And yet he could not give his aid or sanction to a violation of treaties made with even such faithless murderers ; nor disobedience to the orders of superiors. He had much love for General Washington, and some confidence that there were good political and diplomatic reasons why a war should not be carried into the homes of the savages. Let us not drive them into a united warfare, and by no means into closer intimacy with the Spaniards. The French Revolution will cause Spain more trouble at home than will be pleasant. The number of Spaniards here is small; the Indians will, erelong, of this be convinced, and they will never fail to join the nation that has the strength, and best supplies their wants. Our Government will shortly satisfy them upon these points. Our lot is a hard one, but let us abide in it.

For the first time politics were warmly discussed upon the Cumberland. But there were too frequent occurrences of Indian murders and thefts to allow any other topic to absorb attention ; for it will be seen in the summing up of the killed and wounded, captives, and thefts of the year, that these outrages continued from beginning to the end.

At this juncture the " Spaniards gave umbrage to the Creeks," by giving aid to the collection of debts and reclamation of property which refugee tories and thieves had taken into their nation ; sustaining the favorite traders, McGirt and Panton, in their speculation in property and recovery of debts. Agents of the United States assured them of very friendly dispositions on the part of our Government.

Another favoring coincidence was the arrival in our country of that rabid red-republican, Genet, a man alike destitute of wisdom, prudence, and politeness, who knew not Washington or the American people; who could insult both, and set about the organizing of Jacobin societies and military companies within our own territory, to make war upon a nation with which we were at peace, (although she deserved war at our hands.)

Fortunately, the Spaniards apprehended much danger from this French influence and movement, and, to conciliate the good will of the United States, promised their best exertions to induce Creeks and Cherokees and others to be at peace. They dreaded very much an invasion of Spanish territory on the Mississippi, by people from Kentucky and Cumberland. They also feared that these same Cumberlanders, (whom they had for so many years sought to exterminate,) now, having, as was reported, fully one thousand able-bodied men who were good marksmen, were about to accept aid from those same Kentuckians or Virginians, and, cutting their way through the Indian nations, attack and capture the Spanish town of Mobile, and other towns.

Catching up the language or soubriquet used by some of the Cherokee chiefs in their joint letter of complaint to the Baron de Carondelet, this noble and learned Baron, with other Spanish officers and agents, in trepidation, address our Government upon the dangers to which *their allies* (the Indians) and the Spanish settlements are exposed; and, as though they knew no other title for him, they complain of " a *certain* Robertson, who, with his companions, coming upon the Cumberland *secretly, had taken possession!*" This haughty Baron and his officers at the Spanish posts could not only intrigue with Indians, but could encourage and listen to their complaints, justify them, stir them up to ill-blood; "promise and give guns, swords, saddles, blankets, powder, lead, hatchets;" promise, but *not give* them protection, or a restoration of their lands. This same haughty Spaniard could ignore the title of General Robertson; and yet he, (Gayoso, Portell, Mero, De Villemont, and others, could humbly crave his good offices, and hold correspondence with him as the acknowledged head and representative of a political society and Government they had long dreaded. "A certain Robertson," indeed!

General Robertson, and these "Three Estates of Cumberland," are drawn into prominence by Gardoqui, Carondelet, and Dons without number, who finally attempt to justify their wicked interference by reference to a treaty which their nation had made ten years previously with the Creeks, in which, " forasmuch as the Creeks acknowledged his Catholic Majesty for their only sovereign and protector, his Majesty had agreed and felt bound to protect them directly and indirectly; especially by furnishing them with goods, arms, and other needed articles."

This acknowledgment now extorted from Gardoqui, was a confession of wickedness that had long been suspected by our Government, and by none more early than by General Robertson. He had often used the expression, "The hand of Providence is in it!" and he took shelter and consolation under this conviction not only in the midst of greatest afflictions, but when the night of despair seemed to shut down in horrors around the settlements.

It would extend this chapter to an unreasonable length, were we to introduce a notice of the policy and diplomatic correspondence of our Government in relation to the Cumberland settlements, and of the positions which were assumed and points argued. The result was, the *justification of General Robertson*, of the people on the Cumberland, the acknowledgment of our rights, the elevation of the dignity of our Government, and of the character of American citizens; and final peace, in the humiliation of the Indians, the repulse of the schemes of Spain. England, and France, and illustrating of the ways of Providence in this portion of the Western Continent.

But as, in this sketch of dealings between our General Government and other great nations, though originating with or relating in some degree to affairs and people in this then isolated colony in the woods, we have glanced through the year, it is now our purpose to resume our especial narrative of what was done and suffered here.

We have designed this chapter to be rather introductory to the more immediate history of the stations and settlements during the year 1793; at the same time presenting a few incidents by way of entertainment, as well as for instruction and elucidation.

The "Academy" gave hopes of becoming a permanent institution. Distinguished men manifested interest in its character and success. " Mr. President" had applied to the County Court and procured license to establish a ferry across the Cumberland, and it was leased this year for one hundred dollars !

General Smith said to General Jackson, "that is enough to pay the passages of all the Trustees across the river Styx." " I want but one *stick* to make my way," replied the then young Hickory.

There were no less than three Generals in the original Board of Trustees—Robertson, Smith, and Williamson, and three Colonels, Polk, Bledsoe, and Hays. And now, Colonel William Polk having removed, " Mr. Andrew Jackson" is elected his successor.

A ride of six miles to " Spring Hill," crossing the river morning and evening, is considered " rather inconvenient," and " the school ought to be moved to town."

The description given by some of "the boys of that day," of their *equipments* for school; the races, going and coming, the actual verification of the " *Tityre, tu patulæ recubans sub tegmine fagi;*" and of the patriotic remark of " the Parson," their preceptor : " Boys, your fathers never deserted their country, and you will never say '*patriam fugimus*' or '*linquimus,*' " following up the quotation from Virgil, is natural and simple.

" We were bare-footed or moccasined, with linsey pants and hunting-shirts, and if we had on another shirt under that, it was of tow-linen, with *shives* enough all through it to justify our exemption from any worse kind of hackling ; though it did not always avail us. . . I have seen lots of broken limbs and stumps of switches in my day. When we used to go through ' scuff ' and on the ' road to Buchanan's Mill,' up to ' the Academy,' we talked of college, of professions and politics, and the girls, and wrote poetry on paper, and carved names on trees. . . One thing we did, we took good care of our books, and drove the cows home after we were dismissed from school. On Saturdays we used to think ourselves 'set up,' when astraddle of a bag of corn going to Buchanan's Mill, to catch fish and swim in the pond, bring home the bag of meal and a string of fish; have our backs greased with cream, where they had been blistered by the sun, when we were in a-swimming in the creek. Then the shives hurt some, but we didn't mind it—we were growing, and soon got well."—*Conversations of E—— H——.*

There was another mill in the opposite direction, and on the other side of the river. "It was a very good mill, *considering.*" It was on White's Creek, and belonged to "the prosperous old Dutchman, Frederick Stump. Mr. Stump was not satisfied with the legal or established rate of toll for grinding corn, and therefore helped himself to a little more than the law allowed or customers approved.

Here is the record of the result:

October Term, 1793.—"Frederick Stump fined 1ᵈ *paper money*, for taking the *sixth part of corn* ground at his mill, as toll.—1ᵈ."

That wasn't much of a fine, but it was pretty much of a lesson.

In the same report of "Fines received by Andrew Ewing, Clerk," and accounted for to the treasury, may be seen several instances of the "25s. fine" under the old act of 1741. "Mormonism could not be countenanced here by the decent portion of society, in no way they could fix it."

Some of the penalties are made "payable in hard money," but usually in "paper money," or "proc."

CHAPTER XXV.

1793.

As we mentioned near the opening of the first chapter of this year, the Governor entertained so favorable an opinion of the pacific disposition of the Cherokees, that he, on the 8th of January, dismissed most of the troops under Generals Sevier and Robertson, and invited the chiefs to another friendly conference at South-west Point, 17th of April.

The Indians smiled at his credulity, and rejoiced at the clear paths they would have to " gather hair and steal horses :" *id est,* " take scalps, and run with six legs."

Watts had for some time fallen into disgrace, or, at least, lost some of his popularity among his tribe. His participation in the attack on Buchanan's Station, and its failure—notwithstanding the two wounds he there received—seems to have been the cause of this diminution of authority. His people, for a time, deserted him in reality or in pretence. They said they were afraid the white people would come and destroy their town, in retaliation for what Watts had done; that the speech which was reported to them as having been made by General Robertson, was not an unmeaning speech—that " he would come suddenly and destroy them and their town." They urged Watts, or else it was his own cunning policy, to make humble confession of the error and wrong he had committed. He did so. To comfort him, and to confirm him and his people in good resolutions, the Governor, in February, sent Watts and Talotiskee and the Glass a number of presents; and " cast his pearls before swine."

The game of " kill and steal" was soon renewed, not only in East Tennessee, but among our afflicted settlers on the Cumberland. The number of killed in Mero District this year was at least fifty. The accounts vary from forty-nine up to seventy-nine. And if we take the names given by Haywood, which are near the lowest number, and then make only a moderate allowance where he mentions *entire* families killed—such, for instance, as that of the " Widow Baker and all her family except two, which was a numerous household"—" many persons were killed in Sumner county, whose names are not remembered"—and "twenty persons were killed between the 20th of May and 13th August," we cannot much hesitate to adopt the *higher* estimate. An awful account of murdered persons is this, and the wounded enumerated are fourteen! But we will be more definite.

Early in January Mr. Gower was mortally wounded on White's Creek, yet he escaped to Hickman's Station. Two of this family had been killed a dozen years ago. On the same day another person was wounded near the river several miles below Nashville. A party of Indians were pursued from the neighborhood of Bledsoe's Station. They had stolen horses, on which they effected their escape, but dropped some guns and plunder.

January 16th. Mr. Hugh Tenin was killed when at work at his fence. He had erected his cabin, and was clearing off undergrowth, and making a fence, when Indians in ambush shot him, seized his horse, and fled. The persons who were with Tenin escaped. This was on Red River, but a few miles from Clarksville.

January 18th. As Major Evan Shelby (brother of General Shelby, of Kentucky) was returning from the Falls of the Ohio in a large canoe, laden with salt and various articles of prime necessity and value, the Indians fired upon the crew. How many persons were with Major Shelby, whether they were attacked when encamped at night, or when propelling the boat against the current in the day, and the place at which the attack was made, we have not been enabled to ascertain. We conclude it was near Dover, and on the west side of the Cumberland.

Three persons were killed: Major Shelby, James Harney, and a negro man belonging to Moses Shelby. The Indians stripped the dead, and put on their clothes. The gun, sword, and other personal property of Shelby, were appropriated by the leader of the party. They found more in the boat than they had need for. They wasted and exposed what they left in the boat and on the land. Other boatsmen gathered some of what remained.

Evan and Isaac Shelby were sons of General Evan Shelby, of North Carolina. They inherited much of the military and patriotic spirit of their heroic father, whose services in the desperate battle at Point Pleasant have been always highly commended, as were those of Isaac in his association with Valentine Sevier, for which he was honored with command of the fort at the mouth of the Kanawha until Lord Dunmore ordered it to be abandoned, lest Shelby should make it a strong-hold for the American Revolutionists, or Whigs.

Evan Shelby, Jun., served as an officer and ranger for the Watauga settlements, and was repeatedly engaged in conflicts with the Indians. " He had a brush or two with some of the Tories."

When his brother Isaac removed to Kentucky, Evan came and settled on the Cumberland. He filled several positions here with credit to himself and usefulness to the public. His death, and the destruction of property in his charge, were regarded as a double calamity.

The Indians were on the constant lookout for boats on the Cumberland, preferring to attack the ascending boats, for very evident reasons. On board of such the men were busily engaged in propelling the boat, and not on watch. These boats also had valuable cargoes. Several persons were killed near the Red River Stations, whose names have not been recorded.

January 22d. Overall and Burnett were killed as they were returning from Kentucky, having nine horses laden with goods, salt, and whiskey. Overall was one of the earliest settlers here, and we suppose had acted as a spy; therefore the Indians " cut the flesh from his bones." Whiskey, salt, and goods were not only packed to the settlements on horses, but brought by water.

On 24th January, a boat and pettiauga laden with salt and other articles, when ascending the Cumberland, were attacked. The boat belonged to French traders. In it two were killed instantly, and one mortally wounded. In the other boat or pettiauga two were killed and three wounded, one of these mortally. The killed were Gaskins and David Crow; the wounded, Wells, Milliken, and Pruit. Pruit died from a wound in the knee, whilst Milliken, with five balls in various places, survived. This Milliken lost a brother here at an early day.

January 26th. Anthony Bledsoe, son of Colonel Bledsoe, and Thomas Heal, were killed opposite Nashville.

February 17th. Thomas Bledsoe, another son of Colonel Anthony Bledsoe, was fired on and wounded, and chased to within fifty yards of the stockade at Greenfield, in Sumner county. On the same day two negroes belonging to James Clendennen were killed close to the house.

February 22d. Two sons of Colonel Saunders were fired on, both wounded and scalped : one died instantly ; the other after several days' suffering. These were in Sumner county.

February 24th. Captain Samuel Hays was killed near the door of John Donelson's house, (*west* of the " Hermitage.") Hays' own station was a mile east of the Hermitage.

March 19th. Mr. Nolan was killed on Harpeth, about ten miles from Nashville.

In this month two parties of Creeks passed from these settlements with the scalps of three white persons and of two negroes, having with them a negro of Mr. Parker as captive, and several horses. Pursuit was made, but the Indians escaped.

By letter from Governor Blount to General Robertson, under date March 28th, he gave the General warning to look out for an attack by parties from the Upper Creeks and Lower Cherokees; that they would come about the 25th of the month of April, or at the "full moon." "It seems," says he, "you may expect the greatest danger from them; and to guard against them, you will order out a full company of mounted infantry or cavalry, of eighty men, exclusive of commissioned officers. Let them waylay the Indian paths leading to the settlements, explore the woods in search of their camps, and, wherever found within the limits of *fifty miles* from the settlements, treat all but women and children as enemies."

By this authority the limits for the range and pursuit by the troops were extended.   The Governor recommends to General Robertson to engage active, enterprising officers and men, and gives other advice and directions, for which, indeed, there was little necessity.   In case of *imminent* danger, the troops *might* pursue the enemy to the Tennessee River! "We can construe that," said General Robertson.

He also mentions that small parties of Creeks are daily crossing and recrossing the river, killing the people and stealing horses.   In conclusion, he gives General Robertson liberty to supply the Chickasaws with corn, necessary for their support.

"In eight or ten days I shall set out for Philadelphia, if General Smith arrives safe."

He did so proceed, and General Smith, as Secretary of the Territorial Government, attended to public affairs, and communicated with General Robertson.

April 9th. Colonel Isaac Bledsoe, when working in his fields near his house, was killed.   And thus have the Bledsoes been cut down, one after another.   Earliest among the explorers and settlers on the Cumberland, conducting or attracting valuable emigrants to the country, honored by their fellow-citizens and by State and nation with positions of trust, civil and military; making the first field and planting the first seeds in the rich soils of the Cumberland; leaving a name to that spot and Lick which should never be changed, they have identified their names and deeds with the people and the country so as never to be obliterated.

April 10th. The house of Mrs. Simpson was set on fire, but there being several men within, who shot at the Indians, and made them retreat, they extinguished the flames.

April 11th. Hammond and Dowdy were killed near the mouth of Sycamore Creek.

April 14th. Howdishall and Pharr were killed near General Rutherford's, bear-hunting.

April 18th. John Benton, killed near Cragfont, the residence of
Colonel Winchester; and not far off two men killed, on Kentucky trace.

April 19th. Two men killed at Clarksville.

April 20th. Richard Shaffer and Mr. Gombrell were killed, and
James Dean wounded while engaged in ploughing.

April 27th. The station at Greenfield was attacked by a party at first
supposed to consist of only sixty, but it was afterward ascertained that
the entire force was two hundred and sixty strong.

This was regarded as one of the best prepared stations in the settlement, recently built and with lookout station and palisades. It was
saved in this attack by the signal bravery of William Neelly, William
Hall, and William Wilson, aided by one or two others. These men
killed two or three Indians, and wounded several others. "Neelly and
Hall had each lost a father and two brothers by the savages; and were
ready and nerved for a desperate fight, whenever opportunity was
afforded."*

The Greenfield Station was regarded as one of the strongest of recent
defences. A small force was stationed there. During the day-time most
of the people, white and black, labored in the adjacent fields under the
watchfulness of sentinels or lookouts. At night all assembled at the
station. This was customary at all the stations.

During the night of the 26th, the Indians had formed an ambuscade
near the pathway to the fields. The negroes went out early to their
work, and had hitched their horses to the ploughs, when the savages
in ambuscade between the negroes and the fort, showed themselves and
commenced firing at a distance, at the same time raising a most fearful
war-whoop. A number of the men in the fort were ready to proceed to
the field to assist in work and to act as guard. Such men always had
their guns loaded and within arm's-reach; and at the cry of "Indians
about," or at the crack of a strange gun, they were instantly upon their

---

* The present writer has conversed with each of these worthy men, now deceased. Mr. Neelly resided about seven miles east of Nashville, and General Hall
about ten miles from Gallatin, or two from Bledsoe's Lick. They were worthy
men, highly esteemed in life, and their memories are cherished by all who knew
them. General Hall filled several positions in political and legislative, as well as
military life.

feet with rifle in hand. So it was in this instance; and as the negroes and many of the Indians were in full view, and most of the Indians with their backs toward the fort, a sudden sortie upon them was calculated to startle them. The movement from the fort was as quick as thought, and it was by men who had long wished for the encountering of these mur- derers; they cared little how much they might outnumber them. With utmost swiftness these four or five men rushed out and fired upon the Indians, at the same time raising the yell, and calling upon others to come on. "Come on, twenty of you, and we'll fix them." Some of the Indians turned upon the whites; a fence being between them, each party sought for such a covert. The Indians yielded it, and, having secured the horses, they were ready to depart, still firing occasionally at the small party of whites, but at such a distance as to do them no harm. They kept up the war-whoop as they left, seeming as much gratified at the capture of the horses, as if they had killed so many white men. One of the negroes was mortally wounded, and Mr. John Jarvis killed. A ball passed through the hair of Mr. Hall, leaving a slight impression upon the skin. Hall had not waited to put on his hat, and Neelly said " he knew not whether *he* then owned a hat; was sorry he could not furnish Hall with an Indian's scalp for his exposed head."

It appears by this and other instances of threatened attacks of forts, that they had such dread of these strongholds, that few of them would ever boldly approach one of these castles or fortified places. " You keep big gun and dogs," said the Indians.

Whether the cry of these five men, and the bold shout for " more to come on," had any good effect or not upon the foe, could not be decided. There were always in such companies of Indians some half-breeds, who understood our language. The Indians, however, soon discovered the ruse, and made such a formidable display, that Wilson, Hall, and Neelly dis- covered that their own safety and that of the station itself required them to retreat; otherwise, before they could reload their guns, retreat might be cut off, themselves killed, and the station entered. They made good their escape, therefore, amidst the firing of at least fifty guns; leaving Jarvis and one negro man to be scalped. There were but three or four other men in the fort; the "twenty" were women and children.

April 28th. On the next day the Indians killed Francis Ransom in Davidson county. The discovery of so formidable a number of armed savages in the very centre of the settlements, was cause of great alarm to the settlers. It will be recollected that the people had been thrown off their guard; that the troops had been mostly withdrawn; that the military orders came from afar, and were vacillating and disheartening;

27

that now, in the midst of their planting season, every man was driven from his labor, families were compelled to herd together on a sudden in the stations, all implements of husbandry were to be laid aside, and every man to hold his gun constantly in hand, and look on all sides and at all hours for the murderous foe. That some of the people should be greatly alarmed, that others should be excessively enraged, is not at all to be wondered at.

But now an additional cause of excitement is presented.

Shortly before this time, the letter was received from Governor Blount, dated April 14th, notifying General Robertson of the large bodies of Creeks which had crossed the Tennessee for war and plunder; that they "had declared war against the United States," which everybody here said, meant "the united settlements on the Cumberland."   .

The Governor's "expectation to order to their relief a force of one hundred and sixty to five hundred mounted infantry," could not be realized. The call for troops was urgent in East Tennessee likewise, so that the extent of help from that quarter was a troop of one hundred and twenty men. Major Beard was in command, but required to receive orders from General Robertson during his short service in Mero District, for the order was to General Robertson not to detain him more than thirty-one days.

In this same letter were several paragraphs which were bitterly censured by the people. The Governor says, "It has been here reported, on the authority of Colonel Buford, of Kentucky, that General Logan was about to raise a party to invade the Lower Cherokee towns. Such a measure would be totally destructive of the plans and measures of the President, and would destroy the hopes of returning peace.

"Should he attempt to march a body of men through the District of Mero, it will be your duty to command him, in positive terms, to desist from his object of invading the Cherokee nation or towns, and to warn him of the evil consequences that will attend such a measure.

"This you may do verbally if you please, but you must also do it in writing for your justification.

"I have written to Gov. Shelby on the subject.

"In this I do not mean to prohibit the General from ranging the woods as far as permitted by my order of the 28th of March, nor from chastising Indians within those limits."

Here was a dilemma for General Robertson. The people had long complained, and they had a thousand causes for complaint, one for every life taken or body maimed among them. When is this to end; where is the expected and promised aid and protection? Where are the benefits of the Union? Is every ear deaf to our complaints, and every heart callous to our sufferings?

No: here are our neighbors and friends in Kentucky, who have shared in our woeful experience. They sympathize with us. They know our afflictions are real, and that we have endured them far too long already. They know we have stood in the breach, that the pathways of their and our enemies were through our woods and across our borders; and now, when they volunteer to leave their more secure and improved homes, and to come, at their own expense, to chastise those enemies, here arrives an order from head-quarters, absolutely, and "in positive terms," forbidding "any such measures."

This prohibition seemed like a death-knell. What now cares the Government for us; what care we for the Government and its prohibitions? So intense was the excitement at the moment, that we doubt not, had General Logan appeared with a respectable force, and expressed a wish or willingness to be joined by good hunters from Cumberland, he would not have called in vain.

If Governor Blount was possessed of the secrets of the General Government, and if some of those secrets were communicated to General Robertson and a few other leading men, it is certain the people did not know or understand them. To talk to them about diplomacy, policy, and peace, when there was nothing but the most cruel and savage war, was like talking to the whirlwind.

However, the efforts to restore and keep the peace were not wholly neglected. On the very day of the attack upon Greenfield, a letter was issued by the "War Department" to General Wayne, at Fort Washington, (now Cincinnati,) an extract of which was forwarded to Governor Blount, and by him to General Robertson. (Duplicates in vol. i. of General Robertson's Correspondence.) In that it is announced as it had been before: "It is the policy of the Government to endeavor to preserve peace with the Creeks; *the articles now forwarded are put upon the footing of* SERVICES *rendered to the United States!*"

Here was another firebrand thrown into this magazine. "For services rendered the United States!" Yes, yes, how, and what kind of services? and by the Creeks too! Killing our fathers, mothers, wives, sisters, brothers, and leaving others *crippled, mangled, and peeled!* The voice of these maimed ones joins with the voice from the dead, for vengeance. O God, who shall stay our hand? "Give us help from trouble, for vain is the help of man."

Of all the strange things done by Government, this, to many people here, seemed the strangest. We have tried to be at peace with them, we have treated them with hospitality, we have made them presents, we have paid for our lands once and again, and we have entered into treaties, but of what avail are all these? The Creeks and the Cherokees are daily murdering our people, robbing us, and destroying our property. And yet here are presents of blankets, clothing, guns, and ammunition to the amount of thousands of dollars furnished by our own Government to these very murderers, "upon the footing of services rendered the United States!" Why not state the true reason, and say at once, "upon the footing of exterminating the people of Cumberland?" They and the Spaniards have sought to accomplish the destruction of this settlement for years past; but having failed, our own Government now steps forward to furnish the means *to prolong the conflict.* An hundred thousand dollars has been given to McGillivray after he waged an unprovoked and deadly war upon us; annuities and pensions have been given to the chiefs, but there is yet no peace; there is "no footing for the dove of peace" in all this region; war, only war!

We think it not at all strange there was this excitement, and that a large proportion of this suffering people reasoned and clamored as they did. There was a combination of acts and a concurrence of communications or reception of intelligence, which served greatly to kindle and keep alive the commotion. They looked at these dates as significant and ominous.

On this same 27th April an order was issued from the War Department to furnish the Chickasaws with various articles. These were, indeed, friendly Indians, so far as Indians could be called friendly; and Mr. Portell, who knew them well, had said, "*none* of them can be trusted." And so it is : we must be constantly in doubt and on the watch, and incessantly buying the doubtful friendship. But there seems some excuse or plausibility in putting liberalities to the Chickasaws "upon the footing of services"—in abstaining generally from injuries to these settlements. But the proclamation is for peace with all; "the policy of the Government is peace." It is like saying to us, "Patience, good friends, patience; they have endeavored to destroy you *only for fourteen years!* They will surely weary at it erelong, or yield up their blood-thirsty spirit for pay. 'Though the vision tarry long, wait for it.'"

It was impossible for the mass of this people to approve such policy or yield their assent to arguments in its favor. General Robertson, General Smith, and some others, argued for peace, whilst their hearts reluctated. That worthy and learned divine, Rev. Thomas B. Craighead, talked and preached the same doctrines: "Avenge not yourselves, but rather give place unto wrath." With very sour tempers and surly dispositions, the maddest among the people agreed to "stay their hand for a little longer."

To let the reader understand what kind of articles were usually furnished these Southern Indians, we copy entire the order for

"SUPPLY FOR THE CHICKASAWS.

" 500 Stand of Arms.
"2000 lbs. of Powder.
"4000 Flints.
"1500 Bushels Corn.
" 50 lbs. Vermilion.
" 100 Gallons Whiskey.
"Armourer)
"and Tools. ∫
" War Department, 27th April, 1793."

This armorer or gunsmith was sent to put and keep the arms in order and as a common smith.

The "peace-talk" of "President Washington to the chiefs and warriors of the Chickasaw nation of Indians," was also dated April 27th, 1793, and being received here by General Robertson about the same time with other documents and concurring acts, attracted attention; General Robertson retained a copy, and soon started his runners to make it known. Half-breed and sometimes full-blood Indians were employed as the mail or news-carriers. We may mention Findleston, George Augusta, Jo. Derogue, Tom Blount, and McClish. But these were not always implicitly confided in. From subsequent exposure of Spanish intrigues, it became evident that more than one of the above-named informers and secret agents of Governor Blount and General Robertson may have been in the pay of our enemies at some period.

The office of a spy is surely one of danger and deceit; and the remark of General Robertson is worthy of him and creditable to the pioneer settlers: "We have good common sense, and we must use it against all the arts of learned diplomacy, the wiles of the devil, and cunning craftiness of the Indians."

Rains or Sampson Williams said, "Give us but half the quantity of arms and ammunition Government gives to the rascals, and we'll knock the hindsights off every one of them, and make them soon cry out 'Poc-i-mav-i-mus!' the rascals!"

We may as well proceed with the usual and sad tale of suffering—the enumeration of the killed and wounded. In the course of the next eight months, there were killed and wounded in the District of Mero no less than thirty persons. The names of several have not been transmitted to us, but we give the following imperfect list "for the month of May."

"In May, four boys wounded, one scalped, and one escaped the hands of the Indians, by stripping off his jacket and leaving that instead of his scalp. This was within two miles of Nashville. The Indians laughed and yelled at the little fellow, but did not pursue him.

"On the 4th, A. Fleener, Richard Robertson, and Mr. Bartlett were killed; Young and Mayfield, wounded.

" 20th, John Hacker, killed on Drake's Creek."

It was well known there were many parties of Indians on this side of the Tennessee River, and that some of them had gone into Kentucky to steal and kill there. This diversion and division of the large force which had crossed the river between the 1st April and middle of May, afford us the explanation why no large parties of them were discovered by Major Beard and his troop in their explorations between the settlements and the Tennessee River. They discovered a number of deserted camps, killed only three Indians, and wounded as many more. Beard returned to Knoxville early in June. This system of "scouring the woods," way-laying the traces, and searching for the enemy at a distance from the settlements, was, no doubt, productive of alarm to them. Hitherto the incursive parties could come into the settlements, commit their outrages, and, if they were successful in stealing horses, could very generally re-pass "the ridges" and the lines to which pursuit was restricted.

"Numerous parties, however, almost daily recrossed the Tennessee in June, with scalps and horses, which they had taken from Tennessee and Kentucky settlers."

At the same time that Major Beard was on his tour back and forwards south of the settlements, General Robertson had out his favorite, Captain Rains, accompanied by Captain Johnston, in command of one hundred cavalry. They discovered very few Indians, killed no more than Beard; but as these troops ranged separately and passed rapidly, the savages could enjoy no rest or safety at their camps; therefore they deserted them.

In June, James Steele and daughter were killed, and a son wounded.

In July, Jacob and Joseph Castleman were killed, and Hans Castle-man wounded, at a short distance from Nashville, near Castleman's Station. William Campbell badly wounded, as also Mr. Joslin and Mr. Smith—all within short distances from town to the north-west and south-west. There were several other persons killed and wounded, in the very heart of the settlements. This seemed strange and daring; but the truth is, these invaders divided into very small parties, took routes for some time unfrequented, or sought out new ones through the cane, and thus entered the settlements in rear of the scouts and cavalry. Rains' scouts were the only ones now out to range through the woods for three hundred miles in extent.

The prospect for crops was good, and they required much attention. A large portion of the people seemed disposed to practice the lessons of "resignation and forbearance inculcated by the Government," and not disregard the orders given to General Robertson. That old hunter, Abraham Castleman, however, could not longer be restrained. General Robertson, sympathizing in his afflictions, permitted him to raise a company of volunteers, and take his own measures for retaliation. Some of his men had volunteered to accompany him "to any point on this side of the Tennessee." Not having killed any Indians "worth naming," within that boundary, the old man determined to find them at home, in their own country across the river. Ten of his men there parted with him, and took their route of search back to the settlements. Castleman, accompanied by five brave fellows, all good shots, dressed and painted as Indians, crossed the river a little below Nickojack. Intending to proceed to Willstown, they had not gone far before they came in view of a party of near fifty Creeks, seated upon the ground, two and two, painted black, evidently going out to war. No squaws were with them. As the advancing party was so well disguised, the Creek warriors allowed them to approach quite near, continuing to eat their rough meal, and only expecting to be called upon by the rules of politeness and hospitality in the woods to share liberally with the visitors.

But, suddenly, "Old Abe" planted down his left foot and threw his rifle into position, as did his five companions, and at once all fired, taking deliberate aim at separate couples, and each killed his man, and *Abe* his two. His gun had a double charge of buck-shot. So sudden and unexpected was the fire, and so fatal, the Indians were greatly alarmed, and broke into the woods. During this confusion and dispersion of the savages, Castleman and his companions made good their retreat.

This daring and successful onslaugh was on the 15th day of August. "Pretty hot work in a summer's day!"—so they said. Frederick Stull, who was one of the party, used to preface his ludicrous description of the expedition with, "Mortal Report of a Naked Affair!" or "Naked Report of a Mortal Affair." They had hid their clothing on the east side of the river, and in the attack they were *in puris naturalibus minio infecti, cum breech-cloutibus!*

The party consisted of Abraham Castleman, leader, Frederick Stull, Zach. Maclin, Jack Camp, Eli Hammond, and Zeke Caruthers, "right-hand men, dare-devils." They were all from the neighborhood of Nashville. They returned in safety on the 21st, having been absent just three weeks, "well satisfied with what they had done."

In the very evening of the day in which these men reached home, the Indians killed the Widow Baker and her large family, (with exception of two who made their escape into the woods and concealed themselves until the next day.) Mrs. Baker was living on the creek, where her husband had commenced his improvements at an early day, and which is known at the present day as "Baker's Creek." He was one of the earliest hunters and explorers of the country along the Cumberland. When or how or where his life was ended, we know not. But persons of another name occupy the grounds where "the Widow Baker and her children were slain."

Not two more days had passed, before Samuel Miller "was cut in two," near Joslin's Station, (on Charlotte Pike,) and the wife of Robert Willis and her two children, near the same place, were killed and scalped. Pursuit was made of the Indians who had massacred the Baker and Willis families, but with what results we know not.

These were awful tragedies. Some of the stationers entertained the opinion that the party of Indians which had been attacked by Castleman and his five "right-hand men," had pursued their bold assailants in their retreat; and, not overtaking them, or knowing how much easier and safer for them it was to kill women and children than to encounter the daring spies, had avenged themselves in this destruction of helpless families. Castleman said that the murderers of Mrs. Baker could not be of the party he had attacked; they could not have out-travelled him and crossed the Cumberland to do the bloody deed on the 21st of August. General Robertson and others were convinced that this band had been in Sumner county for weeks previous.

About 1st December, James Robertson, another son of General Robertson, and John Grimes, were killed by Cherokee Indians. They were engaged on Caney Fork, trapping for beaver. This was a very sad blow to General Robertson. On the 4th, Colonel Winchester ordered Lieutenant Snoddy in pursuit of Indians who had come into Sumner county from the direction of Kentucky, having many horses well packed, and to which they added others, stolen in Sumner. Snoddy with thirty men made quick march, and surprised their camp on Caney, near Rock Island. The Indians mounted the horses and fled to some distance. Snoddy's men gathered up the valuable articles left in the camp, consisting of twenty-eight good Spanish blankets; two match coats; eight new brass kettles; one firelock; three new swords, Spanish blades; one bag of vermilion; powder and lead, a goodly supply; several bayonets, spears, war-hatchets, bridles, and saddles, etc., etc.

It was evident the Indians had not continued their flight very far, and would attempt a recapture. Snoddy, therefore, removed to an eminence, a mile off, where he encamped, his men sleeping on their arms, and trusty eyes and ears open to see and hear the approach of the returning foe. And sure enough, towards the dawn of day they were discovered approaching, like cats and wolves, crouching near the ground. They came within thirty yards of the whites before either fired; and then each party fired their every gun. The Indians fired nearly all at the same time, as Castleman and his party had done. After receiving the fire of the whites, they retreated, carrying off their wounded, leaving one dead near the white encampment. They removed several wounded. Snoddy had two men killed and three wounded. He retained the blankets, swords, and other property taken.

"About this time several persons were killed in Sumner county, whose names are not recollected."

And it may truly be said that the record of deaths in no one year, in either of the three counties, is full and complete. But such as it is, there is enough to keep up our amazement, and to make us again and again exclaim, "Were ever sorrows like theirs?" How could they endure so much, and so long!

And now another of the Castlemans is killed, and another wounded; also James McCune, and Mrs. Anthony Bledsoe and her companions, fired at. So were John Nolen and William Montgomery. The latter received two balls, one in the thigh, the other breaking his arm. Then Samuel Blair and Thomas Wilcox. And, to close the catalogue of the killed, (whose names are recorded,) John Dier and Benjamin Lindsey; these two near the mouth of Red River.

Before concluding this page and the record of the year, we must inquire after those who, though living, perhaps would prefer death to their situation as prisoners among our savage enemies. We can now give the following names: Mrs. Williams and child; Alice Thompson, of Nashville; Mrs. Caffrey and child, of Nashville; Mrs. Brown, of Mero District; Miss Scarlet, Miss Wilson, a boy and little girl—another boy five years old. At the Big Tallassee, one or two boys and a girl. At Pocantala, a boy twelve or thirteen years of age. In Oakfuskee, a lad fifteen years of age; a man called John; boy, age unknown. "At the villain Lesley's," a young woman; at another's, Mrs. Crocket and son.

Some of these captives had been now for years in the nation. The most reliable evidence they had of visits having been made to the settlements by those who held them prisoners, and of friends having been seen at such visits, was the exhibition of their scalps, their clothing, or their horses. Whatever other information they received, was only calculated to aggravate the distress and misery of their seemingly hopeless condition.

We have intimated once and again, that it was with the greatest reluctance General Robertson yielded to the "policy of the Government," "to bear and forbear," to endure these outrages year after year, until he had seen nearly all his early friends and many of their children cruelly murdered, and hundreds of worthy settlers of more recent date, cut down in all parts of the settlements, his own life constantly imperilled, fired at he knew not how often, and twice wounded. Had the people not seen and known how much he had suffered in his own person and family, and marked his calmness and noble bearing, they would long ere this have spurned at his peaceful counsel and defensive measures. They would have risen, *en masse*, to throw off his authority, and have gone forth to war into the heart of the nations. As Sevier did across the French Broad and Tennessee, on the other side of the Cumberland Mountains, so would they have done here. But, "alas, alas," said Robertson, "for many years we have been barely able to maintain our few and feeble little stations! If we march with four or five hundred men, we take the strength of our male population. Who shall defend our wives and children and little property while we are gone? Who make and secure provisions for them in our absence, and for us if we should return? They have the numbers in East Tennessee to justify such expeditions, we have not. The time will come, when we shall be able to press the cup of afflictions to their own lips. Were the savages not encouraged and supplied by the Spaniards, we could the more easily cope with them. By aid from Kentucky, which I know we can have at any moment the Governor shall feel himself but half justified in allowing a force to be organized and leave his State to join us for such a purpose, we could punish them well. But, in Kentucky as well as here, people suffer greatly from the power which the Spaniards possess over the navigation of the Mississippi, as well as by the influence they exert over the Indians. We all have had abundant reason to judge and pronounce the exercise of such power and influence to be 'evil, only evil, and that continually.' They have tempted us to abandon our settlements; failing to accomplish by their specious offers their sinister designs, they have enraged and backed our savage neighbors to a war of extermination upon us. We despise them for their duplicity, we scorn their allurements, and we abhor and curse their savage cruelties. We can never trust them, and never prosper in any alliance or business with them. Heaven will avenge our wrongs some day. And even should we ourselves be cut off in the struggle, let us hold fast our faith, our innocence, our integrity, our honor, our government, and our possessions. The devices of the wicked shall not always prosper; Heaven will avenge us yet!"

And with these words, scarce restrained he the fury of the people.

So delicate and intricate was the situation of the Western people, so jealous and crafty the Spaniards upon the Mississippi and the Gulf of Mexico, it became particularly desirable to our Government that all acts of irritation toward the Spanish Government, its colonists or its officers at Natchez, New Orleans, and Pensacola, should be most carefully avoided. In these views many prominent citizens zealously concurred.

And now our *great scheme* for the advance of the Anglo-Saxon race and the extension of republican institutions—the "wheels within a wheel," *Rotulæ in rotula rotantes*—is clearly brought out to view in regard to these very little settlements—" these small estates on the Cumberland."

It became more and more manifest that the Spaniards had long traded with Indians within the boundaries of the United States; that they had instigated them to make war upon these settlements; that they had attained this influence by threats and by promises; by monopolies in trade and largesses to the chiefs; by presents of arms, tomahawks, and all the instruments of war, to the braves; by premiums for scalps; and by all the other means and artifices to which that nation had trained its agents for two hundred years—their "GENIAL SYSTEM !"

They had long violated the comity and courtesy which should exist between nations at peace; they looked upon and treated ours, not only as newly introduced into the rank and company of nations, but as being yet so insignificant and ignorant, that the etiquette and obligations of an international character did not belong to this republican intruder among the royal governments of earth!

Both France and Spain had given countenance and some material aid in our war for independence; rejoicing more at our separation from England, and the diminution of her great territory, than at the birth of a nation and the establishment of a new and vigorous power by the side of their American colonies. They each soon grossly insulted our Government and people. These insults were most glaring here and in Kentucky.

SPANISH ORDER CLOSING THE MISSISSIPPI.

"*Advertisement.*—Under date of 16th inst., the Intendant-General of these Provinces informs me that the citizens of the United States of America can have no commerce with his Majesty's subjects, they only having the free navigation of the river for the exportation of the fruits and products of their establishments to foreign countries, and the importation of what they may need or desire.

"As such I charge you, so far as respects you, to be zealous and vigilant, with particular care that the inhabitants neither *purchase* of nor sell any thing to the shipping, flat-bottomed boats, barges, or any other smaller vessels, that may go along the river, destined for the American possessions, or proceeding from them; that they shall be informed of it, for their due compliance to the same.

CARLOS DE GRANDPRE.

"BATON ROUGE, Dec. 22, 1802."

When this notice was issued, it was construed as the deliberate act of the Spanish and French Governments, after a full consideration and understanding between those Governments. It was pronounced illiberal and in disregard of the treaty recently concluded between Spain and the United States relative to the navigation of the Mississippi. It was *felt* here as it was nowhere else; and was placed in the long enumeration of evidences of contempt shown by the "old Governments of the old world" to the "new Republic of the new world;" and "the small Estates on Cumberland" regarded the indignity and wrong as a *personal matter*.

The "policy of nations," and the destiny of our race, had placed this little confederacy on the Cumberland in *eminent* though *perilous position*. It attracted attention from the "high places of earth!" The map of America was examined by distinguished persons in Europe, desirous to ascertain this *small locality*. It was spoken of as a stronghold and an invincible fastness in the wilderness; having unsurpassed natural advantages and defences, and as affording the Americans a sure entrance into the valley of the Mississippi from all the Eastern and Southern States. "By this and the Kentucky routes the whole Mississippi valley would be inundated with the rebels against the Divine rights of Kings."

The pretensions and demands of this "nest of adventurers," together with the like from those in Kentucky, for "space for locomotion" and for "*commerce*," were regarded as presumptuous and arrogant. Small settlements within a vast wilderness, wishing for room! A people yet living upon wild game, and "from hand to mouth, day by day," to demand the free navigation of the greatest rivers of earth for the benefits of commerce! This seemed ridiculous! But here were little wheels within the great machinery rotating wisely. These were "full of eyes within and on the outside." At times these moved with a rapid whirl, but ever in their place. They were *there*, and *there ordained to be*. They could never be detached or displaced. There have they worked in furtherance of the grandest of purposes, the advancement and glory of these United States. Destiny, destiny, is God's will, which none can countervail.

In France, the old monarchical machinery was broken, and a new motive-power attempted. It drove the hastily and badly constructed machinery with *furore*. Spain felt the jarring of its motion, and heard its dreadful and dreaded clattering. Uneasiness was there. And when she saw the dangerous agents at work upon this continent, she knew that it boded no good to her American colonies.

In April of this year, Genet, as Minister from the new French Republic, arrived at Charleston. His short but disreputable career within our country need not be traced on these pages, further than to say that the dislike long entertained by some of the Western people toward the Spaniards, was certainly not *diminished* by the publications and measures of this madcap Minister from France. Every admirer of Washington was the more opposed to foreign influence and intermeddling.

There can be no doubt that the project of invading the Indian territories, whence came the chief troubles to the settlements, had long been discussed; and, as inseparably connected therewith, to inflict some blow upon the Spaniards, the real instigators to mischief. The agents of Spain had violated treaties with us, and long had such agents acted against our peace and lives, coming within our territory, as we have often said, and using the savages living within our own borders. We had too long endured this. We were growing strong, and the shadows of coming events were visible.

And now, Spain is greatly concerned for " the dignity of this Government!" for the inviolability of treaties ! " Certainly, the United States will not permit a *foreign* Government to have agents there, who shall call for and organize troops within American territory, to invade the territory of Spain !"—a nation at *peace* with them, and which has *always* manifested the *most friendly* disposition toward them !" What consummate impudence for Spain thus to remonstrate !

At such a time and in such exigency, the people of Cumberland, and "a certain Robertson," could not be overlooked.

Among other communications upon this subject, we introduce an extract from a letter addressed to General Robertson by the Spanish Agent and Commander of the post at New Madrid :

" It is to be hoped that the *majesty of the American people will not tamely suffer a foreign Minister* to exercise within their territory the *powers of sovereignty*, by issuing commissions and levying armies to be sent against a nation at peace." A very good sentiment to come from Lance de Grace !

General Robertson most highly approved this sentiment. Had it been observed, he should have passed his life in peace; his children, relatives, and friends would not have been butchered around their firesides, in field and pathway, and this in scores and hundreds; and these settlements would have grown and flourished in quiet and abundance.   But now his sorrow must remain and the regret for ever endure that these principles had not controlled the conduct of Spain and her officers, and thus have withheld the savages from murder.   Robertson had suspected at an early day the schemes and wicked, deceitful workings of Spanish agents; this we noticed years since.   He was politic, observing, reserved, as he knew something of the policy and practice of the Administration.   In recent years he had expressed himself with less caution, and now he openly denounced them in terms almost as strong as those used by Captain Rains.   He felt certain the day was not far distant, when Spanish deceit-fulness would be exposed; and Spain, as well as France and England, would yield to our advancing population this vast, yet vacant territory.

> "Look forward what's to come, and back what's past;
> Thy life will be with praise and prudence graced;
> What loss or gain may follow, thou may'st guess;
> Thou then wilt be secure of the success."

England devised and wrought long and carefully to accomplish the separation of her colonies from maternal care; France and Spain had labored for the like deliverances.   Not one of them desired the results towards which a thousand acts were driving.   "Rough-hewn," as were many of the measures, "there was a divinity that shaped their ends."

During the last ten years there was no moment in which an authoritative word from the Spanish Government to "be at peace with these settlements," would have been disregarded by the Creeks or Cherokees; and her officers and traders well knew it.   Therefore did General Robertson read this flattery of "the majesty of the American people," as an insult and gross hypocrisy.   It was left to Thomas Jefferson, Secretary of State, to expose this hypocrisy, and to bring home to the Spanish Government (by her agents) the memory of wrongs and sufferings she had caused, which were enough to cover her with shame for ever.

One or two remarks from Jefferson will here suffice: "Are we to understand that if we arm to repel the attacks of the Creeks on ourselves, it will disturb our peace with Spain?   That if we will not let them butcher us, Spain will consider it as a cause of war? . . We love and we value peace; we abhor the follies of war, and are not untried in its disasters and calamities. . . . We confide in our strength, without boasting of it; we respect that of others, without fearing it."

The language of Monette is appropriate and correct, and suitable here:

"France and Spain were now at war; French emissaries sought, through the prejudice that had been roused against the Spaniards relative to the navigation of the Mississippi, to instigate an invasion of Louisiana and Florida by the people of the United States; and, if practicable, even a separation of the Western States, and an alliance with Louisiana under the dominion and protection of France."

The agents of the French Minister made their appearance among the Cumberland settlers, where "they found heaps of live coals but partially covered, and which it was no difficult labor to fan and blow into a glowing heat." Old grudges and old memories were here. A thousand insults and wrongs committed directly and indirectly by the Spaniards, were brought fresh to mind and talked of in the spirit of exaggeration and revenge. The Baron de Carondelet was fully aware of all this, and greatly feared the outbreak and the consequences to Spanish possessions. In his anxiety to strengthen his defences, he not only increased his forces at the military posts along the Mississippi as high up as Madrid, but "added insult to all former injuries," by entering into a treaty with some of the Chickasaw chiefs, by which there was granted to the Spaniards the right to the Fourth Chickasaw Bluff, whereon a fort was hastily erected and strongly garrisoned. This was American soil, and these Indians were within acknowledged American territory. Fort Barancas or Echore Margot was erected upon the peninsula formed by the junction of the Margot and the Mississippi.

But for this provocation, how long would American progress have been stayed?

CHAPTER XXVI.

1793.

WHILST negotiations were lingering, murders and insults accumulating, the purposes of wisdom unfolding, and men only straining to discover the future by looking through a confused atmosphere beneath a stormy sky, there were consultations between leading men here, upon the Holston and in Kentucky, as to what measures were justifiable, and should be adopted, by the pioneer settlers to terminate these acts of the savages. They deliberated long and anxiously.

To the questions asked by the Secretary of War : "Cannot the Indians be appeased by gifts? Have not most of their acts been provoked and done in retaliation? Will not a hundred mounted men, ranging through the woods and along the dividing ridges and the boundaries to which they have assented, be all that need be done? Is it not most important of all to restrain hunters, spies, and speculators from intrusions upon Indian territory?"—to each and to all of these questions, every pioneer would have replied with indignation and with scorn, "No! no!"

They felt it to be an insult to be asked such questions; humiliating to have to answer them. They had practiced forbearance until it was no longer a virtue. That and all their largesses were interpreted to the prejudice and contempt of the settlers. Who asks if we have not in all instances, or in any, been the wrong-doers? Only one who is so ignorant as to inquire whether a squad of cavalry cannot detect and arrest, or pursue and punish, hosts of skulking savages creeping through the dense forests and thick cane-brakes, over a border of many hundreds of miles in extent! Who would require of the settlers to stay an avenging hand at a boundary over which the murderers and robbers are, in their daily and nightly hunts, passing with impunity; taking back with them the scalps of our relatives and friends, to be hung up in their cabins as trophies—proofs of *their* daring and of *our* cowardly or inactive character?

These men were indignant, mad; and some of them grasped an instrument of death, and *swore*—swore vengeance against the savages and all who should be known to "*agg* them on."

Shelby, Logan, and Wheatley, in Kentucky, Sevier in East Tennessee, and Robertson and his neighbors, on the Cumberland, concurred in this one sentiment: "The Indians must be whipped at their own homes. . . . We can never quietly and safely attend to our stock and corn-fields, until they are made to feel how terrible it is to scatter arrows, fire-brands, and death! We can never catch them in these forests."

The remarkable figure of speech used by Esquaka, exhibits the very idea and truth of Indian secrecy. When asked if he or Coteatoy were present upon a certain occasion, he calmly dipped his finger in water, then withdrawing it, asked, "You see him there?" The waters had closed—there was no mark. The thick bushes and the rank grass might be parted by the dashing or the creeping foe, but the bending limb and the yielding herbage, not rudely thrust aside, recover their natural position, "retain no trace, and tell no tales."

We have shown how very restive General Robertson has been for years; that in his heart the fire burned; that he entertained the most exalted opinion and regard for General Washington, for law and order, and superior authority. He would not be rash and hasty in any matter; he had an ambition to be consistent, moderate—temperate in all things, and at all times. He, if any man, actually gloried in the merits of Washington. Holding a commission from the father of this new country, and having taken the oath of office, "he would suffer torment before he would violate his oath or disgrace his commission." He felt it was devolved upon him, in an especial manner, to teach by his example the duty of respect and obedience to superior authority. "No one could tell how extensive and injurious might be the results of one act of disobedience, by an officer occupying the position of General Sevier and himself. Robertson and Sevier felt themselves to be identified with Washington and "the noble army" of patriots of the Revolution. They had aided, and were yet working and suffering, to save the richest country on earth from foreign and from savage rule, and to put in operation a system of government and laws for the weal or woe of the millions who should come after them. They knew they were doing and were called to do a great work; they had an abiding consciousness of this position: they wished to act up to it. If they failed, it was not because they undervalued or set lightly upon the duties or responsibilities, nor because their heart was not in it. Men of very different blood, temperament, appearance,

28

and manners, their early experiences, allotment, and training were not unlike, and their position, trials, and closing lives not dissimilar.

Sevier had resources, opportunities, and calls to devise, prosecute, and accomplish measures upon the theatre where his active services were required, which were denied to Robertson—wisely denied, as could easily be shown.

The one had the nervous vivacity of the Frenchman—all honor, quick and dashing, and yet elegant, polite, and fascinating; the other the staid sobriety of the Scotchman—calm, patient, uncomplaining, yet resolved to go ahead; ever in the line of duty; of few words, but well considered and weighty.

He was now "in a strait betwixt two." He agreed with all these counsellors that the western settlers had endured beyond all example elsewhere—beyond all that could have been expected or asked of them, and that the deafness of the Republic to the cries of sufferings from the western settlements was sufficient to justify many of the complaints and censures cast upon the Administration. But then he reminded the complainers that their own more immediate friends and neighbors, and their parent State, had long treated them in the same way, or worse. That the machinery of government was yet new, and these stations were at a great distance from the central power. We were, however, enjoying many advantages under the Territorial Government which had not been experienced prior to its organization. We were acquainted with our own officers; they are identified with us. The energy and devotion of the Governor, none can doubt; but he is not supreme.

Robertson wished to have "the tormentors tormented," "the hornet's nest burned down," "the wolves smoked out of their den."

A year ago he had proposed to Governor Blount the propriety of resigning the commission of Major-General, which he held. The Governor replies in substance: "I have noticed what you have said about your resignation, and the object of it; delay it—the time is not yet."

It had repeatedly been suggested to him to throw up his commission and join his fellow-sufferers in one of the oft-contemplated parties, and go in force to destroy the Indian towns whence the marauders and murderers came.

Sevier had often done this, and destroyed towns and many of their warriors, and made his name a terror among them. To all this General Robertson could reply: "We once were without law, and organized a government for ourselves, but we are now under a well-devised and sacredly recognized Government. General Sevier and the people of

Green were pushed to do things in their own way for a season, but the necessity being past, he holds a commission as do others; and it is to be hoped that the rebellion will not extend from Fort Pitt down here. There is too much of it now on Holston and French Broad. Sevier was once denounced and hunted as the Rebel Governor of Franklin. Positions are now changed, and those who pursued and persecuted him may be pursued in turn."

Robertson and Sevier, and others, had endeavored to convince the President that an invasion of Indian territory, and offensive war, would alone procure peace and safety. Governor Blount concurred; but as Washington received no sanction for such measures by Congress, and his Secretary of War sympathized with the savages, the Administration positively refused to authorize any such measures, and so informed Governor Blount. General Washington himself concurred in this view or policy, in warring with savages; but receiving his information as to the nature and extent and causes of these complaints through his Secretary, who cherished a foregone conclusion and condemnation, and "the Congress alone possessed of power to declare war," having adjourned without taking action on the complaint of the sufferers, they must be left "to their long experience," and suffer still. Will they do this patiently? We shall see.

In November General Robertson addressed a letter to General Sevier, couched in somewhat mysterious yet significant terms.

"When will the Lower Towns get their deserts? Governor Blount *hints* that it will be in the spring. I *suspect* it will be before that time. It may be immaterial *to us*, considering our exposed situation, and the little protection *we have*."

Therefore he urged General Sevier to carry an expedition of *fifteen hundred men* into the Creek country, and "to do this *before* the ensuing spring."

This was intended to be a chastisement upon those who merited it— had been and were still at war with the whites in Georgia and Carolina. Such an invasion would alarm the Cherokees generally, and probably employ some of the amalgamated Creeks and Cherokees of the Lower Towns in a direction opposite to and afar off from the Cumberland—an advantageous diversion. Sevier was willing to render this aid to his distant friends, and to punish savages who merited it. But delay was inevitable, or advisable. The Governor did not assent, although the provocations were so many and so aggravating. There were some things said in confidence, and so remain.

"The views of prominent men," the result of the "conferences" announced to the people on the Cumberland, were to delay such offensive measures; perhaps they may be *authorized*, and then no one will fail in duty.

The conclusion was to postpone such steps until September of the next year. The Governor, however, declared (at least publicly) that he should authorize or countenance no such measures, unless he received full authority from Government.

General Robertson, however, had announced to the people that his mind was made up; that if these outrages continued, as he believed they would, he would aid in equipping, and sanction the marching of a strong force to the Lower Towns, and destroy them totally. Then, if his conduct should not be approved, he would resign, or be cashiered, or endure whatever disgrace or punishment might be inflicted.

With this "set purpose" freely published, General Robertson continued actively engaged in the discharge of the many duties of his position. His private affairs needed more of his attention than he could bestow, or withdraw from public concerns, and the multiplicity of calls upon him personally, and by letter, relative to the interests and business of others.

He had secured the services of a number of friendly Indians, of the full and half blood, who passed to and fro, making discoveries, bringing in reports, and fresh meat and skins. The remark of "the said Hood" was, "Words and venison both come under fresh parchment." His meaning was, "A friendly runner, or trot-Indian," who had obtained information he wished to communicate, deemed it sometimes safest to enter the white settlements with something to sell. Deers were brought in "gutted, but not skinned," and when he threw down his load of meat, he delivered himself also of his burden of words. Usually, however, these trotters went and came with light equipments, and "never minded the wild game."

General Robertson repeatedly received knowledge of some of the Spanish dealings with the Indians, through the agency of these (not always trusty) friends.

And there is reason to believe the Spaniards and Indian chiefs learned of transactions among the whites by the like conveyances.

An abbreviated statement may serve to explain the grounds upon which the Spaniards attempted to justify some of their acts, and the complaints made to our Government of the conduct of General Robertson. We need make no further remarks on the treaty they had formed with Indians living within our territory, offering protection to them, having agents and traders among them, etc.   This was an offence which would have justified warlike measures against Spain at any moment.

In the spring of this year a deputation of chiefs, Delaware and Shawnese, from New Madrid, (by the advice of Portell, the commandant there,) visited the Choctaws and Creeks, for the purpose of exciting them to war against the United States, and whilst on their way these chiefs stated they were to meet the Cherokee nation in full council at Estanaula, and expected to induce them also to join in the war.   They informed the Cherokees that the Shawnees had resolved to destroy the Chickasaws for joining the army of General St. Clair.   There were alleged grievances which the Creeks also avowed a wish to avenge upon the Chickasaws.

At the conference at Nashville, (to which they had not been invited, but where they came as spies,) they stole horses from the Chickasaws. The latter pursued the thieves, demanded their horses, (which the Creeks refused to give up,) and in an altercation which ensued, several of the Creeks were killed.   The Creek chiefs justified the theft of the horses with good Spanish diplomatic argument: "We found the horses upon the lands of our enemies, the whites, and if they were your horses, you were there in friendly conference with our enemies."   To which the Chickasaws retorted, " And you were there, enemies, under the guise of friends, and partaking of hospitalities as well as we."   This is the head and front of the offending of the Chickasaws to the Creeks.

Here was now a formidable league to destroy this small nation; and because of their friendship to the United States.   It became the duty and the true policy of our Government not merely to supply them with provisions when they were ready to perish with hunger, but to furnish them with ample means of defence, and to embrace the opportunity so to do it, as to convince all their and our enemies, we were friends who could be relied on; that we had an abundance of provisions, an abundance of fire-arms, and a determined will, which they had best not provoke.

Under these threats and preparations of their enemies, the Chickasaws were driven to defensive measures.   On the 13th of February, a letter, signed by twenty-nine of their chiefs, was addressed to General Robertson, in reply to one of sympathy and encouragement from him.   In their letter they say, "We, head-men, have held you fast by the hand, and have told our young warriors to do the same.   And they will, as long as they are able to lift a hatchet.   We have sent you a war-club.   When we both take hold, we can strike a hard blow. . . . .   Send expresses to every head-man in America, particularly to General Washington; . . . . to the head-men in Kentucky. . . . . .   Let them know our agreement was to be as one man in regard to our enemies and friends. . . . . The Creeks say, all the Virginians are liars, and no dependence is to be placed in them, and that we Chickasaws are fools. . . . . Their talk did not alter us. . . . Speak strong to your young warriors; let us join to teach the Creeks *what war is.*

"You make whiskey; send us some; it is good to take a little at war-talks. . . . .

"We believe the Choctaws will join us, and not our enemies. They need ammunition and guns as well as we. . . . . Muskets, rifles, smooth bores will do. . . . . As we made no crop last year, we are in a starving condition. Send us quickly fifteen hundred bushels of corn, two barrels of flour, one hundred bushels of salt, one hogshead of tobacco, fifty bags of vermilion—as it is greatly wanted in war. Do not forget the whiskey. And we desire that General Washington will station a garrison at the Muscle Shoals, or Bear Creek."

It was in this exigency that Piomingo determined to visit General Robertson and Governor Blount, to deliver to the Governor a speech expressive of the same sentiments as those in the letter to General Robertson.

Knowing the dangers to which these friendly Indians were exposed, and that they were suffering for food, General Robertson promptly decided to send them relief. Fortunately, Mr. Portell, the commandant of the Spanish post at New Madrid, had written to General Robertson to supply him with corn. The General, therefore, resolved to ship such a load as would greatly exceed the necessities of Portell, and the surplus could readily be taken a little lower down the river to those who most needed, and whose wants he preferred to supply.

The boat was easily filled—the settlers had "enough and to spare;" and on the 23d April the boat left the shore at Nashville, under the charge of Jonathan F. Robertson, eldest son of the General, and landed at New Madrid on 7th May. A small swivel or brass cannon was mounted on the boat for its defence.

On the 9th, Mr. Portell wrote to General Robertson, regretting that he had not been advised of his intention to send him the corn—he had supplied himself, and could take but one hundred bushels, for which he had paid his son the money. This small sale was no disappointment to young Robertson, who cheerfully proceeded to the Chickasaw Bluffs and landed his cargo, and "the little piece" or swivel.

Portell "expressed," by canoe, the information of these facts to Carondelet, at New Orleans, who instantly transmitted the intelligence to the Spanish agents at Philadelphia. On the same day, 21st May, the Baron presented his information and sentiments upon this subject to General Robertson. After a number of preliminary and complimentary remarks, he proceeds, " I have felt the greatest concern on account of the measures taken by you to comply with the request of the Chickasaw nation, sending them such supplies, and at the same time *a little piece,* an arm too dangerous in the hands of Indians. . . . . The policy of the United States and of Spain is carefully to conceal from them its use, etc., etc. This had been his conduct toward the Cherokees. And really, (so he ventured to assert,) he had prevailed upon them to stop all hostility against the Cumberland settlements! This they would observe, unless forced to take up arms in their own defence."

He then insultingly speaks of his gracious Majesty *"mediating* with Congress to fix certain boundaries, which, being advantageous to both nations, might prevent further controversy ! The same rule had been observed toward the Creeks, whom *he had* turned from their hostility toward the Georgians! He asserted that he had refused Creeks and Chickasaws, at a conference at Natchez and Walnut Hills, a supply of arms ! . . . . It is probable that a general peace will shortly take place, without which the Cumberland settlement cannot flourish. He wished for an opportunity to see the General, and convince him of the great esteem in which he held him."

The agents of the Spanish Government at Philadelphia entered warmly into the discussion of this affair, and made to our Government their bitter complaint.

Our Government did not condescend to notice these inferior and querulous spirits. Mr. Jefferson, Secretary of State, addressed a dignified and scathing rebuke and refutation, directly to the Spanish Government, through the American minister at Madrid.

It was left to General Robertson, in his own defence and defence of the Cumberland people, to reply to the Baron de Carondelet; and as that reply has never been published, we give it from the original manuscript, vol. i. of Robertson's Correspondence :

"MERO DISTRICT, Nashville, 9th December, 1793.

" SIR :—I had yesterday the honor of receiving yours of the 21st of May, and am happy to find your Excellency's sentiments so congenial with my own, relative to the treatment proper to be given our Indian neighbors. When we reason from general principles, a small degree of reflection will show us the impropriety of enlightened nations furnishing savages, even in time of war, with weapons that a few months may turn against themselves; much more so in a time of peace. This, sir, is, however, an idea that did not occur to me at the time I sent the piece to the Chickasaws; but that step was merely the effect of an effusion of friendship for them in consequence of their faithful adherence to our interest, and perhaps will appear less reprehensible when it is considered, they were then at open war with the Creeks, who have been our constant and inveterate enemies. I must, however, observe, that this was altogether a transaction of *my own*, and must not be charged on our General Government, to which application was made for several more, which was refused.

"I can assure your Excellency that every opportunity has been made use of to impress on the Indians the idea of friendship subsisting between Spain and the United States, and particularly by his Excellency the Governor of this Territory at a treaty held by authority of the United States with the Choctaw and Chickasaw nations at this place in 1792, and it has been my particular care at every conference to hold out the same idea.

"Various reports have circulated with us of the Spanish Government having incited the Indians to war against us, of which I held it my duty to inform Government; though, at the same time, I knew not how to reconcile this with information I received through the channel of correspondence with several Spanish officers, and other corroborating circumstances, wholly incompatible with such measures, which also I remarked in my representations to Government.

"The establishment of peace is indeed a very important object, especially for our infant countries; and it gives me the greatest pleasure to find the measures of your Government directed to that end, and the more so as, if sincerely pursued, which I doubt not they are, they cannot fail of success.

"The honor of an interview with your Excellency, though it would afford me real satisfaction, is what I rather wish for than expect; yet it may still be in our power to correspond, which I flatter myself will be done."

The Spanish Government had sent very artful and energetic agents to the United States, and to her colonies of Louisiana and Florida. They were incessant in the use of all conceivable craft and schemes to embarrass the Government of the United States. The enmity and hypocrisy of the Baron de Carondelet could not always be concealed, his professions of friendship could not always be credited; his attempt (and that of his two vulgar advocates and apologists and defenders, Jaudenes and Viar) to justify interference with and arming of Indians within the territory of the United States, was sufficient to make him distrusted ever after by all prudent and upright men. These artifices were not practiced alone by an inferior governor and commandant and his emissaries, but by so high a functionary as the learned and elegant Guardoqui, whilst representing his Government as minister to the United States, and not less when he returned home and occupied a position next to the all-powerful Alcudia, and there dictated in the affairs of Spain in North America. Even he continued his many professions of devotedness to the prosperity and greatness of our country, when he could not hide his measures or counsels for decided hindrance and opposition. The claims to territory within our treaty limits, and to the exclusive navigation of the Mississippi, were boldly advocated by these representatives of Spanish arrogance. And, as we have intimated, they found much encouragement from the divisions and jealousies in our own country.

In confirmation we may quote a few sentences from the communication of Messrs. Carmichael and Short to Thomas Jefferson, Secretary of State, dated Aranjuez, May 5th, 1793, after the return of Mr. Jay to the United States. During his residence as minister to the United States from Spain, M. Guardoqui had witnessed dissensions, divisions, and jealousies among our States and citizens, and a very inefficient government, and he, like the representatives of England and France, would have never grieved at any continuance or aggravation of such an unsettled and unhappy condition of American affairs, if the aims of his own Government could be promoted.

After his return to Spain, the impressions made on his mind in this country were evident. He retained those impressions, and was unwilling to admit there could have been any improvement after he had left the United States; and especially as he saw the Revolution in France productive of so much bloodshed, wickedness, and disorganization.

"He conversed with some individuals in America who expressed their wishes to see the navigation of the Mississippi *prohibited and our limits narrowed*, in order to have the productions of the western country brought through the Atlantic States, and to have our population more concentrated. . . . He also saw some individuals of the western country, or going to settle there, who treated their *adhesion* to the rest of the Union as *visionary*. . . . From hence he had formed his opinions, that the United States did not desire this navigation and the limits which the Commissioners asked, or at least did not so generally desire it, as that they could be brought to make any united effort to obtain it. . . . And also that the western inhabitants, whenever they shall acquire force, will separate from the Atlantic States."

preserve its *ancient limits* on which they agreed with the British. They pray you to employ all your force to obtain from His Majesty this favor, if it be possible ; and if it cannot be obtained, they *insist that the settlement at Cumberland* alone shall be *removed at all events.* Without this, nothing will satisfy the Cherokees and Talpuches.

" Cumberland was settled towards the conclusion of the last war by a certain Robertson, and some companions of his, who, concealing their journey and designs, took possession, by force, of those lands. Perhaps the Americans will make it appear that they possess these lands by free and lawful treaties ; but it is not so. . . . .

" Robertson and his companions are the real and true cause that so much blood has been spilt ; and the confusion which has subsisted, and still subsists, is owing entirely to this settlement ; and while it remains in this place there is no hope of a solid peace.

" This settlement taken away, the Cherokee nation declares that it does not desire to be an enemy of the Americans : it declares, moreover, that it does not entertain this solicitude from caprice or pique ; that they never questioned the legality of their treaties under the British Government."

These documents bear upon the face unquestionable evidence of Spanish origin ; they are portions of the mass of proof of the presumptuous intermeddling and mischievous designs of Spain against this feeble settlement. Nations, savage and *civilized,* (?) thus combined and made war—a cruel and bloody war—for many years upon " Robertson and his companions." A war of extermination was contemplated, and the agents of Spain urged and aided its prosecution. None can read the history of the sufferings of these hardy Americans, and refrain from expressing surprise that they were not driven away, or annihilated. Were not that period noted for the insolence, insults, and intermeddling of England, France, and Spain, we might express astonishment that Spain should have dared to enter our own territories and arrogate to "the great King of the Spains" the right to protect "all the colored people," "*reclaim and secure ancient limits,*" and "remove the Cumberland settlers !"

The Spaniards urged these Indian warriors to violate the treaties made with the Americans, and this not in such a covert manner as to prevent detection. From the king on his throne, through all the ranks of Spanish nobility and officers, there was vexation, irritation, and subterfuge. They saw the fading away of the glory of their nation. The prestige of her power and greatness was gone. Her immense and rich colonies were rapidly escaping her grasp. She must see that what thus passed from her would but add to the greatness and overshadowing glory of the new Republic of America.

Therefore they prevaricated; resorted to petty and mean artifices; and were guilty of acts which would have justified an active and hostile position on our part.

This was continued down to the actual invasion of our territory across the Sabine, near Nacogdoches, from which they had to retire in disgrace, and surrender all of the French Louisiana to our possession. This same feeling and course of annoyance were continued in Florida until there too we had the pleasure of seeing their last bow, and hearing their fare-well.

In General Robertson's intercourse as a citizen, and as Indian agent, he found it advantageous to conciliate the good will and services of influential Indians, by presents of clothes, hat, cap, and plume, by epau-lettes, and large brass buttons; and, as the mark of highest distinction, by the donation of "silver medals."

This had been the practice of England, France, and Spain. It had ever been regarded as a legitimate and cheap mode of securing the good will of the savages; and unless it was done to corrupt and bribe, and alien-ate the Indians who lived within the territory of a friendly power, there was no cause of offence. But so querulous was Spain, so very jealous, watchful, and anxious to find cause of complaint with the United States, she complained of such presents being made by our Government to chiefs, head-men, and warriors of tribes living within our own limits, to Creeks, Cherokees, Chickasaws, and Choctaws.

Those "polite and sensitive" officers, Jaudenes and Viar, made it a matter of complaint in their letters to Secretary Jefferson that Governor Blount and General Robertson had been the immediate agents in " giving gifts" to the poor savages; that this and that one was flattered with some high military title, with a coat and brass buttons, with an epaulette, hat, and plume; and some were made " Great Medal Chiefs," and offensively displayed on the breast a silver plate, with the effigy of the President, and at the bottom, "George Washington, President, 1792;" and others with the *legend*, " Friendship and trade without end." These cheap dis-tinctions sometimes purchased valuable friendship, or subdued a bitter and dangerous enmity.

> " Spite of all the fools that pride has made,
> 'T is not on man a useless burden laid;
> Pride has ennobled some, and some disgraced—
> It hurts not in itself, but as 'tis placed:
> When right, its views know none but virtue's bound;
> When wrong, it scarcely looks one inch around."

CHAPTER XXVII.

1793.

THE British and Spanish emissaries were busily engaged in machinations and mischief to the western settlements for many years. Without wearing out our own, or the patience of our readers, by attempts to unravel the schemes of diplomacy, or the workings of plots and counterplots, our narrative presents the sufferings endured by those against whom some of these agents of mischief assiduously labored, and the final working out of wonderful deliverances, "through their much tribulation."

We shall throw together some correspondence in a form more full than has been woven into our narrative. This will exhibit again a fact to which we have called attention elsewhere, that the settlers here and in East Tennessee were for years in situations, *naturally* and *politically*, separated by mountain barriers, and virtually cast off by the parent State, so that they were compelled to act very independent parts. As General Sevier was the recognized leader in East Tennessee, and surrounded by able and worthy men, and a host of devoted fellow-citizens, so was Robertson looked up to by the stationers on Cumberland as a worthy leader, by whose side stood Bledsoe and all others; and between these men and Sevier there was a friendship which distance and the mountain-heights could not cool or sever.

There was a strange vacillating, embarrassing, and irritating course pursued both by Virginia towards her western country when the people asked for and needed a separate and independent form of government and to be admitted into the Union; and by North Carolina towards her western territory advancing to a like necessity. In Kentucky they were driven to the holding of nine or ten conventions before they succeeded. North Carolina "ceded" and afterwards "revoked the cession act," neglected them, cast them off, taxed them, granted away their lands, seized the "chief citizen," "outlawed" him, and then gave him up to the people, who delighted to do him honor.

But towards "the small estates on Cumberland," and towards Robertson and his peers, no such harsh measures were pursued. These were too far away, too feeble—and the others intervened. The Creeks and Cherokees waged war against these settlements on both sides the mountains; and for years, if they had been fully recognized as independent States, they could not have been left to manage their own defences by themselves more absolutely than they were, though counties of the State of North Carolina.

But why should these Indians be induced or provoked to come so far and seek the destruction of settlers who had never disturbed them? Have they any real or presumed cause for their hostility? There is no land on this side of the Tennessee to which they have ever had any claim or right. These settlers have done no act by which the Creeks have been damaged, except in self-defence or when attacked.

The machinations of Spanish officers and emissaries were strongly suspected. Robertson and Bledsoe, and others, had long distrusted the honesty of professions which had been repeatedly and lavishly bestowed. They had some information — which caused them to be guarded and watchful. They had corresponded with Spanish officers; they now resolved to send a joint letter and by a full embassy, two distinguished citizens; not to a Spanish officer, but to the chief and most potent agent of Spanish officers among the Southern hostile tribes. Therefore, they addressed a joint letter to McGillivray, the Creek chief, and transmitted it by Mr. Hoggatt and Mr. Ewing, inquiring the cause of continued Creek hostility. To this the Creek chief replied:

"I will not deny that my nation has waged war against your country for several years past, and that we had *no motives of revenge* for it, nor did it proceed from any sense of *injuries sustained from your people;* but being warmly attached to the British people, and under their influence, our operations were directed *by them* against you, in common with other Americans. After the general peace had taken place, you sent us a talk, proposing terms of peace, by Samuel Martin, which I then accepted, and advised my people to agree to, and which should have been finally concluded in the ensuing summer and fall.

"Judging that your people were sincere in their professions, I was much surprised to find that whilst this affair was pending, they attacked the French traders at the Muscle Shoals, and killed six of our nation who were trafficking for silver-ware. These men belonged to different towns, and had connections of the first consequence in the nation. Such an unprovoked outrage raised a most violent clamor, and gave rise to the expedition against Cumberland which soon after took place.

"But as that affair has been since amply retaliated, I now, once again, will use my best endeavors to bring about a peace between us. Indeed, before I received your dispatches, I had given out strict orders, that on the return of all hunting-parties, none should go out, on any pretence, until the first general meeting, which I expect to hold in May next, when all my influence and authority will be exerted in the manner you wish. I shall take leave of this subject, referring you to Mr. Hoggatt, to whom I have freely explained my sentiments.

"I have seen the Resolves of Congress respecting Indian affairs, as early as the beginning of January last, besides being notified of the same by General Pickens. I have yet heard nothing of a Superintendent or Georgia Commissioner. Relative to the business of their commission, I had received his Excellency, Governor Caswell's letter and duplicate, only a short time before the unlucky affair of the Muscle Shoals ; so that I deferred writing an answer until I could be satisfied in my own mind that he might depend on what I should say to him.

"As I abhor every species of duplicity, I wish not to deceive. If I were not decided in settling and terminating the war, I would not now write.

"I have hitherto only seen my friend, Colonel Hawkins, ('Indian Agent,') *on paper*, and I highly honor and esteem him on this kind of acquaintance. The excellent character everybody gives him, makes him a valuable advocate for your cause. Chance may put us in each other's view one day or other, and I shall rejoice in having the opportunity of saluting him as my friend."

Upon this letter Judge Haywood remarks, "A personal avowal of one's own candor, sincerity, or probity, is seldom the best evidence to be had, or on which to rely."

And it is true, that by other letters which this learned chief wrote about this time, it is clearly proven he was guilty of that very duplicity of which he uttered such abhorrence. And it is beyond question, he was *not* "decided to terminate the war at that time," but to prosecute it to the extermination of the settlers on the Cumberland — *if possible*. It was not wholly owing to the disinclination of the Creeks for peace; it was not that the command of this chief would have had no weight with his chiefs and warriors ; but it was, that he was yet a pensioner of one or more foreign Governments, and that he was instigated more by pecuniary considerations than by other motives or inducements. He was determined to obtain money from some source. If he could not gratify this ambition by sharing in the spoils of the privileged trading company of Panton, and through him from his own people, he would make use of the warlike spirit of that people, to plunder their neighbors and commit murders, until his coffers were filled and his "duplicity" supplanted—supplemented, *complimented* by the gift of one hundred thousand dollars in gold, his shoulders ornamented with golden epaulettes, a sword by his side, and a commission in his pocket, ranking him with Brigadier-General Robertson himself. He received the promise from the King of Spain to "make him a greater man than Congress had made him," and his "duplicity" could enjoy that compliment.

"If I were not *decided in settling and terminating* the war, I would not now write!" This he writes in reply to Colonels Robertson and Bledsoe; and within less than five days after his letter, so boastful of honesty and good will, had been received by Colonel Robertson, his friend, Colonel Bledsoe, was shot dead at his own door by the prowling murderers of this "man of probity."

It became the duty of Colonel Robertson to reply to this letter of the Creek chief. How to do so, and not expose his "duplicity;" how to do so, and not reproach him and his savages with wilful murder of one of the best citizens whom he had just then addressed in terms of friendship; how to do so, and not aggravate the troubles then almost past endurance, were questions of exceeding difficulty. Colonel Robertson held a long consultation with his "cabinet officers." The two "Ministers to Tallassee, Ewing and Hoggatt," were consulted as to the character of this influential chieftain: Messrs. Ewing and Hoggatt had studied his words and scrutinized his conduct attentively. The conclusion to which Ewing arrived was unfavorable: he did not believe in his exemption from "duplicity," nor in his indifference to presents. After due deliberation it was agreed that Andrew Ewing, "late Minister Plenipotentiary to the Creek Nation," should, as "Secretary of State of the small Estates on Cumberland," draw up the important document.

At the "Cabinet meeting," Colonel Robertson remarked, that in the joint letter addressed by Colonel Bledsoe and himself to the Creek chief, the then recent murder of his son, *Peyton*, was mentioned, and lamented; but "we uttered no threats of vengeance. . . . My heart could have given him up as a sacrifice, to secure permanent peace. It should have been enough: I could have given my own, if due to atonement for wrongs we have done them; but they have waged an unprovoked and bloody war against us. And now they have killed our best citizen, and they constantly seek my life."

There are greater rascals than these roving savages, or than McGillivray. The Spaniards are at the bottom of it—they are the instigators! It was known that Colonel Robertson *hated* the Spaniards—"never did love

29

them" or believe in their professions of friendship, although in his position he was required to correspond with them, and "repeat the empty compliments," of which they were so lavish. After their own example, from time immemorial, he had to make use of some of their arts of diplomacy.

Mr. Ewing fully concurred with Colonel Robertson, that there was a close intimacy and understanding between McGillivray and the Spanish Governors. He said that McGillivray was a well-educated man, and he thought very shrewd, seemingly bold and frank, yet evidently cautious and guarded. Mr. Ewing prepared the following reply, which was approved and signed by Colonel Robertson, and forwarded to McGillivray. The original draft, or a copy, in the peculiar handwriting of Ewing, may be seen in the first volume of letters and correspondence of General Robertson. From this Haywood copied quite accurately. We give the letter entire:

"NASHVILLE, August 3, 1788.

"SIR:—I received your favors by Messrs. Hoggatt and Ewing, which have given great satisfaction. I transmitted copies to Governor Caswell, and have since seen them published in the Kentucky Gazette.

"The Indians still continue their incursions in some measure, though trifling to what we experienced in the spring. I imagine it must be Cherokees, or some outlying Creeks, who are not acquainted with your orders.*

"Colonel Anthony Bledsoe was killed by a small party, about two weeks ago.†

"It is reported that the inhabitants of Holston and the Cherokees are

---

* This reference to the "incursions in the spring" is made without any harsh expression, without any manifestation of revengeful feeling, although it included the murder of his son, Peyton Robertson, the breaking up of Asher's and Wilson's Stations, on Station Camp Creek, the cruel murder of the Widow Neely near the place where her husband had been killed and daughter captured, eight years before.

We presume neither the writer nor Colonel Robertson had much confidence that McGillivray had given any "orders," or that they were of such an authoritative character as to have restrained his savages from their "incursions."

† Had we not witnessed the calm self-control of Colonel Robertson in his first letter, written a few days after the slaughter of his son, we should be amazed that he could now mention the murder of Colonel Bledsoe without threats of vengeance. "Keep your temper, but don't be idle," was one of Andrew Ewing's sayings. It was observed in the preparation of this letter.

at war, but we have not received any account that may be depended on ;*
nor whether you and the Georgians are likely to terminate your disputes.†

" From Mr. Hoggatt's account, we have expected some of the Creeks
in from you, but none have yet arrived.‡

" I have provided a gun, which Mr. Hoggatt thinks will please you.§
I have caused a deed, for a lot in Nashville, to be recorded in your name,‖
and beg you will let me know whether you will accept of a tract or two
of land in our young country.¶

---

* In the letters to Colonel Sevier which precede these remarks, the reader will
learn the views which Robertson and Bledsoe entertained of the grounds and
necessity of the warfare between the Franklin people and Cherokees.

† The war between the Georgians and Creeks was fierce and revengeful, the
Indians even going to the length of putting to death the "Indian agent."

‡ Mr. Ewing, in writing this letter, omits his own name in reporting "an expected visit from some of the Creeks" on a friendly mission. It is from "Mr.
Hoggatt's account," and not from "Hoggatt and Ewing." This is in further confirmation of the inference we have derived from various small items, that Mr.
Ewing "did not believe in McGillivray or the Indians," and that "if the Creeks
came, it would be but to kill and to steal, to burn and to destroy."

§ "A gun in that day was no insignificant present, even to an Indian chief. Mr.
Hoggatt and Mr. Ewing concurred in the opinion that the Creek chief would not
be offended by the offer of some tokens of good will, which he could see and handle.
And as he had manifested some better liking for Mr. Hoggatt than for Mr. Ewing,
it was prudent to have the gun commended by the former. In fact, Ewing was of
the opinion of Castleman and Rains, that there were only two things which
should be given to Indians, "something to eat, and a whipping."

‖ We have not been successful in our search for such "a deed on record."

¶ Nor do we find any grant of land to McGillivray in this "young country."
These evidently were presents proposed to be made by Colonel Robertson, and
which, we doubt not, he would cheerfully have given, could he have placed confidence in McGillivray. We find nothing said in his future correspondence, either
accepting or declining what was thus offered to him.

However reluctant Colonel Robertson and his friends may have been to take
any part in crafty diplomacy and artful intrigue, they were drawn into it. Others
sought to play the game with them, and for them as the stakes, in which they were
to be won or lost. It became the part of wisdom, therefore, for the party most
deeply concerned to use policy likewise.

If their own country gave them up, they never intended to belong to another.
There were some men who thought of such a step, hinted it, suggested it, dared to
recommend it, but who subsequently dropped it "in hot haste," denied, denounced,
and abhorred it. Perhaps they had been deceived and ensnared.

James Robertson was not one of these ; nor was there one in the party of emigrants which came with him ; nor in that of Donelson, nor in that of Eaton, the
Bledsoes, or of Rains, or of Mansker. These were brave men and true—Americans all and always.

"I could say much to you concerning this same country,* but am fully sensible you are better able to judge what may take place in a few years than myself.† In all probability we cannot long remain in our present state ; and if the British, or any commercial nation, who may be in possession of the mouth of the Mississippi, would furnish us with trade, and receive our produce, there cannot be a doubt but the people on the west side of the Appalachian Mountains will open their eyes to their real interests.

"I should be very happy to hear your sentiments on this matter.

"Myself, and the inhabitants of this young country, return you our most grateful thanks for your very polite treatment of Messrs. Hoggatt and Ewing, and shall always be happy to render you any service in our power.

"I hope you will honor me with a correspondence, and shall do myself the pleasure of writing by every opportunity.

"I am, Sir,

With great esteem, your most obedient,

JAMES ROBERTSON.

HON. ALEXANDER McGILLIVRAY."

It should be borne in mind that at this period there was virtually *no American Confederacy, no American Union,* but really what this very Indian chief aptly and expressively called, *"An Interregnum."*

The old Confederacy was dissolving and without power, and the present

---

* The language used to the Creek chief is quite complimentary to his intelligence and foresight. "*You* are better able to judge what may take place in a few years than myself!" Now Robertson felt assured (and so did Ewing) that this letter would be seen by others than the "great King of the Creeks," as he was sometimes called ; and it was deemed proper to "throw dust in the eyes of all of them."

† No doubt McGillivray was far better informed of the views of the Spaniards than was Col. Robertson. He knew their desire to arrest the advance of American settlements upon the western waters ; he had consented to become the agent of their policy to annoy and destroy the Cumberland settlements ; he knew the obstacles which would be thrown in the way of navigation of the Mississippi ; that "no stream would be left unstopped, or stone unturned," to cause distress to these pioneer settlers.

Here they were, "children in the woods," "over the hills and far away," occupying a most important post, to which they had attained "in journeyings often, in perils of waters, in perils of robbers, in perils by their own countrymen, in perils by the heathen, in perils in the wilderness, in perils among false brethren, in weariness and painfulness, in watchings often, in hunger and thirst, in cold and nakedness."

form of United States Government was not fully adopted. North Carolina had rejected the Constitution, and was neither in the Confederacy
nor in the *Union*. And well might the State of Franklin and the Compact of the Judges on Cumberland (of which the Quarter Sessions Court
was but the successor) hold some anxious consultations.

On the 17th September, 1788, our present form of United States
Government was agreed upon in Convention, but only made known and
submitted to the States for ratification by resolution of the 28th. And
on this same 17th September, the Fourth Convention at Danville, Kentucky, had resolved unanimously in favor of separation from Virginia;
and again to ask admission as a State into the Union. And yet so many
obstacles were thrown in the way of her attainment of this distinction,
that the question was seriously discussed, "whether it would not be for
the interest of her people to unite with others upon the western waters
in the formation of a separate government."

The conduct of some of the Eastern States served greatly to urge this
question upon the people of Kentucky and Cumberland. Measures were
there proposed to discourage emigration to the West. Even such a statesman as Governeur Morris expressed decided opposition to sowing seed from
home on the broad lands west of the mountains, which would, in time,
grow into such a population as to control the parent States. One scheme
or proposition was, "so to fix and settle the ratio of representation in
Congress, that the old States could, in all coming time, preserve and
enjoy the *political ascendency*."

Therefore, we find there a willingness to yield for a number of years,
or to sacrifice entirely, (as some construed the sentiment,) the navigation
of the Mississippi. We need not doubt that these expressions among
politicians on the other side of the mountains, were artfully used by some
designing persons in these new settlements to alienate them from the
parent States. Many here did believe that the purpose with those who
had the power was to secure their own commercial advantages on the
Atlantic Ocean, wholly regardless of the small present or prospective
interests of the few adventurous settlers in these western wilds.

If we consider all the elements then in commotion, all the intrigues on
foot, all the influences at work, all the threats and fears, all the interests
at stake, all the difficulties oppressing, all the embarrassments and
dangers accumulating—how many and how varied were all these, and
with what artifice and ingenuity they were urged upon the western
people—we can only be surprised that the Alleghanies were not made the
western limit to the old Confederated States, at least for a time.

Consider for a moment a few passages in the speech or report of Mr.

Monroe to the Virginia Convention, which ratified the Federal Constitution:

"There was a time when even Virginia in some measure abandoned the Mississippi, by authorizing its cession to the Court of Spain.

"The Southern States were overrun and in possession of the enemy; the Government of South Carolina and Georgia prostrate, and opposition there at an end. North Carolina made but a feeble resistance. And Virginia herself was greatly harassed by the enemy in force at that time in the heart of the country; and by impressments for her own and the defence of the Southern States.

"In addition to this, the finances were in a deplorable condition, if not totally exhausted; and France, our ally, seemed anxious for peace; and as a means of bringing the war to a more happy and speedy conclusion, the object of this cession was the hope of uniting *Spain* in it with all her forces."

Fortunately for us, Spain was too *intriguing*, too *avaricious*, too *diplomatic*. She desired more than the control of the mouth of the Mississippi: she aimed at the suppression or control of the American settlements upon the great streams which empty into that mighty river. Her schemes worked her own utter overthrow. By urging an unjust claim, she endangered her all. "The wise are taken in their own craftiness." The spirit of the Americans was aroused, their watch was more vigilant, their resolution the more determined. No foreigner could rule here; none should.

Mr. Monroe further said: "The Northern States were inclined to yield the navigation; that it was their *interest* to prevent an augmentation of the Southern influence and power; and they would relinquish that river in order to *depress* the Western country, and *prevent* the Southern interest from *preponderating*."

Such a sentiment was quite prevalent in the New England States. The immense territory north-west of the Ohio River had been *Southern property*, yielded up for new States; and the prevailing idea was, that the intercourse and interests of its future inhabitants would chiefly be with the Southern people, going with their business down these great natural highways to the Gulf and to the ocean. No one then foresaw the construction of railroads, which now afford facilities of travel and business over and through the mountains to all the Atlantic shore, surpassing the many rivers on which were then any American settlements, or in contemplation. These have created, and sustain, a sympathy, a prejudice, an interest, tending more to the East (from whence also most of the population has come) than to the South.

The great and populous States north-west of the Ohio have now a common interest with Kentucky, Tennessee, and other Southern States, in the navigation of this vast inland sea; and should not forget that the pioneers at a few and feeble stations in Kentucky and Tennessee, suffered keenest anxiety and remonstrated boldly against the suggestion, the proposal, indeed, to deprive them of the use of waters upon which now annually passes a commerce far greater than was then conducted by all of the United States on sea and land.

But let us turn again to this first settlement and first port on Cumberland, and to the letter of Colonel Robertson, who saw and watched the Spanish aim, and lived to see it wholly counteracted, frustrated. He is now in correspondence with the most dangerous agent of Spanish craftiness and the willing tool to work the destruction of the Cumberland settlements under the care of Robertson. Colonel Robertson seems to say, "Great Indian chief, I know you have entered into treaty with the Spanish governors to kill me and the people with me. You may be in need of the suitable weapon: we are well supplied, have guns to spare; 'I have provided a *gun* which Mr. Hoggatt thinks will please you.'"

If there was not a covert meaning in this intimation, it was no empty compliment. A good rifle, at that day, was an article of value, and highly prized by chiefs and warriors. "I have also caused a *deed* for a *lot* in Nashville to be recorded in your name, and beg you will let me know whether you will accept a tract or two of land in our young country."

This great Indian Chief had commingled in his veins the blood of the Scotchman, the Frenchman, and the Spaniard, with the noble blood of the "Wild Wind," or "Wind Family," the most aristocratic and influential family in the Creek nation.* In intellect and learning he was a Scotchman, in politeness a Frenchman, in diplomacy and craftiness a Spanish Indian. During the war of our Revolution he took sides with England. The warlike spirit which he had indulged at that time and nourished in his nation, was long afterwards manifested towards the Georgians, and extended — under Spanish influence — to the distant "Robertson settlements" on the Cumberland. With all his haughty pride and lofty ambition, he was a man to be *conciliated*—who could be flattered with honors, gained by douceurs. Rich and powerful as he was, or was supposed to be, Hoggatt, Ewing, and Robertson thought he would not be insulted by offering him an interest here. Evidently there was a sly innuendo in this offer.

---

* McGillivray: the name seems to be compounded of the Scotch *McGill*, and of the French *Vrais*.

To our mind, Colonel Robertson seems to say, "Mr. Indian, this is a new settlement, 'a young country,' but we are a great people. We already have a town here, and we intend to make that great. We have rich lands in this, 'our young country,' and we intend highly to improve them. *We* will give *you* a lot in our town, and 'a tract or two of land in this, our young country,' if you will command your rascally hunters to remain at home—not to cross the Tennessee to steal our cattle, to kill our people, to disturb us in our possessions and operations!

"We know your intimacy with the Spaniards, who are seeking to draw or drive us away. We understand something of your agency in the murders and depredations committed here and on the Holston; but, be it known unto you, that we *are here* and *here intend to remain*, that we have already a town and town lots. *We* can *give you a deed* with a title which shall be warranted good against all the world. We would be pleased to be at peace with all the tribes; you can exert much influence upon their predatory and warlike spirit; and now, if it may be any inducement, say so, and what we have offered shall be given.

"Will you have a lot in our town, a tract or two of land in our young country?"

We cannot assert that these proffers had much influence with McGillivray, nor can we find that any such deeds for lot or land were ever executed or registered. Other measures were soon adopted; other and larger grants were soon to be made to him and his sub-chiefs, which should withdraw them from the influence of English, French, and Spanish agents, and restore peace.

Alexander McGillivray was unquestionably a man of superior mind, good education, commanding influence, bravery, and diplomatic tact. His grandfather was a Scotchman, his mother a Creek, of the Wind Tribe, having some cross of European blood. He was educated in Charleston, by his uncle, a Protestant clergyman, and at an early day and age he assumed the position at Indian councils to which his talents and his influential family entitled him. Throughout the War for American Independence he was devoted to the measures of England. At the close of that war he entered into close alliance with the Spanish authorities of Florida and Louisiana. In that conference and treaty he represented the Creeks and Seminoles; and engaged to use his influence and artifice with Chickasaws, Cherokees, and Choctaws, against the people of the United States in their advancing western and south-western settlements.

This alliance and engagement was formed in 1784, soon after the termination of the war, and the acknowledgment by Spain herself of our territorial boundaries and admission into the family of nations. The parties endeavored to keep the existence of such a treaty a secret. When it became known, McGillivray justified his engagement in it, and his acts of hostility, by assertions that the Whigs of the Revolution had confiscated estates to which he would have been entitled.

As well might the children and grandchildren of other tories have claimed indemnity for losses or restitution to forfeited estates as this man. As rightfully might Spain have engaged all the old tories and refugees to continue their hostility towards the Americans, and to have furnished them with arms and ammunition. Her conduct was deceitful and wicked.

The settlers upon the Cumberland had no certain knowledge of the engagements into which McGillivray had entered; but that Colonel Robertson and others were suspicious, thoughtful, careful, distrustful of his sincerity, as well as of his friendship, we are confident. At this time the Spanish officers were *lavish* of their expressions of kindness, proffers of liberality, and guarantees of favors.

But in letters and documents which have since come to light, we discover that the Spaniards had engaged this very Indian chief to "persecute these settlers, annoy these stationers, break up these Cumberland settlements." The Spanish agents offered lands and privileges to withdraw them from connection with their friends on the other side of the mountains; and resolved that if such "fair means" would not accomplish it, they would resort to "foul!" therefore they engaged the Creeks especially to "annoy and destroy" the settlements.

In a letter which McGillivray addressed to Colonel Pickens, in September, 1785, he makes a remark about the "settlements on the Cumberland, and that people there would do well to show a regard to the rights of others, and avoid *further aggressions!*"

Whence comes such a suggestion? Upon whose lands or rights had they "aggressed?" They had trespassed upon no territory or claims of the Creek nation.

Did the Cherokees acknowledge themselves as under the protection of the Creeks? Did the Chickasaws ask the Creek chief to stop "further aggressions" by these stationers?

These last certainly had the best of all the pretentious claims to this wild region; and they were the most friendly to the settlers. Then who put these words into the mouth of this powerful chief?

As Robertson and Bledsoe suspected, and as Hoggatt and Ewing on their return said, "the mark of the beast is easily seen; the screen does not wholly hide the Spanish agency: trust them not, even *dona ferentes.*"

In further proof of the spirit of McGillivray, and of the Spanish complicity and hypocrisy, we quote a remark from a long letter which he wrote in September, 1788, to *Panton*, the Spanish merchant to whom he, as chief of the nation, had granted most profitable and exclusive trading privileges, and who had acquired immense wealth by his dealings. It will be noticed that this letter bears date only a month later than the one which we have copied, as addressed to Colonel Robertson and Colonel Bledsoe. Speaking of proposed terms for peace and boundaries, he says, "Experience has proved that such matters are only to be attained by the *longest fire, and point of sword*, particularly with Americans!"

Rains's commentary upon this expression was, "The longest pole knocks down the persimmons." Rains, Castleman, and Mansker had each, by experience, known the advantage of "the longest fire;" the point of the sword" they had not yet found the enemy who would adventure sufficiently near to test. Not one of them but would gladly have encountered this Creek chief at "long shot," or with "the butcher-knife."

In this same letter McGillivray speaks boastfully of "an attack made by a party of Cherokees on a body of the *Franklin* troops," and rejoices that the latter were completely routed; and adds, "This being the first check they ever got in that country, the drooping spirits of the Cherokees were thereby revived."

Colonel Robertson had said, "It is reported that the inhabitants of Holston and the Cherokees are at war." The sharp sword of Sevier, and of the true Franklin men, discussed "such matters" with the Cherokees, and proved the truth of what could be attained by "the longest fire."

"The State of Franklin and its patriotic Governor!" was a toast received with much enthusiasm in its day. "The Cumberland Stationers!" and "Government of Notables!" was drank with equal gusto.

In another letter to Panton, August, 1789, he says, "I have, in a letter to Governor Mero, *approved his* policy of settling Americans on the west side of the Mississippi, and I truly wish it was in compass of our power to *drive them all from the Cumberland* and Ohio, to seek the *new asylum out of our way!*" These words tell the secret of the many depredations of the Creeks upon the settlements on the Cumberland.

> "Will you walk into my parlor?
> Said the spider to the fly."

The Americans continued their "buzzing around," broke the web, and the spider withdrew or famished. At this date, (1789,) Commissioners were appointed by the United States Government to negotiate with McGillivray, as "King of the Creeks," and they proposed to pay him for his confiscated property about $100,000. With this he was pleased, and promised to visit President Washington at New York and Philadelphia.

In compliance with such promise, he did, in August, 1790, make such a visit, and a treaty was concluded : a treaty of peace, for protection of the Indians, establishing of boundaries, and cession of a large territory; an annuity of $1500 per annum to the Creek nation, and presents and annuities to sub-chiefs, the companions and friends of McGillivray. It was at this time that he received the rank and commission of *"Brigadier-General,"* with the yearly pay of $1200.

He promptly manifested his gratification with this military honor, and was seen proudly to "don the dress, epaulettes, sword, hat, and nodding plume" of a *General* of the United States.

At New York, Philadelphia, and elsewhere, he had been received with marked attention. He returned to his nation proud of his honors, his equipments, his equipage, but there to encounter his old associates, and succumb to those influences which had for many years tempted him to hostility to the Americans.

In the summer of 1792, he was persuaded to visit Governor O'Neille, at Pensacola. It was at this place he had met O'Neille, Mero, and Navarro, and entered into the secret treaty of 1st of June, 1784, to which we have referred.   And, either with treacherous or sinister designs, the hope of other rewards, or a willingness to be tempted into his former habits, he encounters this crafty Spanish Governor and his artful and practiced favorite in commercial transactions, the noted Panton ; and there he is assailed by the ridicule and arguments which such men knew how to bring to bear upon one who had been long entangled in their meshes.

Panton had sent his traders into the Cherokee nation.   They had induced Watts—or Bloody Fellow, or Esquaka—and Little Turkey—or Scola-cutta, or Hanging-Maw—and other chiefs, to come to Pensacola with their "Pack-horses," and there receive supplies of arms and ammunition, as also costly presents of goods.   These chiefs, with their desperate bands of robbers upon and near the Tennessee River, were thus supplied to wage the war of destruction, to carry "fire-brands, arrows, and death" into the Cumberland settlements.   The practices of former years were to be continued.

But will the proud " Brigadier-General" throw his commission in the fire ? Will he break that sword, doff that uniform, and show his contempt of all titles and honors and salaries ? He was in a dilemma. "The Spanish Governor pledged the word of his master, the King of Spain, to make this Creek chief a greater man than Congress had made of him." McGillivray had some confidence in these promises: he hoped such a wonder would be performed, such a glory overshadow the Brigadier-

General, such a post of *preëminence* be attained by the "King of the Creeks," through the gracious and wonder-working power of the "great King of the Spains," as Jardennes calls his "Catholic Majesty :" the same person whom Ewing and Rains so often identified, in name, deeds, and character, with his "Satanic Majesty."

The faithlessness of McGillivray began this year to be strongly suspected, and more and more uncovered. He has been pronounced "the greatest man ever born upon the soil of Alabama," and this was in eulogy by an Alabamian. It will not be difficult to arrive at *our* estimate of the Creek chief.

CHAPTER XXVIII.

1794.

IT having been ascertained that in all the Territory there were over five thousand male inhabitants, elections had been ordered to be held in all the counties, to elect members of the Territorial Assembly and Legislature. This body consisted of thirteen members; the counties of Davidson, Sumner, and Tennessee being each entitled to one. Four counties in East Tennessee were entitled to two members each, namely, Knox, Jefferson, Washington, and Hawkins; and Green and Sullivan each one. These elections took place on 22d and 23d December, and on the 1st day of January, 1794, the Governor issued his proclamation to convene the Assembly at Knoxville, on fourth Monday of February, 1794. The Representatives from the Cumberland District were General James White from Davidson, David Wilson from Sumner, and James Ford from Tennessee Counties; Wilson, of Sumner, was elected Speaker. All suitable measures were adopted to put the Territorial Government in operation. Until this time the Governor and Judges had discharged the varied powers, legislative, executive, and judicial.

It was the duty of the Assembly to nominate *ten* persons, from whom the President of the United States would commission *five*, who should constitute "A Legislative Council:" they were Griffith Rutherford, John Sevier, James Winchester, Stockley Donelson, and Parmenas Taylor. This Territorial Government was soon duly organized and at work.

The Assembly adopted and forwarded to Congress, by their Representative, James White, a memorial upon the Indian war, which had so long distressed the people of this Territory. And to it they annexed "a list of the names of persons *killed*, wounded, and captured, and horses stolen, *since* the 26th day of February, 1794." It is an awful summary; at least we, in our day, would think so:

"Killed,   67.
"Wounded, 10. } 102.
"Prisoners, 25.

"Horses stolen 376, valued at $18,800, if valued at only $50 each."

It seems incredible that the patience of the people could endure so much and so long. Never did a people manifest higher regard to the name of a beloved patriot, and to his wishes and perplexities in setting forward the great movements of our Government, than did they who lived and suffered in this Territory. This was clearly announced in a resolution adopted at the close of the Legislative Assembly, 24th September, as follows:

"*Resolved*, That James White, Esq., the Representative of this Territory in Congress, be instructed to take an early opportunity of exhibiting to the President of Congress the *additional list of one hundred and five* of our fellow-citizens who have suffered by the Creeks and Cherokees, *since our memorial to Congress in the spring*, in addition to the former innumerable and cruel acts of hostility with which this Territory has been insulted by those Indians; and to assure his Excellency that if the people of this Territory have borne with outrages which stretch human patience to its utmost, it has been through *our veneration for the head of the Federal Government*, and through the hopes we entertain that his influence will finally extend to procure for this injured part of the Union that justice which nothing but retaliating on an unrelenting enemy can afford."

Thus they told in much simplicity the sad tale of their horrible sufferings, and of their unexampled patience and forbearance, and why they had endured so much and so patiently. "It has been through our veneration for the head of the Federal Government." *All for Washington!* And there can be no doubt of this; it was a Heaven-implanted sentiment, and saved an empire.

So great were the perils from the savages, that the Governor was called upon and ordered a guard of soldiers to escort the members from Mero District to their homes.* And thus the first session signalized its veneration for Washington and care of its members.

As to small local affairs, we find that "Black Bobb's Tavern" was yet *the* place in Nashville where the thirsty and the hungry could resort and be satisfied. His was never a disorderly house.

---

* To the application for a guard, the Governor replied:

"Mr. President and gentlemen of the Legislative Council, and Mr. Speaker and gentlemen of the House of Representatives:

"The guard you request for the members of Mero District returning home, and for the families moving to that district, will be ordered as you request, and will be in readiness early on Monday.

"WM. BLOUNT."

"The Court, on motion, agree that a certain negro in the town of Nashville, called *Bobb*, be permitted to sell *liquors and victuals* on his good behavior, until the end of the term of the ensuing County Court."

Bobb retained his soubriquet of "Old Good Behavior," and persons yet living have some recollection of him.

The tax list of Davidson shows for this year as follows :

"800,555 acres land, at 25c. per 100 acres.

"412 White polls, at 25c. each poll.

"549 Blacks, at 50c., (between 12 and 60 years of age.)

"101 Town lots, at $1 each.

"15 Stud horses, at $4 each. = $2535 89.

Early in this year Governor Blount had proposed to the Cherokees an exchange of prisoners, and had urged them to be at peace. At the same time he gave them warning, that if the murders and thefts did not cease, their country would be invaded, their towns destroyed, and ample vengeance taken. The peace required must be general, and allowances could no longer be made for predatory and murderous parties coming from the nation into the settlements. A block-house nearly opposite the mouth of Tellico, and other defences, were erected in East Tennessee, and General Sevier had the supervision of them.

Judge Haywood remarks, "The Governor had so far succeeded with the General Government, as to induce it at last to believe that the people of Cumberland were exposed to *some danger* which they had not drawn upon themselves by any misconduct of theirs." Therefore he was authorized to raise from the militia of Mero District *one hundred men*, allowing twenty-six privates for Davidson, the like number for Tennessee, and seventeen for Sumner, besides subaltern officers, sergeants, and corporals, and a mounted troop of thirty men to range throughout the district. But in despite of these measures the savages continued their deeds of slaughter, as we have already intimated.

January 1st. During the past week the settlers had enjoyed quite a merry-making. "From Christmas eve till the dawn of the New Year," they had visited from house to house, station to station ; the girls and the fiddles being the liveliest and sweetest accompaniments. We have heard the "Hutchinson Family" sing the gleesome song of the "Yankee Gathering :"

"There is quite a considerable number of us,
    A considerable number of us,
    All standing in a row."

We doubt not they were a "happy family," and happily represented many a "Yankee gathering," where "the gals are sweet as candy." But we do believe, if there ever were

"Happy families in a cage,
The wild beasts ravening round them,
And savage men all in a rage,
With whetted knife and loaded gun,
All furious to devour them,"

they were here, in the holidays of 1793–4.

The winter was warm, open, delightful ; provisions were abundant, nobody sick, several weddings, and dinners and dances and suppers, "a constant round." When the company passed from one station to another, the men were on horseback, gun in hand, and

"Sweetheart on behind them,
Well balanced on the *pillion*."

"The compliments of the season" had passed round and round with hearty entertainments, and now "*the* dance of the season" was to be on Drake's Creek. The good housewives thought fresh venison and a few fat gobblers would add much to the variety of dishes of meat for the supper. "The men agreed to whatever the women said, whenever they talked about things in their line of business," especially about cooking and eating. Therefore, John Drake, with three other good hunters, made an early start for one of the licks. They had heard the morning call of the turkey gobblers, and had secured enough of them. They must hasten to the lick before the deer should come to quench their thirst and taste of salt. They had not been long in ambush near the spring before they had a buck and doe ready for "the skinning operation." They were busily engaged in skinning, to obtain the saddles and hams from one to take home then, intending to hang up the other and send with a horse for it.

As they were thus busily engaged, they were fired upon by Indians, who also rushed towards them with uplifted battle-axes. So many guns were fired that each white man believed his companions must be killed or wounded ; could not believe that all should escape alive. And when they found that not one had received even a flesh-wound, they were amazed, and mad with themselves that they did not stand by their game and turn upon the enemy, who, no doubt, would have fled before them. But now they had lost not only the deer and turkeys, but their guns.

Fortunately, some other persons had brought in a deer and some turkeys.

So the supper was provided, and the evening's entertainment was cheerful and uninterrupted.   Gamble* was there.   Mr. Drake and his com-

---

* James Gamble was the most distinguished fiddler in all the District of Mero. Indeed, the people here believed that there was not the equal of Gamble west of the mountains, and his superior not in the United States, if there was, indeed, in all the world.

He usually stayed at Bledsoe's or Greenfield in Sumner county. But they often sent for him to come to Eaton's, the Bluff, and to Freeland's, as well as to other stations. He and his fiddle (and they were inseparable) were always welcome, and everywhere. He had a sack of doe-skin, in which he placed "his fiddle and his bow," when not in use or when travelling, and under his arm it was always safe: "He loved it," as he said to the women and the girls, "but never squeezed it so as to break down the bridge or put her out of tune."

" He could make his fiddle laugh and talk. There was such potency in its music, that he often charmed away pains of the body and silenced the groans of the sick. The sweet strains and the thrilling tones of that fiddle filled the air, the ear, the soul. It seemed sometimes as if they could not die. Every nerve in the human system was in symphony with those sweet sounds; there was a delicious feeling and enjoyment in the soul, that always did one good. You could not be angry, ill-natured, or crabbed, where there was such ecstatic and soothing music. It lasted so long, too! you could hear it and feel it the next day, and wish to hear it a thousand times. It would not have done one harm to hear it always."

" We had other fiddlers in the district—indeed, a great many of them, and some remarkably good ones, too; but Gamble excelled them all." Whenever there was to be much of an entertainment or considerable dance, the girls would say, "O, get Gamble! Do get Gamble! We know he will come." And Gamble was, indeed, always willing to come. This was his pleasure; he had no other business, he did nothing else, he knew nothing else, than to play the fiddle. He fiddled as long as he lived, and he fiddled his life away. He was a good-natured, happy man, never hated anybody, never made an enemy. He was married to his fiddle. He and his wife entertained and gratified a great many persons, men, women, and children, in their day.

In our childhood, (towards the beginning of the present century,) we heard "Fiddler Green," whose praise was in all the stations from Fort Harmar to Farmer's Castle, and down on either shore of the Ohio, from the Little and Big Muskingum to the Little and Big Kanhawa; and we can yet sometimes find the traces of the sweet "long-drawn notes" of his celebrated violin, upon our memory's music-book. And there are persons yet living who retain the memory of the celebrated fiddler of Sumner county, and of the delicious music he used to discourse in the Cumberland settlements, "when their old hearts were young."

When the great revival came, the "dancing," involuntary and without ease or grace, was continued; but instrumental music was condemned as unsuitable, and, indeed, sinful to be practiced or heard by professors of religion, and several of the fiddlers of Mero laid their instruments on the shelves or among old trumpery, and a few *broke them in pieces.* James Gamble (we hope) was also a Christian, a devotee to his science of sweet sounds upon horse-hair and cat-gut, but never a

30

panions were the only persons who could not talk to the ladies in a lively and entertaining manner, and use the tender and affectionate term "*dear.*" "They were rather silent that evening! And when they saw 'the gentlemen, every man and boy with his gun,' and theirs, . . . they begged to be excused, didn't want any supper, were not hungry!" "Everybody was sorry for them." But they "went home with the gals in the morning."

January 3d. Miss Gray was passing between two of the stations, about four miles west from Nashville, when several Indians attempted to capture her, but as she was swift on foot she fled before them; therefore they fired at and wounded her, but not so as to stop her flight. Her name was *Deliverance.* She escaped death, captivity, and a scalping.*

January 7th. John Helen, who was at work for General Robertson, half a mile from the house, was shot, killed, and scalped. He ran some hundreds of yards and made a desperate struggle for life, as was "evident by the signs." General Robertson ordered Captain Murray to take twenty men and pursue these Indians.

Murray discovered they had several horses, (no doubt well packed with stolen property,) that there were several squaws with them, and that their route was south-west, towards the Tennessee. He was convinced the party had been so successful by their incursion into the settlements, they were returning to the nation and would cross the Tennessee. After the second day they were travelling quite leisurely, and Murray determined to pursue and attack them when preparing to cross the river. "There were eleven Indian men and five squaws. Murray's pursuit was so cautious, the Indians entertained no apprehension of the whites being so close upon them. Doubtless they believed no one had tracked them."

They encamped somewhat late in the evening at the edge of the river, upon the slope of a ridge "which jutted a little into the river." Here they had gathered some cane for the horses, and kindled a large fire,

---

bigot. He read his Bible, and fiddled: he prayed, and he fiddled; asked a silent blessing on his meals, gave thanks, and fiddled; went to meetings, sang the songs of Zion, joined in all devotional services, went home, and fiddled. He sometimes fiddled in bed, but always fiddled when he got up. We doubt not he indulged in fiddling to excess, but if all men were as innocent of harm and contributed as much to the pleasure of their fellows as did James Gamble, the world would be better than it is.

* "The said Hood" used to remark to Miss Gray, "That's a mighty good name of yours, Miss Gray: you were delivered out of the hands of your enemies."
"Yes, the Lord delivered me, and I did n't 'play Possum.'"
"And the Lord delivered me, too, and I did 'play Possum,'" said he.

evidently a signal fire for friends on the other side of the river. They fired several guns also, at intervals; they imitated the howling of wolves and the calling of the great owl. They sent no alarm-cry across the river, but all was indicative of cheerfulness and success.

The point of the ridge was free from cane and underbrush, and exactly suited to Murray's views of "hemming them in at the water's edge." Fortunately the horses made sufficient noise to prevent the Indians hearing any steps taken by the whites, while examining the grounds and the position occupied by the sleeping Indians.

Captain Murray and Jonathan Robertson undertook this examination, and ascertained all they desired, then retreated to their companions, gave them the information, and the plan of attack for the break of day. At the hour agreed upon, they marched along the ridge, forming a semicircle, extending across the narrow promontory from water's edge to water's edge. They had the enemy completely enclosed. The soldiers crept near to the savages, and as soon as two or three of the Indians began to show signs of being awake, the signal was given, most of the guns fired, and a rush made upon them with tomahawks and knives. Two or three jumped into the river, and were shot by those whose fire had been reserved. Two squaws only remained alive, and as prisoners; all the others, eleven men, three women, had been killed. Not a man in Captain Murray's company was wounded. "A cleaner sweep had not been made than this since the country was settled." Captain Murray and Jonathan F. Robertson were satisfied without promotion, and the men with what they had done, and a division of the spoils. And the way in which they divided and distributed these trophies, was by restoring to the owners such as could be identified, and giving to some, who were destitute, articles to which no one set up ownership.

January 20th. Small parties of Indians appeared in various parts of the frontiers of Mero District, killing or wounding several persons, and stealing horses or shooting the cows. "In several instances they left the divided limbs of the slain *scattered* over the ground." "Every pathway, and many plantations, were marked with the blood or carcasses of the slain."

Of Jonathan F. Robertson, eldest son of the General, Haywood says, "that in all his contests, he returned as good as was sent." "He had many a brush with them."

He had been at home but a few days from the expedition under Captain Murray, until he, in company with three small boys of the name of Cowan, enjoyed what he called "a very nice little skirmish." These lads, from ten to fourteen years of age, each had his gun. They were near to Robertson, passing in the open woods upon a ridge, some miles north-west of General Robertson's residence. They had killed some game, and had it swung across their shoulders, but were "wide awake" for more game of whatsoever kind.

One of the young Cowans observed a movement in some low bushes, and instantly threw his gun in position to fire. Robertson's quick eye detected the barrel of a gun by the side of a tree, and cried out, "Indians! Tree, boys, tree!" At the word, two of the boys jumped behind their separate trees, Robertson and the other boy behind another, which was too small a cover for two persons, and he determined to seek another, telling the boys to "be very careful how they looked out, and not to throw away their fire."

He had but jumped behind the tree with young Cowan, when one of the Indians fired, and wounded the lad who was treed with him, slightly in the thigh. Robertson told him to "lay low," and soon learned from the youth that he "was not hurt bad enough to lie down." He stood up, and "had a crack at them." From Robertson's anxiety to see the foe, and obtain a shot, he exposed his head so much that an Indian put a ball through his hat, immediately above his left ear. His hat fell, and he himself almost fell. Perhaps the slight concussion made him take a step in the direction in which he was leaning. However, when in that position, "he saw the body of an Indian plainly, and let drive." Instantly he jumped behind his tree, and handing his gun to young Cowan, caught up his, while Cowan should reload the one just fired. In this way he fired three times, his partner once, and in full belief that two of their shots had done good service.

The two other Cowans each fired twice, and at least one of their shots was well aimed. The Indians began to run, when Robertson and his young soldiers ran from tree to tree in pursuit, obtaining two or three more cracks at them. But as the Indians escaped into a place where the trees were more numerous, and considerable undergrowth, he forbade any further pursuit.

One of the Cowans passed by a tree behind which the Indian stood at whom he had fired, and picked up a gun. From this fact, and seeing some of the Indians helping others in the retreat into the bushes, the Robertson party was certain they had not wasted all their powder and lead.

An examination of the ground was made a week afterwards, when the remains of two Indian bodies were discovered, the dogs finding them very readily.

Prior to the 27th of February, and within a week of that date, there

was an unusual number of persons killed.   They were killed in all the
settlements—here and there one.   Of the number we may mention Benjamin Linsey, Daniel Read, Edward Caruthers, Jacob Evans, Frederick
Stull, Jacob Morris, and James Davis.

And "between the 27th February and 27th of March, four men were
killed, and many horses stolen."

Of those hunted or killed by the Indians in March, we may mention two
or three.   On the eighteenth, the house of Thomas Harris (a short distance from Clarksville) was set on fire by the Indians.   The chimney was
large, and "out of doors," made of split timbers or puncheons.   This
wood was drier than any other belonging to the house, and here the
enemy could most secretly approach.

They had gathered dry sticks and heaped them against this wooden
chimney, and it was easily set in a blaze.   Fortunately, Mr. Harris was
awakened by the noise made in piling up the fuel which the Indians had
prepared, and the purpose was at once perceived.   There were two guns
in the house, both loaded.   There was no light or fire kindled in the
house, but very soon the blazing heap on the outside caused a state of
horror among the family.   The awful question was presented : "Shall
we stay in and be burned, or go out and be shot down and tomahawked ?"

At the foundation of the chimney-stack were two or three courses of
round logs, upon which the drier split sticks forming the chimney had
been placed, and in order to kindle the fire against these, the Indians
had heaped up a small stack of light dry sticks.   This was the pile which
had commenced to blaze when Mr. Harris, with gun in hand, and dread
perplexity in his mind, looked between the logs of his house to ascertain
if any thing could be done affording hope of escape.   He saw how the
brush had been piled up, and instantly resolved to thrust something
through the chimney, and push off the brush.   In this he partially succeeded, when an Indian ran towards the fire, or came within the light
made by it, and Harris instantly shot him down.   Some of his companions ran up to drag him away, and were in the act of removing the
wounded Indian, when another shot was fired among them, and they disappeared.

With the aid of his family he pushed the chimney from the house, and
in its fall the pieces were much scattered, and the mud or earth which
had been plentifully used in daubing it, fell upon the burning brush
placed by the Indians.   The upper half of the chimney being thus
thrown off from the house, the few shingles which had caught were
easily removed, and all danger of being burned up was for the time
removed.   Day dawned : the incendiaries had fled, and the family escaped.

On the 20th, James Bryan, as he approached one of the deer-licks, about four miles from Nashville, was fired at by Indians lying in ambush. He was within fifty steps of them, and yet they missed him, only piercing a few bullet-holes through his hunting-shirt. He wheeled and ran, the Indians after him. At one time they "headed him," and were close enough to "make a grab at him." He made a very narrow escape. On the same day they killed Charles Bratton, and scalped him. This was done near the house of Major White, in Sumner.

On the next day the same party (probably) approached and concealed themselves at a stone-quarry at a short distance from the spring and house of Searcy Smith, on Drake's Creek. A negro man of Mr. Smith's was engaged in hauling rock from the quarry. Two youths, who by their energy and sprightliness gave great promise of usefulness, were boarding at Mr. Smith's, attending school. Returning from school, they went with the wagoner to the quarry. The Indians rushed upon them: the negro man surrendered, and was taken as a captive, but the white boys resisted *unto death.* They were killed and scalped, and partially stripped of their clothing. They lay near each other in that mangled condition, the scions of a noble stock, the male heirs of worthy men, slain, as their fathers had been not long before, not afar off, by the prowling savages. Earliest among the pioneers, the bosom friends of Robertson, patriots and true men, the fathers were early sacrificed, leaving these beautiful representatives of all their greatness, talents, and worth, to be cherished, guarded, and educated for the society and State in the laying the foundations of which they had toiled, and for which they had been made martyrs. And now these sons are slain; the cousins lie side by side. As kindred blood had ever flowed through their veins, so now the death-blows have mingled their blood upon the earth. "In death they were not divided."

There are the two Anthonys, sons of Colonel Anthony Bledsoe and Colonel Isaac Bledsoe. They were buried by those who loved them, and the places where they fell, and where they rest, are sacred.*

Shortly before the 2d of May, Colonel Samuel T. Chew (who had been tempted by the liberal offers of the Spanish Government to settle near Lance de Grace) had left there to become an inhabitant of one of the counties on Cumberland, and with his pirogue, four white men and eleven

---

* These are pointed out in view of the residence of Mr. Harry Smith, son of Searcy Smith, and grandson of General Daniel Smith, the associate and friend of Robertson, and trusted Representative and Senator of these Cumberland settlers. "Rock Castle," and its historic memories and its present interests, are worthy of examination.

negroes, had ascended above the dividing ridge between the mouths of the Tennessee and Cumberland Rivers, and therefore when he landed was not on Indian territory.

Colonel Chew and his party were there attacked, and, as is believed, were all killed. His body was most barbarously mangled. This murder was committed by the Creeks.

"The prevailing sentiment among the Cherokees was in favor of peace. They gave great credit to the Chickasaws for so engaging the attention of the Creeks, that the Cumberland settlers enjoyed more security than they otherwise would have had.

"The stealing of horses, however, was most successfully practiced in all directions."

May 26th. One of the spies on Bledsoe's Creek was wounded. On the same day they killed the son of Mr. Strawder, and wounded his wife on Station Camp Creek. In this month General Robertson visited Governor Blount, at Knoxville, by request, to adjust some transactions relative to lands; to consult about the interests of the district; to settle some territorial accounts; and, as we believe, to convince the Governor that there would be no end of the Indian ravages until the Lower Towns were destroyed, and heavy blows struck upon the Creeks.

Governor Blount hoped that some recent warlike movements between the Chickasaws and Lower Creeks would keep the latter so engaged that they would not much annoy the Cumberland people during this summer. General Robertson assured him, however, that the chief crossing-places for the Creeks were at those towns; that there the invaders of Cumberland assembled, coming and going; that they found supplies there, and whatsoever property could be stolen in the District was received there and passed off into the Indian country beyond; "that there never would be any safety or peace for Cumberland as long as those infernal nests were allowed to exist."

We incline to the belief that the Governor concurred in these opinions, but may not have given his approbation to the then contemplated measures to do what General Robertson had for years at heart desired to do. He wished that the Governor's range of "vision might, for a time, be confined to his side of the mountain."

The "shadows of coming events" passed before him, and he was exceedingly desirous not to be committed by any decided participation or distinct knowledge which would affect his official character. General Robertson was willing to leave him "a wide margin." He had himself long participated in the embarrassments and misery resulting from the restrictive orders from the War Department, and he knew that Governor

"CRAGFONT, 21st July, 1794.

"DEAR GENERAL :—On the melancholy and unfortunate fall of my brother George, I ordered Captain Blackmore, with about fifty mounted militia, to pursue the trail, if possible, until he came up with them. He had just returned after a long and fatiguing march of near two weeks, without effecting any thing.

"On this unhappy occasion I rather attended to my own feelings as a man, a brother, than to my duty as a soldier and an officer. I, however, trust and hope, if it is in your power, you will permit me to have these men mustered, and let them be paid for their services. The inhabitants of this county are very desirous that the spies may be continued as usual. If it can be admitted, give me orders for that purpose as soon as possible.

"Captain McEllwrath and Mr. James Clendenin, whom I sent to explore Cumberland River from the mouth of Caney Fork to the Salt Lick, 'Report, that the hills set in very close to the river from the mouth of the Caney Fork for a considerable distance up the river. That the only eligible place for a station is at the mouth of a small creek about three and a half miles below the Salt Lick Creek, and in sight of the mouth of Martin's Creek.'* Here, they say, the ground is somewhat broken, but there is the appearance of two or three springs in the neighborhood, and they believe a road may be got from it to the present Holston Trace, though it will not be much nearer than the Salt Lick.

"I am, dear sir, your most obedient,
                                    J. WINCHESTER.
"Genl. James Robertson."

When the intelligence of the death of Major Winchester reached "the Court-house" of Sumner, the citizens were convening for the business of the Court-day, and for other purposes which usually attract a crowd. Fifty men were enrolled under Captain Blackmore, to pursue the murderers at daybreak the next morning. Being mounted on good stolen horses, and having a day and night in advance, the Indians escaped.

No one can fail to approve the conduct of Colonel Winchester, and to admire the calm and tender expressions in regard to his murdered and scalped brother; and how highly he appreciates the dignity of the military position which he occupies.

We ought not to omit all notice of a communication to General Robertson of this same date, (9th July,) dated "Fort Massac," from Major Doyle, informing the General that, "pursuant to instructions from

---

* Here "Fort Blount" was established.

Government, he had begun to establish a garrison at that post." "From information received," he says, "this will be an eyesore to the Cherokees;* permit me to tender you any services from here, and let me rely on intelligence of Indian movements. . . . I shall find pleasure in being in any way useful to the people of your settlement."

As was "supposed," Fort Massac became somewhat of an eyesore to the Cherokees and Shawnees, and a sort of a thorn in the side of the Spaniards; and this more from its advanced position, than from any acts of aggression or defence done by the garrison stationed there. More deserters from United States garrisons and marching troops were caught or brought there, than all the Indians which the soldiers at Massac ever pursued or shot at. It was a sickly place, and had to be abandoned in 1808. It was gratifying to General Robertson and to the people of Cumberland, as it was to those of Kentucky, to see the Government planting a garrison thus in advance of the settlements, and so nigh to the Spaniards. Thousands would have rejoiced to learn of a collision between the regular troops and Indians and Spaniards "mixed up." And yet at this time, and notwithstanding the many causes of offence received from the Spaniards, there were native and naturalized citizens who were pensioned officers of Spain, and secretly working discontent in Kentucky.

There had been several Creek and Cherokee prisoners in the Cumberland settlements for some time. An exchange was agreed upon through Mr. Seagroves, the United States agent at Tuckabatche, (Upper Creeks,) and some of these captives were consequently returned to their nation. They had been very kindly treated by the whites; they were youths, boys and girls. Several of the captives had been kept by families in Kentucky. Captain Rains had one, whom he had captured in "a hard fight and tight race."

The Governor continued to urge upon General Robertson the duties of strictest economy, as an especial virtue in a Republican Government: "*Keep down expense*, is a command from the Secretary to me, and I enjoin on you the observance of it." And yet he is compelled to admit that the people of Mero have been but poorly aided, whilst none have suffered as they have. He continued to have great confidence in his conferences and negotiations. "An attack of Cumberland by a *large party* of Indians, either Creek or Cherokees, or both, is not to be apprehended this summer. Small parties, however, I fear, will yet infest your frontiers." "I entreat and command you to let neither *importunity* nor distant appearances of danger induce you to order out any party

---

* "To the Cherokees," as friends and allies of the Shawnees.

unnecessarily large. . . . Economy is a Republican virtue, which, from the injunction laid on me, I feel myself bound to enjoin on you the observance of. It appears to me that the expense afforded Mero District, since the 1st January last, in comparison with that incurred for the defence of Hamilton and Washington Districts, is more than four to one." ,

The Governor should have remembered, that in all these protracted wars, "*large parties* of Indians" had never, when so embodied, done much harm; and he certainly knew that these "small parties" had done an incalculable amount of mischief. Near the close of this letter of April 15th, the Governor is under the necessity to justify himself from some suspicions of having failed to make a full representation of the sufferings of Mero District.

"I can assure you my official communications to Government are strictly consistent with fact, as to the appearances both of peace, murder, theft, etc." It seemed to many incredible, that if full and fair statements were made, the Government could so long look upon these thousands of acts of murder and rapine, and do no more to arrest them or punish the wrong-doers.

The murder of Colonel Chew and his party of fifteen, the murder of the young Bledsoes, and now that daring one of Major Winchester, together with the many others, had so enraged the people that it was *determined* to destroy the Lower Towns this year, and wait no longer.

Joseph Brown* (the youth who had witnessed his father's head cut off at one of these towns, and had long endured imprisonment there, then living about four miles below Nashville, near the river, on the east bank) was intrusted with a detachment, or rather accompanied one under command of Colonel Roberts, to scour the head-waters of Elk; but with the especial and secret purpose of discovering a route for an army to the Nickojack and Running-Water towns. Such a route was found and reported.

The Governor well knew that such a measure had long been in contemplation. General Robertson had opened the subject verbally and in writing, and seems to have entertained the opinion, (which was very prevalent with others,) that he ought to give not only connivance or sanction, but positive orders, for the chastisement of those brigands. In one of his orders, and communicated to General Robertson, he says, "With respect to destroying the Lower Towns, however vigorous such a measure might be, or whatever good consequences might result from it,

---

* Yet living in Maury county, 1858.

I am instructed specially, by the President, to say that he does not consider himself authorized to direct any such measure, more especially as the whole subject was before the last session of Congress, who did not think proper to authorize or direct *offensive operations.*"

The people could endure these injuries no longer. Talk to them of defensive measures, of keeping at home and watching or working, await the creeping savages, and allow usually the *first fire*, then pursue them to a "limited distance;" if the enemy could reach and pass that line, with the fresh scalps of kindred or friends, and all your property, *there stop* —*go no farther*, don't cross the ridge! These people had already endured the "conflict of ages." The resolution was taken. General Robertson no longer hesitated to approve it.

Sampson Williams, Esq., visited Kentucky and prevailed upon Colonel Whitley to unite in the measure. There was no reluctance there; they had suffered greatly by incursions of Indians from these same towns, or of others which had ever found friends there. The place of rendezvous was agreed on, and the various forces to meet at the block-house two miles east of Buchanan's.

Colonel Ford levied troops between Nashville and Clarksville, on the east side of the Cumberland. Colonel John Montgomery came with a company from Clarksville, and General Robertson raised volunteers in Davidson county, west of the river. In the mean time, Major Ore, of Hamilton District, had been ordered with a command of mounted men, for the protection of the frontiers of Mero District, and very *opportunely* arrived in Nashville at the very time the other troops were assembling! He seemed not to be surprised when he learned the object of the expedition, but heartily concurred, and marched his troops also to the place of rendezvous. Here a council of officers was held and plans agreed upon.

The question of command was a difficult one to adjust, but being settled among those who held the rank of "Colonel," it extended to the "Captains," where the like harmonious result was not attained. Robert Weakley (who resided some three miles east of Nashville) had used much exertion in preparation for the expedition, had prepared a liberal supply of provisions, and had it on pack-horses at the place of rendezvous; was a candidate for "Captain," but not being chosen by the soldiers to this command, he resolved to return home, which he did, in despite of remonstrances from every one. He was so indignant, that he would neither leave his pack-horses nor provisions for the use of others.

The excitement ran high, and some words quite offensive must have been used, to induce a person who ever after enjoyed the esteem of his fellow-citizens, to have taken the "back-track," as he did. In due time he held the rank of "Colonel," was a member of the Legislature, and ever a valuable and respected citizen. The poet, Clarke, celebrates the retreat of Weakley from Nickojack.*

In Ramsey's "Annals," a feather is stuck in the cap of *Andrew Jackson*, which ought not to be there. Old soldiers are yet living who assert that "Jackson was not in the Nickojack expedition."†

As the troops of Major Ore were the only ones levied under public authority, it was agreed, in order to give the expedition the sanction of such authority, and so entitle the volunteers to a claim for pay, and the outfit and equipments from the General Government, to confer the command on Major Ore, and call it "Ore's Expedition."

When Colonel Wheatley arrived with his respectable force, it was agreed that he should have "the chief command." Colonel Montgomery was to be in immediate command of the troops raised in the Territory. Thus these matters were arranged; and yet the order from General Robertson was to be addressed to Major Ore, for the reasons before given It is as follows :

"NASHVILLE, September 6th, 1794.

"MAJOR ORE :—The object of your command is, to defend the District of Mero against the Creeks and Cherokees of the Lower Towns, who I

---

* The following lines which the Homer of Cumberland frequently rehearsed, are from his martial poem, "The Nickojack Campaign." They are not in his "Miscellanies in Prose and Verse," but we have them from a gentleman and lady, yet living, and deem too good to be omitted.

> "Colonel Weakley, he turned back,
> And *would* not go to Nickojack :
> Weakley was his name, and his back—
> He *could* not go to Nickojack :
> And his horses, with their pack,
> *Should* not go to Nickojack.
> Not in courage did he lack,
> Though he took the homeward track."

† "Andrew Jackson, then a private, was one of Ore's men, who then showed his love of country and his fitness for command. His judgment in planning the attack on Nickojack, and his good conduct generally in the campaign, impressed those who witnessed it, favorably." ("Annals," pp. 614, 615, and refers to "Willie Blount's Papers.")

There is abundant evidence in the Tennessee Historical Society to justify the assertion that General Jackson was not in that expedition. The testimony of the late Captain John Davis, Colonels Wm. Pillow and Brown, Charles and Beale Bosley, yet living, is concurrent and unquestionable, and wholly in opposition to the statement in the Annals. We insert this note to "sustain the truth of history." No one ever questioned the bravery or patriotism of Jackson; and his not being in that expedition, is only proof that other duties prevented.

have received information are about to invade it, as also to punish such Indians as have committed recent depredations. For these objects, you will march, with the men under your command, from Brown's Block-house, on the eighth instant, and proceed along Taylor's Trace, towards the Tennessee; and if you do not meet this party before you arrive at the Tennessee, you will pass it, and destroy the Lower Cherokee Towns, which must serve as a check to the expected invaders; taking care to spare women and children, and to treat all prisoners who may fall into your hands with humanity, and thereby teach those savages to spare the citizens of the United States, under similar circumstances. Should you in your march discover the trails of Indians returning from the commission of recent depredations on the frontiers, which can generally be distinguished by the horses stolen being shod, you are to give pursuit to such parties, even to the towns from whence they come, and punish them for their aggressions in an exemplary manner, to the terror of others from the commission of similar offences, provided this can be consistent with the main object of your command, as above expressed, the defence of the District of Mero against the expected party of Creeks and Cherokees.

"I have the utmost confidence in your patriotism and bravery, and with my warmest wishes for your success,

"I am, sir, your obedient servant,

"JAMES ROBERTSON, B. G."

On the next day, the 7th, the army marched to the Black Fox's camp,* (Murfreesboro',) the next day crossed Barren Fork of Duck River, near the ancient stone fort, (now Manchester;) thence to Fennison's Spring; thence crossing Elk River and the Cumberland Mountain, they reached the Tennessee River about three miles below the mouth of the Sequatchee.

It being night when the troops reached the river, most of them encamped upon its bank until daylight. A small force of eager warriors were allowed to cross and guard the bank upon the opposite side of the river; they went over before the break of day. The river at that point is nearly three-quarters of a mile wide. A part of the men remained on the north side of the river with the horses.

Preparations were being made, long before the troops arrived at the river, for crossing. Some of the men gathered dead and dry logs, brush, and cane, and carried these pieces of wood with them to the river's edge. In the morning they commenced the construction of rafts

---

* The Indian word for *Black Fox* is *"Enolee."*

and floats, upon which they placed their guns, ammunition, and clothing, and to which indifferent swimmers were also allowed to "hold on with one hand." Judge Haywood says, that "some crossed upon bundles of dry cane, some upon *chumps*."* This is well understood in all our new settlements. There were good swimmers who needed none of these helps.

The troops having thus passed in safety, were soon formed in line under their respective officers, and under the trusty guidance of Joseph Brown, who was now "at home again;" and of Findlestone, the half-breed, who was well "acquainted with all the region there." Very short addresses were required, or to be listened to, at that time. All were anxious to march, and the advance was to move with their officers, attending to motions and signs rather than to words, until they should reach the town or see the enemy.

And thus they marched up the mountain between the point of which and the river was the town of Nickojack. A mile higher up the river, after passing through a very narrow strait—formed by the river on one side, and the mountain jutting into and projecting over it, on the other—they came to a spacious plain of low-lands, on which stood the town called Running-Water. They penetrated into the heart of Nickojack before they were discovered, and first alarmed the Indians by the report of their guns.

Nickojack was a small town, inhabited by two or three hundred men and their families. A considerable number of warriors were killed within the town. The whole population fled towards the river, to enter their canoes and escape. Many crowded into these frail boats, while others leaped into the river, to swim beyond their pursuers. The troops had now the foe unsheltered before them, and made a general havoc in their destruction in the canoes and in the water. All were within the range of the fatal rifle, and were not spared. Some good swimmers turned down the current with utmost exertion, but were "headed off;" some dove under the water, but when they reappeared, the rifle-ball made them sink to rise no more. Eighteen prisoners were taken in this town—two boys, fifteen girls, and one woman. A great number of the enemy were killed, amongst whom were fifty-five warriors.

When the Indians of Running-Water heard the firing, they instantly

---

* Johnson and Webster define it, "A short, thick, *heavy* piece of wood, *less* than a block." This definition would not buoy up a powder-flask. The Bosleys and others, who were in the expedition, state that the troops carried with them several canoes made of dry hides ; which were used chiefly for the safe transportation of guns and ammunition, and short supply of provision.

ran to the place of action, and met their terrified neighbors flying to their town. From this place of meeting they began to return, but made a stand at the narrow pass before·described; taking their positions behind the jutting rocks and the trees, along the side of the mountain. From such points and defences they fired, but without execution, probably in much haste and trepidation and without aim. The Cumberland troops soon drove them from their hiding-places.

In the town of Nickojack were found two fresh scalps, recognized as from Cumberland, and a number that were hung up in the houses as trophies. Many articles of property which were known by some of the militia to have belonged to relatives and friends, and taken within a few months past, were also discovered. A quantity of powder and lead just received from the Spanish Government, as also a commission to the Breath, the chief of the town, were found in Nickojack. This chief was killed among his warriors. Some horses were captured, but the difficulty of taking them across the river was such as to induce their captors to turn them loose again.

The prisoners gave information that there were sixty Creek and Cherokee warriors then out in the settlements; and that only two nights previous, a "scalp-dance" was held in Running-Water, at which Watts, the Bloody Fellow, and other chiefs were present; where it was resolved to prosecute the war with greater activity than heretofore.

Such is the substance of the narrative, as given by Haywood. In the "Annals" some particulars are added from the recollections of Joseph Brown and others, (yet living,) who were in "the army." We shall copy into the next chapter without abbreviation, and then conclude with the "official report" made to the Governor.

31

CHAPTER XXIX.

1794.

"The troops were landed before day. At daylight they fell into ranks, and were counted by Captain John Gordon, and the exact number who had crossed over was ascertained to be two hundred and sixty-five." At the back of Nickojack field, the men were formed into line of battle among the cane. Colonel Whitley was on the right, and struck above the mouth of the creek that rose in the field. Colonel Montgomery was on the right of the troops from the Territory. Orders were given for the two wings to march, so as to strike the river above and below the towns. On the march, two houses were found standing out in the field, and about two hundred and fifty yards from the town : expecting that from these houses their approach would be discovered by the Indians, the troops were here directed to push with all speed to the town. The corn was growing close up to and around the houses. Near the house on the left the firing commenced, and was returned by the Indians, one of whom was here killed. From one of the houses already mentioned, a plain path was seen leading to the town. William Pillow got into it, and ran rapidly along it, till he reached the commons. Perceiving that he had got in advance of such of the troops as had come through the corn-field, Pillow halted till others had come up. The march, or run, was then continued by the doors of the houses, which were all open. The Indians, at the report of the first gun, had run off to the bank of the river. The troops pursued the leading way to the landing. Here they saw five or six large canoes, stored with goods and Indians, and twenty-five or thirty warriors standing on the shore, near the edge of the water. At these Pillow fired, and soon after him a whole platoon sent a volley of rifle-balls, from the effects of which scarce a single Indian escaped alive. A few by diving, and others by covering themselves over in the canoes with goods, escaped, and got out of the reach of the rifles. About the same time the havoc took place at the landing below, Colonel Whitley attacked the Indians above the mouth of the creek. They were not more than a gun-shot apart. Fifteen men had been directed to stop near the two houses in the corn-field and waylay them, until the firing had taken place in the town. When the report of the rifles was heard, this detachment attacked the houses. A squaw had remained outside to listen. A fellow came to the door, and was shot down. Those within drew him inside, and closed the door, leaving the squaw on the outside. She attempted to escape by flight, but after a hard chase she was taken prisoner. The warriors within made holes through the walls, and made a desperate defence. The squaw taken prisoner was carried up to the town and placed among the other prisoners in canoes. As they were taking them down the river to the crossing-place, the squaw loosed her clothes, sprang head foremost into the river, disengaging herself artfully from her clothes, and leaving them floating upon the water. She swam with great agility, and was rapidly making her escape. Some hallooed, "Shoot her; shoot her!" But others, admiring her energy, her activity, and her boldness, replied, "She is too smart to kill," and allowed the heroine to escape.

After the troops got on the mountain on the other side of the town, Joseph Brown was sent back with twenty men to head and intercept the Indians at the mouth of the creek below the town, when the main body of the assailants should have driven the enemy to that point. This he effected successfully, though his return was resisted the whole way down, about a quarter of a mile, by the constant fire of the Indians. Brown and his men guarded the mouth of the creek, while the troops above were killing and capturing those between the two parties. When Brown met the main body, he inquired if they had taken any prisoners, and was immediately conducted to a house in which a number of them had been fastened up. When he came to the door he was at once recognized by the captives, who appeared to be horror-stricken, remembering, no doubt, that they had murdered his people in the same town, five years before. At length one of them ventured to speak to him, reminding Brown that his life had been spared by them, and importuning him now to plead in their behalf. He quieted her apprehensions by remarking that these were *white people*, who did not kill women and children. Her answer was, "O, that is good news for the wretched!" "O, Co-tan-co-ney!"

These land-pirates had supposed their towns to be inaccessible, and were reposing at their ease in conscious security, up to the moment when, under the guidance of Brown, the riflemen burst in upon them and dispelled the illusion.

The number of the killed was greater than that given by Haywood. Brown conversed with a chief afterwards, at Tellico Block-house, who informed him their loss on that occasion was seventy.

"Seventy warriors!"   Jack Civil was there, but neither killed, wounded, nor captured.   "The said Hood" was not there, being prostrated by fever, from which he never recovered.   He was buried near the Spring, not acting "opossum" now.

Nickojack and Running-Water towns were the principal crossing-places for the Creeks in their war excursions over the Tennessee, and in which they, with the warriors of Lookout Mountain and Will's Town, had heartily coöperated for years past, boasting of their perfect security, not less from their situation than from the number and desperate character of their warriors.

This battle was fought on the 13th of September; and on the evening of the same day the troops recrossed the river, having but three of their number wounded.

Major Ore immediately returned to Knoxville, (instead of continuing to scout in Mero District,) and made to Governor Blount the following report:

"KNOXVILLE, September 24th, 1794.

"SIR:—On the 7th instant, by order of General Robertson, of Mero District, I marched from Nashville with five hundred and fifty mounted infantry under my command, and pursued the trace of the Indians who had committed the latest murders in the District of Mero, and of the party that captured Peter Turney's negro woman, to the Tennessee.   I crossed it on the night of the twelfth, about four miles below Nickojack, and in the morning of the thirteenth destroyed Nickojack and the Running-Water, towns of the Cherokees.

"The first being entirely surrounded and attacked by surprise, the slaughter was great, but cannot be accurately reported, as many were killed in the Tennessee.   Nineteen women and children were made prisoners at this town.   The Running-Water town being four miles above Nickojack, the news of the attack upon the latter reached the former before the troops under my command, and resistance was made to save it at a place called the Narrows; but after the exchange of a few rounds, the Indians posted at that place gave way, and the town was burnt without further opposition, with all the effects therein, and the troops under my command recrossed the Tennessee the same day.

" From the best judgment that could be formed, the number of Indians killed at the two towns must have been upwards of fifty, and the loss sustained by the troops under my command was one lieutenant and two privates wounded.

"The Running-Water was counted the largest, and among the most hostile towns of the Cherokees.   Nickojack was not less hostile, but inferior in point of numbers. At Nickojack were found two fresh scalps, which had lately been taken at Cumberland, and several that were old were hanging in the houses of the warriors, as trophies of war; a quantity of ammunition, powder and lead lately arrived there from the Spanish Government, and a commission for the Breath, the head-man of the town, (who was killed,) and sundry horses and other articles of property were found, both at Nickojack and Running-Water, which were known to have belonged to different people killed by Indians in the course of the last twelve months.

"The prisoners taken—among whom was the wife and child of Richard Finnelson, my pilot—informed me that on the fourth instant, sixty Creeks and Lower Cherokees passed the Tennessee for war against the frontiers. They also informed me that two nights before the destruction of Running-Water, a scalp-dance had been held in it, over the scalps lately taken from Cumberland, at which were present John Watts, the Bloody Fellow, and other chiefs of the Lower Towns, and at which they determined to continue the war in conjunction with the Creeks with more activity than heretofore against the frontiers of the United States, and to erect block-houses at each of the Lower Towns for their defence, as advised by the Spanish Government.

"The prisoners also informed me that a scalp-dance was to be held, in two nights, at Redheaded Will's Town, a new town about thirty miles lower down the Tennessee. The troops under my command generally behaved well.

"I have the honor to be your Excellency's most obedient humble servant,

"JAMES ORE.

"GOVERNOR BLOUNT."

As this invasion of the Cherokee country and the destruction of these towns was not authorized, but in fact prohibited by the instruction from the Secretary of War to Governor Blount, the latter was placed in a dilemma from which he (to us) seems to have made some awkward attempts to extricate himself. We shall copy from Haywood, who quotes the correspondence fairly, and may then venture to give our own opinion.

This certainly was a severe, but merited, chastisement to these towns; and we have noticed in Governor Blount's letters to General Robertson, prior and subsequent to this date, that his opinion decidedly was, that "there never would be peace with the *Creeks*, until the most hostile towns were *destroyed*." What better were these Lower Cherokee Towns than dens for Creeks?

But this chastisement humbled the Cherokees. "Beneficial as was this affair to the people of the South-western Territory, the principal officers of it were obliged at least to pretend ignorance of its commencement and progress.

Major Ore, with sixty men, had been ordered by the Governor on 19th August, 1794, to range the Cumberland Mountains in search of hostile Indians, and *somehow or other* he left the mountains, and found himself at Nashville, just about the time the troops from Kentucky, and those raised in the District of Mero, were about to rendezvous.

Governor Blount, in his letter to the Secretary of War, dated 22d September, informed him of "a report in circulation, which he believed, of the destruction of these two towns;" stating that he understood it was done by order of General Robertson, to whom he, the Governor, *had given no orders for such purpose.* And on the 1st October, the Governor stated to General Robertson the report made to him by Major Ore, of the irruption across the Tennessee, which had been made by a detachment of General Robertson's brigade, sanctioned by his orders; and requested of him a copy of the order which he had given to Major Ore for that purpose.

General Robertson, before he had given the order, had been informed by the Chickasaws that two hundred Creeks might daily be expected on the frontiers of Mero. As early, however, as the 5th August, 1794, a few days only before Ore was dispatched with sixty men to the Cumberland Mountains, General Logan and Colonel Whitley, of Kentucky, had been represented to the Governor as planning an expedition against the Cherokees; they were the most popular leaders on the frontiers of Kentucky, and were publicly announced as the leaders of volunteer companies to be raised against the Indians; and it was apprehended by the Governor, "that this spirit" would diffuse itself amongst the disorderly part of the frontier people, not only into this Territory, but to the mouth of the St. Mary's. His presentiment was correct as to the people of this Territory, but the Governor forgot to give any directions to Major Ore on this subject when he gave orders a few days afterwards to raise men and scour the mountains. It seems as if everybody was tired of being scalped and robbed and cooped up in stations, and was willing to let pass, without scanning too nicely, every thing that was done or intended, to see whether it was exactly according to prescribed rule. Revenge was sweet, and they stole it; protection was valuable, and they inspired the savages with fear to insure it. The event proved that fear was effectual when persuasion was proverbially otherwise.

During the time the men were raising in the Cumberland counties, *so much caution* was used that the Governor *did not hear of it!* and only received intelligence after the lapse of time which intervened between the raising of the troops and the 9th of September, and then it was too late to interfere; he could only communicate intelligence to the Secretary of War! But the Governor, *by some means*, had received information that General Robertson gave encouragement to Colonel Whitley to raise troops, and to be on the Cumberland as early as the 9th of September; for, on that day, he wrote a "private" letter to General Robertson.* It commences:

"You can't conceive my surprise and mortification on being taught to believe that you have so far countenanced the lawless attempt of Whitley, as to give conditional sanction to musters of troops going with him. You have surely paid less respect to yourself on this occasion than on any other since my acquaintance with you.

"It is not possible that the Representatives in Congress from Kentucky can have had so little understanding as to have entertained the most distant hope that the perpetrators of such lawless, unauthorized acts, could expect the least pecuniary reward for their *trouble*—for *services* I cannot call them.

"He hoped the conditional order of muster was *not in writing*. I know not the price I would take to report such an order to the War Office. Your letter of 30th *instant* (he meant ult., or August) will be *destroyed*, that it may *never rise in judgment!* Don't suppose this too severe; it proceeds from my personal esteem and the high value which I set upon your public character. No good consequence can arise from such unauthorized expeditions; and if such must be, let them be made by the States, who have Senators and Representatives in the public councils. You cannot conceive the pain I feel on the occasion."

In another letter of the same date, he writes to General Robertson, "There appears to me to be an impropriety in the President's filling the commission of Brigadier-General of Mero District, until you make a formal resignation to him, and not a conditional one. I shall not write to the President respecting your resignation, until you send forward one more formal."

In another letter to General Robertson, under date of 1st October, the Governor says, "None of your letters heretofore written will appear, so that you have it in your power to take up the subject at large. and state your reasons. Ore's report will go to the President by Doctor White."

With much pleasure we copy the following comments by Judge Haywood:

---

* This letter marked "private," no doubt was sent by "Captain Evans, the bearer" of another of the same date.

"What are the feelings excited by this scene, in which we see an old and tried patriot, who never once failed to fly to the succor of his country in distress, so chided and reproved for an act which actually put an end to Indian incursions, and wrested from their hands the tomahawk and scalping-knife ? We shall be obliged to say, if an error was committed, it was on the side of virtue and patriotism; and reproof should be administered with a great portion of kindness and respect intermixed. Shall one be the saviour of his country, and for that be chagrined into retirement? The regrets of that country will follow his exit, and the glow of affection shall rise at the tale.

"Whoever admires the man that loved his country more than himself, at the same time that he acknowledges the correctness of that policy of government which is inflexible for disobedience of orders, will say, with the graceful sincerity of truth, that, in this instance, I wish it were otherwise."

On the 8th of October, General Robertson transmitted to the Governor a copy of his order to Major Ore, and assigned his reasons for issuing it. We will give the chief of those, at the same time remarking that they are ample for his justification, though he could easily have added a thousand more; and that the destruction of those towns was as right and justifiable as would be the destruction of a hornet's nest that might be hanging upon a branch of a tree near your door, though that tree might have its roots in a neighbor's ground.

If there is a den of wolves across that stream, and they issue forth by day and by night, and kill and carry off my sheep and pigs, shall I be permitted to follow them to the water's edge, see them rioting in blood and whetting their teeth upon the opposite bank, and some stern fiat stay me from crossing and slaying the destroyers of my flocks ? There could be no humanity in the order which forbade the people of Cumberland to pursue and slay the murderers at Nickojack and Running-Water.

General Robertson says, "I had received two expresses from the Chickasaws, one by Tom Brown, a man of unquestionable veracity, and the other by a common runner, giving information that a large body of Creeks, with the Cherokees of the Lower Towns, were embodying with a determination to invade the District of Mero. And not doubting the truth of the information, I conceived that if Major Ore should not meet the invaders, it could not be considered otherwise than defensive to strike the first blow on the Lower Towns, and thereby check them in their advance." Nor could he suppose that the pursuit of the Indians (who had recently committed murders and thefts) to the towns from which they came, and there striking them, could be considered as an offensive measure, unauthorized by the usage of nations in such cases. It surely cannot be necessary to add as a justification, the long, repeated, and almost daily sufferings of the people of Mero District, at the hands of Creeks and Cherokees of the Lower Towns. He states that the destruction of those towns was on the 13th of September, and then recounts murders and robberies committed by savages of those hostile towns, at various places on Cumberland, extending over the country from the mouth of Red River to near Sumner Court-house—places more than forty miles apart, and done on the 13th, 14th, and 16th.

The General was thus "convinced that at that very time there were three distinct parties committing ravages within the district, and must have been here before Major Ore marched." He cites other testimony in confirmation of that given by the Chickasaws, and then *plumps* this question to the Governor: "Is not the old Maw's information to yourself in the latter part of August to the same effect?"

It will be proper to quote the part of the Governor's letter of August 6th, referred to by this interrogatory of General Robertson:

" It now appears probable that a war may be brought about, through the Maw's party, between the Creeks and Cherokees; and it is my secret wish, since the Creeks will have no peace with us, that you encourage, in such ways as you judge best, both the Chickasaws and Choctaws to fall on the Creeks."

" Set the Chickasaws and Choctaws to fall on the Creeks; encourage a war in such ways as you judge best between the Creeks and Cherokees;" but *you* must neither fall on them yourselves, nor encourage or countenance others *whom they have injured* to fall on them! Push others into the fire, but keep yourselves "this side the line," at a distance!

This policy did not accord with the sentiments of humanity or views of chivalry entertained by General Robertson; therefore we regard his reference to the letter of the Governor, and the question he propounds, as having some little *sarcasm* in it, and very suitably given in answer to the harsh remarks of the Governor.

General Robertson continues his letter : " If I have erred, I shall ever regret it. To be a good citizen, obedient to the laws, is my greatest pride ; and to execute the duties of the commission with which the President has been pleased to honor me, in such manner as to meet his approbation, and that of my superiors in rank, has ever been my most favorite wish."

Previously to the march of Major Ore from Nashville, Colonel Whitley, with about a hundred men, arrived here from Kentucky, saying they had followed a party of Indians who had committed depredations on the south-western frontier of that State. That in the pursuit they had a man killed by the Indians, and several horses taken; and they were determined to pursue to the Lower Towns. They were attached to Major Ore's command, which augmented the number to five hundred and fifty men.

He should be happy, he continued, if his apprehensions of a Creek invasion were removed, but they were not, for William Colbert and other Chickasaws informed him that they yet threatened Mero District, not in large numbers, but in small parties, which are equally dangerous, as there is no possibility of guarding against a number of small parties invading the frontiers at different places at the same time. He enclosed a letter from John Watts; and, "from my experience," he said, "in Indian affairs, my hopes are that, from the scourging the Lower Cherokees have received, we shall receive less injury from them than heretofore." He also enclosed Major Doyle's letter from Fort Massac, in consequence of which he had ordered to his relief an ensign, sergeant, corporal, and five privates of mounted infantry.

The Spaniards, the Shawnees, and the Delawares, were all jealous of this American post. " This is another coil of the boa-constrictor winding his way into the valleys of the Mississippi; ere long he will crush us all within his folds. The Robertson people have enjoyed *too much quiet!* they have been there too long: the Creeks and Cherokees must cut in twain the serpent there—crush the head by blows, or put out his eyes by poisoned arrows. All we have done is little worth : he is but scotched, not killed."

They "did their worst," and it was bad indeed. For years, many and heavy blows had been aimed at the life of this American monster. They could not wound the head or touch the heart; here and there a few scales were knocked off, which only caused him to "move his slow length along."

Surely the manner of opposition to these American settlements was "provoking"—but it provoked to further advances. The Spaniards and the Indians rolled on the "wheels within the wheel," and the mighty chariot in which patriots and republicans were securely seated. They accomplished better things than they intended.

The Station of Captain John Donelson was picketed in. It was near the Spring, by the residence of Esquire Wm. Donelson, about one mile from the " Hermitage :" that of "Granny Hays" was at a spring a short distance south of the " Hermitage Church."

Mrs. Hays was an elderly woman, who "never knew fear," or how persons felt when frightened. She was the mother of Colonel Robert

Hays, a brave and active officer. When the attack was made upon her house, there was but one white man there, and he "a half idiot and half cripple." He was in the garden at a short distance from the house, when the Indians fired at and slightly wounded him : he ran to the house, screaming, "Murder! murder! I'm killed, I'm killed!" with a voice loud enough to have alarmed a neighborhood a mile in extent. He left the gate and door wide open, as he rushed in, and fell upon the floor. "You frightened fool," said Granny Hays, "you are not hurt, or you could not hallo so loud. Get up and take your gun and follow me. Be quick, before they have time to reload their guns." Tim Dunbar was thus aroused, and quickly accompanied the aged heroine to a favored position near the gate, from which they fired at some Indians in the bushes, and "wounded one," said Tim Dunbar, "for the red spots were on the leaves."

Having had their "crack at the red rascals," they closed the gate and barred it, reloaded their guns, and reserved their fire for a nearer approach of the Indians. But the enemy kept at a distance, and foolishly fired at the house-logs. This seemed to be their aim and sport, for they hit nothing else. They ventured not to force an entrance; nor did they burn the place, as stated in Haywood. They may have burned some small out-building.

There was no white person within the Donelson Station when it was burned, and so no life was lost in that conflagration. There was, however, some one near, or passing in the woods, who discovered the fire, and promptly conveyed intelligence to Captain Caffrey and the people at his station, which was at the base of "Todd's Knob," near the mouth of Stone's River. Caffrey and others, believing "Granny Hays" was in danger, hastened to afford relief. The Indians had been there, and departed. It was with difficulty she was persuaded to leave her castle, and accompany her friends to what was deemed a more secure place, at Mansker's.

September 28th. Instead of murders, we have the pleasure to record acts far more agreeable—the restoration of some of the captives who had long been in the hands of the Creeks. This exchange was effected by Mr. Seagrove, United States Agent in the Southern Department of Indians. Mrs. Caffrey and Miss Alice Thompson, who had been prisoners for more than two years, were restored. The son of Mrs. Caffrey, Mrs. Brown and son, and young Mayfield, were still detained as captives in the nation.

Miss Thompson was purchased from her captors for eight hundred pounds of deer-skins, valued at about two hundred and sixty dollars.

She married Mr. Collinsworth: A daughter is the wife of "Mark R. Cockrell," whose name has gone to the ends of the earth as the grower of fine wool. Mrs. Caffrey was treated as a slave, and with shocking cruelty, and then compelled to leave her child with the savages.

October 2d. Thomas Bledsoe, son of Colonel Anthony Bledsoe, was killed and scalped near the house of the late Colonel Isaac Bledsoe. His father, brother, uncle, and cousin, had all suffered under the Indian tomahawk and scalping-knife.

On 24th October a party of Indians fired upon John Leiper and his sentinel, near Leiper's house, on the east fork of Red River, in Tennessee county, and on the same day another party killed and scalped Evan Watkins, near Colonel Winchester's mill, in Sumner county. These two places are seventy miles distant from each other. Thus the presence of several parties of Indians within the settlements was evident.

On 25th, a party of Indians was discovered near Bledsoe's Lick ; were pursued, but escaped in the cane. They fired upon Cornet Evans the next day, near the same place, and again escaped, after hot pursuit. This, or another party, was pursued across the Cumberland River, on the 29th, above Gallatin. Although so often seen and pursued, these parties remained in and near this part of the settlements until they succeeded in supplying themselves with horses. Various small parties fired upon the settlers in different parts of the district.

It became exceedingly hazardous for persons to work in the fields, search for their cattle in the woods, or even go out to give them salt, or milk their cows. Neighbors in visiting were often fired at, and it became advisable for most of them to resort to the stations for safety. Intercourse ceased among the settlers for some time, except by patrols, or under their protection. Such a state of alarm had not existed for a long time. "The people again cried out that Congress could not know of their sufferings, and have the feelings of men, or more effectual measures would be taken for the defence and lives of persons here."

On the 5th November an awful havoc was made of the family of Col. Titsworth, on Red River, in Tennessee county. It was one of the most destructive assaults the Indians had yet made in these settlements. Parties of Indians concentrated near the residence of Colonel Titsworth, to the number of fifty, and made a sudden attack, in which they killed and scalped seven white persons, wounded a negro woman, took prisoners one white man, three children, a daughter of Colonel Titsworth, and a negro man.

Pursuit was made by the neighboring militia. The Indians discovering their approach, tomahawked the three children and scalped them, holding on, and dragging them along, until they took off the whole skins of their heads. "It is supposed they killed the white man, the daughter, and the negro fellow." "These murders were imputed to the Creeks."

So inefficient were the patrols, so small the companies of troops which had been authorized, that these parties of Indians remained within, or near the Cumberland settlements, throughout the months of October and November.

We have, for the third time, to introduce the early companion and now aged and bereaved friend of General Robertson, to notice. Although he had suffered so much by the slaughter of his three favorite sons, yet Colonel *Valentine Sevier* determined to maintain his position near the present site of Clarksville. He had opened fields and made convenient improvements, but he was not to enjoy the fruits of his toil in safety or in peace.

On the 11th of November, the Indians made an attack upon his station, killed Mr. Snyder, his wife, and one child, also one of Colonel Sevier's children, and mortally wounded and scalped another. The people in Clarksville heard the firing, and a few of them ran over to the help of Sevier, who, with his wife, was returning the fire of the Indians. In the town were many women and children. As the few men had gone to the relief of Sevier, "the bustle and consternation and crying exhibited a scene which cannot be described." Indeed, had the strong force of Indians attacked the houses in town, the slaughter might have been general and total. But they hastily fled when they discovered men coming to the relief of Sevier.

Colonel Sevier began immediately to remove. All in Clarksville made preparations to evacuate the place the next day, unless assurances of succor should be given them.

On the 12th, John Covington was killed within the limits of Kentucky, north-east of Clarksville, and others on Red River. Many proofs were furnished that these parties of Indians (Creeks, as they were believed to be) were rapidly passing around and through the settlements, and yet escaped the whites with impunity. The Governor was informed of these frequent depredations. And, as General Robertson was absent, he wrote to Colonel Winchester that he had no doubt the Creeks would *continue* to kill and steal as usual, until the United States marched an army *into their country*, and they in turn felt the horrors of war. When this wished-for period would arrive he could not say, but it was clearly his opinion, the sooner the people decided in favor of being admitted as an independent State into the Union, the better it would be for their interests.

On the 27th November the Indians killed and scalped Colonel John Montgomery, wounded Julius Saunders with four balls, and Charles Beatty through the arm, in the northern frontier of Tennessee county. On the 29th, another party, on the northern frontiers of Sumner county, killed and scalped John Lawrence, William Hains, and M. Hampton, and wounded a fourth man whose name is not reported. These Indians were believed to be Creeks and Lower Cherokees.

The excitement in the settlements became intense, and messengers were hastened to Kentucky for such force as they should see proper to send. Resolutions were passed, "no longer quietly to endure these outrages."

On 20th December, Colonel Hugh Tenin, of Sumner county, and John Brown and William Grimes, lately from North Carolina, were killed and scalped on Harpeth River, in Davidson county. These were newly arrived emigrants and heads of families.

Complaints were made in North Carolina and Georgia of long-continued insults and injuries from the Indians; of injustice done to many individuals, by depriving them of entries and purchases of lands, and restoring them to the savages, with the vain hope of conciliating their friendship. So it was in East Tennessee, where many good citizens were denounced as intruders and ordered to abandon their homes, that the Indians might peradventure find a deer in a much larger extent of forest. In reference to such cases, Judge Haywood says, "If in those quarters the long continuance of unchecked devastations by the Indians had a disheartening influence, can it be a matter of surprise that the afflicted population of Mero District should also entertain a sentiment of dissatisfaction at the cruelties which they had never provoked, and which, *like a strong current of mighty waters*, was suffered to beat upon them incessantly, by night and by day? Still they submitted with patient resignation to the arrangements of national authority, and gave to the world a signal proof that as genuine bravery as any age or country could boast of, was not incompatible with the most perfect subserviency to national councils. Every day they had to grieve for the loss of their dearest relations, the victims of savage vengeance; yet they believed that the ways of Government were wiser than their ways, and carefully followed the course which Government prescribed. From the incompetence of the late Confederation to the adjustment of national affairs, they perceived that numerous difficulties had arisen to embarrass the operations of the present Government, and that from all quarters of the earth there came something which claimed attention."

They were bayed by the Spaniards, by the Indians, by the English, teased by the French, disturbed by insurgents, besieged by public creditors, and murmured at by those who were excluded, for a time, from their lands by Indian treaties. Perceiving all this, they yielded to the necessity of circumstances, and hoped with confidence for better times.

Governor Blount having learned of another invasion of the Lower Creek Towns being in contemplation, and that General Logan was advancing from Kentucky with a considerable force, and that Major Ore had just passed through Knoxville to join Logan, addressed to each of them a letter to dissuade them from the project. In these letters he says, "I have received a letter from Double-Head, a principal chief of the Lower Towns, to which I have replied, and had them published in the newspaper of this place, from which you will understand these towns, as well as every other part of the Cherokee nation, are considered in peace with the United States!"

These letters are dated Knoxville, November 1st, 1794, and this, when numerous parties of Creeks and Cherokees were committing many and awful murders in Mero District! The Governor *still* cherished strong hopes from *conferences* and *treaties*. Having a treaty in contemplation, to be held at Tellico Block-house in this month, he was only *anticipating* by a week or more the results of such a conference and treaty : "hoping against hope," for good results by "talks."

After the destruction of Nickojack and Running-Water towns, General Robertson wrote to John Watts, the great chief of the Cherokees, and very plainly intimated that another expedition would soon become necessary if he did not surrender the captives then in the nation, and restrain his warriors from their ravages on the Cumberland. We doubt not the Cherokees had received other information in confirmation of what General Robertson had thus made known, and that the Cherokees were rightly apprehensive that such warning was in real earnest. Therefore the chiefs should attend the conference to which they had been invited.

Such a conference was held at Tellico on the 7th and 8th November, "between William Blount, Governor in and for the Territory of the United States of America, south of the Ohio River, and *Colonel* John Watts, of Will's Town, (one of the Lower Cherokee Towns,) Scolacutta, and other chiefs of the Cherokee nation, at which were present about four hundred warriors, and several citizens of the United States." The notes of this conference, extending over seven pages of foolscap paper, were furnished to General Robertson by Governor Blount, accompanied by a letter dated 12th November, in which he says, "I assure you, *upon my word and honor*, that not only in the public talks, but in a long private one with Watts, he appeared truly *sincere*."

In the conference Watts had commenced his talk or speech thus:
"This meeting appears to be ordered by the Great Spirit, and affords me
great pleasure.   Here is Scolacutta; he is old enough to be my father,
and from my infancy he was a great man, and is now the great chief of
the nation.   In the spring of the year he sent a talk to the Lower Towns,
telling them, he and the Upper Towns had taken the United States by
the hand," etc.   He admitted that the Running-Water and Nickojack
deserved the treatment they had received, and said, "I know General
Robertson to be a good man," etc.

Scolacutta : "I am the head-man of my nation, as Governor Blount is
of the white people.   It was not the fault of either that those towns were
destroyed, but their own conduct brought destruction upon them; the
trail of murderers and thieves was followed to those towns.   Nevertheless,
I cannot neglect the request they have made to me to make peace for
them."

They all dreaded the invasion by General Logan, but promised that
however much damage he and his troops might do in the nation, his
conduct should not prevent the exchange of prisoners demanded by
General Robertson.   They admitted that the ridge which divides the
waters of Mobile and Tennessee was the boundary of the Creek nation,
and that when any of that nation attacked the Cumberland settlements,
they had to, and did, pass through Cherokee and Chickasaw lands to
arrive there to kill our men at their ploughs, and women and children in
their houses !

Logan's expedition was abandoned.   Orders were given, through
Colonel Winchester, to make allowances to persons who had supplied the
Indian captives, rations equal to what had been customary to the guards
or soldiers in Mero District.

The acknowledgments made by Watts and Scolacutta fully exculpated
General Robertson from all just censure for the destruction of the two
towns on the Tennessee.   Governor Blount himself wrote down such exculpation, and we should feel greatly relieved if he had taken this opportunity
to have withdrawn the harsh language used in his letter of 9th of
September, expressive of his "surprise and mortification."

The assurances of peace were many and most earnest from the chiefs
of the Cherokees.   But the Creeks still seemed determined to provoke
the whites to come and destroy them utterly.

It is due to the steadfast friend of General Robertson, Colonel Valentine
Sevier, that we should insert a portion of his letter to his brother,
General Sevier, giving an account of the second attack upon his station,
and the new griefs to which he had been thus subjected.

"CLARKSVILLE, December 18th, 1794.

"DEAR BROTHER :—The news from this place is desperate with me. On Tuesday, 11th November last, about twelve o'clock, my station was attacked by about forty Indians. On so sudden a surprise, they were in almost every house before they were discovered. All the men belonging to the station were out, only Mr. Snyder and myself. Mr. Snyder, Betsy his wife, his son John, and my son Joseph, were killed in Snyder's house. I saved Snyder, so the Indians did not get his scalp, but shot and toma-hawked him in a barbarous manner. They also killed Ann King and her son James, and scalped my daughter Rebecca. I hope she will still recover. The Indians have killed whole families about here this fall. You may hear the cries of some persons for their friends daily. The engagement, commenced by the Indians at my house, continued about an hour, as the neighbors say. Such a scene no man ever witnessed here before."

This early soldier and adventurous pioneer, and his heroic and devoted wife, could not long survive such shocks as they had received. Mrs. Sevier had learned to use the rifle. She stood by the side of her husband, gun in hand, but relied more upon the use of an axe, when attempts should be made to enter the door.

At his first settlement on the Cumberland, Colonel Sevier took his position as an outpost, the farthest in advance of the adventurers. We know not if any of his immediate posterity are living.

The course pursued by Governor Blount, his letter of "surprise and mortification," and the disavowal and disapprobation by the Government of the expedition thus ordered by General Robertson, induced him to tender his resignation.*

---

* In April, 1798, a petition, signed by Stephen Cantrell and others, was pre-sented to the Congress of the United States by W. C. Claiborne, member of the House, asking for compensation for services in the Nickojack expedition. This petition was referred to the Secretary of War, James McHenry, who reported the facts as furnished by the letters of Governor Blount, and of the officers who ori-ginated and conducted the expedition, stating that "The destruction of the Lower Cherokee Towns *stands upon its own footing.* That it was not authorized by the President, or this department, is certain ; that the services for which compensa-tion is asked were performed on an expedition *offensive, unauthorized,* and in *direct violation* of orders to Governor Blount, by whom also they were *not sanctioned.*"

With this report decidedly adverse to the claim, it may be supposed it would most certainly be rejected, but the House regarded it favorably. The members had learned the history of that protracted and cruel war, and they duly appre-

32

Soon after making his report he visited Knoxville, and whilst there, wrote the following letter to Governor Blount:

"KNOXVILLE, October 23d, 1794.

"SIR :—Finding it incompatible with my private avocations any longer to perform the duties of Brigadier-General of the Militia of Mero District in the territory of the United States south of the river Ohio, with which appointment I have been honored by the President of the United States, I beg leave to resign that commission, at the same time assuring you that it is not through any *disgust* with the public service or officers of Government that I am induced to take this step."

But, as Judge Haywood says, he was "chagrined into retirement." It is exceedingly to be regretted that we have neither the original letter nor a copy of the letter of which Governor Blount says, " I will destroy it, that

---

ciated the character of General Robertson. They had confidence in his prudence, patriotism, and truth. That he would not have advised any measure which was not proper or necessary, was a general conviction.

Mr. Claiborne made a suitable speech in behalf of the petitioners. Said he, " The expedition was authorized by General Robertson, and it remains now for us to decide whether soldiers shall or not be entitled to pay until they have previously assured themselves of the legitimate authority of their commanding officer. At the time when this expedition was set on foot, a *war* raged between the United States and the Cherokee nation of Indians, the horrors of which bore hard upon the District of Mero—*the very existence of the settlement was threatened.* Scarcely a day passed without some one of the inhabitants being murdered. Information was received that the Indians were embodied, in order to carry the war into the settlement.

"What was the General to do? Stand still? Make no effort to avert the danger? He was not the man to do that; they were not the people to endure *for ever.* Already had they suffered and had patience beyond all former example. The safety of the people required him to act, and he struck the *first blow,* which was a *defensive* one—a defensive measure fully authorized by the usages of all nations. Citizens obeyed the command of their officer; . . . they had served under him before; . . . they did not falter now."

The opinion of Congress was that a just and wise construction of the orders justified the measures pursued by General Robertson, and that even the term "*defensive,*" upon which such reliance had been placed, required the very course which was pursued. The resolution was agreed to *without opposition,* and a bill reported and passed accordingly.

We notice that in proceedings in Congress, Benton's Abridged Debates, the name of the commanding Major is spelled Orr, and not *Ore,* as it is uniformly by General Robertson and Governor Blount.

it may never rise in judgment;" for, as that letter was dated August 30th, we believe it made known fully to the Governor the plans then on foot to destroy the two hostile towns.   The conduct of General Robertson was open and avowed ; he had no cause to be ashamed of any act, or to fear that any thing he had said, written, or done, "would rise up in judgment against him."   There was but one sentiment among the people of Cumberland—that judgment was all in his favor.   Long ere this the cry of this people had been for vengeance.• But *out of respect* to the President, and the intricacy of negotiations and embarrassments in which the Administration was involved, General Robertson had besought the people yet longer to forbear, and yield to the rigid construction of the "restrictive orders."   Such patience and forbearance were no longer virtues. The demands of humanity and proper self-defence were for the destruction of those dens of murderers.

Had the Bledsoes, the Shelbys, Hays, Winchester, and other noble spirits not been suddenly and cruelly extinguished, they would have cheered and sustained the resolution of General Robertson; they would have been active counsellors, aiders and abettors in every step for this invasion.

It was not long before this event that good news, as from "a far country," reached these settlements.   Some of the Chickasaws had joined General Wayne's army in the territory north of the Ohio, and on their return home added to official reports of his great victory over the Indians and Canadian militia, on the 20th August.   "Wayne's victory" was gained on the banks of the Miami, in the vicinity of a strong British fort.

That battle, the destruction of Nickojack and its neighboring town, together with the manifestation of preparations to repeat these blows, humbled and broke the spirits of the Indians; and the pernicious influence of English agents being counteracted or ceasing, the Indians asked for peace.   Hitherto our Government had invited and urged the chiefs to attend conferences, and enter into treaties.   From these solicitations the savages inferred our weakness, or our dread of their power. But now the peace-talks, the belts of wampum, and the pipe of peace, are presented by the other party.

Watts admitted to Governor Blount that some of his people had been in the battle, and fought against General Wayne, and he knew how complete was that victory.   The Creeks, however, were less inclined to peace than any tribe north or south.

The "Mountain Leader," always the steadfast friend of the United States, of the Cumberland settlers, and of General Robertson, had long been hunted by the Creeks and Cherokees, and they finally (in this year) "wreaked their vengeance upon him. His death was much lamented by the people of Cumberland. It is believed that the Cherokees from some of the Lower Towns were the successful party in the hunt for this chief." (Such was the rumor of the day!)

The negotiations with Spain were greatly embarrassed by the officious intermeddling of the French in various parts of our country, as well as in Europe. Organizations of troops were again reported as taking place in Kentucky, and that citizens in Mero District were disposed to join in the movements. The Spaniards apprehended a warlike invasion of their territory, and were in great trepidation. Their guilty consciences made them tremble.

Governor Blount addressed Governor Shelby, of Kentucky, and General Robertson, urging them to discountenance all such organizations. But as the Governor's letter to General Robertson properly belongs to the next year, we shall here notice it no further.

In the last month of this year the Governor held another conference with chiefs and warriors of the Cherokees, at Tellico, to effect an exchange of prisoners, and adjustment of terms for peace. But as that conference was extended into the year 1795, we also postpone further notice of it in this chapter.

We shall insert the memorial to Congress of which we have spoken, and call attention to the two paragraphs preceding the last, as happily expressing the matured opinions of men who had been familiar with Indian character and feelings.

Treaty annuities, liberal gratuities, and concessions, only awakened in their minds an idea of their consequence. By many of the acts of the State and national Governments in the last century, (and in this,) the Indians were induced to believe that the whites were afraid of them.

The patience with which the Cumberland stationers endured their robberies and murders, had the effect of disseminating among the savages the belief that the Americans were too feeble or too cowardly to expose themselves much beyond their palisaded log-stations.

"Fear, not love, is the only sentiment by which Indians can be governed." General Sevier was incessant in publishing this sentiment, and, as far as he could, he enforced it upon the savages, and with good results. General Robertson was of the same opinion, but his position was so remote, so isolated, and his numbers and supplies so limited and inadequate, that he could seldom invade and strike terror where it was needed and would crush them.

THE MEMORIAL OF THE LEGISLATIVE COUNCIL AND HOUSE OF RE-
PRESENTATIVES, TO THE CONGRESS OF THE UNITED STATES OF
AMERICA.

TERRITORY OF THE U. S., SOUTH OF THE OHIO RIVER.

It appearing from the proceedings of your late session, upon the memorial of the representatives of this Territory, that both the Senate and
House of Representatives agreed in the propriety and necessity of extending effectual protection to the exposed frontiers of this country, though
they differed in the mode; we are induced to hope the subject will again
be taken up at an early day of the approaching session, and that unanimity, as to the mode, will take place.

We have now to inform you that since the date of that memorial, (Feb.
26,) the Creeks and Cherokees have not ceased to kill the citizens of the
United States, resident in this Territory, nor to pillage the country; but
have continued to do both, as usual, with an unremitting hand. In proof
of which we refer to the annexed list of murders and thefts committed
since that period.

We are truly sensible that the motives of Government in forming
treaties with those Indians, and in giving them large presents and annuities, have been—not the love of the Indians—but with the hope that
such proofs of friendship would produce a return of it on their part
towards the citizens of the United States, and thereby a real peace and
good understanding would be established between the parties.

But, alas! we by dreadful experience know it has had a contrary
effect.

Instead of viewing such conduct on the part of the United States as
an evidence of friendship towards them, they have considered it as an evidence of fear, or as a tribute paid to their superior prowess in war; and
thus viewing it, it has served to encourage them to kill additional numbers of your exposed fellow-citizens.

Fear, not love, is the only means by which Indians can be governed;
and until they are made to feel the horrors of war, they will not know
the value of peace, nor observe the treaties they may form with the
United States.

In discharge of the duty we owe our constituents and ourselves, we
have made to you this memorial; confiding that you, in discharge of that
which you owe to yours and yourselves, will take measures to punish
those two faithless and bloodthirsty nations, the Creeks and Cherokees,
according to the usage and custom of nations; and to secure the persons

and property of the citizens of the United States, resident in this Territory.

GRIFFITH RUTHERFORD, P. L. C.
DAVID WILSON, S. H. R.

A LIST OF THE NAMES OF PERSONS KILLED, WOUNDED, AND CAP-
TURED SINCE THE 26TH FEBRUARY, 1794.

March 9.—Sam Martin, killed on a path leading from Henry's Station to his father's house. James Ferguson also killed.

March 12.—Four men killed on Kentucky road, and one wounded. Four killed in Tennessee county—day not known.

March 16.—John Wood wounded with four balls; (leg amputated.)

March 21.—The two young Anthony Bledsoes killed and scalped. Secretary Smith's negro captured by same party.

In March, Double-Head, a Cherokee chief, killed the family of Mr. Wilson, on Rolling Fork : believed to have been eight in number—holds one boy a prisoner now. Many others killed on southern frontiers of Kentucky.

April 1.—T. S. Spencer killed by Double-Head. James Walker wounded.

April 2.—W. Green, a soldier, killed at Fort Grainger, mouth of Holston. James R. Robertson and John Grimes, killed on Cumberland.

April 8.—Four killed ; one negro woman captured.

April 21.—Casteel, his wife and four children, killed, seven miles from Knoxville ; another child dangerously wounded. James McCown killed at house of *Widow* Hays, ten miles from Nashville. Mrs. Hays' husband had been killed a few months previous.

May 26.—One of the spies on duty was wounded on Bledsoe's Creek on same day, on Station Camp Creek, in midst of a thick settlement. A party of Indians fired on Mr. Strawder and his son, at work, within one hundred yards of his house; killed and scalped the son; pursued the father to the house, and wounded his wife as she opened the door to let him in.

June 11.—The wife of Mr. Gear was scalped by Indians within four miles of Nashville, on her way to church. Hugh Webb and Jos. McAdams : the first killed; second wounded with four balls. Robert McRory killed in pursuit of Indians who had killed Mrs. Gear. William Scott, John and James Pettigrew, Mr. Tate and Mr. Young, and another man, and three women and three children killed on Tennessee, on board boat going to Natchez; twenty-two negroes taken prisoners.

July 3.—Isaac Mayfield killed, four miles from Nashville.

July 9.—Major Winchester killed and scalped in Sumner.

August.—Killed near Crab Orchard, on the road, P. Cunningham, Dan. Hitchcock, Wm. Flanagan, and Stephen Renfroe; and wounded Abraham Bird.

Aug. 20.—Allen Nolan killed, four miles from Nashville, on his father's plantation. His father had been killed on same place six years before.

Aug. 24.—Robert Brigance killed on road in Sumner county.

G. Simson killed, six miles from Nashville, in early part of July, on his father's farm, where his father had also been killed.

Sept. 6.—Negro woman, property of Peter Turner, captured near Bledsoe's Lick.

Killed, 67; wounded, 10; captured, 25.

Horses stolen, 374, at $50, = $18,700.

We are reminded by Mr. John Carr, that the favorite fiddler, James Gamble, made a narrow escape in the summer of this year. He knows that Gamble was severely wounded, and with great difficulty made his escape from the Indians, who were on each side of the path on which he was riding.

Had he lost his fiddle, he would have died of a broken heart—a broken fiddle.

Great as the influences of his strains were known to be over the civilized race, he stayed not to test the declaration of Congreve's Mourning Bride,

"Music hath charms to soothe the *savage* breast,"

but made all possible speed, and reached Morgan's Station, where his wound was dressed.

With perfect cheerfulness he lay on his back for some weeks, "all the time a fiddling," trying to make his instrument imitate the surprise, the firing, the screaming, the race, the escape, his bandaged condition, and his hopes for the future. That fiddle was instrumental of much good in its day.

CHAPTER XXX.

1795.

AFTER the conference at Tellico had closed, the Governor, by request of the Executive Council, and urgent solicitation of General Robertson, and others of Mero District, addressed the Secretary of War, and presented such a statement and argument as ultimately "opened the eyes of the blind, by removing the films of prejudice, or the colored glasses from his nose."

General Robertson, as we have shown, desired General Sevier should invade the Creek and Cherokee nations. Governor Blount now recommends an expedition into the Creek country, suggesting the plan and time of invasion. He asserts that the Upper Creeks had killed and robbed the citizens of the United States from the day of the Declaration of Independence to the date of his letter, and this without cause or provocation, and regardless of the treaty of New York, or other pledges. They had done this almost with impunity. Very seldom have the citizens done any act but in self-defence, or in punishment of those who had killed their wives and children, or were fleeing with scalps or stolen horses in their possession. They believe and boast that they are superior to the citizens of the United States in war. Until the Creeks are made to feel the horrors of war, and learn the value of peace and realize their inferiority, there can be no reason to hope they will pursue a more peaceful conduct.

One certain effect of the Upper Creeks having been permitted to kill and rob with impunity, may be seen in the fact that more or less of the Cherokees, (generally of the Lower Towns,) and of the Lower Creeks too, have attached themselves to the Upper Creek warriors, and aided them in the murders and thefts. The danger is that even the Chickasaws and Choctaws, seeing the others enriching themselves with plunder so easily acquired, and also gaining the reputation of warriors, will be induced to follow their example. If this should be the case: the advanced settlements on the Cumberland must be annihilated, unless Government shall come to their aid and defence. A chastisement of the warlike Creeks and Cherokees will tend greatly to confirm the friendship which the Chickasaws and Choctows now profess. He and others had thoroughly studied the Indian character.

The Government was very far from according with these sentiments. At least the new Secretary, Mr. Pickering, who presented the views of the Administration, made them known in such terms as to produce a most unhappy feeling among the settlers on Cumberland, as also in Hamilton and Washington Districts on the other side of the mountains.

The Secretary informed the Governor that all ideas of offensive operations must be laid aside. And, as Judge Haywood says, "to make this purpose the more striking and impressive, money was sent to Colonel King in the spring of this year, to pay the militia; and a very offensive exception was made, so as to exclude General Sevier's brigade, which in 1793 pursued the Creeks and Cherokees who had killed the Cavitt family, and the officers and men who had served in the Nickojack expedition, from all pay whatsoever. The Secretary, in truth, represented the Government as believing that the white settlers on the frontier were the aggressors; and that the Indians stood more in need of protection against them than they against the Indians."

It was saying to the whites, "The Indians do right and are justifiable in committing murders and robberies among you, for you intrude upon their hunting-grounds and steal their wild lands and wild game." That is the substance of Pickering's reasoning. And if he could aggravate the matter, it would be by making known to the savages themselves that the Government looked upon these murders and outcries in this light.

Now, says Haywood, "the people must give up their heads to the scalping-knife, and die with resignation, in hopes of better times. The worried patience of the people began to spurn the inanimate recommendations of the Government, and to question its title to the character of wisdom."

At Knoxville the Grand Jury "presented, as a grievance, that the executive officers of the General Government withheld the pay of the militia who served under Sevier, 'in the case mentioned;' that this Territory had not received protection, or sympathy, or hearing, as in other States and portions of the country, where they have Representatives in Congress."

There was some pretty "sharp shooting" between the Governor and Secretary of War.

"After enumerating many improprieties in the conduct of the Governor and of General Robertson, and saying that no assistance should be given *to the Chickasaws,* the Secretary says: "Upon the whole, sir, I cannot refrain from saying, that the complexion of some of the transactions in the South-western Territories appears unfavorable to the public interests. It is plain that the United States are determined, if possible, to avoid a direct or indirect war with the Creeks."

(There, Spanish influence was more extensive and longer established and more certainly known to our Government, than it was as affecting the Cumberland settlements. The secrets were, however, coming to light as to the covert and wicked devices against these settlers.)

General Robertson received a copy, *one copy,* of this insulting letter, and was industrious to let it be read in the hearing of the people at and near the various stations. The exclamation was, "We have asked for bread, and they have given us a serpent. We have prayed for a blessing, and have received cursing. Our miserable condition is now made more hopeless. We have insult added to unendurable injuries." A slight mildew was gathering on the name of Washington, who had ever been first in the hearts of all early stationers and leading men here. Who can tell how the heart of Robertson was grieved? Who will fail to understand why Andrew Jackson, in the House of Representatives of the United States, voted "*No*" with the very small number, (12 to 67,) upon the resolution of confidence and thanks to the Administration? Who, of all these settlers, "with the lights before them," remembering all the sufferings endured now for so many years, and the very insignificant aid ever rendered, and now the words of insult, could have voted hearty and unreserved approbation of the entire Administration?

But this discussion need not be prosecuted here. It is more in accordance with our work to copy from documents, and present the current acts of the people most interested; closing with this remark, that the members who voted in the *negative* upon the occasion referred to, were from North Carolina, Kentucky, and Virginia, with Lyman of Massachusetts and Livingston of New York; the two last dissenting from an endorsement of the conduct of the Administration in foreign relations, (with the French Republic;) and the others on account of "domestic affairs"—western frontier affairs, with the Indians and Mississippi navigation.

The conference with the Cherokees was renewed at Tellico, 28th December, 1794. The main purpose was to effect exchange of captives. This was accomplished to some extent, and the professions of a desire for peace were many and seemed to be sincere on the part of the Indians. There were some things said and proposed at this conference that are so novel and curious that we shall note them here.

The Governor referred to the last meeting, 7th and 8th November, and the assurances of friendship and peace then given, upon which, he said, he had confidently relied; but that since that time, only sixty days, thirty persons have been killed and wounded in Mero, and one on the borders of Knox county. "The President, our great father, sends word, through the Secretary of War, to your nation, that you must not permit the Creeks to pass through your country. Your Lower Towns are so near that powerful nation, that I fear you cannot stop them in their passage to Cumberland. But I am going *to propose a thing* to you that you can do, that is, to permit a party of your young warriors to go with some white men to the frontiers of Cumberland for the protection thereof. The number I would suggest is sixty, and the term of service three months, for which they shall be paid by the United States."

Scolacutta, in his talk, said the Cherokees were greatly exposed to the enmity of the Creeks; and as the Cherokees and Chickasaws were now becoming good friends, he besought the Governor to "say something to the Chickasaws, who are the greatest friends of the United States. Tell them to join us to assist the white people against the Creeks. I hope the Chickasaws will come to Cumberland and live in the houses with our white brothers!"

"Good talks come from Philadelphia, (the President,) and from Congress. They speak of 'peace with all nations,' and these good talks are sent also to the Creeks, but they will not listen. For many years they have been killing the people of this country. Is it true that this country (Cumberland, etc.) is not under the protection of the United States? Or is it, that the President is uninformed of the many murders and thefts committed by the Creeks?"

These surely were "pointed interrogations." This wily Indian needed not to have heard similar questions asked by the settlers on Cumberland in order to propound them on this occasion. He and others had presumed a negative answer, and had long acted under the impunity of such a presumption. The Governor felt it his duty to reply to such questions, and said: "In answer to the question of Scolacutta, whether the people of Cumberland are under the protection of the United States, I say, all citizens of the United States (of which Cumberland is a part) are under the protection of the Government, and full information has been given to the President of their sufferings."

Scolacutta took no notice of the Governor's hint to permit the young warriors to unite in the defence of Cumberland, but made a proposition which looks very much like a set-off. He said, "I will now tell you, I have heard of your killing one of my people and sending the scalp to

General Robertson ; *if you will kill a Creek for it,* it shall not spoil our good talks !" General Robertson used to quote this as a good joke.

We do not see in the minutes, (which cover over twenty pages of fools-cap paper,) that the Governor "opened his mouth" in reply. In all probability he deemed the caution of Esquaka, in his opening speech, as very suitable for himself in this instance. That wily old chief had thus spoken : "I am happy to hear your talks ; but it is improper to speak *before one thinks;* therefore, I will not speak *now.*" The Governor seems to have taken a similar course. He learned something *ab hoste.*

But here is our old friend Piomingo, the Mountain Leader of the Chick-asaws, *redivivus!* The report and belief of the last fall was that he had been killed by the Creeks, and that his young warriors, in seeking for retaliation, had killed a Cherokee instead of a Creek, which act the Chero-kees proposed to let pass unavenged, if the Chickasaws would unite with them in the war against the Creeks. The life of Piomingo had been threatened by the Shawnees and Creeks. He had been "hunted as a partridge on the mountains," and his absence had given currency to the report that he had been killed.

He and the notorious Colbert were fast friends of the United States : they hated the Spaniards. They had received pay and distinction from our Government; they dressed in full uniform, with epaulettes, hat and plume, and dangling sword. These chiefs visited General Robertson, each with some sixty warriors, to receive instructions from him, or from Governor Blount, as to the route to join General Wayne's army. They marched to Fort Washington, were received into service, and did some execution upon the northern Indians. Yet before the battle of 20th August, 1794, they received information of a contemplated invasion of their nation by Creeks and Shawnees, and some of the warriors hastened home.

On 28th March, " the inhabitants of Clarksville" signed and forwarded an address and petition to General Robertson, setting forth the dangers to which they were exposed ; reciting and commending the faithful services of Peter Christian as a spy, and asking that he may be continued as such, and be entitled to full pay, etc.

This is signed by nine persons, "the inhabitants of Clarksville : James Adams, William Montgomery, Philip Lilbert, A. Bird, Robert Dunning, Hugh McCallam, John Brownlee, Bn. Hawkins, Andrew Snoddey."

In a "private" letter from Governor Blount to General Robertson, under date May 4th, among other matters he says, "You have long wished to resign your Brigadier's commission. This would be a good time, (the meeting of the General Assembly.) In your resignation you might follow the example of the Secretary of War and Treasury, that is, fix a day on which you would cease to exercise the duties of that appointment, say a month, so as to give time to instruct the oldest Colonel."

We take the following paragraph from another letter of Governor Blount to General Robertson, dated May 4th :

" Whatever may have been the motives of the people of Mero District for going with Major Colbert, the Chickasaw Chief, to his nation, with a determination to aid him in the defence thereof against an expected attack of the Creeks, it is certain, judging from the general tenor of the letter of the Secretary of the 23d March, *that their conduct in so doing* will meet the disappointment of the President.

" It will be your duty, sir, to use your authority, in you vested, to prevent the repetition of such acts.

" I know, sir, the difficulty with which you labor, instructed on one hand to use all possible economy in the administration of your office as Temporary Agent to the Chickasaws and Choctaws, and on the other frequently visited by parties of those two friendly nations expecting and soliciting from you a variety of presents, which must be procured only at a high price.

" The Cherokees on this day are to meet in council at Estanaula, at which sundry Creek chiefs are expected to attend."

By a letter from General Robertson to Governor Blount of 13th May, he gave notice that he did not intend to act as Brigadier-General after the 15th of August : " I shall inform the Secretary of War accordingly."

Judge Haywood has used some very expressive terms to describe the nature of the treatment which General Robertson received on account of the Nickojack expedition, teased, pestered, snarled at; and in his last reference to it, and the resignation of the General, he says : "Although it actually put an end to the war of the Cherokees, yet was he *snarled* at by the Secretary of War, Pickering."

In August of this year General Robertson received a peace-talk from Alexander Cornel, Deputy Agent of Indian Affairs in Tuckabatches, (a tribe of Creeks,) to the Chickasaws, in which "he wished the General to send to the Chickasaws for all the Creeks they held as prisoners, and forward them to the Creeks in exchange," and expressing earnest desire for peace on the part of the Creeks whom he represented.

He says, " The Spaniards take every opportunity to exasperate the Indians against your settlement."

These chiefs, " in commission and uniform," were often troublesome and exacting. Colbert had been made a "General," and wished to travel in style with a body-guard, at the expense of the United States. In

August he visited General Robertson, and desired to be furnished with
means to proceed to Philadelphia to pay his respects to the President.
At the solicitation of Governor Blount, General Robertson was required to
put to the test all his skill and ingenuity to divert "the General" from
proceeding farther. "Turn him back from Nashville, if you can. His
brother Major Colbert's visit to me was very unacceptable; he has
persisted in going to see the Secretary of War, to whom I presume his
visit will be not more acceptable than it was to me. He complains that
his wife and family have not been well supplied with provisions, and re-
quests that they may be well supplied in his absence to Philadelphia."
He directs General Robertson to attend to "the lady (squaw) and her
family," whose name is "*Jacsie Moniac*."

"The Chickasaw, Red Shoes, is dissatisfied that he has not received as
large presents as Colbert and other Chickasaws, particularly that he did
not receive a *saddle*, bridle, and saddle-bags! Give them to him, or
other goods of equal value."

This affords us an "inkling" of the troublesome character of the
friendly Indians, and of how much General Robertson and others had to
endure from them to keep them in good humor.

But more than this, although General Robertson had ceased to act as
Brigadier-General, he still retained his office of Temporary Agent to the
Chickasaws and Choctaws. The Governor had desired General Robertson to go himself to the Chickasaws and communicate to them the sincere
wishes of the Creeks for peace, and an exchange of prisoners; also to use
all "the great power and influence of his name and presence" in the furtherance of the true interests of the Indians, and the citizens of the Territory! He advised the General to "call on Colonel Winchester, Commandant of the Militia of the District of Mero," for an escort of a sergeant
and twelve mounted militia, which he did by his requisition, dated
August 20th, 1795. He set out on this mission, as in all other instances,
without hesitation or delay.

The shocking massacre of the family of Colonel Titsworth has been
related. It was the opinion of the white people that Miss Titsworth had
been killed by her captors, and we have preferred to give the impression
then prevailing among the settlers, as it exhibits the state of alarm and
condition of society, and is the more correct narration and history than if
we had anticipated the fact that her life was spared, that she was retained as a servant, and finally was restored to her bereaved father.

Colonel Isaac Titsworth, it seems, was not at home when the attack was
made upon his house, and that of his brother, which stood at a few rods'
distance.

In the summer of this year, learning that the Creeks were desirous of peace, and to exchange prisoners, and that his daughter was probably alive, Colonel Titsworth, having received letters from General Robertson and Governor Blount, and a passport from Mr. Seagrove, went directly to the Tuckabatches. He was there hospitably entertained by Cornel, during the period necessary to make inquiries. He ultimately recovered his daughter and the negro woman.

On his return in August he gave answers to many interrogatories propounded to him by Governor Blount, full copies of which were furnished General Robertson. Some of these questions and replies are interesting, and we give them:

" Did they carry your daughter and negro immediately to the nation?"

" No: they kept them in the woods at their camp upon the Tennessee, near the mouth, many months, and carried her into the nation about the first of June. The same party of Creeks fired upon white people and Chickasaws as they passed the Cumberland River last spring, and had one of their party killed.

" They delivered my daughter and servant readily, and without price."

" Did you discover who it was that attacked and killed Colonel Sevier's family, near Clarksville, and attacked the camp of Colonel Montgomery?"

" I did. They were Creeks, who live at a town called Tuskega, (the old Alabama Fort.) They have yet in their possession the scalps and property of Sevier's family, and Montgomery's gun. The same Creeks killed Thomas Reason and wife, and Betsy Roberts, at her father's house in the Cow-pen; and they also burnt my house four years past.

" The same party killed an old man and a young man, whom they decoyed by speaking the Chickasaw language. They said the young man was very handsome. They also killed Major Evan Shelby, and his negro, and have his gun, shot-bag, and scalp.

" They have many horses; and the Creeks, from the number they have stolen from Mero District, call the Cumberland settlement, " The Horse Stamp," and inquired if any horses were yet left there!

" The chiefs and warriors are sincerely for peace; but there are a few called 'bad young men,' who yet threaten depredations upon the Cumberland settlement; and therefore they advise that guards be still kept upon the frontiers."

" Did you see the Spanish agent, resident in the Creek nation?"

" I saw and conversed with him frequently, and stayed at his house two days. I was informed by himself and others, that he had offered the captors of my daughter four hundred dollars for her. I asked him why he would pay such a price; he answered that ' he wanted to send her to

New Orleans to school, and that the King was to pay all the expenses. Such sums (said he) are nothing to the King of Spain.' "

" How was your daughter treated by the Creeks ?"

"At the camp in the woods, she and the negro cut wood, made fires, brought water, etc.; and upon her arrival in the nation, she pounded corn and made meal, and was whipped, and in other respects treated as a slave.

" The Creeks were assembled in large force—say to the number of five thousand warriors—with promises of five hundred to eleven hundred from the Choctaw nation, to invade the Chickasaw nation. . . . . But through letters from the Spanish officers, Mr. Seagrove, the Choctaw nation, and the Chickasaw nation itself, and with my own assurances of the wish of your Excellency, and of the President of the United States, that they should not proceed, they abandoned their purpose."

Colonel Titsworth takes this occasion to do justice to the conduct of Mr. Seagrove : that in his distant post he had been " so misinformed or uninformed as to the sufferings of the Cumberland people; that now, having more reliable and ample information, he could not and would not justify or extenuate the cruelties, but use all his exertions to stay the Creeks from further depredations upon its citizens."

He adds in a note : " The Creek that was killed at the attack upon Joy's boat last spring, had in his hand Major Shelby's gun, and his shot-bag round his neck."

The Spaniards, under orders from Governor Gayoso, had taken possession of the Chickasaw bluff, and posted some three hundred men there. General Robertson, in his mission to the Chickasaws, informed them that the United States Government would not permit it to stand, but would destroy it. He authorized the Chickasaws to assure the Cherokees and Creeks that the reports which the Spaniards had put in circulation that the Americans intended to seize those bluffs, establish a fort there, and drive the Cherokees from their lands, " were not true," and only " put in circulation to make their own act in taking possession the less offensive to the red people."

The mission of General Robertson was productive of very happy results. As we have mentioned, " Major Colbert" and a few other Chickasaws proceeded to Philadelphia. General Washington delivered to them a " talk" on the 22d day of August, 1795, a copy of which was forwarded to General Robertson, having the veritable autograph of G. Washington thereto.—Vol. i. General Robertson's Correspondence.

We quote one or two paragraphs from this talk :

" MY CHILDREN : I sincerely regret the difficulties in which you are involved by the mistaken opinions which have been entertained of the intentions and obligations of the United States towards their friends the Chickasaws. It was never the design of the United States to interfere in the disputes of the Indian nations among one another, unless as friends to both parties, to reconcile them. In this way I shall do every thing in my power to serve the Chickasaw nation. The Commissioners at the conference at Nashville had no authority to promise any other interference. General Robertson did wrong in telling your nation, last year, that he expected the United States would send an army against the Creeks this summer. Your strong expectation of seeing such an army, and probably other encouragements of support, may have led you to strike the Creeks, which now occasions so much distress. It seems, also, that the commissions which were given to a number of the Chickasaw chiefs were not truly interpreted. They were expressly confined to operations against the Indians north-west of the Ohio. . . .

"The act of the Spaniards in taking possession of the Chickasaw bluff is an unwarrantable aggression, as well against the United States as the Chickasaws, to whom the land there belongs. I shall send talks, and do what else shall appear to me proper, to induce the Spanish king, or his governor, to remove their people from that station, and to make no more encroachments on your lands."

This fort was erected by order of Governor Gayoso, of Natchez, and he took formal possession of it about the 1st of July. It was within the acknowledged boundaries of the United States, and not only a gross usurpation, but daring insult to the United States.

President Washington directed notice to be given to Gayoso to abandon and destroy the fort and buildings erected at the bluff; but as he knew the negotiations with Spain were in progressive and favorable condition, he adopted no immediate and harsh measures to drive off or punish the intruders. The western people, however, complained bitterly—held public meetings, passed resolutions, and were fully intent upon aggressive movements against the Spaniards. This Spanish governor had manifested his jealousy of the western settlements in many instances, and even in this year, 25th March, had written very inflammatory letters to Creeks, Cherokees, Choctaws, and Chickasaws, accusing the Americans of trespasses upon Indian lands, and of a design to possess the whole country. "Then," said he, in his letter to the 'Mad Dog' of Tuckabatche, "what will become of the red men, should they be deprived of their hunting-grounds? The French, who are your enemies, as they are also the enemies of the Spaniards and the English, are to settle on the lands of the Creeks on the Alabama and the Tallapoosa, and instead of a union of all the four Indian tribes against them and your other enemies, (meaning the western

33

people,) you fall out—you go to war against the Chickasaws. Open your eyes to the ruin and destruction which threaten the red people. . . . . Make peace with the Chickasaws. Be you, the Chickasaws and Choctaws, united ; and should you be attacked, your faithful friends and allies, *the Spaniards*, will support you, and give you as many arms and as much ammunition as you may want!" His other talks were of like temper, and as artful and wicked as could be devised. They furnished now undeniable evidence of Spanish complicity in the outrages for so many years committed upon the people of Cumberland. This exposure was made at a moment when the shame and resulting influence of it would be the greatest : when it would most contribute to break and overthrow, and ere long to show up, with ineffaceable ignominy, the career of deception and enmity of the Spaniards in America.

But a month later, and at about the same time that General Robertson and Governor Blount were reading and criticising these incendiary and wheedling letters, the Spanish Governor probably received distinct intimation from his sovereign in Madrid, that all the Indian nations with whom the Spanish Government had any influence, should cease from wars among themselves, and maintain peace and friendship with the United States. This change was brought about by the negotiations between the United States and Spain, which soon thereafter terminated in the settlement of the vexatious questions of navigation of the Mississippi, boundaries, etc.

Governor Gayoso, in a letter to Piomingo, (and which this Mountain Leader promptly forwarded to General Robertson,) endeavored to explain and give satisfactory reasons for seizing the bluff and establishing a fort there. He wished to wheedle the old chief.

In September the Spanish emissaries and partisans, who had kept alive the evil spirit in "the bad men of the nations," began to learn that "other and better counsels prevailed, and the ways of peace were to be pursued."

The ferment, however, was great in Kentucky, and perhaps no less on the Cumberland, due allowance being made for the physiological fact, that but one epidemic of decided character can prevail at the same instant among the same people, and that here on the Cumberland were old chronic cases of Indian wars, murders and robberies, by hundreds and by thousands, committed by enemies on their immediate borders, although there was much of Spanish *virus* in all these. In Kentucky, however, numerous and large meetings were held throughout the State; and in May there met at Lexington representatives from different parts of the State, who "took into consideration the deserted and degraded state of

the country, resulting chiefly from Spanish and British aggressions,"
(they omitted all notice of or reference to the insults and violation of our
national honor and rights by recent measures of French emissaries *in
their very midst,*) and they "insisted that Spain should be compelled immediately to acknowledge our right to navigate the Mississippi; that it
is the common cause of the western people, and that they would unite
with them in *any* measure most expedient for the attainment of that
object."

The messenger or representative of the United States Government,
Mr. Innis, who had been directed to be present, addressed the convention
or assembly of delegates, happily explaining the policy of the President,
and his steady pursuit of the object they desired, and giving assurances
of his confident belief that all would be secured, and this more certainly
and early if the western people refrained from all acts of aggression and
insult, by language or otherwise.

Mr. Jay was instructed to urge forward the negotiations, and, in decided terms and uniformly, to insist upon the free navigation of the great
river.

In the early stages of the negotiation, France favored the pretensions,
and selfish, exclusive claims of Spain; but, being advised that if we
enjoyed fully that navigation her own commercial interests would be
benefited, her eyes were opened, kinder sentiments were in her heart, and
friendly words were spoken to her cousin of Spain.   But other words were
also uttered, and the wild riot of the French Revolution alienated for a time
these neighbors.   Interruptions to the negotiation took place, and delays
were unavoidable.   Suddenly Spain and England joined hands, and
united in the confederation or "Holy League" (!) of despots against the
popular revolution in France.

After most vexatious excuses and delays, the questions were settled by
a treaty, signed 27th day of October, 1795.

Day dawned upon the western settlements; light gilded the mountain
heights; joy gladdened all the valley; the western streams sparkled in
gladness.   Peace, peace, was confidently expected, and the tide of prosperity was fully in view.   A population which should be unsurpassed for
industry and progress set strongly and irresistibly towards the Pacific.

"All ranks of people in the western country plainly perceived that
the patience of the United States, when these western people were enduring such sufferings, was the dictate of a wise and good policy, and not of
indifference or insensibility."

The mischievous Spanish influence being diverted from the Cumberland settlements, large parties of emigrants arrived, especially in the fall

of the year, and farms were being opened in all directions from Nashville. But as the year has its record of a few Indian outrages in its earliest months, we here give them, and then conclude with the troubles in which our allies, the Chickasaws, were involved.

On 5th January, 1795, Elijah Walker, one of the mounted infantry on duty for the defence of Mero District, while acting as a spy on the frontiers, about twelve miles south of Nashville, was killed by the Indians.

On 5th March a party of Indians, supposed to be Creeks, at Joslin's Station, seven miles from Nashville, fired upon Thomas Fletcher, E. Baldwin, and his little brother, who were at work in their field. The first two were wounded with balls; the third was knocked down with a war-club, skull broken, and scalp taken; the two wounded men escaped.

On 14th a man was killed by Indians, within five miles of Nashville, and a number of horses taken.

April 6th, John Wiro, a soldier on duty at the ford of Cumberland, was killed.

About 13th May four men were wounded as they passed down the Cumberland in a boat.

About the 20th the Indians attacked Captain Logan, who, with two soldiers, was escorting a family; they killed one of the soldiers and a little girl, and carried off one woman, whom they killed.

On 5th June old Mr. Peyton was killed, near Bledsoe's Lick, and a negro man of Mr. Parker's dangerously wounded.

This is the last of the fearful record of murders by the Indians.

"The Horse Stamp" at this time had indeed but few horses "left:" they were in great demand, brought high prices, notwithstanding the risk of their being stolen. A right to a "two-forty" would sometimes be traded for a horse. and thus the new emigrants often procured good tracts of land, which the Indians could not steal.

There was a disposition to favor the growth of the town of Nashville and the raising of colts. We find that these two kinds of property are usually classed together, we know not why. The County Records say: "Town-lots and stud-horses not subject to tax this year;" and upon the tax rolls, town-lots and stud-horses are commonly placed in the same category. We notice one exception, somewhat remarkable, and it is in the case of a somewhat remarkable man, Christopher Stump, who "gives in, himself, one town-lot in Waynesborough, and one stud-horse." This. we believe, is in 1796. This new town was laid out at Eaton's Station, a rival to Nashville, and so called in honor of General Anthony Wayne.

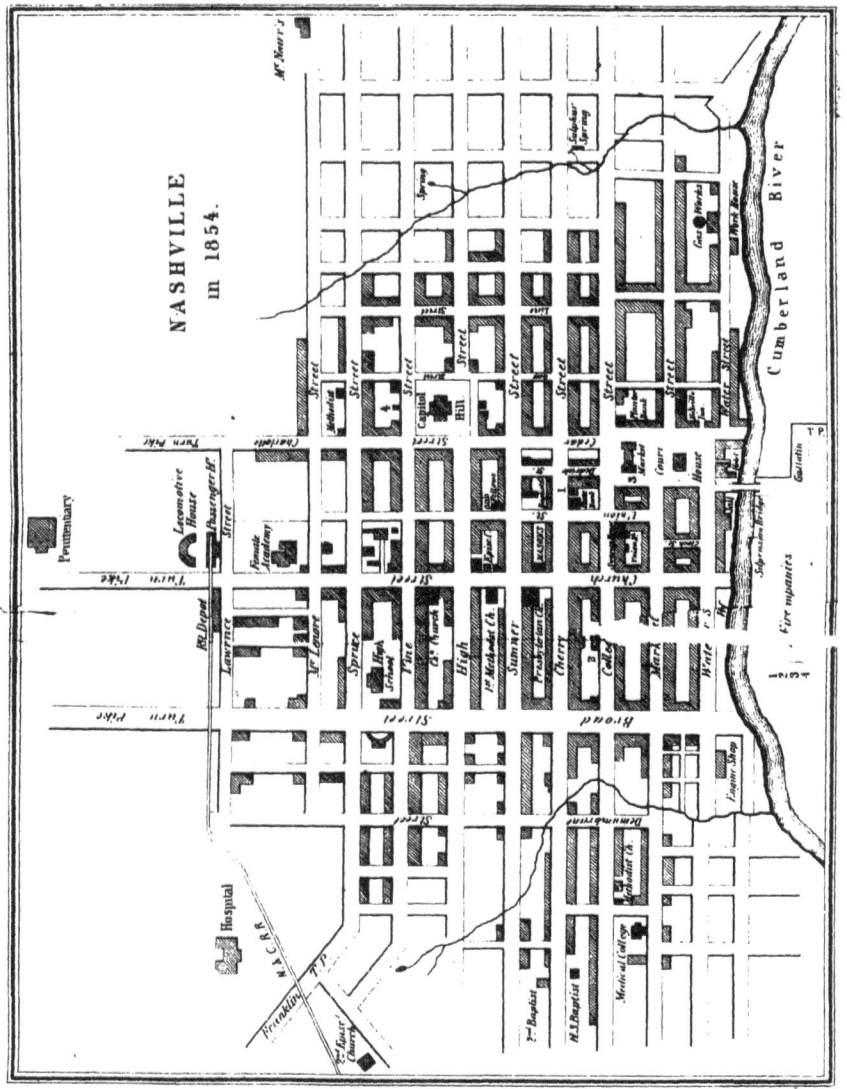

NASHVILLE
in 1854.

Cumberland River

CHAPTER XXXI.

1795.

BEFORE concluding our sketch of the events of this year connected with the Cumberland settlement and the active life of General Robertson, we must more fully present the affairs of the Indian nations in their proper connection.

Early in January, 1795, General Robertson received intelligence, by runners from Colbert and other chiefs, (of whom Underwood was one,) that they, with seventy warriors and some women and children, would visit him at his station near Nashville; that they had five Creek scalps,* which they had taken on Duck River from Creeks who were on their way to kill and plunder the people of Cumberland. The leader of the Creeks was a noted brigand, and had done much damage to these settlements. The Chickasaws surrounded the entire party of Creeks at night, and at early dawn killed them every one. They asked for provisions, ammunition, and artillery. They claimed now to be citizens of the United States, and, as Colbert and others held commissions from the President, they were ready to engage in active service, and prove that the commissions, titles, uniforms, and equipments granted to them had not been unworthily bestowed. They intended to make a long campaign against the Creeks in the spring; but, in the meantime, they required advice and aid in constructing some posts in their country.

General Robertson feared the loss of their friendship, should the Creeks succeed in doing them much damage before support should be given by the United States. They were very urgent for such aid, and pressed him to give assurances that it would be granted. He could, however, only say to them, that from the exalted opinions he entertained of the councils of his Government, and from the view he took of the claims they had upon the United States, he expected that an army would march against the Creeks in the summer: at the same time that he thus ex-

---

* Shall it be said scalps constituted a currency, and that therewith purchases could be made?

pressed himself, he disclaimed having any authority to pledge such support and active aid.

There were more than a hundred Chickasaws with General Robertson at this time, and the expenses of their entertainment were very heavy. Some few persons voluntarily contributed corn, corn-meal, and meat. A few of the chiefs and their squaws were lodged in the homes of the whites. In Nashville, a grand dinner-party was gotten up by subscription to do honor to "General Colbert." It was quite an affair for that day : no such jolly time had been witnessed at the bluff since the days of Mountflorence and Gerard.

And then on the Sabbath (not much like a day of rest either) there was preaching twice at least. That steadfast pioneer soldier of the cross, instructor of men and teacher of boys, Rev. Thomas B. Craighead, was here and had remained here throughout all these troublous times, and one or more pioneer preachers or missionaries of the Methodist denomination appeared and announced the "glad tidings of peace on earth and good will toward men." Mr. Craighead had secured the erection of a small church near his residence east of Nashville some five miles, but preached in the grand Court-house in town. The Methodist minister began in this year to secure means for the erection of a church building upon the square by the side of the Court-house.

On the Lord's day Colbert and some of his staff appeared at church— as many people gathered round the little building and under the shed, or, as the records call it, " *lentoc*," that is, lean-to, or lean-unto, which the Court had directed to be added in 1793.

These Indians being here, they had to be entertained and well treated; they must also be well provided for, whenever they should please to depart; (which would have caused regret to the settlers and General Robertson at no time, provided they left in good humor.) Governor Blount admitted that supplies must be continued, and every show of hospitality, lest they should take offence and be converted into enemies. They were urged to an exhibition of their ball-play, and other games and athletic amusements, and the whites had to manifest much gratification and enthusiasm. Indeed, it was a jolly time all round. When the sound of *the horn* was heard in one direction, all knew that the "red heifer" was ready for the milching; when the horn sounded from another quarter, it was understood there was something to eat "over there;" and when on the Lord's day the sound of the horn was heard at the Court-house door, some of the people "supposed there was going to be preaching."

In the course of this spring the war between the Creeks and the Chickasaws was waged with considerable fury. The latter had been so well armed with good guns and such an abundance of ammunition, that the fierce Creeks became very much alarmed. The Creeks had good reason to apprehend that the whites would not only sympathize with, but aid, the Chickasaws, and that the intimation from General Robertson of the invasion of their country by an army of the United States, such as that of General Wayne's, was not a mere hint or idle intimation. There were some very sad and savage acts among the Creeks, as the result of this war between them and the Chickasaws.

Before the hostilities began, a number of Creek men had married Chickasaw wives; but when the war broke out, *they killed the women and their children.* "They count relationship only on the mother's side; hence the children were as much Chickasaws as their mothers, and equally the victims of Creek vengeance." Some few were allowed to escape to their own nation, and some we presume to the beloved town, or city of refuge.

Colbert and other Chickasaw chiefs had Creek wives, but were too humane and civilized to entertain the thought of such horrid murders. Their visits here were well calculated to have a good influence upon them, and to awaken among them the desire for some of the arts and advantages of civilized life, which were soon thereafter granted.

The Cherokees had been urged in the spring by the agents of our Government to be at peace with the Creeks. They were disposed to accept the advice, and in April sent a deputation to the Creeks with such proposals, which met with a somewhat favorable reception ; but no sooner had these emissaries of peace reached their homes, than there arrived Creek runners with a war-club and earnest invitation to join them in a war against the Chickasaws. A very sensible and significant reply was sent back to the Creeks, from the Little Turkey :

"You had best forbear war upon the Chickasaws until you have made peace with the United States !" The Creeks deemed this good advice. The Choctaws also desired peace with the Creeks ; and the desire of most of the Indians in each nation was for peace. There were some the death of whose relatives had not been avenged, and there were "bad young men," whose thirst for blood had not been satisfied. These continued the question of peace and war in an unsettled condition among all these nations until December.

The threats and organizations against the Chickasaws were such that General Robertson sanctioned and encouraged the enlisting of two companies to go to their relief. In this measure the views of General Robertson were fully concurred in by General Daniel Smith, and indeed by all the settlers.

Captain David Smith, General Colbert, and some fifteen or twenty men, marched by land, and reached Log-town, in the Chickasaw nation, about the 1st of May. Colonel Mansker and Captain John Gwyn, with another party, took boats and reached Log-town about the 10th of May. On the arrival of Colonel Mansker, Captain Smith surrendered the command to him, and acted as lieutenant in Captain George's company.

Information was received that a strong force of Creeks was coming, and the defences were strengthened under the directions of Colonel Mansker. Although the invading force was represented to be very large, the Chickasaws were in good spirits, having the countenance of skilful white men, and the "little piece," or swivel.

On the 28th May the Creeks, numbering two thousand warriors, as was supposed, made their appearance. They found two women who had gone out for wood, at a short distance from the town, whom they killed and scalped. Although the army was so strong in numbers, no attack was adventured by it. There evidently prevailed among them great dread of cannon and fortifications.

Captain Smith proposed to General Colbert to make a sortie, Smith in command of the white men, and Colbert of the Indians. Colbert objected, saying, "That is what they wish, to draw us from the fort, and then they will rush in and destroy the women and children." Nevertheless, a party of Indians who were relatives of the two murdered squaws, rushed out, sprang upon the Creeks at an unexpected place, fired upon them, but had to retreat, leaving one of their number killed and scalped by the Creeks. When Captain Smith saw these few Chickasaws in such peril, he again proposed to Colbert to go to their aid. Now Colbert promptly assented. The Creeks seeing this, and other demonstrations at the fort, hastily retreated. Colbert and Smith's men rushed up near enough to the retreating foe to kill and wound quite a number of them. And thus they came, and thus made haste away.

Colonel Mansker remained some ten or twelve days. The Creeks giving no further evidences of hostility, other than killing cattle, he returned to Nashville without interruption.

This expedition by land and by water was wholly voluntary on the part of these magnanimous men from Cumberland. General Robertson had said they ought to go, and they ought to be paid for their services. General Colbert had said, "If the United States Government does not pay you, the Chickasaw nation will."* In after-years the Creeks were

---

* The first appearance of General Jackson on the floor of Congress, was on 29th December, 1796, advocating the claim of *Hugh Lawson White*, for pay as a soldier

greatly ridiculed for killing two women with an army of two thousand men !

General Robertson had seen the orders from the Secretary of War, discountenancing military aid to the Chickasaws; but truly, as Judge Haywood says, "his honest soul lamented in silence the unapproved restraint." He found pleasure in the performance of all possible acts of kindness to these friends and former allies. He had been authorized to send them more corn, and to supply those who visited him, with victuals, salt, and whiskey, and some other articles. Availing himself of a liberal construction of this permission or order for supplies, General Robertson, on 27th April, shipped to the Chickasaw Bluffs, under the command of Major Coffield, with twenty white men and fifteen Chickasaws, *five hundred* stand of arms, powder, lead, vermilion, whiskey, corn, and other articles. These boats were fired upon when passing Dyer's Island, twenty-five miles below Clarksville, by a party of Creeks; Major Coffield and two others were wounded.

An additional supply of arms and ammunition was placed, by the order of Government, (or through the agency of Colonel Henley,) at the disposition of General Robertson, say about the 1st of July; among these were six small howitzers, ten quarter casks of rifle powder, five hundred pounds of lead, one thousand flints, ammunition for one hundred rounds complete for each piece, besides grape-shot, agricultural implements, *et cetera.*

All the Indians probably had learned something in regard to this large supply of formidable firearms, and they had heard of the havoc

---

under General Sevier, when he pursued the Indians who had murdered the Cavitt family and other settlers in East Tennessee. His second was, on presenting a petition of *George Colbert,* one of the chiefs and warriors of the *Chickasaw* nation of Indians : in which the petitioner set forth as cause of complaint, a non-compliance of stipulations entered into in certain *talks* held with Governor Blount and other agents of the United States, in which they agreed in defensive support of *each other's rights ;* that their nation was invaded by the red people (Creeks) when they applied, according to treaty, for aid; that their brother, James Robertson, said he had no orders to send them any assistance—that he must first have orders from their father, the President of the United States. "However, [proceeds the petitioner,] a detachment of *volunteers,* under command of Colonel Mansker, came to their aid." He asked compensation for supplies furnished to that detachment during sixty days.

The Secretary of War had declined acting on the claim; referred the parties to Congress, who passed it over to the Committee on Claims; and an allowance was made. The Colberts had not forgotten their promise, "The Chickasaws will pay you if the United States will not."

made by the use of them in the great victory of General Wayne. This manifestation of an intention to introduce them into Southern warfare, together with the mission of peace and peace-talks of General Robertson in May, had much influence in arresting the savage warfare.

About the same period when General Robertson visited the Chickasaws to promote peace with the Cherokees, Governor Gayoso likewise visited them and urged peace with all Indian nations. A Chickasaw assembly or council was held and an address agreed upon to be sent to the Creeks. This was made known, and in order that Gayoso might add the weight of his name to it, a copy was sent to him on the 13th of June. On the 27th of July the Creeks returned a favorable answer: "We have smoked your tobacco in token of peace; we desire to bury the war-hatchet for ever; let war cease among the red men. As a proof of friendship, do you deliver to General Robertson all Creek prisoners, and restrain your young men from rash acts. We will do likewise."

The Choctaws cast their influence in favor of peace, but gave unexpected proof of having been in close alliance with and yet greatly under the influence of the Spaniards: saying, "The Spaniards promise us guns and ammunition to defend ourselves. Our father, Governor Gayoso, has told us that the Americans have sold us and our lands. If so, let us be all united, and they cannot take them; but if we kill each other, who will be left to defend them? . . . Send this talk to your brothers, the Cherokees, that they make peace also."

Much of the year was employed in these conferences, talks, and missions; many goods were distributed. The Creeks dissembled and again deceived Governor Blount, as they had done in former years. So did they deceive the United States agent, Mr. Seagrove. Governor Blount finally became "so pestered" by them, the Chickasaws, and others, that he openly expressed a wish "that he might never see any of them again." And yet he soon deemed it prudent to advise General Robertson "to pester himself" in efforts to give them satisfaction. "Give some more of them saddles and bridles and *saddlebags;*" and doubtless he would have added "spurs" if there had been a supply of such equipments. The Indians would have highly prized these incentives to speed, and have proudly fastened them to their naked feet, (as the writer has often witnessed.)

But, besides the attentions to be given to the men or warriors, General Robertson was required to pay courtly attentions to *Mrs.* General Colbert, to Mrs. General Piomingo, and to this and to that squaw-*tyke* of some half-breeched and blanketed warrior.

And such a time as he had of it! If Governor Blount became "tired and pestered," how did General Robertson feel! He had not only to entertain them at his station, but to accompany them or provide escorts, and again and again undertake long journeys into their nations. He made two such during this year.

He brought about a conference on the 10th of October between the chiefs of the Cherokees and Chickasaws, and some of the Creeks. Here were preliminary measures discussed. At a more general meeting, on the 30th of November, the terms of peace were adjusted, and then the Creeks said: "We now look to the white people [meaning the Americans] with clear eyes and straight hearts, and wish for peace with all mankind." And thus hostilities between the Indians were ended.

On 29th of June, in the following year, a treaty in due form was made with the Creeks by the United States, through the agency of a very distinguished commission: Benjamin Hawkins, of North Carolina, George Clymer, of Pennsylvania, and Andrew Pickens, of South Carolina.

Here was a manifestation on the part of the then Administration of as much respect to this Creek tribe of demi-savages as was shown in our negotiations for national independence. This was as formal a commission for negotiation as has ever been adopted to treat with the most powerful nation on earth. These commissioners were regularly nominated to the Senate, and received confirmation. Such was an exhibition of the regard paid by the Administration of Washington to the treaty-making power; such the respect to an Indian nation or tribe, roving over a portion of the unmeasured forests of America. It certainly was a needless delicacy, a waste of etiquette and diplomacy. A single commissioner has often since that day made a treaty with Indians, settling many difficulties and acquiring territory of millions of acres. The several missions of General Robertson had prepared the way for these three plenipotentiaries on the part of the United States to the Creek nation.

We have quoted Haywood's remark, that "Governor Blount was so pestered by the visits of the Indians, that, losing hold of his usual equanimity, he sincerely wished them all"—away off on their last hunting excursions.

He expected more from General Robertson than he could perform himself. We have never heard of such "marked" and flattering attentions paid by him to these more than half-naked savages, as were sometimes given by General Robertson, to tame their savage natures and secure their good will. They uniformly called him a "good man;" and such a scene as was exhibited at the last Chickasaw visit to the General, might well employ the skill of a Hogarth.

Beneath the lofty and beautiful maples which surrounded General

Robertson's Station, might be seen a variety of the copper-colored race, mostly crouched upon the ground. The best dressed of the females have a sack, (not overly long,) yet long enough to hide the strip of "stroud" or baize around the waist and hips; with moccasins and leggins, ornamented by beads and tinkling bells; and across the shoulders a dirty blanket. The hair is braided and hangs down like a mandarin's.

Such was the attire of Jacsie Moniac, the wife of "General Colbert." She had around her a full representation of the half-breed "General"— the parent's "small-arms." Near by sat Molle-tulla, the tall wife of the Mountain Leader, "Captain Piomingo," whom General Robertson had instructions to equip with clothing and ornaments. There were others, "the better halves" of chiefs and warriors of great pretensions and little worth.

If we could transfer another group of Creeks, and stand or seat them not afar off, and such as General Robertson not long before entertained, we should see the partner of the Mad-Dog and "her whelps;" the Turkey and her brood; the Hanging-Maw, and all that set of gourmands.

And now, with all this crew, unwashed, uncombed, unclouted, and—unhung, seated or moving around that tall and sedate person, mark how he pats their heads, and smiles at their recognition. Who else but General Robertson would pause in such a group, and, dipping his finger in the vermilion which the squaw held in one hand, and the black paint in the box, would give to the faces of these not naturally ill-looking urchins the wrinkled appearance of a monkey, the head of a cat, of the wily fox, or sly raccoon! But to have the lines of such a head or face drawn upon the breast or stomach, and a tail traced on the back, as if it belonged there—such limning highly gratified these children of the woods and their parents. This rude and nude painting was regarded by them as "the perfection of art."

General Robertson is again greatly annoyed by Pitchlyn, a Choctaw chief, who had quartered on him, accompanied by fifty of his dirty* people; and he came with a desire to obtain permission and means to travel on to Philadelphia to "see the President."

People in our day have been and are "beset to visit the gold diggings," or to see "the elephant" somewhere, and will abandon homes and comforts to gratify this auri sacra fames, or this "furor for sights;" and surely we need not express surprise that a similar rage prevailed among

---

* We make this remark with a knowledge of its truth. The Choctaws are a dirty race; there are no exceptions, but such as have been produced by the influence of the Missionaries.

the savages to see "their Great Father, the President," and the "seat of his power." It was "something" to see General Robertson; but this only increased the desire to see one whom he and Governor Blount, and all Americans, acknowledged to be "The Great Medal Chief," and Head of all these United States.

Pitchlyn insisted upon permission to make the visit, and to take a suitable escort of his breeched and blanketed crew. General Robertson started a "trotter" to Knoxville with a letter to the Governor, informing him of the presence of these Indians at his residence, and of their wishes. To this the Governor replies by letter of 24th August, urging the General " by no means to let them proceed. The expense will be large, and the use and benefit nothing."

It required no little artifice and influence on the part of General Robertson to dissuade Pitchlyn and his party from continuing their journey. He made them such presents as he and a few citizens could spare, and to these were added some articles from the public stores. With these and other persuasives he succeeded, much to his own and the Governor's gratification.

We believe that by the hands of Pitchlyn, the Mountain Leader forwarded to General Robertson a letter which he had received from Governor Gayoso, dated July 10th. Piomingo had visited the President in the previous summer, received pledges of friendship from the head of the Government, attention from heads of the departments, was "*Nock-en-e*"ized, or, as we say, *Lionized*, made a big man of, clothed, dubbed with a title, loaded with presents, and sent on his way to his nation a gratified Indian; but to excite the jealousy and stir up the ambition of others.

Soon after Piomingo had returned, Bill Colbert insisted that it was time for him to see the President; that he was of as much consequence among the Choctaws as Piomingo was among the Chickasaws.

Colbert had already received a commission as an officer in the army. He strutted in regimentals, wore epaulettes and a sword. We believe these were conferred on or promised to him when at Nashville, in 1792; but he had not been escorted to Philadelphia—he had not shaken hands with Washington. He now comes to General Robertson's: notice is sent on to the Governor that nothing less than a visit to him at Knoxville will satisfy this old "*pyrite*"* of the river Tennessee, (the head of "Colbert's

---

* Whether this spelling was intentional, or from ignorance or carelessness, it describes the man—a half-breed, in looks and smell, "a combination of sulphur and copper, presenting a yellowish lustre," with all the impudence of a bad white man.

gang.") The "*avant courier*" having thus forewarned the Governor, he was forearmed. He gave him a formal reception on "a set day"—made him a speech, and listened to a "talk" in reply.

One of the best things he said to the Governor was : "In your talk, delivered to us at Nashville, in the summer of 1792, you said Choctaw and Chickasaw blood, and *your* blood, (American blood,) is the same. You want tyke; you get him. Me want tyke; me get him. All same blood !" *Id est :* Each of them had his own wife, but "the same blood" made nearly related. "Indeed," he added, "we are brothers, and must assist each other. I am a warrior, and entitled to speak : Chickasaws fight Creeks for Robertson people." He praised the Chickasaws for what they did in their war with the Creeks, and especially because that warfare contributed to the quiet and safety of the Robertson settlements.

Nothing the Governor could say or venture to promise would satisfy him : he must, he would, and he did, visit the President.

At the beginning of September, General Robertson received messages from Piomingo, expressive of anxiety at the threatened invasion by the Creeks, and that his people were not properly provided to resist the enemy.

General Robertson in person visited the nation. He met Piomingo at Log-town. He was actively engaged in efforts to establish peace between the Creeks and Chickasaws. The Creeks expressed such regard to him and his wishes, and the purposes of his mission, that their chiefs forbade the young warriors to make any attack upon the Chickasaws during his visit. Yet some of them were so incensed at the grossly insulting language used toward them by the Chickasaws, (when speaking of their grand invasion, and killing two women, then flying in trepidation,) that conflicts were repeatedly at the point of occurring.

The Chickasaws called the Creeks, "Nockiny-ho-bocks:" not *men*—the meanest sort of women. This was "an offence, to be washed out with blood."

About the middle of the month, General Robertson returned to his house, and had been there but a short time when he received a letter from Piomingo, (written by his white secretary,) giving an account of an affair which had taken place soon after the General's departure.

"About a thousand Creeks came to destroy the Chickasaw nation. They had some white people with them : they came with drums, and had ammunition, and preparations to make a siege and capture of Log-town, and of other places. A great many came on horseback. The Chickasaw warriors of Big-town fell on them, put them to rout, pursued them about five miles, took all their baggage and clothing—*except their flaps*— the only clothing they had on when they began the attack !

"The baggage consisted of their blankets, leggins, and other articles—
except their flaps—their ammunition, kettles, and their provisions." He
is careful to repeat " all except their flaps," proving the *rout*.

The Chickasaw loss was six men and one woman killed. Twenty-
six Creek men were found killed, and many more must have been
wounded.

After this defeat, General Robertson said to the Chickasaws : "You
now can propose to them terms of peace." This was done; and it was
agreed to refer questions arising upon an exchange of prisoners to Governor Blount. And thus the measures for a general peace seemed to be
progressing satisfactorily.

In the summer of this year a wagon-road was opened from Knoxville
to Nashville, direct, so that loaded wagons could pass; and the number
of emigrants became like a constant stream. Such use of the road, and
the hauling of goods thereon, soon made it a good thoroughfare. So great
was the increase of population, that before the end of the year it was
confidently expected that the new census would show a population of at
least sixty thousand inhabitants in the Territory. They came from the
Carolinas, from Georgia, Virginia, Maryland, and from other Atlantic
States. Although thousands stopped along the Holston, French Broad, the
Clinch, and Upper Tennessee, and some tarried by the way in the mountains, yet the great ambition was to reach this *ultima thule*—these rich
lands on the Cumberland, with hopes of early purchases of Indian titles
to all the region to the Tennessee River.

Money had been placed in the hands of the disbursing agent, to
settle for military services. Being clothed with a little brief authority,
Colonel ——— seemed fearful his dignity would not be suitably recognized if he should accept advice from General Robertson, or even information, which any gentleman would have *first* sought of him in preference of all other persons. But the Colonel took it into his head—as far
as it would admit any idea with safety—that forged testimonials or certificates would surely be presented to him; therefore, out of abundant
caution, he made his election of persons entitled; and because General
Robertson remonstrated, or, perhaps, plainly censured and ridiculed his
conduct, he was informed that "no money was retained for his services !"
Judge Haywood says, "Suggestions were afterwards made, that everybody
was paid except General Robertson, but that no moneys were retained for
the satisfaction of his services."

In a letter from Governor Blount to General Robertson, dated August
1, 1795, he says : "The agent, since your departure, has paid all officers
in the Indian department their salaries for the two first quarters of the

present year. . . . His refusing to pay you, and paying others under similar circumstances, accords well with his regular system of inconsistencies!"

It is proper to mention this withholding of pay from General Robertson as something intended as a petty annoyance; but the name of the man who did it cannot appear on these pages other than as *Colonel Blank*. "The Colonel" had to "back water," and General Robertson was paid, without having to accept it through such an agency.

Upon this affair, Judge Haywood makes this sounding figurative remark: "He who knows that the town-bell will ring, even upon suspicion of his motives, will take care not to give cause for alarm by his conduct." Colonel ——— perhaps had not such prudence. The bell rang, when no one was known to have pulled the rope.

"At the close of this eventful year, the Spaniards had become reconciled to the people of this Territory. Their limits on our borders were fixed; the free navigation of the Mississippi was yielded to the United States; the northern and southern Indians had suspended their incursions; emigration flowed in full tide upon the country; the people were about to make for themselves a new constitution, and to assume the rank of an independent State.

" James Robertson, the first settler, both of East and West Tennessee, and the political father of the latter, who had shared in all the dangers and sufferings of the first settlers, still lived, and saw the country which he had fostered with so much care, smiling for the blessings it enjoyed, and for the still greater blessings which Providence seemed to have in store."—*Haywood*.

CHAPTER XXXII.

1796.

In the preparation of measures for the organization of a State, General Robertson was often consulted. He was urged to attend the meetings of the Assembly, at Knoxville, as a member or adviser. Governor Blount addressed him to come: "The public interests, and your own and my interests, require that you and I, and other public men, should meet and consult together. Come on to Knoxville.

"I trust, sir, this infant country, particularly the people of Mero District, of which you may be said to be the political father, will long retain a grateful sense of your services."

As Judge Haywood says, using a very expressive word, "Although the Nickojack Expedition had actually put an end to the Cherokee War, yet the Secretary (Pickering) continued so to *snarl* about it, that the General sent in his resignation," to take effect, as has been stated in the last chapter, on 15th of August, 1795. Although he now desires no longer to be regarded as in commission as Brigadier-General, he is still willing to act as Indian Agent.

He could well say, and it is a just sentiment, that "he never claimed perfection or preëminence for any of his acts: he sought only the perfection of good or best endeavors."

Angels who have kept their first estate have never rendered better service than that: the perfection of best endeavors; the best endeavors of the best affections; the entire consecration of their highest powers.

In the winter of this year the Chickasaws were so destitute of food that they sent most urgent supplications to General Robertson and Governor Blount for corn. The Governor writes to General Robertson: "If corn is not supplied, the women and children may starve to death."

Such calls were never heard and disregarded by General Robertson. The corn and some salt were forwarded to them.

The General continued to have his hands full of public affairs, and the business he had to transact of a more private nature was most astonishing. A large amount of land papers had been intrusted to him. He

34

was called upon to have warrants laid, lands surveyed, to give descriptions of the lands, and to reply to a thousand questions propounded by persons at a distance, many of whom were very desirous that the General and the people of Mero should give the Indians "a sound drubbing," and thus secure a peace, and *then* they would hasten out to occupy and improve their lands, "and enjoy peaceful homes!"

These people thought not how such letters sounded to the ears of these old warriors. But the work was done for them. And then they came, peaceable, industrious, good citizens; *glad that the savages were whipped before they came.*

We have sometimes been amused in the perusal of old letters and documents, written by persons who could not conceive of or appreciate the labors and perplexities of those to whom they addressed themselves.

Governor Blount never "rested upon a bed of roses," as Haywood has well said; and General Robertson more frequently had no bed at all, or it was one so exposed that to attempt to seek rest thereon, was at the peril of life. As to "taking rest in sleep," seldom was it possible, unless "with one eye open"—a good sentinel at the bedside.

He was "pestered" by our good friends, brothers, and allies, the savages; he was pestered by our "treaty friends," the Spaniards; he was pestered by others, who thought it not. Governor Blount made the same complaint, and the high officials at Philadelphia made most laughable and ridiculous lamentations of being "pestered" there too, by these same "teasers and blood-suckers."

A letter from Pickering, Secretary of War, says: "Six Indians, Chickasaws and Choctaws, have *strolled* to Philadelphia without an interpreter or guide. We cannot tell the object of their journey, except that they might expect to be clothed, and to receive presents. They have been clothed, and each furnished with a rifle-gun and accoutrements, and sent home with a guide. Do keep them at home!"

If in Philadelphia they were worried by the presence of *six* Indians, who had strolled there, how would they have survived the presence of sixty or six hundred, and these to be squatted on the ground at their very door for weeks?

They could not "stand it" at Philadelphia, and therefore a circular was addressed to Indian agents to "keep them in the nation; don't let them come on here, unless in very small deputations, and these to be only of the principal chiefs, and most influential of their nation."

They continued to annoy General Robertson and Governor Blount with their applications for leave to visit the President, all at the expense of the Government.

In April General Robertson was instructed to inform the Creeks, Cherokees, and Choctaws, that they might visit the President in the autumn, and to inform Piomingo, and other chiefs of his nation, to be in readiness to come on at the same time. The President desired to have them all there at the same conference, to settle all matters of difficulty.

Many communications were made to General Robertson by the chiefs and their people relative to stolen horses, which they had promised to have delivered. Frequent excuses, however, were made for non-compliance or delays. These matters were very troublesome indeed, but patience, with General Robertson, was a virtue that had astonishing endurance.

The Chickasaws had become restive at the continuance of the Spanish fort. In April preparations were made to dismantle and destroy it.

But we must notice the change in the form of Government—the transition from a Territory to a State.

Under the influence of Governor Blount, and "General Sevier and his Captains," (all strong advocates for a *State*,) the preliminary measures were taken, and they finally "had it all their own way."

An enumeration of the inhabitants was taken in the fall of the preceding year, in pursuance of "An Act of 11th July." The total was seventy-seven thousand two hundred and sixty-three, including ten thousand six hundred and thirteen slaves. The returns from the Cumberland counties were as follows :

DAVIDSON COUNTY.*—Free white males, sixteen years and upwards, including heads of families, 728 ; free white males under sixteen, 695 ; free white females, including heads of families, 1192 ; all other free

---

* For the benefit of the "dear people," and of the "poorly paid officers" of the present day, we furnish the compensation received by the three Sheriffs, N. P. Hardeman, Reuben Cage, and J. B. Neville, for taking the census of their respective counties.

Davidson county—population, 3613 ; compensation, $18.06½. Sumner county—population, 6370 ; compensation, $31.85. Tennessee county—population, 1941 : compensation, $9.70½. Eighteen dollars and six and one-half cents for enumerating the inhabitants of Davidson county.

And they were men "content with their wages," not "concocting schemes whereby to rob the treasury of county or State !"

And we furnish herewith an exact copy of a *warrant*, with its guarantees of correctness, and call the attention of public men to its formalities, assuring them that it is written in the large bold hand of Governor Blount. Very few of them were printed. The one which we copy is written upon a half-sheet of coarse strong paper, (but such as the Blounts commonly used for letter and business pur-

persons, 6; slaves, 992; total amount, 3613; for State, yeas, 96; against State, nays, 517.

SUMNER COUNTY.—Free white males, sixteen years and upwards, including heads of families, 1382; free white males under sixteen, 1595; free white females, including heads of families, 2316; all other free persons, 1; slaves, 1076; total amount, 6370. No vote cast for or against State.

TENNESSEE COUNTY.—Free white males, sixteen years and upwards, including heads of families, 380; free white males, under sixteen, 444; free white females, including heads of families, 700; all other free persons, 19; slaves, 398; total amount, 1941; for State, yeas, 58; against State, nays, 231.

The returns from the eight counties in East Tennessee, together with the votes in Mero, exhibit a strong vote against the formation of a State Government. In Sumner county this question was not voted upon, or doubtless we should have had an expression equally as unfavorable as was that in the two adjoining counties.

In Davidson and Tennessee the vote was as four to one, there being but ninety-six in Davidson and fifty-eight in Tennessee counties voting "for a State."

On 28th November, 1795, Governor Blount issued his proclamation for an election to be held in each county on 18th and 19th days of December, for members of Convention to adopt a Constitution and permanent form of government. The elections were held, and the Convention assembled at Knoxville on 11th day of January, 1796.

---

poses,) *fourteen inches long* and *nine inches wide*, and the writing covers nearly the entire of one side.

(SEAL.)

WILLIAM BLOUNT, GOVERNOR IN AND OVER THE TERRITORY OF THE UNITED STATES OF AMERICA SOUTH OF THE RIVER OHIO.

To Howell Tatom, Esquire, Treasurer for the District of Mero:

Pay to Nicholas Perkins Hardeman, Esquire, Sheriff of Davidson county, eighteen dollars six and one-half cents, being the sum allowed him by law for taking the enumeration of the inhabitants of said county, the number being three thousand six hundred and thirteen, for which this shall be your warrant.

Given under my hand and seal at Knoxville, this 4th day of December, 1795.

By the Governor: WM. BLOUNT.

    WILLIE BLOUNT,
        Pro. Secretary.   (Endorsed,)

                                        " Received, January 8th, 1796,
of Howell Tatom, Treasurer, the full amount of the within warrant.

                                        "N. P. HARDEMAN."

The members from Cumberland were:

From Davidson County—John McNairy, Andrew Jackson, James Robertson, Thomas Hardeman, and Joel Lewis.

From Sumner County—David Shelby, Isaac Walton, Wm. Douglass, Edward Douglass, and Daniel Smith.

From Tennessee County—Thomas Johnston, James Fort, William Fort, Robert Prince, and William Prince.

In the Convention, General Robertson moved the appointment of two members from each county to draft a Constitution: McNairy and Jackson from Davidson, Shelby and Smith from Sumner, and Johnston and Fort from Tennessee, were on that Committee. General Smith of Sumner reported the Bill of Rights; this was duly considered in committee of the whole, General Robertson being in the chair; and on the 6th of February "the engrossed copy of the Constitution was read and passed unanimously."

They did not fail to give an expression of their opinions relative to one of the questions which had so long and so greatly excited the western people. The 29th section of the Bill of Rights is as follows: "That an equal participation of the free navigation of the Mississippi, is one of the inherent rights of the citizens of this State; it cannot, therefore, be conceded to any prince, potentate, power, person, or persons, whatever."

The suggestion had often been made prior to the Convention, that some euphonious Indian name should be adopted for the State, such as Sewanee or Tennessee. The latter was preferred, and adopted without opposition. Tennessee county yielded her sweet-sounding name to the State.

The first session of the Legislature was opened on the 30th of March, and proceeded to business; John Sevier being Governor. Howell Tatom was elected Attorney-General for the District of Mero. At this first session Tennessee county was divided into the counties of Montgomery and *Robertson.**

It is suitable to give here the summary of the character and services of General Robertson in the language of Willie Blount, who knew him intimately and loved and honored him sincerely: "He treated the Indians, when known enemies, as the enemies of his country; when

---

* Robertson county is bounded north by the State of Kentucky, east by Sumner county, south by Davidson, and west by Montgomery counties. It is about forty miles long from north-east to south-west, with a mean width of sixteen miles. It is watered by Red River on the north-west and by the Cumberland on the south, and Sulphur Fork in the middle. Sulphur Fork flows by *Springfield*, the county-seat.

The "first fire" occurred in Nashville in this year. The records speak of "the late fire," and there are several orders and notifications spread upon the records in consequence.

Before the termination of the Territorial Government, to wit, April 16th, 1796, the County Court met pursuant to adjournment: present, James Robertson, Robert Hays, John Gordon, and Samuel Barton. The last entry upon these records is in these words:

"The Court appoint John Castilion Guardian to Richard and John Low, for the special purpose of receiving deed of conveyance from Gen[l] James Robertson to s[d] orphans, and to defend ag[t] all suits whatever that may affect the interest of said orphans.

"Sam[l] Barton,
"Ja[s] Robertson,
"John Gordon.

("N. B.—Rob[t] Hays is wanting.")

Here and thus did James Robertson lay aside his *judicial robe,* having officiated as such from May, 1783, to April, 1796. He retained no commission as a General, none as a Justice; the duties of his "temporary Indian agency" were about to cease; he remained only as an "original and faithful trustee of the institution of learning, Davidson Academy," to 31st May, 1805, when he resigned.

General Robertson was now a private citizen, no less beloved and honored than when power and office were his. He had gathered honors; they ever clustered round him; they sought to rest upon him, and there they never withered or grew dim. He had lived long, very long, counting the number and the greatness of his deeds, and yet he had a score of years to add to "the days of the years" through which he had already lived and toiled as a public servant. But he was gratified to witness the peace, the happiness, and prosperity of the people around him, and to see so many thousands of industrious and thrifty settlers upon lands whereon he had been of the first of the race of white men to tread, and, in the subduing of which from the roving savages, he had endured privations, hardships, and perils known and suffered nowhere else.

---

that the Court ordered the sheriff to fasten his feet between the fence-rails, and there detain him until he should be sober. The fence was near the court-house, and Netterfield contined to curse the Court and throw stones at the court-house. "I saw him in the act, and in this position," says Mr. Bosley. "I have seen a great many men, especially politicians, 'on the fence,' some ridden on a rail, and many more who deserved to be, but Netterfield was the only one I ever saw *between* the rails."

The thought and wish here arise, Now he will have rest; surely he must be weary, and is entitled to cease from his labors; the memory of his deeds will be pleasant and cherished by thousands.

In the fall of this year there arrived from Virginia some very worthy emigrants, and a large accession from the Carolinas and Georgia. They are too numerous to be particularly named.

1796. "By consent of the Court and Bar, Mr. Thomas Stuart is permitted to practice as Atty. until *some law is passed* on this subject." (Davidson County Court Records.)

"Whereas Elijah R. was heretofore allow^d by the Worshipful C^t $60 for a horse furnished *a certain Indian*, on his journey"—the amount is allowed in part of his taxes.

This "certain Indian," no doubt, was one of the *runners, spies* or *guides*, or *trotters*, of which there were several employed by General Robertson and the County Court.

On these records there are a number of entries having reference to "the late fire in Nashville," and the destruction of sundry papers, public and private.

"Ordered, that the Sheriff take no certificates in payment of taxes, where credits that may have been entered thereon appear erased or defaced, unless good proof shown why the same were erased. By reason that numbers of the papers which would have shown the just credits, are burnt in Capt. Williams' and Black's store-house."

Here is the first instance occurring in these settlements of an attempt to defraud the public revenue—the commencement of peculation and forgery: great had been the public gain had this been the last.

The "Homer of Cumberland" commenced his public rehearsals in prose and verse in this year. He vainly essayed to describe "the conflagration of the store;" failing in this, and rejected in his addresses to the fair daughter of one of these merchants, he gave vent to the venom which was in his heart in his published verses to "Miss Susan Black:"

> "You are no beauty, that I know;
> Look in the glass, you'll find it so.
> . . . .
> "And now, Miss Susan Black,
> On you I turn my back."

In the "History of Literature," by our late departed friend, Wilkins Tannehill, Esq., no mention is made of "Clarke's Miscellany, in Prose and Verse"—the *first* book published in Nashville.

If mentioned at all, it would have been classed with the "Curiosities of Literature." Clarke was also "a talking politician," and just as worthy of attention as any of the class, and—*no more so.* He greatly feared a war with France and Spain, and yet was fiercely opposed to an increase of the navy and the existence of a regular army. He professed the utmost confidence in the militia, and "militia musters." At such parades he found idlers ready to listen to his martial odes, his ditties, and prose-y recitals. He was "a standing candidate" for any office in the militia, from "captain down to fourth corporal;" but we believe his military aspirations were never gratified. How much good service was lost to the public by this want of appreciation of his merits will never be known.

"Gideon Davis Pendleton and Jno. Brown are admitted as Attys. by consent of the Court and Bar, *and took the oaths necessary for their qualification*—[until otherwise ordered by the Court."]

This entry is worthy of notice. The words in italic constituted part of the original entry or order; they were stricken out, and the words in brackets interlined. Was this from "abundant caution?" Were they admitted without "the oaths necessary for their qualification?" Was it in anticipation of the order made five days thereafter?—"until otherwise ordered by the Court!"

On the 15th, being Saturday, the Court order the name of Gideon D. Pendleton to be stricken from the roll, and Mr. G. D. P. "stood aside"—*outside* that bar. Five days an attorney of the County Court!

> "Honor and shame from no condition rise:
> Act well your part; there all the honor lies."

A peculiar and significant by-word among hunters received such an application in this instance that it became quite familiar: "Shoot at the *hump.*" Hunters of buffalo used this expression in satire. They knew that "hitting the hump never killed the bison." "The hump" and "the horn of pride" are excrescences with very little sensitiveness. Buffaloes are probably unconscious of having such malformations as humps. Many of the two-legged wild bulls have them of enormous size, in seeming ignorance. Some are even *humped all over.* No shot, no wound will hurt them. Their pride is not like wind in a sack; then it could be let out. Gristle and fat have no sensibility and little blood: why, then, shoot at the hump?

It is probable that the Honorable Court did not hurt anybody by this expenditure of ammunition. A thick hide protects the rhinoceros: some men are as well defended as the hippopotamus.

NASHVILLE

urging them not to seek revenge; to send some of the relatives of the deceased to his house and he would make them presents of corn and other articles, adding, " I have now no authority to speak as an Agent; Colonel Hawkins and Mr. Dinsmore, who are Agents, will do all in their power to secure the ends of justice. I have taken care of a gun, some money, five skins, and some other articles of the two Indians who were killed. Send to me for them, and you shall get them."

General Winchester issued military orders for the arrest of these murderers, and pronounces it "an infernal act, for which the perpetrators should suffer death."*

We notice in General Winchester's letters the Indian name of Obed's or Obey's River : it is *Oo-coo-i-oustehc*, in the Cherokee language.

Horses were now occasionally stolen by Indians from the Cumberland. Colonel Hawkins informed General Robertson that some Indians were engaged as regular *traders*, with licenses; these had their stands or *stamps.* Some of these traders complained of their horses having been stolen, but they did not accuse the whites. However, the practice of horse-stealing was on the increase, and likely to revive hostilities. Colonel Hawkins, nevertheless, was confident of firmly settling peace between the Creeks and Cherokees.

"In the winter, Mr. Forbers, a partner in the trading-house which supplied the Southern Indians under the authority of the Spanish Government," passed some days in the family of General Robertson, and made many professions of friendship for the United States; but the General believed that he and all others — the Spanish traders—would use their influence to delay and prevent the running of the line between the United States and Spain, as its settlement might lessen their trade or break up their monopoly there.

He had also, more recently, another visit from Pitchlyn, a Choctaw chief, who, at parting, begged so earnestly for a *piece of stroud* and a *piece of calico*, that the General had supplied him out of the Government stores in the hands of Mr. Overton, "not being able to procure them elsewhere," and from those stores they ought to have come. As might be supposed, there was a woman who needed a strip or two of that stroud, and a dress from that piece of calico.

Another woman, daughter of half-breed McClish, wanted not only stroud and calico, but a horse which one McGee had in his possession, to which she, "Nancy McClish," laid claim. The horse was procured and delivered to "Miss Nancy," who straddled the animal like a man,

---

* Manuscript letter, 8th November.

"guiding the beast with a rope for a bridle," and using her calico and other "plunder" as saddle blankets. Nancy McClish dressed and rode, as was the fashion then and now among the Indians, (unless where the wives and daughters of missionaries have introduced a different custom,) "a leg on each side." She kicked the horse with her heels and whipped him with the rope, "until she moved him into a canter," at the tune, "Off she goes, Miss Nancy."

In the question of politics the opinions of General Robertson were well settled. He was the political friend of General Sevier, the Governor, as also of the election of William Cocke and Andrew Jackson to the United States Senate. In his letters and conversations, he spoke very kindly of Governor Blount, and with utmost delicacy of the affair in which the Governor had unhappily involved himself, and which caused his expulsion from the Senate. In regard to the letter of the Governor to "Dear Carey," which formed the principal ground for charges against him, his arrest, impeachment, and expulsion, General Robertson, on 8th of August, 1797, uses this very sensible remark: "I never could have judged the letter to have been so criminal, but supposed it would have operated against my friend, as being a public man." How gentle is that!

In this opinion we think posterity will concur, and that Governor Blount was hastily and harshly dealt with. We are much inclined to regard him as being made a sacrifice, an offering, a martyr, upon the altar of his country, that the Government might more easily accomplish its great aims of peace and adjustment of many perplexing questions.

It is certain that in Tennessee his long and arduous labors for his fellow-citizens could not be, and were not, forgotten or lightly esteemed. When such men as General Sevier and General Robertson used no harsher expression than "the letter was ill-advised," "his conduct was very imprudent," "perhaps allowances ought to be made for his very embarrassed circumstances," we feel, at this day, disposed to demand a removal of much of the odium that was heaped upon Governor Blount by his impeachment and expulsion. The people of Tennessee welcomed his returned to Knoxville; he was, indeed, "a fallen politician," pitied, but not despised; *never* spoken of or looked upon as a *traitor*. The sympathy of such a man as General Robertson must have deeply affected the heart of Governor Blount. He certainly could not have forgotten the time and the occasion when he pierced the soul of this "good man" by his expressions of "astonishment and mortification" about the Nickojack expedition. That cause of quarrel was hushed, to attend to the urgent affairs of their fellow-citizens and the calls of their country.

Joseph Bishop, who was here during two or three of the last years of the Indian War, (and who is yet living, 1858, in Smith county,) had a ferry near Hartsville.   He had often to ferry persons across the river and then find they had no money, or the change could not be made, and his labor went unrewarded.   He was tired of this treatment, and resorted to various devices for satisfaction.   He relates the following :

"I saw a gentleman approaching the ferry, whistling a very lively tune as he came.   As he approached me he unpuckered his mouth, and with a very honest look and earnest face he said,

"'Mr. Ferryman, I wish to cross the river, but really I must tell you, I have no money.'

"I thought him honest, but as it might be that he, like others, wished to save his twelve and a half cents, I asked, 'Can you sing ?'

"He replied, 'I can sing a little.'

"I said, 'I am very fond of singing, and if you will sing all the way across the river, I will ferry you over for nothing.'

"'Agreed,' said he.

"He began to sing, I began to shove off and row leisurely.   He got through the first song, and his voice ceased ; the oars fell from my hands.

"'I just stopped to get breath,' said he.

"'I just stopped to spit on my hands,' said I.

"He raised the tune again, I raised my oars.   When the second song was done, my labor with the oars ended.   I could not work without music.   He saw how it was and began again, and so did I.   At the end of a third song he seemed really disposed or under necessity to 'give out,' and stopped ; and my arms and oars rested.

"'I'm tired," said he.

"'Then let's rest awhile,' said I.

"And the boat was floating down the stream.   He began the fourth time to sing, and my labors at the oars were renewed ; and so we continued.   When he sang, I pulled ; when his music gave out or was faint, so did my energies.   He harped away upon jigs and reels until the boat touched shore, when he instantly jumped to land, exclaiming :

"'That ferriage cost me much breath !'

"'It was the longest voyage I ever made across the Cumberland,' said I.

"'I'll bring the money with me next time," said he.

"'Do !' said I : 'or a new set of tunes.'

"And we parted in good humor."

In the month of May there arrived in Nashville three young gentlemen, who attracted more than usual attention.   They were Frenchmen.   Old Monsieur De Munbrune was "excited, like one affected with St.

Vitus's dance :" "he could not keep his hands, his feet, or his tongue still." They were the three sons of the Duke of Orleans. The eldest was subsequently known as *Louis Philippe,* King of France; the two others were his younger brothers.

They were introduced to General Robertson and others of the principal citizens here; and after a delay of a few days, in which time a boat, oarsmen, and provisions were secured, they descended the Cumberland, whether to St. Louis or New Orleans, we know not, but certainly to a life of vicissitudes and extremes, to the throne of royalty and to the flight of fools. It must be confessed that "these sprigs of royalty found very little sympathy among these hardy republicans, for their fallen greatness." It was said,

> "They came astraddle,
>   Riding badly,
> And went with paddle,
>   Looking sadly,
>   In their canoe."

CHAPTER XXXIV.

1798.

WE commence this chapter with an original letter from *Andrew Jackson*, one of the Senators in Congress from the State of Tennessee, to General James Robertson :

"PHILADELPHIA, January 11th, (or 21st,) 1798.

SIR :—Congressional business progresses slowly ; all important questions postponed until we are informed of the result of our negotiation with France.

" The Tennessee memorial has attracted the attention of the two houses for some time. Many difficulties presented themselves, and many delays thrown in the way. Policy dictated to us that the only thing that could strike at the root of opposition, and secure success, was a nomination of Commissioners by the President, for the purpose of holding a treaty with the Cherokees. This was fortunately brought about ; and I believe will have the desired effect. Opposition is on the decline, and I have no doubt but a treaty will be ordered. The Senate agree in the expediency of the measure, but differ with the President in the number of Commissioners necessary. This has occupied the Senate to delay in agreeing to the nomination of the President ; and as those in nomination may be withdrawn, and others presented, I am not at liberty to give you their names.

" It appears to be the wish of the President, by the treaty contemplated, to purchase all the land from the Indians that they will sell ; and I do hope that Tennessee (river) will become the line. When this is completely acted upon by both houses, I will write you more in detail ; and should it be carried into effect, of which I have no doubt, I trust it will be acknowledged that the delegation have done their duty so far as related to that object.

" France has finally concluded a treaty with the Emperor, and the King of Sardinia, and is now turning her force toward Great Britain. Bonaparte, with one hundred and fifty thousand troops, (unused to conquer,) is ordered on the coast, and called the army of England. Do not then be surprised if my next letter should announce a revolution in England. Should Bonaparte make a landing on the English shore, tyranny will be humbled, a throne crushed, and a Republic will spring from the wreck, and millions of distressed people restored to the rights of man by the conquering arm of Bonaparte.

" I am, sir, with sincere respect,
" Your most obedient servant,
ANDREW JACKSON."

Thomas Hardeman, Senator from Davidson County, having resigned his seat in the Assembly, General Robertson was elected to fill his place. Andrew Jackson and Joseph Anderson were Senators in Congress.

By letter to General Robertson from the agent of the United States to the Cherokees, he was urged to attend a council to be held at Tuske-gee, opposite Tellico Block-house, on the 1st of March. Mr. Dinsmore says, "Your presence and influence will be needed, and will be of much service in pacifying them relative to the two Indians killed on Stone's River, about which there will be excited discussion."

The introduction of another letter addressed "to Mr. Robertson and Cumberland," "by Billy Buckles," from " John of Coosa," will be ex-cused as presenting a good specimen of Indian style in conversation and writing, when done by themselves. It seems that Billy Buckles and others wished to hunt and trade near the Cumberland settlements, and brought this letter of introduction and testimonial of good character :

"COOSAW, Aprile 25the days, 1798.
" this winter I hear you see my young people, and telle me, says good man and he people, all good men says.

" and my old cousins, by him name billy Buckles; he want to see you this summer, and deer, he hunt em, and sell meet, says I thinkg 20 or 30 men, all good men.
"You humble servant,
" JOHN O'KELLA, of Coosaw."

"I think a creek Indian, he see you this summer and winter. You see you friend and Sam Bota, he want rifle, rifle gun he want him."

The number of " begging Indians" so increased as to become an annoyance and pest, not much less to be dreaded than when engaged in open war. General Robertson had long suffered from such plagues,

35

as we before mentioned. Benjamin Hawkins, the chief Indian agent, in writing to the General on the 5th of June, says: "I have visited many of the Lower Towns of the Creeks, and I *now begin* to understand their character. They have two blacksmiths furnished to their nation, who have hitherto worked *for nothing,* and they have had a serious debate in a council of the whole nation whether they will accept of them even on those terms. They have been so long accustomed to be courted and caressed by the British agents, that they think they do a favor to a white man, when they condescend to accept of clothes and food when they are naked and starving." If they have received hospitality, food, or clothing from any benevolent person, they send the report through the nation, that all others may go and beg, or rather demand, similar articles from the same person. General Robertson had his experiences of this kind years before this, and for years after this.

Another conference with the Indians was proposed. Governor Sevier wrote to General Robertson and urged his attendance at the treaty. He gave assurances, on the 6th of May, that he would attend if his health should justify the journey. Governor Sevier, Governor Blount, and many of the people of Tennessee, distrusted the disposition of some of the Commissioners appointed on the part of the United States Government to use all proper and strenuous exertions in obtaining a relinquishment of Indian titles to lands which it was believed the Indians had repeatedly sold, and the possession of which was essential to the growing population of the State.*

The Commissioners appointed by the United States were Alfred Moore, George Walton, and John Steele. The meeting of these Commissioners

---

* *Extract of a letter from the Agents on the part of this State, to the Commissioners on the part of the United States, dated Tellico, near the Treaty Ground, July 12th,* 1798.

"Gentlemen:—It has been stated that some citizens of Tennessee had been engaged in either embarrassing your negotiations with the Cherokees, or exercising some influence calculated to interrupt the success of those measures which your duties, and the happiness of the people we represent, equally rendered necessary to accomplish.

"On us it has been imposed as a duty to inquire into the authority of this report, to the end that (if founded) such characters may be held up to the deserved execration of their country, the just reward of conduct replete with so many mischiefs to the community. Should their measures be so cautiously guarded as to place them beyond the reach of legal severity, (or if otherwise,) that unworthy suspicions may not attach to the innocent and the deserving.

with the Cherokees was regarded with so much interest and concern, and as of so much importance to Tennessee, that Governor Sevier appointed three agents to attend the meeting, to protect and promote the interests

---

" In this instance the authority of the charge against the citizens inculpated stands highly vouched, having issued from your secretary, Doctor Hall, of whose talents we think much too favorably to suppose it possible he should have hazarded the charge on vague and unauthorized report, or that it would have been communicated but with your approbation.

" Under this impression, it has been required of us to obtain the names thus implicated, and, if not incompatible with your duties, to solicit the data on which this charge was founded.

" We have the honor to be, gentlemen, most respectfully,

"Your obedient humble servants,

(Signed)   "JAMES ROBERTSON,

"JAMES STUART,

" LACHLAN M'INTOSH.

"Alfred Moore, Geo. Walton, and ⎫
    John Steele, Esquires,   ⎬

" Commissioners on the part of the United States, for holding a treaty with the Cherokees."

THE ANSWER.

" The Commissioners of the United States present their respects to the agents of the State of Tennessee, and in acknowledging the receipt of their favor yesterday, they beg leave to assure them that they have neither received, made, nor authorized any charge of the nature the agents mention, respecting any citizens of Tennessee.

" (The Honorable)

" JAMES ROBERTSON,

" JAMES STUART, and

" LACHLAN M'INTOSH,

"Agents of the State of Tennessee, to attend the Cherokee Treaty.

" Tellico, July 13th, 1798."

" I do certify that the foregoing is a true copy taken from the file, of the original letter of the agents on the part of the State of Tennessee, to the Commissioners and their answer.

"JOHN SMITH, Treaty Secretary to the Agency."

CIRCULAR.

" By the answer of Mr. Parrington to the inquiry of Major M'Intosh, and the note signed Campbell, to Mr. Parrington, bearing date August 1st, 1798, and pubof the State. These persons were James Robertson, James Stuart, and Lachlin McIntosh, all or either of whom possessed more knowledge of Indian character, Indian troubles, Indian traditions, Indian treaties, and

lished in the Genius of Liberty, No. 9, it appears that David Campbell, the same who is one of the Judges of the Superior Court of law and equity, is the author of the piece published in No. 8 of the same paper, under the signature of 'the committee of suffering citizens who have been inquiring into the causes of the failure of the treaty;' it then appears that Judge Campbell, of his own accord, unauthorized by any person, is the author of a piece handed to the public under authority of *the committee of suffering citizens.*' To speak in the gentlest terms of such conduct in Judge Campbell, it must be called a very unjustifiable liberty taken with the persons whose authority he assumed, and a gross imposition upon those to whom it was addressed. To such persons as are well acquainted with the Judge or his writings, nothing further is necessary to prove how little respect is due to either; but to such as are not in that situation, it is judged proper to offer the following state of facts, with some observations respecting the conduct of the agents of Tennessee in writing to the Commissioners of the United States the letter of the 12th of July, a copy of which is hereto annexed. It is not the object of the writer to reply to any other part of the Judge's writings.

"Shortly before the late attempts of negotiation commenced at Tellico Blockhouse, between the Commissioners on the part of the United States and the Cherokees, Mr. Hall, (commonly called Doctor Hall,) the secretary to the Commissioners, came directly from Tellico to Knoxville on official business, as was presumed, and whatever he reported respecting the prospects of the approaching treaty could only be understood as authorized or countenanced by them. Secretary Hall, (for in that character he was,) during his stay in Knoxville, took occasion to give people with whom he conversed to understand that citizens of Tennessee had been taking measures to prevent the success of the approaching negotiation, and designated some of those to whom he alluded. One of the persons thus designated by letter to the agents, to wit : General Robertson, James Stuart, Speaker of the House of Representatives, and Major M'Intosh, of Knoxville, requesting them to embrace some means, during the negotiation at Tellico, to inquire what foundation there was for the report spread by Secretary Hall to the injury of the citizens of Tennessee—a report not only injurious to the particular citizens whom he had been pleased to designate, but to the State generally : the agents accordingly, duly impressed with the importance of exonerating the State from so injurious a charge, if false, or, if true, to fix upon the individuals who were guilty, on the 12th of July addressed a letter on the subject to the Commissioners of the United States, which they showed to the Governor, who was at Tellico, and approved it, a copy of which has been published in the Genius of Liberty, No. 6, together with their answers, both of which are hereto annexed for the better information of readers—especially such as have not had an opportunity to see the paper in which they were before published. The two afford a complete proof that the charges of Secretary Hall were not founded in truth. Thus, the agents, by their prompt and proper conduct, under the eye of and sanctioned by the Governor, obtained an unequivocal exculpation from the Commissioners of the United

Indian boundaries, than these men would have learned had they lived to the age of Methuselah, and remained without the teaching of these " Masters in Israel."

It is by no means unusual, when any great measure is engrossing public attention, to find "busy-bodies, tattlers, and blockheads" thrusting themselves forward, presuming to represent themselves as very wise and serviceable. Persons with high-sounding titles, and commissions from the

---

States—not of an individual only, but of all the citizens of Tennessee, from the malevolent and false charge of their secretary, Hall. The reader is desired to take notice, these charges were spread by Secretary Hall, who rode post-haste from Philadelphia to seek the office: had they been disseminated by Elisha J. Hall, they would not have deserved nor received the notice of the agents. The agents took up the inquiry not merely at the request of an aspersed individual, by a confidential servant of the Commissioners, and in which, if they had, there was nothing but what was highly proper, but by the authority of the Governor, the guardian of all the citizens. Not in behalf of an individual citizen only, but in behalf of all and every citizen, can any person say, upon this state of facts, the truth of which is vouched for, that it was not the duty of the agents to have made the inquiry they did? They made it as was their duty, and the result is that the falsehood and malevolence of Secretary Hall, and the innocence of the citizens of Tennessee, is proved; yet in the eyes of Judge Campbell this appears to be a mighty offence!! Can Judge Campbell be offended at the innocence of the citizens of Tennessee, or ought it to be cause of offence to a judge that Secretary Hall is convicted of a malicious falsehood propagated to their injury!! To every citizen of common sense it will be cause of exultation. The Judge, in one of his pieces, to wit, that signed the committee, etc., says, 'and the agents addressing the Commissioners on the subject, (alluding to Secretary Hall's injurious aspersions,) is certainly a novelty in the annals of history.' Let those who best know the extent of the Judge's reading *in any thing*, determine how capable he is of discovering *novelties* in history. Can it be novel that the agents of a State representing all the people thereof, and acting under the immediate eye and approbation of the Governor, their common guardian, should attempt and actually succeed in obtaining from the Commissioners of the United States an unequivocal declaration of the innocence of all the citizens of Tennessee, of the malicious charge of their secretary? He, certainly, for the Commissioners, owed it to themselves, to their characters as gentlemen, and to their public situation, to make the declaration they did, since it was true, and no doubt rejoiced in the opportunity afforded them by the agents of so doing. To redress injured innocence is a godlike act. The Governor, the agents, and the Commissioners have deserved well of their country, but it is left to the reader to apply appropriate terms to the conduct of Secretary Hall and Judge Campbell. If Judge Campbell or Secretary Hall wish to know the name of the author, for any personal purpose, and so declare, the printer is authorized to give it to either of them, but to nobody else, as none else can apply but from sheer curiosity.

"August 25th, 1798."

President and Congress, sometimes "put on airs," and desire to be courted.

Some correspondence and publications took place in July of this year, of a very angry character. A Doctor Hall so pushed himself into affairs which did not concern him, that both Governor Sevier and Governor Blount ordered suits against him, desiring, as they stated, a "legal investigation into all their official acts, rather than to recover damages from such a quack." General Sevier himself was implicated, and made a publication. But Hall disappeared, and so soon "vanished into airy nothings" the statements he had made. Hall hastened home to Philadelphia. They said he did not belong there, but, like another fellow, "went to his own place." We need not concern ourselves further with the paper warfare.

"The great document" produced on the occasion is one which belongs to these sketches, and to the life and character of General Robertson. We commend it to the perusal of the student of Indian history, and to all the citizens of Tennessee, or admirers of the character of General Robertson. The copy before us is *not perfect*, and we know of none other in existence.*

"MONDAY, July the 9th, 1798.

"The agents, feeling considerable doubt of the result of pending negotiations terminating well, in the manner they had been and were likely to continue to be conducted, transmitted a second communication to the Commissioners of this morning, to the following effect:

"TELLICO, (near the Treaty-ground,) July 19th, 1798.

"GENTLEMEN :—In our last, announcing to you our arrival at the seat of negotiation between the United States, on the one part, and the Cherokee Indians on the other, we stated our earnest desire to forward, by every means in our power, the objects of your mission.

"In conformity to this engagement, we have now the honor of laying before you, so far as it may be gathered from the best sanctioned authorities, a true state of the claim of that tribe or nation to lands owned by the inhabitants of Tennessee.

"We request you to believe that we do not mean to call in question your sincere disposition to extinguish such claim, as far as may be effected, yet we deem it a duty to show the operation of contract, aided by the force of moral obligation on the Government, to release from the

---

* 1858. The Tennessee Historical Society has received a copy, by which we fill a few blanks.

use claimed by the Indians, all lands held by the citizens of the United States, and lying within the limits of the State of Tennessee, whether founded on entry, right, grant, or otherwise, originating under the laws of North Carolina.

"In the first place, it will appear by reference to such documents as can alone throw light on the subject, that the Cherokees, until a very recent date, never had, nor affected to have, a claim on any lands north of the Tennessee, in proof of which we beg leave to cite to you the deposition of Colonel George Croghan, a copy of which we enclose. This gentleman resided nearly thirty years among the Indians, in the character of Deputy Superintendent, and seems to have possessed more general knowledge of the state of their claims, and the history of their wars, than any other who has been drawn into public observation. It is, perhaps, not unworthy of remark, that the point intended to be established by this deposition, at the time it was taken, was wholly different in its nature from that to which it is now applied. And therefore the deponent must be deemed free from any bias, as it respects the present question, that might even, with the best intentions, have swayed the mind to give a coloring to truth. By this deposition it appears that the Six Nations claimed all the lands on the south-east side of the Ohio, down to the Cherokee River, which they ceded at the Treaty of Fort Stanwix, held by Commissioners on the part of His Britannic Majesty with them, November, 1768. An incident which took place at that treaty, and of which proof might be adduced, affords conclusive evidence of the sense entertained by the Cherokees of that claim the Six Nations were then about to surrender. We beg leave to state the fact, although we mean to rely on documents only. Some visiting Cherokees at the treaty had, on their route, killed game for their support, and on their arrival at Fort Stanwix, they immediately tendered the skins to the Indians of the Six Nations, saying, 'They are yours; we killed them after we passed the Big River.' The Cherokees have always designated the Tennessee by this name. But to return. The Treaty of Fort Stanwix passed away from the Six Nations (the sole sovereigns of the soil) all their rights south-east of the Ohio, and down to the Cherokee River, which, to use the language they have recorded in that transaction, '*is their just right*,' and vested the soil and sovereignty completely in the British King. The war that followed between Great Britain and the United States, and its consequences, the inchoate right of conquest in the latter, and this right, were made perfect by the Treaty of 1783, which acknowledged their independence, confirming to each of the States engaged in that controversy the complete sovereignty and soil within the bounds originally assigned them (as) colonial establishments.

"Thus it appears that this formidable claim, destructive of the best interests of the people of Tennessee, is a mere nugatory sound. Yet admit, for a moment, they might consider the delay of settlement as an abandonment of right, either in the State within whose limits this tract is situated, or in the United States, on which a right of occupancy might take root, and by possession become perfect in them. We will examine this right independent of the claim and cession of the Six Nations before stated, and in this examination we believe their every right will shrink into a mere usufructuary of particular limits. At present, however, our objects go no farther than the River Tennessee.

"Their traditionary account of their tribe or nation is, that they are conquerors of the first possessors, and not the aborigines of the soil. We will suppose the abandonment of the conquered tribe the evidence necessary to perfect the title; perhaps it is the only one to be relied on in unlettered and savage negotiations. Their right, therefore, (of their own showing,) is that of conquest, which, always originating in violence, is yet acknowledged perfect among nations, where such right is secured to the conqueror by treaty, at the close of the war.

"These are principles that we believe will not be controverted; and if they are not, they will be found to operate conclusively to the destruction of the entire fabric of the Cherokee claim, as founded on right, leaving open for discussion the question of convenience only, as to the bounds by which they may in future be limited. And we now solicit your indulgence to the recapitulation of some historical facts respecting the Cherokees, which, though universally known, have not (we believe) heretofore been applied to the present controversy: from which, however, we deduce principles carrying with them all the force of moral obligation binding on the Government, to ripen into occupancy the rights the people of Tennessee hold to all lands north of that river.

"At and for a length of time previous to the commencement of the Revolutionary War, the Cherokees were an *appendage* of the British Government, regulating, it is true, the little internal policy of the tribe within themselves. But all their external connections were moulded to the wish of ministers appointed to superintend their interests; and they fought or negotiated as instructed by the agents of that power. We believe it unnecessary to call your attention to features that characterize the dependence of nations, satisfied that we have it fully in our power to develop them by recital in the present case. When the contest became serious between Great Britain and the then associated Colonies, the Cherokees were found arranged as parties in the war on the side of the first—not in the predatory mode usual in Indian warfare, but *levies* were made and *regular enlistments* carried on in the interior of the nation, composing companies, officers, and privates, altogether Cherokees. Which companies were attached to Brown's British regiment of Florida Rangers, receiving the *same pay*, subject to similar regulations with other troops in the service of His Britannic Majesty; the Colonel of which regiment was the Superintendent of their affairs. We know not what further is necessary to establish the doctrine of *appendants*, in a national sense; and if we admit this, the following consequences will inevitably result : that their nation or tribe having embarked as parties with and appendages to the British nation in the war, *they had risked every right on the issue.* And expulsion of the principal from the limits of the United States, established in the latter that inchoate right derived from conquest, coëxtensive with the limits so obtained, unless where restricted by particular compact. And we believe no restriction of this kind exists favorable to the Cherokee claim. What remains necessary to complete the entire prostration of even the semblance of right in them, and to perfect the title in the several States within whose bounds they hold a use, is found in the unequivocal language of the definitive treaty with Great Britain.

"It may, however, by possibility be denied that they were an appendage of the British Government, notwithstanding the proofs that have been adduced. We mean not altogether to rest upon this, but shall now proceed to examine their rights as an independent nation; in which light they will be found to settle still into mere *temporary* use, founded on *indulgence.*

"And to this end, we shall be compelled to call your attention again to the early periods of the Revolutionary War, and the repeated invasions of the frontiers of the four Southern States by the Cherokees. Their depredations, continuing throughout the year 1775, and part of 1776, compelled the United States at length to turn their attention to them. The invasion of their country was meditated and effected. A powerful force was ordered on this service, and they entered the Cherokee country, in the autumn of 1776, by four different routes. One of the divisions, commanded by Col. Christian, consisting of one thousand eight hundred men, crossed the Tennessee, at the Virginia Ford, (near Fort Loudon,) to the south side, and there destroyed the towns of Toquo, Temotle, the Island Towns, the Little Carpenter's Town, and Coyatee, whose strength, as then estimated by persons best acquainted with them, was from eight hundred to one thousand warriors. He then marched to the beloved town of Chota, which he spared, continuing thence until he received the submission of those and a number of other towns.

"A second army, commanded by Brigadier-General Rutherford, and consisting of two thousand four hundred men, passed the French Broad at the mouth of the Swana-noe, and from thence penetrated, by the route since distinguished as Rutherford's Trace, into the nation, to the midst of their settlements and valley towns, carrying devastation into the interior of their nation. They destroyed thirty-six towns and villages, cutting up and wasting the growing and gathered corn, and driving off or destroying at will their flocks.

"A third division, commanded by Col. Williamson, and consisting of a powerful force, penetrated the settlements bordering on the Keowee, and destroyed the Seneca towns, at that time very numerous, wasting the Cherokee country as far as the Unaka Mountain, sparing or destroying towns at his will.

"A fourth division, under Col. Leonard Macbury, entered the settlements on the Tugaloe, and, having defeated the Indians, destroyed all their towns on that river.

"Thus an entire conquest was effected in the course of a few months, in the autumn of 1776, of the whole Cherokee country. And thus the right it bestows, obtained by the arms of the United States, extends to every village of the nation. All, therefore, that remained to perfect this title in the conqueror, was the submission or abandonment in the first possessor by treaty at the close of the war. And that this was done, we proceed to show.

"Waiving submission to individual States or their officers, we shall take a point at which the United States were represented in their national character on the one part, and the Cherokees, in full assemblage of their tribe or nation, on the other.

"The first treaty held by the United States with the Cherokees, after the conquest we have stated, was at Hopewell, on the Keowee, bearing date November, 1785. In this instrument we shall find every right of the nation or tribe merged in the mere use, and this use specially appointed. The language of the treaty is: 'The Commissioners Plenipotentiary give peace to all the Cherokees, and receive them into the *favor* and *protection* of the United States, on the following conditions.' On these conditions, therefore, we rest the proof of that position we have taken, without trespassing on your time by comments on the language, which is unequivocally that of *victors* to the *vanquished*. We shall show an express surrender of all the rights of sovereignty, and no less explicitly of soil.

"Article third of the Hopewell treaty is to this effect: 'The said Indians, (speaking of the Cherokees,) for themselves and their respective tribes and towns, do acknowledge themselves under the protection of the United States of America, and of *no other sovereign whatsoever.*'

"In consideration of this surrender, the United States grant to the Cherokees, 'FOR HUNTING-GROUND,' certain boundaries designated by the treaty. The power (or right of granting) thus conceded, settles all controversies respecting right, and points indubitably to him in whom it is vested. Neither the language of treaties nor of reason affords us terms more definite, or which more fully define the several objects each of the parties held in view, than those used on this occasion. The Cherokees, yet in the hunter-state of society, required an extensive scope. They had, by repeated aggressions, drawn on their nation that war which terminated in their entire conquest, without hope but in the clemency of the conqueror. They exchange rights for the usufruct; and this use they accept indiscriminately, on bounds over which, prior to the surrender, their rights did most unquestionably run; and also of limits which, as has been shown, they have no other claim on, either as derived from nature, from conquest, or usucaption.

"The United States, advanced in improvement, rich in the extent of her limits, and rapidly increasing in population, having secured, in terms too obvious to be misconceived, every right thus acquired, yields the use until her growing settlements, or an interference with the personal rights of her citizens, might render it necessary that it be restrained within narrower bounds; and for this reason we find the duration of such use undefined.

"A short recapitulation of what has been shown, will afford this result: that the claim of the Cherokees, as founded on right, is limited by the Tennessee River; that within those limits such right is not original, but acquired; and that, whether they are considered as an appendage of the British Government or an independent nation, the right of conquest is equally operative, and their abandonment in the one and submission in the other treaty, at the close of the war, resolves every right into the use before stated, founded on indulgence only.

"By recurrence to dates we shall find, that at the time this surrender was made by the Cherokees, each State retained an undiminished sovereignty, neither acknowledging nor admitting of any paramount power within her limits; and though associated for mutual defence, yet associated under this restriction: 'That no State be deprived of Territory for the benefit of the United States,' nor 'the legislative right of any State, within its own limits, be infringed or violated.' Of course, then,

right, one of those requiring no succession of events to accomplish, but complete once for all and perfect on the spot; and thus, when valid, carried with it an irrevocable and unalterable effect. For we find the State of North Carolina . . . . immediately passing portions of them to individuals. Thus she placed them beyond the reach of reclamation, while she held the Union under its then existing form, the guaranty of title.

"We would not be understood to deny the right of the United States to acquire lands in any part of America, or of the world; and, when not within the bounds of some one of the States, *to revert that right*, however acquired, fully to the first possessor. On the contrary, we should feel the exercise of such power to be at all times the proper subject of diplomatic negotiation. But surely it will not be contended that this may be done on the fair extinction of that subordinate claim, held by the Indians on the soil, *within* the chartered limits of the several States, without first rescinding that part of our fundamental laws which inhibits such construction of the powers of Government as shall prejudice the claims of the individual States.

"We beg you to believe we possess entire confidence in your desire to do away any difficulty, and accredit us, that our warmest wishes for success are attendant on your exertions.

"Accept our respects:

"JAMES ROBERTSON,
"JAMES STUART,
"LACHLIN M'INTOSH.

"Alfred Moore, George Walton, and John Steele, Esquires, Commissioners on the part of the United States, for holding a treaty with the Cherokees."

DEPOSITION OF COLONEL GEORGE CROGHAN.

"George Croghan, being duly sworn on the Holy Evangelists of Almighty God, doth depose and say, that the Six Nations claim, by right of conquest, all the lands on the south-east side of the river Ohio down to the Cherokee River, and the west side of the Ohio down to the Big Miamis River, (otherwise called Stony River,) and that the Six Nations never had a claim of any kind, or made any claim, to lands below the Big Miamis or Stony River, on the west side of the Ohio; but that the lands on the west side of the Ohio, below Stony River, were always supposed to belong to the Indians of the Western Confederacy. That (Colonel Croghan, the deponent) has for thirty years been intimately acquainted with the above country and the Indians and their different claims to territory; and never heard the Six Nations claim, and knows they never did claim, beyond the above description, nor did they ever dispute the claim of the Western Confederacy.

"And further saith not.

"GEORGE CROGHAN.

"Sworn to the 20th October, 1781, before me, John Miller.

"By this deposition of Colonel Croghan, it appears that all the land *north* of the *Tennessee* belonged to the Six Nations; consequently it *cannot* belong to the Cherokees."

We have mentioned that the Treaty of Holston yielded the claims of the white people to such an extent of territory as caused surprise and dissatisfaction; that it was done under peculiar circumstances and in the vain hope of peace; that it so reduced the territory on the Cumberland as to encourage the Indians in the attempt to annihilate such small settlements. It was subsequently seen and admitted to have been an error in judgment and a wrong in fact.

We know not the character of the United States Commissioners very particularly; but it certainly is not surprising that the people of this State felt the greatest anxiety in these negotiations, nor that intelligent and influential citizens should have been appointed to be present at the treaty. Indeed, we think Governor Sevier would have been very remiss, had he not appointed suitable persons to attend. And, indeed, we should have supposed the United States Commissioners would have rejoiced to meet with such citizens there, giving attention to the negotiation; men, in every accomplishment, certainly their equals, and in some, greatly their superiors.

But so it happened, that the presence of agents from the State of Tennessee, in the opinions of some persons, derogated from the character and dignity of Commissioners on the part of the United States. The idea of "two sets of Commissioners," greatly troubled somebody. One of the United States Commissioners is spoken of as "the most lofty, imperious blockhead who ever filled so important a position;" and that the treaty progressed and resulted favorably "more from the *good sense* of the Indians than the wisdom and good conduct of the Commissioners of the United States."

There can be no doubt that the presence of Generals Robertson and Sevier contributed greatly to whatever promises and prospects of favorable results arose from these interviews with the Indians. These men understood in what way to touch the secret springs in the Indian character, and how, wisely, to deal with them, in the attainment of important ends. And it became very evident, at an early day in the conferences, that if the "utterances of Doctor Hall," their Secretary, were reliable indications of the qualifications and dispositions of the United States Commissioners, the people of Tennessee had nothing valuable to hope from any treaty which should be made through their agency.

We have a word to say in regard to the indifference so often manifested by General Robertson about pay or compensation for his services. He expressed upon this, as upon other occasions, utter unconcern; and to an intimation from some injudicious youth who perhaps had taken his "cue" from the consequential Doctor Hall, "Some men can always have office and pay," he replied: "If there are persons who *desire* any office ever conferred here, *for the sake of pay*, they ought to die of starvation on that foolish desire."

The question will be asked, Who was the author of this "Great Argument?" Who was the man possessed of such evident legal ability and learning as are evinced in this communication? To us, there appear many indications of the presence and work of Governor Blount and General Sevier. The principal facts, traditions, and pretensions of Indian title were familiar to General Robertson; he had discussed them frequently with Indian chiefs, and his friends in the settlements. That he and General Sevier were present, suggesting and aiding in the preparation of the document, we are confident. We do not claim for either of them the entire composition. Two copies may be seen in the State Historical Society. "The Journal of the Agents," whose names are attached to it, is yet in possession of the worthy writer of the "Annals of Tennessee," and the Argument is copied therein.

The United States Commissioners acknowledged the ability evident in the paper, but regarded much of its contents as irrelevant to the purposes and interests of their negotiation. They said it would be their duty and pleasure to transmit it to the Government.

This set of commissioners agreed upon no terms for a treaty. Another meeting was held, and the treaty of 20th September resulted. The United States Commissioners were George Walton and Thomas Butler. McIntosh and Stuart had resigned, and General Robertson could not attend; therefore General White was appointed to attend on behalf of Tennessee.

CHAPTER XXXV.

1799–1805.

AT the close of the last chapter we had occasion to mention the contempt which General Robertson entertained of all mercenary motives in any of the services which he rendered to the country : it is suitable to give further proof of it, as it was manifested in the early part of this year.

It seems that in the year 1797, he had furnished two parties of Chickasaws with provisions, ammunition, and clothing; that he gave to one "a big coat," to another "a coat," to one "a horse," to several "articles of different kinds," etc.; and says of these Indians : "Although they know that I am no more authorized than any other person to supply them, yet they *fixed themselves on me*, and *here they stick*. All such trouble and personal services I may be able to render my country, will be fully compensated if my conduct meet with approbation." Such was General Robertson ! such his heart, his life, his character !

General Washington, unequalled, unapproachable in the grandeur of his character, and in the consecration of his services to the great cause of American liberty, was not alone in possession of this pure, disinterested, self-sacrificing spirit.

In the settlement of some of General Wilkinson's accounts, these advances by General Robertson were made known, and brought into the accounts at the Treasury Department, in 1799, and were settled, and without his application.

Another instance occurs which we may mention : In the year 1795 (as has been related) he furnished corn to the Chickasaws and Choctaws, the accounts for which he did not render. But in December, 1804, he was induced to have his accounts verified by the depositions of Col. Henley, (Indian Agent,) and by other persons, and forwarded to the accountant's office of the War Department. It could not be allowed at so late a day, and the Secretary advised a petition to Congress for a special act for compensation. We doubt if he ever troubled himself or others with this matter at any period thereafter.

In the adjustment of accounts for military services, and in the investigations and settlement of the many questions arising from early transac-

36

tions among the settlers upon the Cumberland, the presence, testimony, and opinions of General Robertson were often required. He, Smith, Jackson, Weakley, Davis, Edmonson, Ewing, and others of the early settlers, yet lived to give such testimony, and to act frequently as umpires in disputes about land-titles, boundaries, and other matters. The intelligence and weight of character of such men were of incalculable service to the community. They had the knowledge and firmness which were requisite, and which justified them in speaking in an authoritative tone. The extent to which society is now indebted to them on this account cannot be computed.

During the years 1799 and 1800, "political questions" were discussed more earnestly among the Cumberland settlers than at any former period. General Robertson never had any necessity to seek for office; he hunted not after fame; he was always (and, as his friends often said, strangely) averse to mention his own services. Never would he speak disparagingly of the services of others; there was no place in his enlarged soul for jealousy or envy; he loved to tell what others did in early times. Although decided in his political sentiments, he was no rabid or brawling politician, nor did he sanction political enmities.

At this date the institution of learning at Nashville occupied much of his attention. The population of the town was on the increase, and many of the new settlers had sons whom they desired to have educated.

Joseph Anderson and Daniel Smith were the Senators in Congress from Tennessee. General Smith received the executive appointment to fill the vacancy occasioned by resignation of Andrew Jackson.

The exciting political questions of the day arose upon the alien and sedition laws, and relations with France. A people so independent in manners and habits were certain to discuss all such questions "without fear, favor, or affection." Their thoughts and opinions had life in them; they spread their wings to the breeze, and every man's sentiments were known to his neighbor.

Here and in Kentucky the political friends of Jefferson were very active, and they greatly rejoiced at their success. The controversy waxed fiercely from the time of the election of John Adams by the House of Representatives until it became certain that Jefferson had received the popular vote for the next term.

These discussions brought forth a multitude of politicians in Tennessee, "too numerous to mention." The theatre for action is rapidly enlarged; the ramifications and interests of society are greatly extended; and events and actors are too nearly connected with our own day to be brought into the prescribed limits of our work.

CIRCULAR.

KNOXVILLE, September 22, 1799.

SIR :—Impressed by our duty, as Representatives, to convey to our constituents all the information connected with the object of our delegation that comes within our notice, we are under the necessity of making use of printed letters as the only mode by which that information can be generally diffused.

The attention of the Legislature has, as yet, been occupied by matters of private or local concern. Nothing of moment that has a general influence has, as yet, been done, except the qualification of his Excellency, John Sevier, as Governor for the ensuing term of two years, and the re-election of William Maclin, Esq., as Secretary of State, and Landon Carter and Robert Searcy, Esqrs., as Treasurers.

The Report of the Committee of Finances, relative to the Treasury Department of Mero District, for your information, is hereto subjoined :

DAVIDSON COUNTY.—Amount of taxes on lands, white and black polls, town-lots, stud-horses, and billiard-tables, for 1797 and 1798, $2426 39. Paid into the Treasury, $2064 22. Balance due, $362 07. Amount arising from probate of deeds, from October 1st, 1797, until January, 1799, paid in by the Clerk, $165. Amount arising from ordinary licenses and law process, $146 87½. Amount arising from original grants and deeds in same period, $116 87½.

SUMNER COUNTY.—Amount of taxes on lands, white and black polls, etc., $2365 95. Paid into the Treasury, $1988 95. Balance due, $377. Amount from probate of deeds and law process, $342 12½. Amount paid in by Register for 1797, $96 25.

ROBERTSON COUNTY.—Amount of taxes on lands, polls, town-lots, stud-horses, $715 24. Paid into Treasury, $504. Balance due, $211 24. Amount from probate of deeds, etc., $61 54. Amount from deeds and grants to October, 1797, and paid in, $13 12½.

MONTGOMERY COUNTY.—Amount of taxes on lands, polls, town-lots, stud-horses, etc., $1197 91. Paid in, $566 76. Balance due, $631 15.

Amount received by Robert Searcy, Esq., Treasurer, $6420 60. Amount accounted for per vouchers filed, $6442 85.

Whatever information shall hereafter occur, worthy of notice, we shall communicate.   Your humble servants,

R. WEAKLEY,
JOEL LEWIS,
WM. DICKSON,
GEO. M. DEADERICK,
WILLIAM NEELLY.

There was no necessity for "another academy" in the town, yet political sentiments had some influence in an effort to establish the "Federal Academy." This was an ephemeral institution, and soon merged in Davidson Academy, or Cumberland College.

The great companies of emigrants were impatient of the narrow limits to which the settlements were yet confined. The citizens of the State became anxious for the Indian claim to lands within the limits of the State to be extinguished. The discussions and publications which took place at the Treaty of Tellico, July, 1798, and especially the "great argument" of General Robertson, Stuart, and McIntosh, produced entire unanimity of sentiment among the people in regard to the right of the State to all the lands which had been yielded to the Cherokees at Holston. The opinion now prevailed that the Cherokees had *no right*—that if we should have purchased of any one of the Indian tribes, it should have been of the Chickasaws. But many disclaimed all right, title and claim of any of the tribes of Indians, insisting that they should rather be considered "tenants at will," roving hunters by sufferance, and never the owners of the soil. They were not even *nomads*.

These ideas had been presented by General Robertson and others, but in the year 1804, (to which date we may descend without the charge of having overlooked or omitted any matter of importance,) there appears another advocate, learned and decided, of these views. This is *Return J. Meigs*, who had received the appointment of Indian Agent, and took up his residence near the Cherokees at South-west Point, from which place he addressed a letter to General Robertson, under date 21st December, 1804. Portions of this letter we consider to be so clear and satisfactory, that we shall quote them without apology. It seems that General Robertson had written to Colonel Meigs three letters, (two in November and one in December,) in which he had presented his views of this Indian question. In his letter of 11th December the General had furnished "a copy of the instrument from President Washington, under the seal of the United States, acknowledging the *Chickasaw* claim to lands on the north side of the Tennessee," pointing out the boundaries, and pledging protection of the same to them.

General Robertson, Colonel Meigs, and others, now resolved to make good use of this instrument, and *under it* (if they could not prevail by the title from conquest and right of sovereignty) they resolved to gain a title, which the government itself should also "guarantee" to Tennessee.

There was science in this counsel of General Robertson; there was ability and skill in Meigs and others who came to the advocacy. But to these extracts:

"I thank you, sir, for all the exertions you have made in procuring the wished-for information. I am now satisfied that the Chickasaws have an undoubted right to sell those lands, and am fully convinced that there was an error at that early period in the treaties at Hopewell and Holston, *in ceding* a great part of these lands to the Cherokees.

"At that time accurate information was with difficulty obtained of the rights of the Indian tribes. The clashing of their claims may give some trouble to the United States; but we must make the best arrangements we can, and do justice to both parties.

"The Chickasaws had better sell their right as soon as they can; for until this is done the Cherokees will talk about their claim. When the sale is made, there will be an end to the extravagant claim of the Cherokees.

"The more I reflect on this business, the more I am convinced that the Cherokees have no just claim or right to these lands.

"When I first came to this agency, the Cherokees sometimes called this land theirs; at other times they called it the 'Middle Hunting-Grounds,' the 'Hunting-grounds of the Four Nations,' etc. Their conduct for several years past indicates that they are doubtful of the validity of their claim. They have but recently had a few settlements on any part of this land. The settlement made by Double-Head was, I believe, projected by the Cherokees as an essay 'to try their title.'

"The Cherokee chiefs once sent to me a *remonstrance* against our garrison placed at *Bear Creek:* this was another essay to try their title. I sent them the treaty held in 1786 with the *Chickasaws* at Hopewell, showing the grant of a place for a garrison or trading-post. *This silenced them;* and they have never since opened their mouth to me on the subject! All these circumstances confirm me that they have only partial claim, at most, for any part of that land.   .   .   .

"I wish (to save expense) that we could have assurances that the Chickasaws will sell; at all events, we ought to have a treaty. . . . . I concur in the opinion expressed in your letter of 11th instant: 'The purchase of the Chickasaws will hasten the extinguishment of the Cherokee claim to the lands between East and West Tennessee.' If the Chickasaw chiefs should make a visit to the seat of government, which you mention as about to take place, perhaps the cession will be made there; but this is uncertain, and I think a treaty should be called in the spring."

(He presents arguments to be urged upon Congress to make an appropriation for such a treaty.)

"The purchase of that land will much relieve a great number of persons who have invested their money in those lands, and who are justly looking up to the Government for an extinguishment of the Indian title."

A memorial was forwarded to Congress from the Legislature of Tennessee, urging an extinguishment of these Indian claims, and the policy was then INITIATED of giving the Indians lands on the west side of the Mississippi, in exchange for those on which they hunted here. (See Report in favor of Tennessee Memorial.)

The services of General Robertson were required as usual in the preparations for these negotiations, and at the conferences or treaties.

The Cherokees were invited to a treaty at Tellico Block-house on 10th October, at which they urged the Chickasaws to be present.

Major George Colbert (a chief of the Chickasaws) was opposed to a sale—unless a reservation should be made in his favor of a tract of land on each side of the Tennessee River, at his ferry. After the departure of General Robertson to the treaty, Colbert and several other chiefs arrived at Nashville, and had an interview with William P. Anderson, Esq., (who had only two days before returned from the Muscle Shoals, where he had been to promote the objects of the proposed treaty.) Colonel Anderson was desired to forward a talk to General Robertson from these Chickasaw chiefs, which was as follows:

"The Cherokees have sent to us a talk, and desired us to attend the present treaty, in order there to investigate their different titles to the disputed territory. Colbert answers, that if the invitation came from the United States it would be attended to. He further says that you, General, know the extent and boundary of their claim; that when the treaty was held at your house it was all talked over, and therefore he hopes you will not now stand by and see the Cherokees do him injustice."

"Double-Head says he is opposed to any sale. He asked me if the Chickasaws would sell their land on this side of the Tennessee; I told him they would: at this he seemed *thunder-struck*.

"It is a fact: the Chickasaws will sell. Keep alive this idea; it will alarm the Cherokees into measures that are right.

"Double-Head is a great *rascal*, and Chisholm and others who dictate to him are no *no better*. . . . All such villains have *their price*, as their own *doom* also awaits them. . . . Keep these ideas to yourself, and mix not my name in it."

These ideas and suggestions were not new to General Robertson; but some of the information thus communicated was of service in future discussions, for at this conference not much of a decided character was attained.

General Robertson now was the more confirmed in the opinion he had entertained and expressed, that they were making use of the right kind of "*thunder*" to frighten the Cherokees, and that it was wise to keep up a constant *report.*

After General Robertson returned home from Tellico, Colonel Meigs and General Smith urged Governor Sevier to write General Robertson to visit the Chickasaws, and to consider well the policy of encouraging the Chickasaws to insist upon their claim to the lands, and "not permit the Cherokees to get all."

General Robertson promptly engaged in this business, or, we should rather say, he *continued* to exert himself for the accomplishment of all the great ends so desirable to his fellow-citizens.

He had interviews and entered into correspondence with some of the Chickasaw chiefs. The original letter in reply, from Chin-nubbe, (King of the nation,) Major George Colbert, Okoye, and Charles, is before us, and, as it contains important historical information, we shall make free quotations therefrom. It is dated "Chickasaw Nation, January 25, 1805."

" If we were disposed to sell that land, we would not sell by whole-sale ; when we sell, it will be by the acre—same as white people sell. It is true the game is scarce; but that is the only place my children and warriors get their living, and hunt.

" You mention that Cherokees and my people joined in war on the Shawnees. We never was : it is not so.

" When the Shawnees first came, they came up the Tennessee, and then up Bear Creek about thirty miles, and there left their canoes, and came to war with the Chickasaws, and killed several of our people.

" The chiefs and warriors of my nation turned out against them, and drove them off. From thence they went to the Creeks, and lived there awhile, and then they returned back, and crossed at the ' Chickasaw Old Field,' above ' Muscle Shoals ;' from thence they went on to Duck River, and Cumberland River, and settled there. The Chickasaws found them out, and two of our principal chiefs in those days, *Opoi Meti-hah* and *Poushy-Metihah,* raised their warriors—went against the Shawnees, and defeated them—took all their horses, and brought them into our na-tion.

" *The Cherokees had no part in the war. We d*:*ove them ourselves,* without any assistance from any red people.

" Some day we will sell that land ; we will let you know."

Here were some rather "hard cases to deal with ;" but " these four did not constitute the nation." And, besides, it was thought that Gen-eral Robertson could " manage even them."

They soon applied to Colonel Meigs and General Robertson to have a road opened from the Cumberland settlements by the Muscle Shoals on to Georgia; and that the white people should have a fort and a settlement somewhere between the Chickasaws and Cherokees, to *preserve peace.* "*This precaution*" was approved by General Robertson and Col. Meigs. The idea *originated* with them.

And thus the leaven was working, and left to work during the remainder of the year 1804, and to swell and rise higher in the year 1805.

CHAPTER XXXVI.

1805.

In March, General Robertson made his preparations to leave home and proceed to the Chickasaw, and thence to the Choctaw nation. He had in view important negotiations. Clothed with authority, a commission and instructions from the War Department, this thoughtful public agent mounted his horse, (accompanied by one servant and a pack-horse,) quit the comforts of home, the endearments of his family, and journeyed through the forests and the cane-brakes to the accomplishment of an object upon which his mind had been intent for the last five-and-twenty years : a purpose to attain which he had studied and toiled long— for which he perilled his life many a time; in the securing of which he had suffered greatly, and witnessed sufferings and sacrifices by others which we have endeavored to record to his and their lasting honor.

His mission was to secure a relinquishment of the Chickasaw claim to Middle Tennessee. He carried with him but few presents. He used none of those artifices too common in negotiations, none of those appliances which corrupt the heart, pervert the judgment, and debase the soul of civilized and savage men. He had no ardent spirits with which to " drug the souls of men ;" his gifts were few and simple, and of little cost. But his own presence, frankness and kindness, and long-known integrity, secured him a kind reception and ready communication with the chiefs and warriors. He was not a stranger among enemies, but a tried friend among those who respected him.

In May he met Mr. Silas Dinsmore, (Indian agent,) who by the Government had been directed to associate with General Robertson in this interview for a treaty. The chiefs and head-men of the Chickasaws came together, and conferences and talks were continued from day to day with these two United States Commissioners, until, on the 23d of July, 1805, they gave a quit-claim and total relinquishment of their title to all lands from the Ohio and mouth of the Tennessee, up the main channel of that river to the mouth of Duck River, up Duck on the left bank to the Col-

selves make intrusions.   Some of your people have expressed a desire to
go where the game is more abundant.   The Shawnees, the Delawares, and
other Indians across the Mississippi, find the game there 'like cattle in
a field, so numerous and so tame.'   From the woods between the Tennessee and Cumberland you and the white people have destroyed or
driven off the buffalo, elk, and deer; from Cumberland to the Ohio 'the
Virginians, with their long knives,' have got entire possession, and it
will be so to the Tennessee."

These negotiators knew the doubtful character of the claims of these
Indians to any of this region, but they "resolved to hush them up for
ever," and they did it.   And in so doing, neither of them can be charged
with deceiving or imposing upon them.   They allowed the compensations
which were asked, and there remained to the hunters their usual ranges
for "fire and still-hunts."

General Robertson remained some time among the Chickasaws, to
secure their good will, and to harmonize all views upon the compact or
treaty of July 23d.   There was, indeed, little or no opposition to that, or
to a sale of their claim.   The point was to obtain as much as they could.
It was, on both sides, the driving of a bargain between parties, one of
whom was anxious to buy and the other to sell.   It cannot, however, be
charged, upon either Robertson or Meigs, that they intended to or did
"drive a hard bargain !"   We have shown that neither of them regarded
the claims of these Indians as of such validity as to be beyond dispute.
Both of them were disputed; had long been in dispute.   Neither had
possession or felt willing to contend with each other with all their force
and to the last extremity for possession.   If it was not neutral ground,
it was so lying waste that a good Providence evidently called for the proper people to step in, take possession, and put an end to the wasting
savage warfares.   The white race was called upon to end this strife.

General Robertson, having accomplished his work among the Chickasaws, proceeded to the Choctaw nation; and there he met with Silas
Dinsmore, the United States Agent in that nation.   General Robertson
was personally known to several of the head-men in this nation.   His
good name had preceded him, and there, as in the Cherokee country, he
was met most cordially.   The tokens of welcome were "shaking of hands,
offering of the pipe, and ten times as much ash-cake, big-hominy, and
mixed meats as he and his party could *stomach*—with squaws' cooking."
He skilfully managed to have his meals prepared by his own cook, and
give no offence.

What one of the company said, we *know* is not the worst slander that
was ever uttered, in regard to "Choctaw" omelets and ollapodrid--

"We do not remember the term or word in Choctaw used to express these 'confounded mixtures;' but whatever it is, it concentrates in its meaning all the essences and all the odors which would make a delicate stomach 'abhor all manner of meats,' and induce one to vow, with St. Paul, that, as these 'brethren offend me with their meats, I will eat no more meat as long as the world standeth, lest I encourage these my brethren to sin.' After one of these dishes, I tried to turn myself inside out, and I came within an inch of doing it, and within half an inch of losing my life."

But there were exceptions; they prepared some really savory and palatable dishes—for a hungry soul.*

After consultation with Mr. Dinsmore and several of the Choctaw chiefs, it was resolved to call an assemblage of the nation, or of the head-men and warriors, to confer about terms of cession of a portion of the Choctaw lands. They agreed to convene at Mount Dexter, (as Dinsmore named the eminence,) in the portion of the country known by the poly-syllabic name of Poo-sha-puk-a-nuk.

Goods were packed to the place of meeting; corn, meat, salt, and con-diments were prepared—shelters and a council-house; and the Indians, with their tykes and their pappooses, came. The result was a relinquish-ment of the Choctaw claim to a large extent of country on the Homo-chitto, and other streams in the Mississippi Territory. This treaty was concluded on the 16th day of November, 1805.

We thus see at what distances, and to what great and valuable pur-poses, General Robertson has been laboring. He did not enter into these treaties and purchases ignorantly; he prepared himself to reply intelli-gently to the many inquiries which he knew would be made of him as to the country thus purchased; he travelled over much of it.

After the accomplishment of the business of that mission, adjusting matters as far as was then possible, and setting in train measures and applying influences which were sure to work out a further cession of lands, General Robertson returned to Nashville, early in August. He thus travelled, going and returning, probably eight hundred miles, be-sides his extensive explorations of the country. But he had to make another journey from Nashville to Poo-sha-puk-a-nuk, and resort to "the influence of such *reasonable* presents [under the authority of a letter

---

* David, the cook, used to say, that "an Indian *omelet* was a mess into which they let all sorts of things drop." We will not repeat his description of a Choc-taw or Chickasaw imitation of the Spanish ollapodrida. It leaves a long disgust of lizards and land-terrapins.

from the Secretary of War] as circumstances might require." He well understood these.

Mr. Dinsmore had written to General Robertson, "The heart of old Puck-shu-nub-be is crooked," and it demanded the skill of General Robertson and "reasonable presents" to "take the kinks out."

A journey to the moon, we have often heard of, but this journey to Poo-sha-puk-a-nuk had reality in it. The way was in the forest, through dense cane-brakes, through low swamps, and across deep bayous, and travelled almost as much by moon as by sunlight, in the hot weather of the season. But yet he was asked to make it a second time in this same year.

Mr. Dinsmore wrote : "Though the fatigue and inconvenience have been great, yet they have not been *the greatest* ever endured by man." General Robertson was accustomed to fatigue and inconvenience, and would not refuse to go again, though, from the "fall which he had some time since received from his horse," he should find it very painful to travel. He thought the distance and wearisomeness of the journey were fully expressed in the Choctaw name, and that, if a meeting could be held at *Poo-sha*, it would be only half the distance to *puk-a-nuk*. He wished to divide the distance and the word. He had, however, to go the whole distance and the entire name, the "*Poo-sha*" and the "*puk-a-nuk*."

He had written to the Secretary of War on 8th August, after his late mission, that he and Mr. Dinsmore were decidedly in favor of holding another treaty with the Choctaws, as they believed them "well disposed to sell a large scope of country on the Alabama and Tombigby Rivers. Expecting to return to the Choctaws, we preferred to keep the Chicka-saw treaty open until fall," (and further instructions from the Govern-ment.) "The Indians desired time for consultation," and "they wish and expect another conference."

But the system of rigid economy which characterized the Administra-tion was strongly opposed to "so many of these Indian treaties !" The Secretary of War (Henry Dearborne) thought it proper to "express some surprise, and to ask an explanation of General Robertson and Mr. Dinsmore, of the items furnished for those treaties. The supplies seem very large where there were only two Commissioners. Some of the articles, one would suppose, must have remained on hand at the close of the treaties, and the Department would respectfully inquire what was done with them ? . . Among *other extraordinary* articles for an *Indian treaty in the woods*, for *two Commissioners*, may be noticed *raisins, an-chovies, cinnamon, nutmegs, pickles*, etc., amounting to near two hundred dollars. . . . The department presumes that the supplies were furnished

under the directions of Mr. Dinsmore, and the only motive for mention-
ing this subject *to you*, sir, is to show that such things do not pass without notice." This letter is addressed to the General, but to give *Silas* a
rap over his friend's shoulders.

These friends had a hearty laugh over this letter of the War Department. They sat down thoughtfully, with great respect and much deliberation, and wrote "an explanation of their *anchovy* and *pickle account*."

The order had been given (as usual at such treaties) to have a supply
of provisions, groceries, and liquors. The contractor was liberal enough
to agree to take back and make allowance for what should not be used.
"But," say the worthy Commissioners, "we claim to be temperate men,
both as to eating and drinking. It is true there were *only two of us*, but
we never had less than twenty-nine at table, and this for many days.
When Indians eat, they eat indeed; and when they drink, they know no
law which says ' enough is enough !'"

Mr. Dinsmore says : "As for myself, I find that, in this climate, a little
wine or brandy is as important in my drink as bread and meat for my
food. We all have good appetites here ' in the woods,' and it would do
the heads of Departments good to see how we relish our meals, seasoned
with cinnamon, anchovies, and pickles. . . . An Indian can eat enough
at one meal to last him a week. Whoever should see Puck-shu-nubbe,
old Mussula-tubbe, old Push-mata-hoy, or a score of these Falstaffs in the
woods at a feast, would suppose they were indeed eating a last meal—one
that they intended should outlast the present moon, and the next show
her horns, and wax and wane; and when they drink, they do it with
hearty good-will."

On the 12th of October, Mr. Dinsmore wrote to General Robertson,
most earnestly urging him to meet him at *Ho-bu-kin-toop-a*, in the
Choctaw nation, for " they are disposed to sell a larger scope of country
than we had asked of them ! We must meet their present liberal disposition. I believe we can obtain a tract of country fifty miles wide
on an average, connecting this district with Natchez, containing at least
four and a half millions of acres. This opportunity must not be lost;
there may not be another such for years. Meet me here or at Pitchlyn's by 1st of November at farthest."

And in a "P. S." he adds : "We shall have it in our power to
wipe out the remembrance of the anchovies, by the success of this treaty.
I hope the fall from your horse will not prevent your coming."

On the 26th of October, General Robertson wrote to the Secretary of
War—" Being convinced that his presence at the proposed conference with

the Choctaws was important, he would set out immediately, notwithstanding his lameness, occasioned by a fall from his horse."

On the 25th of this month (October) a treaty was concluded with the Cherokees at Tellico, by Colonel Meigs, assisted by General Smith, ceding lands commencing at the mouth of Duck River, as heretofore mentioned. All the lands north of a line drawn from the mouth of Duck, up the same to the junction of the main forks, thence to bank of Tennessee River, opposite mouth of Hiwassee River, etc., etc.

During all of the year 1806, General Robertson had taken charge of two Chickasaw boys, whom he desired to have educated. He made application to the War Department, and, through the Secretary, to the President, in behalf of these lads. In the fall of the next year, the Secretary replied that "your account of expenses for the two Chickasaw boys will be settled by this Department. It is hoped, however, that hereafter the expenses for their clothing will be less!"

General Robertson could well reply—" They are clothed in *home-spun*, like my own boys; they have also had clothes given them, for which no charge has been made. We are, indeed, pretty well accustomed to the sight of Indians in nature's state; but we have a feeling of pride, and shame—if you will—to accustom these to clothes."

We mention these "little things" said or done by the high officers of a great nation towards men in every way their superiors, who had done, and were intent on doing, a work utterly beyond the comprehension or accomplishment of common men, however elevated and dignified in office and title.

The pioneer great men of the West have never been duly honored. They served with insignificant pay all the days of their lives. The amazing advances and high improvements of the present day throughout the valley of the Mississippi, are but the morning rays of the glory that shall shine upon the names and deeds of these early patriots and philanthropists in coming time.

Was not Robertson right then to say, "I know I am getting old; these long rides are fatiguing; but I claim no exemption from labor until I can do no more good!"

CHAPTER XXXVII.

1806.

In the fall of 1806, General Robertson was requested to go, and did go, to Colbert's Ferry, on the Tennessee River, and make an estimate of the value of buildings there, with a view of settling with Colbert. The Colberts, who in 1783—4 were regarded with great distrust, and "denounced as pirates," (with the view of avoiding difficulties with the Spaniards,) have conducted themselves in so orderly a manner, and evinced such friendship for the United States and these stationers, that they have now been deemed worthy of titles of honor, of pay or annuities and compensation for expenditures and losses, real or simulated, at their Ferry Reservation.

In the Legislature of this year, several measures were proposed which arrayed the members from Washington and Hamilton Districts against those from Mero. One measure urged by the Mero delegation was the retaking of the census, or a new enumeration of the inhabitants, and a fair adjustment of representation based on population. The proposition was defeated (so alleged) chiefly by the vote and hostility of the Washington members.

We merely refer to this matter to introduce the name of a very worthy citizen—the progenitor of a numerous posterity of worthy men. This is none other and no less than *Robert C. Foster*, of Davidson County. Being a member of the Legislature, he addressed a long letter to General Robertson, in which he says: "East Tennessee, so denominated in the phraseology of the law, having long brandished the arm of power in the council of State, feels an awful struggling at laying it down. As the symptoms of her malady increase, her agonizing paroxysms become more exquisite. The great moderation of Mero amidst the storm has not escaped the observation of all around."

So rapidly did population increase in the Middle, and anon in the Western District of Tennessee, that East Tennessee no longer claimed to "brandish the arm of power" alone, but, with hearty good will and commendable grace, united with the two other portions of the State in all

37

the wisdom of counsel and in all the power of law. A triple force, happily united, now "brandishes the arm of power." "A three-fold cord cannot be broken," saith the Scriptures, and Robert C. Foster, Sen.

The Legislature had passed an act for perfecting titles to land, which gave considerable dissatisfaction to some of the holders of warrants and settlement rights. This sentiment was rife in the Cumberland settlements, and the discontented parties were desirous for an extra session of the Legislature to repeal the law. Application was made to Gen. Robertson to use his influence with Governor Sevier to call an extra session. In compliance with these solicitations, he wrote to the Governor, setting forth the objections which were urged to the law, (not expressing them as his own,) and requested to be informed " whether, upon petitions from each county, he would convene the Legislature ?"

To which the Governor made an admirable reply, dated Knoxville, 18th October, 1806, which may be read in the " Impartial Review" of 1st Nov., 1806, discouraging such a call, because of the expense; because of his doubts whether the same Legislature would repeal the act complained of; because there are certainly many who, like the majority in the Legislature, deem it a wise enactment; and because it is problematical whether one better and wiser could be suggested and agreed upon. But yet, if there shall be proven to be a *general desire* of the *people of each county* by *their petition*, he will conceive it his duty to obey their request.

General Robertson had the letter published. Then followed among the discontented one of the usual devices of great and small politicians, to *manufacture* or *gather* " public sentiment."

Little cliques came together and nominated *two persons* in each county, (known to favor the views of the opponents of the *fourth* section,) and that such persons should inform the Governor of the *popular opinion* and wish.

" Before this *trick* had gained, a better hand was shown." The manœuvre was exposed; calls were made upon the voters in each military beat, and delegates appointed to meet in Nashville. On 22d November, most of the committee assembled, and although unanimous in dissent to the law, they yielded to the suggestions of the Governor.

General Robertson was a member of the committee. The questions were (we believe) between persons holding warrants, and real occupants. " John Armstrong entries" " Pigeonites," (entries on waters of Big Pigeon,) " Hobgoblin and Legerdemain Gentry."

One "ignoramus living in Mero District," took up the cudgels and belabored "A Citizen," "One of the People," and "Another of the People," who wrote and published whole columns in every paper for weeks. As we know that General Robertson was at least amused by some things said by Ignoramus, we make a few quotations : " Do, Mr. Editor, request them to write again ; especially 'A Citizen,' for the people begin to think that Bugaboo, the Land Law, is not so very much of a *Boo*, and if they will continue to publish, the people will soon get satisfied with it." He then gives " our committee here" a dig or two under the short-ribs ; and as the " committee" have concluded with the Governor against " a called session," the whole matter, so far as the legerdemain gentlemen east of the mountains are concerned, now rests upon the efforts of "A Citizen." " Do urge him to get upon a stump, turn the hind part of his wig before, let his eyes look like a couple of comets, seen through their tails, and bawl out to the people : don't spare them ; don't mind the waste of breath." Then, as to " One of the People :" " Is it come to this, that our Legislature will not undo in a hurry what they did upon mature deliberation ! . . . . . The members of the Legislature might have known that an attempt to pull out the bristles would put the whole sty in an uproar !"

" Good-lack-a-day ! what business had members of the Legislature to think of equity, generosity, to mere occupants ? They constitute but one-tenth of the population of the State, and they will have to pay only $50,000 a year for ten years, (as proceeds of lands sold to them,) and $50,000 is not quite *four* times the amount of the whole revenue of the State. So that in fact they have to pay into the treasury only forty times as much as any other citizens, that's all. . . . The poor Algerines in Blount, Sevier, etc., could, should, would certainly do this, and make no complaint of counterfeit warrants, or entertain further thought of clipping the Legerdemain Gentry, or rubbing up their dander."

In this year Aaron Burr visited Tennessee twice. The last time he arrived at Nashville was on 20th December, after he had been arrested and discharged in Kentucky. His departure hence is thus announced :

" Dec. 27th : Col. Burr embarked from this place for New Orleans on Monday last, with two large flat-boats which did not appear to be loaded."

These boats were built on Stone's River, at the Clover Bottom, under contract with General Jackson. The original account, in the hand-writing of General Jackson, was in existence but a few years since, filed in court at Natchez, Mississippi.

In the Nashville "Impartial Review" of Jan. 3, 1807, there is a " communication" describing " the burning of the effigy of Col. Aaron Burr, last night at nine o'clock, by the citizens of this town." *Another, fiercely* denouncing Burr as a *traitor !* and proceedings of a public meeting in the town of Franklin, of which William Neelly was chairman, and Thos. H. Benton, secretary, Dec. 27, 1806.

The "Silver Grays" now make their appearance. The correspondence is published in the Review of Jan. 10, 1807. The correspondence
is *without date,* and hence have arisen doubts (in recent years) whether
it had reference to apprehended difficulties with France, (there being
an endorsement by some unknown hand—"a tender of services, 1798,")
of war with England, after the English battle-ship Leopard fired into
the Chesapeake, or to the traitorous movements of *Aaron Burr.*

The question is not difficult of solution. The endorsement is mani-
festly wrong. Many of the parties were not living here at that date,
1798. The signature of "Joe. Coleman, Mayor of Nashville," limits the
period to 1806–7 and 1808 — the only years in which Mr. Coleman
could justly and truly have added such title to his name. He was the
first Mayor, and this was in 1806.

Independent of the language of the tender, and the reply of General
Jackson accepting their services, there are expressions in his address
dismissing the troops which had volunteered, or been called out by his
"military order," that determine these questions.

It is due to these *Invincibles,* or *Silver Grays,* that their "tender of
service" should appear on these pages.

"To MAJOR-GENERAL ANDREW JACKSON:

"At a moment when great sensibility, and even fearful apprehensions
for the welfare of our country, have been excited from one end of the
continent to the other—when our Government, the best calculated of all
others for the attainment of individual security and happiness, has
sounded the tocsin of alarm to be on the alert in *suppressing combinations*
of men hostile to the *integrity* of the Union and interests of the country—
it becomes all men, whether aged or youthful, to coalesce in their attachment to their country.

" In the affections of the citizens our Government exists—not in oppressive and unnecessary coercion, as in other countries.

" These principles, which eminently characterize republican institutions,
clearly demonstrate that every citizen, whatsoever his situation may be,
ought to contribute in some mode to the support of the Government
under which these inestimable blessings are enjoyed : the infirm, by
their opinions and exhortations, as to them experience belongs ; they
know the incalculable blessings of freedom of thought, speech, action,
and security of person and property. Patriotism is their claim, though
not exclusively in a country of freedom.

"This is an important crisis, when the limits of legal active exertion
ought not to be sought with a microscopic eye. So far as our bodily

powers will admit, we cheerfully submit to the rigors of military institutions. Our country will require nothing unnecessarily of us. The thread of age will not be broken, but it will be used to the extent of its strength.

" Under these impressions we agree to embody ourselves, aged and infirm as we may be, and to offer our services to our country in support of its laws and constituted authorities :

*General James Robertson,	*Robt. Hays,
Wm. Deckard,	*Jno. Parks,
*Jas. Tatum,	*Clem. Hall,
*How. Tatum,	*Stephen Cantrell,
*Thos. Overton,	Wm. Tait,
*Joel Lewis,	Thos. Talbot,
Geo. Poyzer,	*Wm. T. Lewis,
John Beck, Sen.,	Anthony Winston, Sen.,
Jas. Hennen, (if surgeon, 't is well;	*Robert Edminson,
if not, as a private, if necessary.)	Thos. Dillon,
Will Lytle, Sen.,	Thos. Dar,
*Jos. Hadley, } By W. L.	Geo. Wharton,
*Wm. Walton,	Wm. Wharton.
Joe Coleman, Mayor of Nashville,	

General Jackson's reply is very complimentary, but need not be copied. From his public order dismissing the troops, after referring to the President's proclamation against Burr, and the letter of the Secretary of War, and other matters, he says :

" When the insolence or vanity of the Spanish Government shall dare to repeat their insults on our flag, or shall dare to violate the sacred obligations of the good faith of treaties; or should the disorganizing *traitor* attempt the *dismemberment of our country*, or criminal breach of our laws, let me ask what will be the effects of the example given by a tender of service made by such men as compose the *Invincible Grays*, commanded, too, by the *father* of our infant State, *General James Robertson ?*"

In the western country the impression, to some extent, prevailed, that Burr's movements and purposes had some sanction of the General Government; and that in so far as they were directed against the crafty enemies of western settlements, they deserved to meet here with coöperation. It has never been proven that to any one did Burr openly suggest and urge *a separation* from the States east of the mountains. In this respect

---

* Those marked * are old Revolutionary officers or soldiers.

he never committed himself to the extent to which General Wilkinson had done years before.

In *our* opinion General Jackson retained an old grudge, as did almost every other early settler on the Cumberland and in Kentucky, against the Spaniards, and felt, very much like Rains, "an itching to whip the don'd rascals."

This same sentiment was nourished in the bosom of Governor William Blount, (as far as warlike feelings could be entertained by him,) and this was *the secret* of his interviews and correspondence, which resulted in his *expulsion* from the *Senate* of the United States.

Burr and Blount were sacrificed to State craft and State policy. They lived half a century too soon. The *treason* of their day has been lauded as patriotism in ours.

The fault of Jackson, Wilkinson, and others, was in denouncing Burr, making him a traitor, without any overt act. Had he not killed Hamilton, he would never have known such a storm as raged around his head, nor been so pursued as one with the mark of Cain upon his brow, bad man though he was. He lived to see Texas reännexed, Mexico revolutionized, and continued as a quasi nation only through American sufferance.

Burr, it is true, had vices enough to destroy any public man, and his overthrow furnishes a valuable lesson and warning.

CHAPTER XXXVIII.

1807–1811.

GENERAL ROBERTSON was engaged during much of this year in opening a mail-road from the Tennessee River through the Indian nations to
the "Grind-stone Ford," of the Bayou Pierre, about eight miles from
Port Gibson, and fifty miles from Natchez. This was opened under order
of the Post-office Department, and known as " the Robertson Road."

He had two other appointments, to the duties of which he gave due
attention : the one, as sole Commissioner to run the Chickasaw boundary line; the second, in conjunction with Colonel Meigs, to run the line
as agreed upon in the Treaty and Convention with the Cherokees. The
Commissioners and Surveyors met at the Chickasaw Old Fields, and proceeded with their work, a delegation of Indians being present.

They had a very scientific mathematician and surveyor with them,
Thomas Freeman, and from the correspondence with General Robertson it
would seem that there was with them a person of somewhat "rollicking,
boisterous character." Colonel Freeman writes : " Mr. Strother is yet
with me, and I shall detain him as long as I can. I cannot live alone,
and you know that even the old adage, 'Want of company, welcome trumpery,' will not apply to our acquaintance, Mr. O——e, for he is too trashy
even for trumpery. What a life a savage lives! How far removed are
we ? What trash, what worthless worms are all !"

These lines were run and completed by the last of October, and much
to the satisfaction of the Indians of both nations. On the first of September General Robertson, by invitation, met Mr. Meigs and Mr. Freeman near the mouth of Elk River, to complete some surveys. The
Indian Agents had invited several chiefs to attend, and it was hoped that
General Robertson could exert a happy influence in quieting the excitement which had arisen from the death of Prigmore and Cash, who had
been killed by some Creeks at a Cherokee encampment, near the Muscle
Shoals.

It is very probable that these two white men were of the class called "lawless," and had committed outrages, for which they were pursued across the Tennessee, and here lost their lives when enjoying the hospitality and protection of a Cherokee.

The Creeks had thus, however, given offence to the Cherokees and to the whites, who deemed it somewhat a duty to avenge the insult and punish the murderers.

"The parties were dissuaded from any acts of retaliation :" so it was *hoped.*

We have stated that "the first patch of cotton" planted west of the mountains by American settlers, was by Colonel John Donelson, on the east side of Stone's River, opposite Clover Bottom. This was at the instance of his wife. In the attempt to collect it for her, he and his party escaped destruction by the Indians.

Other prudent housewives may have had cotton planted in one corner of the garden, or in the field; but if so, the fact is nowhere recorded of that year, (1780.)

Before the close of the long Indian War, however, little fields of half an acre or an acre of cotton were to be seen at most of the "improvements" or settlements. The women took the almost exclusive care of "the cotton patch:" dropped in a seed at a time, as they would beans or peas in the garden, watched it as it grew, freed it from weeds, pulled off the bolls into their aprons or baskets, seated themselves with children, white and black, around them, with busy fingers gathering the cotton from the bolls, and separating the seed from the staple. Many a busy housewife had pockets for bolls, picked cotton, and for the good clear seed, and would have her fingers as mechanically employed "picking cotton," or "seeding," as others with their knitting.

The usual evening's employment for idle hands around a blazing log-fire, was the seeding of cotton, "one seed at a time." Such was the *culture* and *ginning* of cotton in the last century, and during a few of the first years of the present.

Ultimum et maximum telum, necessitas, says a Latin historian. "Necessity is the mother of invention," is the vulgar apophthegm, and evidenced in constant improvements, and the developments of science.

To-day, while I write, the civilized world, Europe and America, are exchanging thoughts, messages and compliments, instantaneously, by the scientific control of an all-pervading element which God only had hitherto used for his own purposes. He had flashed it in the face of science for thousands of years, but human knowledge had not discerned its uses—human necessities had not required its subserviency. The constant increase of the latter gives occasion for the exertion of the former. The developments of knowledge are concurrent with the demands of the world. And many a hidden power may yet be brought to light, and many now known be found applicable to purposes yet unimagined.

But not further to digress, we must refer to the construction of the ingenious mechanism which has superseded the slow process of "fingering each cotton seed, to clear it from the pile."

Eli Whitney invented the *cotton gin*, from which have resulted a thousand advances in the growth and manufacture of cotton. He offered the privileges of his patent to the States in which cotton was cultivated.

The State of Tennessee, by act of Assembly, dated October 22d, 1803, "purchased of Eli Whitney and Phineas Miller the right of a machine or new invention for cleaning cotton, commonly called the saw-gin," agreeing to pay the patentees thirty-seven and one half cents for each saw used in ginning for the years 1804, 5, 6, and 7.

The total amount paid by the State for the use of the gin in the counties of Middle Tennessee, or Mero District, was four thousand five hundred and seventeen dollars and forty-nine cents, after deducting two hundred and eighty-eight dollars and thirty-five cents for sheriff's commissions.

Gins were used in ten counties: Davidson, Sumner, Williamson, Montgomery, Robertson, Smith, Stuart, Dickson, Wilson, and Rutherford.

Among the twenty-four owners of cotton-gins in Davidson county, in the year 1804, were John Stump, Andrew Jackson, William T. Lewis, using gins with fifty or sixty saws, on which the tax was about twenty to twenty-two dollars.

In Sumner there were nine gins, owned by Isaac Walton, Joshua Hadley, James Saunders, and others.

In Williamson, six gins: owners, Samuel Crocket, John Wilson, David McEwen, and others.

In Montgomery five gins: Amos Bird, Ebenezer Frost, Benjamin and David Weakly, and others.

In Robertson, five: two owned by James McFarlan, one by Archer Cheatham, others by E. Hughes and J. McMillon.

In Smith, five: Tilmon Dixon, William Sanders, and others.

In Stuart, one: Sterling May, owner.

In Dickson, one: George Ross, owner.

In Wilson, four: (owners not mentioned.)

In Rutherford, four: James Rucker, William Lytle, James Morton, and John Howell.

After the year 1807, all persons who saw proper might have a gin, exempt from taxation.

Indian conferences are not ended; the business of making treaties is still to be carried on; and General Robertson's "occupation is not gone."

Governor Sevier writes to him, under date 24th March, 1808 : "Our Assembly, at their last session, passed a law for the purpose of holding a treaty with the Cherokees, provided the Executive of the United States acceded to the measure. I am informed that permission is obtained, and Colonel Meigs appointed on the part of the United States.

"The Executive of Tennessee is empowered to appoint one or more commissioners, as he may deem necessary. I shall myself attend, and shall only appoint one commissioner, and that one will be yourself, provided it will be agreeable and suitable for you to attend, which I hope it may."

In another letter he suggests his views of the most politic course to be adopted prior to and during the proposed treaty. General Sevier, General Robertson, and Colonel Meigs all concurred in the opinion that there were "certain influential Indians" "who desired to have the customary emollients applied to reduce the inflammatory state of their opposition," and that the usual means should be resorted to, in moderation : *ergo*, somebody must provide guns and ammunition, stroud, calico, vermilion. and beads, some little bells, and *antifogmatics*.

As one of innumerable instances of small occurrences requiring the attention of General Robertson, we may mention the case of a young Indian, who had sought protection, or rather hospitality, with Captain Outlaw, in Hickman county. He had quite a variety of skins and articles prized by Indians. In reckless sport, certain persons there greatly frightened him, and he fled, leaving all his property. Instead of hasting to his nation, he came in his terror and destitution to General Robertson's residence. He stated his case with so much earnestness as greatly to excite the General. He immediately wrote to Colonel John Holland in regard to the matter. The Colonel replied that the Indian had been unduly alarmed, but the conduct of the whites was such as to make it proper to inquire into it, and prevent the recurrence of acts which might result in mischief. The property was secured and restored to the young Indian, who concluded that "General Robertson was not only a good man, but a great man."

A year or more expired, when an Indian (with his squaw, and pappoose laced to a piece of bark) appeared at General Robertson's, and offered Mrs. Robertson a fine saddle of venison as a gratuity, explaining that he was the young Indian who had been befriended by the General when he fled from Hickman county.

We have seldom alluded to the heated political agitations of our population in a way to present General Robertson as an active participant; for he was not a partisan, and never a demagogue. He stood up always a lover of his country, a lover of good men, stern in his rebukes of all disorderly conduct, and of all attempts to disparage the services of pub- lic servants. He was calm and quiet, and, as far as the necessities of his fellow-citizens and his position would admit, he was a domestic man, at- tentive to the affairs of his family and his farm. When he came to town it was on business, and never to "lounge in idleness." Always temperate in eating and drinking, he required the like good habits in his children. He had one rule at his table with his children, which he enforced, and thus put a prompt end to all squeamishness and murmuring: "If any one complained of a want of variety in dishes, or of weariness with the same diet," his remark was, "Your mother has superintended these things; no child shall ever complain of her management: eat it, or go without." And he would quote the Scripture: "Eat what is set before you, asking no questions." That was the law, and no modification allowed but in sickness.

General Robertson was wholly exempt from profanity and irreverence.

Although often appealed to and addressed by letter in regard to politi- cal questions and political men, we find that he usually avoided all "en- tangling alliances, all malign influences, and all ultra measures," all malice and bitterness.

We trust we may be excused for introducing a politico-religious letter from one of General Robertson's warm admirers and devoted friends, William Martin.

"BELLVIEW, 13th Jan., 1809.

"MY DEAR FRIEND:—Our political hemisphere wears a gloomy aspect: shadows, clouds, and darkness rest upon it; every thing portends war; we should be prepared for the worst result.

"I did very much wish to be at the Democratic meeting at Nashville, but other engagements prevented me that pleasure.

"I fear that the Quids and Feds in that vicinity will attempt to with- hold from the President that declaration of public approbation which is his due, and which ought unequivocally to be avowed at your meeting. But I trust that there are Whigs enough among you, impressed with this important duty, (at this momentous crisis,) to prove to others that the people of West Tennessee are grateful, patriotic, and capable of making proper distinctions. [Middle was then known as "West Tennessee."]

"I did hope that when the proceedings of the Administration, as respects foreign nations, were brought to open day, that every mouth would be stopped, and every tongue confess the righteousness of the proceedings; but, behold! we now hear the opposition cry out that we ought to declare war against those powers which have provoked our just indignation, without taking any intermediate steps.

"Strange and perverse man! prone to do wrong; when once avowed a sentiment, (often evil,) persists in that sentiment against the most pungent convictions of his wrong. Such is the false pride which drives many on the rocks of destruction. For my own part, I do not know what more could have been done for this nation than has been done.

"But I think the opposition are influenced by something of the same spirit that the ancient Jews were: the greater the miracles, the louder the cry, 'Crucify him! crucify him!' Their hearts are hardened, their eyes are blinded, they choose darkness rather than light, because their deeds are evil; they appear to be given up to false delusion, that they might believe a lie; that they may all be (politically) damned; who believe not the truth, but have pleasure in unrighteousness. . . .

"Now, may the Great Disposer of all good avert the dangers which threaten us. To this end may we all repent for our sins, and do our first works."

The disposition to relinquish their lands east of the Mississippi, and accept others on the west side, was greatly on the increase among the various Indian tribes. To this policy the President gave his sanction, and, as it became the settled and successful policy of the Government, proper credit should be given to those who suggested it, and moved the Indians to a peaceable and glad acceptance of such an exchange.

The mind of General Robertson had long been made up, and his views made known in regard to this measure, and we believe that the opinions of no man had more influence with the Cherokees, Chickasaws, and Choctaws, than had his.

If he was not a Commissioner, his presence was desired and asked both by white and red men at the conferences and treaties. It was very much the case with General Sevier, from his acquaintance with the Upper Cherokees and Creeks. These savages held in admiration distinguished military men, men of portly bearing, with titles, epaulettes, swords and plumes. Their own great men were "warriors and braves."

And the frequency with which General Robertson appeared among them as their friendly adviser, or as the Representative or Commissioner of the State or nation, and bearing the title of Brigadier-General, exalted him in their estimation. "He was a brave."

In February of this year he received frequent letters from Governor

Sevier on Indian affairs, and to hold himself in readiness to attend various conferences with them, as also the running of lines. The Upper and Lower Cherokees desired a divisional line between themselves; and should this be done, the prospect of negotiating for lands would be none the less plain and promising.

In March and early part of April, General Robertson travelled through the nations, having some goods and money with him, which he was permitted to use in clothing the naked, in adorning some of the proud young warriors, and the copper-colored belles " in the woods," or in relieving the chiefs who were annoyed by debts they owed to *traders*.

On the 11th of April General Robertson informed Governor Sevier of the success he had met with in his tour. To this the Governor replied in very complimentary terms, and says, "What use to make of the small balance of money you report to be in your hands, you are the best judge."

In a report subsequently made by General Robertson, it appears he had used but two hundred and ninety-two dollars, (in silver;) the banknotes he retained and accounted for to the treasury. Who has followed this example?

The General had also written a letter to the chiefs in the Chickasaw nation; to which they returned an answer, dated April 18th, 1809, from which we shall make a quotation, because of the matter of history contained in it relative to the Seneca Indians. It is addressed to Gen. Robertson, by Chin-nubbe, (king of the nation,) Hattashimeco, Ematamica, O-koye, Mattaha, and others. In pursuance of treaties with these various southern Indians, the Government had ordered all white settlers to remove from lands within the Indian limits, and to enforce such a measure the aid of the military was in some instances required. Colonel Meigs writes to General Robertson that most of the settlers were of respectable character—worthy citizens—a valuable acquisition to any State. "Our riches and our strength consist of such citizens." Many of them settled on these lands on the east side of Elk, without the thought of giving offence to the Chickasaws, being assured by Colbert and others that the title would soon be relinquished. They said, "As there is very little game there, and no Indian settlements, the Indians will not look upon the white settlers as intruders." " But now," says Colonel Meigs, " the conduct of Colbert is so marked with unsteadiness and duplicity as to cause much inconvenience and loss. I have removed two hundred and one families off the Chickasaw, and eighty-three families off the Cherokee lands; not less than seventeen hundred or eighteen hundred persons in all. Let them 'bide their time,' and they may return to places of permanent habitation.

"We ought not to lose a single man who desires land to live and work on. A disposition to migrate seems to pervade the whole eastern part of the United States; we invite that emigration here; obstacles ought to be removed. The tendency is as uniform as the law of gravitation, and can no more be restrained *until the shores of the Pacific Ocean make it impossible to go farther.* Within seven years, stations and settlements will extend to the mouth of Columbia River!" Such was the prophecy of this intelligent and far-seeing patriot.

We would be pleased to add much of this worthy and useful man: intelligent and laborious, exemplary in all the walks of life; fond of his books, and of educated society, yet for years secluding himself in the forests, and living among the savages.

We can only account for such a person finding society and enjoyment in loneliness, by taking a look at his writing-desk, and at the rude shelves in his unhewed-log-cabin.

He is frequently interrupted and annoyed by the presence of Oconos-tota, Atta-culla-calla, and the Hanging-Maw, and glad when they wrap their old blankets around them and depart; but he is never wearied with Thucydides, with Herodotus or Homer, with Cæsar and Livy and Virgil, closely bound in leather.

"Canst thou speak Greek?" "Yes, and also Cherokee." "I dwell among the living and the dead, but prefer the dead."

The State of Tennessee should rejoice in the erection of one grand, glorious cenotaph at the seat of Government, made of her own choice marble, whereon should be carved the names of distinguished pioneers— "the noble army of martyrs"—the patriots and public men of the last century, "who prepared the way for all her greatness." Statues of Sevier and Robertson should be the first to occupy niches in the Capitol.

From these digressions we must return to our friends the Chickasaws, and listen to their address to General Robertson:

"FRIEND AND BROTHER:—We have received your letter. The nation is very grateful to the President for the favor of having intruders ordered off our land; as our breath has been gone for some time; but it is now restored to us again. When friends and brothers are too near each other, their friendship is not so apt to continue; but when at a distance, friendship always remains firm and secure.

"We have understood that the President did purchase this land that you name in your letter, and we suppose you know as well as *us* that it was not of the Cherokees, but of the *Senecas*—a nation who thought to *destroy all the white people*—and, in their wars *with the whites, lost all their land;* therefore they had no land to sell. We believe you know as well as ourselves that where General Pickens now lives was formerly their country.

" The Little Turkey and his party, and all who live below the Lookout Mountain, have no land; they are all *of the same Seneca nation,* and are beholden to red people like ourselves for land to live on.

" This nation does not consider that it is by order of the United States Government, but that they are rather urged and insisted on to sell their lands by the *contrivance* of some *individuals in Tennessee State,* who urge it for their own private interest. We have understood that the Cherokees have been persuaded by these individuals to sell their land; and in consequence of this there were four or five Cherokee chiefs *broke* by their own nation. This was on account of their not being true and honest men to their nation.

"As to any prejudiced person advising us, it is not so. We had friends among the Cherokees that attend their councils, and from them we get the information which makes you suppose we are advised by prejudiced persons.

" We have long suspected that the Government of the United States was advised by those individuals to purchase this land. We never suspected the Cherokees of selling this land; and if the Government has purchased, it has not been of the right owners, but of people who had no right to sell.

"This nation is not disposed to sell land at present, as it is people of a loose, bad character that are the first, generally, to settle a new country, and, of course, may not be good neighbors."

Whoever dictated or wrote that address to General Robertson was "well posted;" and from some of the remarks and words *underscored,* we judge he intended to *hit* certain individuals, and point to certain well-known measures and influences. But if Walpole could utter it as a truism among enlightened and civilized nations, "All men have their price," could not American Commissioners easily ascertain that all Indian Mingoes, headmen, and warriors, are not above price?

George Colbert (a half-breed Chickasaw) was a cunning Indian, and afraid to hold talks and interviews alone with General Robertson. He would not visit the General, or come to the Cumberland: he knew he had " acted with two hearts and two faces," and that General Robertson could "turn him inside out."

Colonel Meigs therefore urged the General to visit him at Hickory Flat, where Colbert could be induced to be present, and have his own interpreter.

An invitation to the Cherokee *Chiefs* (leaving out head-men and warriors) was sent by Colonel Meigs and Governor Sevier to come to the "Garrison on the 20th of August," and General Robertson "must attend—his presence is very important. We may hope for a favorable treaty, unless prevented by some persons who find their interest in preventing such measures, and there are some such persons."

The 20th of August was the day agreed on between Colonel Meigs and the chiefs; and General Robertson made his preparations to leave home on the tenth day of August; but as he was about to start, he received a letter from Governor Sevier, stating that Colonel Meigs had informed him the chiefs could not, *or would not,* come before the 25th of September! This postponement was regarded as the work of persons inimical to the treaty.

The day thus named was one when the Governor would be compelled to be present with the Assembly, and when the presence of General Robertson also was important there; hence Colonel Meigs was desired to have the day set for the last of November.

Colonel Meigs approved of the 30th of November, saying, "A little delay will do no harm—perhaps it will whet their appetite: their minds are never fixed, but are always vibrating like the pendulum of a clock."

Governor Sevier wrote to General Robertson to the same effect: "It has always been my opinion that the longer the treaty could be put off, the greater would be the success, provided we seize time by the forelock, when his head hangs invitingly down. *The reasons* will naturally suggest themselves to you!" "Delays" are not always "dangerous."

Colonel Meigs was not able to notify the Indians of the day proposed by the Commissioners, and a little confusion and some dissatisfaction resulted. Some of the chiefs attended, were dissatisfied at not meeting the Commissioners, and because proper provisions had not been supplied. The merchants of Kingston furnished supplies, and the chiefs were pacified. The emigration of Indians to the west of the Mississippi was greatly on the increase. Indeed, as was remarked, the tide of white emigrants settling upon the borders of Indian territory caused heaving and rolling waves of the red population to move onward, and across the great Mississippi.

The Cherokees and Chickasaws were disappearing from the lands for which the whites were impatiently waiting. "The buffaloes had long preceded the migration of the red men; the red men must follow them."

General Robertson and a few others, now aged and care-worn pioneers, had witnessed the entire process. They had seen these forests filled as a well-stocked park with game of all sorts: they had heard the savage

war-whoop, and endured savage hostilities as no other people had endured; they had lived until wild beast and savage men had almost disappeared, and were permitted to welcome industrious and intelligent citizens
by thousands; to see towns laid out, roads opened, farms in good cultivation, and yielding in great abundance; society and government,
schools and churches, well organized; and the initiatory settlements and
governments at Watauga and Cumberland extended, and built up to
become a State in the great American Union, and ere long to furnish
Presidents to all these States bordering upon both the Atlantic and the
Pacific Ocean. Such "days of small things" are never to be "despised."

> "This is thy work, Almighty Providence!
> Whose power, beyond the reach of human thought,
> Revolves the orbs of empire, bids them sink
> Deep in the dead'ning night of thy displeasure,
> Or rise majestic o'er a wondering world."

The question was often asked at this very early date, Is not West Tennessee (which then included and meant only the Cumberland settlements
and others upon adjacent waters) entitled to the honor of furnishing a
Governor? "Why may not Robertson be nominated and elected?" There
were two answers: East Tennessee far outnumbered in voters, and General
Robertson had no idea of being a candidate. He could truly say, in the
language of Governor Willie Blount, as used in a letter to the General,
under date March 8th, 1810: "The trade of political governing does
not suit my genius, as well as retirement. I am tired of it."

It was well that his last days were not to be made miserable by party
politics and the annoyances of office.

During this year portions of the State *south* of Cumberland were in-
fested by an organized band of lawless men, under one *Lowrey*. The
Indians and whites were often greatly annoyed by these banditti, and especially on and near Battle Creek. Colonel Meigs says: "Notwithstanding
the infamous character of Lowrey, he has sufficient influence to keep up
his troop of marauders. He fears not the military, as his adherents know
every movement of the troops from the garrisons. Unless the arm of
civil power is laid upon them, they may soon lay the whole country under
contribution." A call is therefore made upon General Robertson and
Major Anderson to awaken the civil officers to unite with the military,
under Colonel Purdy, and arrest or disperse this "gang of outlaws."

The correspondence of this year between Governor Sevier and General
Robertson evinces the wisdom of some of the measures they had proposed and adopted. They said one to the other, "Keep alive the treaty;

38

but as the Indians began the game of evasion, delay, and postponement, let it be played out: they know we must eventually win: they are becoming more and more anxious to treat and sell. We will 'make haste slowly,' let them press it upon us as they will."

General Sevier says to General Robertson, August 5th, 1810: "The Cherokees wish to remove over the Mississippi, and will most certainly do it, if not *prevented* by Government. Two years will carry them chiefly off, which will be the most effectual treaty for Tennessee, as well as a very cheap one. They say they are becoming more and more in love with that country, and cannot be kept out from it."

Governor Willie Blount and Colonel Meigs were in favor of holding the treaty, and the former had invited some sixteen of the principal chiefs of the Cherokees to a conference with him, and to prepare for a full treaty in the fall; but after having the views of Generals Robertson and Sevier in favor of a postponement, there was a full concurrence in sentiment, and no treaty was held this year.

In December Governor Blount addressed to General Robertson a long and very able argument in favor of the claim of the State of Tennessee to these lands, the want of title in the Indians, and the illegality of the transfer or relinquishment made by the treaty of Holston. He took up the positions assumed in the address of General Robertson and others to the three "pompous" Commissioners of the United States, in July, 1798. General Robertson had presented the strong points in that printed address, and they are ably handled by Governor Willie Blount. But to discuss them now (at so late a day) seems like fighting a shadow, when the substance is in our possession, and is the very thing we were contending for. There could be little need of argument when the Indians yielded possession.

There are remarks in these letters of Governor Willie Blount which we should delight to quote and publish, but they are unnecessary to the main purposes we have had in view. The memoirs and writings, public and private, of Willie Blount should be presented to the public in a form worthy of him and creditable to the State. He was "a voluminous writer;" wrote much on political and religious topics.

In the fall of this year, "his children being grown and living and acting for themselves," as he says, General Robertson applied to the War Department for the situation of Agent to the Chickasaws. He said "he was at leisure, and thought that, at a time when British agents were endeavoring to seduce the southern Indians into alliance with that Government, and hostility to the United States, he could do some good, and use some influence to counteract their machinations!"

Here was this aged servant, "with *leisure* on his hands!" the first time in his long and laborious life that he had been thus troubled and "pestered;" the first time he had ever solicited office; but it was to counteract the "machinations of enemies of his country." Of course, the office was gladly conferred. He is now sixty-eight years of age. The care of his family does not trouble him, but the perils of his country do. Wisely does he conclude that his name and presence among the Indians may stay the progress of mischievous machinations. He, sooner than any other white man, can discover the true state of feelings among these southern tribes.

The influential Shawnee chief, Tecumseh, and his brother, "The Prophet," were making vigorous efforts to arouse all the Indians, north and south, to war against the United States. This movement originated with agents of the British Government, and was one of the many provocations to the war of the next year.

A national council was held on 10th September at Tuckabache; and before it closed there arrived a party of Shawnees, in number seventeen, accompanied by one Creek, and one or two from two other tribes, evidently intent on war. They had sent to the council, before their arrival, a war-pipe and hatchet. The council refused to receive these tokens of war, and disapproved of the proposed coalition.

General Robertson had anticipated some measures of this kind, and therefore sought the appointment of agent, as we have seen.

Governor Blount soon learned that eighty to one hundred Creeks were persuaded by these emissaries to join the Prophet's party.

General Robertson received a number of letters very complimentary upon his acceptance of the agency; but the one which he probably prized as highly as any other, was from Colbert, whose influence had now become paramount among the Chickasaws, and was very weighty with the Cherokees and Choctaws. The letter is in reply to one from the General, and in acknowledgment of a "talk" he had sent to Colbert for the nation. As it evinces the esteem in which General Robertson was held among the Indians, we quote from it:

"MY OLD FRIEND AND FATHER:—I am overjoyed with the word you send, that you are to be the guide of our nation, as you have been the life of this nation; and every chief of the Chickasaws, I make no doubt, will feel the same as I do. I hope every thing will prove satisfactory in every council. When you go by my house, I will take my horse and ride to the King's house and the agency with you."

Chin-nubbe was the King of the Chickasaw nation. He is the same person who, with Colbert, Okoye, and others, wrote to General Robertson, in 1805, that "when they sold land it must be by the acre, in the mode adopted by the United States."

They used to think that the fee simple and absolute sovereignty of all the trackless forests were in the Indians; but the civilians and warriors of Holston and Cumberland have argued those points, and overthrown those pretensions. These same pioneer warriors and statesmen initiated a new theory and a new policy of dealing with and for the disposal of all the savage tribes. Government has adopted it.

Destined to melt away before the white settlements, their existence has been prolonged by removals west of the Mississippi, and by the introduction of husbandry and many of the arts and comforts of civilized life, yet utter extinction seems to await them all ere the close of this century.

Early efforts were made to change the habits of the Chickasaws, Cherokees, and Choctaws. Implements of husbandry had been furnished, and an intercourse and friendship established, which was deemed advantageous to the white as well as to the red people; but the decree had gone forth in regard to them, as well as to all others: "Passing away! passing away!" The Fourth of July toast expressed the truth: "The Indians: like saleable goods, going, going, gone!" "Knocked down [as Williams said] by the three great generals, General Sevier, General Robertson, and General *Providence.*" (This was not original with Williams.)

CHAPTER XXXIX.

1812–1814.

THE Creeks had yielded very much to the persuasions of the emissaries from the "northern tribes." Their ancient hostility was revived, to some extent, towards the settlers between the Cumberland and Tennessee. A number of persons were murdered by them in this year, near the mouth of Duck River. Repeated acts of a hostile character were done by them. The 'Governor, Willie Blount, made a requisition upon the War Department for a company of United States Rangers, to perform duty on the frontiers of the settled parts of Tennessee, and to range between the Tennessee and Mississippi Rivers, to cut off or check the intercourse between the Creeks and northern Indians. A company, under command of Captain David Mason, was ordered to perform this duty.

War having been declared against Great Britain on 12th June, the military and warlike spirit was at once aroused in this State. Nowhere was there a more general approval of the declaration, and a greater readiness to engage in its prosecution. It pervaded all classes. Old warhorses champed the bit and pawed the earth when they heard the drum and saw their country's flag unfurled; aged citizens were fired with the enthusiasm of youth, or would teach their juniors that patriotism could not die—that in old age they would resent and punish insults, and defend the rights of the country.

Most of the "Invincibles" or "Silver Grays" were yet alive, and were ready to reörganize and tender such services as they could perform. They were left, however, by their own happy firesides, there to fight their old battles over in martial words.

General Robertson was not of the number of those who sat down quietly at his own hearth-stone. He desired no command, and he could not serve in the tented field. He had selected his proper sphere. There was a place prepared for some important character, and Providence, which had prepared the place, also prepared the man suitably to fill it, and discharge all appropriate duties.

His mission was still to go "unto the heathen." The chiefs and warriors of several of the southern tribes were much interested in the declaration of war. They said there would be something for them to do, other than hunt game.

Some who were friendly to the United States had met with others whose minds were unsettled. Good advice came from the friendly party. They said, "General Robertson by visiting the agencies might exert a happy influence. It was a good time to fix the wavering."

Among the many Indian chiefs of General Robertson's acquaintance—all of whom greatly respected him—none had a higher regard for him or was more in his confidence than John Pitchlyn, of Oak-tibbe-ha, in the Choctaw nation. The General had "in his heart the hearts also of" other chiefs with sonorous polysyllabic names, such as Push-mata-ha, Mush-ula-tubbe, Puck-shu-nubbe. They were the friends of the United States, and "kept the hearts of the people straight." This is one of the tribes which never did make war upon the citizens of the United States. Most of them are lazy and stolid.

At this time there were "banditti of Muscogees, and of other tribes and towns of equivocal character," roving through the country between the Tennessee and Cumberland, stealing horses, producing alarm, and "stirring up the demon of revenge." Unfortunately, Captain Mason and his party of rangers killed a Choctaw without provocation, asserting—what was never believed—that he was taken for a hostile Creek. For this act, the brother of the Choctaw waylaid the Natchez trace, and killed a traveller by the name of Thomas Haley. The Choctaw who thus retaliated the death of his brother was a very small lad, some ten or twelve years of age, not more : so ingrained was the *lex talionis*—so "dyed in the wool" were the very children.

There were several other events about this time of an unhappy tendency, and it required all the skill of General Robertson, Pitchlyn, and others, to keep some of the nation from acts of open hostility. The agents of the United States had persuaded some of the chiefs of the Cherokees to meet the Chickasaws in council at Itala, on 15th September, at which they desired General Robertson to be present.

The council continued for a week, and General Robertson preserved the "short talk of Too-tuma-stubbe, the great *medal* chief of the Choctaws," who was present by invitation. He did not like the white rangers very much : said, "My heart is straight, and I wish our father the President to know it. Our young warriors want to fight. Give us guns, and plenty of powder and lead. We fight your enemies; we fight much ; we fight strong. I do not like white rangers : make trouble in our country.

Our Father don't want to make us trouble. Our warriors good Americans—fight strong. You tell him so. You, General Robertson, know me ; my heart straight. Choctaw soldiers good soldiers. Give epaulettes and guns and whiskey—fight strong !"

General Robertson approved the suggestion to enlist and equip several companies of Choctaws, Chickasaws, and Cherokees, to be in the pay of the United States—well supplied with "guns and epaulettes," who should act as rangers upon the borders, to prevent interviews between the northern and southern Indians, and particularly to stop all hostile Creeks from passing through any of their territories. He knew the character of these Indians—the springs of action—their military pride ; how to sustain their integrity and preserve their friendship. This advice was deemed judicious, as also to engage some of them in the war now to be waged against the Creeks.

The atrocities committed at the North, and the few outrages at the South, (together with many indications of increasing hostility further south,) awakened very angry feelings in Tennessee. Inflammatory meetings and publications were calculated to alienate all the Indians, compel them into a coalition and alliance which it had cost General Robertson and others long and earnest efforts to prevent, and which had induced him in advanced life to seek an office and to proffer his services as an agent among the Indians. Having so happily quieted their minds, and found their "hearts straight," or "straightened them," he was much concerned to learn the character of these measures among the "people at home." He therefore left his agency and returned to Nashville.

On the 20th of October he wrote out his views, and earnestly expressed his sentiments and wishes. He protested against all unkind treatment of Cherokees, Chickasaws, and Choctaws. He pledged himself for their friendship, and its continuance, unless the whites themselves should destroy it. He knew they occupied an important position between the Shawnees and other tribes west and east of the Mississippi and north of the Ohio, and the Creeks and Seminoles at the South. As to the sincerity of the Chickasaws and Choctaws, he had no doubt whatever. In the declarations of the Cherokees he placed much more confidence than in former years. He intended to return to his post at the "agency," and hoped that his fellow-citizens would not do or suffer any thing to be done which might increase his labors, or defeat all his efforts and wishes, and sadden his last days.

We have mentioned the migration of Cherokees and others to the west side of the Mississippi, and the satisfaction with which this movement was viewed by the white settlers near the Indian borders. But there commenced an ebb-tide. They came in haste—as fugitives—with terror depicted in their faces. They were not afraid of men; they had met no warriors, white or red; none of their friends had fallen in battle; they had not suffered by pestilence or famine; the game was much more abundant than they had ever seen in their native country. "But," said they, "we deserted the bones of our chiefs, our warriors, our forefathers, and the Great Spirit is angry with us. The earth is ready to swallow us up: it trembles under our footsteps; it heaves and labors to vomit us forth. We cannot remain there. We return to sit down, cover our heads, and weep by the graves of our ancestors."

The *earthquakes* alarmed others besides these ignorant children of the forest. Those who returned came not with hostile feelings, but rather with spirits troubled and broken. Some few, no doubt, were ready to listen to any advice and to engage in any measures which wily persons might suggest. The condition of most of them was miserable and desperate. But the kind attentions of United States agents were not wanting, and much good was thus done in time of need, the happy influence of which was seen in after-years. This kindness was not thrown away.

There were white persons in the settlements who were somewhat disturbed of their equanimity by this return of Indians. They contended that the reception and attentions given to them were encouragements for all to come back; and that they would "have to be paid liberally again in order to *rid* the settlements of their annoyances."

The system or practice (as since understood and pursued by Government agents with so much profit to themselves, and expense to our treasury) of removing the Indians at so many dollars *per capita*, and then, by sub and counter agents, paying and inducing the poor wanderers to return to their old haunts and hunting-grounds, that these same "agents for emigrating Indians" might renew their applications to Government and obtain further liberal appropriations to remove "these pests to white settlements"—this game of defrauding our Government was not then initiated, or so often and so successfully practiced as it has since been. Millions of dollars have thus been filched from the treasury.*

* "CHICKASAW AGENCY, August 10th, 1812.

"CAPT. JOHN DAVIS:—I arrived at this place 23d of last month. I was sick the day I left your house and the next day; have been tolerably healthy since.

"I am well pleased with my berth, and have had the greatest council that ever was in this nation.

"The Chickasaws profess to be as well pleased with me as I am with them.

The many murders and outrages committed by the Creeks on the Mobile, and in the Mississippi Territory, aroused the military spirit of Tennesseeans to the highest state. A very large assemblage of citizens from the different counties in this, then Western District, was convened at Nashville, on Saturday, 18th September, "to devise means whereby speedy and effectual aid should be afforded those distressed citizens, and to punish or exterminate their nation and abettors.

"The Rev. Mr. Craighead was conducted to the chair as President, and in an eloquent and impressive speech stated the object of the meeting."

The resolutions, passed unanimously, were in favor of instantly raising five thousand troops, to march under the command of General Jackson. This was the beginning of the famous Creek war under General Jackson. With its details we shall not concern ourselves in this work.

"A copy of Mr. Craighead's eloquent Address" was requested for publication, and appears at the close of the proceedings of the meeting.

When General Jackson, at the head of his brave Tennesseeans, was gaining victories and wreathing laurels around his brow, Robertson was accomplishing the great work committed to his charge. He urged forward such organizations among "the friendly Indians, our allies," as were authorized by the War Department; and encouraged the Chickasaws to watch against and prevent any communications between the Creeks and northern Indians, who were taking sides with England. And they maintained a vigilant police, and made frequent reports to the Agency.

The services which General Robertson rendered during his agency in the years of the war with England, are to be reckoned among the very

---

There cannot be a people more determined to observe peace with the United States than the Chickasaws.

"If the professions of the Creeks are sincere, there will be no danger with the southern Indians.

"This nation is determined to put their law in force in the strictest manner, should horse-thieves or murderers pass through this country. And the Choctaws have ordered all out of their nation.

"You will see in 'The Clarion' the letter from the Creeks to these people, and the proceedings of our council.

"The death of the Choctaw killed by the rangers will cause much trouble, but will not be any great national crime. His brother has killed a Mr. Thos. Haley on the Mobile road, (in retaliation.)

"I have invited the two Indians who lost their companion and property to accompany me to Nashville, the last of September.

"JAMES ROBERTSON."

valuable ones rendered by him in a series of forty years, in not one of which years did he omit the discharge of many acts of important and disinterested patriotic service. He was indeed almost sovereign and unopposed in influence among the Chickasaws. And well was it for them, and well for the American settlements on or near their border.

Among distinguished and successful lawyers in Tennessee who rapidly advanced in public consideration as politicians, we notice now *Felix Grundy*. He was a man of quick discernment, acute discrimination, firm decision, learned, ingenious, eloquent. He was a member of Congress in this year, and promptly "made his mark," and assumed a position of distinction.

In writing to General Robertson, in February, 1813, General Sevier, then a Senator in Congress, speaks in terms of highest commendation of "this your friend Grundy: he ought to be reëlected; the district will never find a better representative should he be changed for another."*

With pleasure would we insert suitable sketches of many other men of talents, men of worth, occupying various stations of usefulness in Middle Tennessee at this date, but our prescribed limits forbid the indulgence of such notice.

In April, the suggestion which had been made to employ companies of Choctaws and Chickasaws to defend the frontiers and to protect travellers,

---

* In a letter from General Robertson to Captain John Davis, dated "Chickasaw Agency, March 9th, 1813," he writes: "The Chickasaws are in a high strain for war. They have declared war against all passing Creeks who attempt to go through their nation. They have declared, if the United States will take a campaign against the Creeks, that they are ready to give their aid. They consider the United States at war already with the Creek nation, as they say that, to their knowledge, one of the ten who did the mischief near the mouth of the Ohio has been a principal leader for upwards of twenty years, and that there was another chief present; so that the Creeks can no longer say that it is their young men only who are at war. The Chickasaws do not believe that the Creeks will give up those [murderers] to the United States. They hope the United States will humble the Creeks and bring them to their own terms. They have requested Government to send them two full companies of horsemen, to protect them until a campaign can be undertaken. The women seem much alarmed; but the war is popular with the warriors, and war seems to be certain.

"Mrs. James Colbert wants, by the first of July, one hundred pounds of feathers, and to be put in a new tick, or two ticks!   .   .   .

"Is it not strange that Colonel Cannon should oppose *Mr. Grundy*, when he does such honor to the State? His equal is not in the State. You Harpeth people ought to turn out and keep up the credit of the State."

was taken up by Pitchlyn, and urged upon the United States Agents; and he says : "When the Creeks have to fight the red and the white men together, they will learn it is a *national* affair, and will prove the ruin of the Creek nation; and *then, I think,* there will be *an end* put to their further proceedings." So every one would suppose.

Pitchlyn was active and faithful and intelligent. (We had some personal acquaintance with him.)

General Robertson had returned to his post and duties as agent among the Chickasaws.

The war was waging with the British on land and sea and lake, and with Indians north and south. Savage murders and horrible outrages were committed in the settlements in Alabama and other sections, and the call was made for five thousand volunteers, to march under General Jackson to the "Florida War."

The war with England, and the campaigns of General Jackson, require and have their own histories. (We would here express our wish, that persons who have information or documents relating to those campaigns, may intrust the same to the State Historical Society.)

Our patriot, hero, statesman, negotiator, "peace-maker," was at his post. He had endured hardships all his life long; he was not known hitherto to complain of either "hard bread or a hard bed," but in this agency he found "too much of both and too little of either"—the bread and the bed too hard, and the bread and the bed *too scant.*

He wrote to his wife to send by Mr. Cohee some feathers and bed-clothes, and very fairly and kindly offered her, "should she come that way, the very best chance for rest and sleep which the bed would afford, provided, always, that he should retain a part of the same." And, as a dutiful and devoted wife, she accepted the offer or permission as though it had been a command. How strange that this aged couple, seventy-one and sixty-three years of age, should leave their hard-earned but now quiet home, their beautiful and comfortable residence near Nashville, to go again into the wilderness and among the savages, and there patiently, yea, cheerfully, "submit to all sorts of inconveniences and annoyances!" Before he departed the last time on this mission or agency, he said : "I know I am getting to be an old man; I cannot delude myself with the idea that I am young, or with the hope that in this life my days and being will turn backwards, and carry me from age through reversed stages down to childhood again. I may not do all the good I design. My heart is warm and full, though my limbs are not so very supple. As some of you have said, I may not live to return and settle down again quietly at home. Older men than I have found the post of duty away from their pleasant firesides, and where duty calls, there is home."

And he remained at that post. "Every person and every act having a suspicious appearance, were sure to have eyes of suspicious scrutiny fixed upon them." The old and familiar system of spies and "trotters" was revived, and the General was quite well posted in the affairs going on near and afar off. The news of the capture of Washington City distressed him very much, and surprised some of the chiefs who had visited that city.

During the residence of General Robertson at the Chickasaw Agency, he had his eye upon some persons and movements at and near Fort Pickering, (or Memphis.) Colonel Richard Sparks, a son-in-law of General Sevier, was in command of the United States troops at that post, and his suspicions had been aroused by information from the post-master, Mr. Allen, and others, as to the friendly influence, by speech and conduct, of one Judge Fooy, who had been "an old *residenter* in the Chickasaw nation, and whites and red people both speak of him as a man in whom there can be no dependence; and that he will take sides with that government that bids the highest, and with *two* at the same time if he can be paid by both."

If Judge Fooy was indeed inimical to the United States, and received pay as an agent of Great Britain, he gave some proofs of friendship, and many professions, as if he had been in the pay of ours.

General Robertson continued in his agency, to the great satisfaction of the Indians and of the United States Government; but his friend, Silas Dinsmore, long the agent among the Choctaws, continued not in favor with the Administration. Colonel John McKee was a greater favorite at head-quarters, as he also became with the Indians.

In writing to General Robertson of this sudden revolution and overthrow, and of the pleasant interview between himself and his successor, who had also been his *predecessor*, he says:

"This is the Fourth of July. Colonel McKee and I have just finished our dinner, and are ready to drink a toast to the retreat of Bonaparte. . . . . We laugh at the coincidence in the fortunes of *Bony* and *myself*. When I superseded the Colonel, Bony superseded the Bourbons, or made himself Emperor. The Bourbons now supersede him and are reinstated: McKee supersedes me and is also reinstated. 'Nos poma natamus!' 'How we apples swim!'"

The services of General Robertson as a member of the Legislature have not been stated in chronological order, nor have we made even a reference to them all. We have found it difficult to avoid extending our work by notices of many other worthy men who were the contemporaries and co-laborers of Robertson. None of them or their meritorious services are disparaged by this unavoidable omission.

General Robertson had been long subject to violent attacks of *neuralgia*. From these he was indeed a great sufferer. With his advance in years the attacks became more frequent and distressing. If they lasted less than twenty-four hours, he escaped not without much debility and the appearance of a month's illness from ordinary fever.

He had repeatedly said that his life would end in one of these attacks. He knew he could not survive many more of such as he had recently endured. But he was calm and resigned, and "might as well die there [in the Indian nation] as anywhere, if the will of God was so."

In August he seldom passed a day exempt from this affliction. He had given up his rides on horseback ; light and noise were painful to him ; he had an indisposition to converse ; his brain was racked ; there was great inflammation of the brain ; he was sinking ; his breathing was heavy and distressing ; and he became insensible. On Thursday, the 1st day of September, 1814, he ceased to breathe. His wife was by his side. Henceforth her name is to be written "a widow." She is a widow indeed. Her children are not around her. These aged parents had not called them to forsake the duties and cares of their respective positions to attend them afar from their families and homes. Sooner than do this, he would have surrendered his agency, and have returned to his own home, and to the pleasant neighborhood, where his many friends and most of his children were settled ; who would have been happy to visit him and minister to his wants, or weep around his death-bed. But he dies where duty called—he dies at his post. In this he was content, resigned.

On Friday, the 2d September, his remains were interred at the Agency. There they remained until the year 1825, when they were removed to the cemetery at Nashville. A very large concourse of citizens attended. An eloquent tribute and just historical oration was delivered by the Honorable Judge Haywood, (which, it is to be regretted, was not preserved.)

A plain tomb covers the spot where rest the remains of this pioneer to the Cumberland, who has been called by Blount, and Haywood, and Jackson, and Ramsay, and "the truth of history," *the Father of Tennessee !*

By his side rest the remains of his wife. On these tombs may be read these simple records :

"GENL. JAMES ROBERTSON,
THE FOUNDER OF NASHVILLE,
WAS BORN IN VIRGINIA,
28TH JUNE, 1742.
DIED
1st SEPT., 1814."

CHARLOTTE R.,
WIFE OF
JAMES ROBERTSON,
WAS BORN IN NORTH CAROLINA,
2d JANY., 1751.
DIED
11th JUNE, 1843."

The following notice of the death of General Robertson appeared in "The Clarion and Tennessee State Gazette," Thursday, September 8th, 1814:

"Each hour Death warns us by an awful call;
Each hour our fellow-mortals round us fall.
Father of lights, O guide and guard our way,
Through life and death, 'to heaven's eternal day.' "

"It is with unspeakable emotions that we discharge a heart-rending duty in recording the death of *the Father* of his country.

"*General James Robertson is no more.* His spirit took its flight to the regions of bliss on Thursday last. On the 1st inst., while at the Chickasaw Agency discharging his duty as the United States Agent to that tribe of Indians, he was attacked with a violent inflammation in the head; and on the first instant the complaint triumphed, and left us to mourn the loss of our friend and patriot.

"The important and long faithful services of the deceased, the sacrifices he made of time and health to promote our prosperity, require that we should not omit a tribute of respect to his memory at this distressing moment.

"We fear our feeble attempt will fall far short of the worth of the man. We could wish, for the honor of our State, that some abler hand had undertaken the painful task of detailing the actions of him whom we all mourn.

"Our remarks will be imperfect, for we had not the honor of sharing with him the toils and privations which earned him a character that endeared him to the people; nor have we access to written records of the early transactions of the founders of this section of the Union; consequently, as there is a necessity for something being said on the occasion, we are obliged to be brief, and depend entirely on the impression made on our minds by conversations with different persons some years ago.

"It is a subject of regret to us that no individual, of leisure and talents for the purpose, has attempted to collect the items necessary for a history of the settlement of this country. It would be an employment that would give young politicians a knowledge of our State policy, and qualify them for public trusts, and, as such, would be both honorable and profitable.

"General James Robertson was a native of North Carolina, but before he arrived at the age of manhood—about the year 1760—he embarked his all in company of some acquaintances who were emigrating to the rich regions of the West.

On the banks of the Watauga River, a branch of Tennessee, then a frontier, he made a settlement, and tarried for many years. In this settlement the character of the deceased was developed. The continued marauding butcheries of the savages called forth the vigilance of the whites: rencontre after rencontre took place. In common with others, it became his duty to sally forth to chastise the foe, and protect the frontier from the tomahawk and scalping-knife. Success generally attended his movements, and, by dint of hard fighting and good management, he acquired a reputation for bravery and judgment that insured him the confidence of his fellow-citizens.

"A few of the many anecdotes that might be inserted will suffice to show his character. In July, 1774, when politics ran high, a British Captain by the name of Nugent, recruiting on the Watauga, used some provoking language respecting the colonists. General Robertson and Colonel Cocke heard his insolence, and determined to punish him for it. They seized and tarred and feathered him. This resolute conduct taught him the propriety of behaving better in future, and he profited by his experience. Shortly after, General Robertson turned out against the Indians, and was *the first man shot at*, or *who shot an Indian* at the bloody battle at the Point, (Point Pleasant,) in October of that year.

"In 1776 he was chosen to command a fort built near the mouth of Watauga, which he did with skill and judgment, and repulsed an attack of the savages, who lost a considerable number. The Indians retreated with the greatest precipitation, but were pursued by the General and

Colonel Cocke until night overtook them; they then struck fire, and with torches continued the pursuit until they came to Camp Creek, where they found the Indians' camp. With a daring never excelled, they penetrated between the guard and main body of Indians, and recovered ten horses they had stolen, and returned in safety.

"About the year 1778, a few who had seen the Cumberland country returned to the Watauga frontier, and gave such an account of the richness of the soil, the luxuriance of the growth, and the incredible quantity of game, as fired the desire of many to emigrate there. Time after time the people projected schemes for effecting their object, but they all failed until a company mostly composed of those who had fought by the side of Captain Robertson made ready to start, some by water, others by land. In September, 1778, (9?) the emigrating colony set out. Captain Robertson was chosen to command the expedition.

"After encountering delays and innumerable difficulties, the company arrived where Nashville now stands, on the 24th of December, 1778. (9?)

" To a traveller from Watauga to Nashville now, the route seems nothing ; but when we go back to the time spoken of, and recollect that the company had an untracked wilderness of several hundred miles to explore, mountains and rivers to pass, provisions to hunt, and a vigilant guard to keep out constantly to be prepared for surprises by a savage foe, the undertaking will not be considered a contemptible one.

" The few brave men who thus commenced a settlement several hundred miles from the parent State had an incredible number of difficulties to encounter. They had to hunt food, work to erect a shelter or gain provisions, or stand guard alternately.

" The parent State, for causes best known to a speculating junto, discouraged all emigration, and enacted laws which operated very oppressively on the few here. Emigration, however, continued, and time effected a change in the policy of North Carolina towards us, much to our advantage.

" In the course of the summer and fall of 1779, from ten, the company counted about two hundred. Early in the year 1780, the Cherokee Indians appeared and commenced their work of destruction. It seems it was their intention to entirely destroy the settlers. Frequent rencontres took place. The savages were in many instances successful; and station after station was abandoned, until only one or two were left occupied ; the people flying before the foe in every direction towards the station erected where Nashville now stands. The panic produced by the persevering movements of the enemy was so general, that serious preparations were made for abandoning the Cumberland country entirely. In this emergency, the zeal and active spirit of General Robertson showed itself. He was everywhere, using every argument that love of country, honor, or danger in retreating could suggest. He had partially succeeded when fortune accomplished his dearest object.

" On the 15th of January, 1781, the Indians attacked Freeland's Station. The people had been wearied down with continued fatigue, and had retired to rest. General Robertson accidentally happened there that night. The noise at the gate aroused him ; he looked out and saw the Indians had removed the fastening of the gate, and were entering the station. He immediately gave the alarm. The whites sallied forth, and a vigorous assault obliged the enemy to retreat with considerable loss. This unexpected repulse of the enemy cheered the settlers much. Many of them consented to stay and trust for better times. They were gratified.

"As had been predicted, the successes of the whites induced fresh emigration. The spring of the year, however, seemed to offer new stimulus to Indian effrontery. Their naked limbs were no longer benumbed with cold ; the thick foliage of the forests afforded protection. The Indians from attacking smaller stations could not satisfy their desire for plunder, but by a bold stroke thought to possess themselves of the principal, and, except one, the only one remaining station of the whites.

" The 2d day of April, in the year 1781, will be ever memorable in this country.

" The largest body of Indians ever known to be collected in any war expedition in this State, amounting to over seven hundred warriors, arrived the evening before on the ground where the Cumberland College now stands, (which was very thick with privet and other undergrowth,) and made the following arrangements : The main body was divided ; one half were to conceal themselves in the branch where the street crosses from Nashville to the college, a little above Demunbrune's Spring. The other was placed on the side of the hill about where Mr. Claiborne now lives, with the purpose of cutting off the retreat of the whites, should they leave the fort, and then endeavor to force the gates.

" The arrival and arrangement of the Indians was with so much circumspection that the whites suspected nothing of the magnitude of the attempt. In the night, about one o'clock, Jonas Manifee, who was on a block-house, saw an Indian spying out the fort, and shot at him. This Indian disappeared, and between day and sunrise two others showed themselves at a distance and shot at the fort. The whites immediately (as had always been the practice) prepared to pursue them ; and a little after sunrise they (twenty-one in number) left their friends in the fort.

39

"These brave men were divided. Captain Leiper commanded the advance, and General Robertson the main body. They pursued the way the Indians took, until they arrived within thirty feet of where the enemy lay concealed, when a few of the Indians rose, and, contrary to their usual method, remained standing until the whites alighted from their horses and shot. The Indians then instantly rose from their concealment and rushed on the whites.

"The whites were defeated; and but for the gallantry of General Robertson and a few others, not an individual would have escaped. As it was, only thirteen returned to the fort.

"The Indians laid siege to the fort; and on the second day fired upwards of a hundred rounds at it, but without doing any damage to the inhabitants. It seems the Indians found they could not storm or surprise the fort, and therefore divided into small parties to plunder the inhabitants and burn their property. These parties stole all the horses and stock they could find. After the failure of the attempt to possess themselves of the fort, they only attacked single individuals as they could find them. The whites were very cautious, and nothing of much importance occurred for some time. The few pioneers who continued to stand as a bulwark against a host of savages were decreasing; and the probability was that the settlement would be depopulated in a few years, when the peace with England, in 1783, changed the " face of appearances." The savages, no longer lured by the gold of England to imbrue their hands in the blood of the whites, abandoned the country, and for nearly two years molested no one of the settlers.

"As soon as this was known to the old settlements, emigrants flocked in, and the heretofore threatening forests 'were converted into fields of blooming corn, which abundantly rewarded the toil and abstinence of the tillers.'

" The State of North Carolina took the colony under its protection, and laid off the county of Davidson, appointed courts, officers of militia, and other public functionaries.

" General Robertson was shortly after elected to represent the county in the North Carolina Legislature, which he did for many years to the satisfaction of the people and benefit of the country.

"In 1790 the Constitution of the United States being adopted, and North Carolina having ceded her western lands to Congress, the 'Territory of the United States south of the Ohio River' was formed.

" In organizing the Territorial Government, the immortal Washington selected General Robertson for Brigadier and Commander of the Militia of the Territory. This mark of confidence and respect was not lost on the General.

"He took incredible pains to organize the militia and train them for service.

"The Indians began to harass the settlers. General Robertson was informed that the Cherokees, who were the most troublesome, belonged to a town on Cold Water, a small stream a few miles below the Muscle Shoals, and he therefore determined to expel them from it. Accordingly, at the head of a few brave lads, he started for that place. When they came to the Tennessee, the men divided; one part continued on this side, and the other swam the river at the Shoals, and approached the town with so much caution that they took it by surprise. The warriors and squaws were all sitting on a green near the town, drinking, etc., and the first intelligence they had of the whites was the discharge of their pieces. Never was there a more complete victory. Not an Indian ever returned to his country to tell the sad tidings.

"Want of accurate information compels us to pass over several years of General Robertson's life, with only stating, that whenever a treaty was desired with any of the southern tribes, he was sure to be selected to hold it. He possessed the confidence of the whites and Indians. The former sometimes were almost tempted to consider him a particular friend of the latter; but he was never so at the expense of justice. When he saw the Indians imposed on, he would correct the procedure if he could.

"To the confidence placed in him by the Indians, we attribute considerable part of the success that attended his conferences with them, for obtaining grants of land and for other purposes. At one treaty he obtained the country now occupied by at least one hundred thousand souls.

"As the spirit of discontent began to manifest itself among the southern Indians, the Government of the United States, impressed with a just value of the influence of the General with the southern nations, tendered to him the appointment of Agent to the Chickasaw tribe. He accepted the appointment, and continued to discharge the duties attached to the office until the close of his long life of usefulness.

"For half a century he has been an active public servant, discharging every office in the gift of the people, either in the cabinet or in the field. He was repeatedly, in particular, honored with a seat in the electoral college for choosing a President of the United States, and uniformly voted for a republican candidate.

"As a politician he was correct. He always uttered the sentiments contended for by the fathers of the Revolution. As a man, he was humane and just. As a member of society, he was hospitable and generous. He had enemies, and, no doubt, had faults. Where is the man who has been in public life half a century who had not both?

"A long list of public services of the most important kind obliterate the remembrance of his errors, and his name will be handed down to posterity with reverence, when the names of his enemies will be lost in the vortex of time.

"This tribute to departed worth is not such as we could wish it to be, but the best our time and feelings will permit us to offer on the lamented occasion."

We shall add only a few remarks upon this tribute by Mr. Bradford in the Clarion. The paper is in full mourning. There are several inaccuracies in the historical statements, which may be readily detected by persons who will refer to documents and dates we have used.

We call attention to the error as to the place of his birth, and to the year stated in which the Robertson party arrived here. Bradford says 1778, whereas it was 24th December, 1779. But the sketch, as a whole, is correct, and in every way creditable.

DONELSON FAMILY.

Our sketches would be inexcusably imperfect were we to say no more of Colonel John Donelson and his family than by quotations from Haywood. We would gladly furnish biographical outlines, if nothing more, of many other worthy pioneers and stationers on the Cumberland; but, having before us some reliable information of this family, which presents them in a most favorable light, and unfolds some of the great designs and instrumentalities in regard to this south-western country, and intimately connected with the small theatre whereon our chief personage acted his important part, we shall avail ourself of this to furnish our addenda to the chapter for the year 1786.

Colonel John Donelson was a native of Pittsylvania county, Virginia. His father (and grandfather) had been engaged in commerce and the shipping business from London, England. At what date the ancestor of Colonel Donelson came into the colony of Virginia we know not.

It is very evident, from the memorandum-book and field-notes which he kept as a surveyor; from his journals and letters, as well as from more public documents, and the important positions to which he was repeatedly called, that he was an educated man; not only a theoretical, but scientific and practical *surveyor*. In his day the knowledge of surveying was the most important and reputable attainment in education. It is enough to say that Washington was a surveyor; and so were Jefferson, and Henderson, and Fry, and other distinguished Virginians with whom Donelson was well and personally acquainted.

It is supposed that Colonel Donelson was born in the year 1718, and was, therefore, about fourteen years older than Washington, as General Sevier, another Virginia surveyor, was about eight years younger than Washington. It is well worthy of notice, that Sevier and Shelby and Robertson, Donelson and Bledsoe, Henderson and Cartwright, were born and educated in the same section of country; that they were personally acquainted; that they were all devotedly attached friends; that they possessed constitutions, energies, qualifications for high offices and great affairs; and that, leaving Washington as the central sun, they went forth upon their respective missions, moving in most suitable orbits.

These all received their noblest impulses among the great Virginians, and the no less wise and independent spirits of North Carolina. These men were ever unfaltering friends, and unswerving *Washingtonians*.

This last-mentioned fact must not be overlooked or lightly esteemed, when we study the progress of the Anglo-Saxons, westward and southward. The life and times of Sevier and Robertson show clearly the importance of their devotion to and confidence in Washington, for the extension and triumph of the American Union and republican government, from Virginia and North Carolina, westward to the Mississippi, southward and onward to the Gulf of Mexico, and yet onward to the Pacific Ocean. The character and services of Colonel Donelson, his descendants and connections, have an important bearing, and serve happily to illustrate this same sentiment and its value.

There was a potent virtue in the name of Washington. Esteem for and confidence in him were important elements in the patriotic sentiment of America, contributing to our national independence, to the adoption of the Federal Constitution, and to the suppression of a disunion sentiment west of the mountains.

It was a wise ordination of Heaven, that so many of the officers and soldiers of the Revolution, who loved and venerated Washington, emigrated at an early day to the western wilds. This fact obtrudes itself upon the notice of the student of our history at a thousand points. They came with a fervent love of freedom, a lofty sentiment of independence, and an unbending purpose not to allow the rich fruits of their great victory to prove "apples of Sodom."

What they had gained they could not themselves long enjoy, but they determined that their posterity should possess an inheritance more valuable than had ever before been bequeathed to any people.

It was to make these possessions doubly sure that these wise, brave, patriotic men moved westward, and unfurled that flag under which they and their great leader had acquired glory and undying honor.

The fact that Washington was interested at a very early day, even before the Declaration of American Independence, in large grants of land upon the waters of the Ohio, is not to be overlooked or lightly esteemed, as one of the *preludes* to a far greater interest in all the western and southern country. The territorial rights of Virginia north of the Ohio, and especially the conquest by her brave soldiers of the British forces in Illinois, and the organizing of that territory into a *county* of the Old .

Dominion, are other items in the grand summary of historical incidents in favor of the union of the western with the eastern territories.

As the *Ficus Indica*, the marvellous banyan tree, spreads forth its branches, which, bending to the earth, take root and form new, vigorous, and fruitful trees, covering "broad acres," so the great American live-oak, the tree of Independence, has shot forth its strong limbs, imbedded deep its marvel-working roots, whence have arisen gigantic oaks, with all the majesty, strength, and glory of the parent stock. Though distinct and noble trees, as they spread out, beautify and bless the land, they are united at the root, partaking alike of the richness and fatness of the soil, and yielding alike to the shelter and happiness of the one great and united family, the American people.

Never may these roots be severed; never may one tree become barren; never one yield other than healthful fruit, or be covered with other verdure than that which is perennial in its greenness : leaves from the tree sanctified for "the healing of nations!"

Prior to the Declaration of Independence, Colonel Donelson had served as a Member in the House of Burgesses, and it is believed that he was once or twice a Member of the Assembly of Virginia subsequent to the Declaration. Jefferson and Henry were his personal friends; he held commissions under each of them, to execute important trusts, such as the survey of State lines, the negotiating of treaties with Indians, or establishing the authority of the State over distant territory.

In the year 1772, Colonel Donelson was appointed to survey the State line west, to designate certain limits for the Indians, and to secure a route for emigration to Kentucky. He met some of the Cherokees at the Long Island of Holston, and there formed a treaty, or obtained their approbation of a certain line which he had already run, or which he immediately thereafter traced more distinctly.

He formed the acquaintance of several chiefs, who answered his many questions as to the character of the lands on the great Tennessee, and the navigation of that river. The Great Bend and the Muscle Shoals were described. He was induced to believe that few if any Indians were settled on the east side of the river, and that if the white people desired to acquire possessions there, and establish trading-posts, they would meet with little opposition.

Other adventurous land-hunters had obtained some knowledge of the extensive body of rich land in that Great Bend; and there was a desire among prominent men in Virginia, North Carolina, and Georgia, to secure some portions of it. We know not with whom it originated, but the project was not many years thereafter formed of establishing a colony there, of which Colonel Donelson was an active participant. With him General Sevier was associated. At an early day they visited that country together.

The boundary line between Virginia and North Carolina had been the cause of much contention between the two colonies from the year 1700, and various sets of Commissioners had been appointed to run and determine the same, but it remained in dispute for one hundred and twenty years. It was never settled as between Virginia and Carolina; and only as between Kentucky and Tennessee in 1820.

In the year 1777, another meeting was held with the Indians at the Long Island of Holston.

Governor Henry, of Virginia, had notified Governor Caswell, of North Carolina, that he had appointed Commissioners to meet with the Cherokee chiefs at Fort Patrick Henry, near the Long Island, in the spring, and that the desire of Virginia was to obtain an alteration of the line run by *Donelson*, and to have a road to and through the Cumberland Gap included in a cession then to be obtained from the Indians. Emigrants to the county of Kentucky must needs pass through the Gap.

Either from the unsuitable time selected, or want of due notice to Governor Caswell and the Indian chiefs, there was no meeting in the spring, or so small a representation that the assembling of Commissioners from the two States and the chiefs was fixed for the 26th day of June, 1777.

At the time appointed the parties met. The Virginia Commissioners became satisfied that Colonel Donelson was very nearly right; that he had not run his line too much to the north; and they gave way to the North Carolina Commissioners to conclude the treaty, knowing that through whatsoever territory that State acquired, the citizens of Virginia would have the liberty of passage. The result was the treaty at Fort Henry, near the Long Island of Holston, July 20th, 1777, signed by the chiefs of that part of the nation called the Overhill Cherokees.

In the fifth article, a line (called Brown's, being near his settlements) was designated as " agreed upon between Virginia and the said Overhill Cherokees," which is made the " beginning-point" for the boundaries now established. And thus were the wishes of the Virginia Commission attained, and satisfactorily settled *there* for a short distance.

Colonel Donelson was present at this treaty, and acquired further knowledge of the country on the Tennessee and Cumberland.

All the men of note who had commenced settlements upon the Nollachucka, Holston, and in adjacent regions, were present on some day of the three weeks' assemblage at the Fort. There were others from

Carolina and Georgia, who had an eye upon the lands in the Great Bend. The conception of the great "Tennessee Land Company," subsequently known as "Cox's," in all probability originated with persons who met at this treaty.

Here were Robertson and Sevier, Boone and Bledsoe, Shelby, Henderson, Hart, and others—all men of worth, of nerve, of enterprise— "men who feared God, but obeyed no earthly king."

They talked freely of the Declaration of Independence, as it had been announced at Mecklenburg, in North Carolina, by Patrick Henry and the Virginians, and by the Continental Congress just twelve months before. They did not think of giving notoriety out there to the Fourth of July; but they all heartily concurred in the renunciation of allegiance to the King of Great Britain, and in the resolution to make "these States free and independent." They talked proudly of Washington. The border county in Virginia was "Washington County." But the Carolinians could say more than that : the whole territory now constituting the State of Tennessee had been erected by the Assembly of North Carolina into "Washington District."

The men were there who had first honored themselves and their country by applying the name of Washington to particular localities. Who can be at a loss to understand the character of these men, and of their political sentiments ? Who can be blinded as to the special origin and tendency of this and other acts and associations?

We could continue the enumeration of incidents all concurring in the "wonder-working Providence" to wrest the great valley of the Mississippi from the savages, and especially from the dominion of all foreign governments. It is an interesting trace of American history.

But before we proceed with the memoir of Colonel Donelson, and a development of the purposes which were to be promoted through his instrumentality, we must deepen and confirm the impression in the minds of our readers, that Donelson enjoyed the acquaintance of and was early associated with the truest and earliest advocates of "the private, natural and inalienable rights of the people, as men and Christians," and of "American Independence."

We must pay our respects to some of the Commissioners from North Carolina who negotiated the treaty of Long Island, 20th July, 1777.

The first commissions for that purpose were filled with the names of Brigadier-General *John McDowell* and Colonel *John Sevier*. They, however, effected nothing of much consequence with the Cherokees.

Then followed the appointment of Waightstill Avery, William Sharpe,

Robert Lanier, and Joseph Winston, who concluded the treaty with Ocon-os-tota, and other chiefs.

The Commissioners from Virginia were Colonel William Christian, Colonel William Preston, Colonel Evan Shelby. What an assemblage of *patriots* in the fastnesses of the Cumberland Mountains, in July, 1777! And how incalculably great the influence they sent forth in behalf of American independence !

Let us mention again, and in this connection, the names of other pa-triots who were there, or had been there, for they were to be considered as stationers there, ere long to advance farther west, step by step, station by station.

There were John and Valentine Sevier, Daniel Boone, Isaac Bledsoe, (a witness to the treaty,) Anthony Bledsoe, Isaac and Evan Shelby, Rich-ard Henderson, Thomas Hart, James Robertson, James Eaton, Robert Cartwright, John Rains, and many others who " blazed their way through the wilderness, fought for the liberties of the country, and planted the institutions of civil and religious order," where

> "None but savage men,
> And beasts almost as wild,
> Kept worthless and untilled
> The richest of our earth."

But who were these Commissioners?

WAIGHTSTILL AVERY

was a resident of Wake County, North Carolina, but born in Norwich, Connecticut. He settled as a lawyer at Charlotte, in 1769. He was a bold advocate of liberty, a member of the " Mecklenburg Convention," and a signer of that notable " Declaration of Independence, May 20th, 1775." This was "glory enough," and proof unquestionable that he was ready to " die in his country's cause." " He was an exemplary Chris-tian, a pure patriot, and an honest man." He died in 1821.

WILLIAM SHARPE

was a distinguished patriot of the Revolution. Born in Cecil County, Maryland, in 1742, where he studied law: removed and settled in *Meck-lenburg*, where he married a daughter of *David Reese*, one of the *signers* of the Mecklenburg Declaration. He was a member of the *Continental Congress* at Philadelphia, in 1779, and served till 1782. Died in 1818.*

---

* The file of the Georgia Gazette, possessed by the Tennessee Historical Society, was once Dr. Sharpe's.

He left a widow and twelve children. · A son bearing his own name resides near Murfreesboro, Tennessee.

ROBERT LANIER.

We have no distinct information of this member of the Commission. Our impression is that he remained upon the Holston for some years, and that his descendants are well and reputably known in Davidson County, Tennessee.

JOSEPH WINSTON

was a native of Stokes County, North Carolina; an early and devoted friend of American liberty. In 1775–6, he was an active member of committees and patriot meetings. He was a *Major* in the battle of King's Mountain, and, with McDowell and Sevier, commanded the right wing in that fierce and bloody fight. He was a Member of Congress from 1793 to 1795, and again from 1803 to 1807. Died in 1814.

Such were the men with whom Colonel Donelson delighted to associate, in whose patriotic sentiments he heartily concurred.

At this important meeting, information was received from Boone, Rains, Mansker, and others, who had hunted and explored in 1769–70 upon the Cumberland. The reports which they gave of the country, and its marvellous herds of buffalo and deer, awakened very considerable interest; and in 1771 some of the same pioneer hunters, accompanied by John Montgomery, Isaac Bledsoe, and Joseph Drake, again visited the country, and returned in 1772. Such parties continued to visit these hunting-grounds, acquiring more and more information at each visit, and increasing the favorable opinion of the country.

In the spring of 1779, as we have stated elsewhere, a party of friends on the Holston determined to visit the Cumberland and commence a settlement, as a nucleus for other settlements. They planted corn near the French Lick, and returned to bring out their families in the fall of the year.

Mansker arrived here with another party before Robertson's companions had started back. He and his friends selected lands on the east side of the river, and returned for their families.

In October the various parties again set out from the Holston settlements to come by way of the Gap through Kentucky. The wives and children, with much of the household property of these emigrants, were to come by way of the River Tennessee "to the upper end of the Muscle Shoals," where, according to the journal of Colonel Donelson, the Robertson party were to have marked some trees and left signs which should indicate, not only "that they had been there," but "that it was *practicable* for Colonel Donelson and his party to go across by land" to the Cumberland. Such were the arrangements and agreements for these emigrating parties.

Colonel Donelson was a devout man; indeed, no attentive student of the character and conduct and language of most of the early settlers, can fail to notice how often and how decidedly they recognize "Divine Providence." That they were accomplishing "purposes wisely ordered," in their respective spheres, we have no more doubt than we have that General Washington was "the great power," the specially ordained instrument in the hands of God, to accomplish the independence of these United States, and to set in operation our happy form of government.

Colonel Donelson had constructed at "Fort Patrick Henry, on Holston," a very comfortable boat, which he properly named "the good boat *Adventure.*" With his own family, which was large, (and a goodly number of servants,) with the wife of Colonel Robertson and her five children, and others, as mentioned in the Journal of Colonel Donelson, he set sail on the 22d day of December, 1779. They proceeded but a short distance, when, by reason of the low stage of the water, and severity of the cold, they stopped for two months, near the Poor Valley Shoals. Here they were joined by other boats, filled with emigrants, bound on the same voyage, or for the Illinois, or Natchez. According to the statement of Mr. Cartwright, who was with Colonel Donelson, there were "about forty boats in the squadron."

Colonel Donelson was regarded as the principal person among these voyagers. He is the only person who is known to have undertaken the keeping of a Journal of the voyage. As that Journal is given under the date of 1780, in chapter iv., we shall make no quotations from it here, other than the expressive, reverential, and proper acknowledgment in the *caption*, that the "voyage" was "intended by God's permission;" and we may truly say it was by God's good favor they passed through so many dangers, and arrived so safely at "the end of their journey, at the Big Salt Lick, on Monday, April 24th, 1780."

The causes which prevented Colonel Robertson and his companions from going "across to the Tennessee, and leaving signs above the Muscle Shoals," we have shown in the appropriate place. But it is now proper to recur to the consideration of some of the inducements and aims of leading men in these parties of emigrants.

John Rains and his friends set out with intention to go to Harrod's Station, and settle in Kentucky; but falling in company with the Robertson party when on the route, they were persuaded to accompany the latter to the Cumberland; and here he acted an important and useful part.

The Robertsons, Bledsoes, Mansker, Eaton, Freeland, Neelly, and others, had long cherished the purpose of permanent settlements here for themselves and their posterity; (really to extend the name, the influence, the power of the United Colonies upon the Cumberland, as others were doing upon the Kentucky rivers.) They toiled, they suffered, some of them perished, but the great purposes were accomplished; if not in all instances "so much for them," they were for thousands of others who have since lived and shall hereafter live.

It is not the men who *design* and *lay* the *foundation* that always live to behold the magnificent edifice erected and completed; but they are the men who should possess both the physical and the mental energy to brave toils and trials, and dig deep and lay firmly the entire basement. Then "other men may enter into their labors; other men may build thereon;" other men may answer well the purpose of scaffoldings, or the carriers of brick and mortar, or to give the finishing embellishments. Each design and structure needs a variety of workmen: God has a purpose, a use for them all, "each in their own order."

The men of whom we write were trained and fitted for the important positions which they occupied, and none of them lived in vain or lived alone unto themselves. It was not permissible or possible for such men so to vegetate, and wilt, and rot: they were gifted of Heaven with talents which could not be hid in a napkin and buried; they were called to make their mark here, and *they did it.* Colonel Donelson was, to use his own language, "intended by God's providence" to a position of honor.

In the spring of 1780, very soon after his arrival, Colonel Donelson commenced the search through the forests and cane-brakes for land. His aim, like that of others, was for a location on rich land, and where there should be combined other natural advantages. He passed up the west bank of the Cumberland to the mouth of Stone's River, thence up that stream until he came upon a beautiful body of bottom-land, and rich upland gently descending towards it. In a number of open spots there was discovered a luxuriant growth of native white clover; but the low and uplands were mostly covered with timber and cane. This place has become known as the "Clover Bottom."

Here Colonel Donelson determined to make his location. He selected a gentle eminence, which was about one hundred and fifty yards to the north-west of the bridge across Stone's River on the Lebanon Pike. The place is yet partially covered with the native forest. The descent is gradual towards the river and bridge.

He moved there with his family and servants, erected some shantees with open fronts, or "half-camps." In one of these his daughter-in-law, the wife of Captain John Donelson, Jr., gave birth, on 22d June, 1780, to a son, whom they named *Chesed.* We have no doubt this was the first white child born on the Cumberland. He died within a short time after birth.

The name given to this child is somewhat remarkable; is certainly not familiar to any modern ears. It is a *Hebrew* word, all the significations of which are not very pleasant. The prominent meaning is "a destroyer." By the adoption of this name was there intended to be an acknowledgment or an intimation that the "destroyer" was nigh? What did it indicate? There was none of the family named Chesed. "The great destroyer" soon marked this child as his victim; and other destroyers continued the work of destruction—cheseds indeed of the worst signification.

The work of cutting and burning cane, and opening the rich, virgin soil with the hoe, was progressed with rapidly. Colonel Donelson had a number of able-bodied negro men and women, and instead of first erecting log-houses and defences for his own family and his servants, he gave his attention almost exclusively to the preparations for various crops. There being so much open ground in the bottoms, enabled him to get in his corn crop in a very seasonable time. Some small trees were cut down, which, with the brush and tops of fallen timber, were converted into temporary fences.

There were immense herds of buffalo, deer, etc., ranging through these forests, and the expectation was to watch and frighten them from the growing corn, rather than to keep them out by such rude enclosures. It was very evident these wild animals were accustomed to resort to this locality to graze upon the native grasses.

This settlement was called "Stone's River," or "Donelson's Station," as may be seen upon the records of the Provisional Government of the 13th May, 1780. It was entitled to one Representative in the Assembly of Notables at the Bluffs.

The name of Donelson is the fifth on that roll of noble pioneers who adopted the anomalous government, 1st of May, with the amendments and additions of 13th May. His name precedes that of Gasper Mansker, as Mansker's does that of John Caffrey, who came in the "Adventure" with Colonel Donelson. It is written "Jno. Donelson, C." Colonel Donelson always abbreviated his christened name, whereas his son wrote his name in full—John Donelson.

Having planted his corn on the south side of the river, he planted "a small patch of cotton" on the north side of Stone's River, (a few rods below where the bridge spans the river,) and where the exposure to the sun and adaptation of soil to such a plant were deemed more favorable.

These crops were growing rapidly, and giving great satisfaction, exciting hopes of abundance, when an event occurred which was viewed, at the time, as the most disastrous which could befall them. Some time in the early part of July the entire bottom was overflowed to such a depth as to cover the corn. It was then regarded as a total loss, and, with his large family soon to be in want of bread, caused very great anxiety to Colonel Donelson and his son. Added to this calamity, it was known that savage Indians had appeared on the Cumberland, and had already killed some of the pioneers.

The danger from Indians and this destruction of his corn by the flood, at once decided him to remove his family to Mansker's Station. This removal he accomplished in his boats before the water had entirely left the bottom-lands wherein his crop of corn was planted. The flood, deemed at the time a great calamity, was afterwards viewed as a most fortunate circumstance. All were under the impression that the crop was a total loss. Had Colonel Donelson known the true state of the case, or have supposed that the corn would have lived and flourished as it did, after the subsiding of the waters, he would unquestionably have adhered to his position, though it was then totally without defences. He had neither block-house, stockade, nor sentinel in regular station.

In such exposure, his whole family must have fallen under the Indian tomahawk and scalping-knife. Already one or two white men and Colonel Henderson's negro (Jim) had been killed, the latter near Clover Bottom. And very soon after this removal to Mansker's, several irruptions into the new settlements were made by the Indians.

Although much disposed to look for suggestive and guiding indications from the events transpiring around him, yet was he a man firm in his purpose, set in his resolutions, and not easily diverted. He disliked exceedingly to abandon his settlement and lose his crop, but the crop having wholly disappeared beneath the flood, and other events concurring, the intimation seemed plain and sufficiently urgent for departure.

Such are the facts in regard to that station and its abandonment; and yet there was to be a return thither, and the enacting there of the greatest havoc of this first year of settlement on Cumberland.

Having become stationers at Mansker's, the Donelsons were not idle. Other lands were sought out, which were not subject to inundation; but the season having too far advanced to open ground and plant other crops, which could mature before the frost, the best which could be done was to aid in the cultivation of such crops as others had planted. But no one at Mansker's had a crop beyond his own ability to cultivate, and far too limited for such a force and family as that of Colonel Donelson.

He had learned that at the stations in Kentucky the prospects of abundant crops would justify additions to their population. He had friends there, and calls to transact business there, and yet he tarried at Mansker's until the fall of the year.

Then it was ascertained that, instead of his corn having been destroyed by the overflow, it had sprung up and grown and eared most astonishingly; and, strange to say, neither Indians nor wild beasts had wasted much of it. Perhaps the Indians had watched it, and awaited the time when the owners should come to gather it, that then they might destroy both it and them!

Colonel Donelson was highly pleased to learn that there was such prospect of bread; and knowing that the stationers at the Lick, or Bluff, had likewise lost much of their crops by the inundation and other causes, and were in great destitution, he generously proposed to divide with them whatever could be gathered from his field. Indeed, it may be said of these pioneers, as of the early Christians, "they held all things in common:" a generous hospitality and cheerful liberality characterized them all. Call it prudence, call it friendship, call it necessity, call it what you please, it was a sentiment in which were combined prudence, friendship, and need—elements in the formation and development of good character and good society; an overruling principle and purpose, which housed, herded, and huddled these pioneers together: "a fellow-feeling, which made them wondrous kind:" not very unlike to pleasure to

"Share each other's woes;
Each other's burdens bear."

It is not fabulous, nor an exaggeration, to say, that if there remained but *one dried buffalo tongue*, or but *one knife*, they divided that tongue and broke that knife, making as equal a division as possible for each one's separate necessity. They were often just in those circumstances in which the development of character was prompt and inevitable; wherein evil dispositions were restrained, and the kindest sentiments drawn out and strengthened.

The offer of Colonel Donelson having been accepted, and the day agreed upon, and the mouth of Stone's River designated as the place for meeting, each party complied with the agreement. The company from the Bluff was under the command of Abel Gower. He had with him his son, Abel Gower, Jr., John Randolph Robertson, a relative of Colonel Robertson,* and several others, white and black, seven or eight in all.

---

* Haywood says, "John Robertson, the son of Captain James Robertson."

The party from Mansker's was under the direction of Captain John Donelson, second son of Colonel Jno. Donelson. He was a young man of about six-and-twenty years of age. Robert Cartwright, an aged gentleman, was also in this company.

The history of the Clover Bottom defeat, as preserved distinctly in the family, is as follows:

The parties having ascended Stone's River, and fastened their boats to the bank, (between the present turnpike bridge and the small island a few hundred yards below,) commenced gathering the corn, packing it in baskets and sacks, and upon a sled to the boats.

Captain Donelson had brought a horse for the purpose of dragging the rudely constructed "slide," as also in towing the boats up the stream.

They were encamped for several days and nights upon the ground. During each night their dogs kept up an almost incessant barking. They had with them more dogs than men. Some of the party had suggested that the dogs scented or discovered Indians in the surrounding woods and cane. But the prevailing opinion was, that, as there was much fresh meat at the camp, and offal left in the woods where some buffalo had been killed, the wolves were attracted thereby, and the dogs were barking at these wild beasts.

During the last night of their continuance at the place, "the dogs rushed furiously in every direction around the camps, as if actually mad, making the woods ring and echo with their barking."

In the morning they made no examination for Indian signs, but hastened the completion of their loads and preparations for departure. Very early in the morning Captain Donelson pushed his boat across the river, and began to gather the bolls of cotton and deposit them in heaps upon the corn in his boat. It was thought this would cause but a short delay. But when Captain Gower's party had finished their breakfast, they became impatient to start. Donelson had expected Gower's boat also to cross the river, and his people to share in the crop of cotton.

Great was the surprise of Captain Donelson and Mr. Cartwright to discover Gower's boat passing down the stream instead of coming across. Captain Donelson stepped to the bank of the river, hailed them, and asked if they were coming over, or going to leave them behind.

Gower replied: "We are not coming over; it is getting late in the

---

There was then no son named John. Haywood is again in error in asserting that Colonel Donelson was there. It was *John, Jr.*, known as *Captain*, the father of our friends William and Stockley, who yet reside near the Hermitage, and from whose family Bible we obtain the names and ages of the family.

40

day; we wish to reach the Bluff before night. I think there is no danger."

Captain Donelson remonstrated, but added, "If you can risk it, so can we; we will first gather the cotton."

By this time, and while they were yet conversing, Captain Gower's boat had drifted into the head of the narrow island shute, when the Indians, who were in ambush on the south side, (supposed to be several hundred in number,) opened a desperate fire upon the men in Gower's boat.

Captain Donelson saw the attack plainly. He immediately ran down to his own boat and secured his rifle and shot-bag. Upon rising the bank he saw the Indians in pursuit of several men, who had jumped from the boat at the first fire. The water did not exceed three or four feet in depth.

He also discovered a large party of Indians making their way up the river bank to a point opposite to his boat. There, however, the river was too deep to be forded. Upon that party Captain Donelson fired, and then endeavored to join his own party. They had all fled into the cane upon hearing the guns fired and the yells of the savages.

It was with considerable difficulty he was enabled to rejoin his friends. The horse was given up to Mr. Cartwright, who otherwise could not have escaped, being aged and infirm.

Some of the party of Captain Gower were killed at the first fire, others were overtaken in the water and tomahawked. That every man was not shot dead in the boat, and pierced with many bullets, can only be accounted for by the fact we have had to state or suggest in other instances of the Indian warfare against the Cumberland settlements, namely, that such guns as they had were almost worthless, that they used very light loads of powder and ball, and that most of them were armed only with the primitive Indian weapons, bow and arrows, and the blow-gun and arrows.

Another fact is to be noticed: the river's bank by the side of that narrow channel is naked, destitute of bushes near the shore, and afforded an ambush or covert only upon the top of the bank, at some distance from the water, and the foe would have to shoot *down* at such an angle or aim that most of them would be apt to miss.

One white man and a negro escaped into the woods. Another negro, a free man, known as *Jack Civil*, was slightly wounded, and surrendered. He was taken to the Chickamauga towns, remained, and moved with that roving, murderous, thieving set farther down the Tennessee River, and gave name to the town of *Nick-a-Jack*, or Nigger-Jack's town.

The white man and negro who jumped from the boat and escaped into the woods, wandered for twenty hours. At length they reached the station towards morning, pushed aside some of the pickets, and entered the enclosure at the Bluff undiscovered by any one in the fort, "although the dogs gave the faithful alarm."

Gower's boat, as we have elsewhere mentioned, floated down the river, the corn and some of the dead being on board undisturbed, except by some of the dogs which continued therein.

The opinion prevailed for some days that the Donelson party had fallen victims to the guns and tomahawks of the savages. It was hazardous to pass between stations so distant as Mansker's and the Bluff.

James Randolph Robertson was among the slain. Thus early was Colonel Robertson made to taste of the cup of affliction, which, in after-years, was so often filled and pressed to the lips of these pioneers.

There was no alternative for the Donelson party : they must abandon the boat and all it contained and flee into the woods. They could render no assistance to their friends, now overwhelmed; they could not pass out with their own boat; and they might well suppose that the savages, flushed with an easy victory over half the harvesters, would speedily be in pursuit of themselves.

After Captain Donelson had overtaken the fleeing party, they hastily agreed upon the direction to be taken, so that they might assemble the next day upon the bank of the Cumberland, some miles above the mouth of Stone's River, where they would attempt to cross and escape to Mansker's Station. It was deemed advisable to separate, *not all to go together*, lest thereby they should make such a trail through the cane and bushes as the Indians could easily follow.

Having continued their course until sunset, Captain Donelson discovered a large hickory tree which had fallen to the ground, and, as it had a thick top and large supply of leaves, he called in the wanderers, and they huddled together there for the night. They did not attempt to kindle any fire, though they greatly needed it. The night was passed in quiet, but with very little sleep.

Captain Donelson informed the party of the slaughter he witnessed of the Gower party. He believed they were all killed, and that the Indian force was sufficient to besiege and capture any of the stations.

The situation of this little squad was also very critical. The savages might be in search of them, and they had the river between them and their friends at the Mansker Station, and there was no boat to be had. How should they get over ? or what should they do ?

Having convened upon the bank of the river, they endeavored to construct a raft upon which to be floated across. They had left the axe in the boat, and no light and suitable material could be found to answer the purpose. Yet they gathered sticks, and fastened them together with withes and vines, and made several attempts to go over, but the current invariably drove their rude float back to the side of the river whence they had set out. They had to abandon all efforts thus to get over, and permit their raft to be carried away by the current. What now shall be done? At this juncture, Colonel Donelson's faithful servant, Somerset, volunteered to swim the river, with the aid of the horse, and ride to the station and give information of the situation of the party. He succeeded in crossing, ascended the opposite bank, and hastened in the direction through cane and woods. Safely arriving at the station, he gave the first information of the disastrous defeat. It was indeed sad news, disheartening to every one.

Immediately a few active men returned with Somerset, taking axes wherewith to cut and prepare a float for the relief of their friends, who were suffering with cold and hunger. It was chill November weather, and the rain had fallen during a part of the night and morning. They were all passed over, and safely arrived at the station.

Colonel Donelson had delayed his departure to Kentucky on account of the prospect of obtaining this supply of corn. He now determined to carry into effect his previous purpose, and made immediate preparations for moving. Having packed his horses, and given the best conveyances to the women and children, and the men being furnished with such utensils and weapons as were most needed and serviceable in their hands, the party set out for Davis's Station. They arrived there without interruption by the savages, or more toil and suffering than they had anticipated.

The family of Captain Rains was already there, or arrived near the same time; so did some other of the early Cumberland stationers. Indeed, there was quite a "stampede" at this period, and very disheartening to the few who *would* not or *could* not also remove; for some there were who determined never to abandon their stations, and a few who may have been inclined to depart, but could not, owing to the incumbrance of wives, children, or property, which could not be transported, or attachment to friends whose lives would be the more endangered by further desertion.

The few persons who remained at Mansker's were urged to leave the place; but there was much reluctance on the part of some, and such delay to do so that the lives of two or three were lost there. Then there was an entire desertion of the place. Mansker and his wife took refuge (we believe) at Eaton's Station. Colonel Henderson and his brother,

Captain Hart, and a number of others, had already gone to Kentucky in advance of Colonel Donelson.

The early emigrants to Cumberland, who were natives of Virginia, had relatives or friends already in Kentucky; so had many of the Carolinians.

The destitution of corn, and deficiency of powder and lead, operated strongly upon the minds of many of the persons who departed in the summer and fall of 1780, and winter of 1780–81. A few removed their families to more secure positions, and then returned to stand by their friends in defence of the stations at Eaton's, the Bluff, and Freeland's.

Colonel Donelson had Virginia claims in his own right and for friends which could be located only in Kentucky. To attend to and secure these was another object to be attained by going to some Kentucky station. Having placed his large family (white and black) in safety at Davis's Station, he extended his visits to several of the other settlements, and obtained intelligence from Virginia of a much later date than any possessed upon the Cumberland. He learned the sad news from South Carolina and Georgia : the surrender of Charleston, the defeat of General Gates, and the rumored submission of the largest number of the people to British rule. But then there soon came the intelligence of the victory at King's Mountain, attained by his own personal friends, Campbell, Sevier, Shelby, McDowell, and Cleveland.

If Gates had captured Cornwallis at Camden, the heart of Donelson would not have so swelled with joy, as it did when he heard what had been done, so suddenly and so completely, by these his personal friends over the skilful partisan leader, Ferguson. It was a joint victory attained by Virginians and North Carolinians, and brightened and strengthened the chain of friendship between all the early settlers in Kentucky and on the Cumberland.

We should mention that Colonel Robertson was at some of the stations in Kentucky at this time, acquiring information of the strength of their defences and number of the population. He also procured a supply of ammunition for his fellow-adventurers now remaining at Cumberland. With this stock of powder and lead he arrived, as we have shown in its proper connection, at Freeland's Station most opportunely, and gave the first alarm of the entrance of Indians into that fort, and aided in their repulse.

But of Colonel Donelson we must say, that in leaving his friends on Cumberland he did not "go out from them because he was not of them ;" because he was indifferent to their safety and welfare ; or because he was willing or intended to abandon his locations near the Cumberland, or had yet lost all his *yearnings* for the Great Bend of Tennessee.

The fact is, that the removal of his large family was a relief to the stations on Cumberland. He had proposed to divide whatever might be secured as the product of the labor of his hands. The people at the Bluff had, indeed, obtained *their share: that boat-load had floated to their very shore,* and the number of mouths to be fed had been reduced at that point; whilst Colonel Donelson, and his own family and friends at Mansker's, were deprived of every ear of corn and every boll of cotton. There was a necessity, therefore, for his removal; and a necessity perhaps almost as urgent justified the departure of others, though some of them went in spite of appeals and remonstrances.

And yet the appearance of Donelson in Kentucky may have served a better purpose than he could have accomplished had he remained on the Cumberland, with an abundant supply of provisions. Let us search for such evidence. He had not been there twelve months before he was called upon to enact a part which is the culminating point in his history.

In all companies and everywhere he had been the decided advocate of the American Revolution; always and everywhere had he spoken in terms of warmest eulogy of Washington; always and everywhere did he urge and contend for the union of the Colonies.

With his family and friends he had crossed the mountains, resolved to make their permanent homes upon some of these western waters. He was still a Virginian on Virginia soil; an American, and at home in this far west of that day.

The idea of *expatriating* himself had never entered his mind. The thought of placing his children under bigoted, Spanish, papal rule and influence, would have been abhorrent to his soul; to distrust and denounce Washington, and plot *treason* against his country, in his estimation, would have been "worse than the sin of witchcraft, and next to the unpardonable sin."

Aged as he was, brief as had been his sojourn in Kentucky, he hesitated not to declare his opinion, that Virginia of right claimed and would maintain her dominion over this transmontane territory; that no "State of Transylvania" could be set up in defiance of her sanction; and least of all would she submit to an alienation of any portion of her western territory and people, that England, France, or Spain might here establish a foreign rule.

It was strongly suspected that Spain at this early day, while professedly aiding in the war of Revolution, and for our separation from England, was secretly working up a spirit of discontent and alienation among our exposed, harassed, and embarrassed and adventurous pioneer population.

Donelson and some others were ready to declare, that if there were

"Americans born" who would yield to any of these dishonorable suggestions, "not only their bodies but their souls needed to be purged, as
with fire." He did not indeed wish an *auto-da-fé* in old Spanish fashion,
but rather that the flame of patriotism might burn so fiercely "that no
old tory or *new traitors*" could live in all the land.

He found in Kentucky some true-hearted Virginians, Washingtonians,
adherents to the Confederacy; but he heard also of others, "whose hearts
were not as his heart."

It is strange, but yet true, that the "Spanish Kentucky conspiracy,"
which, in its various devices and struggles to separate the western country
from the Eastern States, caused our early Administrations so much trouble, and the true lovers of the integrity of the Union so much anxiety,
had its inception years before the termination of the War of Independence. Of that conspiracy we have elsewhere written; and we say now,
what we have said or intended to say in its proper connection with this
whole matter, that there was much to induce, we can almost say justify,
suggestions, consultations, and wishes for a separate and independent
government west of the mountains; yea, that it is strange the people
went no farther than discussions and bitter words. But of this we also
feel as confident as of any other position we can assume in relation to the
whole subject, that not one native American, however much he may have
said, at heart desired or could long have endured a close alliance with
Spain, or any of her officials in Louisiana or Florida. As General
Robertson once said, "They and their entire system, political, diplomatic,
and ecclesiastic, have too strong a smell of Tophet and garlic."

The earliest manifestation of this western Spanish intrigue, perhaps,
may be discovered in the year 1781, the first year of Colonel Donelson's
residence in Kentucky. The project seems to have been started several
years before the arrival of General Wilkinson in the western country.

We have had to show, that in the correspondence of General Robertson with some of the Spanish officers, he felt himself justified in the use
of words which "palter in a double sense." He took hold of their own
diplomatic weapons; he spoke graciously to them, when his very soul
abhorred all manner of deceit and the deceivers.

That in those early times, and doubtful and perplexing circumstances,
there may have been most worthy, true, and loyal republicans in Kentucky who yielded for a moment, or seemed to yield, to some of these
projects, is very probable; and that some of the early settlers believed
that, of necessity, the people west of the mountains must institute a government independent of and separate from that which was not yet fully
organized on the Atlantic side, cannot be denied. This sentiment was

not novel and wholly repudiated among the people of the Eastern States: the topic was discussed there, as well as in these wild woods and "rank barrens."

And now, when we read such an assertion as this—"In the fall of 1781, Colonel Todd, with about fifty or sixty of his adherents, assembled at Harrodsburg to deliberate on this scheme, [the Spanish scheme for a separation of the western from the eastern country :] *Colonel Donelson*, a *firm* supporter of *the Union of the States*, having heard of their intentions, convened a much larger party, and broke up their meeting, *in a manner, by force*, rather than persuasion"—we are ready to say, in so doing Colonel Donelson did no great violence to any of these *supposed conspirators* or *traitors*.

Of this we are confident, that Colonel Todd, with the majority of those who were in consultation at Harrodsburg about the condition of these new and exposed settlements, their prospects and policy, was uncorrupted and incorruptible by malign foreign influences. He was as true a patriot, as brave a soldier, and as accomplished a gentleman as could be found among men, who, in that day, were generally preëminent in the possession of each of these qualities.

It should never be said of Colonel Todd that he was "a traitor." His vigorous exertions for the defence of his fellow-citizens, and his dashing heroism at the sad affair at Blue Licks, on 18th August, 1782, in which rash attack upon the Indians he lost his life, furnish abundant proof that his American heart had never been soiled by the thought of treason.

The accusation made by Humphrey Marshall, Esq., which we have quoted, is without the least qualification. We cannot, therefore, let it pass without some further remark. Mr. Marshall, who was not inferior to others of that intellectual family, was apt to use very strong terms "even bitter words," to express his views and sentiments. He had no respect for the man who withheld praise from Washington, and to utter a word of censure against his administration, was to insure Marshall's unappeasable hatred. The charge he makes against Colonel Todd was unquestionably made when actuated by such a feeling, or from ignorance, or from rash misjudgment.

At the time of this assembly at Harrodsburg, (in which Mr. Marshall says they were concocting treason,) the land-office was opened, and crowds of emigrants were urging their applications for land. Historians of that period say there was "a rabid passion to enter lands."

The defences of the stations were neglected; emigrants exposed themselves in all directions; the savages easily surprised and destroyed many, and then escaped with impunity. To embody any suitable force and pursue the offenders was a task requiring much persuasion, so long as the land-office remained open. The topics of conversation were "the rich lands," "the growth of corn and tobacco," and "a market at New Orleans." They had little anticipation of any trade to the States across the mountains; and yet every man had friends and relatives and cherished remembrances among the citizens on the Atlantic side.

We say, then, there was no criminal intent in this meeting at Harrodsburg; and our opinion is, that when such a suggestion was made to Colonel Donelson, he found no difficulty in embodying "a larger party," (as Mr. Marshall says,) and aiding in suitable deliberations, so as to calm the disquieted, and extend confidence in the purposes of Government.

The presence and conduct of Colonel Donelson, no doubt, produced good results; and in these, it is probable, Colonel Todd ultimately rejoiced as heartily as any other man. Judge Innis was, at a subsequent period, sent by the Administration for the same pacific purposes to the excited people of Kentucky.

The alternative resorted to in the time of the land mania, was to call on General Clarke to exert "his military authority" to close the land-office! This done, the Indians were pursued and punished, and peaceful homes secured.

In the year 1783, Colonels Donelson and Martin received appointments from the Governor of Virginia to hold a treaty with "the southern Indians," especially with the Cherokees and Chickasaws. These Commissioners deemed the French Salt Lick or Nashborough the suitable and convenient place for holding the treaty. They accordingly sent runners into the nations for this purpose; and whilst they awaited the arrival of the Indian chiefs and head-men, Colonel Donelson visited his first encampment, and examined the choice body of lands at and around the Hermitage. Here he made entries or locations of some of the best lands in Tennessee, and commenced the erection of his block-house. The site of this new station was near a large spring, a mile west of the Hermitage, (being the spot now occupied by his grandson, William Donelson, Esq.)

Objections were made by the settlers on the west side of the Cumberland to the treaty being held there. The question was submitted to vote, and the people on the east side, or at Eaton's Station, deciding for the treaty, it was held, as we have elsewhere stated.

This being done, Colonel Donelson returned to Kentucky, but with the avowed intention to move back to the Cumberland as soon as he adjusted some matters of importance in Kentucky and Virginia.

Colonel Donelson remained in Kentucky until the year 1785, when he visited Virginia to communicate with his friends about the many land claims intrusted to his management. He had large interests offered him in grants or military warrants to be located in Kentucky. He had, however, resolved to return and settle on his locations near the Cumberland. In view of such return, he had procured the planting of another crop of corn on one of his tracts near Stone's River.

Information of such intention on his part was received by the Cumberland stationers with much satisfaction. The return of the Colonel and his son, Captain John Donelson, with their families, would encourage others to return, and attract new emigrants.

"In this year, 1785, the Assembly of Georgia, by an act passed for the purpose, established a county by the name of Houston, opposite the Indian town of Nickojack, in the bend of Tennessee, opposite the Muscle Shoals, including all the territory which belonged to Georgia on the north side of the river. Colonels Hord, Downs, Donelson, Sevier, and Mr. Lindsay were appointed Commissioners, with full authority to organize the new county. They opened a land-office there, appointed Colonel Donelson surveyor, and authorized the issuing of land-warrants. These Commissioners, with eighty or ninety men, descended the river to the point where it was intersected by the State line. They appointed military officers and justices of the peace, and elected Valentine Sevier, the brother of Colonel John Sevier, to represent them in the General Assembly of Georgia. The warrants were signed by John Donelson and John Sevier, and were dated 21st December, 1785."

The Commissioners and their party remained there but two or three weeks. The threats of violence, and the preparations by the Indians to attack these land-hunters, were such that it was deemed advisable to return to the Nollachucky and Holston, and abandon the project, for the present at least.

A well-sustained settlement in the Great Bend would have saved the stationers in Kentucky and on the Cumberland from such formidable invasions and havoc. It was a grand idea, a magnificent project. These men gave it notoriety: others were not slow to realize in princely estates the visions of these earliest pioneers.

A plat and deed for ten thousand acres, located at the mouth of the Blue Water, opposite Muscle Shoals, "to John Sevier, one of the Commissioners of the Tennessee Land Company," may be seen in our State Historical Rooms.

About the year 1827 the Congress of the United States granted to the heirs of these Commissioners five thousand acres each, to be selected from any vacant lands of the Government in Alabama or Mississippi, in lieu of their ten thousand, and in full satisfaction for their services as such Commissioners, surveyors, and explorers. A time was limited within which these lands were to be located. All but the Donelson heirs made their selections within the specified time; so that the perils and labor of Colonel Donelson remained without compensation, and his long-cherished scheme and hope of acquisitions there were frustrated and fruitless.

During his absence to Virginia and to the Muscle Shoals, in 1785–6, the families of Colonel Donelson and of his son had returned to the Cumberland, and were again identified with the stationers there. The Indian wars were not ended, perilous times continued, and they came once more to witness and experience sufferings in this great "slaughter-pen" of the pioneers.

Colonel Donelson had owned extensive iron-works in the county of Pittsylvania, Virginia, which he sold to Colonel Calloway, (perhaps during this his last visit to his native State.) He had repeatedly represented some of the western counties (Campbell and Pittsylvania) in the House of Burgesses prior to the Revolution. And while in such office, and associated with eminent men, he signed that address which advocated the placing of American industry upon a footing more independent of the jealous and restrictive policy of the mother country. That address was signed by Washington, Jefferson, Henry, Lee, Randolph, Donelson, and other members of the House of Burgesses. Here was another of those links in that golden chain which bound him to the patriots of Virginia. Here was infused through the great deep of his soul sentiments which gave a right direction to all his subsequent life, and made him ever ready to "pledge his word of truth and honor, that whatever Washington and his associates advocated or did was the wisest and best in the circumstances." He never could doubt of this. He was exceedingly anxious that other persons should entertain the like implicit confidence. And we verily believe that the strong faith he had, and the earnestness with which he delivered his sentiments, for the Father of our country, and "the like precious faith" cherished by Generals Sevier, Robertson, Smith, and other leading spirits in Tennessee, had a most happy and conservative influence over all the population of Tennessee; and that there were men of eminent talents, actuated by the same spirit, who stayed or hushed the storm of discontent in Kentucky.

Ah, there were giants in those days: *pigmies* are an inferior race and far more common. *Anacharsis*, in his travels, says "he found them everywhere; so he did, women and children, but *men*, real, intellectual, and moral great men, only where God had need of them." That accords with our view; such the lesson we learn in American history.

It is stated in Filson's History of Kentucky, also in Butler's, that "Colonel John Donelson, in behalf of Virginia, negotiated a treaty with the *Five Nations* for the country between the Kentucky River and the great Kenawha; the consideration of which was five hundred pounds sterling."

This, in all probability, like the treaty at Nashville in 1783, and Henderson's in 1775, may have been finally regarded as a private negotiation. We find it not among the colonial records, nor in any volume of Indian treaties; but, like Henderson's and others, it had some "virtue in it." The great men of Virginia did not disdain such "color of title."

It was upon the banks of the Ohio and of the Great Kenawha (near the junction) that Washington and Lewis, the Randolphs, Lees, and others, obtained large tracts of land. Donelson had been there before them, and had extinguished the nomad "squatter sovereignty." The doctrine of "Indian squatter rights" lost its potency when discussed by some of these pioneer jurists. "The Great Argument," which we have presented in chapter xxxiv., might furnish some new ideas to judges, however "learned in the law" as taught in the Institutes and Blackstone.

We are enabled to copy from the original, in the Tennessee Historical Society, the last letter written by Colonel Donelson to any member of his family:

"CAMPBELL COUNTY, VA., 4th Sept., 1785.

"DEAR JOHNY:—I have the happiness to inform you that I am in health at present, with the most sanguine hopes that by the first opportunity I shall be made happy by hearing of the health, happiness, etc., of yourself and our dearest connections.

"I lately saw Capt. Ewing, who told me that several warrants from the Military Department were sent out to your care, to locate on the usual terms; I think he said to the amount of 10,000 acres.

"I wish amongst those warrants you could spare me one small warrant to secure the vacancy against my lands on the south side of the Cumberland.

"I have had some conversation with Stockley Donelson concerning our locations with Col. Blount. He says that he has reason to trust the warrants for those lands have issued, and that we need not fear the consequences thereof.

"However, I shall start to-morrow morning over to Carolina, in order to be satisfied in that business. I purpose returning to Richmond from Carolina, in order to see if it is in my power to get some goods for our families' use, and to return to you and my family as soon as possible.

"If you should find it convenient to remove to Cumberland before my return, if my family can remove at the same time, I shall have no objection.

"I shall have some debts to settle in Kentucky in my way out. . . . . I hope to be at home next month. . . . .

"I entreat you to take particular care so to provide that no waste may be made in my corn at Cumberland. A plentiful stock of provisions is the 'main chance.' Give every assurance to your dear mamma that I shall use every endeavor for her happiness, and for every branch of the family.

"Your mamma's ease and happiness in every comfort of life, your and your brothers' and sisters' well-being and happiness, and more, if I could say more, is the constant petition and most ardent desire of your most affectionate father,

"JNO. DONELSON."

We give this letter, not only because there is historic interest in it, but because it presents the tender sentiments of the husband, father, and Christian; and to avail ourselves of this occasion to assert, that "such as was Colonel Donelson in these characteristics, so were *most* of the leading men in the Cumberland settlements."

May their descendants, and all others, receive the knowledge of this fact, and glory in it, and do honor to such example!

Colonel Donelson had forwarded this letter by private hand, and soon thereafter started for Kentucky. He pursued the usual route by the Gap, and on to Davis's Station. There he learned that his family had removed to Mansker's Station. Delaying only a few days to settle some business, he renewed his journey on horseback to rejoin his family.

Two young men joined him and proposed to travel in company, having in view, as they said, a settlement at Nashville. These young men arrived safely, and gave the following statement:

They had travelled together until in the heat of the day, when they "stopped to take a drink from a spring." Colonel Donelson rode on, saying he was anxious to reach home. He had not gone far, and but a few moments, when they heard several guns fired. Their impression was that his sons had met him, and had fired a *feu de joie*.

After some further delay, they resumed their journey, and finally overtook him, when they found him dangerously wounded and in great agony. He was, however, proceeding on his journey. He had been wounded by a ball, which passed across the abdomen in such a manner as to cause a ghastly wound. They continued in company. "In their opinion, he had been wounded by Indians;" but they said not what was Colonel Donelson's opinion.

They encamped on the bank of Barren River that night, and there

Colonel Donelson expired. In the morning they buried his body as best they could; then, taking his horse, saddle, and saddle-bags, they crossed the river; but in crossing, the saddle-bags were washed off the saddle, floated down the river, and were lost.

Such was their statement. He had many valuable papers belonging to himself and friends, and it was supposed he had some money.

"Suspicion rested strongly for some time on these young men, but no proof of guilt being found, they were released and cleared of the charge."

The sons of Colonel Donelson, taking one of the young men with them, returned to Barren River in search of the body and the saddle-bags. The body was found in position to verify their statement, and the saddle-bags were recovered, with some papers, but so damaged as to be of very small value.

Such is the mystery in which the end of Colonel Donelson is shrouded.

In sentiment, and, we believe, by profession, he was a Presbyterian, a religious man, and we trust he was not taken unprepared away.

Taking Colonel Donelson as the *radix*, and tracing out the descendants and connections for the last fifty years, we find, especially in the South and South-west, the alliance to be extensive and influential in political and military position.

The sons-in-law of Colonel Donelson were Colonel Thomas Hutchings, Captain John Caffery, Colonel Robert Hays, and General Andrew Jackson. The ramifications down to the present day are too numerous and wide-spread to be inserted in this work.

Volumes of genealogical and biographical sketches could be written of the pioneer settlers of Middle Tennessee, rich in anecdote, illustrative of history, replete with valuable instruction for the present and future generations. We would take pleasure in such study, composition, and publication; are not averse to the undertaking, nor wholly unprepared with materials.

We could say of many a one, as Cicero did of a person whom he eulogized: "*In oculis civium magnus, intus domique præstantior:*" Distinguished, not only in the estimation of his fellow-citizens, but more excellent *at home*, in the "family circle." Of such it is pleasant to write; of scores of such we would willingly be encouraged to write—*pro bono publico.*

UNIVERSITY OF NASHVILLE, MEDICAL DEPARTMENT.

ORIGIN AND EARLY HISTORY

OF

The Nashville University.

1785. By an act of the North Carolina Legislature, passed 29th December, 1785, entitled "An Act for the promotion of learning in Davidson county," the Rev. Thomas Craighead, Hugh Williamson, Daniel Smith, William Polk, Anthony Bledsoe, Lardner Clarke, Ephraim McLean, Robert Hays, and James Robertson were appointed Trustees, and constituted a body politic under the name of "President and Trustees of *Davidson Academy*," with authority to receive, by *bequest*, *gift*, or *purchase*, land, tenements, and property or money for the purposes of the Academy. The last clause or section is in the following words :

"And be it further enacted by the authority aforesaid, that *no* lands, tenements, or hereditaments which may be vested in the Trustees of the Academy of Davidson, for the sole use and behoof of the said Academy, shall be subject to any tax for the space of *ninety-nine years.*"

Two hundred and forty acres were granted by this act, adjoining the town of Nashville on the Cumberland River. This body of land lies south of Broad street, all now within the city limits, most of it highly improved. Individuals also made subscriptions of land of various amounts. The act itself encouraged "bequests, gifts, and purch es."

1786. *The first meeting* of the Trustees took place 16. august. "Messrs. Williamson and Clarke not present. Rev. Thomas Craighead chosen President; Ephraim McLean, Treasurer; Daniel Smith, Secretary."

One of their first orders relates to the two hundred and forty acres of land adjoining the town of Nashville, which, with the ferry, caused the Trustees much care and trouble for years.

At this first meeting it was "ordered that William Polk and Ephraim McLean be appointed in behalf of the Trustees to superintend the surveying of the two hundred and forty acres of land which is given them by the State. They will notify the Trustees of the town of the time of their doing the business, and make such division between the Academy lands and the town lands as shall be just and lawful," "to be done by first day of October next."

"Ordered, that subscription papers in the following form be drawn and circulated, to have donations made to the Academy."

This form is for subscriptions in *lands*, with covenant to convey by deed within twelve months after a title can be procured from the State, or sooner, if conveniency will permit.

September 25th.—"Ordered, that the tuition for each student be at the rate of £4 per annum, to be paid in *hard money*, or other money of that value."

"Ordered, that *Spring Hill Meeting-House* be the place where the school be taught."

Among the many mutations in name, place, and circumstances which this institution has undergone, this surely is worthy of notice. Few persons know that the University of Nashville had its birth in Rev. Thomas B. Craighead's little church or "meeting-house," six miles east of Nashville, "in the suburbs of the town of Haysborough." There is the burial-place of some of the early dead of Middle Tennessee; there rest the remains of the founder and first President of this institution of learning.

The construction of the turnpike has destroyed the foundations of that primitive academy. A stone from its walls should have been inserted in the substantial structure (of which a good view is herewith furnished) on College Hill in our city.

Another entry is of above date:

"Ordered, that £5 hard money, or the value thereof in other money, be paid for each scholar per annum."

"Messrs. McLean and Hays authorized to *rent out* the Academy lands."

October 5th.—"Board agreed that Mr. President make a motion to Court for a *ferry* just above the town lands."

(This ferry was established just above the east end of Broad street.)

1790. May 31st.—"Robert Hays reported that he rented the field at the ferry landing to John Boyd, Sr., for —— years; Boyd agreeing to put it under good fence as a consideration. Also, he rented part of the

Lick Field (Kasper Mansker's Lick?) to Daniel Hay, Jacob Castleman, Jr., and Robert Thompson, for the year 1787, they agreeing to give thirty bushels of corn for said field for one year, and leave it in good repair," etc.

Mr. McLean reports that "he rented all the cleared arable lands belonging to the Academy to L. Clarke, for four years from 1st December, 1787. He was to put all the cleared arable land under good fence, and to leave it so, and to pay 10s. per acre in current money every year, only deducting half the price of *mauling the rails*, except that he agreed that one half of the 10s. should be paid in corn at current price of the country."

"Messrs. Hays and McLean appointed to employ some one to keep the *ferry*, build ferry-house, boats," etc.

"Ordered that a fine of $1 be imposed on Trustees who fail to attend meeting, or give good excuse to exculpate themselves."

1791. October 8th.—"Board met at Spring Hill. Adjourned to meet at Mr. Clarke's, in Nashville, at 10 o'clock, Monday, 10th inst."

Met accordingly.

"Ordered, that *Mr. Andrew Jackson* be appointed a Trustee in the room of Colonel William Polk, removed."

"The Board adjourned to meet at Mr. Clarke's, in Nashville, on *Friday, 4th inst., next*, to survey the *cleared* lands in the lands of the Academy, and to settle with Mr. Clarke."

These are strange duties for Trustees of a literary institution! Mauling rails, making fences, building houses, keeping ferries, surveying lands, clearing and renting, collecting, measuring, and selling corn!

But these truly great men were not above any such duties. Some of these very persons have filled the highest positions in this State, and in this great nation, and they would never have merited the higher, had they despised the lower place of service and of honor.

November 8th.—"By order, John Boyd exonerated from his debt, by paying Mr. McLean one hundred bushels corn, part of our debt to the latter for building the ferry-house. Be it remembered that Colonel Hays paid thirty bushels of corn rent, which he had received in part pay for procuring the ferry-boat to be built."

"Colonel Hays authorized to sell the *Academy's small boat*, and to request the 'Commissioners of the Licks' to make us a title to *Kasper's Lick*."*

---

* By act of the Legislature of North Carolina, December, 1789, it was ordered that salt licks and springs, and lands adjoining, be sold. And the County Courts of Davidson, Sumner, and Tennessee were directed, at their April Term, 1790, to make a list, signed by their Chairman, of all licks at which salt could be made,

41

1794. March 4th.—There are large accessions to the population of the District.   Ferries became places of much notoriety, and yielded handsome incomes.

"The Academy ferry leased to Abram Boyd for the term of five years for two hundred dollars per annum, payable in *certificates* on 1st June next," etc.

These certificates were issued to officers and soldiers who had served as guards to escort emigrants from Clinch to Cumberland.   They constituted a reliable paper currency—were receivable for taxes due the county; the State of North Carolina having very *graciously* allowed these counties to defray all these expenses.

And here are these Trustees accepting guard certificates as of equal value with "hard money!"   (We know some persons who would be quite rich if the "good old North State" should redeem her old issues at half the value of these guard certificates.)

"Ordered, that a deed be made to Elijah Robertson for a small parcel of land lying within his fence, computed to be about half an acre, lying along the southern line of the tract adjoining Nashville, belonging to said Academy, for which he is to pay *three* dollars."

A fixed sum for very indefinite boundaries!   How much is it now worth?

"The South Field" leased for five years.   (This is now the most highly prized portion of the city for private residences—south of Broad street.)

"'Dutch John's Field' is leased to William T. Lewis for four years, at sixty bushels of corn per year.   Three or four acres leased to Timothè De Mon Bruen *for the fencing* thereof, and agreement to leave it with the houses in good repair."

"The same committee report that they had sold one hundred and eighteen bushels of corn to John McNairy at twenty-five cents, payable

and especially naming Eaton's, Denton's, Kasper's, Neelly's, Drake's, Madison's, Stoner's, and Bledsoe's, which were directed to be sold.   The Court should declare what licks should be sold, or reserved from sale, or be subject to entry.   The Commissioners were to have surveys completed, and lay off six hundred and forty acres adjoining each spring at which salt could be made, and offer the same at public sale.

Two of the licks thus reserved, with the adjoining land, were to be for the use of Davidson Academy.   Kasper's or Mansker's was one of these; the other was—I know not where.

(*A Question:* Are not these, or any lands "donated, bequeathed, or sold" to the Academy, as much exempt from *taxes* under the last section of the act of December 29th, 1785, as the two hundred and forty acres now within the corporate limits of the city of Nashville?)

in certificates last July; and that William T. Lewis is indebted eighty bushels corn for last year's rent of Dutch John's Field."

Then follows the appointment of a committee to collect and sell corn. etc., and another to collect debts and purchase *books* for the use of the Academy. Here is the beginning of the *Library*.

We notice that Mr. Craighead attended all the meetings of the Board, and that Generals Robertson and Jackson were seldom absent, though they each resided several miles from town.

"A piece of land belonging to the Academy, *joining* Nashville, sold to John McNairy at *six dollars per acre*, payable in cash or certificates 1st July next!"

What rate of interest on six dollars, compounded every six months for sixty-four years, (1794 to 1858,) would make an aggregate equal to the present value of those acres?

April 8th.—Authority and directions given to an agent to procure a patent from North Carolina for the two hundred and forty acres of land given by the State.

1796. The Territorial Government ends: the State of Tennessee is organized.

1797. There are sundry unimportant entries in these years.

1798. "Rev. Thomas B. Craighead and Andrew Jackson are appointed a committee to draft a memorial to the Legislature of Tennessee, to *repeal* the act entitled 'An act to amend an act for the promotion of learning in the county of Davidson.' "

The memorial was adopted, and forwarded to General Robertson to lay before the Legislature. The act therein alluded to was passed 15th April, 1796, and attempted to intrude *new Trustees* into the old Board; to appoint *auditors*, to whom the old Board should account; to oust the old Trustees from office; institute suits against them if they refused to account to these auditors, and to substitute and install in their places these newly appointed, clothing the latter "with the same powers, rights, and privileges that are by law vested in the whole Board!"

The old veterans were not thus to be moved from their propriety or their places; they had passed through more trying times than these; they had never been known to falter, and they shrunk not back now. They met these *ten* would-be Trustees, and *three* auditors, at the threshold, and withstood them there.

The Board had already resolved to comply with the last section of the act in which these aspirants to academical places and honors were mentioned, and designed to be foisted into supremacy. That section is in these words:

"Be it enacted, that the buildings of the said Academy shall be erected on the most convenient situation on the hill immediately above Nashville, and near to the *road leading to Buchanan's Mill*; and that the Trustees aforesaid shall proceed to erect buildings, and employ tutors to proceed to the business of tuition, as soon as the funds will permit."

The boys had many a rhyme with the words,

> "The Academy on the hill,
> Near the road
> Leading to Buck's Mill;"

and such queries as, "At which place the best grinding was done?" etc.

On 24th December, Board met at the house of Thomas Talbot, (Talbot's Tavern,) in Nashville.

"Ordered, that Thomas B. Craighead and Daniel Smith be continued a committee to receive books from Mr. Deadrick for the Trustees, and settle for the same as soon as convenience will admit, after the *General's return from Congress*."

In this order there are several noticeable facts for the year 1798 : Additions to the library through the agency of *Merchant* Deadrick, and that *General Smith* was then a Senator in Congress.

"Ordered, that H. Tatum, Esq., be and he is hereby invested with full and ample power to settle with William T. Lewis for rents due by him, . . . and for all damages the Trustees have sustained by reason of said William not complying with the terms of his lease; . . . . also to receive all moneys due from said William, John McNairy, and all others, and report accordingly."

1799. April 10th.—Met at house of Robert Hay. A long entry about a lease to Abram Boyd, neglect of fences, repair of boats, loss of paddles, etc., and a compromise.

"Ferry rented at $100, to Peter Johnston, who is to *find a chain*," etc. Another chain is linked to this.

It may be presumed, from the act of 15th April, 1796, that there was dissatisfaction among some of the citizens with the old Trustees and their management, and a wish, by the introduction of the new ones, to infuse more life and energy, or another spirit, into the Board and the operations of the institution.

What particular grievances were alleged, or negligences charged, we venture not to suggest. How far *political* and *religious* sentiments were operative, need not be mentioned. The history of that period is full of incidents connected with both topics. Flashes broke forth on every side from the surrounding darkness. There was gathering a political tornado; there was coming a religious frenzy.

As connected with the Academy, *politics* seemed to have more influence than religion. Some of the citizens set up and patronized a rival institution. The flame assumed for this new school is indicative and significant. They called it " *The Federal Seminary.*"

Population did not require, the wealth of the citizens could not sustain, two schools; therefore efforts were made by some calm and judicious persons for a union: that "the two should be consolidated."

A conference was had between Rev. Mr. Craighead and Mr. George McWhirter on the part of Davidson Academy, and Judge McNairy, William T. Lewis, and Dr. Henning on the part of the Federal Seminary, about 9th August, at which the latter Trustees proposed a union, and that the institution should be incorporated and viewed as belonging to Davidson Academy, "together with its teacher!" that it should be kept near Nashville, and the funds united; in which case, they would give us all the assistance in their power."

This is the substance of the report of this conference, as spread upon the records of Davidson Academy.

The consideration of the report and proposition was "deferred to some other meeting." The old soldiers were in no great haste: they pass to the consideration of other matters. There follow various orders. "Members *generally*, and Daniel Smith in *particular*," are directed to make inquiries about lands belonging to the Academy.

1800. June 16th.—Proceedings relative to rents, leases, repairs of river bank at ferry-landing, fences, etc. These matters being attended to, repairs made, and fences put up, they let down the bars and admitted the United States Federal Judge.

A consolidation of the two schools, Academy and Seminary, had taken place; and what we remark as somewhat peculiar, the points of discussion and controversy are kept off the record; and not a word is said of the day or the manner in which this rivalry is terminated.

At this meeting of the 16th June, Judge McNairy is present, and so is David Shelby, and the old Board admit them very politely to seats, and give them something to do.

1801. February 25th.—"Judge McNairy and Mr. McWhirter are appointed a committee to rent lands, complete contracts, and *sell rails!*"

These two gentlemen had not "pulled evenly together," or worked in the same "political traces," in years gone by; but now, in the cause of education, they work like good "wheel-horses." Such were the figures used.

Mr. William T. Lewis had been associated with Judge McNairy in the Federal Seminary movement, and as there was a matter of a little delicacy between the old Board and Mr. Lewis about "the East Field," the matter of settlement was committed to the "Hon. John McNairy, Judge of the United States Court," and he obtained the corn and pumpkins!

"Colonel William Donelson, who lived on adjoining land, was empowered to manage the Kasper's Lick tract of land."

1802. "Richard Boyd rented the ferry at five hundred dollars per annum; but on 25th February, 1803, he is reported as having failed to give proper security: whereupon *General Robertson* leased it, at three hundred dollars per annum, for the term of two years. He enters into bond to keep ferry-house, boats, and landing in good condition, and that the ferry should be faithfully attended to for public convenience, and to deliver all in good repair."*

Here is the chief citizen, the first man in Middle Tennessee, "the father of the country," (so acknowledged by all,) engaging that this important "crossing" should be "faithfully attended to for *public conven- ience.*"

General Robertson's residence was about five miles from the ferry; but he engaged a trusty steersman, and put old Jack at the oars, and emigrants, travellers, and citizens "were all ferried over."

But all matters are not settled quietly and permanently in favor of the Academy. Some discontented Trustees and subscribers desired to remove the school to *Sumner county!* It seems to have been agreed that this question should be decided by and in favor of the largest amount subscribed in favor of either place—Nashville and Montpelier.

William P. Anderson was appointed to obtain subscriptions in favor of Nashville, and Colonel Edward Douglas for Montpelier. The result was in favor of Nashville, and therefore Nashville has *the University.* And now the Trustees resolve to erect buildings.

July 15th.—General Jackson and General Robertson are appointed to superintend the erection of the Academy."

"Resolved, that a number of lots be laid off ready to be sold on 24th October next, under the direction of General Robertson and General Smith, *reserving ten acres for the use of the Academy.*"

This first effort was to sell lots *subject to a ground-rent.* That was an idea which the people of a new country could not countenance. Land here was almost as free as air and water. The aim and purpose of emigrants was to possess an *unencumbered freehold*—a fee-simple title to farms and town-lots. Hence these two Commissioners report, (on October 26th,) "The lots will not sell, subject to a ground-rent;" therefore, "Ordered, that they be sold on 28th November next, at nine months' credit, giving a fee-simple title."

November 28th.—This day sixteen lots were sold, at from $40 to $150 per lot. Amount of sale of sixteen lots, $1263 50. The sale was continued the next day, when twenty-three lots were sold, at from $16 to $71 per lot. Amount of this day's sale, $2129 50.

A comparison of the present value of these lots with the sales of 1803, would be interesting. The difference between half a million and less than thirty-four hundred dollars, would perhaps cause a momentary regret. But without sales, the town could not have been enlarged, population increased, nor the Academy sustained.

Nov. 29th.—"Ordered that lots of one acre be surveyed on Market street, First, Second, and east side of Third street, and all the land to the westward, into four-acre lots; leaving a street (Broad street) between Nashville and the Academy lands, and sales to commence on second Friday of January next. Mansker's Lick tract to be sold on the last Tuesday of December."

"General Winchester authorized to close contract with undertakers of the building."

1804. January 19th.—"On the question : Will the Trustees proceed to business under the late law of the State of Tennessee, entitled "An act to amend an act entitled an act to establish a *College*, and incorporate the Trustees thereof, in Davidson county ?

"It was carried unanimously, after mature deliberation, and taking the opinion of counsel learned in the law, *in the negative.*"[*]

1804.—Judge McNairy resigned; Moses Fisk appointed Trustee in his place.

Craighead and Smith a Committee on Memorial to Legislature, setting forth ill effects of their late law, and its illegality, as the Trustees are advised.

Messrs. Fisk and Shelby to draft a Petition to Congress, praying for a grant of lands to the Academy.

"Adjourned to meet second day of *Federal Court !*"

"Academy building to be 45 *feet wide* by 40 *feet long !*" And Messrs. Craighead and Robertson restricted to these dimensions for the building !

1805. May 31st.—General Robertson, General Smith, and Colonel Hay resigned. They had served for nearly twenty years, and were seldom absent from the meetings. Robert C. Foster, David McGavock, and Joseph Coleman chosen to fill these vacancies.

Ferry leased for seven years to Josiah Horton at $650 per annum.

---

[*] An act passed at Knoxville, 25th October, 1803. This act was repealed by act of 4th March, 1804.

Nov. 26th.—Andrew Jackson resigned; Judge Robert Whyte elected in his room.   Jackson was seldom absent.

Charles Cabaniss has contracted for building the Academy building at $10,890.

1806. January 21st.—"The Bunker-Hill farm sold for $255." Where was this farm?

The Board purchased the relinquishment of the claim of Tait and Stothart to twenty-one acres of land between Johnson's Spring branch at the Academy ferry, and Manifee's line near the river.   Part of lot 16, a large one, is reserved perpetually from sale and improvement.

The limits of the lots and square reserved for the buildings of the Academy are specified, and considered *binding between* the Academy and the *purchasers of lots adjoining.*

(Here may arise legal questions of much perplexity and importance at some day.)

The margin of the river is also reserved from sale—say from low-water mark to the top of the bank.

"Lot No. 27 is conveyed to the Cedar Street Church, on condition that they cease to use lot No. 7 as a burying-ground."

March 29th.—"Out-Lot No. 26 to be conveyed to the Presbyterian Congregation to be used as a public burying-ground, instead of the Meeting-house lot."

July 19th.—A petition to the Legislature prepared, praying that Davidson Academy may be erected into a *College,* contemplated by the late *Act of Congress,* to be established in West Tennessee.

Dec. 2d.—"At a meeting of the Trustees of the LATE Davidson Academy at Nashville—present, Rev. Thomas B. Craighead, President, James Winchester, Robert Searcy, R. C. Foster, David McGavock—after the execution and acknowledgment of sundry deeds, "The Board adjourned without day."

And now Davidson Academy is to be merged in *Cumberland College.*

NASHVILLE CITY HOSPITAL.

CHAPTER II.

1806.

By an act of the Congress of the United States, passed 18th April, 1806, the State of Tennessee was authorized to issue and perfect titles to certain lands therein mentioned; and the General Assembly of this State, by an act to establish a College in West Tennessee, incorporated a body of *nineteen* trustees—placing the Rev. Thomas B. Craighead as the first named in the list, "by the name of the Trustees of Davidson College," in the preamble of the act, it being stated to be upon the petition of the Trustees of Davidson Academy—vesting all the property, real and personal, of said Academy in the Trustees of the *College*.

By the 6th section it is provided that one moiety of proceeds of the sales of one hundred thousand acres of land described in the 23d section of an act for the appointment of a Register of the Land-Office, and sale of lands south of French Broad and Holston, agreeably to the Constitution of this State and provisions of the act of Congress therein referred to, etc., etc.

1806, Sept. 11th.—The first meeting of Trustees of the College was at Talbot's Hotel, Nashville, when Joseph Coleman, first Mayor of the city, was chosen to preside, until a president should be duly elected. Mr. Craighead was not present at this meeting—perhaps the only absence in twenty years; but at the next meeting, July 21, he is unanimously elected President. And thus he is honored in the Collegiate as he had been in the Academic Board: an honor which he deserved.

First Term in College: "*Resolved*, that the College be opened for reception of students on 1st day of September next." Books and apparatus to the amount of $1000 purchased.

From the "Rules and Regulations" adopted by the Board, we copy the following:

"It will be improper to suffer the students to attend assemblages, balls, theatrical exhibitions, parties of pleasure and amusement, and more to frequent gaming-tables, taverns, and places of dissipation.

" They should seldom indulge themselves *in going to town*, except on necessary business, which should be dispatched hastily, that they may return to College without delay."

The foregoing rules have ever been respected—pretty much after the example set in the observance of the prescriptions of the following regulation:

" Your Committee further recommend that the tutors, in all their official duties, wear a College habit, or loose upper garment, made of some light black stuff or *fille model*, after the manner of the surplice or gown worn by gentlemen of the literary professions, distinguished by black *tossels* on the shoulders or sleeves, as badges of office; and that the students also wear black gowns of similar material, but *without the tossels* when they attend on recitations, prayers, public speaking, public worship, and when they walk into the town !"

1809. — By act of Legislature : "No ordinance, rule, or by-laws shall ever be made or entered into so as to give a preference to any one denomination of Christians."

October 19th.—" Board met: Rev. Thomas B. Craighead absent. Committee appointed to confer with Dr. James Priestly, to know whether he will accept the office of President."

October 24th.—" Dr. Priestly unanimously elected President."

Mr. Craighead served as President of the College two years and three months. The assertion that " he never was President of the College" is unfounded.

1810. January 15th. — " Ordered that College lot be enclosed by cedar post and rail fence; and that Messrs. Foster and Lewis have plank steps made to the doors of the College; and that Treasurer pay Joel Lewis $5, for conveying two letters to Black and Perkins : adjourned, to meet *at the College* 29th inst."

January 30th.—" Dr. Priestly appeared, and took his seat as President of this Board."

1811.—Nothing worthy of note.

1812.—Nothing worthy of note. Students desire to witness military parades; and break some windows.

1813. January 8th.—Full Board; unanimous vote : Two students, of good capacity, expelled, for non-compliance with rules prescribing course of study: one of these has attained eminence as a politician in Tennessee, served much in Congress, as a Postmaster-General, Bank President, and in other positions.

All boys are not ruined by discipline: expulsion does not always disgrace, or destroy friendships; and yet they are *few*, whose energies are so aroused and exerted by such discipline that "they were then awaked to greatness."

January 20th.—The students in College disapproved this act of the Board, which led to the adoption of the following effort to " kill off sympathy :"

"*Resolved*, That when a student is expelled or suspended, he must quit the College *immediately*, and not return to it on *any occasion* without permission of the Board or Faculty; and it shall not be lawful for any *society* or *student* in College to give a certificate to any one who is expelled, suspended, or under censure."

This was spoken of as a restraint upon the right of private opinion— an infringement of the liberty of speech; and the students declared, " though they have turned Cave out, we will not ' cave in.' " But when there came " a sober second thought," better counsels prevailed, and quiet was restored; though some " wished to be expelled and join the army." War was then in progress.

April 13th.—Committee report sale of the Ferry and reserved land at $7005 25.

May 22d.—A committee of lawyers—Messrs. McNairy, Haywood, Grundy, and Beck—requested to report what ought to be done to *recover the property* of the College.

Here is something which should be posted at the corners of the streets for the consideration of the citizens of Nashville :

"*Resolved*, that as it is the duty of all the citizens, so it is especially the duty of the Trustees, to countenance and encourage students by all means in their power, that so our country may have the benefit of as much knowledge and virtue as possible, and that, consequently, to *neglect examinations* and commencements, is to show a disregard of public good."

August 30th.—At this meeting Rev. Thomas B. Craighead appears as a Trustee. *Nomen indelebile*. President Priestly was not present. Board adjourned to September 3d.

September 3d.—Degree of A. B. conferred upon several graduates— among whom appears Ephraim H. Foster, " the noblest Roman of them all."

The Honorable Robert Whyte is added to the committee of able lawyers—to report " what measures should be adopted to recover the funds of the College."

Here end the Records, (as far as we have seen them,) and the connection of Thomas B. Craighead, the founder of the institution, therewith.

Others, Priestly and Lindsley, enlightened Christians, ripe scholars, and accomplished gentlemen, came as successors.

We shall not attempt the history of the changes which have taken place in these recent years, resulting in the improvements and prosperity of the present day.

The view of the College buildings which we present is correct. The buildings of the Medical College are not shown in this view.

MILITARY INSTITUTE, NASHVILLE, TENN.

TENNESSEE ASYLUM FOR THE INSANE.

H. BOSSE SC

TENNESSEE HOSPITAL FOR THE INSANE.

THIS is a noble charity, in every respect creditable to the State. The buildings, arrangements, and conveniences are not surpassed in all the country. The body of land is rich, and happily varied in surface and soil. There are four hundred and fifty-five acres in this farm, and in its management it yields largely to the pleasure, comfort, and support of the inmates or patients.

The whole edifice presents a front of four hundred and nine feet, and will accommodate three hundred persons.

These buildings, (of which we furnish a correct view,) front on the Murfreesboro' Turnpike, and are six miles from Nashville.

The rooms are warmed and ventilated by steam. Provision is made to board, clothe, nurse, and watch over one hundred indigent patients at the expense of the State; all other patients are charged at moderate rates, according to their condition mentally and physically, and their wants, as may be required by their friends or guardians.

Counties, when erected. Towns, when Incorporated or Organized.		Population of Towns in 1850.	1790.	1800.
Bedford,	1807			
Shelbyville, .	1809–1819			
Cannon, .	1835			
Cheatham, .	1856			
Cumberland, .	1855			
Coffee,	1835			
Davidson,	1783–1784		3459	9965
Nashville,	1784–1806	11,520		
De Kalb,	1837			
Dickson,	1803			
Fentress,	1827			
Franklin,	1807			
Giles, .	1809			
Grundy,	1844–1848			
Hardin,	1819			
Hickman, .	1807			
Humphreys, .	1809			
Jackson, .	1801			
Lawrence,	1817			
Lewis, .	1843–1848			
Lincoln, .	1809			
Macon,	1842			
Marshall,	1835			
Maury,	1807			
Columbia,	1807–1817	3000		
*Montgomery,	1786–1787		1387	2899
Clarksville,	1795–1819	2600		
Overton,	1806			
Putnam, .	1842–1854			
*Robertson, .	1796–1797			4280
Springfield,	1796–1819	400		
Rutherford, .	1803			
Smith, .	1799			4294
Stewart,	1803			
Sumner, .	1786–1787		4616	2196
Gallatin,	1801–1815	1000		
Warren, .	1807			
McMinnville,	1813–1833	1500		
Wayne, .	1817			
White,	1806			
Sparta, .	1809–1813	500		
Williamson, .	1807			
Franklin,	1815	1000		
Wilson, .	1801			
Lebanon,	1802			
Van Buren, .	1847			
			9462	23,634

* These counties were formed from the original "Tennessee County," which contained at the "First Census" a population of 1387.— Wherever there appears a decrease of population at any decade,

1810.	1820.	1830.	1840.	1850.	1858.
8242	16,012	30,444	20,546	21,511	
			7193	8982	3173
					7000
					4000
			8184	8351	
15,608	20,154	28,089	30,509	38,882	supposed
	3400	5566	6929		32,000
			5868	8016	
4516	5190	7260	7074	8404	
		2760	3550	4454	
5730	16,577	15,644	12,033	13,768	
4546	12,558	18,920	21,494	25,949	
				2773	
			8245	10,328	
2583	6080	8132	8618	9397	
1511	4067	6189	5195	6422	
5401	7593	9902	12,872	15,673	
			7121	9280	
				4438	
6104	14,761	22,086	21,493	23,492	
				6948	
			14,555	15,616	
10,359	22,140	28,153	28,186	29,520	
8021	12,219	14,365	16,927	21,211	
5643	7128	8246	9279	11,211	
					Recently organized county.
7270	9938	13,302	13,801	16,145	
10,265	19,552	26,133	24,280	29,122	
11,649	17,580	21,492	21,179	18,412	
4262	8397	6988	8587	9719	
13,792	19,211	20,606	22,445	22,717	
5725	10,341	15,351	10,803	10,179	
	2459	6013	7705	8170	
4028	8701	9967	10,747	11,444	
13,153	20,640	26,608	27,006	27,201	
11,952	18,730	25,477	24,460	27,443	
				2674	
160,360	283,588	377,693	426,884	499,424	

it is owing to the organization of new counties. The Metropolis and several of the county towns have grown rapidly since 1850.

TABULAR STATEMENT OF THE

COUNTIES.	Town Lots.	Value.	Acres of Land.	Value.
Anderson, . .	62	$ 26,500	209,426	$ 859,830
Benton, . .	68	21,060	260,367	611,110
Blount, . . .			389,359	1,837,644
Bedford, . .	376	475,785	297,769	5,284,075
Bradley, . .	319	217,460	211,216	2,066,685
Cannon, . .	87	37,525	159,533	1,304,929
Campbell, . .	59	12,525	392,526	647,190
Carter, . .	76	34,000	270,247	770,749
Carroll, . . .	249	108,715	367,164	2,284,977
Cheatham, .			189,982	843,955
Coffee, . . .	33	107,925	328,662	1,405,251
Cocke, . .	6	26,375	243,597	1,192,125
Cumberland, . .			278,921	241,705
Davidson, . .	4734		310,978	19,122,420
Decatur, . .		*		668,090
De Kalb, . .	200	38,375	181,516	881,590
Dyer, . . .	*	81,285	389,967	1,659,546
Fentress, . .	69	*	*	326,148
Franklin, . .		7,140	397,504	1,869,185
Gibson, . .		209,980	393,134	3,186,239
Grainger, . .	60	33,900	187,811	1,625,550
Greene, . .			438,908	2,687,876
Grundy, . .	75	8,072	205,477	596,913
Hamilton, . .		625,641	379,754	2,115,703
Hancock, . .	55	14,950	108,878	560,807
Hardeman, . .		270,395	414,829	3,223,222
Hawkins, . .	76	80,900	330,705	1,971,962
Haywood, . .	244	201,910	388,069	3,452,130
Henderson, . .	149	82,955	383,452	1,617,688
Henry, . .	307	315,510	356,233	2,980,637
Hickman, . .	61	24,775	374,568	1,126,945
Humphreys, .	47	29,450	357,935	779,218
Johnson, . .	40	16,400	198,944	480,664
Knox, . .	791	1,073,125	310,709	3,249,710
Lauderdale, . .	118	31,980	293,223	1,212,586
Lawrence, . .	133	72,954	400,162	1,144,804
Lincoln. . .	218	188,720	408,446	3,907,758
Madison, . .	*	723,450	382,590	3,561,305
Marion, . . .			455,968	954,680
Marshall, . .	173	57,375	213,627	2,525,059
Maury, . . .	557	594,050	376,675	6,128,093
McNairy, . .	201	87,920	385,757	1,325,288
McMinn, . .	270	128,160	276,295	2,000,990
Meigs, . .			132,355	913,615
Monroe, . . .	160	58,200	435,483	1,773,410

TAXABLE PROPERTY OF TENNESSEE—1857.

No. of Slaves under 12 and over 40 years.	Value.	Value of all other Taxable Property.	Total Value.	State Tax on.
250	$ 208,400	$ 91,975	$ 1,186,705	$ 1,661
204	164,450	15,949	812,469	1,137
577	464,700	261,766	2,564,110	3,599
3004	2,345,50)	579,726	8,655,086	12,117
501	348,950	116,810	2,749,905	3,849
387	337,578	75,253	1,753,285	2,454
152	126,800	47,904	834,419	1,545
170	124,150	34,323	963,222	1,348
1823	1,435,100	197,334	4,056,526	5,685
782	609,525	96,173	1,549,653	2,169
612	480,010	59,283	2,052,469	2,873
370	290,750	64,972	1,574,222	2,203
60	45,150	8,070	294,925	412
6599	4,286,415	1,681,769	25,090,604	36,636
	299,080	29,919	1,035,464	1,449
375	314,750	84,588	1,362,213	1,907
976	740,860	57,652	2,468,058	3,958
70	46,850	15,608	395,806	857
1514	1,082,250	136,656	3,088,091	4,323
2302	1,719,060	129,219	5,244,398	7,342
504	340,200	151,881	2,151,531	3,012
542	304,075	238,577	3,230,528	4,522
121	99,600	289,511	794,196	1,272
749	568,100	170,596	3,480,040	4,872
118	100,250	40,685	716,992	1,365
3621	3,439,770	517,337	7,450,727	11,163
891	568,750	269,534	2,891,146	4,047
5249	4,489,800	392,016	8,535,856	12,708
1559	1,269,500	112,899	3,093,042	4,330
2501	1,991,975	279,934	5,568,056	8,781
938	688,270	146,227	1,986,217	2,780
606	478,100	28,019	1,314,787	1,840
93	54,900	47,173	599,137	838
1122	846,770	328,058	5,497,663	7,697
1129	980,070	32,861	2,257,497	3,160
590	461,150	241,609	1,930,517	2,702
2896	2,128,990	475,944	6,699,412	9,379
4547	3,793,950	149,665	8,228,370	12,461
348	264,750	38,585	1,258,015	1,761
1928	1,441,388	270,105	4,293,927	6,679
6326	4,549,300	606,039	11,877,482	16,542
801	655,675	113,734	2,182,617	3,055
880	705,220	210,038	2,129,150	2,980
272	221,100	63,201	1,197,916	1,677
685	534,000	187,029	2,552,639	3,573

42

TABULAR STATEMENT OF THE

COUNTIES.	Town Lots.	Value.	Acres of Land.	Value.
Morgan, . .	50	$ 6,770	401,439	$ 226,214
Overton, . .	105	37,525	328,591	1,256,598
Perry, . .	74	14,620	434,301	904,883
Polk, . . .	218	26,275	198,076	3,073,597
Putnam, . .	106	11,483	333,217	637,512
Robertson, . .	*	106,320	273,490	2,592,355
Rhea, . .	65	7,030	149,874	605,320
Rutherford, . .	364	556,522	352,972	4,937,735
Sevier, . .	45	9,200	533,557	672,945
Shelby, . . .	*	10,423,513	539,947	11,663,905
Smith, . .		69,100	230,173	2,383,737
Stewart, . . .	88	39,215	396,173	1,314,431
Sullivan, . .	319	124,230	278,007	2,458,372
Tipton, . . .	250	51,625	278,498	2,207,938
Van Buren, .	85	10,170	348,249	209,341
Warren, . . .	144	188,785	247,998	1,721,600
Washington, .		150,300	302,677	2,031,540
Wayne, . . .		50,015	403,617	899,496
Weakley, . .			361,410	2,582,906
Wilson, . . .	233	361,085	363,681	5,377,206
Williamson, .		240,630	361,514	6,357,516
White, . . .	104	44,020	219,971	855,215

* Not given.

TAXABLE PROPERTY OF TENNESSEE—1857.

No. of Slaves under 12 and over 40 years.	Value.	Value of all other Taxable Property.	Total Value.	State Tax on.
57	$ 28,500	$ 5,276	$ 266,760	$ 373
525	426,350	90,936	1,811,409	2,535
215	189,200	34,544	1,143,247	1,600
258	215,930	29,739	3,345,541	468
295	237,538	274,671	1,161,254	1,625
2223	1,730,196	442,567	5,314,005	7,541
245	169,050	45,767	827,167	1,158
5518	3,945,462	524,314	9,963,033	14,884
225	144,350	69,137	895,630	1,253
7919	6,411,302	717,321	29,344,967	43,482
1980	1,393,290	284,734	4,130,861	5,783
1844	1,238,805	99,414	2,691,865	3,768
489	301,800	253,629	3,138,031	4,393
2463	2,134,550	231,425	6,475,732	6,939
125	98,450	19,217	337,178	472
1034	820,600	106,057	3,971,858	3,971
496	350,050	145,783	2,677,673	3,748
574	482,439	78,211	1,510,161	2,114
1730	1,333,640	277,643	4,194,189	5,871
3570	2,888,220	647,508	9,373,019	14,330
5826	4,564,150	1,041,002	12,203,298	17,084
565	412,700	119,436	1,431,371	2,003

CITY OF NASHVILLE.

1787 AND 1858.

In 1787—Twenty-six "Acre Lots," price £4, North Carolina currency, Tax $1 = $26.

In 1858—Valuation of City Lots, $9,983,399; 1715 Slaves, $1,419,800; Carriages, $28,885; Stocks, $209,341; Plate and Jewelry, 20,884; Pianos, $45,060; Watches, $47,536; Total, $11,754,905.

Corporation Tax, $123,425 80; School Tax, $26,189 83; Total, $149,615 63.

1794.

"McNairy John,	640	acres in Tennessee County.
	640	" Davidson " Richland Creek.
	200	" " " French Lick.
	477	" " " " where I now live."
1000, 1000, 1000,	640	" On Stone's River.
	640	" S. side of Cumberland River.
	1622	" Sumner County, first fork, Obed's River.
	1000	" Davidson County, on Hickman Creek.
	640	" Tennessee County, where Virginia line crosses the Cumberland.
	1000	" Davidson County, on waters of Stone's River.

10,499 acres.—7 Slaves, 1½ Town Lots.
Total Tax, $31 49¾."(!!)

We give this as an illustration.

At the first assessment of real estate, (1787,) the principal property-holders were, the Boyds, Bosleys, Buchanans, Blackemore, Cartwright, Carr, Conrad, Castleman, Clarke, Donelson, Drake, Dunham, Ewing, Espey, Elliott, Foster, Frazer, Guise, Gillespie, Hogan, Hay, Heaton, Hays, Hornbarger, Loggans, Lanier, Lancaster, McFarland, Mayfield, Molloy, Menees, Manifee, Neelly, Nevill, Prince, Pirtle, Payne, Robertson, Ramsey, Stuart, Shaw, Shannon, Stump, Shelby, Thompson, Titus, Todd, Walker, Wells, Williams.

The McGavocks purchased in 1788–1790. Colonel Weakley, the Hydes, Hoopers, and others, appear on the Tax List in 1789; and so does "*Jordan River.*"

INDEX.

CHAPTER I.
1742–1774.

CHAPTER II.
1774–1777.

CHAPTER III.
1777–1780.

CHAPTER IV.
1779.

CHAPTER V.
1779–1780.

CHAPTER VI.
1780–1781.

CHAPTER VII.
1781.

CHAPTER VIII.
1782.

CHAPTER IX.
1782.

CHAPTER X.
1783.

3 M

ERRATA.

PAGE 29—"Hoste" for "Hostes."
'   92—Change letter *a* to *e* in "dependances;"
"   121—Change letter *e* and read "agged," 14th line from the top
"   124—Change letter *e* to *a* and read "tantas"
"   134—Read "hoste doceri."
"   183—Read "at" for "as," 9th line from bottom.
"   184—Read "then" for "them," 4th line from the top.
"   220—"Immigration" for "emigration," and so in several places. "immigrate."
"   242—Erase "have been" and read "be " 9th line from top.
"   279—Read "they" for "then." 7th line from top
"   281—"Adapted to."
"   377—"Adapted to."
"   365—"Tumuli" line 20 from bottom.
"   378—Erase "the" line 6th from top.
"   393—Change "third" to "second;" line 15 from bottom.
'   400—Read "equitum" line 7 from bottom.
"   405—Change "from" to "for." line 2 from top.
"   429—Change "with" to "cum." line 3 from top.
"   480—Change "Dove" to "dived," line 6 from bottom.
"   537—Change "are" to "is," line 16 from top.
"   541—Change "Return" for "returned," line 9 from bottom.
"   543—Read "King of the French," line 3 from top
'   597—"18th of June."

hardcover

www.ingramcontent.com/pod-product-compliance
Lightning Source LLC
Chambersburg PA
CBHW020242010726
47475CB00001B/12